ADDRESSES AND PUBLIC PAPERS

OF

JAMES BAXTER HUNT, JR.

ADDRESSES AND PUBLIC PAPERS

OF

JAMES BAXTER HUNT, JR.
GOVERNOR OF NORTH CAROLINA

Volume II

1981-1985

JEFFREY J. CROW, *Editor in Chief*

JAN-MICHAEL POFF, *Editor*

Raleigh
Division of Archives and History
Department of Cultural Resources
1987

DEPARTMENT OF CULTURAL RESOURCES

Patric Dorsey
Secretary

DIVISION OF ARCHIVES AND HISTORY

William S. Price, Jr.
Director

NORTH CAROLINA HISTORICAL COMMISSION

ISBN 0-86526-221-7

STATEMENT OF POLICY

Section 121-6(b) of the *General Statutes of North Carolina* requires that a copy of "all official messages delivered to the General Assembly, addresses, speeches, statements, news releases, proclamations, executive orders, weekly calendars, articles, transcripts of news conferences, lists of appointments, and other official releases and papers of the Governor" be provided to the Department of Cultural Resources. From these records a selection is made by a "skilled and competent editor" who "shall edit according to acceptable scholarly standards, the selected materials which shall be published in a documentary volume as soon as practicable after the conclusion of the term of office of each Governor."

For the introductory biographical sketch, each governor is privileged to select an author. This essay, not to exceed twenty printed pages, represents views of the person selected to write it and is a supplement to and not an official part of the documentary.

PREFACE

Every governor of North Carolina since Locke Craig, 1913-1917, has had a selection of his public papers and addresses edited and published. The North Carolina Historical Commission, forerunner of the present Division of Archives and History, assumed responsibility for editing and publishing the governors' papers with the issuance of *Public Letters and Papers of Thomas Walter Bickett, Governor of North Carolina, 1917-1921* in 1923. In the decades that followed, the state's historical agency, as a tradition, continued to compile, edit, and publish each chief executive's public papers. Finally, in 1971, the General Assembly of North Carolina gave the then State Department of Archives and History statutory authority for producing the series; Volume II of *Addresses and Public Papers of James Baxter Hunt, Jr., Governor of North Carolina*, is the most recent addition to this series.

This second volume of the Hunt papers contains a lengthy appointments section. Under a state constitutional amendment approved in 1977, North Carolina's chief executive is permitted to serve two consecutive terms in office. Governor Hunt won reelection in 1980; Memory F. Mitchell, editor of the first Hunt volume, wisely determined to publish that documentary without an appointments section since many of the governor's appointees to boards, commissions, and other bodies would likely continue in their posts. Volume II thus includes Governor Hunt's appointees during both administrations.

Beyond that sizable addition to Volume II, the editors have tried to follow as closely as possible the excellent editorial standards established in earlier collections of the governors' papers by Mrs. Mitchell. Selectivity—gleaning from available resources those documents that most accurately reflect a governor's term in office— is always essential. But because of the appointments section it was necessary to be even more discriminating in choosing which addresses and public statements to edit, annotate, and publish. Many excluded speeches have been excerpted, summarized, or mentioned in notes accompanying published remarks on similar topics. A list of omitted items is included.

The speeches of Hunt have been lightly edited to assure consistency of spelling, capitalization, punctuation, use of numbers, and the like. Most abbreviations have been expanded, and typographical errors in the originals have been corrected. Lack of uniformity in the textual mechanics of addresses is the norm. A modern governor depends on many speechwriters, in every department of state government, to generate accurate and reliable copy in terms of content; with so many different hands producing texts, editorial inconsistencies frequently appear.

Every effort has been made to identify individuals the first time they were mentioned, by the governor, in this documentary. Where such persons could not be identified from standard biographical directories, letters requesting biographical information were forwarded to them; those who failed to reply were not footnoted. Likewise, extensive measures were employed to locate and cite laws and reports to which Hunt referred and to check the source and accuracy of quotations he used. Not every one could be verified.

During both terms of the Hunt administration the staff of the Historical Publications Section had the full cooperation of the governor's press office, which provided copies of the governor's schedules, speeches, public statements, and news releases on a timely basis. In particular the helpful assistance of Gary Pearce, Wanda Parker, and Brent Hackney is hereby acknowledged. Other individuals who eased the labors of the editors and contributed substantially to the completion of this volume are listed in the acknowledgments. To all, the editors offer their sincere thanks.

Jeffrey J. Crow
Historical Publications Administrator

July 1, 1986

ACKNOWLEDGMENTS

Late in 1983, Jeffrey J. Crow, administrator of the Historical Publications Section, Division of Archives and History, suggested that I assume the editorship of the second volume of the *Addresses and Public Papers of James Baxter Hunt, Jr., Governor of North Carolina.* As editor in chief, Jeff offered timely, indispensable advice, served as a liaison, and, just as important, placed an enormous amount of trust in my discretion by allowing me considerable autonomy over this project. The benefit of both his experience and his confidence is gratefully acknowledged.

Many people, in many ways, assisted with the preparation of Volume II of the *Addresses of Hunt,* and all deserve hearty thanks for their contributions. While it is regrettably impossible to list everyone who joined in this endeavor, the following individuals merit special consideration for their most generous cooperation: Judy Barnhill, Leslie Bevacqua, and Wanda Parker, of the Office of the Governor during the Hunt administration; Rabbi Martin P. Beifield, Jr., Temple Beth Or, Raleigh; Stevens H. Clarke, Institute of Government, University of North Carolina at Chapel Hill; Carolyn Q. Coleman, North Carolina field director, National Association for the Advancement of Colored People, Greensboro; Alice R. Cotten and staff, North Carolina Collection, University of North Carolina at Chapel Hill; Marla Cramer, Raleigh, who was executive assistant to First Lady Carolyn Hunt; Ted Darling, president, Rex-Rosenlew International, Inc., Thomasville; Sharon E. Denitto, General Affairs Section, American Institute in Taiwan, Taipei; Charles Ellertson and staff, Tseng Information Systems, Inc., Durham; Robert L. Fry, director, North Carolina Zoological Park, Asheboro; Mary M. Hilley, research director, *Business Week* Management Group, New York; Doris Holloway, Margie King, and Cheryl McLean, Documents Branch, Division of State Library, Raleigh; Bill Humphries, North Carolina Agricultural Extension Service, North Carolina State University, Raleigh; Frank Long, professor of science and society, emeritus, Cornell University, Ithaca; Bill D. Moyers, CBS News, New York; Melvin Nadell, UJA-Federation Campaign, New York; Park Jong Seh, attaché, Korean Information Office, Embassy of Korea, Washington, D.C.; Gary Pearce, State Capital Services, Inc., Raleigh; the Reverend Cedric D. Pierce, Jr., Pleasant Grove Free Will Baptist Church, Pikeville; David E. Price, professor of political science, Duke University, Durham; James A. Rogerson, University Archives, University of North Carolina at Greensboro; Maurice S. Toler, archivist, and Virginia Hughes, University Archives, North Carolina State University; and Izaak Wirszup, professor of mathematics, University of Chicago. Finally, this book could not have been completed without the duties so ably performed by Historical Publications

Section proofreaders Lisa Bailey and Sally Copenhaver; secretaries Rose Ennemoser, Trudy Rayfield, and Stephena Williams; and 1983 student intern Charles Francis, then a rising junior at Princeton University.

Jan-Michael Poff

July 1, 1986

TABLE OF CONTENTS

LIST OF ILLUSTRATIONS

GOVERNOR JAMES BAXTER HUNT, JR.

By Gary Pearce*

It was a coincidence that North Carolina became the nation's tenth-biggest state while James B. Hunt, Jr., was serving his second term as governor. It was no coincidence that it started acting like it then.

For much of its history, North Carolina has lived in the shadows of other states, "the vale of humility between two mountains of conceit." But between 1977 and 1985, with Hunt as governor, it stepped out of the shadows and achieved a national and international reputation for economic growth and educational innovation. The state's emergence was fueled by Hunt's vision and energy. His unprecedented two four-year terms, combined with his vigorous and purposeful use of the powers of office, gave North Carolina something it had never had: a sustained period of continuity and authority in executive leadership.

That he served two terms was, by itself, revolutionary. That he served eight years enabled him to put his stamp on the state as no other governor had.

Hunt boldly committed North Carolina to a future as a "high-technology state." He believed state government had a responsibility to help make the transition to a modern economy based on technological development, scientific research, and world trade.

He believed the state's future depended on its public schools. So the son of a schoolteacher brought about sweeping reforms: smaller classes; better pay and training for teachers; and rigorous standards and better instruction, especially in the sciences and mathematics. He called it "education for economic growth," preparing North Carolina's youngsters for the requirements of a modern economy.

Better schools and better jobs were Hunt's twin passions. But his restless intensity and active style left his imprint on the state in other ways: its courts; its land, air, and water; its roads; its hospitals; its prisons; its universities and community colleges; and its libraries. Most of all, he changed the way North Carolinians looked at their state.

He believed in government's ability, and responsibility, to help people. That was not always popular in an age when the nation's president called government the problem, not the solution. As the federal government drew back from involvement in domestic prob-

---

*James Gary Pearce (1949–   ), native of Ahoskie; resident of Raleigh; B.A., North Carolina State University, 1976. Reporter and editor, *News and Observer* (Raleigh), 1970–1975; press secretary to Governor Hunt, 1977–1984; communications consultant since 1985. James Gary Pearce to Jan-Michael Poff, November 25, 1985.

lems, Hunt saw an opportunity for state governments to become, what he called in his second inaugural address, "true laboratories for democracy." So he began new initiatives in health care, day care, environmental protection, and criminal justice.

He was willing to risk his political capital when he believed the state's progress was at stake. In the first year of his second term, he demonstrated his mastery of the legislative process by passing an unpopular gasoline tax increase to finance highway maintenance and repairs. But the tax, and the accumulated bruises of eight years, took their toll. His political hide was toughened by battle and scarred by his first election defeat when he tried unsuccessfully to unseat incumbent United States senator Jesse Helms in 1984. The national Republican tide that Hunt defied in 1980 drowned him four years later.

Through it all, Hunt remained an optimist. He whistled when he came down the Executive Mansion steps to work in the morning, and he was still whistling, albeit wearily, when he returned, usually late at night. When he moved out of the Mansion in January, 1985, he naturally was disappointed by his own election defeat and his party's failure to hold the Governor's Office, but he delighted in the way his policies and initiatives continued to set the state's political and legislative agenda even after he left office. He plunged into his new life as a corporate lawyer with characteristic relish and enjoyed uncharacteristic time with his family. In September, 1985, after the former governor passed up another run for the U.S. Senate in 1986, the Raleigh *News and Observer* reported: "Nothing could be more symbolic of Hunt's changed attitude than his recent construction of a swimming pool and a Jacuzzi at his Rock Ridge farm. His friends are amused at the thought of the workaholic and decidedly untrendy Hunt relaxing in a Jacuzzi."

* * *

When Jim Hunt took the oath of office as governor on January 5, 1977, North Carolina faced a crucial turning point. The temper of the times to come would magnify his impact on the state.

He was able to make North Carolina look both to its history and to its future. He enthusiastically organized a statewide observance of the 400th anniversary of the first English settlement in America, an event that took place on North Carolina's shores. A full-sized replica of a ship, similar to one that made the first voyage, was constructed in Manteo, and Princess Anne of England lent a royal touch to the opening ceremony. At the same time, Hunt put to work a citizens' commission to look ahead to the year 2000, discern what the future would bring, and recommend how to meet it.

The Commission on the Future of North Carolina, chaired by William C. Friday of the University of North Carolina, found a state in transition. For generations, North Carolinians had worked on the farm and in the mill, but national recessions and foreign competition had closed many of those doors by the mid-1970s. The industries upon which the state traditionally had relied—textiles, tobacco, and furniture—survived by modernizing and automating. But thousands of jobs were lost, and for a time, North Carolina suffered the nation's highest unemployment rate.

It was clear that the state needed to broaden its economic base and find new sources of jobs. Hunt grew convinced, from his five overseas trade missions and countless industry-hunting trips and calls around the nation, that Research Triangle Park and the state's excellent public and private universities provided an ideal base for attracting new, growing, "high-tech" industries. So he turned his 1980 reelection campaign into a referendum on the state's economic future. He preached the virtues of North Carolina's being on the leading edge of scientific research and technological development. From a sometimes-reluctant Council of State and legislature, he obtained the money to establish the multi-million-dollar Microelectronics Center of North Carolina, a keystone of the state's efforts to recruit the new industries. He persuaded the General Assembly to support research in biotechnology and its applications to agriculture. Engineering instruction was beefed up at the state's universities and job training expanded in the community college system.

Hunt's strategy paid immediate dividends, and North Carolina's industrial growth was remarkable: $15 billion in capital investment and a quarter of a million new manufacturing jobs. By 1985, the state was as famous for the Research Triangle and microelectronics as it was for tobacco and textiles. In sharp contrast to a decade before, North Carolina boasted one of the nation's lowest unemployment rates.

During his second term, Hunt developed the idea of "education for economic growth." In 1982 he became chairman of the Education Commission of the States and plunged it into a national debate over public school reform. The commission published a report, *Action for Excellence*, that called on the fifty states to make investments in education that would prepare their youngsters for jobs that required brainpower more than muscle power.

North Carolina set the pace. It established the first tuition-free, residential high school, with a focus on science and mathematics, for gifted and talented students. The North Carolina School of Science and Mathematics was Hunt's brainchild, and he liked to brag that it produced more National Merit scholars per capita than any school in the country. And when the governor targeted the state's startlingly high dropout rate for extra attention and resources, the number of students who failed to complete school each year declined by 5,000.

Hunt sought to enlist not only public support for educational reform but also active involvement by parents and citizens in the schools. Every Monday morning, the governor and First Lady Carolyn Hunt would leave the Mansion for a public school in Raleigh where they did volunteer work. The Office of Citizen Affairs, which he established in his first term to promote volunteerism and citizen involvement, recruited businesses, churches, and other organizations to "adopt" individual schools. Each year, at special awards ceremonies across the state, Governor and Mrs. Hunt honored more than 1,000 citizens for volunteer activities.

The governor singled out business leaders for a key role in education reform. He formed a committee of business executives to work on math and science instruction. He appointed business people to a task force that recommended a sweeping package of reforms promoting "education for economic growth" in 1984.

Although 1984 was supposedly Hunt's lame-duck year as governor, he won legislative approval for the largest education program in North Carolina history: $281 million to reduce class sizes, upgrade the teaching profession, and raise the quality of education statewide. One year later, even with Hunt out of office, the report still dominated the legislature's debate on education.

Hunt's innovative approach to economic and educational challenges won North Carolina national attention. One author called it the nation's newest "megastate," reflecting the 1980 U.S. census's official determination that, with a population of 6.5 million, it had surpassed Massachusetts and had become the tenth most populous state. A book entitled *Global Stakes* said, "Jim Hunt is an aggressive and successful promoter of North Carolina as a home for a new generation of high-technology industry. He personifies the public sector at its best in conceptualizing and moving toward a future-minded growth strategy."

Hunt became a leader in regional and national governors' organizations, especially on education, technological innovation, health care, and criminal justice. In 1984, the Education Commission of the States presented to him the James B. Conant Award as the public leader in the nation who had contributed most significantly to educational progress. He became a national figure in the Democratic party, chairing its Commission on Presidential Nomination which wrote the party's rules for the 1984 presidential campaign.

Much of that visibility was made possible by repeal of the one-term limitation on governors. Hunt, who led the 1977 effort to remove that vestige of colonial suspicion of royal governors, found that the change sometimes brought him into conflict with a General Assembly determined to assert and expand its own power. But it gave him an unprecedented opportunity to exercise the powers of office and influence the course of the state.

He made thousands of appointments, bringing women, blacks, and Indians into key positions in executive agencies and, especially, the state's courtrooms. He took a special interest in the judges he appointed. One hopeful recalled his interview in the Capitol: "I went in expecting a courtesy call and a nice chat. Hunt pulled out a legal pad full of questions and grilled me for forty-five minutes. I was exhausted."

Throughout his second term, Hunt continued to deliver special messages on crime to each session of the legislature. In one, he launched a statewide volunteer program to combat juvenile crime. In another, he mobilized public support to pass a tough law against drunken driving. The state also felt the full impact of the criminal justice reforms enacted during his first four years: a speedy-trial law, a more uniform system of criminal sentencing, and more emphasis on requiring offenders to pay restitution to their victims.

Confronted with the less-desirable effects of North Carolina's growth, the son of a farmer and soil conservationist responded. Governor Hunt established the first statewide program to manage hazardous wastes safely. He signed orders protecting prime farmland and forests against the bulldozer. He supported restrictions on damaging development along the state's beaches and mountain ridges. He strengthened the state's protection against pollution of its lakes and rivers.

As the state's population grew, it grew older. Hunt saw to it that more in-home health aides and senior activity centers were provided.

More children were growing up in poverty. Hunt wielded his power as director of the budget to provide more health care and nutrition services to pregnant mothers and families with infant children. The state's infant mortality rate declined. For the first time, state money was put into child day care.

Prisons had become overcrowded. Hunt put more than $100 million into modernization and construction. The dungeon-like Central Prison in Raleigh gave way to a modern, single-cell facility.

He pioneered advanced training for state government managers and executives. He even brought a touch of Hollywood to North Carolina, establishing a film office that attracted major productions to the state. Producer Dino DeLaurentiis built a huge studio in Wilmington. Actress Natalie Wood made her last film in North Carolina, and when she and her costars visited Hunt, it was the best attended of the weekly press conferences he held throughout his second term.

Hunt lent strong support to more traditional Tar Heel cultural pursuits. The state symphony, buffeted by budget and management problems, was put on a solid financial footing. The new state Art Museum was opened. Libraries and arts programs in communities throughout the state received financial boosts.

North Carolina developed a state zoo that was becoming recognized as one of the nation's best. An aviary and African plains area were opened.

The state ports at Wilmington and Morehead City were thriving. North Carolina's roads and highways, the largest state-maintained system in the country, received a long-overdue injection of maintenance and repairs. Hunt put the construction of Interstate 40 from Raleigh to Wilmington at the top of his transportation priority list, and the project was well under way when he left office.

All of this activity by state government reflected the vitality of North Carolina itself. New industries, new offices, and new homes dotted the landscape. Attention shifted from how to attract good growth to how to manage it. By 1985 the transition Jim Hunt had foreseen was upon North Carolina, and he had succeeded in getting the state about the business of meeting the challenge.

* * *

The final judgment of history on Jim Hunt's governorship remains to be written. Academics and politicians will debate endlessly the consequences of gubernatorial succession. The economic transition was by no means complete when he left office. But there can be no doubt that Hunt brought his state a new dimension of leadership. He had the vision to look to the future, the courage to try to change it, and the will to inspire others to join him.

Every governor brings policy priorities to office; some have more success than others translating them into reality. Every governor finds himself impelled by events, issues, and problems he cannot predict or select. Every governor signs hundreds of orders, makes thousands of appointments, and faces countless decisions about human beings—from who is invited to a Mansion reception to who lives and dies.

The character of a governor's service to the state is determined most of all by the human qualities he brings to the office. Every day, Hunt brought a bedrock of integrity, a personal incorruptibility that was never in doubt. He brought a restless intellectual curiosity. He had the rare talent of listening, and learning from what he heard.

He took a patient amusement in the inconveniences of office, the omnipresent security men, and the inevitable stir and stares when he drove his family to church on Sundays.

Hunt was a perfectionist and an exacting, but never demanding, boss. He had a disconcerting habit of asking his cabinet or staff for an answer or a fact or a detail they had not anticipated.

He was tested, as all governors are. Twice during his second term he received formal requests to commute death sentences. Each time, after an exhaustive review, he refused to block the executions. The 1984 Senate campaign took a heavy personal and political toll. Hunt faced a relentless assault on his record and character. Defeat was harsh, but he bore neither bitterness nor regrets. He said, "My nature is never to dwell on disappointment. I just move on to the next thing in life."

The cares of office never slowed his step or silenced his whistling. He would recharge himself on the family farm with his fishing pond and the ducks, dogs, and horses. He could escape the chores of office with the chores of farming: the fences that needed fixing, the barn that needed painting, the fields that needed mowing. And he set aside each Sunday for his family.

The man who was governor never left behind the boy who was the son of James B. Hunt, Sr., and Elsie Brame Hunt. He was a product of family, church, farm, and school. From his parents, he inherited a love of learning and a love of the land. He inherited a fierce sense of justice and fairness, and nothing angered him more than prejudice and discrimination. It was a belief for which he paid dearly politically, but he never regretted it.

Most of all, he inherited a conviction that government existed to help people. When others flagged, he talked about the kids—the ones who didn't have a loving family, didn't get a hot meal, didn't see a doctor, or didn't get a good education. As governor, he touched thousands of them. It was the legacy he wanted most to leave.

Above: Governor Hunt confers with U.S. Senator Robert B. Morgan at a meeting of western North Carolina Democrats in 1980. Of candidates engaged in "big three" races on the state's ballots that year—U.S. president, U.S. senator, governor—Hunt was the only member of his party to win the endorsement of a majority of Tar Heel voters, defeating Republican opponent I. Beverly Lake, Jr., by a substantial margin. Morgan lost a close battle to challenger John P. East. (Unless otherwise specified, photographs furnished by the Governor's Press Office.) *Left:* The Hunts prepare to enter Reynolds Coliseum, North Carolina State University, for their second inaugural ball, January 9, 1981.

Above: Chief Justice Joseph Branch, of the state supreme court, administered the oath of office to the governor on January 10, 1981, as First Lady Carolyn Hunt looked on. Hunt was the first North Carolina chief executive to seek re-election under a state constitutional amendment approved in 1977. (Photograph from State Archives, Division of Archives and History, Department of Cúltural Resources.) *Below, right:* Hunt at work in his Capitol office, 1982.

INAUGURAL ADDRESS

As I take this oath of office for a second time, I am humbled and honored by the responsibility entrusted to me by the people of North Carolina. I thank you, and I pray that I will be worthy of you.

Today is a day of celebration—a celebration not merely of the inauguration of a governor and a Council of State, but a celebration of North Carolina, our future, our hopes, and our vision. We have much to celebrate. The nation envies North Carolina's natural beauty and our quality of life. We lead the South in the struggle to open the doors of progress and opportunity for all our people. And as the tenth most populous state, we stand poised now to lead the nation.

Yet we hear it said by some people that North Carolina's "image" is otherwise. We hear it said that our state's reputation is tarnished and our good name is lost. I stand here today and declare as clearly and strongly as I can that those people are *wrong!*

We believe in our state motto, "Esse Quam Videri—To *Be* Rather Than to Seem," and we know what we can be. We are not satisfied to rank forty-first in per capita income, and we must change that. We are not satisfied to rank forty-seventh in infant mortality, and we must change that. We are not satisfied to have one out of every three teenagers drop out of school, and we must change that. We are not satisfied to see our great rivers become polluted and die, and we must change that.

Our history has prepared us well for this moment. Our heritage is one of independence and initiative. We have faced hardship before, and we have overcome it.

Almost 400 years ago English settlers established the first colony in the New World—on North Carolina's coast.

Almost 200 years ago North Carolina led the fight for a Bill of Rights.

Over the last 100 years North Carolina led the South in recovering from the scars of war and building a prosperous, fair, and progressive society.

Fifty years ago Governor O. Max Gardner[1] and North Carolina led the way to recovery from the Depression.

Now, in the last twenty years of this century, it is time for North Carolina to lead again. The nation is searching for new answers and new directions. The role of the federal government is properly diminishing, and the states can again become true laboratories for democracy.

We are keenly aware of the state of America's economy today. This is a time for leanness. This is a time for government to reexamine itself and reduce its burdens on the people. But this is *not* a time to abandon the work of compassion. This is *not* a time to turn back from progress. Across the nation the winds of retreat are blowing, but North Carolina must sail against the wind.

This is a time for courage. This is a time for vision. This is a time for leadership.

I believe North Carolina is ready. I believe North Carolina can show the nation how to create new opportunities for all our people, how to create new jobs and new wealth by building our economy through hard work and free enterprise.

A historic opportunity lies before us, and we must seize the moment. The tide of the Technology Revolution is coming in throughout the world, and North Carolina can rise with it. Let us resolve today to meet that future. Let us resolve to develop the full potential of our people. Let us resolve to build our future in our great universities and our public schools. Let us resolve to provide a good job for everyone who wants to work. Let us resolve to be more faithful stewards of the land, the water, and the air that God has given us. And let us resolve not to tolerate those who preach hatred and bigotry among us.[2]

These are not the tasks of only the governor or of government itself. They require the dedication of all of us as citizens. Will you join me in this time of testing? Will you pledge anew your love of North Carolina and your devotion to its future? Will you volunteer yourself personally—to help a child learn to read or avoid juvenile delinquency, to protect your neighbors from crime, to give assistance and comfort to a lonely senior citizen? Will you give something back to this state for all it has given to you? If you will, and if we do this together, we shall achieve our vision.

There will be setbacks and sacrifices in the years ahead, but we have met them before and we shall overcome them now. With God as our helper, we shall light the flame of human brotherhood, and we shall make North Carolina a beacon of hope and progress throughout the land.

---

[1]Oliver Max Gardner (1882-1947), native of Shelby; B.S., Agricultural and Mechanical College (now North Carolina State University), 1903. Attorney; state senator, 1911-1916; lieutenant governor, 1917-1921. During his administration as governor, 1929-1933, aid to schools was increased, a workman's compensation law was adopted, and the state took over county road maintenance. Designated U.S. ambassador to Great Britain by President Truman, Gardner died before arriving in London. John L. Cheney, Jr. (ed.), *North Carolina Government, 1585-1979: A Narrative and Statistical History . . .* (Raleigh: North Carolina Department of the Secretary of State, second, updated edition, 1981), 423, 424, 488, 492, 493, 495, hereinafter cited as Cheney, *North Carolina Government*; Beth G. Crabtree, *North Carolina Governors, 1585-1974: Brief Sketches* (Raleigh: Division of Archives and History, Department of Cultural Resources, third printing, revised, 1974), 122-123, hereinafter cited as Crabtree, *North Carolina Governors*; *Who Was Who in America*,

Volume II: *1943-1950* (Chicago: A. N. Marquis Company, fifth printing, 1966), hereinafter cited as *Who Was Who in America*, with appropriate years.

[2]According to William D. Snider, Hunt's call to North Carolinians to thwart persons inciting hatred and bigotry was a reference to the November 3, 1979, Klan-Communist shootout in Greensboro. Snider, *Helms and Hunt: The North Carolina Senate Race, 1984* (Chapel Hill: University of North Carolina Press, 1985), 78, hereinafter cited as Snider, *Helms and Hunt*.

MESSAGES TO JOINT SESSIONS
OF THE GENERAL ASSEMBLY

STATE OF THE STATE ADDRESS

JANUARY 15, 1981

State of the Economy

I believe we should begin our deliberations with this question: What can we do this year, as governor and as members of the General Assembly, to help North Carolinians in a time of economic hardship? Our nation faces its most serious economic problems since the Depression fifty years ago: sluggish growth, high inflation, high interest rates, and high unemployment.

North Carolinians have suffered with the nation. We also have persistent economic handicaps: low per capita income, too much poverty, and not enough good jobs. Let us pledge tonight that we will overcome them. Let us pledge that our agenda this year will be to open the doors of economic opportunity to all North Carolinians. Let us pledge to make it possible for all North Carolinians to earn a good living and provide adequately for their families.

Let us also count North Carolina's blessings. In the 1970s the average pay of our people increased at a rate seventh-highest among all the states. In the last four years we have enjoyed unprecedented economic growth. Industries have decided to invest $8.1 billion in new and expanded plants—more than in the previous eleven years combined. That is an achievement North Carolina can be proud of.

Despite the national recession, 1980 saw North Carolina reach the second-highest level of industrial investment ever—$2.24 billion, second only to the $2.4 billion recorded in 1979. That is an achievement North Carolina can be proud of, and that investment over the last four years will bring North Carolina more than 122,000 new manufacturing jobs. That is an achievement North Carolina can be proud of.

So we have a strong foundation on which to build. Now we need a strategy for strengthening our people and overcoming our human handicaps. We need a strategy for economic development and for human development, and we need to recognize that the full development of our people is essential to the development of our economy.

Human development means infant health care and child day care. It means education and skill training. It means a good job and a good retirement. It means full and equal opportunities for *everyone*.

Economic development means more than just convincing industries to come to North Carolina. It means good roads and public transit and ports and airports. It means a good energy supply. It means safely disposing of hazardous wastes. It means protecting the air, the land, and the water that God has given us.

Let us commit ourselves to a strategy that will develop the full potential of our people and unlock the full potential of our economy. Let us commit ourselves to making North Carolina all that it can be and ought to be.

Responsible Government

But as we do so, let us remember this: We must be responsible with the taxpayers' money. We must make wise investments that will yield better jobs and better education and a better future. We must be conservative *and* progressive. We must cut out the fat but build the muscle.

We have kept state government on a strict diet. The number of state jobs has increased only 10 percent the last four years, while it grew 20 percent the previous four years. This year, the growth in state jobs is the smallest in more than a decade—0.8 percent. But we can do something in the coming budget year that hasn't been done in a long time, if ever. We can actually *reduce* the number of state employees. You will do that if you approve this budget.

I recommend that we eliminate 1,002 jobs from the state payroll. That can save the taxpayers $13 million in salaries. It will shrink the size of state government by almost 2 percent. If you do that, it will mean that over the last four years we will have abolished almost 2,200 jobs—almost 1,000 of them in the Department of Transportation.[1]

The rest of the nation is just now waking up to the wisdom of restricted government growth and responsible taxation. That has been the North Carolina way for decades. We have had no state tax increases in the last eight years. For this year, dependent exemptions have been increased by $200 each. Standard deductions and personal exemptions have been raised 10 percent.[2] This General Assembly can be proud of that. We rank forty-sixth among the fifty states in our combined state and local taxes. We pay $711 per person per year, while the national average is $934. The difference is $223 per person in North Carolina.

In keeping with that tradition of responsible taxation, we should consider tax relief carefully targeted to help those hit hardest by inflation—families with children and the elderly. I recommend the elimination retroactively of the early filing deadline that cost many elderly people their homestead exemption on property taxes last year. I also support raising the income limit and exemption amounts to reflect inflation. But the state should reimburse the counties and cities for any loss in tax revenues.[3]

I also recommend helping low- and middle-income working parents by providing a child-care tax credit instead of the present deduction.[4]

We should recognize the burden that property taxes put on our citizens and the restrictions they place on local governments. Those governments have made great progress in their strength and effectiveness. The budget I am presenting to you would provide new and continued assistance of $14 million to local governments for Medicaid, health, and social services costs. This legislature might also properly examine the long-run financial needs of local governments as compared to their revenues from present tax sources.[5]

We must be fair to the fine employees who work for state government. This budget provides $106 million for their salary increases. I urge the legislature to look at various ways to pay this, but I hope you will especially consider maximizing take-home pay to teachers and state employees by having the state pick up 5 percent of the 6 percent retirement contribution made by state employees. This would permit an average increase in take-home pay of about 7 percent.[6]

I recommend that retired employees get the same increase in their benefits as the active workers get. That principle of equity should now be firmly established for the future. In addition, oversights in the retirees' benefits that were enacted by the last legislature should be corrected this year.[7]

High-Technology Strategy

The very leanness of the budget forces us to clarify our strategy for economic growth and to establish clear priorities. I believe we should seek a future as a high-technology state. We should emphasize productivity, ideas, and innovation.

We should target high-wage, high-growth industries like microelectronics.[8] One microcircuit smaller than your fingernail can process huge amounts of information that once required computers the size of this hall. These tiny "chips" will be the crude oil of the 1980s. This is the Information Revolution, and it has hit the world with the impact of a second Industrial Revolution. We can ride that wave to build a more prosperous economy and become a more productive state.

Microelectronics isn't the only industry in our future. Thanks to our universities and research institutions, North Carolina can pioneer in molecular biology, photovoltaics, and other sophisticated technologies.

We are attractive to those industries. Look at General Electric's decision to locate its major new microelectronics research and development facility in North Carolina after looking at many other states. This week, we read where the governor of California is worried by our competition for that industry.[9] Well, let's give the governor of California something to really worry about. Let us resolve that no state will be more innovative and aggressive than North Carolina in pursuing this good growth. Let us boldly commit ourselves to making North Carolina the East Coast center for this industry.

I am asking this legislature to commit $24.4 million over the coming biennium to develop the Microelectronics Center of North Carolina.[10] The center is a unique partnership of government, education, and industry. It will tie together the scientific and research resources of five great universities—North Carolina State University, the University of North Carolina at Chapel Hill, Duke University, North Carolina A&T State University, and the University of North Carolina at Charlotte—as well as our community college system and the Research Triangle Institute. It will train the minds and the skilled hands that are the lifeblood of this industry. It can be the magnet that will attract microelectronics-related industries and good jobs to all parts of North Carolina—from the mountains to the coast.

This high-technology future can further our goal of balanced growth. We are committed to that principle in law.[11]

Venture capital and utility services are needed throughout North Carolina to help bring good jobs to where the people are. Small businesses and minority-owned firms stand to benefit from this balance.

Human Development [12]

Meeting the goal of a productive, high-technology state requires the full development of our people.

We must begin by raising up healthy, well-educated children who will grow up able to hold high-technology jobs. We cannot afford to do otherwise. It costs us as taxpayers $36,000 per year for a mentally retarded child at Western Carolina Center. It costs us $38,000 a year for a mentally ill patient at Dorothea Dix. It costs us $31,000 for a juvenile at C. A. Dillon School.

Every year 26,000 teenagers give birth in North Carolina. Half of their babies are illegitimate; many are retarded or handicapped. It is a shame that North Carolina ranks fourth highest among the states in the number of babies that die before their first birthday, and we must change that.

We have made a good beginning these last four years. We have provided better infant and maternal health care. Hospitals are screening babies at birth, and doctors and nurses are following up with those who have defects and diseases.

Now we must mobilize all our resources to save the children. For them we must expand our infant and child health programs. As they grow older, we should continue to put state money into private day care. This General Assembly took that bold step in 1979.[13]

The state should do more to help those of all ages who need help. For the mentally ill, I ask you to provide a $2 million reserve to improve community treatment. For the mentally retarded, I ask you to provide more money for group homes. For the severely and profoundly retarded, I ask you to provide additional specialized treatment. For those who suffer from alcoholism and drug abuse, I ask you to provide more community treatment and prevention programs.[14] For older adults, I ask you to provide more assistance for senior citizen centers.[15] And for all of us and for our future, I ask you to make the same commitment to education that Charles Brantley Aycock made in his Inaugural Address in 1901 when he said: "I pledge the state, its strength, its heart, its wealth, to universal education. . . . I pledge the wealth of the state to the education of its children."[16]

North Carolina has made great strides in its public schools the last four years. Our teachers, principals, superintendents, and all educators deserve tremendous credit. We are focusing on the basic skills and developing competency for life.

For years North Carolina has been way down in the national education scores. But now, for the first time ever, our students in grades one through six have scored at or above the national average in reading, language, spelling, and math. Our students' SAT scores are up, while they are dropping in other parts of the nation.

Our minimum competency test has had a powerful impact throughout the school system. The passing rate has increased each year it has been given. The greatest gains have been made by black and Indian students.

I appeal tonight to two groups in particular. First, our teachers. They have the toughest and most important jobs in our state, and this General Assembly recognized that last year by enacting a fairer salary schedule for them. I appeal to our teachers to commit themselves to nurturing every young mind in their classes and to making our public schools the best in the nation.

I appeal to you, the members of this House and this Senate, to make the wise investments that will mean true excellence in education.

This year let us begin a new quest in education. Today, one out of every three teenagers drops out of school before graduating. That is a tragic waste that North Carolina cannot afford. Let us commit ourselves in this General Assembly to perhaps the biggest and most important goal we have ever set: to help every child in North Carolina graduate from high school.

We should build on our proven Kindergarten and Primary Reading programs. They have produced those exceptional test results.

I urge you to appropriate the money needed to reduce class sizes in grades four through six from one teacher for every thirty students to one teacher for twenty-six.

We should put the same emphasis on individual help for students in the basic subjects—reading, language arts, and math—in grades seven through twelve. Our goal here should be to reduce class size to one teacher per twenty-five students. Because of the tight budget, I can only move halfway toward that goal in the coming biennium. But we must make that full commitment in our hearts.[17]

In addition to reducing class size, our program to reduce dropouts includes additional remedial instruction, vocational guidance counseling, and a greater emphasis on teaching writing throughout the school grades.[18]

But our schools and our students need more than tax dollars. My goal during the next four years will be to get more people helping to make their schools excellent. We will work to get every single school "adopted" by a church or organization that will provide volunteers and support, and we will expand the Community School program to every local school system, opening the doors of the schoolhouses to the community.

The preparation of our young people for careers in high technology will require a greater emphasis on math and science. Our North Carolina School of Science and Mathematics has focused national attention on our state, and I urge you to approve the items in this budget for operations and major renovations of its buildings.

To achieve a productive state, education and skill training must go hand in hand. Our goal must be to develop in each citizen the job skills necessary to get a good job and provide a good living for his or her family. Over the last twenty years this legislature has provided the funds for building one of the finest community college systems in the country. Today, that system has strong, new leadership and its own governing board composed heavily of industry leaders. I ask you to give it the tools and support it needs to do its job, and its primary job is to train people to work. This budget provides $18 million for better training equipment and programs in our fifty-eight institutions.[19]

In addition, we need a comprehensive state policy on skill training. I promise you that as chief executive of this state we will soon develop a policy to use more efficiently the training funds available in our community college system, the public schools, the university, the Employment Security Commission, and, most important, private industry. All of these parts must work together to train the hands that run the wheels of industry and agriculture.[20]

The high-technology future we seek in North Carolina will come about only as we maintain and build our great university system. It is more than just an educational enterprise. The University of North Carolina and all of its campuses are the major attraction for scientists, engineers, medical researchers, and other top people in their economic fields. The university system is part and parcel of our microelectronics development now under way and our efforts to develop new energy sources. I urge you to give it your loyalty and strong support.

I also remind you of the superb private colleges and universities in our state and their heroic battle to provide resources for their special educational functions. Because of limited revenues, this budget increases our per-student allocation by only $50.00 each year, and that is not adequate for their needs. I will be pleased if this amount can be increased.[21]

We must also nurture and develop our cultural resources. We should give all our people a chance to experience the richness and fullness of music, art, drama, and literature. We must take them to the people. North Carolina's business community has been generous in its support of our cultural activities. Corporate contributions to those purposes totaled $7.4 million in 1979. Volunteers have given countless hours. State government owes it to our people to make the same level of commitment and dedication.

All of this—health care, day care, education, our cultural resources—is part of our human development strategy. But it will be in vain if we do not open the doors for full participation in our society by all of our citizens. Let us make that commitment today, the birthday of Dr. Martin Luther King, Jr. We must not tolerate discrimination in our state—against blacks or Indians, women, the mentally retarded or mentally ill, the elderly or the handicapped. I ask this General Assembly to join me in actively searching out and putting a stop to discrimination and, further, to affirmatively offering full and equal opportunities to everyone.

As the father of three daughters and a son and as governor, I continue to believe that the Equal Rights Amendment to the United States Constitution is morally right and that we ought to ratify it.[22] We must also provide justice to the one half of our population that is female by correcting unfair state laws. It is high time that wives in North Carolina—who work as equal partners on farms, in businesses, and in the home—be treated equitably in the distribution of marital property. They helped earn it, and they should share in it fairly.[23]

We cannot expect people to believe in and support our free enterprise system unless they have a fair chance to get into it and progress on their merit. Therefore, I will support enactment of a fair employment bill to give state government the authority to resolve complaints of hiring discrimination.

We must guarantee that our system of justice is fair to minorities. When I deliver my "Special Message on Crime" to this General Assembly, I will ask you to pass legislation designed to provide fair representation of minorities on jury lists. I will also speak to a number of issues relating to one of the most important of all freedoms—the freedom from crime and physical violence. I will especially emphasize the importance of helping young people avoid being drawn into a life of crime.[24]

Economic Development

Just as we have a strategy for human development, we must also have a strategy for economic development. It may be tempting to look at the record of the last four years and want to relax, but North Carolina can't do that. We have too far to go, and the competition is too fierce. North Carolina will fall behind in the race for better jobs if we don't build the muscles that keep us competitive.

A healthy economy requires energy. North Carolina can lead the nation in developing and using alternative sources of energy. We must make that commitment.

Because of the action by this General Assembly, our state has one of the most effective systems of utility regulation in the nation. Our Utilities Commission and the Public Staff have kept the increase in electric rates below the inflation rate the last four years. Both Duke and Carolina Power and Light provide power at a cost lower than most utilities across the nation, and they deserve our praise. At the same time we must take whatever action is necessary to guarantee fair rates for the people of northeastern North Carolina, and I am prepared to do that.

But a good energy policy should do more than regulate. It should produce more energy, and that requires three things: investments, innovation, and incentives—investments in research, innovations in how we use energy, and incentives that will encourage people to adopt alternative forms of energy.

North Carolina is already a national leader in blazing an alternative energy path. We are proving that the future does not have to be cold and dark. We are proving that, while the world may be running out of cheap oil and gas, it is not running out of energy.

North Carolina is a national leader in energy conservation. We are using solar power, wood, and waterpower. We have under way a Revolving Solar Trust Fund designed to finance the construction of one solar demonstration home in all 100 counties. We have created the North Carolina Energy Institute and the Alternative Energy Corporation. Both are pioneering in the search for new forms of energy.[25]

This year I will ask you to enact a package of tax incentives that will encourage our citizens to use those new sources. This will include a passive solar tax credit. It will include restoring the tax credit for insulation. It will include investment credits for businesses and farms that install alternative energy sources. I will also propose legislation to establish a program that will help people obtain low-interest loans to install solar energy equipment in their homes.[26]

One of the most crucial issues facing our state today is the safe management of hazardous and low-level radioactive wastes. We are the fourth largest generator of low-level radioactive waste in the nation—202,000 cubic feet in 1979—and the eleventh-largest generator of hazardous waste—more than 120 million gallons in the same year. The generators of these wastes are the backbone of our economy. The textile industry generates varsol solvents,[27] dye sludges, and lubricating and hydraulic oil wastes. The furniture industry can generate waste solvents. Our printing and publishing industry generates solvents and metal residue wastes. Important health tests use radioactive elements.

Last July I appointed the Governor's Task Force on Waste Management, composed of representatives from state and local governments, higher education, environmental groups, and industries. They have worked long and hard to arrive at the best solutions to this problem. The draft report of this task force is being circulated throughout the state now for public comment, and the final report is due in February. It will call upon us for some hard decisions—decisions that will determine our future and our children's future, decisions about who will be ultimately responsible for a comprehensive and safe management system, decisions about how it will be accomplished. These are decisions that must be made if North Carolina is to move ahead in the 1980s.[28]

We must strengthen our program of monitoring air quality. We are in danger of losing good industry if we don't.

We must continue our work to clean up the Chowan River and save our other rivers from pollution.

We must maintain strong protection of our precious and fragile coastal region.

Just as we must maintain our natural resources, we must maintain our capital resources. We cannot let our roads and highways and bridges fall into ruin and disrepair. We cannot leave a legacy of neglect to future generations. The responsibility to prevent that is *yours* as members of this General Assembly. All of our efforts to build our economy will fail without a good system of transportation to supply our farms and homes and industries and to transport our products across the state, the nation, and the world. I will not make any recommendation to you on this issue until the spring. I will be working until then to determine how much of our current revenues we can save.[29]

We must remember that North Carolina's economy cannot be strong if agriculture is not strong. Every day in the United States 12 square miles of American farmland are lost to shopping malls, housing development, and highways. We must develop a way to protect our prime farmland from unnecessary and unwise development, and I will propose legislation to do that.[30]

We must provide greater support for our farm exports and our marketing facilities, and we must expand our agricultural research and extension efforts.

Conclusion

Let me conclude tonight with this: I have sought to present you and the state of North Carolina with more than a budget. I have outlined a program for progress, a strategy for the future. Across the nation we see other states laying their plans. Many are content to stand still, or even to turn back, but North Carolina cannot afford to stand still or to turn back. We cannot hide from the future. We must not be afraid to swim against the tide, to sail against the wind. We must move ahead.

I have a vision for North Carolina. It is one in which we face the future without fear. It is one in which we live together in safety, peace, and harmony. It is one in which every human being is free to be all he or she can aspire to be. It is one in which no child goes to bed sick, or hungry, or hurt. It is one in which older adults live in dignity and comfort.

Does that sound like an idealistic vision? Certainly it is, but we can achieve it. I believe in North Carolina, our people, and our promise.

Last Saturday I was sworn in as North Carolina's forty-first elected governor. This week you convene as North Carolina's 134th General Assembly. What we do this year, we do for 400 years of history that come before us and untold generations that will follow.

What will we leave for them? It can be a legacy of hope and progress. It can be a North Carolina in which, truly, the weak grow strong and the strong grow great. Let us—General Assembly and governor together—leave that legacy this year.

---

[1] North Carolina General Assembly, *Report of the Joint Special Committee to Review the Department of Transportation. Submitted to the 1983 General Assembly* ([Raleigh]: North Carolina General Assembly, December 6, 1982), 6-7, outlines staff and crew reductions in the Transportation Department. See also "An Act to Make Appropriations for Current Operations of State Departments, Institutions, and Agencies, and for Other Purposes," ratified July 8, 1981. *Session Laws of North Carolina, 1981*, c. 859, s. 71, hereinafter cited as *N.C. Session Laws, 1981*.

[2] "An Act to Provide Tax Relief for the Citizens of North Carolina," was ratified June 6. *N.C. Session Laws, 1981*, c. 801.

[3] See "An Act to Extend through April 15, 1981, the Period for Applying for the Homestead Exemption for Property Taxes for the Calendar Year 1980," c. 28, ratified February 27, and "An Act to Raise the Property Tax Homestead Exemption," c. 1052, ratified October 10, 1981. *N.C. Session Laws, 1981*.

[4] "An Act to Provide an Individual Income Tax Credit for Child-Care and Other Employment-Related Expenses," was ratified July 9, 1981, and became effective retroactive to January 1. *N.C. Session Laws, 1981*, c. 899.

[5] *N.C. Session Laws, 1981*, c. 859, ss. 14-23.3.

[6] "An Act to Modify Current Operations and Capital Improvements Appropriations

for North Carolina State Government for the Fiscal Year 1981-1982 and to Make Other Changes in the Budget Operations of the State" was ratified October 10. *N.C. Session Laws, 1981,* c. 1127, ss. 6-21.

⁷*N.C. Session Laws, 1981,* c. 859, ss. 42-45.2.

⁸Embracing high-technology industries such as microelectronics and biotechnology, Hunt told the Conference on Technological Innovation for Economic Prosperity, February 21, 1981, would prove North Carolina's "chance of a lifetime, the chance to break away from the anchors of low wages and low income, the chance to give our people a better economic future and a better life. For the nation this is our chance to revitalize our economy and to regain our position as the world's industrial leader."

⁹Having learned that Hunt "'was proposing $30 million for a microelectronics center and that one had already been established in Minnesota,'" Governor Edmund G. (Jerry) Brown, Jr., urged the California legislature to approve $5 million for a similar facility in its state. He added, "'[M]y competitive instincts told me that if these governors continue to come out here and siphon off the new growth in the semiconductor business, that we're going to be in big trouble.'" *News and Observer* (Raleigh), January 10, 1981, hereinafter cited as *News and Observer.* Hunt visited California's Silicon Valley during a business recruiting trip in November, 1980. Memory F. Mitchell (ed.), *Addresses and Public Papers of James Baxter Hunt, Jr., Governor of North Carolina,* Volume I: *1977-1981* (Raleigh: Division of Archives and History, Department of Cultural Resources, 1982), 791-792, 794-796, hereinafter cited as Mitchell, *Addresses of Hunt,* I.

¹⁰*N.C. Session Laws, 1981,* c. 859, s. 2.

¹¹"An Act to Establish the North Carolina Balanced Growth Policy" was ratified April 19, 1979. Previously identified in Mitchell, *Addresses of Hunt,* I, 37, 45n.

¹²Hunt also addressed the points on education, contained in this section, in speeches to the North Carolina Association of Educators (NCAE), April 3; the North Carolina Principals and Assistant Principals Association, October 20; and the NCAE Division of Principals and Administrators, November 10, 1981.

¹³See *General Statutes of North Carolina,* 143B-153 (2) d, hereinafter cited as G.S. "An Act to Amend G.S. 143B-153 to Require the Social Services Commission to Establish Standards and Adopt Rules and Regulations for Payment of State Funds to Private Child-Caring Institutions" was ratified July 10. *N.C. Session Laws, 1981,* c. 961.

¹⁴"An Act to Appropriate Funds to the Division of Mental Health, Mental Retardation, and Substance Abuse Services, Department of Human Resources for the Purpose of Assisting Area Programs in Providing Community Support Services to Chronically Mentally Ill Persons," c. 1007, was ratified October 9, 1981; "An Act to Amend Article 3 of Chapter 122 of the General Statutes to Assure Continuity of Residential Care or Treatment for Persons with Mental Retardation," c. 1012, was ratified the same day. *N.C. Session Laws, 1981.*

¹⁵As an example, see "An Act to Appropriate Funds for an Area Senior Citizens' Center in Charlotte," ratified October 10. *N.C. Session Laws, 1981,* c. 1113.

¹⁶"On a hundred platforms, to half the voters of the State, in the late campaign, I pledged the State, its strength, its heart, its wealth, to universal education. I promised the illiterate poor man bound to a life of toil and struggle and poverty that life should be brighter for him and the partner of his sorrows and joys. I pledged the wealth of the State to the education of his children." R. D. W. Connor and Clarence Poe, *The Life and Speeches of Charles Brantley Aycock* (Garden City, N.Y.: Doubleday, Page & Company, 1912), 232, hereinafter cited as Connor and Poe, *Life and Speeches of Aycock.* Aycock (1859-1912) was governor of North Carolina from 1901 to 1905. Previously identified in Mitchell, *Addresses of Hunt,* I, 40n.

¹⁷H.B. 1281, "A Bill to be Entitled An Act to Reduce Class Size by One Pupil per Year for Four Years Starting in Fall 1983," was introduced June 19, 1981, and received an unfavorable report from the House Committee on Education. *Journal of the House of Representatives of North Carolina, 1981,* 835, 851, 951, hereinafter cited

as *N.C. House Journal, 1981. N.C. Session Laws, 1981*, c. 859, s. 29.9, designated "statutory class size maxima of 26 pupils in kindergarten-grade three, 33 pupils in grades 4-8, and 35 pupils in grades 9-12."

[18]"An Act to Make Students in the Department of Human Resources Institutions Eligible for Remediation Funds for Students Who Fail the Competency Test" was ratified April 13. *N.C. Session Laws, 1981*, c. 205.

[19]*N.C. Session Laws, 1981*, c. 859, s. 35.

[20]See Also "Community College Congress," May 16, 1981, and "Statement on Job Training," March 3, 1982, below.

[21]*N.C. Session Laws, 1981*, c. 859, ss. 37-39.1.

[22]The state legislature twice rejected the Equal Rights Amendment during Hunt's second administration, the first time in 1981, and again the following year. S.B. 102, "A Bill to Authorize a Statewide Referendum on the Equal Rights Amendment to the Constitution of the United States," was introduced February 10, 1981, and dispatched to the Senate Judiciary I Committee, while S.B. 173, "A Bill to Ratify the Proposed Equal Rights Amendment to the United States Constitution," introduced February 27, was referred to the Senate Constitutional Amendments Committee; neither offering reappeared. *Journal of the Senate of North Carolina, 1981*, 71, 118, hereinafter cited as *N.C. Senate Journal, 1981*. In 1982, H.B. 1452, "A Bill to be Entitled an Act to Ratify the Proposed Equal Rights Amendment to the United States Constitution," introduced June 3, was directed to the House Committee on Constitutional Amendments, where it died; a day later both S.B. 803, "A Bill to Ratify the Proposed Equal Rights Amendment to the United States Constitution," and S.B. 804, "A Bill to Ratify the Proposed Equal Rights Amendment to the United States Constitution," were introduced—the latter was declared "out of order" because it exactly duplicated the former, while S.B. 803 was tabled. *N.C. House Journal, 1981, Fourth Session, 1982*, 12, and *N.C. Senate Journal, 1981, Fourth Session, 1982*, 9, 10, 168; see also *News and Observer*, February 27, 28, 1981, and May 21, June 5, 1982, and "ERA Rally," June 6, 1982, below.

[23]"An Act for Equitable Distribution of Marital Property" was ratified July 3. *N.C. Session Laws, 1981*, c. 815.

[24]See "Special Message on Crime," February 2, 1981, below; jury legislation identified in footnote 3.

[25]Executive Order No. 17, signed in January, 1978, created the North Carolina Energy Institute. *N.C. Session Laws, 1977, Second Session, 1978*, 252-255. The North Carolina Alternative Energy Corporation was founded in 1980 after open hearings sponsored by the public utilities commission "indicated the need for an innovative, statewide program to encourage more widespread use of alternative energy technologies. The Commission proposed that all of the state's electrical power suppliers and distributors join to form a nonprofit corporation to fulfill this objective. . . ." *1980-1981 Energy Report, North Carolina Energy Policy Council* ([Raleigh]: Energy Division, North Carolina Department of Commerce, 1982), 20. See also, "Statement on Energy Conservation," November 18, 1982, below.

[26]"An Act to Provide Income Tax Credits for Expenditures for Various Alternative Energy Systems" was ratified July 10. *N.C. Session Laws, 1981*, c. 921.

[27]Varsol is an "aliphatic petroleum solvent." H. Bennett (ed.), *Concise Chemical and Technical Dictionary* (New York: Chemical Publishing Co., Inc., 1974), 1100.

[28]See "Governor's Waste Management Board," December 9, 1981, footnote 1, below.

[29]See "Address to the General Assembly on Highway Needs," April 28, 1981, below.

[30]See "Governor's Conference on Retention of Prime and Important Farm and Forest Land," December 17, 1981, footnote 1, below.

SPECIAL MESSAGE ON CRIME

FEBRUARY 2, 1981

[Governor Hunt repeated much of the following address at the National Restitution Conference, September 16, 1981.]

This is the third time I have come before this General Assembly to deliver a "Special Message on Crime."

During the last four years this legislature has responded, and it has led. You have given North Carolina new weapons in the war on crime:

—A law requiring speedy trials.
—A presumptive-sentencing law.
—Harsher penalties for drug smugglers.
—Mandatory prison terms for armed robbers.

And the people have responded. We have mobilized thousands of North Carolinians to fight crime in their communities and their neighborhoods by preventing it from happening in the first place. But, as these sheriffs and police chiefs seated in the gallery can tell you, we have a long way to go. The crime rate all over this country remains alarmingly high.

Some people say crime is inevitable and we are helpless to prevent it. I do not accept that notion.

I do not believe the people of our state have to be held hostage to terror. I do not believe we have to accept a situation where a family is not safe in its own home, where elderly citizens are afraid to walk on the streets, and where women cringe when they hear a knock at the door. Crime hurts people—the people least able to defend themselves—and we must not tolerate it.

In the last four years we have forged a more effective and more efficient system of criminal justice, but we must widen our war against crime and fight it on new fronts. We can't win that war in the police stations and the courtrooms and the prisons alone. Ultimately, it will be won or lost in the hearts and minds of our people—particularly our young people.

If we save our children, we can save society. If they turn to a life of delinquency and crime, we will lose. If they are guided to a lifetime of respect for the law, we will win. I come to you tonight to propose a strategy to save them and save our future.

Strengthening the System

That strategy builds on the foundation this General Assembly has laid the last four years. Because of the Speedy Trial Law this legislature passed, defendants now must be tried within 120 days. On October 1 that deadline goes down to 90 days.[1] The courts can be ready by then, and the budget I have proposed to you gives them further assistance. Swift punishment is essential to fighting crime, and I will oppose any effort to further delay that 90-day requirement.

Another change that will deter crime, the Fair Sentencing Act, is scheduled to take effect March 1. It reduces the discretion judges have in determining sentences—discretion that is far too great. I urge you to act within the next three weeks to enact simple amendments that would make the law work better.[2]

This year we should make further improvements in how our courts work. We must ensure fairness in selecting juries for criminal trials. I will propose legislation to guarantee that minorities are fairly represented on lists of potential jurors, and I will recommend legislation reducing the number of potential jurors lawyers can reject. In multidefendant trials jury selection often takes too long and costs too much. The Ike Atkinson drug trial in Goldsboro cost our taxpayers $239,352 in legal fees for defendants who claimed to be indigent. Of that figure, $194,676 went to lawyers who took three months to pick a jury.[3] That has to be stopped.

Later in this legislative session, our Courts Commission[4] will come forward with additional proposals to improve the effectiveness of the courts. They will include incentives for bright young attorneys to make careers of criminal prosecution, the decriminalization of minor traffic offenses, and streamlining criminal appeals.

I want to express my gratitude to Chief Justice Joseph Branch,[5] one of the truly outstanding jurists in this nation, for his leadership in bringing about a more efficient administration of justice in North Carolina. He deserves our thanks. I encourage senior resident superior court judges to follow his example. They should meet regularly with court personnel, law enforcement officers, district attorneys, and trial lawyers. These meetings can greatly improve the flow of criminal cases and increase public confidence that the entire system is focusing on reducing crime and using tax money wisely.

Just as we should strengthen our criminal justice system, we should strengthen our laws against crime. We must intensify our efforts against organized and white-collar crime. I urge you to enact a racketeer influenced and corrupt organizations law modeled after the federal statute, and I join with Attorney General Rufus Edmisten in recommending legislation that will make bid rigging on any state contract a felony. We have seen North Carolina's good name besmirched by those who have defrauded the state and cheated the taxpayers. As governor, I intend to see that we punish those who have done wrong and recover the taxpayers' money. The law we propose would make the penalties for that extremely severe. This legislature can pass the strictest law in the country to make sure that it never happens again.[6]

We should make other laws stronger. As part of the Fair Sentencing Act, I will propose longer sentences for habitual felons. I also believe a person who commits a crime while out on bail should face consecutive, not concurrent, sentences. I agree with the district attorneys of this state that those who plan a crime and solicit someone else to carry it out should be subject to the same penalties as those who commit the crime. And we need to remove the provision in criminal law that prohibits spouses from testifying against each other. We shouldn't force such testimony, but neither should we prohibit it.[7]

Many of the proposals I have talked about tonight are the work of the Governor's Crime Commission. That commission is charged by law with officially planning our state's fight against crime.[8] I am committed to keeping it working, despite the loss of federal funds from the Law Enforcement Assistance Administration that it has relied on. LEAA money has helped local law enforcement agencies modernize and try innovative programs. Just as soon as resources permit, we should provide state crime-control grants to help local governments strengthen their law enforcement.

Victim Protection and Assistance

The constitutional rights of the accused must always be protected, but I believe the rights of innocent victims should weigh more heavily on the scales of justice. We should require criminals to pay more restitution to their victims for the losses and injuries they cause. I believe that over the next four years we can double the amount of restitution being paid. I urge judges to require it in every possible instance.

Restitution should be made the *first* priority among payments made by a convicted defendant. The least we can do is pay the poor victim first—before state costs, before court costs, before lawyers' fees, before anything else. I urge you to require that by law.[9]

Whenever we can, we should make the criminal pay restitution to the victim. But it is also time to consider using state funds to help the victim pay for his losses and making the criminal reimburse the state later, and the people we shall start helping right away are the victims of rape. I find it unconscionable that our system requires a rape victim to undergo an immediate and often humiliating physical examination—and then makes her pay for it. We can find the money to do it, and we are going to begin paying for those examinations.[10] And we are going to make the convicted rapists repay the state in full.

We must also extend greater protection to elderly citizens—the people who suffer most from the mental, physical, and financial injury inflicted by criminals. I support legislation that would make it a felony to commit any assault and battery on a person over sixty years of age. I also recommend that judges consider giving longer sentences to criminals who attack elderly victims.[11] Let the word go forth from this governor and this General Assembly: "Friend, if you lay a hand on an elderly person in this state, we're going to throw the book at you."

Citizen Involvement

We can't hire enough policemen and we can't pass enough laws to eliminate crime. We can make a dramatic difference only if we enlist our people—people who care and are willing to volunteer their time and energy to the war against crime.

Community Watch is a proven deterrent to crime. Three years ago, the Van Story Hills area in Cumberland County had ninety-six break-ins. Last year, after residents organized a Community Watch, they had only six. In Buncombe County the 22,000 people who were part of Community Watch have had only six break-ins the last four years. We now have more than 6,500 Community Watch programs operating across North Carolina. Our goal is to double that by 1985.

I believe in Community Watch. I belong. I have Community Watch signs at my farm and at the mansion.

We also have to reach young people. We have to teach them the value of the law—how it holds our society together; how it protects us from a tyranny of terror. We are working now to take educational programs on crime and our system of justice to more than one and a half million youngsters in Scouts, 4-H clubs, and other organizations across North Carolina. And their sharp eyes and ears can be weapons against crime.[12]

Preventing Juvenile Crime [13]

Those young people are where our war against crime will be won or lost. All of the approaches that I have discussed are important, but a commitment to keeping young people out of crime can do more than all the rest put together.

That commitment should start in the public schools. If you doubt it, take note of the fact that 80 percent of the people in prison in North Carolina are dropouts. As we teach children to read, to do math, to get a good job, to become responsible—we prevent crime. That underscores how important it is for you to approve the reductions in class size and other educational programs that I proposed in my "State of the State Address."

When students misbehave, we should use in-school suspension. They should not be given the freedom of the streets. They should be put in a closely supervised classroom, forbidden to talk, and required to study every minute.

For too many young people drug use is the door to a life of crime.

Many steal or become prostitutes to support their habits. Others become pushers themselves. This legislature has provided more SBI agents to attack this problem and enacted jail terms of up to fifty years for drug smugglers. But we should now take another step. I believe people who purvey drug paraphernalia, trying to popularize drug use among young people, are parasites on society. I ask you to pass a tough drug paraphernalia law that will pass constitutional muster and put every head shop in North Carolina out of business.[14]

For those youngsters who get into trouble, I will work hard to develop community-based alternatives to incarceration and better treatment for severe emotional disturbances.[15]

Let me talk to you now about what I believe is the most important idea to prevent crime that I have ever discussed with this legislature.

Over the last two years I have led the National Governors' Association's search for the best ways to prevent crime. I believe we have found it, and I intend to devote my crime-fighting efforts to this cause. It is the matching up of caring adult volunteers with young people who either have committed their first crime or appear headed for it. Right then, *before* they become criminals, we have got to help them.

The help they need is a real friend, someone who will spend time with them, help them work out their problems, encourage their school work, help them develop self-esteem, and help them get a job if they want to work. They often come from broken homes. Many were abused children. Most of them never had a chance. They need someone who will do what a good parent does.

Probation and parole officers work with hundreds of young people in trouble. District court judges and court counselors see dozens come before them. They know what kind of help these kids need, and they know they're not getting enough.

So what are we going to do about it? I suggest that thousands of us can do something about it by volunteering to help a kid who needs help. Yes, it would take some time—as much time as some of us spend each week running or watching a couple of basketball games.

It's not easy to know how to do that. Most people don't feel right just walking into the courthouse and searching for somebody to tell them how to help. That is where those of us in the executive and judicial branches can help. We can show local people how to organize a good, sound program that will match up an adult with a young person and give both of them the support they will need in the months and years ahead. That means pulling together support from citizens, judges, court counselors, and educators.

This approach is being tried by the Volunteers to the Court program in Hertford and Guilford counties and the Partners program in Wake County. Across the nation, whatever you call it—

"Partners," "Friends," "Big Brother/Big Sister"—it works, if it's done right. To help us, I have recruited the man who established the "Friends" program in Concord, New Hampshire, perhaps the most successful program in the country.[16] In that program the adult volunteers and youngsters spend an average of eleven hours per week together. How many of us spend that much time with our own children?

Our goal will be to establish a program like that in each of our 100 counties over the next four years. We will strive to match up every single youngster in trouble with the law with an adult who will love him and help him become a law-abiding and useful citizen.

This is not a government program. Very little, if any, state money will be involved in it, and I ask you for none tonight. Rather, it is a people program. It will need an outpouring of help from the churches of our state, the Jaycees, and other helping groups. I appeal to the good citizens of our state to join in this statewide crusade.

These young people, and this approach to crime prevention, require leadership at the highest level. One of the great problems we face in helping them is a fragmentation of services. Many agencies and many people work with youngsters—the schools, the courts, law enforcement officers, training schools, mental institutions. We at the state level need to pull all of these together into a working team.

I am announcing to you tonight the formation of the Governor's Executive Cabinet on Juveniles. I will personally chair this group, and it will meet monthly. I have asked the chief justice, the attorney general, the superintendent of public instruction, the secretary of human resources, the secretary of correction, the secretary of crime control and public safety, the chairman of the Crime Commission, and the chairman of the Courts Commission to serve on it.

It will be our responsibility to sit down together every month and take a hard look at how good a job the agencies under us are doing. And to get citizens involved. If we aren't satisfied—and we should never be satisfied—each of us will be responsible for going back and talking to the people, whoever they may be, who can make a difference. We will use all the powers we have—hiring and firing, the budget, and just plain persuasion—to see that we do a better job.

Conclusion

I would conclude my message tonight by making this appeal to the people of North Carolina: I appeal to you to learn what you can do for the young people in your communities. I appeal to you to volunteer to develop a one-on-one relationship that will save a kid and bring more meaning to your own life. Love and caring can do more to prevent crime than jails and courtrooms.

If we lose our war against crime, the blame would not rest on the law enforcement officers here tonight, or thousands more working across our state, or the judges or the district attorneys. The blame would rest on all of us who fail to act and fail to help.

The right to be safe is fundamental in our society. It carries with it a responsibility, a responsibility to be involved and to help bring about justice:

—Justice for the victim, in the form of comfort and assistance.

—Justice for the youngster headed wrong, guidance and understanding.

—Justice for the criminal, swift and sure.

I ask the people of North Carolina: What will you do to bring about justice? You can save someone's life. You can give them a future. You can make a difference, and, in doing so, you can make North Carolina a safer place to live—for you, for your family, for your neighbors, for 5,800,000 people.

Two weeks ago I proposed a strategy for North Carolina's future. I said we can build our economy and provide greater opportunities for every single person, and I said we could help our people become successful citizens. But we cannot walk into that bright future if we cannot walk safely on our streets. We cannot dream great dreams if our children turn to drugs and stealing as a way of life. We cannot let criminals tear down what we build. Let us resolve tonight, all of us, to guarantee for all North Carolinians the most important freedom: the freedom from fear.

---

[1]Speedy trial legislation previously identified in Mitchell, *Addresses of Hunt*, I, 24n. See also, "An Act to Amend the Speedy Trial Law," c. 626, ratified June 19, and "An Act to Make Technical Corrections to Chapter 626 of the 1981 Session Laws and Speedy Trial Law," c. 902, ratified July 9. *N.C. Session Laws, 1981.*

[2]Mitchell identified fair sentencing legislation in *Addresses of Hunt*, I, 54n, 716n; it is the "presumptive sentencing law" containing "[m]andatory prison terms for armed robbers" Hunt mentioned earlier. See also, "An Act to Delay the Effective Date of the Fair Sentencing Act," c. 63, ratified February 27 (whereby implementation was postponed from March 1 to April 15, 1981); "An Act to Amend the Fair Sentencing Act, as Amended in 1980," c. 179, ratified April 6; "An Act to Change the Classification for Second Degree Murder and Change the Maximum Sentence for Class C Felonies," c. 662, ratified June 23; "An Act to Increase the Punishment for Stealing Horses, Mules, Swine, and Cattle," c. 664, ratified June 24; and "An Act to Amend the Fair Sentencing Act of 1981 to Make Sale or Delivery of a Controlled Substance to a Minor an Aggravating Factor," c. 889, ratified July 9, 1981. *N.C. Session Laws, 1981.*

[3]See "An Act to Amend G.S. Chapter 9 to Facilitate the Juror Selection Process," c. 430, ratified May 21, and "An Act to Substitute Lists of Licensed Drivers for Taxpayers as a Source of Names for Jury Lists," c. 720, ratified June 29, 1981. *N.C. Session Laws, 1981.*

There is a discrepancy between the length of time the governor states jury selection for the Atkinson trial required and that reported in the *News and Observer*, January 19, 1979, the tabloid stating the process lasted three weeks. As a result of pretrial publicity in Wayne, nearly 500 potential jurors were bused to Goldsboro from

Nash County; the considerable number was necessary because "each of nine defendants has separate counsel and the right to dismiss six jurors without citing any reason. District Attorney Donald M. Jacobs has an equal number of challenges, for a total of 108." Leslie (Ike) Atkinson received a twelve- to twenty-year jail sentence for operating a heroin trafficking ring, from his cell, while serving a forty-four-year term for drug smuggling. *New and Observer*, January 6, 7, 10, 12, 19, and 20, 1979.

[4] Ratified June 8, "An Act to Re-create the North Carolina Courts Commission" became effective July 1, 1979. *N.C. Session Laws, 1979*, c. 1077; see also Mitchell, *Addresses of Hunt*, I, 52.

[5] Joseph Branch (1915-   ), North Carolina Supreme Court chief justice, 1979-1986. Previously identified in Mitchell, *Addresses of Hunt*, I, 568n.

[6] The federal legislation to which the governor referred, "Title IX—Racketeer Influenced and Corrupt Organizations," 84 Stat. 941, c. 96, was ratified October 15, 1970. H.B. 121, "A Bill to be Entitled An Act Creating a Racketeer Influenced and Corrupt Organizations Act for North Carolina," was sent February 3, 1981, to the Committee on Judiciary No. 1; it received an indefinite postponement report July 2. *Journal of the House of Representatives of North Carolina, 1981*, 65, 992, hereinafter cited as *N.C. House Journal, 1981*.

Rufus Ligh Edmisten (1941-   ), was state attorney general, 1975-1985, and also the Democratic nominee for governor in 1984. He lost to Republican James G. Martin. Previously identified in Mitchell, *Addresses of Hunt*, I, 82n; see also *News and Observer*, November 7, 1984.

"An Act to Regulate Contractors, Subcontractors, and Suppliers in Dealing with Governmental Agencies, and to Make Restraint of Trade a Felony" was ratified April 6, 1981. *N.C. Session Laws, 1981*, c. 764.

[7] *N.C. Session Laws, 1981*, c. 179, s. 13. H.B. 117, "A Bill to be Entitled An Act to Establish Consecutive Sentences for Convicted Offenders of Crimes Committed while on Pretrial Release," was introduced February 13, 1981, and referred to committee; it was awarded an indefinite postponement report on May 15. *N.C. House Journal, 1981*, 64, 586.

"An Act to Abolish the Distinction between Accessories Before the Fact and Principals and to Make Accessories Before the Fact Punishable as Principal Felons" was ratified June 25. *N.C. Session Laws, 1981*, c. 686.

H.B. 372, "A Bill to be Entitled An Act to Allow a Spouse to Testify Against the Other Spouse if He or She Desires to Do So," was introduced March 5, 1981; action thereon was postponed indefinitely July 2. *N.C. House Journal, 1981*, 167, 992. "An Act to Permit a Spouse to Give Testimony in a Paternity Action," *N.C. Session Laws, 1981*, c. 634, was ratified October 1.

[8] "An Act to Establish the Governor's Crime Commission Amending and Rewriting G.S. 143B-337 and Renaming, Restructuring and Redefining the Purposes of the Governor's Law and Order Commission" was ratified February 15. *N.C. Session Laws, 1977*, c. 11.

[9] G.S. 7A-304(d) was amended to make restitution the fourth priority among the court-imposed financial obligations of a convicted defendant. See "An Act to Establish Priorities and Procedures for the Disbursement of Funds by Clerks of Court," *N.C. Session Laws, 1981*, c. 959, ratified July 10.

[10] "An Act to Provide Assistance for Victims of Rape and Sex Offenses" was ratified July 10. *N.C. Session Laws, 1981*, c. 931.

[11] Age and physical and mental infirmity were made aggravating factors in sentencing under c. 179, s. 1, *N.C. Session Laws, 1981*.

H.B. 71, "A Bill to be Entitled An Act to Make Abuse of or Injury to An Elderly Person a Felony," was introduced January 27 and referred to the Committee on Aging. It was never reported out of committee. *N.C. House Journal, 1981*, 46.

[12] Governor Hunt announced on April 16, 1981, the "Preparedness Through Prevention" program, a collaboration between state Boy Scout councils and the Department of Crime Control and Public Safety that he hoped would involve over 85,000 Scouts and become a national model for similar campaigns; he also

acknowledged in the same speech the participation of 20,000 Girl Scouts in a separate anti-crime effort. On July 23, 1981, Hunt praised North Carolina 4-H members who took part in Operation I.D. and cited their crime-prevention activities in Stokes, Alleghany, Davie, Alamance, and Union counties.

   [13] Points covered under this heading were also featured in the governor's addresses before the North Carolina Conference on Delinquency Prevention, February 5, 1981; North Carolina Jaycees Luncheon, February 7, 1981; Eastern Regional Conference on Delinquency Prevention, April 24, 1981; Christian Church in North Carolina, April 24, 1981; North Carolina Annual Conference, United Methodist Church, June 8, 1981; the National Association of Volunteers in Criminal Justice, October 12, 1981; and the joint meeting of the Baptist State Convention of North Carolina and the General Baptist State Convention, November 2, 1981.

   [14] "An Act to Control Trafficking in Certain Controlled Substances," *N.C. Session Laws, 1979, Second Session, 1980*, c. 1251, ratified June 25, 1980, lists punishment for drug-related offenses. "An Act to Prohibit the Manufacture, Delivery, Sale, Possession, and Use of Drug Paraphernalia," c. 500, was ratified June 4, 1981, and modified by c. 903, "An Act to Make a Technical Amendment in Chapter 500 of the 1981 Session Laws," ratified July 9. *N.C. Session Laws, 1981*.

   [15] "An Act to Appropriate Funds for Community-Based Alternative Programs for Juveniles" was ratified October 10. *N.C. Session Laws, 1981*, c. 1065.

   [16] Richard G. Maxson (1942-   ), native of Syracuse, New York; resident of Post Mills, Vermont; M. Ed., Antioch University; J.D., University of Denver; advanced graduate studies, Dartmouth College, since 1983. Clerk, U.S. District Court, 1974, and founder, director, Friends Program, Inc., 1974-1980, in Concord, New Hampshire; Governor Hunt's special assistant for juvenile affairs, 1980-1983. Richard G. Maxson to Jan-Michael Poff, May 7, 1984; see also "Friends: A Deceptively Simple Concept That Works," *New Hampshire Times* (Concord), March 16-22, 1977.

ADDRESS TO THE GENERAL ASSEMBLY ON HIGHWAY NEEDS

APRIL 28, 1981

[This appeal is similar to one televised statewide, April 27, 1981, in which the governor explained the need for, and sources of, additional highway maintenance and construction funds.]

   Last night I went on statewide television to talk with the people of North Carolina about our roads—and our future. My speech to you today will not be a rerun.

   You have been in session for more than three months. You know what the problem is. Today I want to explain my proposal to you— how I propose we obtain additional revenues and how I plan to assure the wise and efficient use of that money. But, more than that, I want to talk to you about the responsibility that you and I have together—to act, to face up to this problem, and to do what has to be done for North Carolina's future.

   When I delivered my "State of the State Address" to you in January, I said that we should begin our deliberations with this question: What can we do this year, as governor and as members of the General Assembly, to help North Carolinians in a time of economic hardship? That is the question here today.

I also said then that our agenda this year should be opening the doors of economic opportunity to all North Carolinians and making it possible for everyone who lives in this state to earn a good living and provide adequately for their families. That is our agenda here today.

If we fail to act responsibly this year to protect our investment in our roads and highways, we have failed in our responsibility, and North Carolinians will pay the price for years to come. They will pay the price in lost industry, lost jobs, lost income, lost opportunities. They will pay the price in lost travel business—an industry that brought our people $2.3 billion in income last year. They will pay the price in damage to their own cars and trucks and in higher repair bills. Worst of all, they will pay the price in human beings killed and maimed on the highways.

That is the price the people will pay if we fail them this year. We must not fail them.

Over the years North Carolina has built the reputation as "the Good Roads State," and for good reason. But it wasn't always that way. At the turn of the century Governor Glenn said that North Carolina's greatest handicaps were ignorance and muddy roads.[1]

We pulled our state out of ignorance by building a strong system of public schools, community colleges, and great universities. And we pulled our state out of the mud by building 76,000 miles of roads and highways—enough to circle the Earth at the equator three times. It's the largest state road system in the nation. Many states pay part of their road costs through county property taxes. But we built and we maintain our roads totally through state revenues, primarily from the gasoline tax. And we have built our economy on those 76,000 miles of roads.

Without those roads and highways we could not have enjoyed the record economic growth of recent years—the $8 billion worth of industrial investment announced in the last four years and the 120,000 new manufacturing jobs. Good roads helped us attract Philip Morris to Cabarrus County, Campbell Soup to Robeson County, IBM to Charlotte, Rockwell to Henderson County, GKN plants to Lee and Alamance counties, General Electric to the Research Triangle, and Cummins-Case to Nash County.

We cannot afford to lose the competitive edge our roads give us. We see what has happened in our nation's Northeast, where the roads are crumbling and where industries are closing down and moving away—many of them are coming here. North Carolina cannot afford to go down that same road; that is why the decision we make this year will be critical.

Our roads and highways are in good shape today, because we've done a good job keeping them up in the past. But we're just starting to see and feel the cracks, the little holes that become big potholes, and the crumbling shoulders.

For more than a year our situation was studied by the Blue Ribbon Commission chaired by former Governor and Supreme Court Justice Dan K. Moore. I urge you to read their report carefully.[2] His commission found that our highway revenues have been going down recently about 5 percent a year, while the cost of maintenance and construction has gone up as high as 20 percent a year.

The result? We have fallen behind on our resurfacing. Governor Moore's commission concluded that we need to resurface at least 2,600 miles each year to keep up with normal wear and tear. In recent years we have been doing 1,300 miles. This year we can only afford to do 740 miles. So, when his commission completed its work, Governor Moore wrote in an open letter to all North Carolinians that "we must make a major investment in resurfacing and maintaining our highways or we will face a major and unprecedented expense of highway rebuilding in the near future."[3]

The Moore commission, which included members of this General Assembly, did an excellent job. I am guided largely by their thorough and expert findings.

What I recommend to you today is a *minimum* program—one required of us as good stewards. If we do act this year, we will face a difficult choice between stopping *all* construction on projects in the Seven-Year Plan or falling farther and farther behind on maintenance, leading ultimately to the ruin of our system. Here is what I suggest we do:

First, we need an additional $247 million over the biennium to return to a regular resurfacing schedule of 2,600 miles a year and to catch up on what we haven't been able to do in recent years. To catch up, we need to do an extra 1,000 miles each of the next five years.

Second, we must replace or repair many bridges. More than half of our 16,000 bridges today cannot support the legal weight. More than 4,000 cannot support the weight of a loaded school bus.

Third, we need an additional $18 million to match our share of federal aid funds for the construction of essential primary highways. North Carolina used to be a "donor" state, sending more gas-tax dollars to Washington than it got back. We have reversed that situation in the last four years, and now we get back more than we put in. We must continue to get our fair share.

Fourth, we need an additional $93 million for some badly needed improvements on some smaller roads and for access roads to new industry. Without some safety improvements, certain roads in our state will continue to cause accidents, injuries, and deaths.

Fifth, we must provide adequate support to our airports, bus systems, and ferries. They are all a part of our modern transportation system.

We will provide $40 million for the cities, $11 million more than they are now receiving. An equal amount will be earmarked for secondary roads.

That minimum program will require a little over $200 million in revenue next year. But, before I ask you to provide that revenue and before we ask our people to pay it, we must give them a guarantee.

It is apparent that the taxpayers of this state have been cheated for decades by bid rigging. Those involved are being indicted, prosecuted, and punished. We will fire any state employee who was involved. But we need stronger laws to prevent it from ever happening again.

Earlier this year the attorney general and I proposed legislation that would give North Carolina one of the toughest laws in the nation against bid rigging. This law would make bid rigging of any kind a felony, punishable by ten years in prison. It would prohibit state employees from receiving anything of value from anyone doing business with the state. It's tough, and it's right, and I urge you to pass it just as soon as possible.[4]

Now here is how I recommend we obtain the revenue we need. The first source of that money should be savings in the operation of the Department of Transportation. This General Assembly's Select Committee on Transportation has made many good suggestions, and I appreciate their work.

That department and Secretary Tom Bradshaw have already made changes over the past four years that are saving the taxpayers of this state millions of dollars each year:

—The Department of Transportation has 1,000 fewer positions than it did four years ago and that saves $14.5 million each year.

—The department has 4,000 fewer pieces of equipment than it did four years ago.

—And the department is burning three million gallons of gasoline less each year.

That is a good record, but we need to do more. I have directed the department to take a number of additional new steps. The Board of Transportation will reevaluate the need for every project in the Seven-Year Plan that is not already new construction. Medians and right-of-way will be narrower. We will double the number of prisoners working on the roads. We will reduce the number of people in state maintenance crews. I believe these steps can save $20 million.

I also recommend that you put revenues from the sales tax on automobile parts and accessories into the Highway Fund. That will give us $59 million. To replace that money in the General Fund, I will recommend a 50 percent increase in the tax on alcoholic beverages, a severance tax on minerals mined in our state, and a sales tax on vacation homes that are rented out for less than ninety days.

Trucks should be paying more, and I recommend that you increase their license costs and impose a special charge on overweight and oversized loads. We have a great trucking industry in North Carolina, and I know they expect to pay their fair share. This would give us $16.9 million.

I recommend that you increase the cost of drivers' licenses, which are renewed only every four years, to $10.00 and the cost of chauffeurs' licenses to $15.00. This would give us $14.5 million. I recommend that you increase various miscellaneous fees in the Division of Motor Vehicles. This will give us $7.4 million.

I recommend that you obtain the remaining $90 million that we need by increasing the gasoline tax by 3 cents per gallon.[5] But, as I said in my address to the people last night, I recommend that you do it in a way that will not increase the cost of living for the average North Carolinian but will put the burden on those who use the roads the most.

I propose that we allow an income tax credit for the 3 cents extra paid up to a maximum of 750 gallons of gasoline for necessary personal driving. Those 750 gallons, in a car that gets sixteen miles per gallon, would take you 12,000 miles. That is about what the average family drives in a year, for going to work, taking kids to school, and shopping. By filling out a simple form on their income taxes, people could claim a credit of up to $22.50—the same amount this tax increase would cost them at the pump each year.[6]

I want to commend Senator Kenneth Royall[7] for developing this approach. It meets the twin objectives of providing additional highway revenue and putting the burden on trucks, business vehicles, and out-of-state travelers. I think this approach is reasonable, fair, and affordable. It is consistent with this General Assembly's concern not to raise the cost of living for the average taxpayer. In fact, in 1979 you provided a tax cut for our people by increasing all exemptions and the standard deduction on state income taxes by 10 percent and increasing dependents exemptions from $600 to $800 each. During the eight years that I have had the privilege of working with you as lieutenant governor and governor, this General Assembly has passed no tax increases.

This minimum package of revenues for our roads is also appropriate in a year of lean budgets and spending restraints which you have worked on so hard. You have already cut the continuation budget after close and careful scrutiny, and the expansion budget which I recommended to you for next year does something that not even President Reagan proposes to do in Washington: It actually reduces the number state employees.

The operations of the Department of Transportation must reflect that same hard-nosed approach to efficiency. In addition to the items of savings that I mentioned earlier, there are other good recommendations in the twenty-nine-point report prepared by the select committee of the General Assembly which studied the Department of Transportation. Others have come from the appropriations committees. We are beginning to implement some of them already, and I promise you that we will carry through every single one of them from which real savings and better management can emerge. And I will devote more of my time as governor in helping see that that massive department does even more to operate efficiently.

In particular, we will make an all-out effort to do two things: first, to see that work crews doing maintenance or construction contain the minimum number of personnel needed and that all of them are working. Second, to get every prisoner in our system that we possibly can "working on the roads." They will have to be identified, and we must take adequate security precautions, but I don't want a single idle prisoner in the corrections system of North Carolina on any day when it is possible to have him working on the roads—for his benefit and to help pay his debt to society.

This year I have not presented you with a lengthy legislative program, but I have proposed—and you have proposed as members of this General Assembly—legislation that is critical for North Carolina's economic future. And it all fits together: legislation that affects taxes and our business climate, funds for better technical education and to prevent dropouts, encouragement for energy conservation and alternatives, safe management of hazardous wastes, high-technology research and development. But money to keep our good road system is the most important step we will take by far.

The *Wall Street Journal* recently surveyed 1,200 experts across the nation who are involved in the location of industrial plants. That newspaper asked them to rank the importance of various factors in site selection. "Highway Transportation Facilities" ranked *third*, behind only the availability of labor and a reliable energy supply.[8]

You and I are fortunate to be leading North Carolina, together, at a time I believe is one of the best in our history. The magazine, *Nation's Business*, recently cited North Carolina as one of the top three states in America in which for industry to locate.[9] I believe we can be "Number One." What we do this year on our roads will determine that more than anything else.

Over many decades this General Assembly has had two great hallmarks: a commitment to fiscal responsibility, and a commitment to economic growth. I ask you to reaffirm that commitment this year, by protecting our investment in North Carolina's highways and North Carolina's future.

---

[1] North Carolina became known as the "Good Roads State" as the result of an "unprecedented" highway construction program begun during the administration of Governor Cameron Morrison, 1921-1925. Hugh Talmage Lefler and Albert Ray

Newsome, *North Carolina: The History of a Southern State* (Chapel Hill: University of North Carolina Press, third edition, 1973), 600.

Robert Brodnax Glenn (1854-1920), native of Rockingham County; attended Davidson College and the University of Virginia. Attorney; state representative from Stokes, 1881, and senator from Forsyth, 1899-1900; governor, 1905-1909. Crabtree, *North Carolina Governors*, 113-114. Cheney, *North Carolina Government*, 423, 461, 477. Glenn once remarked, " '[M]ud and illiteracy lay the highest tax on the State,' and he declared that as Aycock should be known as the Education Governor, he desired to stand in history as the apostle of better roads." Samuel A'Court Ashe, *History of North Carolina* (Raleigh: Edwards and Broughton Printing Company, 2 volumes, 1925; Spartanburg, S.C.: The Reprint Company, 1971), II, 1229.

²Daniel Killian Moore (1906-1986), North Carolina governor, 1965-1969. Previously identified in Mitchell, *Addresses of Hunt*, I, 39n. Hunt established the thirty-four member North Carolina Transportation Study Commission on July 31, 1979. Executive Order No. 37, *N.C. Session Laws, 1979*, 1507-1509. *Report of Governor's Blue Ribbon Study Commission on Transportation Needs and Financing* ([Raleigh]: N.p., [1981]), 18-20, hereinafter cited as *Report of Governor's Blue Ribbon Commission on Transportation*, proposed three funding options to generate additional revenue.

³*Report of Governor's Blue Ribbon Commission on Transportation*, ii.

⁴For legislation on bid rigging, see "Special Message on Crime," February 2, 1981, footnote 6, above. Governor Hunt explained more fully the salient points of this bill in a news conference held January 30, 1981.

⁵"An Act to Increase the Gasoline Tax, the Special Fuels Tax, and the Tax on Carriers Using Fuels Purchased Outside the State; to Increase Powell Bill Funds for Municipalities; to Provide for Construction of Secondary Roads; to Transfer Sales and Use Taxes on Motor Vehicle Parts, Accessories and Lubricants to the Highway Fund; to Increase Motor Vehicles Fees; to Increase the Registration Fees on Property Hauling Vehicles; and to Establish Fees for Oversize and Overweight Vehicles" was ratified June 26. *N.C. Session Laws, 1981*, c. 690.

⁶House members determined that the rebate, if enacted, would come to less than $5.00 per driver and therefore did not include the governor's proposed state income tax credit in the final draft of the legislation. *Charlotte Observer*, June 26, 1981.

⁷Kenneth Claiborne Royall, Jr. (1918-   ), state senator and majority leader since 1973. *North Carolina Manual, 1983* (Raleigh: State of North Carolina [issued biennially 1903 to present]), 207, hereinafter cited as *North Carolina Manual*; also previously identified in Mitchell, *Addresses of Hunt*, I, 261n.

⁸*Wall Street* (New York City) *Journal*, March 11, 1980, hereinafter cited as *Wall Street Journal*.

⁹"Corporations: South Most Inviting to Manufacturers," *Nation's Business*, April, 1981, 22.

STATE OF THE STATE ADDRESS

JANUARY 17, 1983

This is the fourth "State of the State Address" I have had the honor of delivering to this General Assembly. To all of you in the chamber, and to all the people of North Carolina, I thank you humbly and sincerely for granting me this opportunity to serve you. My family and I give thanks for all that this state has given us. Truly, North Carolina is blessed by God.

As I have done each time before, I come before you tonight to report what we in North Carolina have done—and what we have yet to do. I come before you to affirm my faith that our best days are not behind us, but ahead of us. I come before you to challenge those who say that our economy is doomed to failure and that our system of government is flawed and outdated and inadequate to the challenges we face, who even say that government itself is the problem. My friends, I do not accept that, and North Carolina deserves better than that!

I come before you to proclaim my belief that the limits on our financial resources do not mean that we have to limit our vision, our dreams, and our aspirations for North Carolina. There are no limits on what we can do, if we do it together. A tight budget is no excuse for wringing of hands, for inaction. To the contrary, the conditions that prevail today *demand* action. We must act, and we must lead!

We don't have to have more money to do what we need to do in North Carolina. We can continue to cut out fat and waste. We can get our priorities in order. We can use what we already have better, and we *can* meet our responsibilities to the people of North Carolina!

You members of the General Assembly come from communities in every corner of our state. You know what is happening to the nearly six million people who live here. As we meet tonight, the cold winds of a national economic recession are blowing through nearly every home in North Carolina. One in ten of our people is out of work. Farms, factories, and small businesses face bankruptcy. Layoffs and loss of income threaten thousands of families. One in every three working families can hardly keep a roof over its head, clothes on the kids, and food on the table. Older people worry about living in decency and with dignity. Their fears and their anxieties must be our agenda this year.

The people of North Carolina need good jobs. They need good paychecks. Their children need a good education. You and I were elected by those people. We have a responsibility to them. It is our duty this year to work for them—cooperatively, compassionately, and courageously. We must help them! I welcome that responsibility, and I welcome the opportunity to work with you on their behalf.

This year, I will submit to you a legislative program that is limited in length, but unlimited in hope for the future. It is based on a careful strategy of investing in education and economic growth, in more jobs and better schools. That is the strategy North Carolina must have to meet the challenges that will confront us in the next two years, the next two decades, and the next century. We can meet those challenges, and we must get to work doing it!

Those challenges come clearly into focus in the report of the North Carolina 2000 project.[1] That effort, chaired brilliantly by President Bill Friday, brought more than 100,000 North Carolinians into the process of planning for tomorrow—a tomorrow that re-

quires strong action to promise a secure economic future, provide
educational opportunities, preserve our communities, and protect
our natural resources. North Carolina has made a commitment to
follow that path to the year 2000, and beyond.

That path has already led us to a national and international
reputation as one of the best places in the nation to live, work, and
do business. It has strengthened and broadened our economy. It has
helped us attract 177,709 new jobs in manufacturing in the past six
years. It has helped us withstand the recession better than other
states. In the 1974-1975 recession our unemployment rate exceeded
the nation's by almost 3 percent. In this recession, fewer people have
lost their jobs in North Carolina than across the rest of the nation,
and we have had 20 percent fewer people out of work than our
neighboring states.

When I travel outside our state, people ask about our universities,
our community college system, our public schools, our North Carolina School of Science and Mathematics, our Research Triangle
Park, and our Microelectronics Center. They ask me, "How does
North Carolina do it?" And I tell them: "Our strategy is to invest in
education and economic growth."

The program I will submit to you will continue that strategy. It is
a program and a strategy that will keep North Carolina moving.

I will propose that you strengthen instruction in our public
schools in science and mathematics and in writing. I will propose
that you strengthen the capacity of our community college system
to teach young people job skills and to retrain adults in new skills.

I will propose that you continue North Carolina's leadership
in attracting the high-technology industries that will create the
greatest number of jobs: electronics, computers, information processing—all of them based on microelectronics technology.

I will also propose, in a "Special Message on Crime," that you
give our people tough protections against the drunk driver. I hope
that the "Safe Roads Act" will be your first order of business. We
must get the drinking driver off the road![2]

The recommended budget that I will submit to you tomorrow will
be the most austere North Carolina has seen in a decade. It will
contain only one expansion item: The people who work for North
Carolina, who educate our children, who help our sick and aged,
who keep our roads safe, do a *good* job. They have paid the price for
the recession of this year. They *deserve* a fair pay raise! Before you
conclude this legislative session, I hope the economy will have
turned up enough to provide each of them an across-the-board
increase.[3]

But even with the tight budget I will present to you, I urge you to
be positive in your consideration and enact what I think should be
the top priority of this legislature: lifting the salary freeze for

teachers and state employees.[4] They also deserve all the help we can
afford to give them in other ways:

—Like giving teachers a duty-free lunch period, a few minutes for
them to refresh themselves and prepare for the afternoon classes.[5]

—Like increasing the travel allowance for state employees.[6] This
year, to help us get through this budget shortfall, they have worked
harder, they have worked longer hours, and they have stretched
everything a little farther.

Since the time this legislature adjourned last year, our revenues
have fallen short of estimates by nearly $150 million because of the
lingering national recession. But we have managed that shortfall in
a way that has avoided the hardships and disruptions that states
across this country have suffered. Michigan had to cut 10,000
employees off the payroll, shut down state government for six days,
and cut salaries by 5 percent. The new governor[7] there has just
ordered that the public schools' budget be cut by $500 million. Idaho
had to put its state employees on a four-day work week, cutting pay
by 20 percent. In Minnesota, the legislature had to raise taxes and
cut out programs to meet a $300 million shortfall. In Colorado, the
state police are laying off almost 10 percent of the force and cutting
out some late-night patrols. In California, the state had to borrow
$400 million from the Bank of America to help meet a deficit of
more than $1 billion.

When we in North Carolina saw what was coming last year—
that revenues might fall short—we did not wait. We cut spending,
across the board, by 6 percent. We put severe restrictions on hiring,
purchasing, and travel. We asked the public schools to save 2
percent of their appropriations. We have managed the taxpayers'
dollar responsibly.

This year, some people will try to tell you otherwise. They will
claim that North Carolina's progress has come at too high a price,
with too much spending and hiring. My friends, those people do not
know what they are talking about!

The fact is that while some people in Washington *talk* about
balancing the budget, we in North Carolina *do* it.

The fact is that the growth in state employment, counting the
public schools, the community colleges, and the universities, has
been held to a total of 5.5 percent since 1977—less than one percent
a year.

The fact is, that is 20 percent less than our average population
growth of 1.25 percent a year in the same six years.

The fact is that, when education is excluded, the growth of state
government since 1977 has been a *total* of 1.7 percent—less than 0.3
percent a year.

The fact is, during the last two years we have cut nearly 2,000 jobs
off the state payroll.

The fact is, that is a remarkable record—and don't let anybody try to tell you that this state and this legislature have done otherwise! And if Washington wants to learn how to run a government with strong economic growth and no deficits, let them come to North Carolina!

This year, I welcome this legislature's help in finding ways to do more with what we have. My administration will be working to do that. We welcome your oversight and partnership.

We will be replacing welfare with workfare.[8]

We will save money by centralizing computer services in all departments under the governor.[9]

We will ask you to give the Department of Revenue more help to see that all of our citizens pay the taxes they owe on time and in full, and I will ask you to pass a statute that will make tax evasion a felony.[10]

I will *oppose* any efforts to erode our tax base, just as I will oppose any efforts to raise general taxes. North Carolina has one of the lowest tax burdens in the nation, and we cannot afford to lose that advantage over other states.

We are competing with states all across this nation—competing for jobs. This year, every legislature in every state is asking the same question: What can we do to get more jobs for our people?

Those are not just states in the Sunbelt. States in the Midwest and the Northeast are taking drastic steps to stop the flow of capital and industry from their borders. They are trying to catch North Carolina. They know we are ahead of them.

We are on the right course and we must stay on it. We must redouble our efforts to meet their competition. We must maintain North Carolina's momentum. We must keep our competitive edge!

Our primary goal must be to prepare our people to work in a modern technology economy. That means basic skills, job training, and research. It means infusing our entire educational system with excellence and discipline. I urge the following ten-step plan for our public schools which we can carry through even with our tight state budget:

(1) We must continue our superb Kindergarten and Primary Reading program with a teacher and full-time aide in every classroom in grades K through three. We cannot afford cuts in this solid foundation of our system![11]

(2) We should retrain teachers who are presently teaching math and science "out-of-field," and prohibit this in future years. In grades seven through twelve in school year 1980-1981, 40 percent of our math teachers were not certified in math. The figures for science were 29 percent. We must change that. The budget I present to you will provide for $1,000 retraining grants to pay the costs of high school teachers taking college and university courses in science and mathematics. It will fund a summer institute program to retrain

1,500 teachers in middle schools and junior high schools. Over the next four years, we can finish this job of retraining and have every teacher teaching "in field." We can achieve this goal.[12]

(3) We should recruit math and science teachers more aggressively by redirecting the Prospective Teacher Scholarship Loan program to those who plan to teach in this critical field.

(4) We should provide funds as recommended in the budget for an additional six weeks of employment for one lead teacher of math or science in each of North Carolina's high schools. This teacher would work during the summer at improving science and math instruction for the entire school for the coming year.[13]

(5) We should develop examples of true excellence in math and science by establishing model projects at elementary or secondary schools in each of the eight educational districts.[14]

(6) We should begin to gradually increase the minimum standards required for passing on the competency test and consider putting some science questions in the competency and annual tests.[15]

(7) The State Board of Education under Dick Spangler's fine leadership should approve quickly the proposals to increase the high school graduation requirements from eighteen to twenty units, including at least two units each in math and science. We must set rigorous standards for high school graduation.[16]

(8) We should increase our emphasis on maximum competency in schools by implementing the proposed North Carolina Scholars program, giving higher recognition to students who complete a more rigorous high school curriculum, including at least three courses in math, three in science, four in English, and two in foreign language.[17]

(9) Our colleges and universities should increase the number of math and science courses required for admission.[18]

(10) We must continue to build the North Carolina School of Science and Mathematics, which is stimulating better math and science teaching in all of our public schools and, in both years since its establishment, has led the nation in the percentage of national merit scholarship semifinalists.

I will also ask you to expand the special institutes in which teachers upgrade their skills in teaching writing. We will add writing to our rigorous testing program.[19] We must strengthen our students' ability to write and communicate.

We have significantly reduced the number of dropouts from our schools over the past few years. Now we must redouble our efforts and stress joint programs between our public schools and community colleges. The state of Charles Brantley Aycock and Terry Sanford[20] should not rest until we help every single North Carolina youngster to graduate.

These will be the new building blocks on top of the strong education foundation that this legislature and this state have already built for our future. We must teach our children the skills they will need to compete with their peers in South Carolina and Virginia and Japan and West Germany and the Soviet Union.

Because we are preparing students for the jobs of tomorrow, we must make business a full partner in educating them. We must make sure the skills they learn today connect to the skills business will need tomorrow. Spending more tax money is not the only way to strengthen education. We need more businesses and individuals giving the schools a helping hand. I applaud the establishment of the North Carolina Business Council on Science and Mathematics Education and the Adopt-a-School program, which has been so successful.

All of North Carolina, led by its governor and General Assembly, must make a new commitment to excellence in education. We ought to hold up good teachers and good principals and good schools as examples. We ought to recognize their accomplishments and issue a challenge for excellence. This is why I have proclaimed 1983 as "The Year of the Public School" in North Carolina.[21] The time has come to rally around the public schools, the time has come to get more personally involved in them, and the time has come to mobilize the forces for education across our state.

The key to economic growth is education—the public schools, the community colleges, and the universities.

I will ask you to strengthen skill training in our state. The primary responsibility of our community college system must be to teach people the skills they need to get good jobs, and we must see that this responsibility is being met. So I will ask you to provide new training equipment for the system and to increase its ability to train employees for new industries.[22]

Very soon, I will sign an executive order spelling out a job-training policy for North Carolina, assigning specific responsibilities for each part of our overall system and mandating a close working partnership with private industry.[23] We are already developing a new Labor Market Information system to identify the new jobs and where they will be in the years to come. I am tired of people having to move to North Carolina to fill certain jobs. I want us to commit ourselves to train our own people to fill every job in the "help wanted" ads of North Carolina's newspapers.

We know where the new jobs will be in the future: in rapidly advancing technological fields related to areas like microelectronics and biotechnology. That is where North Carolina must go! In 1981 this legislature wisely created the Microelectronics Center of North Carolina, drawing together university researchers and students in that field. That action put North Carolina far ahead of most other states in the competition for the jobs of the future.

The Microelectronics Center of North Carolina is our magnet as we move to attract jobs in electronics and microelectronics. Already our fourth-largest industry, this is a field that is relatively recession-proof, that tends to recover very early in an economic upturn, and one in which the United States still has a high degree of world leadership. This year, I will ask you to continue your support of this center, so that we can operate the facilities under construction, buy the equipment needed, and build the communications network to tie together the universities that make up the center.[24]

To survive and to meet the economic and military challenge from abroad, our nation must learn to work smarter. That is how our great textile industry has survived—by investing in technology and automation and efficiency. Ten years ago some people had written the textile industry off as dead. But it met the challenge; it remains North Carolina's most important industry. We should learn the lesson textiles has taught us, and we must continue to support this $15 billion-per-year industry.

There are other things we must do to keep North Carolina competitive. We must finish critically important links in our highway system. You know how great those needs are, especially in certain parts of our state. We cannot afford to let our hard-earned tax dollars that we send to Washington go to build roads in other states. I will ask you to provide the additional funds required to match federal construction aid,[25] and I believe those additional funds should come primarily from an increase in the tax on alcoholic beverages.

Since 1981, under Secretary Bill Roberson,[26] the Department of Transportation has cut out the fat, instituted tough new protections against bid rigging, and increased miles of road being resurfaced by tenfold.

To attract new industry, we must maintain an adequate supply of electrical energy at a reasonable price.

The safe reduction, recycling, and disposal of hazardous wastes is also critically important to economic growth, as well as to environmental protection. The 1981 legislature established a waste-management system that is among the best in the nation.[27] We must maintain that system and strengthen it if that is needed.

We must maintain our strong environmental laws. I will urge you to provide the additional funds needed to keep in place the Coastal Area Management Act,[28] and, although North Carolina has bound itself in the past not to exceed federal environmental regulations, we will closely watch the regulations to govern landfills now being developed by the EPA. If these standards are too weak, I assure you that I will propose legislation to this General Assembly to provide for the safety of our people. We must make wise and full use of our productive resources—our forests and our fisheries. We must ensure that prime farmland is preserved.

We must not squander any of the resources that we have dedicated to meeting the great needs of our people—from the newborn infant to the oldest adult. Washington may be retreating from meeting those needs, but North Carolina will not retreat! We will maintain our commitment to helping mothers and their babies and to preventing mental retardation in children. We will maintain our commitment to day care, and we will give special attention to the problems of working women. I will sponsor a statewide conference this year on women and the economy.[29]

We must find some additional funds and provide more support for community mental health programs.[30]

Working hand in hand with private businesses and individuals, we will continue to bring art, music, drama, dance, and literature into the life of our communities. We will open the new art museum.[31] We will keep our symphony sound,[32] and we will make North Carolina's observance of the 400th anniversary our showcase to the nation.

That observance will be more than a tourist attraction. It will be a time to remind us of our beginnings, to renew our faith in America and in ourselves, and to rededicate ourselves to the ideals of liberty, equality, and opportunity. It will be a time to examine whether we are worthy of the spirit and courage of the men and women who crossed an ocean to make a new beginning and, in time, to build a new world.

It will be a time to recall that America was not built on small dreams and short-sighted vision. It was not built on governments and tax money alone. It was built by men and women who fought and struggled and loved and sometimes lost, men and women who had hope in the face of hopelessness, courage in the face of fear, and faith in God in the face of despair. I believe we are worthy of those who came before us, and I believe we shall be worthy of those yet to come.

It is our turn now. This nation has always lived in the future, believing that today will be better than yesterday, and tomorrow, better still. Let us not allow our children and our grandchildren to lose that hope and optimism. That is our challenge, that is our historic opportunity, and that is the greatest gift we can give all the generations of North Carolinians yet to come.

---

[1] See "Presentation of North Carolina 2000 Report," April 27, 1983, below.

[2] See "Special Message on Crime," January 25, 1983, footnote 6, below.

[3] "An Act to Make Appropriations for Current Operations of State Departments, Institutions, and Agencies, and for Other Purposes," ratified July 15, provided a 5 percent pay increase for all permanent state employees. *N.C. Session Laws, 1983*, c. 761, s. 193.

[4] Automatic increments and merit pay increases remained frozen for the 1983-1984 fiscal year. *N.C. Session Laws, 1983*, c. 761, s. 217.

[5] *N.C. Session Laws, 1983*, c. 761, ss. 87-88.

[6] *N.C. Session Laws, 1983*, c. 761, s. 22.

[7]James J. Blanchard (1942-   ), native of Detroit; resident of Pleasant Ridge, Michigan; B.A., 1964, M.B.A., 1965, Michigan State University; J.D., University of Minnesota, 1968. Michigan assistant attorney general, 1969-1973; member, U.S. House, 1974-1982; elected governor of Michigan, 1982. Barone and Ujifusa, *Almanac of American Politics, 1984*, 657.

[8]S.B. 609, "A Bill to Develop a Program to Enhance the Capability of Certain Public Assistance Recipients to Obtain and Retain Employment and to Become and Remain Self-Sufficient," was referred to the Senate Human Resources Committee on June 13, 1983. A committee substitute bill, approved on July 6, was dispatched to the Appropriations Committee. *N.C. Senate Journal, 1983*, 590, 748. The General Assembly enacted the Community Work Experience Program, also known informally as "workfare," as a county option in 1983. *News and Observer*, September 8, 1985; see also *N.C. Session Laws, 1983*, c. 761, s. 48.

[9]"An Act to Establish a Computer Commission and to Give This Commission Authority over Information Processing" was ratified May 6. *N.C. Session Laws, 1983*, c. 267.

[10]H.B. 717, "A Bill to be Entitled An Act to Raise the Penalties for Tax Evasion," passed its third reading on June 14 and was sent to the Senate for approval. *N.C. House Journal, 1983*, 307, 721, 750. *N.C. Senate Journal, 1983*, 615, 787, 798.

[11]See State of North Carolina, *Summary of Appropriations, 1983-1985 Biennium* ([Raleigh]: Office of State Budget and Management, 1983), 87, hereinafter cited as *Summary of Appropriations, 1983-1985 Biennium*.

[12]*Summary of Appropriations, 1983-1985 Biennium*, 88.

[13]*Summary of Appropriations, 1983-1985 Biennium*, 88.

[14]Model projects in mathematics and science had been organized in each of the state's eight educational districts prior to the spring of 1986. While one such program had been added for junior high school students, most had been initiated at the secondary level. William J. Brown, Jr., special assistant for research, Office of the Superintendent of Public Instruction, to Jan-Michael Poff, May 21, 1986, hereinafter cited as Brown correspondence.

[15]Minimum passing standards for the reading and mathematics portions of the North Carolina Competency Test were not raised. However, a language mechanics component and an essay writing requirement were included as additional skills to be mastered before a diploma could be awarded. Science questions were added, for pupils in grades three, six, and eight, to the Annual Testing Program. Brown correspondence.

[16]C. Dixon Spangler, Jr. (1932-   ), native of Charlotte; resident of Chapel Hill; B.S.B.A., University of North Carolina at Chapel Hill, 1954; M.B.A., Harvard University, 1956; U.S. Army, 1956-1958. President, C. D. Spangler Construction Co., 1958-1986, and of Golden Eagle Industries, 1968-1986; board chairman, Bank of North Carolina, 1982-1986; director, Hammermill Paper Co., since 1982, and of Aeronca, Inc., 1983-1985, and NCNB Corp., 1983-1986; succeeded William C. Friday as University of North Carolina president, 1986. Trudy Atkins, assistant to the president, University of North Carolina, to Jan-Michael Poff, March 7, 1986.

The State Board of Education, in 1983, approved a proposal to raise high school graduation requirements to twenty units beginning with the 1986-1987 academic year. *Raleigh Times*, February 11, 1984.

[17]The state's 1984 high school graduates were the first students eligible for the North Carolina Scholars program, which required participants to complete a twenty-two-hour course load encompassing additional foreign language, math, and science requirements, while maintaining a B average. The program was begun in 1983 by the State Board of Education. *News and Observer*, February 23, 1984.

[18]The University of North Carolina Board of Governors raised minimum admission requirements, for all of the system's campuses, on February 10, 1984. The revised standards, to become effective beginning with the fall, 1988, semester, called for an extra math and science course beyond the requirements for a high school diploma. *Raleigh Times*, February 11, 1984.

[19]The General Assembly earmarked $200,000, for both years of the 1983-1985 biennium, to support teacher writing institutes at eight North Carolina universities. It also provided funding to include an examination of writing skills, for sixth and ninth graders, as part of the state's testing program. *Summary of Appropriations, 1983-1985 Biennium,* 88.

[20]Terry Sanford (1917-   ), governor, 1961-1965, president of Duke University, 1969-1985. Previously identified in Mitchell, *Addresses of Hunt,* I, 149n.

[21]See "Superintendents' Summer Conference," July 9, 1983, footnote 4, below.

[22]*N.C. Session Laws, 1983,* c. 761, ss. 100, 103.

[23]Hunt signed Executive Order No. 93, systematizing and coordinating the state's job-training policy, on June 8. *N.C. Session Laws, 1983,* 1426-1434.

[24]*N.C. Session Laws, 1983,* c. 761, s. 2.

[25]*N.C. Session Laws, 1983,* c. 761, s. 8.

[26]See "Statement on Appointment of William R. Roberson, Jr.," July 9, 1981, footnote 1, below.

[27]See "Governor's Waste Management Board," December 9, 1981, footnote 1, below.

[28]State funding for Coastal Area Management Act (CAMA) programs was increased significantly during 1983 as a reaction to federal budget reductions. For a synopsis of CAMA-related measures passed by the General Assembly, see Ann L. Sawyer (ed.), *North Carolina Legislation, 1983* ([Chapel Hill]: Institute of Government, University of North Carolina at Chapel Hill, 1983), 173-176, hereinafter cited as Sawyer, *N.C. Legislation, 1983.*

[29]Hunt addressed the Governor's Conference on Women and the Economy on October 31, 1983, at the Raleigh Civic Center.

[30]*N.C. Session Laws, 1983,* c. 761, s. 23.

[31]See "North Carolina Museum of Art Opening," April 5, 1983, below.

[32]The 1983-1984 budget established a $400,000 reserve to be used as matching funds for a North Carolina Symphony endowment. Sawyer, *N.C. Legislation, 1983,* 8.

SPECIAL MESSAGE ON CRIME

JANUARY 25, 1983

When I delivered my "State of the State Address" to you last week, I spoke of a strategy to protect the people of North Carolina against the enemy of economic recession—unemployment, loss of income, bankruptcy, and hardship. Today, in the fourth "Special Message on Crime" that I have delivered to the General Assembly, I will speak to you about a strategy to protect our people against another enemy—an enemy that would invade their homes and businesses, an enemy that would take away what they have worked for and earned, an enemy that would threaten the lives of our families and every single person in North Carolina. That enemy is crime.

North Carolina has declared war on crime, and this year, we must step up our offensive.

No state in this nation has had a more impressive record in passing laws to reduce crime than we have. Since 1977 this administration, the General Assembly, our criminal justice system, and the law enforcement officers in this hall today have built a powerful foundation for a safer North Carolina.

We have established a cabinet-level Department of Crime Control and Public Safety.

We have provided the best deterrent there is to crime—swift and sure justice.

We have passed a law requiring speedy trials. No longer can a criminal escape punishment by delaying judgment.

We have passed a law that makes sentences more certain. No longer can a criminal shop around for a slap on the wrist.

We have passed laws that require mandatory jail terms for armed robbers, drug smugglers, and hardened criminals.

We have made drug paraphernalia illegal, and, just as we promised to do two years ago, we have put the "head shops" out of business in North Carolina.

We have put prisoners to work on the roads.[1]

We have reinstated the death penalty for first-degree murder.[2]

We are paying the medical expenses of rape victims, and we are committed to protecting the victims of family violence.[3]

We deal with the white-collar criminal just like we deal with any criminal, and we have passed the toughest law in the country against bid rigging.

The people of North Carolina have organized Community Watch and Crimestoppers programs to prevent crime. They have guided young people away from a life of crime. They have made their communities, their businesses, and their homes safer against crime.

We are turning the tide against the forces of crime. North Carolina is the tenth most populous state in the nation, but our crime rate ranks thirty-ninth among the fifty states.

But we cannot rest on the record. We cannot rest until every single person in North Carolina is safe from the young hood on drugs, the rapist who lurks in the shadows, and the violent criminal who is out on bail. And, this year, we must recognize that the most common murderer in North Carolina is the drunk driver.

In 1981 drunk drivers claimed more lives than all the murders reported in our state. It is time that we cracked down on what has almost become a form of socially accepted murder. It is time that we got the drunk driver off the road in North Carolina.

Last night, I went before the people of North Carolina on state-wide television to explain the Safe Roads Act and to ask for their support.[4] The demands for action are coming from the people— especially those whose lives have been shattered by a horrifying phone call telling them that a loved one will never come home again.

The Safe Roads Act will save lives. It was carefully developed by the Governor's Task Force on Drunken Drivers, which was chaired by Jack Stevens[5] of Asheville, one of the most respected former members of this body and an outstanding attorney. Its members included legislators, leaders in business, civic life, the law, law enforcement, and the clergy. They made an exhaustive study of our present laws. They went out and heard from the people in public hearings across the state.

They have developed a plan that is tough, comprehensive, and effective. If you enact that plan into law, you will be telling the drunk driver that, in North Carolina, the free ride across the center line is over.[6]

The Safe Roads Act makes a series of important changes in our laws:

—It makes it easier to convict a drunk driver and it eliminates plea bargaining.

—It guarantees a jail term for serious offenders.

—It gives judges very strict guidelines for sentencing in all cases.

—It requires jail or community service or loss of a driver's license—plus a fine—in every case.

—It continues the one-year revocation by the state Department of Motor Vehicles.

—It makes it harder for a drunk driver to get his license back.

—It requires the state to publish a report card on how every county, every judge, and every district attorney handles drunk-driving cases.

—It gives the magistrate the power to take away a drunk driver's license for ten days, right on the spot.

—It gives the magistrate the power to detain a drunk driver for up to twenty-four hours, to keep him from hurting himself and others.

—It gives the judge the power to impound a repeat offender's car.

—It requires the problem drinker to get professional help.

I know that some parts of this bill are controversial, but they are constitutional; they are necessary, they are right, and they will save lives.

It is already illegal for a bar to serve a drink to a minor or a person who is already drunk. Making bars subject to a civil suit will hit them where it hurts most—in the pocketbook. These establishments should be more careful about whom they serve, and they are in a position to save lives.

I support raising the minimum age for drinking beer and wine from eighteen to nineteen. I would not oppose raising it to twenty-one, but I think our primary goal should be getting it out of the high schools. And nineteen is adequate, given so many other tough provisions in the law against teenagers driving and drinking. A sixteen- or seventeen-year-old caught with any amount of alcohol or drugs in their blood would lose their license until they were eighteen, and they would get a fine of up to $100 and up to sixty days in jail.

But we have to change more than laws. We have to change minds and hearts and attitudes. This legislature can make a dramatic start this year, and our people will be grateful.

Our philosophy in North Carolina is to make the punishment fit the crime and protect our people. This year, in addition to providing tougher punishment for the drunk driver, I hope you will provide tougher punishment for other criminals—like those who go free on bail and commit another crime, and those young people who are just as tough and as mean as criminals twice their age. Too many dangerous criminals are going free on bail and it is time to put a stop to it.

Today, a judge can deny bail only when an offender is charged with a capital crime. But what about the criminal who is arrested, set free on bail, and goes out and commits another crime? And what about the assailant who threatens to kill a woman he viciously raped if she goes to the police and testifies against him? Those people don't have any business being out on the street. I urge you to give the judge the power to deny them bail and to keep them locked up to protect the people of North Carolina!

And the youthful offender—some of them are just kids who made a mistake and can still be saved. The secret to keeping them out of court and out of prison is to set them straight before it is too late. That is why we created the Executive Cabinet on Juveniles, and that is why this legislature established community-based alternative programs throughout North Carolina. We are committed to helping young people who can be helped and reaching those who can be reached; we will continue reaching out to them with a helping hand.

But some young people are criminals who can be reached only with a strict hand. Since 1976, total arrests of juveniles have declined by 28 percent, but arrests of juveniles for felonies have *increased* by the same percentage. Not long ago, in Fayetteville, a fifteen-year-old boy was charged with abducting a woman at gunpoint in a convenience store, raping her, and almost killing her. A few years ago, here in Wake County, four teenagers—one of them thirteen years old and another, fourteen—beat an elderly woman to death to get her Social Security check. They aren't just kids, they're criminals—and they ought to be treated that way.

But our present law doesn't let us treat them that way. The only choice a judge has today is to send those kids to training school for an indeterminate sentence, which averages about ten months, or to put them in prison with adults. Often, neither choice is a good one. Our judges need to be able to send these young criminals to training school for a set period of time, not an indeterminate sentence that means they can be turned loose right after they arrive.[7]

If a young person commits a serious felony, it ought to stay on his record forever,[8] and the judge should be able to see the juvenile record of an adult offender he is getting ready to sentence;[9] our present laws prohibit this, and they should be changed. We ought to let judges order parents to participate in treatment programs for young offenders,[10] and schools should be required to have strong, tough discipline programs. Discipline must begin in the home and in the school.

When we sentence the criminal, we shouldn't forget the victim. North Carolina does a better job than any other state when it comes to making the criminal pay restitution to his victim. But if we are really going to get serious about putting the victim first, we have got to make the victim first to be paid—before the court costs and before anything else. That is the only way we have of showing the victim that we care. In the last legislature, you moved the victim up to fourth in line to be paid. This year I urge you to put them at the head of the line! And, just as soon as we can afford it, I believe North Carolina should compensate victims of armed robbery for their medical expenses.

A recent decision by the North Carolina Supreme Court demonstrated that we must strengthen our law against armed robbery. Any use of a gun in an armed robbery should put that criminal in jail for a minimum of seven years.[11] Despite hundreds of pleas, I have not commuted *any* armed robbery sentences as governor, except for two cases recommended by the SBI.

The purpose of punishment is deterrence, preventing crime. Sometimes the best form of deterrence is a tough prison sentence. Sometimes it's ordering an offender to do community service work to repay his victim and society.

Sometimes, alternative forms of punishment are best for nonviolent offenders. Our judges are making these alternatives part of probation today. We have nineteen special alternative-punishment programs in place today in North Carolina, and we will have twenty-five by July 1.

We are giving careful study to the report of the Citizens Commission on Alternatives to Incarceration, which was chaired by Judge Willis Whichard, a respected former member of the General Assembly.[12] We ought to use every innovative idea that will keep people out of prison in the first place and help them become taxpayers instead of tax burdens. We should consider using training schools to house several hundred younger prisoners, and we must make better use of existing state facilities, like Dix Hospital, to meet special needs in our prisons.

Since 1977 we have built 5,000 new prison beds in North Carolina. We do not want to build any more prisons than we *have* to, but we are serious about protecting our people, and the criminals need to know that we will build all the prisons we *need* to protect the people of North Carolina against them.

We ought to protect law enforcement officers against criminals, too. We need to plug a loophole in our law that, in some cases, does not make it a crime to use force in resisting arrest. These officers put their lives on the line for the rest of us every day, and they deserve to have the law of the state of North Carolina standing behind them.[13]

To do all of this, to protect our people and our law enforcement officers, to see that the punishment fits the crime and the criminal, we must see that our courts operate efficiently and effectively. We need to take minor traffic cases off the crowded court calendars, so they can be devoted to serious criminal cases, like drunk driving. We need to eliminate unwarranted, costly, and time-consuming appeals, and, when the state and the defendant both agree to trial before a judge, we should not require jury trials.

All of this has one goal: protecting the people of North Carolina against crime. Every single citizen in this state has a right to be safe. No older person should have to be afraid to walk outside in the evening. No woman should have to be afraid to answer a knock at the door. No family should have to be afraid to go to the store.

You and I have a responsibility to those people, and you and I have a historic opportunity. History will remember these years as a time when North Carolina not only taught every child to read and helped adults find good jobs. We will also record that this was the time when we began to turn back a wave of crime that threatened to engulf our entire nation and our entire society.

This is a battle we have fought in the courtroom, in the jailhouses, in the streets, in the schools, in our homes—in these very halls. It is a battle we have fought for the people of North Carolina. It is a battle against fear and for freedom. It is a battle we can win. Let us make it our legacy—a safer North Carolina for our children and all the generations yet to come. Thank you.

---

[1]"An Act to Make Appropriations for Current Operations of State Departments, Institutions, and Agencies, and for Other Purposes," *N.C. Session Laws, 1977,* c. 802, was ratified June 29. Sections 25.35 through 25.37 transferred $500,000 from the Transportation Department to the state Department of Corrections to cover the expense of using medium custody inmates as construction and maintenance laborers on public highways and enabled the classification of minimum- and medium-security prisoners for road work.

[2]"An Act to Establish Procedures for Sentencing in Capital Cases and to Fix the Punishment for Murder" was ratified May 19 and became effective June 1. *N.C. Session Laws, 1977,* c. 406.

[3]"An Act to Provide Remedies for Domestic Violence" was ratified May 14. *N.C. Session Laws, 1979,* c. 561. See also "Governor's Statewide Conference on Crimes against Women and Children," October 31, 1983, below.

[4]See "Statewide Television Address on Drunken Drivers," January 24, 1983, below.

[5]John Shorter (Jack) Stevens (1933-   ), state House member, 1969-1976, and chairman, Governor's Task Force on Drunken Drivers. Previously identified in Mitchell, *Addresses of Hunt,* I, 446n.

[6]"An Act to Provide Safe Roads by Requiring Mandatory Jail Terms for Grossly Aggravated Drunken Drivers, Providing an Effective Deterrent to Reduce the Incidence of Impaired Driving, and Clarifying the Statutes Related to Drinking and Driving" was ratified July 3 and became effective October 1. *N.C. Session Laws, 1983,* c. 435. See also c. 1101, "An Act to Make Technical Changes to the Safe Roads Act," ratified July 6, 1984. *N.C. Session Laws, 1983, Second Session, 1984.*

[7]H.B. 987, introduced in the General Assembly in 1985, would allow stricter

sentences for any juvenile, aged fourteen years or older, who had been adjudicated a delinquent for a nondivertible offense. Robert P. Joyce (ed.), *North Carolina Legislation, 1985* (Chapel Hill: Institute of Government, University of North Carolina at Chapel Hill, 1985), 117-118, hereinafter cited as Joyce, *North Carolina Legislation, 1985.*

[8]S.B. 100, "A Bill to Prohibit Expunction of a Juvenile Record if the Juvenile was Adjudicated for an Act that would be a Class A, B, or C Felony if Committed by an Adult," received an unfavorable report from the Senate Judiciary I Committee. *N.C. Senate Journal, 1983,* 75, 140.

[9]S.B. 184, "A Bill to Allow Inclusion of Certain Juvenile Records in Pre-Sentence Reports," passed its third reading in the Senate on May 23, 1983, and was sent to the House. However, a House subcommittee substitute bill was tabled on July 11. *N.C. House Journal, 1983,* 577, 868, 894, 899, 972; *N.C. Senate Journal, 1983,* 150, 411, 448.

[10]"An Act to Provide Court-Ordered Parent Participation in Treatment on Certain Juvenile Cases" was ratified on July 20, 1983. *N.C. Session Laws, 1983,* c. 837.

[11]The state supreme court, in a four-to-three decision, determined that mere possession of a firearm during a theft did not automatically warrant an armed-robbery conviction. The July 8, 1981, ruling also directed that it was the responsibility of the prosecution to prove that the perpetrator employed the weapon "to threaten or endanger" the life of the victim. *News and Observer,* July 9, 1981.

[12]*Report, Citizens Commission on Alternatives to Incarceration, 1982* (Durham: [The Commission, 1982]).

Willis Padgett Whichard (1940-   ), North Carolina Court of Appeals judge since 1980. Previously identified in Mitchell, *Addresses of Hunt,* I, 344n.

[13]"An Act to Remove the Defense of Unlawful Arrest in Cases of Resisting Arrest by Use of a Deadly Weapon or Deadly Force," c. 762, was ratified July 15, 1983. *N.C. Session Laws, 1983.*

RECOGNITION OF 1982 AND 1983 NATIONAL COLLEGIATE ATHLETIC ASSOCIATION BASKETBALL CHAMPIONS

APRIL 18, 1983

[Devotees of Atlantic Coast Conference basketball, particularly in North Carolina, found reason to rejoice in 1982 and 1983. The University of North Carolina Tar Heels capped a 32-2 season by winning the NCAA Tournament on March 29, 1982. The school's first national men's basketball title since 1957, and the first ever for Coach Dean Smith, came in a 63-62 victory over Georgetown University in the New Orleans Superdome. Not to be outdone by its perennial rival from Chapel Hill, the North Carolina State University Wolfpack kept the NCAA championship in the Triangle area by upsetting top-ranked University of Houston, 54-52, a year later. The April 4, 1983, win in Albuquerque gave Coach Jim Valvano his first national title; it also ended an emotionally charged, four-week period in which his team unexpectedly won the ACC Tournament and continued, thereafter, to defeat opponents that it was not supposed to beat. Art Chansky, with Eddie Fogler, *March to the Top* ([Chapel Hill]: Four Corners Press, 1982), 109-116; *News and Observer,* April 5, 1983.

The governor and General Assembly honored the accomplishments of both teams in a special legislative session held the evening of April 18.]

Of all the occasions I have had to address the General Assembly, this is without a doubt the happiest. Of all the speeches I have delivered to you, this will be without a doubt the least controversial and best received. And, you will be happy to hear, it will also be the briefest.

We have come here tonight to honor two teams and their coaches, for they have proven to the world that, when it comes to college basketball, North Carolina is number one. No state has ever had two of its universities win back-to-back national championships—and I must point out, in all modesty, that since I became governor in 1977, a team from North Carolina has been in the national finals five out of seven years. I'll dare any governor in America to match that record!

Truly it is a remarkable event that brings so many State fans and Carolina fans together in love and harmony, but these are two remarkable teams. To Dean Smith[1] and your national champions, this honor is a year overdue. We honor you for your victory in New Orleans, but we also pay tribute tonight to a coach and a program that, year in and year out, have been the best in America. To Coach Valvano[2] and the "Cardiac Pack," we honor the fulfillment of "the dream." You wrote the most unbelievable Cinderella stories in the history of sports. I don't think the people of this state could stand one more of those heart-stopping, last-second victories, and I don't think Raleigh could stand one more celebration.

These were two very different teams—one ranked number one, the other perennial underdogs. But they were alike where it counted: talented, disciplined, courageous, selfless—*teams* in the true sense of the word.

To the players, let me say this: Some of you are from North Carolina, some are not—but we consider all of you *ours*, now and forever. You have brought pride and honor to this state. Whatever your plans for the future, we hope you will make this your home state, and we hope North Carolina is as good to you as you have been to us. We don't say that just because you are winners; we say it because we have seen the kind of people you are.

That is a tribute to your coaches. More than coaches, really—teachers: Dean Smith, the master of discipline and decency, and Jim Valvano, the master of love and laughter. To Coach Smith and Coach Valvano, nothing I say can speak with more eloquence to the kind of men you are than the courage and character of these young men you have taught and led and inspired.

To all of you, let me say this: North Carolina has a long and proud basketball tradition, from coaches—like Everett Case and Frank McGuire and Vic Bubas and Bones McKinney,[3] to today—and the players: the Ranzinos and Pucillos and Shavliks and Rosenbluths and Moes and Browns and Millers and Joneses and Davises and Hubands and Willifords and Clarks and Thompsons and Towes and Burlesons and Kupchaks and Fords and Whitneys.[4] Today, it is Valvano and Smith and Jordan and Perkins and Worthy and Bailey and Lowe and Whittenburg and all of you.[5] Those are names we will never forget. Tonight, in this session, we honor you. Ladies and gentlemen, how 'bout those Heels and how 'bout that Pack!

---

[1] Dean Edwards Smith (1931-   ), native of Emporia, Kansas; resident of Chapel Hill; B.S., University of Kansas, 1953; U.S. Air Force, 1954-1958. Assistant basketball coach, golf coach, United States Air Force Academy, 1955-1958; assistant basketball coach, 1958-1961, and head coach, since 1961, University of North Carolina at Chapel Hill; guided 1971 Tar Heels to National Invitation Tournament title; coached U.S. men's basketball team to gold medal at 1976 summer Olympics, Montreal; winner of conference and national coaching awards. Smith has more 25-win seasons than any coach in college basketball history, and his teams have garnered more regular-season and tournament titles than those of any other school in the Atlantic Coast Conference; by mid-1985 his record as Carolina head coach totaled 551 wins and 165 losses. Prepared biography from Dean Edwards Smith, June 28, 1985; *Who's Who in America, 1982-1983*, II, 3114.

[2] James Thomas Valvano (1946-   ), native of Queens, New York; resident of Cary; B.A., Rutgers University, 1967. Assistant basketball coach at Rutgers, 1968-1969, and at University of Connecticut, 1971-1972; head coach at Johns Hopkins University, 1970, Bucknell University, 1973-1975, Iona College, 1976-1980, and at North Carolina State University, since 1980; career coaching record: 240 wins, 154 losses (104 wins, 57 losses at N.C. State), as of July, 1985. *News and Observer*, February 6, 1983; prepared biography from Department of Athletics, North Carolina State University, July 9, 1985.

[3] Everett Norris Case (1900-1966), native of Anderson, Indiana; died in Raleigh; teaching certificate, Old Central Normal (later Canterbury) College, 1918; was graduated from University of Wisconsin, 1933; M.A., University of Southern California; U.S. Navy, 1942-1945. Coached high school basketball in Indiana; was assistant coach at University of Southern California, afterward served as head coach at DePauw; head basketball coach at North Carolina State College (now University), 1947-1964, where his teams compiled a 379-134 record and won ten conference titles. Inducted into North Carolina Sports Hall of Fame in 1964. Charlie Harville, *Sports in North Carolina: A Photographic History* (Norfolk, Virginia: Donning Company, Publishers, Inc., 1977), 6, hereinafter cited as Harville, *Sports in North Carolina; News and Observer*, February 25, 1951, May 1, 1966.

Frank Joseph McGuire (1914-   ), native of New York City; B.S., St. John's College (now University), 1936; served in U.S. Navy during World War II. Head basketball coach at St. John's, 1947-1952, and University of North Carolina at Chapel Hill, 1952-1961; record at UNC: 164 wins, 58 losses. Tar Heels won 1957 national basketball championship under McGuire. *News and Observer*, November 27, 1955, August 1, 1961.

Victor Albert Bubas (1927-   ), native of Gary, Indiana; was graduated from North Carolina State College, 1951; U.S. Army, 1945-1946; Member, N.C. State basketball team, 1947-1951; All-Southern Conference, 1949, 1950; freshman basketball coach, and later assistant varsity coach, N.C. State, 1951-1959; head basketball coach, Duke University, 1959-1969, during which time his teams won four conference championships and advanced to the NCAA Tournament final game three times; served as special assistant to the chancellor, 1969-1970, special assistant to the president, 1970-1974, and as vice-president for university-community affairs, 1974-1976, Duke University; installed in North Carolina Sports Hall of Fame, and became Sun Belt Conference commissioner, in 1976. *Durham Morning Herald*, April 1, 1969, April 17, 1970, July 1, 1974, March 14, 1976; Harville, *Sports in North Carolina*, 6, 29; *News and Observer*, March 27, 1980.

Horace Albert (Bones) McKinney (1919-   ), native of Lowlands; resident of Hickory; attended North Carolina State College and University of North Carolina at Chapel Hill; entered Southeastern Baptist Theological Seminary, 1952, and later ordained; U.S. Army, 1942-1946. Played basketball at N.C. State and UNC; played professionally, 1946-1952, for Washington Caps and Boston Celtics; assistant basketball coach, 1952-1958, and head coach, 1958-1965, Wake Forest College (now University). Record as Wake Forest head coach: 122 wins, 94 losses, two conference championships; 1960-1961 team advanced to NCAA Tournament final game. Assistant director, 1966-1967, and appointed director, 1967, of prisoner rehabilitation, State Prison Department (now Department of Correction); inducted into North Carolina Sports Hall of Fame, 1970; head coach, Carolina Cougars, of the American Basketball Assn., for two seasons, beginning in 1971; college basketball announcer. *Charlotte Observer*, February 7, 1970; Harville, *Sports in North Carolina*, 6, 58; *News and Observer*, February 21, 1954, August 9, 1966, April 7, 1967.

[4]Sam S. Ranzino (1927-   ), native of Gary, Indiana; N.C. State basketball player, 1947-1951; All-America, All-Southern Conference, 1949-1951; drafted by Rochester, 1951; inducted into North Carolina Sports Hall of Fame, 1981. Virginia Hughes, University Archives, North Carolina State University, to Jan-Michael Poff, February 26, 1986, hereinafter cited as Hughes correspondence; Ronald L. Mendell, *Who's Who in Basketball* (New Rochelle, New York: Arlington House, 1973), 188, hereinafter cited as Mendell, *Who's Who in Basketball*.

Lou Pucillo (1936-   ), native of Philadelphia, Pennsylvania; N.C. State basketball player, 1955-1959; All-America, 1959, All-Atlantic Coast Conference, 1958, 1959, and ACC Player of the Year, 1959; drafted by St. Louis, 1959. Hughes correspondence; Mendell, *Who's Who in Basketball*, 184.

Ronald Dean Shavlik (1933-1983), native of Denver, Colorado; died in Raleigh; N.C. State basketball player, 1952-1956, holds unbeaten school record for career free throws and rebounds; All-America, 1955, 1956; All-Atlantic Coast Conference, 1955, 1956, ACC Player of the Year, 1956; first-round draft choice, New York Knicks, 1956; inducted into North Carolina Sports Hall of Fame, 1979. Hughes correspondence; Mendell, *Who's Who in Basketball*, 210; *News and Observer*, April 11, 1986.

Lennie Rosenbluth (1933-   ), native of New York City; University of North Carolina-Chapel Hill basketball player, 1953-1957; All-America, 1956, 1957; All-Atlantic Coast Conference, 1955, 1956, 1957, ACC Player of the Year, 1957, ACC Athlete of the Year, 1957; drafted by Philadelphia Warriors, 1957. *Carolina Basketball, 1984-85* ([Chapel Hill]: Office of Sports Information, University of North Carolina at Chapel Hill, [1984]), 61-63, hereinafter cited as *Basketball Blue Book*, with appropriate years; Mendell, *Who's Who in Basketball*, 198.

Doug Moe, native of Brooklyn, New York; UNC basketball player, 1957-1961; All-America, 1961; All-Atlantic Coast Conference, 1959, 1961; played professional basketball; coach, Denver Nuggets, National Basketball Assn. *Basketball Blue Book, 1957-58*, inside rear cover, *1958-59*, 16, *1960-61*, 13, *1984-85*, 61-63, *1985-86*, 82.

Larry Brown, native of Long Beach, New York; UNC basketball player, 1959-1963; All-Atlantic Coast Conference; member, U.S. Olympic team, 1964; played professional basketball. *Basketball Blue Book, 1960-61*, 10, *1961-62*, 11, *1962-63*, 10, *1984-85*, 61-63, *1985-86*, 82.

Larry Miller, native of Catasauqua, Pennsylvania; UNC basketball player, 1964-1968; All-America, 1967, 1968; All-Atlantic Coast Conference, 1967, 1968, ACC Athlete of the Year, 1967; played professional basketball. *Basketball Blue Book, 1964-65*, 9, *1965-66*, 22, *1966-67*, 9, *1967-68*, 13, *1984-85*, 61-63, *1985-86*, 82.

Bobby Jones (1951-   ), native of Charlotte; UNC basketball player, 1970-1974; All-America, 1974; All-Atlantic Coast Conference, 1974; member, U.S. Olympic team, 1972; played professional basketball. *Basketball Blue Book, 1970-71*, 54, *1971-72*, 23, *1972-73*, 22, *1973-74*, 20, *1984-85*, 61-63, *1985-86*, 82.

Walter Davis (1954-   ), native of Pineville; UNC basketball player, 1973-1977; All-Atlantic Coast Conference, 1977; member, U.S. Olympic team, 1976; played professional basketball. *Basketball Blue Book, 1973-74*, 30, *1974-75*, 27, *1975-76*, 21, *1976-77*, 20, *1984-85*, 61-63, *1985-86*, 82.

Kim Huband, native of Wilmington; UNC basketball player, 1968-1972; Academic All-America, 1972. *Basketball Blue Book, 1968-69*, 54, *1969-70*, 20, *1970-71*, 24, *1971-72*, 19, *1984-85*, 61-63.

Vann Williford, native of Fayetteville; N.C. State basketball player, 1966-1970; All-Atlantic Coast Conference, 1969, 1970; H. C. Kennett Award winner, 1969; drafted by Phoenix, 1970. Hughes correspondence.

Franklin S. (Rusty) Clark, native of Fayetteville; UNC basketball player, 1965-1969; All-Atlantic Coast Conference, second team, 1968; NCAA Eastern Regional Tournament Most Valuable Player, 1968. *Basketball Blue Book, 1965-66*, 12, *1966-67*, 13, *1967-68*, 14, *1968-69*, 13, *1984-85*, 61-63.

David O'Neal Thompson, native of Shelby; N.C. State basketball player, 1971-1975; holds six school and three conference records; winner of numerous awards, including All-America, 1973-1975; All-Atlantic Coast Conference, 1973-1975, ACC Player of the Year, 1973-1975, ACC Athlete of the Year, 1973, 1975; National Player of the Year, 1974, 1975; first-round draft choice, Atlanta, 1975; inducted into North Carolina Sports Hall of Fame, 1982. Hughes correspondence.

Monte Towe, native of Converse, Indiana; N.C. State basketball player, 1971-1975; All-America, 1974; All-Atlantic Coast Conference, 1974; drafted by Atlanta, 1975. Hughes correspondence.

Tommy Burleson, native of Newland; N.C. State basketball player, 1970-1974; All-America, 1973, 1974; All-Atlantic Coast Conference, 1972, 1973; drafted by Seattle, 1974. Hughes correspondence.

Mitch Kupchak (1954-   ), native of Brentwood, New York; UNC basketball player, 1972-1976; All-America, 1975, 1976; All-Atlantic Coast Conference, 1975, 1976; member, U.S. Olympic team, 1976; drafted by Washington, 1976. *Basketball Blue Book, 1972-73*, 27, *1973-74*, 27, *1974-75*, 26, *1975-76*, 16, *1984-85*, 61-63, *1985-86*, 82.

Phil Ford (1956-   ), native of Rocky Mount; UNC basketball player, 1974-1978; All-America, 1975-1978; All-Atlantic Coast Conference, 1976-1978, ACC Athlete of the Year, 1977, 1978; member, U.S. Olympic team, 1976; first-round draft choice, Kansas City, 1978. *Basketball Blue Book, 1974-75*, 31, *1975-76*, 26, *1976-77*, 23, *1977-78*, 10-11, *1984-85*, 61-63, *1985-86*, 82.

Charles (Hawkeye) Whitney, native of Washington, D.C.; N.C. State basketball player, 1976-1980; All-America, 1980; All-Atlantic Coast Conference, 1979, 1980; first-round draft choice, Kansas City, 1980. Hughes correspondence.

[5]Michael Jordan (1963-   ), native of Wilmington; UNC basketball player, 1981-1984; All-America, 1982-1984; All-Atlantic Coast Conference, 1982-1984, ACC Rookie of the Year, 1982, ACC Athlete of the Year, 1984; member, U.S. Olympic team, 1984; first-round draft choice, Chicago, 1984; NBA Rookie of the Year, 1985. *Basketball Blue Book, 1981-82*, 20, *1982-83*, 18, *1983-84*, 17, *1984-85*, 61-63, *1985-86*, 82.

Sam Perkins (1961-   ), native of Latham, New York; UNC basketball player, 1980-1984; All-America, 1982-1984; All-Atlantic Coast Conference, 1982-1984, ACC Rookie of the Year, 1981; member, U.S. Olympic team, 1984; drafted by Dallas, 1984. *Basketball Blue Book, 1980-81*, 19, *1981-82*, 18, *1982-83*, 16, *1983-84*, 16, *1984-85*, 61-63, *1985-86*, 82.

James Worthy (1961-   ), native of Gastonia; UNC basketball player, 1979-1982; All-America, 1982; All-Atlantic Coast Conference, 1982, ACC Athlete of the Year, 1982; NCAA Tournament finals Most Valuable Player, 1982; first-round draft choice, Los Angeles, 1982. *Basketball Blue Book, 1979-80*, 21, *1980-81*, 17, *1981-82*, 14, *1984-85*, 61-63, *1985-86*, 82.

Thurl Bailey, native of Seat Pleasant, Maryland; N.C. State basketball player, 1979-1983; All-Atlantic Coast Conference, 1983; NCAA All-Tournament finals team, 1983; first-round draft choice, Utah, 1983. Hughes correspondence.

Sidney Lowe, native of Washington, D.C.; N.C. State basketball player, 1979-1983; All-Atlantic Coast Conference, 1983; NCAA All-Tournament finals team, 1983; holds school career record for assists; drafted by Chicago, 1983. Hughes correspondence.

Dereck Whittenburg, native of Glenarden, Maryland; N.C. State basketball player,

1979-1983; All-Atlantic Coast Conference Tournament, 1983; NCAA All-Tournament finals team, 1983; drafted by Phoenix, 1983. Hughes correspondence.

PRESENTATION OF NORTH CAROLINA 2000 REPORT

APRIL 27, 1983

[Executive Order No. 66, signed June 1, 1981, created the Commission on the Future of North Carolina, outlined its operation, and set guidelines for the composition and duties of its membership. *N.C. Session Laws, 1981,* 1770-1771. For Governor Hunt's assessment of the purpose and progress of the North Carolina 2000 project, see "North Carolina 2000," June 1, 1981, and "Commission on the Future of North Carolina," March 15, 1983, below.

At a news conference held October 1, 1981, the governor announced the appointment of William C. Friday, identified below, and Elizabeth Duncan Koontz as commission chairman and co-chairwoman, respectively. Koontz (1919-   ), lecturer and consultant, served as assistant superintendent of the state Department of Public Instruction from 1979 to 1982. Previously identified in Mitchell, *Addresses of Hunt,* I, 307n; see also Elizabeth Duncan Koontz to Jan-Michael Poff, October 4, 1984.]

You are gathered here today to review a roadmap for North Carolina's future. Dr. William Friday [1] and the Commission on the Future of North Carolina have done an outstanding job. They have involved thousands of our citizens in the process. Their recommendations are too valuable to be left on the shelf. I ask you to join me to see that their report is used to guide North Carolina on the path to a prosperous and progressive twenty-first century. [2]

Let me tell you why this is so important.

Yesterday, I flew to western North Carolina, to Mitchell County, to announce the opening of a new industrial plant. [3] The mountains were still topped with snow. We flew over the stark beauty of Linville Gorge. Pisgah Forest stretched out before us like a green carpet. We saw hawks circling in the sky. The majesty of Grandfather Mountain seemed to reach right up to the heavens.

We flew over piedmont farms where the ground had just been turned. We passed over the thriving businesses of Winston-Salem and Greensboro. We saw yellow school buses going down the roads. I wanted to fly all the way to the coast so we could just stay right up there close to heaven.

My friends, from the mountains to the coast, North Carolina is truly the most beautiful and magnificent spot God put on this earth. We have the finest people you'll find anywhere. We have the best communities in the world to live and raise a family—big cities, small cities, small towns, and little crossroads. We have strong families and churches, growing businesses and farms, and schools that are getting better, not worse. I am tired of people who belittle all that we have, who put it down and do nothing but criticize. My answer to them is that they should get out and see North Carolina.

I know there is much to be done, and our first responsibility is to preserve the strength and beauty and grace that make North Carolina a special place. We are the caretakers for the future. So, today, it is my great honor to present to you a man who can help us see that future.

Since 1956 when he was installed as president of the University of North Carolina, Bill Friday has been an institution in North Carolina education. He has guided the growth and expansion of a state university system that knows no equal, and throughout all those years, Bill Friday has shown a nobility of style and a dedication to excellence in education that knows no equal. His commitment to quality education has gone beyond North Carolina's borders. He has served as president of the Association of American Universities and the American Council on Education. He served as chairman of the National Task Force on Education for Presidents Johnson and Carter, and he was a member of the groundbreaking Carnegie Commission on Higher Education.

Mr. Speaker, Mr. Lieutenant Governor, members of the House and Senate, I want to introduce to you a man who has proudly borne the North Carolina banner of education. He has seen the future. He has seen the joy and prosperity education can bring to North Carolina. His eyes have seen a new day. I have the high honor to present to you President William Friday.

---

[1] William Clyde Friday (1920-   ), president of the University of North Carolina since 1956, retired in 1986. Previously identified in Mitchell, *Addresses of Hunt*, I, 42n; see also *News and Observer*, June 19, 1985.

[2] Commission on the Future of North Carolina, *Report of the Commission on the Future of North Carolina: Goals and Recommendations for the Year 2000* ([Raleigh]: North Carolina 2000, March, 1983), was the report to which Hunt referred.

[3] The governor announced in Spruce Pine, on April 26, that Outboard Marine Corporation would build a $10 million manufacturing plant in the community.

SPECIAL ADDRESS ON EDUCATION

JUNE 7, 1984

[Although Governor Hunt raised a number of budgetary matters, in the following speech, which required legislative action during the 1984 short session of the General Assembly, he urged lawmakers to focus special attention on improving the state's public education system. Many of those school-related recommendations previously had been included in addresses before the North Carolina Commission on Education for Economic Growth, January 17, 1984, its advisory panel, January 31 and April 5, 1984, and its regional briefings in Charlotte, May 1, Smithfield, May 2, Asheville, May 4, and Greensboro, May 11, 1984; the State Goals and Policy Board, January 19, 1984; and in statements to the press, June 23, 1983, and January 9 and April 5, 1984.]

Lieutenant Governor Green,[1] Speaker Ramsey,[2] members of the House and Senate, distinguished guests, and my fellow North Carolinians:

Next Monday evening, I will deliver my only commencement address of this year. It will not be before a major college or university, nor before a large high school. Instead, it will be before the forty-one seniors of Cape Hatteras School, less than fifty miles from where the first English settlers planted their first colony 400 years ago.

I made the decision to deliver my only commencement address there for both personal and symbolic reasons. In 1955, I was one of seventy-six graduating seniors at Rock Ridge High School in Wilson County. I was class valedictorian, right proud of myself and pretty sure that I was ready to set the world on fire. That fall, in my first semester at North Carolina State College, I found out differently. I found that my high school education had not prepared me as well as my new friends from Raleigh and Greensboro and Charlotte were prepared. I found out that I was behind, not because I had not worked hard, not because my parents did not care about education—but because of where I was from.

I promised myself then that if I could ever do anything to see that kids from the country, or kids from the wrong side of town, or kids from poor families, could have a better chance—an equal chance—for a better education, I would do it. So I stand before this General Assembly today and ask you, the elected representatives of the people of North Carolina, to fulfill that hope for the students in a tiny, distant school on the shores of Cape Hatteras and for children in every city and every corner of this state who deserve a decent education, a fair chance to make a success of their lives, and a good job.

This is no ordinary short budget session of the General Assembly. The responsibility for action here surpasses any personal or political agenda we bring to these halls. The people of North Carolina are ready for action for excellence in education. The challenges of a growing economy and a changing world will not wait. The decisions you make during this session will determine whether the next generation will take North Carolina farther than any of us dream, or whether tomorrow will pass us by.

The children of North Carolina deserve a dramatic improvement in their schools, and our generation must meet that responsibility to their generation. Those who came before us—governors like Aycock and Sanford, far-sighted senators and representatives—met their responsibility. Their wisdom and their courage, again and again over the past three decades, have transformed North Carolina.

Today we are building a new economy based on new technologies. We have combined a tradition of agriculture and manufacturing with the promise of science and technology. We have preserved a small-town way of life and productivity, yet prospered from a big-city vitality. We have built something special in North Carolina, and we are the envy of the nation.

As a place to do business, as a place to live, as a place to raise a family, as a place to visit—North Carolina has emerged literally as the nation's leader. But a leader cannot be lazy, for other states are nipping at our heels: Tennessee, South Carolina, Virginia. Still others are spurred on to action: California, Texas, Massachusetts. The competition is fierce—for economic growth, for jobs, for the future. Our state and our children can compete with the best, if we give them the kind of education that tomorrow's economy will require. We have good schools today, and those who deny that don't know what they are talking about. But we must make them better.

North Carolina can afford to make that investment. We have survived the most serious economic recession of the last forty years, when 10 percent of our people were out of work, and we did so without cutting essential services to our people or firing state personnel. We did it by dedicated teachers and state employees accepting limited salary increases. Now North Carolina is leading the nation's recovery. Our economic growth—not higher taxes—has generated the capital we need to invest in our schools, our children, and our future.

There is widespread agreement throughout our state—indeed a mandate from our people—that we must make this investment in education and that we must make it in a way that will bring strong economic growth to every single area of North Carolina. To determine just what that requires, I appointed last year a fifty-member Commission on Education for Economic Growth—business executives, educators, legislators, school board members, labor leaders, parents, students, and dedicated citizens.[3] They heard from more than 250 people during their hearings across this state. They spent countless hours studying what other states are doing. They received advice from representatives of thirty-two organizations that have an interest in North Carolina's schools. I ask you to give their recommendations your serious consideration during this session, and I ask your permission now to have the members of the commission who are present—and its co-chairs Bland Worley and Dick Spangler—to stand so that we might thank them for the contribution they have made to North Carolina.[4]

If we follow their recommendations, many of which are paralleled by the Education Policy Council, which will present its main report to you next January, we can make excellent schools the vehicle to give North Carolina unquestioned economic leadership among the states of this nation.[5] But I caution you: There is no quick fix, no easy road. We must make deep, profound changes in our schools. We must take bold, ambitious strides forward, not timid steps. We must take action in six areas:

First, we must build a team—a partnership—of businesses, churches, civic groups, and citizens, that is excited about, involved in, and committed to improving the schools. And they must have staying power.

Second, we must reform and strengthen our curriculum so that our children are learning the abilities and skills they need to hold a good job and be good citizens. No more "cotton-candy" courses or social promotions. Students should know we have high expectations of them, and a passing report card and a high school diploma should be a guarantee anywhere in our state that essential competencies have been mastered.[6]

Third, we must develop a higher regard for our teachers, recruit the best we can get, train them in the way business trains its best, and pay them like the professionals they are.

Fourth, we must follow up on our nationally acclaimed Primary Reading Program, which has virtually eliminated "non-readers" in grades K through 3, by reducing class size to twenty-six in grades four through six.[7] We should relieve teachers of distracting non-teaching duties and provide them with clerical assistance as soon as possible.[8]

Fifth, we must clearly understand that good principals and superintendents will run good schools. So we must pay them on a level competitive with business and help principals and school administrators develop the management strengths that will inspire and motivate teachers and students alike.[9]

Sixth, we must see that every single child—those who live in the country, those who have special talents, those who have special problems, every single child—has the chance for a good education.[10]

The most expensive investment I am recommending—and the most important—is in the people who teach our children. We must attract the best and the most dedicated people into teaching, and that means paying salaries that are competitive with what those people make in private industry. So I am recommending for all certified education personnel a 10 percent salary increase, and that you as the legislature reclassify them up one grade for an additional increase of about 5 percent.[11] We should aim for a pay scale that offers an experienced and able teacher the chance to make $35,000 a year, or more.

Of equal importance, I am recommending that the state of North

Carolina develop a new way of paying teachers. I urge that the 1985 legislature establish a career development plan to provide extraordinary rewards for extraordinary teachers, not just for reaching the upper levels of seniority, but for reaching the upper levels of competence and effectiveness as well.[12] I want the word to go out here and now that salaries for the best teachers in the future will compare with the best salaries in other professions.

In addition, one of the recommendations I am making to you is to establish free scholarships for students who want to become teachers,[13] and the State Board of Education is already developing a plan to attract the best students into teaching in the years ahead.

I am recommending that we test students in grades three, six, and nine to determine that they have mastered the competencies necessary at that level.[14] If not, students should be held back and provided strong and effective remedial programs, including free summer school, until they have earned promotion.

I recommend that we strengthen vocational programs, math and science laboratories, and that we buy new textbooks and computers.[15] Dropout prevention programs should be expanded,[16] and an Office of Rural Education created to work on behalf of children who live in remote, rural areas.

Finally, two concerns of parents that have been too often ignored should be addressed squarely. An Office of School Discipline should be created at the state level and modest funds made available to every school district to deal with disruptions and discipline problems. Nine pilot projects are working across North Carolina now. We can and we must make every school safe and conducive to learning.

The men who took the beaches and parachuted behind the lines at Normandy made their sacrifices and were successful for reasons far beyond their ability to read and compute and punctuate correctly. They were committed to certain values that this country stood for. We must develop plans to incorporate the teaching of positive values in our public schools. Boards of education should develop materials and methods for teaching these values such as patriotism, responsibility, good citizenship, honesty, courage, compassion and respect for other persons and other cultures, and free enterprise.[17]

This is an ambitious agenda, but it is achievable. As governor, I urge that you pass every recommendation of the Commission on Education for Economic Growth. This is the year to seize the future for North Carolina's schools, but your commitment should not be for this year alone. Many of the recommendations of the commission are for the next biennium and for the years beyond. Indeed, making our schools excellent—world competitive—is a job for the rest of this decade and through the year 2000.

I will ask that you make other investments in our state's future in this session.

I urge you to enact a seven-part package of compensation and benefits to our loyal state employees:

—A 10 percent cost of living salary increase for active employees.[18]

—A 10 percent cost of living increase for retirees.[19]

—More flexibility and funds for salary adjustments (reclassifications).

—Addition of the tenth step in the State Employees' Salary Increment Program for 1984-1985.[20]

—Elimination of the salary grade fifty from the State Employees' Salary Schedule.[21]

—Changing the teachers' and state employees' retirement formula from 1.57 percent to 1.60 percent.[22]

—Recommendation of the reinstatement of the Salary Increment Program in the biennial budget beginning July 1, 1985, in effect reinstating the merit system.[23] (This budget will go to the printer in November or early December of 1984.)

We must pass a Clean Water Budget to protect North Carolina's rivers, streams, and lakes against pollution.[24]

I urge that we improve our juvenile correction programs and that we extend statewide our "workfare" program that has proved effective in getting people off of welfare rolls and into paying jobs.

Let me conclude with a personal word to the members of this General Assembly:

It has been my honor and privilege over the past twelve years to serve with members of this body, past and present. During my eight years as governor we have had a time of challenge and change. We have had to ride out storms of recession and inflation, of political reaction and political renewal. I'm proud that in the beginning of my first year as governor, we had a beginning credit balance of $68.5 million. Today, we enter our eighth year with a credit balance of $225 million—and we have enacted no broad-based tax increases.

Our accomplishments in economic growth, high technology, human development, education, and the preservation of our natural resources have been impressive, and we have made North Carolina clearly one of the leading states, not just of the South, but of the nation.

Yes, we've had our disagreements. And we will always have those who criticize what we did yesterday, doubt what we are doing today, and question what we will be tomorrow.

But North Carolina has cast its lot with the future. We have faced tomorrow with hope—not with fear, with courage; not with hesitation, with belief in ourselves and in each other; not with doubt. That is the spirit that has prevailed in these halls, in the hearts and minds of the men and women who work and serve here. And it is particularly the driving spirit behind two of the finest leaders with whom it has been my honor to serve here: Lieutenant Governor Jimmy Green and Speaker of the House Liston Ramsey. That, my friends, is the spirit that has moved North Carolina forward for 400 years.

For myself and for my state, I give thanks to God for the wisdom and the courage and the vision that has walked in these halls. And I give special thanks for you, the men and women with whom it has been my privilege to serve and whose trust and friendship I shall cherish as long as I live. Thank you.

---

[1]James Collins (Jimmy) Green (1921-   ), lieutenant governor, 1977-1985. Previously identified in Mitchell, *Addresses of Hunt*, I, 167n.

[2]Liston Bryan Ramsey (1919-   ), speaker, state House of Representatives, since 1981. *North Carolina Manual, 1983*, 295; also previously identified in Mitchell, *Addresses of Hunt*, I, 515n.

[3]See "Statement on North Carolina Commission on Education for Economic Growth," October 13, 1983, below.

[4]For recommendations, see *Education for Economic Growth: An Action Plan for North Carolina* ([Raleigh]: North Carolina Commission on Education for Economic Growth, April, 1984), hereinafter cited as *Education for Economic Growth*.

Bland W. Worley (1917-   ), native of Kinston; resident of Winston-Salem; B.S., University of North Carolina at Chapel Hill, 1938; attended Graduate School of Banking, Rutgers University, and Executive Program, University of North Carolina at Chapel Hill; served in U.S. Army during World War II. President, vice-chairman, Wachovia Corp., 1946-1975; chairman, BarclaysAmerican Corp., 1975-1985, and of North Carolina School of Science and Mathematics. Bland W. Worley to Jan-Michael Poff, February 12, 1986.

[5]"An Act to Create the Public Education Policy Council" was ratified July 20. *N.C. Session Laws, 1983*, c. 860. *Report of the Public Education Policy Council . . . to the 1983 General Assembly, 1984 Session* ([Raleigh: The Council], 1984) contained recommendations on public school administration, curriculum, finance, and personnel; many of the proposals were included in "An Act to Enact the Elementary and Secondary School Reform Act of 1984," ratified July 6, 1984. *N.C. Session Laws, 1983, Second Session, 1984*, c. 1103. The primary findings, to which Hunt referred, above, were provided in *Report of the Public Education Policy Council . . . to the 1985 General Assembly of North Carolina* ([Raleigh: The Council], 1985).

[6]*N.C. Session Laws, 1983, Second Session, 1984*, c. 1103, s. 2.

[7]"An Act to Modify Current Operations and Capital Improvements Appropriations for North Carolina State Government for the 1984-85 Fiscal Year and to Make Other Changes in the Budget Operation of the State," c. 1034, was ratified June 29, 1984. Sections 11-13 reduced the student-teacher ratio in grades four through six. *N.C. Session Laws, 1983, Second Session, 1984*.

[8]The Student Information System pilot program was intended to diminish the amount of time teachers spent keeping class records. *N.C. Session Laws, 1983, Second Session, 1984*, s. 14.

[9]The Principals' Management Program was established under c. 1034, s. 54, *N.C. Session Laws, 1983, Second Session, 1984*. See also *N.C. Session Laws, 1983, Second Session, 1984*, c. 1103, s. 5.

[10]See *N.C. Session Laws, 1983, Second Session, 1984*, c. 1034, ss. 19, 20, 25-28, for provisions pertaining to exceptional and handicapped schoolchildren.

[11]*N.C. Session Laws, 1983, Second Session, 1984*, c. 1034, ss. 6, 20.

[12]The General Assembly authorized the State Board of Education to develop a career growth plan for teachers under c. 971, "An Act to Modify Current Operations and Capital Improvements Appropriations for North Carolina State Government for the 1984-85 Fiscal Year and to Make Other Changes in the Budget Operation of the State," s. 4, ratified June 25, 1984. See also c. 1103, ss. 8, 11, *N.C. Session Laws, 1983, Second Session, 1984*.

[13]The Scholarship Loan Fund for Prospective Teachers, established by G.S. 116-171, was authorized to provide 200 loans annually, beginning with the 1984-1985 academic year. *N.C. Session Laws, 1983, Second Session, 1984*, c. 1034, s. 10. See also *N.C. Session Laws, 1983, Second Session, 1984*, c. 1103, s. 13.

[14]*N.C. Session Laws, 1983, Second Session, 1984*, c. 1034, s. 8.

[15]The Basic and Vocational Education Skills Pilot Program was expanded under c. 1034, s. 17. The per-student allocation for math-science education materials and equipment was increased under c. 1034, s. 15, *N.C. Session Laws, 1983, Second Session, 1984*.

[16]Spending guidelines for dropout prevention programs were augmented under c. 1034, ss. 17.1, 18, *N.C. Session Laws, 1983, Second Session, 1984*.

[17]See *Education for Economic Growth*, 36.

[18]*N.C. Session Laws, 1983, Second Session, 1984*, c. 1034, s. 206.

[19]Retirement allowances were increased a maximum of 8 percent. *N.C. Session Laws, 1983, Second Session, 1984*, c. 1034, ss. 222-224.

[20]Joyce, *North Carolina Legislation, 1985*, 238.

[21]Session Laws of 1985, c. 757, raised the minimum salary for full-time state employees, subject to the State Personnel Act, to $758 per month. Joyce, *North Carolina Legislation, 1985*, 238.

[22]The retirement formula was increased, from 1.57 to 1.58 percent, under c. 459, s. 190, Session Laws of 1985. Joyce, *North Carolina Legislation, 1985*, 242.

[23]Chapter 479, s. 226, Session Laws of 1985, provided funds for eligible state employees to receive two, half-step increments in pay during the 1985-1986 fiscal year. Joyce, *North Carolina Legislation, 1985*, 239.

[24]Implementation of and participation in the Nutrient Sensitive Watershed Project was addressed in *N.C. Session Laws, 1983, Second Session, 1984*, c. 1034, ss. 109, 110. Despite stringent opposition from soap and detergent industry lobbyists, the state House Natural and Economic Resources Committee substitute version of H.B. 1603, "A Bill to be Entitled an Act to Provide for the Sale of Clean Detergents in North Carolina," passed its third reading on June 22, 1984, and was sent to the Senate. However, the Special Ways and Means Committee of the upper house reported unfavorably on the measure. *News and Observer*, June 20, 23, 1984; *N.C. House Journal, 1983, Second Session, 1984*, 36, 55, 100, 109; *N.C. Senate Journal, 1983, Second Session, 1984*, 82, 180.

PUBLIC ADDRESSES AND STATEMENTS

[Whether serving as a volunteer in a Raleigh school, advocating improvements in the state's human resources programs or infrastructure, spreading the gospel of education for economic growth to other parts of the country, or conducting trade missions to the Far East and Europe, James Baxter Hunt, Jr., clearly led an active second term as governor of North Carolina. Indeed, there is no better illustration of his high level of visibility than his weekly schedule for 1981-1984, which reveals that the governor delivered a minimum average of 370 speeches a year to audiences from Manteo to Tokyo, from Düsseldorf to Murphy. Were that annual figure to include the majority of Hunt's campaign appearances in his quest for the United States Senate, it no doubt would be higher.

Of the approximately 1,500 speaking engagements listed on Governor Hunt's official agenda, press copies of texts, notes, or outlines for more than 1,250 messages exist; add to them the scores of news releases issued by the governor's press office, and one has amassed a body of material too large to be reprinted in the single-volume documentary permitted each of the state's chief executives, per term of office, by North Carolina law. Materials ultimately selected for inclusion in the *Addresses of Hunt* most accurately reflect the scope of the governor's activities during his second term, discuss the aspirations and accomplishments of his administration, explain policies, illuminate some aspect of his occupational or political philosophy, or contain significant autobiographical elements. Naturally, it is inevitable that some of the same conceptual currents flow through more than one address, thus demonstrating the continuing importance Hunt assigned to specific issues; annotations accompanying documents reprinted herein mention textually similar and thematically identical items that were omitted. Deleted speeches and statements, and messages for which there is no press copy of any kind, are listed by date, title, and place of delivery, on pages 522-569.

Some will question the extent to which materials from Hunt's campaign for the United States Senate appear in this volume, and the absence of his official announcement for the Democratic nomination (Wilson, February 4, 1984) and transcripts of his four televised debates with Senator Jesse Helms might be considered noteworthy. A twofold explanation for these lacunae must suffice: First, because the debate transcripts were published by the Raleigh *News and Observer* (July 30, September 10, 24, October 14, 1984), which is widely available on microfilm, it was decided not to reproduce them here. Second, although state law requires all governors to deposit their official papers with the Department of Cultural Resources— and it is upon official papers, like Governor Hunt's, that documentaries such as this are based—the manner of disposal of personal records is left to the discretion of the chief executive. Hunt's 1984 campaign files have been placed, under protective covenant, among the political papers he donated to the East Carolina Manuscript Collection, Joyner Library, East Carolina University, Greenville.]

JOBS FOR PROGRESS

ROCKY MOUNT, JANUARY 7, 1981

[Partners in the Cummins-Case project—Cummins Engine Company, Columbus, Indiana, and the J. I. Case Company, Racine, Wisconsin—disclosed plans in December, 1980, to erect a 1.1 million square-foot diesel engine factory, situated on 115 acres, at Whitakers, Nash County. Nash, Halifax, and Edgecombe business interests enticed the project (now known as Consolidated Diesel Company) to the area, in part, by presenting 47 acres of land adjoining the proposed location of the plant to accommodate the facility's potential growth. Jobs for Progress, Inc., a nonprofit organization, was established to solicit "tax-deductible business donations" to retire the $1 million loan secured to purchase the additional acreage. *News and Observer*, January 13, 1981.

During an appearance at a Jobs for Progress rally, September 2, 1981, Hunt noted that repayment of the loan had been guaranteed; that construction of the new factory was continuing expeditiously, while Nash County had earmarked $3 million for allied water-sewer projects; and that ground had been broken near Consolidated Diesel for a training center, under the aegis of the then Nash Technical Institute, to provide the plant with skilled employees.]

It's always good to be back home in this part of eastern North Carolina. No other section of the state has contributed more or has more potential than eastern North Carolina, and a major reason for the success we've had is those of you in this room tonight.

We face a great challenge. That is the challenge of assuring that as we grow in North Carolina, progress occurs all across this state. No other state with as large a population as ours has had such balanced growth. We must keep it that way. We've got to seize those opportunities that will bring jobs to this region. In the past, you have been successful in that effort.

Now along comes the Cummins-Case project. It is a once-in-a-lifetime chance to provide a prosperous economic future for this entire region—and let me emphasize region. No question that Nash County will receive substantial tax benefits from this plant, but the benefits of this plant go far beyond tax revenues and the borders of Nash County. For example, the $355 million commitment Cummins-Case has made is the fourth-largest announcement by a new industry in this state's history. In addition, we estimate that new industrial investment related to the Cummins-Case project by other companies will total about $200 million—and we plan to encourage those companies to locate throughout this region.

Cummins-Case ultimately will provide 1,200 to 1,400 jobs. The additional industrial investment combined with normal multipliers could result in over 4,000 new jobs created by the location of Cummins-Case here. That's almost as many jobs generated by this one project as all the industrial jobs announced in Edgecombe,

Halifax, Nash, and Wilson in the last three years combined. There is no way all those jobs are going to be filled by people living in one county. Hundreds of people in each of your counties will fill those jobs.

If that isn't enough, consider the several hundred people who will be employed during the construction phase; the $65 million to be spent, mostly in this region, during construction. Annual expenditures by Cummins-Case for goods and services, mostly in this region, will be $20 to $25 million. Well over $50 million in retail sales throughout the region will be created as a result of the increased employment.

Take away the statistics and it's easy to see that this project will positively affect families throughout the region. Overall, I've never known of an industrial project that will mean more to this state than Cummins-Case. The Cummins-Case project will be an economic anchor for this region—and don't just take my word for it on how important this project is. Consider that New York appropriated $75 million as an inducement for this project. Consider that another state is still making extravagant offers to lure Cummins-Case away from North Carolina.

At the state level we have worked long and hard to recruit this project. Commitments have been made to improve roads in the region and upgrade technical training. Both are steps that will help the region, not just the company.

At the local level cooperation in attracting the company has been excellent. We need that same type of cooperation in developing services for the company to stay here.

There is still a piece of our puzzle missing: a tract of land. The choice of this region is simple—raise $1 million, acquire the land, or lose the project, lose the investment, lose the jobs, lose the economic security this project can provide your communities.

I realize raising a million dollars is a big job. It's a job that can't be accomplished by one community or one county. Perhaps more than any other time in the history of this region, we must unite to turn an impossible task for a few into a solvable problem for many.

The task is a difficult one, but dollar for dollar the payoff will be greater than any other fund raiser you could ever undertake. The million dollars will be returned to this region a thousandfold. No other cause can help so many ways for a similar investment. Five years from now when the poverty and unemployment I know is still in this area stares you in the eye; or you know somebody who just can't find a job; or your business has leveled off; you are going to find yourself asking, "What if we had been able to raise the million dollars and Cummins-Case were here?" Don't put yourself or this region in that position.

I want each of you to give this fund raiser all the support you can. With your support we will be successful. With success we will be a major step closer to making a reality the dream of prosperity for this region. It's a dream I've had while growing up in eastern North Carolina. I know it is one you share with me.

NOTES FOR CABINET SWEARING-IN CEREMONY

RALEIGH, JANUARY 12, 1981

[Eight of the nine persons sworn into the cabinet at the beginning of Hunt's second term held the same posts during his first administration; the exception was James Charles (Jimmy) Woodard, who succeeded Amos E. Reed as secretary of the Department of Correction. *News and Observer,* January 13, 1981. Those taking the oath of office on January 12 included: Thomas Wood Bradshaw, Jr. (1938-   ), secretary of transportation, 1977-1981. Previously identified in Mitchell, *Addresses of Hunt,* I, 397n. Duncan McLauchlin (Lauch) Faircloth (1928-   ), secretary of commerce, 1977-1983. Previously identified in Mitchell, *Addresses of Hunt,* I, 153n; Governor Hunt announced Faircloth's resignation at a news conference held June 16, 1983. Sara Wilson Hodgkins (1930-   ), secretary of cultural resources, 1977-1985. Previously identified in Mitchell, *Addresses of Hunt,* I, 228n. Howard Nathaniel Lee (1934-   ), secretary of natural resources and community development, 1977-1981. Previously identified in Mitchell, *Addresses of Hunt,* I, 90n; see also "Dinner Honoring Howard Lee," July 23, 1981, below. Mark George Lynch (1915-   ), secretary of revenue, 1977-1985. Previously identified in Mitchell, *Addresses of Hunt,* I, 402n. Burley Bayard Mitchell, Jr. (1940-   ), secretary of crime control and public safety, 1979-1982, and state supreme court associate justice since 1982. Previously identified in Mitchell, *Addresses of Hunt,* I, 589n; see also *North Carolina Manual, 1983,* 661, 777. Sarah Taylor Morrow (1921-   ), secretary of human resources, 1977-1984. Previously identified in Mitchell, *Addresses of Hunt,* I, 74n; see also *North Carolina Manual, 1983,* 683. Jane Smith Patterson (1940-   ), secretary of administration, 1981-1985; acting secretary, 1979-1980. Previously identified in Mitchell, *Addresses of Hunt,* I, 241n; see also *North Carolina Manual, 1983,* 591. James Charles Woodard (1915-   ), secretary of correction, 1981-1985. Previously identified in Mitchell, *Addresses of Hunt,* I, 445; see also *North Carolina Manual, 1983,* 639.]

I. Challenge

We have a historic opportunity—to build on successes, accomplishments, and knowledge of the last four years.

II. Teamwork

We must work together—as a team. Work together on tough issues that involve separate agencies. Work with people in our departments—they're good people. Also work with private sector and local governments. And enlist *citizens.*

III. Responsibility

We must carry out commitments I made—we made—to the people in last year's campaign:

   —Economic Development (microelectronics)
   —Education (dropouts, class size)
   —Energy
   —Environmental protection (hazardous wastes)
   —Crime (juveniles)
   —Elderly
   —Children
IV. Summary
   As I said in my "Inaugural Address," it is time again for North
Carolina to lead the nation. We must prove that we can be both
conservative *and* progressive. We must prove that government can
be both lean and compassionate. We must prove that we can be
responsible with the taxpayer's money and at the same time make
wise investments that will yield better jobs, better education, and a
better future for our people.

ANNOUNCEMENT ON
R. J. REYNOLDS TOBACCO COMPANY

RALEIGH, JANUARY 12, 1981

   I am very proud that R. J. Reynolds Tobacco Company is giving a
$1 million grant to North Carolina State University to support
agricultural extension and research programs. This announcement
means a great deal to North Carolina farmers and to the agricultural and tobacco industries in this state, but it doesn't surprise
me. R. J. Reynolds has always been one of our very finest corporate
citizens and has done so much to help the farming industry in
North Carolina.
   It was Reynolds, for example, that took the principles of mechanical tobacco harvesting that had been worked out here at North
Carolina State University and incorporated them into a practical
farm-type harvester. Last year almost half of the total flue-cured
crop in North Carolina was mechanically harvested, saving farmers
millions of man-hours of labor. I personally appreciated Reynolds's
participation in the trip I made to China two years ago to try to
open new doors to trade between China and this state, and since
arrangements have now been made to sell Camel cigarettes in the
People's Republic of China, we have proof that this trip did open
doors for North Carolina tobacco.
   But I want to emphasize, too, that North Carolina State University greatly deserves this million-dollar grant. This university has
tobacco scientists and specialists here on campus and extension
agents out in the counties who help our farmers and agribusiness-
men stay abreast of the technological changes in tobacco production that seem to be coming faster and faster. This grant will

substantially benefit our total program of research and education, and if we are going to continue to move forward in the agriculture field, we must have strong research and education efforts.

I want to single out one new program that will be supported by this grant: the training program for farm women. Women make tremendous contributions to the agricultural economy of this state. They are farm managers, partners, and workers. I'm proud to see that you will have good educational activities geared especially to their needs and interests. It is commendable to target women for this support and help. I think this program will emphasize the importance of women in agriculture.

Reynolds, as you know, started a "Pride in Tobacco" campaign three years ago. Reynolds is showing its confidence in tobacco through this $1 million grant and the $1 billion expansion program the company announced last summer.[1]

I want each of you to know I have pride in tobacco too, and I am proud of R. J. Reynolds Tobacco Company, North Carolina State University, and our North Carolina farmers who grow the best tobacco in the world. With this kind of partnership, the future for tobacco in North Carolina looks bright.

---

[1]The expansion program to which Hunt referred entailed building the world's largest (2 million square feet) and most advanced cigarette factory, in Tobaccoville, and an addition to the Whitaker Park, Winston-Salem plant. Other corporate goals included "the modernization of existing production equipment, and the installation of state of the art technology throughout our operations." Maura T. Payne, Corporate Public Relations Department, R. J. Reynolds Industries, Inc., to Charles T. Francis, July 6, 1983.

CLOSING REMARKS, NORTH CAROLINA CONFERENCE ON SMALL BUSINESS

RALEIGH, JANUARY 28, 1981

[In opening remarks before the North Carolina Conference on Small Business, January 28, 1981, Hunt reminded listeners of the positive impact the state's successful industrial recruiting program had upon the growth of small business and reviewed the advances his administration had made on its behalf: establishment of the Business Assistance Division and the Small Business Development Office of the Department of Commerce; holding statewide buyer-supplier conferences; and increasing the number of minority-owned firms on the vendors' list. Other points made in this speech appear in Mitchell, *Addresses of Hunt*, I, 783-785.]

Chairman Lineberry,[1] I am told that the people participating here today have been rather busy since I spoke this morning. I understand that there has been a lot of spirited discussion about the problems confronting small business in North Carolina. I thank you for the recommendations that have been submitted to me, and again, I want to thank the advocacy council for the tremendous job it has done these past months.

I want to take this opportunity to respond to these recommendations. My positions on many of these proposals will be more detailed and refined as time goes by. Many of them are under study by the Department of Commerce and other agencies. Let's take a look at them now.

First, the issue of taxation. North Carolina has a good story to tell with regard to our tax system, but it is important that small business operators and individuals have full access to information about tax policy. I agree with your recommendation for a tax awareness program, and I will appoint a task force to implement such a program.

I am aware of your desire for phase-out of the manufacturer's inventory tax, and for expansion of the concept to cover retailers and wholesalers, but I must say to you with all candor that this is a particularly tight budget year at both the state and local levels. Fiscal responsibility dictates that I not actively support such a phase-out at this time. The issue will, however, be before the General Assembly for its consideration.

I concur with your recommendation that a study be made of a gross-receipts tax for North Carolina. I would suggest that the General Assembly request information on this concept from the National Conference of State Legislators.

I am aware that there was a lot of comment at your meetings about government regulations and the problems it presents for small business. I was particularly disturbed to learn of reports that, in some instances, regulatory personnel have displayed a less than positive attitude in their dealings with business people. I will not tolerate negative or uncooperative treatment. I will take this matter up with my cabinet secretaries and other state officials, and I want to pause in my remarks right now to sign an executive order directing all regulatory personnel to treat all who come under their jurisdiction in a positive, cooperative way.[2]

Your recommendations for enactment of a regulatory flexibility act and equal access of justice are very attractive concepts. It is likely that many of the objectives of these recommendations will be met with proposed refinements to the Administrative Procedures Act.[3] I urge the Small Business Advocacy Council to monitor the proceedings in this area and report back to me on what they learn.

Your recommendations for a study of franchise law and the Sunset Law have merit. The General Assembly will be reviewing these items, and I think it is important that small business operators have input into their deliberations.[4]

Capital formation and retention are essential to the survival of any business enterprise, and it becomes more difficult during these uncertain economic times. I want to be of any assistance I can in this area, and as a first step I intend to convene a meeting of the chief executive officers of the major financial institutions in this state. I will ask for their cooperation and their suggestions about how small business can get better access to capital.[5]

Your recommendation for the establishment of a Small Business Investment Company is a concept I support. I urge the Small Business Advocacy Council to pursue this idea and get to me all the information you are able to assemble.

This administration is committed to supporting small business by providing education, training, and information to businesses and their employees. In response to your request for a toll-free line in the Business Assistance Division that business people can call for information, I will at my earliest opportunity take up this idea with Secretary Faircloth.

I am pleased with the recommended establishment of high-skill technical training centers, because the Department of Community Colleges is working on this right now. Certain institutions will be designated as advance training centers in specific skills. We will strive to provide these programs with the most advanced instructional aids and equipment.

I support your proposal for expanding high school curricula relating to small business and its role in the free enterprise system. I challenge each of you to become more involved with your local schools and see how you can help accomplish this.

I will consider further the idea of changing the method of funding for community colleges to encourage additional training opportunities for small business. I think our community college system is doing a commendable job in this area. These institutions offer two-year programs in business management; there are course offerings in such areas as computer programming, data processing, taxation, and personnel management.

In the area of procurement and bonding, I want to pursue your idea for a pilot procurement program involving small businesses and our Purchase and Contract people. I am pleased to announce that a specialized buyer-supplier event like the one you suggest will be held here at McKimmon Center on May 21, and it will focus on the electronics industry. In the fall a similar event will focus on the metalworking industry in North Carolina.

I strongly support the idea of a series of meetings aimed at helping small and minority businesses learn how to do business with the state. A series of six workshops will be held on the campuses of six community colleges and technical institutes this year. I support the concept of continued affirmative action in the Division of Purchase and Contract, and I am requesting that that division develop goals that I can implement to maximize the business the state does with minority firms.

Turning to your general recommendations, I agree that we need a directory of state services for business and industry, and I am directing Secretary Faircloth to have such a publication prepared. I will also ask the secretary to pursue the possibility of permanent state funding for the Small Business Development Section.

Having looked at your recommendations, it has become very apparent to me that the work begun by this council needs to be a continuing process. I want the Small Business Advocacy Council to continue in existence and continue to serve as a communications link between me and the small business community. We haven't solved all the problems today, but this great turnout tells me that we've got something very promising going here. I hope this will be the first of many such conferences.

In conclusion, I want to again express my heartfelt thanks to the members of the Small Business Advocacy Council. You have made many personal sacrifices, but you can rest assured that your work is helping make North Carolina a better place to live, work, and do business.

---

[1] Albert Shuler Lineberry, Jr. (1946-   ), resident of Greensboro; chairman, North Carolina Small Business Advocacy Council. Albert S. Lineberry, Jr., to Charles T. Francis, June 24, 1983; also previously identified in Mitchell, *Addresses of Hunt,* I, 785.

[2] Executive Order No. 60, *N.C. Session Laws, 1981,* 1756-1757.

[3] "An Act to Establish Procedures for the Conduct of Proceedings before Administrative Agencies and to Establish a Code of Administrative Regulations" was ratified April 12, 1974. *N.C. Session Laws, 1973, Second Session, 1974,* c. 1331.

[4] "An Act to Repeal the Sunset Law and to Replace the Governmental Evaluation Commission with a Legislative Committee on Agency Review, which will Complete the Process of Reviewing Laws and Programs that were on the Sunset List" was ratified July 10, 1981. *N.C. Session Laws, 1981,* c. 932.

[5] On April 8, 1981, the governor urged a meeting of the North Carolina Bankers Association "to target small businesses as a special market to be developed." He noted, "More than half the people who are working in this state are employed by small businesses. That's where we're seeing the real growth in employment, and we can't afford to let small businesses stagnate because of a lack of financial support."

STATEMENT ON SCA SERVICES, INC.

RALEIGH, FEBRUARY 18, 1981

[SCA Services, Inc., of Boston, received a permit from the Department of Human Resources to construct a $12 million hazardous waste disposal plant in Arrowood Southern Industrial Park, near Charlotte. But allegations that the company was affiliated with organized crime and participated in bid-rigging schemes had drawn scrutiny from both Congress and the state of New Jersey; the charges also aroused the concern of the Mecklenburg County Board of Commissioners, which requested that Governor Hunt initiate an SBI investigation. Construction of the facility was suspended until a suit filed against SCA by Mecklenburg citizens was resolved and the SBI probe into the firm's reputed criminal activity in other states had been concluded. *Charlotte Observer,* February 17, 20, 1981; *News and Observer,* February 19, 1981. Because the case was pending in the North Carolina Court of Appeals, the SBI was unable to comment on the findings its inquiry produced. Haywood R. Starling, director, State Bureau of Investigation, to Jan-Michael Poff, August 14, 1984.]

I am today, with the full concurrence of Attorney General Rufus Edmisten, directing the State Bureau of Investigation to conduct a formal investigation into allegations concerning SCA Services, Inc., which has been granted a permit to construct and operate a hazardous waste disposal facility in Mecklenburg County.

I have been deeply concerned about these allegations since they first came to my attention. My decision concerning an SBI inquiry has been made after close consultation between my legal staff, the North Carolina Department of Justice, and the District Attorney's Office in Mecklenburg County. We feel that an SBI investigation is the best means available to address these issues and provide information to the Department of Human Resources and other state officials.

The safe and effective management of hazardous wastes is of vital importance to the future of North Carolina. It is absolutely essential that firms operating waste-management facilities in this state be law abiding. I want to emphasize that I have no preconceived notions about what will be learned during these inquiries. When sufficient information has been developed by the SBI, the state of North Carolina is prepared to take whatever action may be appropriate.

STATEMENT ON CAPE HATTERAS LIGHTHOUSE

RALEIGH, FEBRUARY 19, 1981

[The contents of Hunt's letter of February 19 concerning the threat of beach erosion to Cape Hatteras Lighthouse, to Joe Brown, southeast regional director of the National Park Service, are summarized below.]

I am releasing today a copy of a letter I am sending to the southeastern regional director of the National Park Service.[1] In it I ask him to take immediate action to carry out the federal government's obligation to protect the historic Cape Hatteras Lighthouse from beach erosion.

In 1958 the state transferred the lighthouse property to the federal government. The federal government committed itself, at that time, to preserving the lighthouse as a part of the Cape Hatteras National Recreation Area. Storms last year brought the ocean to within fifty feet of the lighthouse. Over the years a number of steps have been taken to protect the structure, but it is clear today that the lighthouse will fall into the ocean unless the federal government lives up to its commitment.

Secretary Howard Lee will be meeting with officials of the National Park Service in Atlanta tomorrow, and he will personally deliver this letter for me there.

I am asking the Park Service to conduct an immediate review of five alternative strategies for protecting the lighthouse and to get to work as soon as possible on the plan that offers the most protection. Those alternatives include moving the lighthouse about a half mile, at a cost of $2.7 million; building a mound of rubble around the base; construction of groins; and substantial beach "nourishment."[2]

I understand the difficulties in protecting any structure from the movement of the shoreline. I understand the budget problems. But I also understand that the federal government has a commitment to the state of North Carolina to do everything in its power to save this great lighthouse. I want the federal government to live up to that commitment.

---

[1]Joe Brown (1918-   ), native of Buffalo, New York; resident of Atlanta; received bachelor's degree in forestry from University of Georgia, 1942; served in U.S. Army Air Force during World War II; retired major, U.S. Air Force Reserve. Employed in various administrative capacities by National Park Service, 1965-1977; director, Southeast Region, National Park Service, 1977-1981. Neal G. Guse, acting director, Southeast Region, National Park Service, to Jan-Michael Poff, November 22, 1983, hereinafter cited as Guse correspondence.

[2]Brown's undated response to Hunt indicated that, of the proposed alternatives for saving the lighthouse, his office would suggest to the director of the Park Service "repairing and extending shoreward the three existing U.S. Navy groins; constructing a fourth groin to the south of the existing groin field; and ringing the lighthouse with sheet steel piling. The cost estimate for this work is around 4 to 4.5 million dollars. . . ." Joe Brown to Governor Hunt, ref. no. A3815-SER-SA, included in Guse correspondence.

NORTH CAROLINA ASSOCIATION OF INDEPENDENT COLLEGES AND UNIVERSITIES

RALEIGH, FEBRUARY 25, 1981

I want to thank President Henley[1] and the leaders of this fine organization for inviting me to be here today, along with Lieutenant Governor Green, Speaker Ramsey, and these members of the General Assembly. I think I can speak for all of these people when I say that those of us in positions of leadership in this state consider the private colleges and universities to be an absolutely vital part of our system of education. People like Terry Sanford, John Henley, and all of the campus presidents and trustees here in this room have done an excellent job over the years of making state government aware of just how important the private colleges are.

I am acutely aware of the need for not only preserving the private campuses, but also the need for your academic programs to grow and develop in the years to come. In the last decade North Carolina's financial commitment to private higher education has grown steadily. In the budget presented to the General Assembly by my administration and the Advisory Budget Commission, it is recommended that the per-student expenditure for these institutions be increased by $100 over the next biennium.[2] As President Sanford stated so eloquently last week, our financial commitment needs to be even greater if we are to ensure the long-term survival of private colleges and universities.

These are tough economic times for state government and for the taxpayers who support it; accordingly, the private colleges and almost all state-funded programs are feeling the pinch. But in the coming years, as additional revenues become available, private higher education must have a high priority in the allocation of those revenues. I hope that in the near future we can give serious consideration to the establishment of a funding formula that would allow private colleges and universities to keep pace with increasing costs.

The public funding that goes to private institutions is money well spent.[3] If it weren't for these institutions, the taxpayers would have to bear a larger portion of the cost of educating your students, and some of those students wouldn't even have the opportunity to get a college education. I am as committed as anybody to our great public university system, but as great as that system is, it cannot meet all of our needs in the realm of higher education.

There must be diversity in a truly great educational system — academic diversity, social diversity, and cultural diversity. That is what you make possible. You give students and their parents a meaningful choice in terms of academic programs, campus atmosphere, and educational philosophy.

I think the primary reason why private higher education is becoming more vital to our future is a commitment to excellence in *undergraduate* education. Graduate education and research certainly have their place, but I think educators sometimes tend to forget that most young people who enter college will not go on to graduate school. For most of them their four years of undergraduate work is their primary preparation for a life's work. It is the undergraduate schools that train the vast majority of our teachers, business people, and professionals. The private colleges and universities of our state have never lost sight of this.

The institutions you represent have made an immeasurable contribution to North Carolina. As we continue to move this state forward in the years ahead, your role is going to become even more important. You have throughout your history risen to great challenges. You will have my support in meeting the great challenges and opportunities that the future holds.

---

[1]John Tannery Henley (1921-   ), president, North Carolina Association of Independent Colleges and Universities, since 1979. Previously identified in Mitchell, *Addresses of Hunt*, I, 515n.

[2]*N.C. Session Laws, 1981*, c. 859, ss. 36-39.1.

[3]Speaking February 9, 1982, at Belmont Abbey College, Hunt acknowledged North Carolina's $20 million annual investment in its thirty-seven independent institutions of higher education and noted that the "economic benefit" of those schools "to our state is conservatively estimated at $1 billion a year."

SYMPOSIUM ON ENGINEERING SYSTEMS FOR FOREST REGENERATION

RALEIGH, MARCH 3, 1981

It is a great pleasure to welcome you to the great state of North Carolina and to share some thoughts with you on forest resources— a subject of great importance to this state, to the Southeast, and to our nation. We are very proud to be the host state for this symposium. I am impressed that it has attracted people from twelve countries, indicating the global importance of this topic.

I want to talk with you today about forest resources in North Carolina, a state that is two-thirds forest land.

I see three main reasons why North Carolina, and certainly the Southeast and the nation, must be concerned about our forest resources and must work to ensure the most efficient use of them.

First, we must use our natural resources wisely. In North Carolina, which ranks fifth in the nation in the amount of commercial timberland, our 19.5 million acres of forest land are one of our state's principal assets. But we are by no means realizing the full potential of this land. In North Carolina forest land is producing less than half the growth that could be gained with even a moderate level of management. The majority of our forest land is owned by farmers and others who are not involved in industrial forestry enterprises. Regeneration of our forest land is being practiced on far too few acres.

Second, with inflation taking its toll on all of us, forest production represents a significant additional income to landowners and also provides the very basis for the rapidly expanding forest industry in the South.

Third, the use of alternative energy sources will be the key to a secure energy future. Wood energy can play a big part in that. In this nation, even now, more energy is produced from wood than is generated from nuclear power plants. Wood management and regeneration are critical if we are to fully use our forest resources. We must encourage and provide incentives for forest management on private land.

North Carolina has undertaken a plan of action to put idle forest land to work. We are making good progress:

—We have a Forest Development Program that provides subsidies for reforestation efforts by nonindustrial owners. Our North Carolina Division of Forest Resources offers site preparation and planting services at cost to small woodlot owners.

—I established an Advisory Task Force on Small Woodlot Management to recommend ways the state can help small woodlot owners increase the productivity of their land. We are already seeing good results from some of its recommendations that we have put into effect.

—We have developed county forestry associations that sponsor programs for woodlot owners to help build their knowledge of investment and income opportunities in growing timber. We expect to expand that program from the present thirty-eight counties to all 100 counties within the next year.

—The Small Woodlot Research and Development Program at North Carolina State University develops appropriate technology for small woodlot management that is less costly than industrial systems.

—Tax incentives are also important, and in 1979 North Carolina tax laws were changed to exclude from gross income those payments received under federal and state cost-sharing systems. Reforestation and related costs can be amortized over a sixty-month period, and some landowners can distribute, over a three-year period, receipts received from timber sales in any one year.[1]

—We have a Governor's Interagency Committee on Small Woodlots, consisting of the heads of state agencies and agricultural groups, that has developed good cooperation among agencies dealing with woodlot owners. It has helped bring about the formation of the county forestry associations and has supported their programs.

—In the last year the North Carolina Division of Forest Resources acquired new land that eventually will be able to produce enough genetically improved pine seedlings to plant 100,000 acres annually. Also, North Carolina State University's School of Forest Resources' cooperative work with the forest industry in the field of genetic pine tree improvement has resulted in major gains in wood productivity throughout the South.

—Since good market opportunities for woodlots depend on vital and well-dispersed forest industries, we have become more aggressive in recruiting forest-based industries to North Carolina, as well as encouraging expansion of existing industry.

So we have made good progress, but we have a long way to go. Too much forest land is sitting idle; too much is not used to its full potential. We must continue directing our resources and talent toward development of good management systems for our forests, particularly those owned privately for nonindustrial use.

I know we can be successful in our efforts to more fully use this valuable asset. I hope you have very productive discussions on this subject and help ensure that we develop the diversity in engineering systems for regeneration that will be appropriate for owners of small woodlots as well as those needed for large-scale industrial operations.

---

[1]See "An Act to Amend G.S. 105-164.13 Regarding Certain Exemptions from the Sales and Use Tax," c. 46, ratified February 16, 1979, and "An Act to Provide Tax Relief for the Citizens of North Carolina," c. 801, ss. 32, 40, ratified June 6, 1979. *N.C. Session Laws, 1979.*

TESTIMONY BEFORE U.S. HOUSE COMMITTEE ON ENERGY AND COMMERCE, SUBCOMMITTEE ON HEALTH AND ENVIRONMENT

WASHINGTON, D.C., MARCH 10, 1981

[Campaigning for the presidency in 1980, Ronald Reagan promised to reduce the federal deficit by cutting government spending; by the end of February, 1981, his administration unveiled a program of budget reductions amounting to $48.6 billion in 1982 and worth nearly $200 billion by the close of 1984. A component of the package—the 5 percent maximum cap, above the 1981 level, on federal Medicaid funding—proved to be "one of the most controversial and bitterly fought proposals in Reagan's fiscal 1982 budget." Congress ultimately refused to impose the measure; nevertheless, when H.R. 3982 (PL 97-35) was signed into law August 13, 1981, it cut $35.2 billion from the 1982 budget, $1 billion of which came from federal Medicaid expenditures. See "An Act to Provide for Reconciliation Pursuant to Section 301 of the First Concurrent Resolution on the Budget for the Fiscal Year 1982," 95 Stat. 783-830, Title XXI.

State governments support 45 percent of Medicaid's total financial requirement, with the balance coming from Washington. Were the 5 percent cap on federal spending to be enacted, the amount of the states' contribution to the program would have to increase in order to maintain the current level of service. There were many officials who doubted the difference in revenue could be raised, considering the condition of the economy, at state and local levels. Speaking on behalf of the National Governors' Association before the House Subcommittee on Health and Environment, Hunt offered an alternative to the proposed federal Medicaid spending ceiling that would reduce costs while furnishing acceptable care at reasonable rates.

Congressional Quarterly Almanac, 97th Congress, 1st Session, . . . 1981, Volume XXXVII (Washington, D.C.: Congressional Quarterly, 1982), 256, 477-478, hereinafter cited as *Congressional Quarterly Almanac.*]

I have come here today as chairman of the Human Resources Committee of the National Governors' Association to talk to you about our very serious concerns with the administration's proposal to cap Medicaid expenditures. I also want to offer you a workable alternative, which we believe will save twice the amount the president is seeking.

I am sure that you will be hearing from many special interest groups asking you to cut somebody else's program, not theirs. This is *not* the case with the National Governors' Association's recommendations. We sincerely believe we can offer you an interim solution to the problem of rapidly escalating Medicaid costs without sacrificing essential health care services or denying care to the elderly poor and the needy children of this nation.

Medicaid program costs have risen at an average rate of 15 percent each year. A majority of the forty-nine states that have Medicaid cannot afford to finance even the state share of those costs. Rising unemployment, a growing elderly population, and increased numbers of single-parent families all contribute to the rising demand for and use of publicly supported medical care.

The problem we all face in financing this program will not be solved—not even in the short run—by arbitrarily and drastically limiting the amount of federal dollars supporting this program. The immediate effect of such a move will be to shift costs to the states and local governments, and we simply cannot absorb cuts of this magnitude. I am even more concerned about the effect on the needy as major program reductions take place and eligibility is denied or vital services are eliminated.

The need for health care will not disappear along with the dollars to fund it. Someone will have to meet these needs, and I fear that it will fall to our community and state institutions to care for these people perhaps in a setting or at a level that is both costly and inappropriate, but the only one available to them. My concern, then, is that we reduce Medicaid program costs, but that we do so in a way that will preserve a balanced health-care package for our poorest citizens at the least cost to the taxpayer.

Let's look at where the federal funds are spent. Over 70 percent of all Medicaid dollars go to institutions—hospitals and nursing homes. Physician services and prescription drugs account for less than half of the remaining 30 percent. Hospital outpatient care, clinics, eyeglasses, hearing aids, home health services, and dental care make up the balance. Where would you look for savings if you were faced with cutbacks of 10 percent or more? I believe you would logically consider reductions in the area of institutional care.

Can we really reduce costs by eliminating the noninstitutional services? Will real savings occur if we reduce the support we so desperately need for preventive care for children so that they can grow up without disabilities and become productive citizens? Will we benefit by reducing support for home care for the elderly so that they do not have to spend the last years of their lives confined to an institution? What will happen to our goals of deinstitutionalization of the mentally ill? Of rehabilitation? Can we afford to turn away from these priorities even for a moment? The obvious answer to our immediate fiscal crisis must be found in the way we fund institutional care.

The governors have proposed, and we hope you will support us, that the rate of increase for hospital reimbursement in both the Medicare and Medicaid programs be limited to 10 percent in 1982. If this proposal is accepted, neither Medicare patients nor Medicaid patients will suffer loss of benefits, yet the savings in Medicare expenditures alone would equal $1.7 billion. Medicaid savings would be an additional $200 million or more, reducing federal expenditures by almost twice that of the Reagan[1] proposal.

All of us will have to make sacrifices when the budget is cut. Hospitals will receive less than their expected rate of increase, which in some states has been as high as 18 percent, but we know that hospital costs can be held down, as witnessed in those states which have regulated this industry. I am not proposing that we regulate this industry. I am saying only that we cannot meet our targeted reductions entirely at the expense of the needy. If hospitals protest this limit in increases, they should consider the alternatives that states may be forced to impose, such as limiting the number of days of hospital care that will be reimbursed, regardless of the patient's length of stay.

We must include Medicare in this proposal because in most states Medicaid tracks Medicare principles of reimbursement. Moreover, Medicare purchases about 25 percent of all hospital services, while Medicaid purchases only 10 percent. We must combine Medicaid's limited purchasing power with that of Medicare if we are going to bring about any changes in the way health care is financed or delivered. If private industry joined us and also refused to recognize more than a 10 percent rate increase for its health insurance premium costs, we would achieve considerable leverage in the health-care marketplace.

The second major proposal addresses nursing-home care. Only a few states have in place fully developed and fully funded long-term care plans for their chronically ill population. Yet nursing-home costs have grown faster than any other health-care service in recent years. Almost 40 percent of federal Medicaid dollars are spent for this service. Until now, states have had *limited* resources for at-home or community-based care, and virtually *unlimited* Medicaid funds for nursing-home care. The barriers to funding alternative support services have contributed heavily to reliance on institutional placements.

Because Medicaid pays for more than half of the nation's nursing-home care, we feel that this is an area where we can and should exercise more influence at the state level. We would accept a cap which would limit the growth of nursing-home expenditures to 7 percent in 1982 provided we are given the flexibility to design a rational long-term care plan to meet our needs without federal restrictions on reimbursement principles, service delivery, or definitions of eligible services. We estimate that a 7 percent cap on nursing-home expenditures would yield savings of approximately $400 million. Future increases should be tied to a state's elderly population in need of care. I know, Mr. Chairman,[2] of your interest in this area, and I hope that you would work with us in developing this proposal.

Finally, we want to talk to you about our need for greater flexibility to act as prudent buyers and to manage our programs more efficiently. For many years the National Governors' Association has urged Congress and the administration to reduce the regulatory burden imposed on the states, on local governments, and on the private sector. It is painfully clear to many of us that states are prohibited both by law and by regulation from making decisions in their Medicaid programs that are sound and would result in savings at all levels of government. Whether or not a cap is imposed, and I urge [you] to consider our alternatives seriously, we need— and the taxpayers have demanded—freedom from regulations that prevent us from saving scarce tax revenues.

We can no longer afford to have the federal government dictate to us in detail every process we must follow and ignore the outcomes or the product of our efforts. An excellent example of this is in the EPSDT program—that is, Early and Periodic Screening, Diagnosis, and Treatment for Children. No one is more concerned about raising healthy children than I. We cannot invest enough in this most precious of all resources so that our young people will grow up to be happy, productive citizens. Yet countless hours have been spent and millions of pieces of paper have been wasted in attempts to comply with the ridiculous regulations promulgated by the Department of Health and Human Services. The effect of the regulations has been, in some states, an increase in costs, a decrease in the number of children served, and a growing reluctance by providers to participate in the program.

There are other examples of burdensome and unnecessary regulations that dramatically affect the costs of the Medicaid program, but I believe you already have a copy of the National Governors' Association's proposal highlighting a number of them. What is most important to remember is that we cannot reduce the growth in

Medicaid costs without the flexibility we are seeking. We will work closely with this administration and with this Congress in our efforts to untie the hands of our program managers so that they can get on with the business of managing their programs in the most efficient and effective way possible.

Thank you for inviting me to come before you today. I hope that we can move ahead together in this challenge—to provide needed care at a price we can afford, and to minimize the hurt to those less fortunate than we.

---

[1] Ronald Wilson Reagan (1911-   ), native of Tampico, Illinois; A.B., Eureka College, 1932; U.S. Army Air Force, 1942-1945. Sports announcer, actor, 1932-1966; California governor, 1967-1975; businessman, rancher, 1975-1980; fortieth U.S. president, elected 1980, and reelected in 1984. *Who's Who in America, 1982-1983*, II, 2758.

[2] Henry Arnold Waxman (1939-   ), U.S. representative from California's Twenty-fourth Congressional District, since 1975, and chairman of the Subcommittee on Health and Environment; Democrat. Michael Barone and Grant Ujifusa, *The Almanac of American Politics, 1984* (Washington, D.C.: National Journal, 1983), 134, hereinafter cited as Barone and Ujifusa, *Almanac of American Politics, 1984*; also previously identified in Mitchell, *Addresses of Hunt*, I, 731n.

AYDEN CHAPTER, PITT COUNTY CHAMBER OF COMMERCE

AYDEN, MARCH 13, 1981

[The governor also stressed the consequences of deteriorating roads in speeches to the Travel Council of North Carolina, March 11; North Carolina Traffic League, March 17; North Carolina Aggregates Association, March 26; employees of Kelly-Springfield Tire Company, March 26; North Carolina Bankers Association, April 8; Sales and Marketing Executives Club of Asheville, April 13; Charlotte Optimist Club, May 4; Transportation Week Announcement, May 14; and news conferences given April 1, 2, 3, and 28, 1981.]

It is a special pleasure to be here today with this newly formed Ayden Chapter of your county Chamber of Commerce. I think the reorganization of your county chamber was very wise in light of the great progress this area has made and the need for more special attention to be given to towns like Ayden, Grifton, Farmville, and Bethel. It's particularly appropriate that this Ayden Chapter was the first offshoot formed, excluding Greenville. Your town has grown an amazing 26.9 percent in the last ten years. That points out the need for more attention in your community to areas like economic development, roads, and so forth. And as the first town in eastern North Carolina to switch from electric service by VEPCO to CP & L at a savings of 36 percent, along with your good water supply and your area's aggressive recruiting efforts, Ayden is ripe for further industrial development.

Ayden has grown as North Carolina has grown, and we have come a long way. We have become an industrial giant, and now, if we seize the opportunity, we can become a national and international center for high-technology industry. We have come to this point, in large measure, because of the excellent network of roads and highways that we have built.

North Carolina is known as "The Good Roads State." That is more than a reputation. It is a tradition. Fifty years ago Governor O. Max Gardner took over the old county roads. Thirty years ago Governor Kerr Scott [1] got the farmers out of the mud. We, the people of North Carolina, built the roads that take farmers to their markets and factory workers to their jobs. We built the interstate highways that save us hours of driving—and thousands of lives.

Those roads—from two-lane country blacktops to six-lane super-highways—are the bones that support the muscles of our economy. Everyday I talk with industry executives, persuading them to build their plants in North Carolina. I can tell you that in just about every single case they wouldn't come to North Carolina if it wasn't for the good roads and highways we have. Blue Bell would never have decided to build its plant here in Ayden if it weren't for the good roads in this area. The completion of U.S. 264 from Wilson to Greenville will play a vital role in the continued economic development of this area.

We, the people of North Carolina, have built the largest state-maintained highway system in the nation—75,000 miles. That would circle the Earth at the equator three times. We need that system because we don't have just one big city, with all the problems of a New York or Detroit. We have a lot of smaller cities and towns and communities. People can live here in Ayden or Farmville or Grifton and drive to work in Greenville. They can drive from here to the du Pont plant in Lenoir County where I know many of this area's residents work. They can live on the farm and work in the factory.

In a real sense, our economy—and our jobs—ride on our roads. But I have to give you some bad news today. Our roads and streets and highways are in trouble, and we—the people who built them—are going to have to face up to that problem. We put a lot of wear and tear on those roads. Like anything else, they will crumble if we don't keep them up.

You don't see any real bad potholes or crumbling shoulders yet, because we have done a good job of keeping them up in the past. But in 1970 it cost us only $9,600 to resurface one mile. Today it costs us $25,000 a mile.

Why is that? Inflation, that's why. In 1970 a ton of the asphalt we use in resurfacing cost $31.63. Today that same ton costs $153.23. So we can't resurface as much. In 1970 we resurfaced 2,810 miles of roads. This year we can only do 740 miles—just over one fourth as much as a decade ago.

So you may not see any potholes or bad rough spots yet, but believe me, before long you are going to *feel* them. And it will cost you. I had my staff check around today and get some prices. It will cost $18.00 to get your front end aligned. A pair of shocks will cost you $47.90. A new tire can cost you up to $100.00.

That's not the only way we'll pay. We will lose industries and good jobs. We will lose like Pennsylvania has. There, some of their interstates are in such bad shape that the speed limit on them is 30 miles an hour.

I think of the schoolteacher and another Pitt County resident who were killed in the winter of 1979 near Greenville when a car hit a shoulder that was too low and too soft and crossed over to the other side of the road, hitting another car head-on.

What are we going to do about that? Not just the governor, not just the General Assembly, but all of us, the people of North Carolina. You ultimately will have to decide.

When I gave my "Inaugural Address" a little over a month ago, I talked about the greatness of North Carolina. I talked about our proud history. I talked about the great progress we have made, and I talked about the fantastic future that we can have.

No state is growing faster than North Carolina. While the nation is in a recession, North Carolina is attracting tremendous numbers of new industries. Existing industries are growing and expanding. That means more jobs for our people, more money for their families, a better future for their children. That is the kind of future we want for North Carolina.

But we are at a crossroads today. Will we go down the same road that Pennsylvania took? Will we let our roads crumble and go to pot? Will we lose those industries and that momentum? Or will we face up to the future? Will we make the tough decisions that our children and our grandchildren will thank us for?

North Carolina cannot afford to listen to those people who don't have any answers, who just say, "Don't do anything." They are hiding their heads in the sand, and they would have all of us do the same. But I think we know better than that.

I heard a story once about Frank Howard, the tough old football coach and athletic director at Clemson.[2] Somebody came to him with the suggestion that Clemson add the sport of crew, or rowing, but Frank replied, "We're not going to have anything to do with a sport where you sit down and go backward."

I don't think North Carolina wants to sit down and go backward. It is time to get walking and go forward.

[1] William Kerr Scott (1896-1958), native of Alamance County; B.S., North Carolina State College (now University), 1917; U.S. Army, World War I. Farmer; county agent for Alamance, 1920-1930; state agriculture commissioner, 1937-1948; governor, 1949-1953; U.S. senator, 1953-1958. Over 14,000 miles of secondary roads were paved as a result of Governor Scott's "Go Forward" program. Cheney, *North Carolina Government*, 423, 426, 438n, 726, 727, 749n; David Leroy Corbitt (ed.), *Public Addresses, Letters, and Papers of William Kerr Scott, Governor of North Carolina, 1949-1953* (Raleigh: Council of State, State of North Carolina, 1957), ix-xxvi, hereinafter cited as Corbitt, *Addresses of Scott*.

[2] Frank James Howard (1909-   ), native of Barlow Bend, Alabama; resident of Clemson, South Carolina; educated at University of Alabama. Line coach, 1930-1940, head football coach, 1940-1969, and athletic director, until 1971, Clemson University. Clemson Sports Information Office to Charles T. Francis, July 27, 1983.

NORTH CAROLINA WHITE HOUSE CONFERENCE ON AGING

RALEIGH, MARCH 13, 1981

It is a privilege for me to welcome all of you to the North Carolina White House Conference on Aging. I want to commend you for the hard work you have done in preparation for this conference. I understand that more than 6,000 people have participated in more than 300 community forums across this state. Following this meeting, I think you will be well prepared to submit a report to me in the near future and to make your impact felt at the national conference.

I personally feel a great sense of urgency about the work of this conference. You will be going about your work at a time when we as a state and nation are becoming increasingly aware of the needs of older adults. Generally speaking, older adults have needs and concerns not that much different from those of most Americans. They want to be able to make ends meet in these inflationary times. They want access to good and affordable health care at reasonable cost. They want a decent place to live and a neighborhood in which they can move about freely without the fear of being robbed or mugged or raped.

North Carolina must respond. We are talking here about more than 800,000 people in our state alone. That is 14 percent of our population, and the number of North Carolinians over the age of sixty is expected to exceed one million by the end of this decade. About half of those who are over sixty are living at or below the poverty level, and many others live at the edges of poverty on fixed incomes.

Due in large part to the efforts of many of the people here in this auditorium, [this] administration has reached some important milestones in making North Carolina a better place for older adults to live and work:

—We established a Division of Aging in the Department of Human Resources, and under the great leadership of Nathan Yelton that office has been invaluable to me in formulating policy relating to older adults.[1]

—We have provided $6 million a year in state funds for in-home services to older adults.

—We have provided a one-time exemption from the capital gains tax for the sale of a home.

—We restored dental coverage in the Medicaid program.

—And we provided a $7,500 exemption on property taxes for people over sixty-five and having a disposable income of less than $9,000.

I am proud that the legislature, on our recommendation, acted recently to correct an injustice that cheated many older citizens out of their homestead tax exemption. The General Assembly in 1979 changed the deadline for claiming the exemption, but that has now been retroactively changed; older adults who missed that deadline now have until April 15 to reclaim what they lost last year. We still have legislation pending to increase the homestead tax exemption and make more people eligible for it. I hope the General Assembly will act promptly on that proposal.[2]

I realize that much remains to be done to ensure that every older adult has the opportunity to achieve economic security, good and affordable health care, good housing, and freedom from fear. With the administration in Washington proposing drastic budget cuts in the human services area, the leadership is going to have to be provided at the state level.

I was in Washington earlier this week to testify before a congressional committee. I told the committee that if North Carolina and other states are going to respond effectively to reduced funding from Washington, we have to have greater flexibility in administering human services programs. This is particularly true of Medicaid. If we get greater flexibility and less regulation, we can hold down the cost of health care and do a better job of providing care to older adults.

In the vitally important area of housing, we are about to begin a new program in North Carolina that will assess the housing needs, opportunities, and barriers for older adults. The Governor's Commission on Housing Options for Older Adults will make recommendations to me and the General Assembly on ways to ensure that every older adult has a safe and affordable place to live. And it is my pleasure to announce today that my good friend Buck Buchanan, the retired chief of the Housing Loan Section of the Farmers Home Administration in North Carolina, will be chairman of this commission. Nobody has a better grasp of the problems and the possible solutions, and I am grateful to him for accepting a very demanding assignment.[3]

Our state must make a stronger commitment to protecting older adults from crime. I have urged the General Assembly to enact legislation to make sure that those who commit crimes against the elderly are punished swiftly and severely.

I think the most important thing for all of us to keep in mind is that North Carolina can never reach its vast economic, social, and educational potential until older North Carolinians have full opportunities to reach *their* potential. The 800,000 older adults in this state represent a great reservoir of experience, energy, intelligence, and talent. Thousands and thousands of these people would be willing to give of their time and energy and love in the expanding volunteer programs that we have established—if only someone would ask. We're going to be asking their help.

My charge to you today is to develop innovative proposals for making North Carolina and America a special place in which to grow old. I want you to submit to me a report that tells me and tells the General Assembly what we need to know about the problems of older adults and what we at the state level can do about them. I want you especially to provide information that can be a plan of action for the Governor's Commission on Housing Options for Older Adults, and I want your impact to be felt at the White House Conference when you send delegates to that meeting. The work you do can become a model for the nation.

I am talking about taking a step toward the fulfillment of a possible dream. As older adults become safer, more secure, and more productive, North Carolina becomes a better place in which to live and work and play. The future of older adults in North Carolina is the future of every man, woman, and child in North Carolina. Let's make that future bright.

---

[1] Nathan Hunter Yelton (1901-1981), assistant secretary, Division of Aging, Department of Human Resources, 1977-1981. Previously identified in Mitchell, *Addresses of Hunt,* I, 129n.

[2] "An Act to Set the Same Application Period as Listing Period for Senior Citizens and Disabled Persons Using the Homestead Exclusion" was ratified April 13. *N.C. Session Laws, 1979,* c. 356. It was amended under chapters 28 and 1052, *N.C. Session Laws, 1981,* previously identified in "State of the State Address," January 15, 1981, footnote 3. See also "An Act to Require that Application Need Only be Made Once for the Homestead Exemption for the Elderly and Disabled," ratified February 27. *N.C. Session Laws, 1981,* c. 54.

[3] James O. (Buck) Buchanan (1915-   ), native of Laurel, Mississippi; resident of Raleigh; B.S., Mississippi State University, 1937; U.S. Army, 1941-1945. Real estate loan chief, 1962-1970, and rural housing chief, 1971-1981, Farmers Home Administration, U.S. Department of Agriculture; president, board of directors, North Carolina Rural Rehabilitation Corp., 1983-1984. James O. Buchanan to Charles T. Francis, August 5, 1983.

Governor's Commission on Housing Choices for Older Adults: Report to the Governor, 1981 (Raleigh: Office of Policy and Planning, North Carolina Department of Administration, October, 1981), makes twenty-two recommendations presumed to guide state government in assisting older adults to remain at home in their communities and to provide a variety of domiciliary alternatives for those who must move.

NORTH CAROLINA CITIZENS ASSOCIATION

RALEIGH, MARCH 18, 1981

This is a group that has always been concerned with the economy —in North Carolina and the nation. As we enter the 1980s, it is clear that the United States is at an economic turning point. We hardly know what single-digit inflation and interest rates look like. Unemployment is high. Real income growth is low. Productivity is declining. Resources face disturbing limits. The American dollar has lost world respect.

Last year's presidential election was fought on that battleground, and we see in Washington today an administration committed to reining in federal spending and getting our economy moving again. I support President Reagan's basic approach, but I want to talk to you today about what we need to do in the long term—in North Carolina and the nation.

Our society has always subscribed to the notion that, "I'm doing better than I did before." We have always worked so that our children and grandchildren would do even better, but that notion seems in danger now. Somebody said recently that not even the future is what it used to be.

Well, I'm more optimistic than that. I sense in our nation a willingness to take the long view, to take the bold steps that will mean a better life for our children and our grandchildren. I want to talk to you today about solutions, about what we can do to make our economy stronger in the next twenty years and into the next century. Above all, we must come to grips with inflation. We must recognize that our sagging productivity lies at the root of double-digit inflation. As a society, we must develop a strategy to change that. It will require action by the public and private sectors, and it will require both to work together.

TEXTILE INDUSTRY

We ought to learn from the experience of our great textile industry, the backbone of North Carolina's manufacturing economy. That industry has undergone a revolution during the past decade. The *Washington Post* told that story in its business section Sunday, describing the textile industry of a few years ago as "the Chrysler Corporation of American business."[1]

Well, the textile industry is humming like a Rolls-Royce today. Its plants are outfitted with modern equipment like the high-speed looms I saw when I visited Burlington's new plant in Richmond County last year. Sophisticated computers now keep tight control on plant inventories. American exports have the Europeans clamoring for quotas.

That is a great success story, and it was written by the vision and drive of that industry's leaders. They have invested more than $11 billion over the last decade in modernizing their plants, and they may invest twice that much over the next ten years. We ought to study what they have done and profit from their example, in government as well as in business.

ECONOMIC STRATEGY

Exciting things are happening in North Carolina's economy, and you know of my enthusiasm for new, high-technology industry. But we are not so enthusiastic that we are going to forget who brought North Carolina to the dance. Textiles, apparel, furniture, cigarettes—those are the industries that built North Carolina, and those are the industries that will continue to employ thousands of North Carolinians. Those industries are North Carolina's future, and what strengthens them strengthens North Carolina and its people.

I believe we must develop a strategy to do that.

The first thing—and the most obvious thing—we must have is capital, the money to invest in new equipment and more productive processes. Government must devise tax policies that encourage savings and investments. The administration in Washington is sensitive to this need, and North Carolina must be prepared to make similar changes when it can afford them and to remove barriers to industrial growth and development. But let us not forget that North Carolina's tax structure is already among the most attractive to businesses in the nation, as shown by the fact that we rank forty-sixth among the states in the size of our total state and local tax burden.

We need a true partnership, a triangle formed by government, industry, and education that will be the foundation for development and growth—like the great Textile School at North Carolina State University, which we must reestablish as number one in the nation; like our Microelectronics Center of North Carolina, which would link our universities, our private research institutions, and our community college system for the training of people.

Government has to stop looking on business as the enemy. That has happened too often, and primarily at the federal level. Too often, our society has used government to simply regulate and left private industry on its own to initiate change and growth.

We can learn from Japan. Why is it, for instance, that Americans drive so many Toyotas and watch so many Sony television sets?

Japan uses government to support and enhance private industry, teaming up with industry. Their relationship is not an adversarial one. It is one of cooperation and consensus. Their houses are not divided, and ours do not have to be.

Look at the difference in our two nations' educational output. We are short on engineers and long on lawyers. Our production of electrical engineers has steadily declined to 17,000 a year over the past decade, while our production of lawyers has steadily increased to 33,000 a year. Out of every 10,000 people in Japan, 400 are engineers or scientists and only one is a lawyer. Out of the same sized group in the United States, seventy are engineers or scientists and twenty are lawyers. Now, I can say this because I am a lawyer. There is nothing wrong with lawyers. My point is simply that our system's balance suggests an emphasis on regulation and litigation, while Japan's suggests a greater emphasis on science and technology.

So government has a responsibility to change. Overregulation and tax barriers must be eliminated.

Private Investments

But let us not pretend that simply slashing away at taxes and regulations is going to be the magic formula for prosperity. The private sector has a responsibility, too. Between 1968 and 1978 corporate investment in research and development in the United States increased only 4 percent. This nation cannot follow that path if it wants to be an international leader in technological innovation and economic growth.

I believe the private sector has to look at more than the quarterly dividends to stockholders. Too many corporate managers are afraid to put more money into research and development, to invest in their own future. They seem to think risk is too risky. I would advise them to look to the lesson of their counterparts in the textile industry, who invested in their future and are reaping the real dividends today.

Public Investments

This is my primary concern as your governor: Where should we make our public investments in our future?

The first answer, I believe, is in education. That is why I worked very hard, with this association's support, to establish the North Carolina School of Science and Mathematics. This is a full-time, residential high school that admits the most-talented and brilliant students in North Carolina, and we expect them to become the leading scientists and mathematicians of tomorrow, as well as the engineers and the researchers who may revolutionize your business.

What we learn in that school will help us teach, and inspire, students throughout North Carolina.

But our most important task is to see that *every single* young person in North Carolina masters the basic skills: reading, writing, and math. You know from your own business that a smart employee is a better employee and a more successful citizen. That is why I find it hard to believe that some voices in North Carolina are calling for retreat in education, for taking away the reading aides who have helped youngsters in the first, second, and third grades make so much progress in those national rankings. That would be a tragic mistake for our state.

We must invest in job training, guaranteeing that our people have the skills and the training to be able to operate the sophisticated equipment in your factories. I am in the process of devising a comprehensive approach that will pull together all our resources to do this job, particularly our community college system. We need the active involvement of the private sector in that process.

That triangle of government, industry, and education must work together now to master the problem of hazardous wastes. I will soon be introducing legislation in the General Assembly to establish a system that will emphasize reducing and controlling those wastes, and I need your help to do that.

This year, most important of all, North Carolina must decide how it will maintain the billions of dollars it has invested in its roads and highways. We cannot afford to let that system go to ruin. To do so would be like a businessman whose plant has a leaky roof. If he doesn't spend the money to fix it, the rain is going to ruin more than his roof. It's going to ruin his equipment, his walls, his floors— everything he owns and has worked so hard to accumulate. North Carolina cannot afford to make that shortsighted mistake.

Conclusion

I have spoken at some length today to give you my perspective, as a governor beginning his second term, on what we need to do to successfully meet our economic future. I am talking here about what the nation, as well as North Carolina, must do.

Long before it was a nation, America was an idea—an idea based on independence, self-reliance, and initiative. That idea is as powerful today as it was 200 years ago.

The challenge before our nation, in the last twenty years of this century, is to regain our position as a world leader. That position is not just based on military might or measured by a standard of living. Those are important, but I believe we will be measured ultimately by our ability to harness the power of science and technology to our own future.

It is true that our energy and natural resources are finite, but our imagination is not. The real wealth of this nation isn't in the ground, it's in our hearts and minds. And that is a renewable resource.

---

[1] *Washington* (D.C.) *Post*, March 15, 1981, hereinafter cited as *Washington Post*.

NORTH CAROLINA PUBLIC SCHOOL SUPERINTENDENTS

RALEIGH, MARCH 20, 1981

I'm delighted to have this opportunity to speak to the key educational leadership of North Carolina today. I know what has brought you to Raleigh: your deep concern over what the education cuts proposed by the Reagan administration would mean when they get down to the classroom. I want you to know that the governor of North Carolina stands with you in opposing cuts that will hurt children in classrooms across this state and this nation.

Now, I'm not one of those who doesn't believe education should be touched. We have to take our fair share of cuts. We have to be prepared to eliminate some administrative positions. I have said that I believe we could take a cut of up to 10 percent in federal funds for education—*IF* we are given more flexibility in spending that money. We could take that and not hurt the quality of instruction.

But the deep, deep cuts they are talking about—more than one third in education—would be absolutely devastating. And it would be false economy. We would be saving comparative pennies today at the cost of many, many dollars as our children grow older and seek to become successful citizens.

It is becoming clear what the proposed cuts would mean to our people:

—About 3,200 fewer teachers in North Carolina.

—School lunches will cost families more than $1.00 each across our state. How does that help fight inflation?

And let me take this opportunity, too, to say that I don't like some of the talk I hear in North Carolina's General Assembly. We are hearing the voices of retreat and retrenchment: "Cut out reading aides, cut out teachers for the deaf," they say.

Well, my friends, I say to you today that North Carolina can't afford to retreat in education. The friends of education have fought a long, hard battle in this state. We are making progress in the war against illiteracy and ignorance. Now is not the time to take away the very programs that are helping our children move up those national rankings and that are moving our state forward. Now is the time for the friends of education, citizens and educators alike, to stand and fight and send this message to Raleigh and to Washington: We will not let you sell North Carolina's children—and North Carolina's future—short.

THIRD ANNUAL URBAN AFFAIRS CONFERENCE

CHARLOTTE, APRIL 3, 1981

It's a pleasure to be here in North Carolina's largest city.

I've been thinking over the past few days about how North Carolina is sometimes perceived as a sleepy, rural, agrarian state—when in fact we have just become the tenth most populous state in the union, with more than 5.8 million people.

We are becoming increasingly urban in character, and urbanization brings about problems that have to be addressed. In an urban setting such basic services as law enforcement, transportation, housing, protection of the environment, and education become more difficult and expensive to provide.

But I don't think North Carolinians are afraid of our changing landscape. We have advantages here that the large metropolitan areas of the Northeast and Midwest don't have. We have a magnificent opportunity to develop our state's economy, to provide our people with the kinds of jobs that bring about a decent income and a degree of dignity.

Yes, we are becoming more urban, but our growth has been balanced. That is a trend we have tried to encourage at the state level with my administration's Balanced Growth Policy.

We remain a state of small towns and relatively small cities. Our communities have retained their uniqueness, and our growth has not outstripped our ability to cope with it. State and local governments are hard at work now in a cooperative effort to prepare ourselves for the challenges that come with growth.

Most of you know of my commitment to putting this state in the economic mainstream of America. I firmly believe that Charlotte and other areas of this state are going to realize tremendous benefits from our efforts to attract high-technology jobs to this state. We are going to mobilize the public schools, the community college system, our universities, and the Microelectronics Center of North Carolina to educate and train our people for the kinds of jobs and professional opportunities that are coming.

If North Carolina is to continue its economic growth, we must be prepared to safely and effectively manage the hazardous wastes that are a byproduct of industrial development. Next week I plan to submit legislation to the General Assembly that will give us the tools we need in the management of those wastes.

A good transportation system is the skeleton on which a strong economy is built. We cannot postpone some tough decisions to preserve, maintain, and expand our roads, streets, airports, and mass transit systems. I will be addressing that issue before the General Assembly before the end of the month.

I said earlier that we are a state of small cities and towns. Charlotte, our largest city, still ranks forty-eighth in the nation in population. Winston-Salem has about 150,000 people. That sounds like a lot until you consider that Memphis has more than 600,000.

In some respects, those statistics have hurt us in our efforts to attract large industrial facilities and regional corporate head-quarters. These companies have traditionally looked to larger population centers, and that is a hard habit to overcome. But North Carolina's metropolitan areas do have the services and the population base to support these kinds of enterprises. The Triad area of Greensboro, Winston-Salem, and High Point has a million people. The Metrolina area has 1.3 million people, and did you know that more than a half-million people live within fifty miles of Rock Ridge?

For the first time we are better packaging this information about our urban areas. Our effort is centered on a cooperative metropolitan marketing program involving our Department of Commerce and local leaders in nine urbanized regions of the state. Information about population, labor supply, and transportation facilities will be compiled on a regional basis and made available. We will use direct mail and aggressive salesmanship to attract the top national and international firms to these areas and make them better able to compete for plants, headquarters, and major distribution centers.[1]

Growth does have its pitfalls, but I think North Carolinians welcome healthy, orderly growth and the increased opportunities that come with it. The people of our state are optimistic about the future, and I share in that optimism. I believe that with good, effective leadership, we can do much to shape our destiny. We can bring about the kind of future we want. We can forge a future of better schools, better jobs, a cleaner environment, and happier, more productive lives for our people.

---

[1] Economic profiles for each of the nine regions participating in the Metropolitan Area Development Program were to be completed by the end of November, 1981, according to Hunt's speech before the Governor's Conference on Economic Development, October 27, 1981.

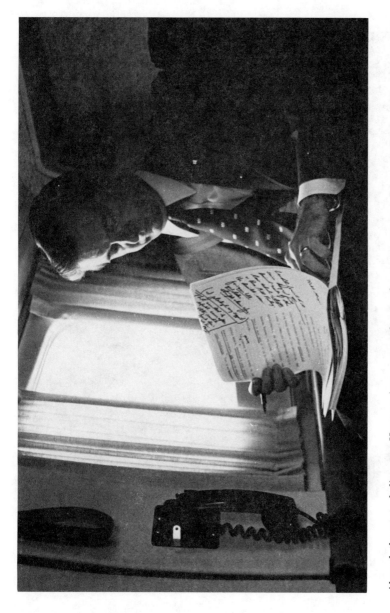

Aboard the state helicopter, Hunt revises prepared remarks en route to a Research Triangle Park industrial dedication ceremony.

Donald S. Beilman, vice-president of General Electric, and Governor Hunt examine a model of GE's Semiconductor Division headquarters, one of a number of high-technology operations attracted to Research Triangle Park by the establishment, in 1980, of the Microelectronics Center of North Carolina. The governor announced Beilman's designation as MCNC's first president in July, 1982.

CHRISTIAN LIFE COUNCIL

RALEIGH, APRIL 7, 1981

It's a pleasure to be here today to talk with you about my Christian faith and how that relates to my job as governor.

During the 1940s and '50s when I was growing up, the most prevalent view of government was that there was something inherently wrong or dirty about it. The common joke was that dishonest persons ran for office and honest persons who did win didn't remain honest very long.

Two major influences prevented that thinking from becoming part of my value system. The first influence was my family. Both my parents were public servants. Mother taught school, and daddy was a soil conservation agent.[1] They worked for government, but I don't know of anyone who had more honesty and integrity. I knew, by their example, that you could be both a public servant and a Christian.

The second influence was my church. We didn't miss church often, and my parents' questions on Sunday afternoon encouraged me to listen to the Sunday school teacher and pastor. What I heard, and continue to hear, at church and home about God is very important to my personal life-style and to my performance as governor.

Let me highlight four of the major themes which have significantly influenced my life.

The first is stewardship. I learned early the seriousness of burying one's talent, of squandering an opportunity, of wasting a life, of destroying a relationship. Doing God's will was a major objective placed before me. It was clearly understood that a Christian was to be faithful with his time, money, and influence. He was to be faithful because what he was and had was entrusted to him by God.

A second theme is "Love Thy Neighbor as Thyself."[2] The Golden Rule was a practical way of showing one's love and devotion to God. Love was the force that guided our ethical system.

There was a strong sense of community and family in my early life. Taking care of the hurts and needs of neighbors was not an option, but it was the woof and warp of the Christian life. The parable of the Good Samaritan was *the* parable in our church.[3]

A third influence is emphasis upon the Christian life. As a boy, my parents often said, "Jimmy, we do or don't do something because we are Christians." I learned early that one gave validity to his words by his deeds. Thus, faith for me became actional. The verbs in the Bible are signposts for me. Do. Be. Follow. Obey. Trust. Go. Work.

One of the most critical insights a young person can learn about Christian life is its breadth. I learned early that God was as concerned about prejudice as drinking, as concerned about pollution as profanity. For me, Christian life did not just consist of a few don'ts. Nor did it center on just a personal life-style. Personal and corporate morality became a tandem which is of great concern to me today. One without the other is totally inadequate.

A fourth theme is transformation of the world. Often, the small number of us in the Baptist church I attended while growing up was compared to the little band of Jesus' disciples. We were told that they turned the world upside down for Christ and that we could too. And you know what? I believed those preachers. They said that changed men ought to change the world.

My life was changed because of my personal faith and commitment to God through Jesus Christ, and all those words about being salt, light, and leaven are the main reasons I wanted to be governor.[4] One person can make a difference. As disciples, we are called not to conform to the world, but to transform it.

As I looked forward to being here and thought about what I would say to you, the tremendous potential for good that Baptists possess in North Carolina excites me. Your numbers are many, and your influence exists at country crossroads and urban intersections, from mountain valleys to sandy seashores.

There is much to be done in North Carolina. Our senior citizens must be assured of hope and security; troubled youth need love and guidance from caring adults; children need quality education; the hungry need food; the criminal needs rehabilitation; the unemployed need jobs; families must be strengthened, and those alienated from God need to come home. The list of needs is almost endless.

I firmly believe that the church and state are partners in the business of helping people. To be sure, we must remain separate, neither dominating the other. Care must be given to prevent forcing the narrow sectarian beliefs of a few upon every one. My good friend, Walter Mondale, who visited our state just a few days ago, expressed this conviction when he said:

"No government can guarantee a perfect life for anyone. No government can substitute for our families, our churches, our synagogues, our neighborhoods, our volunteers. But a progressive government must do two things. It must create the conditions to help all people build better lives for themselves, and it must do so efficiently and honestly and fairly."[5]

Yes, we are partners—partners in helping people. The challenge that is before us both is great. The Christian Life Council, the many agencies within the Baptist Convention, the thousands of your churches have led us in the past and must do so during these difficult days.

Let me conclude with a story which reminds us all of where our ultimate allegiance belongs. It is a story about one of your Baptists, Bill Moyers.[6] President Lyndon Baines Johnson called on Bill to pray at a meal. Right in the middle of his prayer, LBJ roared, as only he could do, "Speak up, Bill. I can't hear you." To which Bill softly replied, "I wasn't talking to you, Mr. President." [7]

---

[1] James Baxter Hunt, Sr. (1911-   ), native of Greensboro; resident of Wilson County; B.S., North Carolina State College (now University), 1934. Tree and tobacco farmer; U.S. Department of Agriculture, Soil Conservation Service, 1934-1966; member, Tobacco Marketing Committee, 1966-1972, and Coastal Plains Regional Commission, 1966-1981; chairman, Mount Olive College Board of Trustees, since 1965.

Elsie Brame Hunt (1903-   ), native of Rock Ridge; resident of Wilson County; A.B., State Normal and Industrial School (now University of North Carolina at Greensboro), 1926. Homemaker, retired public schoolteacher; taught high school English in Johnston, Guilford, and Wilson counties. James Baxter Hunt, Sr., and Elsie Brame Hunt to Charles T. Francis, August 4, 1983.

[2] Mark 12:31.

[3] Luke 10:30-37.

[4] Matthew 5:13-16, 13:33.

[5] "Acceptance Speech to the Democratic National Convention by the Honorable Walter F. Mondale, Vice-President of the United States," *Official Report of the Proceedings of the Democratic National Convention, Madison Square Garden, New York City . . . August 11 through August 14, 1980* (Washington, D.C.: Democratic National Committee, n.d.), 600. Walter Frederick (Fritz) Mondale (1928-   ), native of Ceylon, Minnesota; B.A., 1951, LL.B., 1956, University of Minnesota. Lawyer; Minnesota attorney general, 1960-1964; U.S. senator from Minnesota, 1964-1977; U.S. vice-president, 1977-1981; unsuccessful Democratic presidential candidate, 1984. *Who's Who in America, 1982-1983* (Chicago: Marquis Who's Who, Inc., forty-second edition, 2 volumes, 1982), II, 2349, hereinafter cited as *Who's Who in America, 1982-1983*.

[6] Bill D. Moyers (1934-   ), native of Hugo, Oklahoma; B. Journalism, University of Texas, 1956; graduate student, University of Edinburgh, Scotland, 1956-1957; B.D., Southwestern Theological Seminary, 1959. Personal assistant to Senator Lyndon Baines Johnson, 1959-1960; associate director, 1961-1963, and department director, 1963-1964, Peace Corps; special assistant, 1963-1967, and press secretary, 1965-1967, to President Johnson; publisher, *Newsday*, 1967-1970; editor-in-chief, "Bill Moyers Journal," PBS, 1971-1976, 1978-1981; editor and chief correspondent, "CBS Reports," 1976-1978. Senior news analyst, CBS [television] News, since 1981. *Who's Who in America, 1982-1983*, II, 2396.

[7] Lyndon Baines Johnson (1908-1973), born near Stonewall, Texas; B.S., Southwest Texas State College (now University), 1930; LL.D., Southwestern University, 1943; U.S. Navy, 1941-1942. Teacher, Houston public schools, 1930-1931; secretary to Congressman Richard M. Kleberg, 1931-1935; state director, National Youth Administration of Texas, 1935-1937; congressman, 1938-1948, and U.S. senator, 1949-1961, from Texas; U. S. vice-president, 1961-1963, and president, 1963-1969. *Who Was Who in America, 1969-1973*, 375. Commenting on the dinner episode as Hunt described it, Moyers notes: "The story told by the Governor is true, except that the President did not 'roar.' I don't know the date. We were dining in the private quarters at the White House with the Johnsons and a few of their personal friends. The President himself told the story repeatedly thereafter. He enjoyed it." Bill Moyers to Jan-Michael Poff, August 14, 1984.

GOVERNOR'S TASK FORCE ON
VOLUNTEERISM FROM THE WORKPLACE

RALEIGH, APRIL 8, 1981

I am proud to say that volunteering is a North Carolina tradition. People being good neighbors and responsible citizens not only built the major institutions of our state but also sustains the high quality of life for which we all are proud and grateful. Volunteerism is our best hope for the future. What kind of communities would we have if people did not care enough to help each other?

This spirit of helping is shown by the hundreds of thousands of North Carolinians who are volunteers in the public and private sectors. A lot of these people have full-time jobs but still find time to help their fellow men and women. But we have some challenges before us as we face the 1980s. The stress of a rapidly changing society will change volunteerism as we know it today. Inflation, the energy crisis, and unemployment will continue to cause further human problems. Because volunteering remains critical to our society, we must seek increased citizen involvement in solving these community problems.

Many business leaders today realize the importance of social responsibility. The activity of the Xerox employees who were recruited through Gini Smith's Involvement Program in Winston-Salem is a fine example. The employees volunteered their time to make improvements at the Child Development Center. Your chairman, Brooks Whitehurst,[1] has been part of the loaned executive program at the Texasgulf Chemicals Company. He was appointed by me and Superintendent Craig Phillips[2] to develop a program to involve business and industry people in our public schools.

Some companies in North Carolina, like R. J. Reynolds Tobacco Company, Levi Strauss and Company, Sears, and General Electric, have established opportunities for employee volunteer efforts. You need to look at the things that employers can do to provide volunteer opportunities. Many corporations with successful programs have a full-time staff person available as a liaison between the community and employees in administering strong volunteer efforts. Flex time, employee release time, and loaned executives are viable options to be considered.

I need to know how we in state government can support, recognize, and encourage volunteerism from the workplace in both the public and private sectors. I have recently met with the presidents of twenty of North Carolina's largest corporations who make up the North Carolina Council on Management and Development, Inc. They serve as volunteers in helping me encourage economic development in this state. I have asked each of them to designate someone from their corporation to form an ad hoc committee to pursue volunteerism. These people will be meeting with representatives of the Governor's Office of Citizen Affairs in Greensboro on April 22.

The purpose of this group will be twofold. First, to determine what their organization and employees are already doing to help others. Second, to find ways to encourage and promote the concept of business people helping their neighbors.

I feel good [that] we are vigorously pursuing volunteerism from the workplace. Your support, work, and recommendations will confirm North Carolina's leadership in meeting the needs of our people and communities through every available resource. I look forward to reviewing your recommendations this coming January.

---

[1] Brooks Morris Whitehurst (1930-   ), manager of engineering services, Texasgulf. Previously identified in Mitchell, *Addresses of Hunt*, I, 319n.

[2] Andrew Craig Phillips (1922-   ), elected state superintendent of public instruction in 1968. Previously indentified in Mitchell, *Addresses of Hunt*, I, 41n.

NORTH CAROLINA ASSOCIATION OF ARTS COUNCILS

RALEIGH, APRIL 9, 1981

I am delighted today to be with a group which represents a phenomenon that began here, in our "State of the Arts." The community arts council movement that was born in Winston-Salem more than thirty years ago has changed the face of arts development across the nation.

Let me begin by congratulating you on your theme of advocacy for the arts. Those of you who attended the Arts and the Child Conference know that I am a believer in making people know what you want, when you want it. By that, I don't mean you should put on blinders and talk about narrow issues without considering whole situations; I do mean you should identify areas most important to you, make sure your public officials understand your point of view, and know how to use the political process to make changes you think are needed. That's your right and your responsibility as citizens.

I am well aware that cuts in federal spending will leave holes in your budgets. I am also aware that my own recommended budget, while continuing our current high level of support, has no money for expansion for arts council work. However, this does not mean our state is cutting back on its commitment to community arts councils. Frankly, my recommended budget contains almost no money for expansion anywhere. You read the newspapers. You drive on our deteriorating highways. You know as well as I do that these next couple of years are a time for maintaining the quality we have worked hard to achieve. This is not a time for moving back, but the progress we see must be carefully planned.

I'm optimistic about the progress we're going to make in the arts, even during the next couple of years. One reason is that arts supporters have led the way in understanding the crucial importance of volunteer work. You have long been able to get big results from small budgets, because you are committed to excellence. Another is the fact that you have insulated yourselves from some of the dangers of government dependence by forging a remarkable partnership of arts institutions, government, and the private sector.

Later today I will be in Greenville meeting with my Business Council on the Arts and Humanities and presenting awards to businesses that support cultural organizations. The fact our state has such a program is remarkable. What it is accomplishing, with your help, is even more astonishing. A study just released by the Department of Cultural Resources shows that in 1979 our state's businesses pumped almost $7.5 million into cultural activities. They donated countless hours of volunteer time to boards and fund-raising campaigns, and the study shows most businesses plan to give even more.[1]

But that doesn't mean that government can abandon its share of arts support, confident that private givers will pick up the slack. The state has a distinct role which it has played well thus far and should work to perfect. Because we believe that cultural development benefits all our citizens, we have the responsibility of supporting examples of excellence, such as our arts councils, our North Carolina School of the Arts, our art museum, and symphony. We have the challenge of convincing private givers that culture represents an investment, which returns benefits far beyond its cost.

You know that I care about bringing into our state the kind of businesspeople who know the importance of our quality of life. You know that I care about educating all our citizens, so they can understand and appreciate all that life has to offer. You should know also that I consider all of you partners in my efforts to make our "State of the Arts" the best it can be. Improvements in industry, in education, in transportation can only mean a brighter future for you and your institutions as well.

---

[1] R. Michael Lowder calculates that in 1979 the state's businesses contributed $7.4 million to cultural programs, a figure slightly lower than the one Hunt provides. *Business Support of the Arts and Humanities in North Carolina* ([Raleigh]: North Carolina Department of Cultural Resources, January, 1981), 18, hereinafter cited as Lowder, *Business Support of the Arts and Humanities.*

GOVERNOR'S BUSINESS COUNCIL ON THE ARTS AND HUMANITIES

GREENVILLE, APRIL 9, 1981

I am pleased to be here today. The work you are doing is very important to the state. As you know, we will have to make a renewed effort in the future. Besides maintaining current levels of programs and services provided by the state's cultural institutions, it is imperative that we seek cost-effective ways to expand cultural opportunities to all our citizens.

The arts and humanities in North Carolina have made great progress in the last fifteen years. Those of you who have worked directly with cultural organizations know that most arts groups survive and develop within a very thin margin between success and failure. The cost of performing arts activities has skyrocketed during the 1970s. Both the private and public sectors have increased their support in response to our need for more and better cultural activities, and arts groups have been making a concerted effort to approach businesses in ways which elevate the arts and humanities above pure charity.

Businesses today are very aware of what the arts can do for them and for their communities. The arts attract tourists to our state; they create jobs; they generate taxes; they provide public recognition for businesses. I have found that North Carolina's cultural environment is a strong selling point to industry considering a location in North Carolina.

So we all have a vital interest in maintaining and improving our cultural resources. The Business Council on the Arts and Humanities has done a great deal to promote business support over the past four years. I think the structural changes Ty Wilson[1] has outlined today will enhance the business and the arts movement in the state. But for that to happen, we all must renew our commitment to the arts. You must return to your communities and involve other businesses.

The recently published study of business support to cultural institutions and programs points out that many of the state's small and medium-sized businesses are not providing all the support they can. Some large corporations still provide the bulk of support. This is an issue I recommend you address. The "five percent club" proposal suggested in the report also should be looked at.[2]

The council's aim should be broad in scope. The whole range of nonprofit cultural activities—the visual and performing arts, historic preservation, public libraries, the humanities, the folk arts, public radio and television, history museums, arts education—should be considered by this council. The awards program has been successful. It is important that we continue to recognize outstanding business efforts and to encourage other businesses to become involved.

When the Department of Cultural Resources first approached the National Endowment for the Humanities in 1977 for funding for this model project in public-private cooperation, it was done with the hope that the business community would one day take on the financial costs of operating the council. In response, the task force has recommended a nonprofit structure with fund-raising and spending capabilities. This gives me a great deal of satisfaction and hope for the future of the business and the arts movement in North Carolina.

I know that Ty Wilson will provide the dynamic leadership and innovative ideas necessary in the years ahead. The challenge is immense, but the rewards for our state, its communities, and its citizens are worth the effort.

---

[1] J. Tylee (Ty) Wilson (1931-   ), native of Teaneck, New Jersey; resident of Winston-Salem; A.B., Lafayette College, 1953; U.S. Army, 1954-1956. Group vice-president, Chesebrough-Pond's, Inc., 1972-1974; president and chief executive officer, RJR Foods, Inc., 1974-1976; executive vice-president and director, 1976-1979, president and director, 1979-1983, president and chief executive officer, 1983-1984, and chairman and chief executive officer, since 1984, of R. J. Reynolds Industries, Inc. *Who's Who in America, 1982-1983,* II, 3593; letter, Dorothy P. Boose, executive assistant to J. Tylee Wilson, to Jan-Michael Poff, October 19, 1983; and "Wilson, Horrigan Elected RJR Chairman, President," *Business: North Carolina,* June, 1984, 60.

[2] "The nation's tax laws have encouraged charitable giving by allowing corporations to give up to five percent of their pretax earnings to non-profit causes. But . . . the national average has hovered around one percent. A few cities and states . . . have initiated five percent clubs which honor those businesses . . . which make a yearly five percent donation. Such a 'club' must be considered for North Carolina. Even an increase from one to two percent would have a dramatic impact upon the quality of life in this state." Lowder, *Business Support of the Arts and Humanities,* 21.

TESTIMONY BEFORE U.S. SENATE COMMITTEE ON LABOR AND HUMAN RESOURCES[1]

WASHINGTON, D.C., APRIL 10, 1981

[Hunt also emphasized the potential problems of administering block grants in remarks to a congressional staff members' luncheon, June 4; the Robeson County Elected Officials' luncheon, August 13; and the annual conference of the North Carolina Association of County Commissioners, August 14, 1981.]

I am testifying as chairman of the Committee on Human Resources for the National Governors' Association.

President Reagan's budget recommendations represent a dramatic attempt to cut government spending and to undertake a fundamental change in federal, state, and local government relationships. The nation's governors support both of these broad goals, although we are concerned about some specific aspects of the proposals.

The National Governors' Association and individual governors have long supported block grants, in program areas other than income assistance and medical care financing, as a way of increasing program flexibility and sorting out the appropriate roles of the various levels of government. We have indicated our belief that, if programs are consolidated into block grants with greater state flexibility and less extensive administrative requirements, we could provide a higher level of services with the same amount of funding, or the same level of services with funding reductions of about 10 percent. I would call your attention to the fact that, in a period of double-digit inflation, *maintaining* funding at current levels represents a 10 percent cut in real terms.

While they are tied together in the administration's proposals, the block grant concept and program funding levels are in fact two separate issues.

The burden of the federal budget-cutting effort is falling heavily on state and local government. Of the $48.6 billion in FY 1982 outlay savings proposed by the president, state and local grants will bear $14.6 billion, or about 30 percent of the cuts. If enacted, the Reagan budget would reduce grants to state and local governments in real terms for the fourth consecutive year. The administration's projections show grants to state and local governments falling from 15.8 percent of the federal budget in FY 1980, to 12.4 percent in 1982, and to 9.7 percent in 1986. We estimate that federal grants would drop, as a result, from 26.3 percent of state and local spending in FY 1980 to about 15 percent in FY 1986.

These impacts will fall on state budgets that already are strained by the 1980 recession. At the end of last year, twenty-one states were experiencing revenue shortfalls, seventeen states had imposed across-the-board spending cuts (reductions ordered in Michigan were 20 percent; in Oregon, 10 percent), fourteen states had imposed hiring freezes, twelve states had frozen capital projects, and nineteen states had imposed a total of twenty-eight tax increases in 1980 (ten of them motor fuel tax increases).

Despite these difficulties, the governors support the need for substantial federal budget cuts for two reasons: First, cuts are essential to combat the current inflationary psychology and to return our nation to a course of economic growth and stability; and second, the administration has proposed a substantial increase in flexibility that would allow state and local governments to mitigate, but not eliminate, the harmful impact of the cuts.

The fact that the proposed budget cuts will clearly exceed any reasonable estimate of potential administrative savings, however, combined with the inability of most states to consider offsetting the cuts with state funds, heightens the need to maximize any savings that can be realized so that service reductions can be kept to the lowest possible level.

As I have indicated, the National Governors' Association is pleased with the general thrust of the block grant initiatives announced by the administration in the context of its 1982 budget proposals. Because provisions adopted in implementing the block grants will directly affect the level of services we are able to provide, we are eager to outline the attributes we believe the block grants should have. These are, in fact, the criteria by which we will determine whether the block grant proposals submitted by the administration are acceptable and whether we should enthusiastically support them. We hope that the committee will take our concerns into account as it refines and advances the administration's proposals. I will highlight several criteria and submit others in writing for the record:

1. *Consistency with the National Governors' Association's "Sorting Out" Policy.* The block grants must be consistent with our policies on sorting out appropriate responsibilities for the federal government and for state and local governments. In particular, this calls for full federal assumption of financing and program design for income assistance and medical care financing programs. This is not the case and continues to be of great concern to the states. The governors' policy also calls for a primary state/local role in areas such as education, with the federal government retaining a role with respect to several functions of national importance. As we understand the administration's stated intentions, the block grant proposals to be submitted to this committee largely will satisfy these criteria.

2. *Funding and Spending Issues.*
   a. Consistent with the general purpose of the block grant, *governors must be given the ability to determine how to expend block grant funds.*
   b. Because it would allow maximum flexibility in program development and operation, *states should be allowed to retain and carry over any unused block grant funds from one to the succeeding fiscal year.*
   c. Because it would provide states and localities with the stability needed to plan effectively and operate more efficiently, *block grants should be funded at least one year in advance.* Waste occurs when the amount of available funds is not known until a few weeks before—or even after—the beginning of the state's program year.
   d. To enhance flexibility, *states should be given limited authority to transfer funds from one block grant to another.*

3. *Removal of Existing Categorical Program Regulations.* The existing categorical system is encumbered by unnecessary and unreasonable requirements at three levels—in the legislation relating to the programs; in the regulations implementing the legislation; and in the administrative requirements imposed by federal agencies in carrying out the program. These burdensome categorical requirements must be eliminated, and must be avoided in establishing the block grant system, if we are to have a chance of realizing any administrative savings at all. If you simply repackage existing requirements under a new name, it will cost, rather than save, money. To illustrate the types of burdensome requirements to which I refer I would like to submit for the record a list of unnecessary regulations recently developed by my staff in North Carolina.

4. *Annual or Biennial Review of Block Grant Funding Levels.* Unless inflation significantly subsides, the funding level for major social programs, including block grants, cannot be frozen without further reducing program service levels each year. Some specific means for accomplishing congressional oversight must be incorporated in the block grant legislation —whether by staged increases in annual authorization amounts that will allow Congress to increase program funding if it chooses, or in some other way. We wish to note that, with respect to several of the block grants, you will consider the nation's governors might be willing to consider further reductions in exchange for commensurate full or substantial federal assumption of fiscal responsibility for programs, such as Aid to Families with Dependent Children or Medicaid.

5. *Reduced Federal Overhead.* The federal commitment to the reduction of red tape, duplication, and overhead should be demonstrated by a marked reduction in federal national and regional program and supervisory staff. Savings in federal expenditures achieved by such reductions should be added to the block grant authorizations and appropriations to support the administrative responsibilities newly assumed by the states.

6. *Gubernatorial Administrative Flexibility.* Each governor shall have the authority to establish his own administrative structure for programs funded by block grants. The governor should designate the state fiscal agent of his choice to receive and be ultimately accountable to the federal government for expenditure of the block grant funds. He also should have the authority to delegate to one or more other agencies; there should be no single organizational unit requirements for any block grant.

7. *Audit Procedures.* States should be allowed to establish their own audit procedures, so long as they meet state standards

and broad minimum federal requirements, with audit results to be provided to the federal government annually. In concert with the audit, states should be required to demonstrate that funding received under a block grant was expended only for the broad purposes authorized in the enabling legislation.

8. *No Maintenance of Effort Should Be Required.* States must not be required to maintain a specific level of effort for any one or more of the categorical programs merged into a block grant. Further, when the federal government is cutting dramatically its funding of programs incorporated into block grants, it is inappropriate to prohibit states from making funding reductions if budget circumstances require or increased efficiencies or more appropriate targeting permit.

9. *Freedom to Determine Program Eligibility.* Within the broad guidelines for targeting recipients established by Congress, states should be permitted to develop their own eligibility criteria.

10. *Allocation Funding to the States.* The federal enabling legislation for each block grant should provide that each state's allocation be paid to the state. The state can arrange for allocation of the funding in the manner most appropriate to its needs, circumstances, and traditions and in accord with state law and procedures.

11. *Public Participation.* States must be allowed to determine their own procedures for public participation in deciding how to allocate block grant funds, consistent with state laws and practices. The federal government should not dictate this procedure in any respect; rather, it should require only that public participation be assured, and the means made known by each state to both the citizens of the state and the federal government.

The governors have estimated the administrative savings of block grants at about 10 percent; the administration is proposing inflation-adjusted cuts of about 35 percent. There is thus little doubt that the block grants proposed will result in a reduction of services. Congress should take two major steps, apart from adjusting funding levels, to minimize service reductions. First, it should maximize flexibility and ensure that the flexibility and the funding cuts arrive simultaneously. Second, it should give state and local governments the maximum lead time possible for implementation.

If congressional action on the block grants is not completed until shortly before the federal fiscal year begins next October 1, most state governments will be three months into their fiscal year without firm knowledge on how these important programs will operate. Most state legislatures will have adjourned and will either have to be called into special session or will have to return in January to rewrite state budgets and state laws governing the operation of these programs. The need for state action may further complicate local government adjustments to these programs.

Although these problems are substantial, governors believe that the long-range benefits offered by block grants in terms of increased efficiency and healthier balance among federal, state, and local government responsibilities make tackling the block grant issue now well worth the effort. The alternative is reduced federal funding with proportionately higher overhead costs across a broad range of activities, thereby ensuring that services to people bear the full brunt of the budget cuts.

We appreciate the opportunity to present the specific views and recommendations of the National Governors' Association concerning the proposed block grants. Having been forced in recent months to impose substantial budget cuts themselves, the nation's governors fully understand the serious problems now facing Congress. We are committed to work cooperatively with you in achieving the savings you desire and in minimizing the impact on the people that we represent and serve. Thank you.

---

[1] Orrin Grant Hatch (1934-   ), native of Pittsburgh; resident of Salt Lake City; B.S., Brigham Young University, 1959; J.D., University of Pittsburgh, 1962. Attorney, 1962-1977; U.S. senator from Utah since 1977 and chairman of the Committee on Labor and Human Resources; Republican. Barone and Ujifusa, *Almanac of American Politics, 1984*, 1188.

GROUNDBREAKING FOR LITTLE RIVER NAVIGATION PROJECT

LITTLE RIVER, S.C., APRIL 22, 1981

I am delighted to be here today at the groundbreaking ceremony for the Little River Inlet Project. This event is the culmination of the efforts of some dedicated people in this state and in our sister state of South Carolina. It signifies that all the long, arduous chores of planning, seeking appropriations, and coordinating the efforts of various governmental units are finally paying off.

We are now ready to realize the substantial benefits this project will mean for this region. Now fishing boats will not have to travel thirty-two miles up the coast to Cape Fear River or thirty-five miles down the coast to Murrells Inlet. Now your fishing fleet should grow and produce jobs and income for local people. Now Little River can provide a harbor of refuge for boats seeking safety.

I would like to call your attention today to perhaps the most impressive feature of this project. I am talking about the cooperation among the various governing bodies that made this project possible. This involved both state government, the government of

Brunswick County, North Carolina, and Horry County, South Carolina, the Corps of Engineers, and the United States Congress. This project required careful planning and coordination by the corps and substantial and continuing annual appropriations from Congress. It required sustained commitment and support from local government.

One of the significant hurdles that had to be crossed was determining the exact location of the boundary line between the two states so that our cooperation could be based on an accurate assignment of responsibilities. The location of the state line was particularly important in this case because the chief nonfederal responsibility was to acquire the land on both sides of the inlet required for construction. The Bi-State Boundary Commission, with the help of the U.S. Geodetic Survey and agencies in both states, successfully established the boundary.

After settling that first important point, the sponsoring county in each state and the two state governments patiently and persistently pushed the project through the necessary legal steps, made the financial commitments, and brought us to this spot today.

The Little River Inlet Project is a fine example of good, solid cooperation among all levels of government to accomplish a worthy goal, and the people of this area will benefit from this project for years to come. This is the kind of cooperation I have been stressing throughout my administration, and I will continue to advocate it as long as I hold office. Government at the local level is the most efficient, effective, and responsive of all. The role of state and federal government is to step in and provide assistance when issues cross jurisdictional lines or when the problems are greater than local government can handle, but it takes working together, with cooperation and give and take from all concerned, to accomplish projects like this one we are initiating today.

The water resource development institutions and laws which have made the Little River Inlet Project possible have been criticized for a number of years. Some of the critics have pointed out the extremely long time required to plan and construct a project. Others have opposed spending federal dollars for such projects and called for a retreat from this responsibility by the federal government.

These criticisms have some validity. We do need to find ways to plan and construct high priority projects faster to meet urgent needs. The system for cost sharing and financing of water development projects needs renovation and modernization to meet current needs.

I am convinced, however, that any new policies our nation develops for water resource development should continue to be based upon the type of good intergovernmental cooperation that has been demonstrated here on the Little River Inlet Project. Each level of government has certain resources and abilities that are important to the success of good water management. As we look toward future needs and consider improved policies and financial mechanisms for water development, we should make certain that we maintain the type of practical intergovernmental cooperation that has been demonstrated in the work here.

As governor of North Carolina, I am proud to participate with Brunswick County and our partners in South Carolina in this groundbreaking ceremony. I look forward to continuing to work with you and with the Corps of Engineers during the remaining steps required to complete the project—and I look forward to the day I can return to this place and see fishing boats and other vessels churning through this inlet, safe in the knowledge that their way is clear and confident that Little River will always mean "safe harbor" for them.

GOVERNOR'S DAY DINNER

COLUMBIA, S.C., APRIL 22, 1981

[The Reagan budget cuts, reasons for the outcome of the 1980 elections, and party rejuvenation were also topics featured in the governor's introduction of Walter Mondale at the Young Democrats state convention, March 28, and in remarks before a Democratic dinner on April 6; the Western Democratic party rally, August 4; Russell Walker Day celebration, September 17; Democratic Women's banquet, September 18; and the Union County Democratic party reception, October 20, 1981.]

I want to thank Governor Riley, Chairman Dorn, and the Democrats of South Carolina for inviting me to address this great gathering. The Democratic party is on the move in South Carolina. Under the great leadership of your new chairman, Bryan Dorn,[1] and your new executive director, Bill Carrick, you are laying the groundwork for great victories in 1982.

Of course, a lot of the speculation about 1982 focuses on my good friend Dick Riley.[2] I understand he is still keeping his own counsel about running for reelection. Dick, I managed to get through a reelection campaign last year, and I find I still like the job. I don't want to give you or the voters of South Carolina any advice, but I sure like the idea of having the two Carolinas represented by reelected Democratic governors.

While I'm on the subject of 1982, I'm reminded that South Carolina's delegation to the U.S. House of Representatives is composed of two Democrats and four Republicans. I am convinced that in the next election those numbers are going to change. Ken Holland and Butler Derrick are doing a fine job.[3] They are two of the most able members of Congress today, but let's send them some reinforcements in 1982.

Then there's the South Carolina Rock of Gibraltar, Fritz Hollings.[4] If there is a more able and more respected member of the Senate, I challenge anybody to tell me who that is. As a Democrat and as an American, it makes me feel good to know that Fritz is sitting as ranking member of the Senate Budget Committee. I just want him to be chairman again after the next election.

So here in South Carolina and elsewhere, I see a lot of reasons for optimism as we prepare ourselves for the time when this great party is called upon to lead this nation again. I'm optimistic, for example, about our new national chairman, Chuck Manatt, a man I've known since my college days and one of the best thinkers and organizers I've ever been around.[5] With Chuck at the helm, we are going to be organized like never before. We're going to master the most sophisticated techniques of fund raising, candidate recruitment, and issue development. Never again are we going to let the Republicans mislead the American people about the things the Democratic party stands for. We're going to carry that message across this land on our terms.

I imagine the other party will continue to outspend us. After all, they continue to be the party of the fat cats, while we are the party of the working men and women of America—that's the way it always has been and that's the way it always will be. But with Chuck Manatt carrying our banner, all we have to do is raise a dollar for every two the Republicans raise and we'll whip them every time.

Chairman Manatt has very kindly asked me to chair a national Democratic panel assigned to review our party's procedures for nominating national candidates and selecting delegates to our national convention. What we want to do is look for ways to make that process more attuned to the needs and desires of the American people, and more open to participation by the people who serve our party from positions of elective office.[6] I hope that all of you here tonight will give us your ideas. We will need the benefit of your time, your talent, and energy.

For Democrats this is a time to renew, to build, to examine. We have never been reluctant to do that. That is why we are the oldest political party on this planet; that is why we have time and again led this country and this world through times of crisis. We are the party the men and women of America have always looked to when the chips were really down.

Our Republican "friends"—I almost choked on that word but I'm trying to be diplomatic here—cannot, in the long run, offer people the kind of leadership that is going to be needed during these next two decades and into the twenty-first century.

H. L. Mencken didn't much care for politicians of any stripe, but he once said: "In this world of sin and sorrow, there is always something to be thankful for. As for me, I rejoice that I am not a Republican."[7]

Oh, they win an election now and then and promptly declare themselves to be the wave of the future. But every time, they end up standing on low ground when the tide gets high.

In the last election, they sold the American people on the notion that the Democratic party stood for reckless spending, overregulation, and a weak national defense. The fact of the matter is that the last Democratic administration substantially reduced the federal deficit, deregulated major industries like the airlines, increased military spending in real dollars, and took us a giant step toward a stable and peaceful world by forging a peace treaty between Egypt and Israel. We just didn't do a very good job of getting our message out. The Republicans had the money, the computers, and the mailing lists.[8]

We can't change what happened, but we can learn from it. But all of the organization and effort we can muster will do us no good if we don't offer the American people good ideas and good alternatives. If we are going to tell the American people what it is we are about, we had better know ourselves. It is not good enough to sit back and say, "Well, it's just a matter of time until the Reagan administration starts making mistakes and losing popularity. Then we'll be back in the saddle again." That is lazy, infantile thinking and it doesn't contribute anything to the building of this party and this country.

It is also not good enough to merely cast ourselves as partisan obstructionists—to simply oppose the Republican administration for the sake of opposing, to wallow in self-indulgence and sour grapes. I believe we should be generally supportive to the president's efforts to get the economy on the right track. Deep budget cuts are in some cases going to hurt people, but all of us know that we must get government spending under control.

But Congress must not abrogate its responsibility to scrutinize the president's budget line by line. The American people expect that. Let me give you an example. The other day, Bill Hefner,[9] a Democratic congressman from North Carolina and a member of the House Budget Committee, was approached by a woman who wanted him to support the president's economic program. Then she turned right around and asked Bill to help her daughter get a student loan so she could go to college next fall. She was surprised when Bill told her that student loans were targeted for drastic reduction in the administration budget.

In addition to specific programs being cut, I sense a deepening concern about the possible impact of the tax reductions being proposed. I'm not sure they amount to "voodoo economics" as Vice-President Bush once described them,[10] but we must ask ourselves if such drastic tax cuts are going to fuel inflation and give us a federal deficit from which it could take us years to recover.

The House Budget Committee is asking the right questions and has come up with an excellent counterproposal. The federal budget

proposed by that committee provides for substantial cuts in federal
spending and a healthy tax cut. What it also does is project a deficit
billions of dollars less than the administration budget. That is not
obstructionism. That is a good, commonsense, Democratic alternative, and tonight I call upon President Reagan to accept that
alternative.

As Democrats, we must not exclusively focus our attention on
Washington. The Democratic leadership being provided in the
statehouses is a source of great hope. In North Carolina, if you'll let
me brag a little bit, a Democratic administration and a Democratic
legislature are leading my state on an unprecedented program of
progress—in economic development, in education, and in fighting
crime.

In South Carolina, Dick Riley and the Democratic party are
carrying on the great progressive tradition of Bob McNair, John
West, Fritz Hollings, and all of the other great Democratic governors that have served here.[11] The Riley administration has correctly
placed the education of the children of South Carolina number one
on the priority list. This administration has helped the working
people of this state by leading the fight for reform of the South
Carolina Public Service Commission and by really working to get a
grip on the growth of state government.

With forward-looking Democratic leadership, this state, my state,
and all of the others can truly be laboratories for democracy. In so
doing, we can help formulate a national Democratic agenda.

We can help formulate a policy for the development of alternative
sources of energy at a time when the Republican administration—
along with an energy secretary familiar to most of you[12]—has
virtually abandoned that effort.

We can demonstrate an ability to compensate for reduced federal
dollars by mobilizing citizen-volunteers.

We can and must develop a long-range strategy for reindus-
trializing this country and making it once again the most productive in the world.

Democrats must also take the lead in devising systems for
managing the hazardous wastes that are the by-product of economic progress.

We have the talent to forge this agenda. All over this country the
brightest faces on the political scene are Democrats. This is the
party of Dick Riley and the party of Walter Mondale, the party of
Bill Bradley and the party of Tom Bradley, the party of Jerry Brown
and the party of Jay Rockefeller, the party of Anne Wexler and the
party of Bob Graham, Joe Biden, Fritz Hollings, and Sam Ervin.[13]

We are also the party that has meant jobs and a decent living. We
have put people to work and kept them working. We understand our
people's hopes and dreams for a good job, good schools, and safe
neighborhoods. We are Democrats because, as Woodrow Wilson

said, "It is the Democratic party that releases the energy of every human being." [14]

If the two-party system is to be preserved in this country, it is the Democratic party that will preserve it, because we stand for something. We are not a collection of one-issue groups that get together at election time, then split and spin off in a hundred different directions.

We are an open party that stands for an open society—open to men and women, rich and poor, black and white. We cannot and will not abandon our historic commitment to human equality, to fairness, to justice. If we do abandon that, we are no longer Democrats; we are something else. We must never turn our backs on our belief that every man, woman, and child must have the opportunity to burgeon out all that is within them.

Our roots stretch deeper than those of any political party in the world today—going all the way back to the wellsprings of Jefferson and Madison—because we stand for these things. We understand that *who* leads us is not as important as *what* leads us—what convictions, what courage, what faith. *Who* we are is not as important as *what* we symbolize. Men and women together, wedded to great and timeless principles, can accomplish anything. That is our challenge. We are ready to rise to that challenge and lead again.

---

[1] William Jennings Bryan Dorn (1916-   ), native, resident of Greenwood, South Carolina; educated in Greenwood public schools; U.S. Army Air Force, 1942-1945. Member, South Carolina House, 1939-1940, and Senate, 1940-1942; U.S. representative from South Carolina's Third Congressional District, 1947-1948, 1951-1974. Distinguished lecturer in American politics and government, University of South Carolina at Spartanburg since 1978, and adjunct professor of government at Lander College, Greenwood; chairman, 1980-1984, and chairman emeritus, since 1984, South Carolina Democratic party. *Who's Who in America, 1982-1983*, I, 861; see also William Jennings Bryan Dorn to Jan-Michael Poff, June 1, 1984.

[2] Richard Wilson Riley (1932-   ), native of Greenville, South Carolina; resident of Columbia; B.A., Furman University, 1954; LL.B., University of South Carolina, 1960; U.S. Naval Reserve, 1954-1956. Attorney, 1959-1978; member, South Carolina House, 1963-1967, and Senate, 1966-1977; elected governor of South Carolina, 1978, and reelected in 1982. Barone and Ujifusa, *Almanac of American Politics, 1984*, 1067; *Who's Who in America, 1982-1983*, II, 2807.

[3] Kenneth L. Holland (1934-   ), native of Gaffney, South Carolina; B.A., 1960, LL.B., 1963, J.D., 1970, University of South Carolina. Attorney; U.S. representative from South Carolina's Fifth Congressional District, 1975-1982; legal counsel, South Carolina Democratic party. *Who's Who in America, 1982-1983*, I, 1550.

Butler Carson Derrick, Jr. (1936-   ), native of Johnston, South Carolina; resident of Edgefield; B.A., University of South Carolina, 1958; LL.B., University of Georgia, 1965. Attorney, 1965-1974; member, South Carolina House, 1969-1975; U.S. representative from South Carolina's Third Congressional District since 1975. Barone and Ujifusa, *Almanac of American Politics, 1984*, 1073; *Who's Who in America, 1982-1983*, I, 813.

[4] Ernest Frederick (Fritz) Hollings (1922-   ), native, resident of Charleston, South Carolina; B.A., The Citadel, 1942; LL.B., University of South Carolina, 1947. Attorney, 1947-1958, 1963-1966; member, South Carolina House, 1949-1955; lieu-

tenant governor, 1955-1959, and governor, 1959-1963, of South Carolina; U.S. senator since 1966. Barone and Ujifusa, *Almanac of American Politics, 1984*, 1066; *Who's Who in America, 1982-1983*, I, 1553.

⁵Charles Taylor Manatt (1936-   ), native of Chicago; B.S., Iowa State University, 1958; J.D., George Washington University, 1962. California attorney since 1962; chairman, California Democratic Committee, 1971-1973, 1975-1977; member, since 1976, and chairman, 1981-1985, Democratic National Committee. *News and Observer*, November 9, 1984; *Who's Who in America, 1982-1983*, II, 2121.

⁶See "Statement on Democratic National Committee Commission on Presidential Nomination," Washington, D.C., July 2, 1981, below.

⁷Henry Louis Mencken (1880-1956), native of Baltimore, Maryland; educated in private schools and at Baltimore Polytechnic. Author, critic, reporter, editor, staff member, various Baltimore newspapers, 1899-1956; editor, *American Mercury*, 1924-1933; director, Alfred A. Knopf, Inc. *Who Was Who in America, 1951-1960*, 591. Neither the source nor accuracy of the quotation Hunt attributed to Mencken has been verified.

⁸Poor intraparty relations also jeopardized the outcome of the 1980 presidential election, Hunt asserted on August 4, 1981, at the Western Democratic party rally: "We've got to show that Democrats can work together. One reason we lost last year, regardless of who was to blame, was that President Carter and the Democratic Congress gave people the idea they couldn't work together. And people wanted something done."

⁹W. G. (Bill) Hefner (1930-   ), native of Elora, Tennessee; president, WRKB radio station, Kannapolis. Elected to U.S. House of Representatives, 1974, from North Carolina's Eighth Congressional District, and returned in subsequent elections; member, Conservative Democratic Forum, Congressional Textile Caucus, and Congressional Travel and Tourism Caucus. *News and Observer*, November 8, 1984; *North Carolina Manual, 1983*, 175.

¹⁰George Herbert Walker Bush (1924-   ), native of Wilton, Massachusetts; B.A., Yale University, 1948. Cofounder, director, Zapata Petroleum Corp., 1953-1959; president, 1956-1964, and board chairman, 1964-1966, Zapata Off Shore Co.; U.S. representative from Texas's Seventh Congressional District, 1967-1971; U.S. ambassador to the United Nations, 1971-1972; chairman, National Republican Committee, 1973-1974; chief, U.S. liaison office, Beijing, China, 1974-1975; CIA director, 1976-1977; adjunct professor, Rice University; U.S. vice-president since 1981. *Who's Who in America, 1982-1983*, I, 467. While campaigning for the Republican presidential nomination in 1980, Bush termed the 30 percent decrease in federal income tax rates backed by rival candidate Reagan as "voodoo economics." " 'Not a Cross Word Between Us,' " *Time*, July 28, 1980, 20.

¹¹Robert Evander McNair (1923-   ), native of Cades, South Carolina; resident of Columbia; B.A., 1947, LL.B., 1948, University of South Carolina; U.S. Naval Reserve, 1942-1946. Member, South Carolina House, 1951-1962; lieutenant governor, 1962-1965, and governor, 1965-1971, of South Carolina; attorney since 1971. *Who's Who in America, 1982-1983*, II, 2255.

John Carl West (1922-   ), lieutenant governor, 1967-1971, and governor, 1971-1975, of South Carolina; U.S. ambassador to Saudi Arabia, 1977-1981. *United States Government Manual, 1981/82* (Washington, D.C.: Office of the Federal Register, National Archives and Records Service, General Services Administration, Revised May 1, 1981), 396; *Who's Who in America, 1980-1981*, II, 3485; also previously identified in Mitchell, *Addresses of Hunt*, I, 139n.

¹²James Burrows Edwards (1927-   ), native of Hawthorne, Florida; B.S., College of Charleston, 1950; D.M.D., University of Louisville, 1955; U.S. Navy, 1955-1957. Oral surgeon; governor of South Carolina, 1975-1979; appointed secretary, U.S. Department of Energy, in 1981. *Who's Who in America, 1982-1983*, I, 925.

¹³Bill Bradley (1943-   ), native of Crystal City, Missouri; resident of Denville, New Jersey; B.A., Princeton University, 1965; Rhodes Scholar, Oxford University, 1965-1968. U.S. Olympic basketball team, 1964; professional basketball player, New York Knicks, 1967-1977; U.S. senator from New Jersey since 1979. Barone and

Ujifusa, *Almanac of American Politics, 1984*, 727; *News and Observer*, November 8, 1984.

Thomas Bradley (1917-   ), native of Calvert, Texas; resident of Los Angeles; student at University of California-Los Angeles, 1939-1940; LL.B., Southwestern University, 1956. Officer, Los Angeles Police Department, 1940-1961; attorney, 1961-1963; city councilman, 1963-1973, and mayor, since 1973, of Los Angeles. *Who's Who in America, 1982-1983*, I, 362.

Edmund Gerald (Jerry) Brown, Jr. (1938-   ), native of San Francisco; resident of Sacramento; B.A., University of California-Berkeley, 1961; J.D., Yale University, 1964. Research attorney, California Supreme Court, 1964-1965; attorney in private practice, 1966-1969; secretary of state, 1970-1974, and governor, 1975-1983, of California. Barone and Ujifusa, *Almanac of American Politics, 1984*, 80; *Who's Who in America, 1982-1983*, I, 410.

John Davidson (Jay) Rockefeller IV (1937-   ), secretary of state, 1968-1972, and governor, 1977-1985, of West Virginia; U.S. senator since 1985. Barone and Ujifusa, *Almanac of American Politics, 1984*, 1260; *News and Observer*, November 8, 1984; previously identified in Mitchell, *Addresses of Hunt*, I, 122n.

Anne Wexler (1930-   ), native of New York City; B.A., Skidmore College, 1951. Executive director, Citizens for Muskie, Muskie for President, 1972, and committee on voter registration, Democratic National Committee, 1972; associate publisher, *Rolling Stone*, 1974-1976; served on Carter-Mondale transition planning team, 1976-1977; deputy undersecretary, U.S. Commerce Department, 1977-1978; assistant to President Carter, 1978-1981; president, Wexler and Associates, since 1981. *Who's Who in America, 1982-1983*, II, 3535.

Robert Graham (1936-   ), native of Miami, Florida; resident of Tallahassee; B.A., University of Florida, 1959; J.D., Harvard University, 1962. Vice-president, Graham Company; board chairman, Sengra Development Corp.; member, Florida House, 1967-1971, and Senate, 1971-1978; elected governor of Florida in 1978 and reelected in 1982. Barone and Ujifusa, *Almanac of American Politics, 1984*, 233.

Joseph Robinette Biden, Jr. (1942-   ), native of Scranton, Pennsylvania; resident of Wilmington, Delaware; B.A., University of Delaware, 1965; J.D., Syracuse University, 1968. Attorney, 1968-1972; U.S. senator from Delaware since 1973. Barone and Ujifusa, *Almanac of American Politics, 1984*, 223; *News and Observer*, November 8, 1984.

Sam J. Ervin, Jr. (1896-1985), native, resident of Morganton; U.S. senator from North Carolina, 1954-1975. Previously identified in Mitchell, *Addresses of Hunt*, I, 584n.

[14]President Wilson's original statement was an endorsement of a specific form of government, not a comment on party politics: " 'I believe in Democracy,' " he said, " 'because it releases the energies of every human being.' " Edmund Fuller (ed.), *Thesaurus of Quotations* (New York: Crown Publishers, 1941), 258.

Woodrow Wilson (1856-1924), native of Staunton, Virginia; A.B., 1879, A.M., 1882, Princeton University; Ph.D., Johns Hopkins University, 1886. Attorney, 1882-1883; college professor, 1885-1910; president, Princeton University, 1902-1910; governor of New Jersey, 1911-1913; U.S. president, 1913-1917, 1917-1921; Democrat. *Who Was Who in America, 1897-1942*, 1364.

DEDICATION OF REX-ROSENLEW INTERNATIONAL

THOMASVILLE, APRIL 28, 1981

I am particularly pleased to participate in this ceremony today. I have been following the progress of this project almost since its infancy.

In 1979 I had the great honor of meeting Mr. Rosenlew[1] at a seminar I attended in Switzerland. Last year in my office I joined with Mr. Savander and James Johnson in announcing Rosenlew and Rex Plastics' plans to establish this plant,[2] and I want to especially thank Mr. Savander and James Johnson for their help in promoting North Carolina to other companies in Finland during the last several months. It's good to be here and see those plans put into action and to see North Carolinians in these good jobs.

Rex-Rosenlew today officially becomes another member of the great community of international businesses in North Carolina. Our state has more foreign-owned manufacturing plants than any other in the Southeast. Last year more of those foreign-owned plants were announced in North Carolina than in any other state.

Rosenlew is the fifteenth European company we met either in Switzerland in 1979 or on a 1978 industrial mission to Europe that has decided to locate in North Carolina. Those fifteen companies will invest over $120 million and employ over 1,300 people in our state. That's not a bad return on two trips which cost the state a total of about $40,000.

We are happy that Rosenlew would team up with the fine North Carolina company of Rex Plastics. Rex Plastics has been in North Carolina for over twenty years and provides 300 jobs here in Thomasville. I commend James Johnson and Rex Plastics for being open to this joint venture. Without Rex Plastics' enthusiasm and support we would not be holding this ceremony today. I also want to thank Miles Smith and Kay Lambeth of the state Economic Development Board and the International Division of the Department of Commerce for their help in matching up these two companies.[3] My special thanks to local officials who have provided such great support.

This partnership between Rosenlew and Rex Plastics is an important symbol. Today we not only commemorate this plant, but we celebrate the beginning of a whole new important relationship between North Carolina and Finland. Earlier I mentioned European trade missions. Let me assure you, Mr. Ambassador[4] and Mr. Rosenlew, that on our state's next European mission we will want to meet with companies in your country. We want to visit your country because we know that companies there emphasize technology and quality. As a country with a relatively small home market, you must compete in the world marketplace. The best way to do that is by producing the finest products. We feel combining Finnish ingenuity and experience with the outstanding productivity of North Carolina workers is the perfect match.

Rosenlew has set the example for your fellow countrymen. You have learned that North Carolina provides a central location to a large portion of the United States marketplace. Our good roads make access to that marketplace easy.

We are proud to have your company here, Mr. Rosenlew. Rosenlew has been in business over 125 years and is a name recognized internationally. Having the Rosenlew name in North Carolina adds great prestige to our state's reputation.

This joint venture has proved, once again, that North Carolina can be a place where overseas-owned businesses can operate successfully.

We have benefited not only from your jobs, but from your friendship. These business relations have led to better human relations. We thank you.

---

[1] Gustav Rosenlew (1929-), native of Helsinki; resident of Pori, Finland; B.Sc., Helsinki University of Technology, 1954; Finnish army, 1953-1954. Executive vice-president, 1963-1969, president, 1969-1977, and chairman and chief executive, since July 1, 1977, of W. Rosenlew, Ltd. Ted Darling, president, Rex-Rosenlew International, Inc., to Jan-Michael Poff, November 5, 1984, hereinafter cited as Darling correspondence.

[2] Magnus Savander (1936-), native of Helsinki; resident of Pori, Finland; Master at Law, Helsinki University, 1960; Finnish army, 1954-1955. Attorney, 1964-1967, marketing director, 1967-1969, executive vice-president, 1969-1977, and president, since July 1, 1977, of W. Rosenlew, Ltd. Darling correspondence.

James William Johnson (1928-), native of Guilford County; resident of Thomasville; B.S., University of North Carolina at Chapel Hill, 1951. President, Rex Plastics, Inc., since 1958. Darling correspondence. For more information on the union of W. Rosenlew, Ltd., and Rex Plastics, Inc., see Mitchell, *Addresses of Hunt*, I, 648-649.

[3] Miles James Smith (1927-), native of Greensboro; resident of Salisbury; B.A., University of North Carolina at Chapel Hill, 1950; M.B.A., Wake Forest University, 1976; U.S. Naval Reserve, 1945-1946. President, Carolina Rubber Hose Co.; board chairman, Premtec, Inc., since 1979. Miles James Smith, Jr., to Jan-Michael Poff, November 13, 1984.

Katharine C. (Kay) Lambeth (1917-), president, Erwin-Lambeth, Inc., 1946-1982; secretary-treasurer, Lambeth, Ltd., since 1979. Katharine C. Lambeth to Jan-Michael Poff, November 8, 1984; Mitchell, *Addresses of Hunt*, I, 271n.

[4] Jaakko Olavi Iloniemi (1932-), native, resident of Helsinki, Finland; M.A., 1957. General secretary, Finnish League, 1954-1958, and of the National Union of Students of Finland, 1959-1961; secretary, International Committee for Development Assistance, 1961-1964, director, Bureau of Development Assistance, 1965-1971, ambassador at large, 1972-1973, and director, Political Department, 1975-1977, of the Ministry of Foreign Affairs, Finland; deputy permanent representative of Finland to the United Nations, minister counselor, 1971-1972; ambassador, Finnish Mission to the Conference on Security and Cooperation in Europe, 1973-1975; undersecretary of state for political affairs, 1977; ambassador to the United States, 1977-1983; director, Union Bank of Finland, since 1983. Press Section, Embassy of Finland, to Jan-Michael Poff, November 8, 1984.

EXECUTIVES TOUR OF NORTH CAROLINA

RALEIGH, MAY 5, 1981

[In similar remarks made May 6 before the Telex Corporation Board of Directors, Hunt listed reasons why North Carolina was so attractive to businesses relocating or expanding from out of state: quality of life, corporate income tax rates having remained constant for forty-seven years, the constitution's balanced budget requirement, low state and local taxes, and holding the growth of state government to 10 percent.]

I want to welcome you to the Executive Mansion and to North Carolina. We are proud those of you with companies from out of state have decided to spend some time with us, learning more about our state.

I also want to welcome members of the General Assembly, George Herbert, Lauch Faircloth, Larry Blake, Ned Huffman, and representatives of local chambers here.[1]

I know it's been a busy two days for you. I think by now you can see the importance we place on your industry in this state. We feel the electronics industry is the key to opening the door to future economic growth in this state. I hope you have felt the enthusiastic support of business, government, and educational institutions to make that dream come true.

With the tremendous help of the General Assembly, North Carolina has long supported the necessary laws, regulations, and investments in government and education to stimulate economic growth. We plan to do the same in connection with electronics. Community colleges and universities have already begun beefing up their facilities. We've expanded university instruction in microelectronics and established the Microelectronics Center of North Carolina. I've asked this session of the General Assembly for $24 million to provide the necessary support for that center.

Quite frankly, that proposed investment—just as with the investment in the state's schools, textiles, furniture, design and engineering—isn't made to help only industry. The primary motivation is to assure our citizens the best possible job and career opportunities. This is particularly crucial in electronics. Your industry is undergoing unparalleled growth. You are creating thousands of jobs across this country. Your products are revolutionizing our traditional industries. The future for young people in our schools in large measure will be tied to electronics. For those young people we must move ahead in our support of education now, or the rest of the world may just pass our youngsters by.

The changes have already begun in North Carolina. The electronics industry employs 50,000 people in this state in fifty counties. The output of North Carolina companies like Telex, IBM, General

Electric, Westinghouse, Northern Telecom, Western Electric, and Data General ranks fourth, behind textiles, tobacco, and chemicals and ahead of furniture.

I'm optimistic that we will provide the support needed. I'm confident we will help our students and others upgrade their education and skills. We will make sure that North Carolina continues to be the best place in the country to live and operate a business, and we will do everything we can to make North Carolina the most attractive location for the electronics industry.

---

[1] George Richard Herbert (1922-   ), president, Research Triangle Institute, since 1979. Previously identified in Mitchell, *Addresses of Hunt*, I, 268n.

Larry J. Blake (1930-   ), state president, North Carolina Department of Community Colleges, 1979-1983. Previously identified in Mitchell, *Addresses of Hunt*, I, 531n; see also *North Carolina Manual, 1983*, 637.

Ned E. Huffman (1917-   ), native of Poughkeepsie, New York; educated at Guilford College. Former division manager, Southern Bell Telephone & Telegraph Co.; executive vice-president, Research Triangle Foundation of North Carolina, since 1965. Ned E. Huffman to Jan-Michael Poff, January 29, 1985.

COMMUNITY COLLEGE CONGRESS

RALEIGH, MAY 6, 1981

In recent days I have been reading news stories about some rankings that we should have very much in mind during this Community College Congress. They concern North Carolina's ranking among the states in per capita income. In 1970 we ranked thirty-eighth. Today we rank thirty-ninth. When I became governor in 1977, we actually ranked forty-first.

So we have made some progress since 1977, and I think we will make some more because of the things we have done the last four years. We have seen record industrial growth in that period, but it takes time to build new plants and expansions and to put people to work in them. So I think the lesson to us here today is this: Yes, North Carolina is moving forward, but we need to do a lot more if we're going to bring about real, fundamental changes in the economic well-being of our people.

There is more to that task than just recruiting industry. We have to maintain a good system of roads and highways, and that is why I spelled out a program to do that last week. We have to manage and dispose of our industrial wastes wisely and safely. We have to guarantee our entire state a reliable and affordable supply of energy.

And we have to equip our citizens with the skills they need to get and hold good jobs. That is, I believe, the primary issue before this congress and before this community college system.

I'm tired of North Carolina being thirty-eighth or thirty-ninth or forty-first in per capita income. Our people are tired of it. I believe the best way to escape the bottom is to set our sights on making North Carolina a center for high-technology industry.

High technology isn't just microelectronics. It's also the high-speed looms and automated equipment of a modern textile plant. High technology demands highly skilled people, and those skilled people must be the product of our community college system.

One of the things I am going to spend a lot of my time on in my second term as governor is the development of a comprehensive state approach to skills training. As I have prepared for this, I have had the benefit of the advice of an ad hoc group of state government leaders representing nearly every agency that is involved, one way or another, in job training: public schools, community colleges, the Employment Security Commission, and various state departments. I have asked a group of the state's largest corporations to lend this state some of their best people to advise me.

There is a lot to be done. But one thing has already become clear, and I have already made one key decision on this state's policy: Our community colleges should be the "presumptive deliverers" of skill training in North Carolina. In Rock Ridge language that means we will presume that the community college system is the place training shall be done, unless we find a good reason otherwise.

I am committed to pressing for the state resources that will enable this system to fulfill that responsibility. Our budgets, particularly regarding equipment, will reflect this emphasis on skill training. At the same time we must explore other means of getting better equipment, such as leasing it.

Today I want to outline for you some of the things I think we should do to ensure that we move decisively toward making this system what it can be.

First, we need to improve our coordination with business and industry. That is why I appointed the people I did to the Board of Community Colleges, like Carl Horn.[1]

We need to get business people more seriously involved in helping us design and select the courses we offer. We need to make business participation on our boards more meaningful and rewarding for both the business person and our institutions. And we must draw upon the knowledge of a greater variety of business leaders.

We need to tap the resources of business and industry to help solve our equipment problems and to keep our teachers up to date on modern production and management methods. An indication of what this relationship with the private sector can mean is found in our New and Expanding Industries program. It has enabled new businesses to get the trained employees they need—and North Carolinians get the better jobs they need. It deserves even more attention and support.

Just as we should reach out to business for help, we must do a better job of reaching out to those citizens who need help. The primary and secondary schools have taken impressive steps to improve the education our young people receive before they graduate from high school. I commend the State Board of Education and the Community Colleges Board for turning their attention to the dropout problem and taking steps to help those who have dropped out. I urge you to get involved in these efforts and help show that North Carolina is committed to ensuring that each person be all they can be.

We must also take seriously the need to help minorities and women overcome the unreasonable barriers that have limited them to less productive employment.

The community college system needs to be reaching out to the high school graduates. More of our young people need the additional training they could get from you before they enter the labor force. We need to have each one in the most productive job they can handle, and we need to help them avoid the bitter experience of dead-end jobs.

One tool that all of us need is better labor market information. We need a good, dependable system so that we can determine how many people we should train in a given skill and where those jobs will be in demand. I will soon be ready to announce a plan that will call upon all agencies involved in gathering this information to work together to improve the accuracy and efficiency of their activities. I will designate a lead agency to be responsible for making timely and accurate data available for planners—and to train the planners in how to use it. That will be a major step forward in North Carolina's skill-training program—a program that will depend, in large measure, on the people in this room.

We're giving our community college system a big job. I'm giving you a big challenge. I'm asking you to be receptive to change when change is needed. I'm asking you to be prepared to take brave steps to build North Carolina's future. I want you to know what this governor is expecting of our community college system. It is a new day for this system, and it can help bring about a new day for North Carolina and for all our people.

---

[1]Carl Horn, Jr. (1921-   ), native of Rutherfordton; resident of Charlotte; B.A., 1942, J.D., 1947, Duke University; U.S. Army, 1942-1946. Attorney; vice-president and general counsel, 1959-1971, and president, chairman, and chief executive officer, 1971-1982, Duke Power Company; chairman, state Board of Community Colleges, 1980-1983; executive in residence, School of Business Administration, University of North Carolina at Charlotte, since 1982. Carl Horn, Jr., to Jan-Michael Poff, October 6, 1983; News and Observer, May 24, 1981.

NORTH CAROLINA WORLD TRADE ASSOCIATION

RALEIGH, MAY 20, 1981

[On October 15, 1981, the governor told the International Investors Conference there were 230 foreign-owned manufacturing facilities in the state; that exports of North Carolina textiles and furniture increased 150 percent since he had taken office; and the total value of all state-produced exports exceeded $4 billion annually. However, apart from jobs and profits, he also noted world trade "brings about the exchange of ideas, the establishment of lasting bonds and friendships. As mutual economic ties increase, understanding among people increases. North Carolina and its business community are aware that these economic ties can make a contribution to the goal of international friendship and world peace." Hunt made similar remarks in a speech commemorating International Student Day, March 20, 1981.]

I take special pleasure in addressing this group, because you share my excitement about North Carolina's involvement and potential in international trade. This meeting symbolizes this state's growing involvement in the world economy. There is an increasingly close interrelationship among states and nations. This is due to the communications revolution, the rise of multinational corporations, and a growing awareness of trade opportunities all over the world.

Expanding international trade is going to be vital to the coming reindustrialization of this nation and the rebuilding of our economy. I think President Reagan is on the right track in his efforts to rebuild this country into a productive economic power, and I support his efforts. It is an honor for us to have the president's daughter, Maureen Reagan,[1] with us here today, and I hope she will pass those sentiments along to her father.

I want North Carolina to be an important part of the emerging world trade picture, and during my administration we've taken some important steps in that direction. One of the most important initiatives was creation of the International Division in our Department of Commerce. Last year that office handled over 4,000 telephone calls concerning international trade opportunities.

We supported the creation of foreign trade zones in Charlotte, Wilmington, and Morehead City, and last year we opened a state office in Japan.

I have personally led trade missions to Europe, Japan, and the People's Republic of China. I met with officials of foreign governments to discuss trade between their countries and North Carolina. Those trips have spread North Carolina's name worldwide. More foreign firms announced new plants here last year than any other state.

We're setting revenue records at our ports, and we have only begun to realize the potential they offer. I particularly want to thank the Japan Tobacco and Salt Public Corporation for its longtime support of our Port Authority. With us today is Mr. Kazanori Horai (Kahz ah nor eee-Ho rye), assistant representative in the Raleigh office of JTS. Mr. Horai, I want to thank you for what your firm has done for North Carolina, and I want to assure you that we will continue to provide the kind of service you need.

North Carolina could not be making this great progress in world trade were it not for a strong partnership of government, the universities, and the business community. In Greensboro, for example, we have the District Office of the International Trade Administration. At North Carolina State University we have the [North Carolina] Japan Center and the International Trade Center. A few weeks ago the University of North Carolina at Chapel Hill and North Carolina State University conducted seminars on doing business with Mexico, and I announced at that time that an honorary Mexican consulate would be established in Charlotte.[2]

I am proud that the North Carolina World Trade Association was the first statewide, business-oriented, international trade group in the United States. You're doing a superb job of carrying the story of the expanding opportunities available to the businesses of this state. The message is getting across. Companies are learning that a quality product can and should be marketed worldwide.

The expanding export business has meant the difference between success and failure for some firms. The textile industry, for example, has remained vigorous in this state partly because of its aggressive commitment to exporting its products.

Every $1 million in additional exports creates thirty-five new jobs. That's the most cost-effective way I know of adding jobs to our economy.

I will continue to devote a great deal of attention to expanding our state's role in the world economic community. I have asked the General Assembly to appropriate additional money for the export office and the Japan Center. We intend to go on a trade mission to Mexico, and I hope we'll be returning to Japan in the near future.

We have only scratched the surface in creating a worldwide market for North Carolina products. There is a lot left to be done, but with your support we can one day make North Carolina a household word from Tokyo to Tunisia to Tahiti.

---

[1]Maureen Elizabeth Reagan (1941-   ), eldest daughter of President Ronald Wilson Reagan, was born to Reagan and his first wife, actress Jane Wyman. The

Reagan-Wyman marriage ended in divorce in 1948. *World Book Encyclopedia*, 1982 ed., s.v. "Reagan, Ronald Wilson."

²Governor Hunt further explained the function of the North Carolina Japan Center in a speech before the Southeast U.S.-Japan Association, November 16, 1981. The appointment of Charlotte businessman Wayne Cooper, as honorary consul, was announced April 21, 1981.

FURNITURE, BEDDING, AND ALLIED INDUSTRIES DIVISION OF THE UNITED JEWISH APPEAL- FEDERATION OF JEWISH PHILANTHROPIES

NEW YORK, MAY 27, 1981

[Thanking those attending the Greensboro Bonds dinner, June 16, 1981, for having bestowed upon him the City of Peace Award, Hunt then delivered a speech similar to the one appearing below. He also used the occasion to announce the creation of an endowment study committee to determine sources of permanent funding for the North Carolina-Israel Visiting Scholar Program.]

Madame Chairwoman,¹ Distinguished Honorees, Friends:

I am honored to be with you this evening. I want to extend my congratulations to Stanley Rosenberg, Abraham Stenberg, and Mark Schreiber as recipients of Leadership Awards from the Furniture, Bedding, and Allied Industries Division of the United Jewish Appeal-Federation.² The outstanding examples you have set are now goals for others to reach in the coming years.

I am not at all sure I will be able to match the eloquence of speakers who previously have appeared before you. I have chosen to speak to you about what I know best, and that is North Carolina. As I talk about North Carolina, I will try to draw some broader implications for our nation and for our world.

North Carolina is a big state, now the tenth largest in population. We stretch 600 miles across, from the Atlantic Ocean to the Appalachian Highlands, with much farmland, forest, and open space separating our cities.

North Carolina is a growing state, adding people and jobs at a rate above that of most other states. Our people and jobs, however, are dispersed. We are still considered a rural state. Our jobs historically have been concentrated in three main industries: furniture, textiles, and tobacco.

North Carolina is a clean state environmentally, with pure mountain air, clean waters, and virgin forests. But we are also a poor state, ranking very low in average manufacturing wages and only somewhat higher in per capita income.

The future will bring change. It already has begun to happen.

Our strategy for economic development is based on change. That strategy can be summed up in one word: diversification. At the same time we want to encourage expansion of our traditional industries such as furniture, which we see as a growth industry for North Carolina. We also expect to build upon a base of high technology, which will require a more skilled and sophisticated labor force. Our challenge during the next twenty years of transition will be to join together the traditional and the new in a positive and progressive manner.

Diversity and change is not only a challenge for North Carolina. Coping with its impact upon people and tradition seems to me to be one of the fundamental challenges of our nation and of modern civilization. Yet, it is absolutely clear that diversity and change are what has made us a great nation and what has brought about the advance of civilization since the dawn of mankind.

A famous historian looking backward on history took the position that five centuries into the Common Era, what mankind witnessed was the decline and fall of the Roman Empire—a crumbling of authority and control over a large part of the western world. Another historian, perhaps somewhat wiser and approaching history from the vantage point of looking forward, concluded that what really was significant at that same period of time was the rise of free nations and the beginnings of individual liberty.

Encouraging the growth of diversity and harnessing the creative energy that flows from change, I believe, is the wellspring for progress. Nowhere have I seen this carried out more effectively than in Israel.

I led a scientific mission to Israel in 1978, a mission that included the Speaker of the North Carolina House of Representatives, two cabinet secretaries, several agency division heads, and members of my Economic Development Board.[3]

I went to Israel because I had become convinced that world progress depends upon international exchanges. We all are familiar with the flow of goods and money between nations. What we have tended to overlook is the great importance of the flow of knowledge and the absolutely enormous impact that new ideas have on world progress. Too little of that flow has been encouraged.

I went to Israel because I wanted to see firsthand the visionaries who had begun to realize man's greatest dreams: harnessing energy from the sun, taking fresh water from the sea, and making the desert bloom.

I was not disappointed. The fascinating blend of the traditional and new in the life of Israel has given rise to creative advances that are a beacon of hope to the world.

To bring about a sharing of these advances and to further encourage international exchange, I signed Executive Order No. 21 while at the Hebrew University of Jerusalem, creating the North

Carolina-Israel Visiting Scholar Program.[4] Since that time eight senior scholars and scientists have participated as visiting scholars. And our first visitor from Israel, Professor Moshe Benziman of the Hebrew University, collaborated with Professor Malcolm Brown of the University of North Carolina at Chapel Hill on a pioneering and dramatic breakthrough in the laboratory growth of pure cellulose.[5] Their work was featured as the cover article in the November, 1980, issue of *Science* magazine.[6]

North Carolina, like Israel, will encourage diversity and change, seeking a blend of the traditional and new. As we set about this task, we will draw upon the talents of all of our people, those whose families have lived in North Carolina for generations, those who have come here more recently.

Two persons with us tonight, not born in North Carolina, are an outstanding example of how we encourage and build upon diversity. I am very proud of them, and I would like to take a moment for personal congratulations.

Arthur Cassell,[7] whom I mentioned earlier, recently received the Distinguished Citizens' Award from the Furniture and Allied Industries Society of Fellows, Anti-Defamation League of B'nai B'rith. Arthur, my warmest congratulations.

Arnold Zogry,[8] the deputy secretary of my Department of Administration, recently received the 1980-1981 Promotion of the Cause of Judaism Award from the North Carolina B'nai B'rith Association. Arnold, my congratulations.

Just four weeks ago tonight, at this time of the evening, I stood in silence, watching the lighting of candles at our first State Remembrance of the Holocaust. Six persons lit candles, five survivors and the son of survivors. It was very moving, and I felt a surge of pride in this country and our state which offered a new home and an opportunity to each survivor to begin life again. But I can only barely understand the terror of living an existence in which, as Elie (E-Lee) Wiesel (We-sell) said at the National Holocaust Ceremony, "For the first time in history being became a crime. Jews were destined for annihilation not because of what they said or proclaimed or did or possessed or created or destroyed, but because of who they were." [9]

Yes, we have helped the survivors. But they in turn help us greatly with their presence, their being.

In my "Inaugural Address" last January, I asked that North Carolina not bow to prevailing winds but turn to the direction that is the right one and step forth to lead the nation. Our commitment is one of progress through diversity, opportunity, equality, and excellence. With inspiration from nations such as Israel and with the support of all of our people, we shall reach our goals.

Thank you for letting me share this evening with you. Shalom.

[1] Edith L. Claman (1935-   ), native of New York City; B.A., Barnard College, 1956; M.S., Yeshiva University, 1961. Elementary school teacher, 1961-1973; secretary, 1973-1982, and executive vice-president, since 1982, of Lewittes Furniture Enterprises, Inc.; chairperson, Furniture, Bedding, and Allied Industries Division, United Jewish Appeal-Federation of Jewish Philanthropies, 1977-1983. Edith L. Claman to Jan-Michael Poff, February 8, 1985.

[2] Stanley Rosenberg is president of Stanley Rosenberg Associates, and Abraham B. Stenberg is vice-president of Burlington Industries, Inc. Melvin Nadell, assistant director, Trades and Professions, UJA-Federation Campaign, to Jan-Michael Poff, January 28, 1985.

Mark F. Schreiber (1942-   ), native of Detroit; resident of Villanova, Pennsylvania; B.S., University of Arizona. Executive vice-president, John Wanamaker, Philadelphia. Mark F. Schreiber to Jan-Michael Poff, February 12, 1985.

[3] The scientific mission Hunt led to Israel inspected the country's use of solar technology and was part of an industrial recruiting tour, April 2-15, 1978, that included West Germany, Switzerland, and the United Kingdom. State officials accompanying the governor were Thomas W. Bradshaw, transportation secretary; D. M. "Lauch" Faircloth, commerce secretary; Sara W. Hodgkins, cultural resources secretary; Lynwood Smith, chairman of the state Economic Development Board; board member and Speaker of the state House of Representatives Carl J. Stewart, Jr.; James R. Hinkle, International Division director; and William Arnold, director, and Hunter Poole, assistant director, Travel and Tourism Division, of the Commerce Department. Business executives participating in the tour, on personal funds, included Rep. John T. Church, of the State Ports Authority; Felix Harvey, of Kinston; Seby Jones, of Raleigh; Kay C. Lambeth, of Thomasville, head of the Travel and Tourism Committee, state Economic Development Board; board vice-chairman Miles Smith, of Salisbury, secretary Harold C. Shirley, of Monroe, and Graham Phillips, of Wallace; Rep. Ben Tison; Seth Wooten, of Wilson; and eleven others. *News and Observer*, March 31, 1978.

[4] Executive Order No. 21, "North Carolina-Israel Visiting Scholar Program," April 9, 1978. *N.C. Session Laws, 1977, Second Session, 1978*, 267-268.

[5] Moshe Benziman (1928-   ), biochemistry professor, Hebrew University of Jerusalem. Previously identified in Mitchell, *Addresses of Hunt*, I, 632n.

R. Malcolm Brown, Jr. (1939-   ), native of Pampa, Texas; resident of Austin; B.A., 1961, Ph.D., 1964, University of Texas at Austin. Associate professor of botany, 1968-1973, and professor, 1973-1982, University of North Carolina at Chapel Hill; assistant professor of botany, 1965-1968, and professor, since 1982, University of Texas at Austin. R. Malcolm Brown, Jr., to Jan-Michael Poff, October 10, 1983.

[6] The article to which Hunt referred is "Calcufluor White ST Alters the *in vivo* Assembly of Cellulose Microfibrils," by Candace H. Haigler, R. Malcolm Brown, Jr., and Moshe Benziman. *Science*, 210 (November 21, 1980), 903-905.

[7] Arthur Cassell (1918-   ), native of New York City; resident of Greensboro; A.B., 1939, J.D., 1941, New York University; U.S. Army Air Force, 1942-1946. Chairman, Casard Furniture Mfg. Corp., 1958-1985; member, Advisory Budget Commission, 1981-1985, and of the Board of the Center for Public Broadcasting. Arthur Cassell to Jan-Michael Poff, January 24, 1985.

[8] Arnold Zogry (1935-   ), deputy secretary of administration until 1981. *News and Observer*, November 3, 1981; see also Mitchell, *Addresses of Hunt*, I, 632n.

[9] Elie Wiesel (1928-   ), native of Sighet, Romania; attended Sorbonne, Paris, 1947-1950; honorary degrees. Prize-winning author, humanitarian; naturalized U.S. citizen since 1963; distinguished professor, City College of New York, since 1972. *Who's Who in America, 1982-1983*, II, 3562. Neither the source nor accuracy of the quotation attributed to Wiesel could be verified.

STATEMENT ON "GOOD ROADS" LEGISLATION

RALEIGH, MAY 28, 1981

[The Congressional Club's television and radio advertisements opposing the proposed 3-cent-per-gallon gasoline tax increase criticized the Transportation Department, attributed bid rigging to the Hunt administration, accused the governor of allowing political cronyism to influence transportation-related policy decisions, and wondered why a $200 million revenue boost was necessary when the state had surplus income in excess of a half billion dollars. Although the press copy of Hunt's May 28 news conference, below, demonstrates a relatively restrained response to those allegations, his extemporaneous remarks on the same occasion were more lively. For example, the problem of bid rigging, the governor stated, "has been going on for decades. It is under this administration that we're going to end it. That's something the Republicans didn't do." Furthermore, he labeled as "a distortion" the advertisements' "claim that the state had $537 million in surplus funds. . . . That money, which represents the increase in the state budget over the next two fiscal years, will be used to offset inflation in government costs and essential programs for mental hospitals, prisons and schools." *Durham Morning Herald*, May 29, 1981; *News and Observer*, May 29, 1981.]

The General Assembly will be voting soon on the good roads bill, and I am confident that it will pass. That is a credit to the courage and determination of the senators and representatives who are working for the bill. They are doing it because it is important to the future of North Carolina. It would be a tragic mistake to underestimate how important this issue is.

Every city and every state in this nation is facing serious problems in the deterioration of public services, including roads and highways. The future belongs to those who look ahead and make investments this year that will save millions of dollars and thousands of jobs in the years ahead.

The opposition is looking to furthering its own ends, not to building our future. The Congressional Club is showing its true colors on this issue, just as they did in their smear campaign against Congressman Bill Hefner.[1]

Most of us in North Carolina want to build; they want to tear down. Most of us want to talk sense; they want to spread lies and insults. Most of us want to appeal to the best in people; they want to appeal to the worst.

The issue is very clear. We must have more money to keep our roads in good condition. We can raise the gas tax and make those who use the roads the most pay the most. Or we can take the money out of schools, hospitals, day care, and law enforcement, as the Congressional Club proposes to do.

I believe our plan is the fairest way, and the income-tax credit enables people to offset what the 3 cents will cost them for the driving they have to do.

The people of North Carolina should ask why the Congressional Club is raising millions of dollars from oil companies and other special interests across the nation to oppose a good roads program in our state.

I'm glad to have their opposition, because I frankly feel that it will help us pass our program.

---

[1] According to the *Charlotte Observer*, August 15, 1981, the Congressional Club inundated the constituents of the Eighth District with mail, the previous April, in an effort to persuade them "to put the heat on Congressman Hefner to support the President's budget." Hefner refused to bow to such pressure. Consequently, former Governor James E. Holshouser, Jr., "raided the district with a group of Republicans to advertise 'Preparation H'—a prescription for what they think ails the 8th District. It basically calls for Hefner's defeat. Hefner called both forays 'smears,' and even Holshouser thinks the 'Preparation H' campaign might have been in poor taste."

HUMAN RESOURCES LIAISON COMMITTEE, NATIONAL GOVERNORS' ASSOCIATION

WRIGHTSVILLE BEACH, MAY 28, 1981

[The heads of human services departments from twenty-five states, the District of Columbia, and Puerto Rico convened in Wrightsville Beach to consider avenues for implementation of block grant programs and methods of compensating for funds lost through federal budget reductions. The session was sponsored by the Human Resources Liaison Committee of the National Governors' Association (NGA) and hosted by the North Carolina Department of Human Resources and the New York Department of Social Services. It served as a prelude to a "special seminar on block grant strategies," cochaired by Hunt and Richard A. Snelling, governor of Vermont, to be held at the annual meeting of the NGA, August 9. *Human Services and Federalism: Proceedings of a National Conference on Human Services, Wrightsville Beach, N.C., May 1981, and Summary of States' Strategies for Managing Block Grants* (Raleigh: Department of Human Resources, 1981), i, 41, hereinafter cited as *Human Services and Federalism*.]

I welcome the opportunity to speak to you today. There are few more important groups of government officials at this point in our nation's history than the directors, secretaries, and commissioners of the states' human resource agencies and their senior assistants. We have entered an era of fundamental and sweeping change in the way we approach human problems in this nation. You and the governors of this nation are on the firing line.

Many of the changes being contemplated in Washington bring with them dramatic and perhaps unequaled opportunities for state and local governments to come of age in ministering to human need. In many areas the administration's proposal to convert human resource categorical programs into a set of block grants is a delightful prospect, one we have sought and supported. States would be given the authority to allocate funds based on their own priorities and needs. I believe that we here in North Carolina—my human resources secretary, our legislative leaders, the program advocates and recipients, all of us considering our needs very carefully—can do a better job of running these programs than the federal government has done, if we are given the chance in the right way.

But there is a real danger here. This concept of state responsibility, for which we have worked for many years, could turn out to be a real disaster—not because it is a bad concept, but because the cuts are so deep and because we have so little time to adjust to them.

We may, in fact, find ourselves at the right place at the wrong time. As columnist Neal Peirce noted in a recent *Washington Post* article: "This year's struggle over budget cuts and sharp devolution of power to state and local levels is one that eventually had to come, in the name of sensible intergovernmental management and fiscal prudence." But whether it is being done the right way "is quite another matter." [1]

As Peirce correctly notes, the timing is highly questionable. The block grants can't possibly clear Congress until late summer, when most legislatures will be adjourned for the year or the biennium. Each congressional committee has its own idea as to the form the block grant should take, if indeed the committee can agree there should be one. It is virtually impossible now to anticipate the final product—one that may be handed to us literally a few days before it is to be implemented. I wholeheartedly agree with Peirce's observation that "a year's advance notice would have been a far more responsible way to introduce the block grants."

When you couple with this the depth of the proposed budget cuts in the human services area, you get an uneasy feeling. We are talking about an inflation-adjusted cut of anywhere from 33 to 38 percent in most of the 1982 human resource programs. The governors have estimated we can, by consolidation and careful administration, reduce funding levels by 10 percent and provide the same level of services to the same number of people. But we can't do that with a 38 percent cut. Most states are already in a severe budget squeeze, so there will be few, if any, state dollars available to make up the difference.

Make no mistake about it. Cuts of that magnitude mean that some of the people receiving help this year will not receive help next year. There is going to be real pain and real suffering. That is what these budget cuts mean, and I think everybody should clearly understand that. But, as leaders, as public officials charged with helping those in our society who most need our help, we must make it work.

We must be fair. The public and those affected must understand what we are doing and have a voice in deciding it.

We must minimize the hurt. That means targeting our money where the needs are greatest. It means coordinating federally supported efforts with state and local efforts to get the maximum impact.

We have long denounced the voluminous paper work, the red tape, the data gathering, and the burdensome rules imposed on us by the federal categorical grants. We must not duplicate those burdens. The block grants must give us the flexibility and regulatory reform to accomplish this.[2]

Out of this exercise I think we can see real improvements emerge in the process. We can develop a true partnership with local governments; with nonprofit organizations, such as those that provide day care; and with for-profit companies, such as those that operate nursing homes. We must work with them to set our priorities and to use our resources in the wisest way. We must seek out the best innovative programs and make sure all the states know about them. That is my primary goal as chairman of the National Governors' Association's Human Resources Committee. The frontier of innovation in human services isn't in Washington. It's in the states.

Finally, I think we must encourage and stimulate more private-sector involvement in meeting the needs of our children, our elderly, our poor, our ill and infirm. In our state we have communities where a civic club has "adopted a school" and has taken full responsibility for things like getting volunteers to tutor poor students or getting more books for the library or providing monitors on the school buses. We have churches that provide home care for older adults. We have industries that provide day-care services for working parents and health services for all their employees. We have hundreds of individuals who give hundreds of hours to programs like Partners, which is one of the most effective juvenile delinquency prevention programs in existence today—and which costs our state nothing.

None of these programs are "state" programs. We don't appropriate money for them, but we encourage them, for they are worth thousands upon thousands of dollars and they are effective; they extend our ability to serve far beyond the limits of our financial resources. I believe this is the direction in which we must move.

Despite the real dangers we face, we have a once-in-a-lifetime chance to achieve greater control over our state's efforts to meet human needs, to minimize human suffering, and to move human beings from dependency to self-sufficiency, from the welfare rolls to the employment rolls. This should spur us all on to what may be the greatest challenge and greatest achievements of our careers in public service. And when we are tempted, out of the fatigue and frustration that surely will come from time to time, to slow down or give up, then we must keep in mind that hundreds of thousands of eyes will be watching us: the eyes of the disabled, the impoverished, the children, the elderly, the ill, the infirm, and those who also are committed to meeting their needs.

If we stumble, there will be no shortage of those standing by to criticize and to attempt to wrest control back to the federal government. What to us is a chance to do better things for the most unfortunate of our citizens will be seen by many as a "put up or shut up" test.

We must succeed. We must operate human service programs with minimum waste and inefficiency, with maximum compassion and precision. That is our challenge, and we governors will rely on you.

I believe we can do this. I believe we must do this, and I urge all of you to take the task before us very, very seriously.

Many are skeptical. Many equate the state governments of today with those of twenty, even ten years ago. They are not the same. We have seen great changes throughout this country, and especially in this region where all of us are gathered today.

I would say to the skeptics exactly what I said to Senator Kennedy when I testified before the Labor and Human Resources Committee.[3] I told him I happen to believe there are a lot of people in Washington who simply do not know what is going on in the states around this country and the kind of initiatives that are being taken in the human services area. We have people in our Department of Human Resources who are every bit as concerned about the needy people of our state and their special problems as there are on that committee staff in Congress, or at Health and Human Services, or at any other governmental agency.

I have great confidence that we can do the job. I believe in this concept, and I believe that, no matter how difficult the circumstances, our people deserve no less than the best.

We have much to do, and little time in which to do it. We carry the responsibility for millions of Americans as we go about it. We must meet that responsibility with skill and dedication. We must be equal to the task.

---

[1] Neal R. Peirce (1932-   ), native of Philadelphia; resident of Washington, D.C.; B.A., Princeton University, 1954. Legislative assistant to Congressman Silvio Conte, 1959; political editor, *Congressional Quarterly*, 1960-1969; contributing editor, *National Journal*, since 1969; syndicated newspaper columnist, Washington Post Writers Group. *Who's Who in America, 1982-1983*, II, 2610-2611. Peirce's article, "Block Grants: Doing Right Thing the Wrong Way?" was reproduced in *Human Services and Federalism*, 22.

[2] Hunt repeated to the North Carolina Association of County Commissioners, August 14, 1981, the necessity of reducing bureaucratic restrictions "that wrap us so

tightly and rob our flexibility and responsiveness." He then applauded the commissioners' proposed alterations in more than 400 state regulations and promised his administration would effect those changes, where possible.

[3]Edward Moore Kennedy (1932-   ), native, resident of Boston; B.A., Harvard University, 1956; LL.B., University of Virginia, 1959; U.S. Army, 1951-1953. Assistant district attorney for Suffolk County, Massachusetts, 1961-1962; U.S. senator from Massachusetts since 1962, and ranking Democrat, Senate Committee on Labor and Human Resources. Barone and Ujifusa, *Almanac of American Politics, 1984,* 616. Hunt's comments to Kennedy on state human services programs do not appear in the press copy, reprinted elsewhere in this volume, of his testimony before the Senate Labor and Human Resources Committee, April 10, 1981.

NORTH CAROLINA 2000

RALEIGH, JUNE 1, 1981

It's good to be here today with all my good friends from across the state. I know you're all wondering now, "Why a futures effort?" And, "Why now?"

I've asked you here today so we can address those questions, but first I want you to know how happy I am to see you here. As far as I know, this is the first time that leaders of state boards and commissions have met together for a common goal. This is a remarkable group representing the state's best talent and expertise. I know all of you have visions of what you'd like North Carolina to become. You care about preserving what's best in our state.

We are living in a period of great change. We are faced with choices about how to respond. Some people shake their heads and complain that things are out of control; others want to turn back the hands of the clock and ignore the progress we've made. We must take responsibility for making the world what we want it to be, for ourselves and our children, and that requires looking into the future *now.*

Looking at the future can help us make decisions; anticipate changes; prepare for what lies ahead; and put *us* in the driver's seat, to chart the course for North Carolina. But first we need to know where we're going. The more information we have, the better decisions we can make.

Our future lies in our people. We have some clues about our people in the year 2000 — about where they will live, and how they will live:[1]

—Some experts say North Carolina's population will grow to 7 million by the year 2000, adding 1.3 million people in less than twenty years. Many will be from other states.

—On average, North Carolinians probably will be older. Between 1980 and 2000 the number of school-aged children is expected to remain about the same, but the working-age and older adult populations could increase dramatically. The number of older adults could increase by 50 percent, from 600,000 to 900,000.

—Estimates show that the number of households could grow by 60 percent, nearly three times as fast as the population. The number of two-parent families will be about the same as today, but households with single people and households headed by a female are expected to increase greatly.

So, over the next nineteen years we will grow and we will be different. What we don't yet know is how our growth and change will affect the quality of life in North Carolina. We must start looking ahead, asking ourselves questions. For example:

—We expect to attract 900,000 more jobs by the year 2000. Will that be enough to support the additional 1.3 million people?

—We will probably gain jobs in higher-skill industries and lose jobs in some of our traditional industries as automation increases. How do we prepare our people for those higher-skilled jobs?

—If we continue to lose prime farmland at our present rate, by 2000 we will lose over one million acres. How can agriculture survive as a major industry in the state?

—Three of our major river basins will have less than a 20 percent surplus of water by 2000. Half of our population currently lives in these areas. How can we support continued growth?

—Along with growth in population and the economy, we can expect a growth in the demand for energy. How can we meet these demands through conservation and alternative energy sources?

—The use of our highways for personal travel could increase by as much as 80 percent in the next two decades and for freight movement by as much as 200 percent. How will our highways adequately meet this additional growth?

—School-age population will drop in the 1980s and return to the current level by 2000. What does that mean for public education?

So obviously our future is not fixed. It is up to us to create it. That's what North Carolina 2000 is all about.

North Carolina 2000 begins today, with your help. It will be a major statewide program. It will involve people in choosing directions for the state.

I am convinced that we must look ahead to resolve *today's* problems, as well as prepare for the future we want.

I am establishing by executive order the Commission on the Future of North Carolina. The commission will guide us in developing North Carolina 2000. Members will include some of the real "thinkers" and "doers" in North Carolina, including the members of the State Goals and Policy Board, legislators, and leaders in our academic community, in industry and business, and other areas. North Carolina 2000 will include local meetings and statewide polls to get citizens choosing directions for the future. It will bring together leaders and citizens across the state to develop proposals for action.[2]

Creating the kind of future we want for North Carolina will

require the active participation of each individual. We can no longer afford the luxury of burying our heads in the sand, as individuals, communities, or as a state. We can make a difference. We can shape our future. We can make better decisions if we prepare for change and manage it, rather than letting change control us.

I am asking you to take the lead in this effort. I am depending on you for its success. I call on you to make North Carolina 2000 a priority in your work. I am confident that we can create the future we desire. God has given us the tools we need—nature and our imagination. It is up to us to use them wisely for the greatest good of our state.

---

[1]Statistical projections found in this speech appear with others in *Workbook: Preparing North Carolina for the Year 2000* ([Raleigh]: Policy Development Division, North Carolina Department of Administration, June, 1981).

[2]North Carolina 2000 was not the first statewide goals and policy poll undertaken by the Hunt administration. That distinction belongs to the North Carolina Tomorrow survey, conducted in 1977. Mitchell, *Addresses of Hunt*, I, 39n.

EAST DUPLIN HIGH SCHOOL COMMENCEMENT

BEULAVILLE, JUNE 5, 1981

[Governor Hunt reminded seniors attending the Needham B. Broughton High School baccalaureate ceremony, May 31, that North Carolina's advances in employment, education, health and human services, and the general quality of life, were the result of people committed to progress, "people who by the sheer power of their determination and grit and courage *make it happen.*" He urged them, as he did the participants in East Duplin High School's commencement exercises, to use their education humanely and wisely, thus ensuring the continuing betterment of the state and the lives of its inhabitants.]

I am deeply honored to be your commencement speaker tonight. I am honored to play a small part in one of the most significant moments in your lives. This is the second graduation I have attended this week. On Wednesday night my son Baxter graduated from Broughton High School in Raleigh. That was a proud moment for Carolyn and me, so I think I know what your parents are feeling tonight.

It's been a few years since I graduated from high school, but I can still remember all of the conflicting thoughts and emotions that were there. It reminds me of a story I once heard Senator Sam Ervin tell.

It concerns an old mountain couple, very poor, who lived in an old shack with simple, handmade furniture. One day they decided to buy a beautiful grandfather clock to add to their home and enjoy during their retirement years. They hitched up the mule to the wagon, drove down the mountain to town, and bought a lovely clock they had seen earlier in a store.

They got it home and placed it in their sitting room, and they just sat there, hour by hour, listening to the chimes. When 10 o'clock came, Miss Bessie, the wife, got tired and went to bed. But the husband, Mr. Tom, wanted to stay up until midnight. He heard the beautiful clock chime 10:30, 11 o'clock, 11:30, and waited eagerly for midnight. But when the time came, the clock didn't stop at twelve chimes. It just kept on chiming.

With that, Mr. Tom ran down the hall to wake up his wife. And when she asked what was the matter, he replied breathlessly, "Miss Bessie, it's later than it's ever been before."

It is indeed later than it's ever been before. You've been on this earth less than twenty years, but just think of all that has happened in your lifetime. Most of you were born in 1963 and 1964, the years that saw an American naval blockade of Cuba and the world standing for days on the brink of a nuclear holocaust.[1] John Glenn became the first American to orbit the earth,[2] and President Kennedy's murder in Dallas inalterably changed our society and the world.[3]

You've lived through the war in Vietnam, the end of school segregation, the assassinations of Martin Luther King and Bobby Kennedy,[4] riots on city streets and college campuses. During your lifetime man walked on the moon for the first time, diseases have been conquered, and presidents and governors and senators have come and gone. Events of enormous significance have been beamed right into your living rooms, and these events—the good and the bad—have already shaped your lives more than you know.

It is understandable for you to think that in such a big, complicated, changing and difficult world, one person can't make much of a difference. But let's examine that for a minute. If you just think about it, all of you can probably think of a person who has come into your life and changed it—perhaps a teacher, a friend, certainly your parents.

Most of you probably don't yet know what you're going to be doing five, ten, or twenty years from now. I'm sure some of you plan to go to college, or to a community college or technical institute, or perhaps into the military. But whatever your immediate plans, you must go forward with the knowledge that the future is yours to make what you will of it. You can make a difference in this world, and if you want to make a difference, the most powerful weapon you can have at your disposal is a sincere caring for your fellow men and women, a love for all humanity and a love for family and friends.

It is also very important that you carry with you a commitment to good citizenship. That doesn't just mean obeying society's rules. It means an involvement in the making of those rules. It means reading and learning and keeping yourself informed. It means voting in every election and taking an active part in the political process. If you aren't equipped in later years to make wise, logical choices that are in the best interests of the communities in which you live, then the democratic ideal will be eroded.

You are in a unique position to make a difference by virtue of where you live, here in eastern North Carolina—a historically poor region from an economic standpoint, but a region that is wealthy in its human resources and unlimited in its economic potential.

The last few years have seen the dawning of a new economic era in North Carolina. We are going to see tremendous growth here in the next few years, and this part of the state is going to share in that growth. Agriculture will continue to be a vitally important segment of our economy, but there will be diversification; with diversification will come career opportunities never thought possible just a few short years ago. I hope many of you will stay here, raise your families here, and help bring about this great new era.

Before closing I want to return for just a moment to something I was talking about earlier—the importance of caring for your fellow men and women. Your families and your churches and this fine school you are about to leave have given you a good foundation. You've learned a lot about life, and you have had enduring values instilled in you.

But you must take it from here. I really believe that the reason we are on this earth is to extend a hand to those who need it—the poor, the friendless, the sick, and the forgotten. I believe that every person—black and white, rich and poor, male and female—is entitled to the opportunities that life affords. We must never allow greed and prejudice and cynicism to obscure our determination to help those around us, to make a difference in our own lives and in someone else's.

Young people, the future is yours. It lies stretched out before you like a golden flame. Make of yourselves what you can, and in doing so help shape a better world. God bless you.

---

[1]In response to the Soviet deployment of nuclear missiles to Cuba and the construction of launch sites there, President John F. Kennedy confirmed, October 22, 1962, the beginning of an American naval quarantine of the island. Although Premier Nikita Khrushchev stated his country's ships would disregard the measure and "blustered that Kennedy had pushed mankind 'into the abyss of a world missile-nuclear war,'" five Russian vessels allegedly transporting such matériel refrained, on October 24, from crossing into the restricted zone; on the twenty-sixth, the Soviet leader sent two communiqués to the president—one seeking his promise that the U.S. would not invade Cuba, in exchange for the removal of the offending weapons, and another calling for the withdrawal of U.S. missiles from Turkey. Attorney General Robert F. Kennedy advised his brother to overlook the second message and act on the first; on October 28, Khrushchev announced that the missiles sent to Cuba were to be

recalled. George Brown Tindall, *America: A Narrative History* (New York: W. W. Norton & Co., 2 volumes, 1984), II, 1272-1274.

[2]John Herschel Glenn, Jr. (1921-   ), native of Cambridge, Ohio; resident of Columbus; B.S., Muskingum College, 1939; U.S. Marine Corps, 1942-1965. NASA astronaut, 1959-1965, first American to orbit the Earth, February 10, 1962; vice-president, Royal Crown Cola Co., 1966-1968; president, Royal Crown International, 1967-1969; U.S. senator from Ohio, since 1975; unsuccessful candidate for Democratic presidential nomination, 1984. Barone and Ujifusa, *Almanac of American Politics, 1984*, 909; *Encyclopaedia Britannica Macropaedia*, 15th ed., s.v. "Space Exploration."

[3]John Fitzgerald Kennedy (1917-1963), native of Brookline, Massachusetts; B.A., Harvard University, 1940; U.S. Navy, 1941-1945. U.S. representative from Massachusetts's Eleventh Congressional District, 1947-1953; U.S. senator from Massachusetts, 1953-1960; U.S. president, 1961-1963, assassinated in Dallas, Texas, November 22, 1963. Author, *Profiles in Courage* (1956), won Pulitzer Prize for biography, 1957. *Who Was Who in America, 1961-1968*, p. 521.

[4]Martin Luther King, Jr. (1929-1968), native of Atlanta; A.B., Morehouse College, 1948; B.D., Crozer Theological Seminary, 1951; Ph.D., Boston University, 1955. Clergyman; civil rights leader; pastor, Dexter Avenue Baptist Church, Montgomery, Alabama; founder, president, Southern Christian Leadership Conference; recipient, Nobel Prize for Peace, 1964; assassinated in Memphis, Tennessee, April 4, 1968. *Who Was Who in America, 1961-1968*, 1059.

Robert Francis Kennedy (1925-1968), native of Boston; resident of Glen Cove, New York; B.A., Harvard University, 1948; LL.B., University of Virginia, 1951; U.S. Naval Reserve, 1944-1946. U.S. attorney general, 1961-1964; U.S. senator from New York, 1965-1968; candidate for Democratic presidential nomination, assassinated June 5, 1968, in Los Angeles. *Who Was Who in America, 1969-1973*, 391; *Encyclopaedia Britannica Macropaedia*, 15th ed., s.v. "Kennedy Family."

STATEMENT ON UNIVERSITY OF NORTH CAROLINA DESEGREGATION

RALEIGH, JUNE 20, 1981

[It appeared as though eleven years of legal wrangling between the federal government and the state of North Carolina had come to an end when, on June 20, Hunt announced that litigants embroiled in the University of North Carolina desegregation case finally had reached an agreement. The compromise was contained in a consent decree, dated July 2 and signed by Franklin T. Dupree, Jr., chief judge of the Eastern District of the United States District Court of North Carolina. It included a plan to improve curriculum development at and financial support for state-funded, historically black institutions of higher education and "commitments to increase minority presence, enrollments, and employment" throughout the system. However, Joseph L. Rauh, Jr., principal attorney representing the NAACP Legal Defense and Education Fund, Inc., called the agreement "the worst civil rights sellout of the Reagan administration thus far" and added that it allowed the state to continue operating a segregated system of advanced learning despite a three-decade-old ban prohibiting such practice. Rauh and his clients, convinced of the inadequacy of Dupree's decree, unsuccessfully appealed it twice in 1982 and took their case to the U.S. Supreme Court a year later; on February 21, 1984, the justices declined to obstruct implementation of the desegregation plan and dismissed the request "on a procedural basis . . . [indicating] the defense fund couldn't go court-shopping in pursuing its claims." *Durham Morning Herald,* January 10, October 15, 1982, February 22, 1984; *News and Observer,* June 21, 1981, February 22, 1984; *State of North Carolina, et al., Plaintiffs,* v. *Department of Education, et al., Defendants:* Consent Decree. No. 79-211-CIV-5 (E.D.N.C., filed Apr. 24, 1979), ss. VI, VII; see also Mitchell, *Addresses of Hunt,* I, 520-521.]

I want to congratulate the parties who negotiated the proposed settlement of the University of North Carolina desegregation case. I am hopeful that the proposed agreement will bring an end to this dispute. I especially want to commend President Friday, the Board of Governors, Secretary Bell, Raymond Dawson, Felix Joyner, and Senior Deputy Attorney General Andrew Vanore for their hard work in bringing about the proposed settlement.[1]

I am grateful to the North Carolina General Assembly for its willingness to appropriate funds to upgrade the traditionally black institutions of higher learning in North Carolina, as I recommended during the 1979 legislative session. My administration will continue this commitment to improving the quality of these institutions and to the educational excellence of the UNC system.

---

[1] Terrell Howard Bell (1921-   ), native of Lava Hot Springs, Idaho; B.A., Southern Idaho College of Education, 1946; M.S., University of Idaho, 1953; Ed.D., University of Utah, 1960. Superintendent of public instruction, 1963-1970, and commissioner of higher education, 1976-1981, state of Utah; served with the Office of Education, U.S. Department of Health, Education, and Welfare, 1970-1976; U.S. secretary of education, 1981-1985. *News and Observer,* January 12, 1985; *Who's Who in America, 1982-1983,* I, 224.

Raymond H. Dawson (1927-   ), native of Camden, Arkansas; resident of Chapel Hill; A.B., College of the Ozarks, 1949; M.A., Vanderbilt University, 1951; Ph.D., University of North Carolina at Chapel Hill, 1958; U.S. Army Air Force, 1945-1947. Political science professor, since 1960, and dean of the College of Arts and Sciences and General College, 1968-1972, University of North Carolina at Chapel Hill; vice-president for academic affairs, general administration, University of North Carolina, since 1972. Raymond H. Dawson to Jan-Michael Poff, September 30, 1983.

L. Felix Joyner (1924-   ), native of Savannah, Georgia; resident of Chapel Hill; A.B., Berea College, 1947; U.S. Navy, 1943-1946, and U.S. Naval Reserve. State budget director, 1952-1955, commissioner of finance, 1964-1967, and commissioner of personnel, 1980, commonwealth of Kentucky; consultant, Public Administration Service, Chicago, 1956-1960; executive director, Kentucky Turnpike Authority, 1961-1964; vice-president for finance, University of North Carolina. L. Felix Joyner to Jan-Michael Poff, October 19, 1983.

Andrew A. Vanore, Jr. (1938-   ), native of Brooklyn, New York; resident of Raleigh; A.B., 1959, J.D., 1962, University of North Carolina at Chapel Hill; lt. col., North Carolina National Guard. Law clerk to Chief Justice Susie M. Sharp, 1962-1963; senior deputy attorney general of North Carolina. Andrew A. Vanore, Jr., to Jan-Michael Poff, September 29, 1983.

TESTIMONY AT INTERNATIONAL
TRADE COMMISSION HEARING
ON SCRAP TOBACCO

WASHINGTON, D.C., JUNE 24, 1981

[Acting on information from U.S. Department of Agriculture secretary Bob Bergland that increasing amounts of tobacco imported into the United States imperiled the federal price support system for the domestic, flue-cured commodity, President Carter ordered the U.S. International Trade Commission, January 18, 1981, to initiate an investigation. Four days later Governor Hunt made public a letter to President Reagan in which he recounted the factors prompting Carter's directive, reminded him that if the ITC corroborated the conclusions of the Agriculture Department he (Reagan) could then legally impose import restrictions, and expressed the "hope that your administration will pursue this matter aggressively before the ITC and do everything to protect our farmers and the entire North Carolina economy." Hunt's testimony before the trade commission, supporting federal relief for American growers from foreign tobacco imports, appears below.]

Mr. Chairman [1] and members of the commission:

Thank you for allowing me to appear before you today. As governor of the nation's largest tobacco producing and manufacturing state, I am deeply interested in matters affecting the future of the tobacco industry.

I am here today, at the request of the North Carolina Farm Bureau, to emphasize to you the importance of the tobacco industry —and the tobacco quota and support program—to the people of my state. In 1979 tobacco provided jobs for 148,000 North Carolinians. That includes 44,000 farmers who depend on tobacco for a livelihood. It includes many small farmers. In two recent years (1978 and 1980) the gross income from tobacco on North Carolina farms exceeded $1 billion a year.

In 1978, the latest year for which comprehensive figures are available, North Carolina farmers received gross income of $1.1 billion from tobacco. That was more than Kansas farmers received for wheat—and Kansas is the number one wheat state. It was more than Arkansas farmers received for broilers—and Arkansas leads the nation in broiler production. It was more than Texas farmers received for cotton—even though Texas is number one among the states in cotton production. North Carolina's tobacco farm income was greater than California farm income for eggs—and California is number one in the nation in egg production.

I grew up on a tobacco and dairy farm near Wilson, which has the largest tobacco market in the world. My thesis for a master's degree in agricultural economics from North Carolina State University was the basis for the acreage-poundage controls for flue-cured tobacco.

Since becoming governor nearly four and one-half years ago, I have actively championed the cause of tobacco, working with the state's delegation in Congress when antitobacco forces have tried to eliminate or weaken the quota and price support program. In 1979 I led the first tobacco trade mission to China in thirty years, taking with me a group of twelve farmers, industrialists, and tobacco specialists for several meetings with Chinese trade and tobacco officials. I have worked for lower tariff rates on U.S. tobacco entering the European community and other areas of the world. At my request a group of farmers went to Europe to talk with tobacco buyers and manufacturers as a follow-up to preliminary discussion which I had there.

As you can see, I have a close familiarity with the tobacco program. And I fear that program is endangered today.

The flue-cured tobacco program that we have today has evolved over a period of forty-eight years, and it is a great success story. Since 1965 the control program has been based on both acreage allotments and poundage marketing quotas. This means the grower is limited not only as to the acres he can plant but also the pounds he can sell. These are the tightest controls ever applied to a major farm commodity in the United States. In referendum after referendum, flue-cured growers have voted overwhelmingly to continue their supply control and price support program. Usually the proportion of favorable votes has been between 95 and 98 percent of the total number cast.

Growers have had to make genuine sacrifices in order to keep their program. There have been many times in the past thirty years when they had to accept sharp quota reductions. Just since 1975 the basic flue-cured quota has been reduced by about one third. A 40-acre allotment in 1975 would have shrunk to only 27 acres in 1981. It has not been easy over the years for growers to live with these quota cutbacks, but growers know that the cutbacks were essential in order to make the program work. They have also made it work by continuous fine tuning of various features of the program.

Under the tobacco program growers have efficiently produced an adequate domestic and export supply of quality leaf. All segments of the industry and all sectors of the economy have benefited from the *stability* that the program has brought, stability of supply as well as price. Between marketing seasons, on a year-round basis, buying firms have been able to purchase tobacco from the loan inventory held by the Flue-Cured Tobacco Cooperative Stabilization Corporation. In effect, loan stocks have been used as a reserve supply available to the companies whenever needed.

Prices paid to growers for their tobacco have increased over the years, but not excessively so. Year-to-year adjustments in the support price have been based on increases in farmers' costs. Thus, most growers have been able to survive despite the soaring costs of such production items as fuel, fertilizer, pesticides, labor, machinery, and others. If the price support formula had not been written so as to help growers meet today's highly inflated costs, how could the medium and smaller growers hope to survive?

No one should conclude, however, that returns to flue-cured tobacco farmers for the resources used have been excessive. That simply is not the case. Through the North Carolina State University Electronic Farm Records Program and from other sources, data are available showing that return on investment for a flue-cured tobacco farm in Pitt County, North Carolina, over the past six years has ranged from 5.2 percent in 1975 to an average of 3.7 percent in 1978-1980. For the farm owner who received one-fourth share of the crop as rent, profit as percent of tobacco sales price rose from 2.8 percent in 1975 to an all-time high of 13.0 percent in 1978 and then fell to 11.2 percent in 1979 and 4.5 percent in 1980. These and other data available on the Pitt County farm show that by any standard of measurement used in business today, the profits have *not* been excessive.

In one respect the tobacco program occupies a unique place in the agricultural history of America. It has been in operation for more than four decades, and its cost to the federal government during that period of time has been very small. In fact, tobacco growers have received less than one percent of the federal funds spent on all types of commodity support programs over the past fifty years—or for that matter during the entire history of the country.

I submit that tobacco growers have reason to be proud of their program and of the part they have played in keeping the program on a sound basis. Despite the fact that all segments of the tobacco industry have been caught up in a "technological tornado" over the past thirty years, tobacco growers have been able to maintain the basic principle of their program—control of supply in return for fair, realistic price support—even though structural modifications became necessary from time to time.

In the past few years, however, our tobacco farmers have become worried by the rising tide of imported leaf. According to the North Carolina Farm Bureau, in 1969 imports amounted to 237 million pounds, or only 18 percent of the tobacco used in cigarettes. By 1979 imports accounted for 31 percent (or 478 million pounds) of the tobacco used in cigarette production. The most alarming increases came in the "scrap" category, which increased from 10 million pounds in 1969 to 204 million pounds by 1979.

A number of factors account for the increases in imports:

—The smoking and health issue has resulted in low-tar, low-nicotine, filter-tip cigarettes. Manufacturers have been able to increase the use of imported flue-cured leaf of lower quality than domestically produced flue-cured without the smoker being able to recognize the cheaper leaf.

—The tobacco companies have a responsibility to their boards of directors and their stockholders to make a profit. They have become truly international companies, and they have encouraged the production of tobacco in many parts of the world. At the same time, they have increased their exports of manufactured cigarettes from 29.15 billion cigarettes exported in 1970 to 81.99 billion in 1980, an increase of more than 250 percent.

—Another factor in the increase of imports has been that United States foreign policy encourages the importation of goods from less developed countries. Many of them have the large supply of labor and limited supply of land needed for tobacco production.

—Foreign countries have subsidized their tobacco exports in order to earn the U.S. dollars they need for international exchange. The Office of Monopoly in the Republic of Korea, for example, supplies farmers with fertilizer, seeds, chemicals, covers, materials for drying sheds, and so on. Growers receive the equivalent of $1.64 per pound farm sales weight, and export the tobacco through joint ventures with international leaf dealers to the United States for $1.44 per pound, processed weight. It is obvious that subsidies are involved.

All of these factors have contributed to the flood of imports.

Stabilization loan stocks have increased despite repeated reductions in the national marketing quota, voluntary efforts to limit the harvest of lower-quality tobacco, and the elimination of price supports on eight grades of lower-quality tobacco. The U.S. Department of Agriculture estimates that, because of increased imports, about 140 million pounds of domestically grown flue-cured tobacco have been diverted into Stabilization loan stocks. This tobacco had an estimated loan value of $172 million by the end of the 1979 season. The department estimates that 38 percent of total loan stocks in Stabilization will be under loan because of increased imports.

Recent actual realized losses to the Commodity Credit Corporation, the funding agency for Stabilization, have been small. For the ten-year period ending September 30, 1980, price support charge-offs have been $5.8 million, including a $5.2 million charge-off for fire loss. Gains to the CCC by collateral fees paid by associations have been $4 million. Thus, the net loss for the most recent ten-year period was $1.8 million.

Potential losses to the CCC could be substantial in the near future if excessive inventories are sold at prices that do not cover the value of the collateral plus accrued interest and carrying charges. The USDA estimates that there is a high probability of a CCC loss for existing stocks (1975 through 1980 crops) of at least $96 million over the 1981-1985 period. For future crops, including the 1981 crop, losses associated with sales of loan stocks will depend on the level of imports as well as world and U.S. market conditions. Unless the USDA is wrong in its calculations, it is fair to project that actual taxpayer losses because of imports will be at least $96 million by 1985. Thus, it is clear that the price-support program will soon be monetarily damaged by imports.

Under section 22 of the Agriculture Act, relief is appropriate when imports "render or tend to render ineffective, or materially interfere with, any program or operation undertaken under this chapter . . . or any loan, purchase, or other program or operation undertaken by the Department of Agriculture." [2] We believe this is happening, and that is why we are appealing to this commission for help.

Let me conclude by summarizing my concerns this way: We are talking about a substantial number of people in this nation, an estimated 103,000 full-time jobs in tobacco farming and another 400,000 part-time jobs during the tobacco harvest. In the main they make a fairly modest living. Few of them are affluent. They have worked hard to build an effective system that costs less than other farm marketing systems.

This system is carefully balanced, depending on the cooperation and understanding of the farmers, the warehousemen, the manufacturers, the importers and exporters, the retailers and wholesalers, and local, state, and federal governments. Now this careful balance is threatened by the high amounts of imports. The tariff system must protect the farmers in a reasonable way if they are producing efficiently. The growers need immediate help to deal with the problem of imports. I am here today to ask that they be given all the help possible, as quickly as possible.

---

[1] William Relph Alberger (1945-   ), native of Portland, Oregon; B.A., Willamette University, 1967; M.B.A., University of Iowa, 1971; J.D., Georgetown University, 1973. Legislative assistant, 1972-1975, and administrative assistant, 1975-1977, to Congressman Al Ullman, of Washington; administrative assistant, House Committee on Ways and Means, 1977; vice-chairman, 1978-1980, and chairman, 1980-1982, U.S. International Trade Commission. *Who's Who in America, 1982-1983*, I, 32.

[2] "An Act to Relieve the Existing National Economic Emergency by Increasing Agricultural Purchasing Power, to Raise Revenue for Extraordinary Expenses Incurred by Reason of Such Emergency, to Provide Emergency Relief with Respect to Agricultural Indebtedness, to Provide for the Orderly Liquidation of Joint-Stock Land Banks, and for Other Purposes," 48 Stat. 31-54, c. 25, s. 22, Act of May 12, 1933, and as amended; see also 7 U.S.C. s. 624 (1982 ed.).

STATEMENT ON DEMOCRATIC NATIONAL COMMITTEE COMMISSION ON PRESIDENTIAL NOMINATION

WASHINGTON, D.C., JULY 2, 1981

Thank you very much, Mr. Chairman.[1] I am, of course, both pleased and honored to undertake this very important job. As the chairman stated, we are not beginning, but continuing a process of review and change.

The 1980 Democratic Convention said, rightfully, that "great strides have been made toward assuring that all interested Democrats wishing to participate are accorded full and open opportunity."[2] That openness and that opportunity is one of the principal differences between the Democratic party and the Republican party. It is a dramatic counterpoint to Republican narrowness as embodied in Republican programs.

The task this commission[3] has before it is one that must assure that the 1984 delegate selection process will continue to be open. We will work toward a 1984 convention that will be responsive and meaningful, reflecting a progressive and broad-based Democratic party. I look forward to serving as chair of this very distinguished commission. Our members include drafters of previous reforms and architects of real accomplishments, along with elected officials and party activists who can provide real experience to make changes more helpful to candidates and to campaigns.

We want to structure the Democratic party's delegate selection process so that we choose the strongest possible nominee with the best opportunity to be elected. We want to encourage a positive relationship between state and local parties, the candidates, and the nominating process. Finally, we want to refine our internal political processes so that our nominee, when elected, has greater opportunity to govern.

There are many areas of the process that are open to discussion and potential change. Chairman Manatt has mentioned a few; I'd like to add my own thoughts to his.

One, we must shorten the preconvention campaign. This will not be easy, but the tools provided the party by the Supreme Court in the Wisconsin case make that job more manageable.[4] Concern has been expressed about the number of primaries in the process now. I hope the commission will also consider alternative means of selecting delegates.

Finally, as the chairman stated, we have to provide the means to include more elected officials as active participants in the nominating procedures and the platform process.

We have an exciting task ahead and a relatively short time frame to do our jobs. I am proud to have Doug Fraser[5] and Dottie Zug working with me and I look forward to a most interesting and rewarding experience.

I look forward to working with Democratic leaders across the country in this process. In addition to the meetings and hearings that we will be holding, I invite them to write me with ideas or suggestions they have. I particularly look forward to working with the members of Congress.

---

[1] National Democratic Party chairman Charles Taylor Manatt.

[2] Neither the accuracy nor the source of this quotation could be verified.

[3] Commission on Presidential Nomination.

[4] No. 79-1631, Democratic Party of the United States of America, et al., Appellants, v. Bronson C. LaFollette, et al., *United States Law Week*, 49 (February 24, 1981), 4178-4187.

[5] Douglas Andrew Fraser (1916-   ), native of Glasgow, Scotland; educated in Detroit public schools; U.S. Army, 1945-1946. President, Local 227, Detroit, 1943-1946, international representative, 1947-1951, administrative assistant to international president, 1951-1958, coregional director, 1959-1962, member at large, international executive board, 1962-1970, international vice-president, 1970-1977, and international president, 1977-1983, of the United Auto Workers. "Fraser Leaves Big Shoes to Fill," *Business Week*, November 15, 1982, 118-119; *Who's Who in America, 1982-1983*, I, 1104.

STATEMENT ON APPOINTMENT OF WILLIAM R. ROBERSON, JR.

RALEIGH, JULY 9, 1981

I am announcing today my appointment of one of North Carolina's top businessmen, William R. Roberson, Jr., of Washington, North Carolina, as secretary of transportation.[1] He is the man I will be looking to, as will members of the General Assembly and of the public, to carry out the Good Roads Program that this legislature has authorized.

Of all the candidates I looked at, Bill Roberson is the person who best fit the qualifications I outlined for the new secretary in my memorandum to members of the General Assembly: "a hard-nosed, experienced, and capable business person who will know how to manage the employees of the department, to fully utilize the equipment owned by the department, and to obtain the maximum benefit from every dollar appropriated to the department."[2]

Bill Roberson is a successful businessman with legislative experience himself. I am grateful to him for accepting this position, and I will be working very closely with him.

He has outstanding credentials as a successful businessman who has built and run profitable enterprises in television and radio broadcasting, real estate, a shopping center, and soft-drink bottling.

His stature as a businessman is demonstrated by the fact that he just completed a two-year term as chairman of the National Soft Drink Association.

Bill's four terms' experience in the General Assembly will also be a tremendous asset in this position.

I am confident that he will be a strong and successful secretary in what will clearly be the most challenging time in the history of the Department of Transportation and this state's entire transportation system.

Now that the General Assembly has appropriated an additional $120 million a year in highway funds, it is the responsibility of my administration and of the Department of Transportation to get the job done. That means, first and foremost, catching up on the backlog of maintenance needs by resurfacing 3,600 miles of roads and highways each year. Let me outline some of the changes in the department that I am expecting to be made as we strive to carry out our responsibility:

—The Board of Transportation, the citizens' board that represents the people, must take on a stronger policy-making role. The new board will have the difficult task of completely overhauling the Seven-Year Plan and putting our transportation priorities in line with new realities. I would particularly like to see the board work in committees to oversee various aspects of the department's operations, such as finance, personnel, equipment, cost estimates, contract awards, and secondary roads.[3] I also want the number of out-of-town board meetings reduced to save money.

—I want the department and the new secretary to have a closer working relationship with the members of the General Assembly.

—The new secretary will have great authority to make whatever personnel changes he believes are needed in the department.

—I want the Transportation Efficiency councils that I will be appointing in all 100 counties to give our citizens a stronger voice in improving the operations of DOT, whether it be a complaint or an idea for a new way of doing things. The new secretary and board members should work closely with the councils.

—Management in the field must be strengthened, and decision-making authority should be decentralized.

—Special attention should be given to restoring the morale of the 13,000-plus department employees. They have come under a great deal of criticism, but the vast majority of them are hardworking, dedicated employees who want to get the job done right.

—The department's equipment pool must be scrutinized very closely. We cannot afford to have idle equipment or wasteful purchasing practices.

—Finally, the secretary and the new department will be expected to work closely with the Bid Rigging Oversight Commission to make certain that bid rigging does not happen again.

As you can see, the new secretary has a big, tough job ahead of him. But I know he can do it, and he will have my strongest possible support.

---

[1] William Riley Roberson, Jr. (1918-   ), native of Washington, Beaufort County; educated at Davidson College, 1935-1936, and graduate of Maryland School of Accounting, 1938. Chairman, WITN-TV, Inc., North Carolina Dr. Pepper Bottlers, Inc., and of Smallwood, Inc.; member, state House of Representatives, 1967-1974; transportation secretary, 1981-1985. *News and Observer*, January 8, 1985; *North Carolina Manual, 1983*, 747.

[2] The memorandum from which the governor quotes could not be located.

[3] Restructuring of the state Board of Transportation included the formation of six new committees—Bidding and Audit, Maintenance and Equipment, Secondary Roads, Public Employees and Public Affairs, Ferry Operations, and Programming—that would enable members to become better acquainted with Transportation Department operations and provide a firmer basis for decision making, according to Hunt's statement at a news conference on August 14, 1981.

STATEMENT ON ECONOMIC DEVELOPMENT

RALEIGH, JULY 23, 1981

It's my pleasure to announce today some outstanding economic news. Despite continuing economic uncertainty at the national level, North Carolina's state ports have had their best year ever. Industrial investment announced during the first six months of this year was $1.1 billion, which is up 48 percent from the same period last year, and last year was the second best year we ever had in industrial investment.

The progress we've made at our state ports has been remarkable. For example: When we took over the state ports in 1977, total annual revenues were $7.19 million. Revenues this fiscal year ending June 30 were $12.68 million, a 76 percent increase. Tonnage moved through the ports this year is up 62 percent from 1977. For the third year in a row, revenue and tonnage at both ports set all-time records. And, after a long struggle, we managed to turn a profit at Morehead City for the first time since 1967.

In addition, several shipping lines are upgrading their service to North Carolina. Coal business at Morehead City is providing significant revenue. We have received approval to establish foreign trade zones at both ports.

Good ports mean increased income for North Carolinians. We estimate that tonnage moving through the port will generate more than $500 million in extra personal income for our citizens, and every extra $1 million in exports creates forty jobs.

Obviously, the $1.1 billion industrial investment is of tremendous significance. It will provide much needed tax revenue for our communities. New construction will create jobs in that sector. Suppliers throughout the state will receive millions of dollars in extra business. Service and retail companies will benefit.

Equally important are the types of jobs those industries are bringing with them. Once again, electrical and electronic machinery was the leading category for new jobs announced during the first six months. Fabricated metals ranked second. One out of every four jobs announced were in those two categories, which pay considerably higher wages than the average for North Carolina industries.

Our efforts to increase the diversity of our economy also met with success through announcements by such companies as Reliance Electric, TRW, IVAC, Cooper Group, Lilly, and International Jensen. Plant announcements were for locations stretching from Fletcher to Shelby, to Monroe, Eden, Creedmoor, Lumberton, and Creswell.

Overall the future looks bright for North Carolina's economy. The General Assembly's appropriation of $24 million for the Microelectronics Center was a major step forward. A *Business Week* national survey concluded that North Carolina is the most likely site for industries to consider new plants.[1] Our ports have become internationally recognized as two of the fastest growing on the East Coast.

Those are just a few of the very positive signals that are being sent across this nation and throughout the world. We will keep doing whatever is necessary to strengthen those signals. We must have better job opportunities for our citizens. These announcements today indicate we are making continued progress toward that goal.

---

[1]"America's New Immobile Society," *Business Week*, July 27, 1981, 61.

DINNER HONORING HOWARD LEE

RALEIGH, JULY 23, 1981

[The target of criticism for his department's mishandling of federal Comprehensive Employment and Training Act (CETA) contracts, natural resources and community development secretary Howard Lee tendered his resignation to Governor Hunt on May 20, 1981. Wilbur Hobby, state AFL-CIO president and owner of Precision Graphics, Durham, was sentenced on December 29 to an eighteen-month prison term, five years' probation, and fined $40,000 for "fraudulently obtaining and misapplying" the nearly $130,000 in CETA funds he had been granted to provide the disadvantaged with job skills. The grand jury investigation into Precision Graphics that preceded the trial also resulted in the indictment of Mort Levi (a business colleague of Hobby) and an NRCD employee.

Hunt announced, on May 29, 1981, that Lee's resignation was to become effective July 31. *Durham Morning Herald*, March 28, 1982; *Greensboro Daily News*, December 30, 1981; *News and Observer*, May 30, 1981, July 3, 1984.]

This dinner is one of those occasions that tugs two ways at your heart. I feel a real sadness that Howard Lee will be stepping down after four and a half years as secretary of natural resources and community development—four years of leadership, commitment, and progress. But my heart is also filled by the deepest gratitude for what Howard Lee has meant to me personally, to our administration, and to the state of North Carolina. Howard, I know your friends here will join me in expressing that gratitude to you now.

All of us know there have been critics. I've had mine the last four and a half years, and Howard has had his. A lot of my critics tried to get at me through him, as a matter of fact.[1] But I've worked closely with Howard Lee for four years. I have watched him, and depended on him, and turned to him for counsel. He has never let me down, and he has never given up the good fight. He has shown what kind of man he is.

His tenure as secretary of the Department of Natural Resources and Community Development has been marked by real progress. He has built state government's community development program from the ground up, and I don't know anybody else who could have done it: the Main Street Program, the community development grants, working with community action agencies and other groups, making real progress in strengthening job training, and many other areas. All of them come down to one thing: helping people help themselves, giving people a better chance in life. That is the hallmark of Howard Lee's service here.

I don't think he has received the credit he deserves for the significant accomplishments in environmental protection: developing a plan to save the Chowan River, strengthening our marine fisheries program, firm and fair enforcement of the Coastal Area Management Act, completion of the African phase of the zoo, establishment of a mountain-to-sea trail, and creation of the Office of Regulatory Relations to coordinate and centralize environmental permitting.

The last four years have been tough sometimes. Both Howard and I have some scars to show for it, kind of like war veterans. And, in a way, it has been a war. It has been a hard-fought battle, one that has gone on for many years, for the things that every person in this room believes in: equality of opportunity, social justice, hope, and fairness.

It may be in fashion these days to say the country is turning to the right, to say that compassion for the poor is out of fashion. It may be in fashion to say we should look out for the rich and comfortable and let it trickle down to the poor and uncomfortable. It may be in fashion, but it's not right.

It's people like Howard Lee who have led that fight, who have borne unjust criticism, who have stood up against the odds and fought for people who need help. Howard Lee has fought that fight. He has set that example for all of us, and he is the kind of man who will never give up that fight, all his life.

It has been a long, hard battle. It's not over; it's never over. The struggle goes on. But, so long as there are leaders like Howard Lee and so long as there are dedicated people like you here tonight, the battle will go on, and we shall overcome.

---

[1] I. Beverly Lake, Jr., Republican candidate in the 1980 state gubernatorial election, attempted to use Lee and the CETA issue to persuade voters not to send Hunt back to the Capitol for a second term. *News and Observer*, May 30, 1981.

SOUTHERN LEGISLATIVE CONFERENCE

CHARLOTTE, AUGUST 19, 1981

This is the third meeting of state and local officials that I have attended in the last ten days—the National Governors' Association, the North Carolina Association of County Commissioners, and now this gathering of legislators from across the southern states. Believe it or not, the main topic of discussion has been the same everywhere. You could call it: "Making Do With Less." Whatever you call it, the topic is the federal budget cuts.

State and local government leaders all across the South and the nation are facing the same challenge today: absorbing the budgetary shock waves sent out by the political earthquake that has hit Washington.

Let me say this: I'm a Democrat, and I support the thrust of what President Reagan is doing. I support cutting federal spending. I support balancing the federal budget, and I called for it long before this president was elected. North Carolina balances its budget, just like you do. But cutting spending and cutting taxes are only two parts of what needs to be done and what President Reagan has said he would do. The third part—and the part that hasn't been done yet—is cutting the federal red tape.

The president has said he wants to reduce the role of the federal government and return to the states and local governments their proper resources and responsibilities. Some people are calling that the "New Federalism." There's nothing new about it. That's the way our founding fathers intended our system to work.

I applaud the president's intentions, but I'm disappointed with what Washington has given us. They seem to have forgotten that federalism is a two-way street. Washington needs to know that it can't save a buck by passing the buck, and I think the states and cities and counties of this nation need to tell Washington that we're not going to be victims of a shell game. If we don't speak up and if we're not heard, that's what the block grants and the New Federalism may turn out to be: a shell game.

For many years the governors of this nation have contended that, if Washington gave us more flexibility in spending federal money, we could save 10 percent without cutting back services. That is *not* what Washington has done. They have given us 75 percent of the money, but at least 95 percent of the regulations. They have failed to cut the red tape. The block grants do not give us the flexibility and room for innovation that we need.

The states can't absorb those cuts without cutting services. We can't in North Carolina, and our people need to know that. They need to know that the states can't pick up the costs. They need to know that it's Washington that is cutting the services, not Raleigh or Columbia or Nashville or Montgomery or Tallahassee.

I've been deeply involved in following this as chairman of the Human Resources Committee of the National Governors' Association. We've won some battles, such as preventing the Medicaid cap, and we've lost some. I understand, for example, that the new AFDC law contains twenty-one—count 'em, twenty-one—new regulations.[1]

Now, Vice-President Bush promised the governors last week that the administration would stick with us in our fight for more flexibility. Secretary of Health and Human Services Richard Schweiker[2] and I agreed to appoint a high-level committee that he and I will head to work on reducing and simplifying the paperwork and regulations in that area.

You need to know this. You and your governors need to be heard in Washington. If we aren't, the states are going to be left holding the bag, and this important principle of federalism will be discredited. If that happens, I'm afraid that more than principle will be lost. I'm afraid of what will be lost here in the South.

Let's remember what these cuts in taxes and spending and regulations are really for. It's not just cutting for the sake of cutting. It's for the sake of getting this nation's economy going again. Creating jobs. Encouraging industrial investment and expansion. Helping people be taxpayers, not tax burdens. Providing children a future.

But look what is being cut: the Economic Development Administration and the grants it makes for water and sewer systems, grants that support growth; the Appalachian Regional Commission, which has supported growth throughout that poverty-stricken mountain region. And more cuts are coming. Congress cut taxes over the next three years by $280 billion and spending by only $130 billion—less than half as much as the tax cut. It is widely believed that the federal deficit next year may be $20 million larger than the administration predicted.

Where will the cuts come from? Not from defense. Not, to any great degree, from Social Security and veterans' benefits. Not from interest on the national debt. My friends, they will almost certainly come from the remaining $88 billion that the federal government now sends to the states for education, housing, highways, welfare, revenue sharing, and so on. I say to you that this is a very disturbing prospect for those of us in the South.

This is still the poorest region of the country. Twice as many of our people live below the poverty level. We have 32 percent of the nation's children, but 40 percent of all the nation's poor children. The high school dropout rate is 50 percent higher in the South, and per capita income in the South is only 91 percent of the national average. The South has the most to lose, because we are the poorest region.

Right now we are also the fastest-growing region. We're beginning to catch up because we are the most attractive region to industry. That is partly an accident of climate and location, but only partly. It is also the result of our people—hardworking, honest, productive people. To fully develop those human resources, we need good schools, good health care for infants and mothers and young children, good nutrition, and good job training for adults.

Our progress is also the result of the investments we have made in the muscles and bones that support economic growth—roads and airports and water and sewer. Many of you had to wrestle this year with the politically unpopular issue of raising highway taxes to keep up your roads. Nineteen states raised theirs, just as North Carolina did. It was tough, and it took courage, the kind of courage that legislative leaders in North Carolina like Senator Kenneth Royall showed. But you did it because it was right, and because it means jobs for people.

What will happen to the South now if Washington backs away from those investments in human resources and economic growth? What will happen if Washington stops putting money into highways and schools? What will happen if Washington drops that "safety net"? What will happen if Washington does not give us the flexibility and the resources we need to minimize those losses and the hurt they will surely cause?

Yes, the South and the people who live here will suffer, because we are the farthest behind and we have the farthest to go. But the nation will also suffer. Our states compete with each other for industry, but the competition is not so much with each other as it is with Japan, Germany, and the Soviet Union. We cannot let our nation lose its economic and technological leadership in the world, but how can we compete if Washington drops out of the race and abandons its role of investing in our people and in their economic future?

Fifty years ago Franklin Roosevelt described the South as being one-third "ill-clothed, ill-housed, and ill-fed." [3] Today we have another president who likes to be compared to Franklin Roosevelt.

In the last fifty years the South has come a long way. But we still have far to go. Today too many of our people are ill-paid, illiterate, and ill-prepared for success in life. Let us commit ourselves tonight, as leaders of the South, to seeing that the gains of the last fifty years and our hopes for the next fifty years are not left along the wayside of history.

---

[1] 95 Stat. 843-874, Act of August 13, 1981, Title XXIII, "Public Assistance Programs."

[2] Richard Schultz Schweiker (1926-   ), native of Norristown, Pennsylvania; B.A., Pennsylvania State University, 1950. Business executive; U.S. representative from Pennsylvania's Thirteenth Congressional District, 1961-1969; U.S. senator from Pennsylvania, 1969-1980; secretary, U.S. Department of Health and Human Services, 1981-1983. Who's Who in America, 1982-1983, II, 2988.

[3] "I see one-third of a nation ill-housed, ill-clad, ill-nourished." Franklin Delano Roosevelt, Second Inaugural Address, January 20, 1937, quoted in John Bartlett, Familiar Quotations: A collection of passages, phrases, and proverbs traced to their sources in ancient and modern literature, edited by Emily Morison Beck (Boston, Toronto: Little, Brown and Company, fourteenth edition, revised and enlarged, 1968), 971, hereinafter cited as Bartlett, Familiar Quotations.

Franklin Delano Roosevelt (1882-1945), native of Hyde Park, New York; A.B., Harvard University, 1904; attended Columbia University law school, 1904-1907. Attorney, 1907-1910, 1924-1933; member, New York state Senate, 1910-1913; assistant secretary of the navy, 1913-1920; New York governor, 1929-1933; thirty-first U.S. president, 1933-1945. Who Was Who in America, 1943-1950, 457.

EDUCATION COMMISSION OF THE STATES

Cambridge, Mass., August 28, 1981

[On August 28, 1981, Governor Hunt accepted the nomination as chairman-elect of the Education Commission of the States; that same day, in introducing the speaker at the ECS annual banquet, he declared: "Were it not for Terry Sanford, his boundless energy and his remarkable ability to translate great ideas into reality, we wouldn't be holding this meeting. It was he who seized upon Dr. James B. Conant's suggestion for the creation of the Compact for Education, which in turn created the Education Commission of the States." James Bryant Conant (1893-1978), chemist, Harvard University president, diplomat, and education expert, praised Sanford's initiative in My Several Lives: Memoirs of a Social Inventor (New York: Harper and Row, Publishers, 1970), 649; see also Who Was Who in America, 1977-1981, 121.]

The growth of nonpublic schools and the role of state governments in their operation are issues of great importance. The number and types of students in these schools vary from state to state. Some states have mostly Catholic schools; others have the traditional college preparatory schools.

In my home state of North Carolina we have a strong nonpublic school population in the college prep schools, in Christian fundamentalist schools, and in Catholic schools. The number of students in fundamentalist schools is the greatest.

Although the number of North Carolina students in nonpublic schools is growing, it still represents only about 5 percent of all grade school students in our state. I believe that is because of our outstanding public schools.

We have a responsibility to the students enrolled in independent schools. The state has an inherent responsibility to protect children. We must watch out for their safety and health. We want them to be in the safest possible environment.

All state controls over nonpublic schools were removed by the 1979 General Assembly, except those state regulations concerning health, sanitation, and safety. The legislature did provide for establishment of a student achievement testing program in grades 1, 2, 3, 6, 9, and 11.[1]

As a result of that 1979 legislation and to fulfill the state's responsibility to our children, we established within the Governor's Office the Office of Nonpublic Education. Consultants from that office visit each independent school at least once a year to ensure compliance with the safety and health regulations and to provide any information or assistance needed. Through this office's work, we now know that in 1964 there were about 13,000 children attending 126 nonpublic schools in North Carolina. Today about 58,000 students are enrolled in 377 independent schools.

North Carolina state government has been able to work well with the nonpublic school community. We have a liaison committee with the fundamentalist Christians and a nonpublic school advisory committee. In addition, I appoint observers from these schools to sit in on meetings of our Competency Testing Commission and Annual Testing Commission. They helped us develop our state's testing program, and they continue to advise these committees on the state's program. All in all, we have developed and are maintaining a mutually beneficial relationship between the state and the nonpublic schools.

In the higher education area, North Carolina has thirty-eight strong independent colleges and universities, and we do have a responsibility to the young people in those institutions. The General Assembly has a policy of providing tuition grants to North Carolina residents attending these schools. From an initial appropriation of about $1 million in 1972-1973, funding for our young people in private colleges grew to nearly $20 million in 1980-1981. By the end of 1982 these grants will be up to $850 per student. In effect, our legislature is telling North Carolina's young people that they may choose a college or university on the basis of personal needs and goals, and the state will financially assist them, whether that institution is public or private.

We cannot forget our children and their needs. Education is vital to their development. As Plato said: "The direction in which education starts a man will determine his future life." [2]

---

[1] "An Act to Create an Article to Deal Specifically with Private Church Schools and Schools of Religious Charter," c. 505, and "An Act to Create an Article to Deal with Certain Qualified Nonpublic Schools," c. 506, were ratified May 2, 1979. *N.C. Session Laws, 1979.*

[2] Plato, *The Republic*, bk. IV, p. 425-B, quoted in Bartlett, *Familiar Quotations.*

PROFIT THROUGH INNOVATION CONFERENCE

RALEIGH, SEPTEMBER 10, 1981

I wanted to be here with you today because this conference is about a subject very close to my heart—the whole area of innovation, technology, and productivity.

North Carolina has become a national leader on that new frontier.

More and more manufacturing jobs are demanding higher and higher levels of technological skill—not just the new industries we are attracting, but the vitally important traditional industries like textiles, too.

North Carolina has a lot of advantages as this nation undergoes the Technological Revolution.

We have the greatest university system in the country, with all its research capabilities.

We have the third largest community college system in the nation.

We have the Research Triangle Park, which the *Wall Street Journal* has called "one of the country's most sought-after workplaces." [1]

We have just established the Microelectronics Center of North Carolina, which can make us the East Coast capital for this industry of the future.

The challenge before us is to build on that base. We must master technology and put it to work for us—in our businesses, on our farms, and in government, too.

Sometimes it's tough to do that because people don't want to change. But, to paraphrase an old saying, necessity and competition are the mothers of innovation. To stay ahead requires adapting to change.

I believe the biggest obstacle to innovation and technological progress are children and adults who don't learn: the poor readers, the dropouts, the failures at math and science. If we don't teach our young children to read and write and do math, if we don't train teenagers and young adults on good equipment, and if we don't give them good instructors and career guidance, all the technology and fancy machines in the world won't help your companies. We need industry's help to do that.

Our community colleges suffer from serious shortages of equipment. Some classes are using equipment that dates back to World War II. The entire system's equipment-replacement cycle is lower than once every twelve years; many electronics classes are using early solid state, which is like the stone age compared to today's state of the art. Recently, some industries have stepped forward to help remedy that problem by either donating or loaning equipment to their local community college. There is, of course, a tax break for donations. Perhaps we need to consider a tax break on loaned equipment. Nevertheless, I encourage you and your company to work with your local community college in providing equipment that will bring about more effective training.

Second, we have a tough time keeping enough good instructors at our community colleges. So I am asking all industries in the state to consider establishing an executive or technician loan program to the faculty of their local community college. Dr. Larry Blake, president of the community college system, assures me his institutions will be as flexible as possible in working out any arrangement.

With better equipment and more good instructors we can take a quantum leap in the number of students truly qualified to work for your companies and others. The result will be higher productivity and better profits.

At the same time, we need to encourage industry to replace out-of-date equipment. In this day of rapidly changing technology, the existing state depreciation schedule for manufacturing equipment needs to be revised. I applaud Congress for changing the rates to enable faster write-off of physical assets for federal income tax purposes; I think North Carolina should conform with those improved rates of depreciation. If legislation is needed for our state to conform, I will recommend the introduction of that legislation.

This is all part of what we need to do to get our nation's economy moving again.

One of the most important things we must do [is] to invest in our economic future, in education, in people. We hear a lot of debate these days about whether more is better or less is better. The answer is not necessarily either one. *Better* is better. Smarter is better.

What we need to learn to do in this country is to plan, think, and work smarter. That is how we will maintain our technological lead over the Japanese and the Germans. That is how we will help every person have a chance to be a successful and productive citizen—a taxpayer, not a tax burden. I am convinced that is the key to unlock our state's and our nation's future, and I thank you for coming here today to help us all face that future.

---

[1] "The combination of progressive, quiet plants plus sophisticated yet small-town living nearby had made the park one of the country's most sought-after workplaces." *Wall Street Journal,* April 29, 1981.

NORTH CAROLINA STATE EMPLOYEES ASSOCIATION

WINSTON-SALEM, SEPTEMBER 12, 1981

[The speech reprinted below was also presented on September 12, before the North Carolina State Government Employees Association annual convention. The governor made similar remarks at a luncheon for the NCSEA and NCSGEA membership drive, April 14, 1981.]

This is the fifth year I have spoken to North Carolina's state employees associations. I think it is important for the governor to be with you at these conventions, just as I think it's important for the governor to have an open door to you year-around.

Some of you have been coming to these meetings and working for the state for many years. I doubt there has ever been a more difficult time to be working in government. The nation has been swept up in a fever that says "cut, cut, cut." Washington has undergone a political revolution. You have felt the sting of taxpayer anger personally.

This has been a tough year for state employees. Some things have happened in Raleigh that may have made you feel that you're not appreciated. One reason I wanted to come here today is to tell you that this governor appreciates you. I appreciate what you've been through. I think you're doing a good job. I'm going to keep sticking up for you.

I know the disappointment you felt when the General Assembly left town without approving an across-the-board pay raise. When they return next month, my top priority will be a fair pay raise for you. I will say a little more about that in a few minutes. But, first, I want to talk positively about some things we have done in North Carolina.

The picture is not all bleak. I think this administration and the General Assembly deserve some credit. Every year that I have been governor, employees of the state of North Carolina have received not only the normal automatic, merit, and longevity increases but also an across-the-board pay raise. For this biennium there is already $317.7 million of new money in the budget to support merit raises, longevity increases, and other built-in salary steps, even before an across-the-board raise is given.

Considering what has happened in Washington and in state capitals across the nation, I think state employees in North Carolina have fared pretty well. We haven't taken a meat ax to government here, the way a lot of states have. Our reduction in force [RIF] amounted to 2 percent of the total number of jobs being eliminated. Just about every state in the Southeast cut more than that. In Virginia and South Carolina it was 7 percent. In Tennessee it was 10 percent.

It was worse elsewhere. In Michigan 9 percent of the jobs were abolished, with another 4.5 percent expected to be cut out. Wisconsin has cut 8 percent out of its budget, and the federal cuts have come on top of that in all the states.

We in North Carolina have done our best to carry out that reduction in force in a fair and humane way. We gave supervisors a firm and clear policy on how to go about it. We gave the people who lost their jobs priority for other jobs. Out of the 707 people who were "riffed" in agencies that receive state money, only 137—less than 19 percent—have not been placed yet, and we are working hard on them.

Your leadership, working with my administration and with the legislature, deserves a lot of credit for those good things. I believe that is a story that needs to be told. But, for all that, I understand your concern about an across-the-board pay raise.

You know that I recommended in my proposed budget that $106 million be set aside for a pay raise of some kind. I suggested two alternatives—an across-the-board raise of 4.3 percent, or picking up most of your retirement contribution, which would amount to about a 7 percent increase in your take-home pay.[1] I have had extensive discussions with the legislative leadership on this issue in recent weeks. They share my commitment to a fair pay raise.

But I must be honest with you. Our state's revenue picture is cloudy, and we don't yet see a silver lining in the economy. I stand by our estimate of a 12 percent growth in revenue this year. The legislature projects only a 10 percent growth. The high interest rates and sluggish economy make predicting a risky business, and the General Assembly will have to make a very tough judgment next month. I cannot predict what will happen. I still hope that $106 million can be put into a pay raise. I will stay in very close touch with your leadership and with the legislative leadership on this.

Let me conclude with this: I am not naïve about how state employees are feeling. I understand the frustration and anger I've heard, and I don't mind hearing it from you. I've got a pretty thick skin, and I can take it. But I want you to know that, for all that has happened—the RIFs, the uncertainty over pay, the federal cuts, all of it—I care about you, I know what you're doing for our state, and I appreciate it.

One thing I want to do over the next few months is to develop a way of recognizing outstanding performance by individual employees, to hold them up to the legislature and our people as examples and symbols of the dedication and hard work that you demonstrate every day. I will be appointing a group to do that very soon.

That's part of the job we have to do. Government isn't very popular these days. It's an easy target. We know there are problems, and we understand the anger and frustration that taxpayers feel in tough economic times. That means you have been on the receiving end, and that has been tough, but I wish the people of our state had a chance to know you the way I know you. I wish they could see you working every day. Seeing that firsthand might change some minds and some attitudes.

These are tough times, and you're in the teeth of the storm, but we'll weather it together. I'll stand with you, and we'll fight together for a government that serves the people who pay for it well and treats the people who work for it the same way.

---

[1]*N.C. Session Laws, 1981*, c. 1127, s. 6, authorized a 5 percent raise for state employees.

MAIN STREET PROGRAM

NEW BERN, SEPTEMBER 15, 1981

I am very pleased to visit one of the five North Carolina communities that are participating in the Main Street Program. It is a great honor that North Carolina was one of only six states chosen to participate in this downtown revitalization effort. This program should be a great economic boost to these communities and will show other communities how to revitalize their downtown areas, while keeping in mind the importance of historic preservation. But it will take a public-private partnership for a Main Street Program to succeed. We are here today to announce private help for this exciting project.

NCNB[1] is contributing $50,000 to the National Trust for Historic Preservation. This generous contribution will be used for expenses of the Main Street Program in our five participating towns. Also, NCNB will offer technical assistance to each of the communities. NCNB's credit department is developing a program to help merchants and residents take full advantage of financial incentives now available to them. A Charlotte-based credit officer and a credit officer in each of the five towns will provide this assistance. NCNB says they strive to be the "best bank in the neighborhood," and their commitment to the Main Street Program proves it.

One year into the Main Street Program we are making great progress. Here in New Bern the city has revised zoning ordinances to encourage more downtown residential development. In the last four months four shops have moved into downtown New Bern, and a major developer is interested in the Belk's building and the Bicentennial Park area. Also, two developers will start construction soon on commercial and office condominiums in the Bicentennial Park area, and Branch Banking and Trust Company will build a new bank in this area.

The four other Main Street communities are also making great progress. In Tarboro five storefront renovations have taken place, and five more are under way. Construction will begin this fall on the $12 million retirement center that will be located downtown. An interest-subsidy loan program will be available for property owners who are interested in exterior renovations to downtown buildings.

In Washington a merchant is in the process of developing sailboat slips on the waterfront.

A recruitment packet is now available in Shelby with information on property for sale or rent, marketing data, chamber of commerce materials, and other information about the town.

Salisbury has organized a Main Street Task Force and is providing incentive grants to merchants to match the state's incentive grant program.

These are just a few examples of our towns' progress in the Main Street Program. I am excited about the potential of this program, and I commend these communities for taking full advantage of it.

I would like to make another announcement today of importance to New Bern. I am pleased to announce that New Bern will receive a $10,000 Coastal Energy Impact Program grant to study the effects of vibrations from coal trains on historic structures. Wilmington and Morehead City will also be receiving these grants to look at possible impact of coal transportation in their areas. The grants are from the federal Office of Coastal Zone Management and will be administered by our Department of Natural Resources and Community Development.

As you know, I am committed to building the economy of our state and giving people opportunities for better jobs and better lives. But I am equally determined that economic development come about in such a way that our rich cultural and environmental resources be protected. This is a challenge that I believe we are prepared to meet.

---

[1]On March 31, 1984, NCNB Corporation of Charlotte reported assets of $14.8 billion, making it the biggest bank holding company in the Southeast. *News and Observer*, July 3, 1984.

NICKELS FOR KNOW-HOW
CAMPAIGN KICKOFF

RALEIGH, OCTOBER 14, 1981

It's a great pleasure to be with you today to help kick off the 1981 referendum campaign for North Carolina's unique Nickels for Know-How program.

North Carolina is a national leader in agriculture, and the Nickels for Know-How program is one reason why. This grass-roots program which supports agricultural research and extension efforts is the only one of its kind in the nation.

We all know what this program has meant for North Carolina agriculture. Those nickels have been a boost to every major agricultural advance made in this state in the last thirty years. For example, Nickels funds made possible the setting up of integrated pest-management programs in tobacco to gain on-the-farm experience in controlling the tobacco budworm, green peach aphid, and tobacco flea beetle. The money that individual farmers pay into this program may not seem like much, but those nickels add up, and that "seed money," as Dean Legates[1] calls it, helps you prove to the General Assembly that a particular idea or program deserves state funding.

I want you to know that I strongly support the increase you are requesting this year—from one nickel to two nickels for each ton of seed and fertilizer. As all of us are aware, inflation hits us everywhere, and we must recognize that the two nickels being sought in this referendum are equal to only 3 cents in 1951 money. I am very proud of our Nickels for Know-How program because it is one of the best examples I know of in this state of people helping themselves. People working together for their own good and for the benefit of their neighborhoods. People saying they care about our future and are willing to do something about it.

I am also proud of the strong cooperation so evident in the Nickels program. The program is sponsored by the North Carolina Farm Bureau Federation, the North Carolina State Grange, and the North Carolina Agricultural Foundation. Our Department of Agriculture works with manufacturers of feed and fertilizer, collecting the money and turning it over to North Carolina State University, and the Agricultural Foundation works to find the best uses for the money. Obviously, feed and fertilizer users have confidence in how their money is being handled, or they wouldn't continue to support the Nickels program, with votes often of more than nine to one.

North Carolina must continue its strong leadership in this field, and the Nickels for Know-How program is one of the best ways I know of to help us continue that leadership. With your help and support, I know the 1981 Nickels for Know-How Referendum is going to pass, and it is going to pass big. Thank you for helping us continue this state's great progress in this most vital area.

---

[1]James Edward Legates (1922-　　), native of Milford, Delaware; resident of Raleigh; B.S., University of Delaware, 1943; M.S., 1947, Ph.D., 1949, Iowa State University; U.S. Marine Corps Reserve, 1943-1946. University professor, 1949-1970; dean, School of Agriculture and Life Sciences, North Carolina State University, since 1971. James Edward Legates to Jan-Michael Poff, October 3, 1983.

TRANSPORTATION EFFICIENCY COUNCILS

Raleigh, October 26, 1981

I want to thank all of you for taking time off from your jobs and other responsibilities to come here and meet with us today. I appreciate your personal sacrifice in this, because I know we didn't appoint this many independently wealthy "people of leisure" to help us in our Good Roads Program!

You all are coming on board our transportation team at one of its most challenging times. We talk a lot about teamwork in our administration, and we believe in it. It's because of our teamwork with the legislature, with the administrators and employees of the Department of Transportation, and with our Transportation Board members that we have come through the recent funding crisis with the tools we need to do the job on our highways.

You are going to be key players on our team, and today I want to talk to you a little bit about how our team works and what we expect from all the players. But first I want to give you a little bit of background.

In 1979 we realized we faced a serious crisis in funding our highway program. Declining gas-tax revenues and inflation were eating us alive. I appointed a Blue Ribbon Study Commission, headed by Governor Dan K. Moore, to study the problems and recommend courses of action. That commission reported to me last December that we needed to fund a program that would allow us to catch up on our backlog of maintenance and keep up with current needs—about 3,600 miles of maintenance the first year. To meet that goal, we put together a package of funding methods that included substantial savings by the department as well as a 3-cent-per-gallon gasoline tax. We were successful in getting almost all of our package through the legislature, and I am confident that the last remaining portion of it, about $20 million a year for the next two years, will be forthcoming when the legislature meets next June.

In addition, the Department of Transportation, under the outstanding leadership of former Secretary Tom Bradshaw and our new secretary, Bill Roberson, has achieved great savings in the operation of the department. I won't go into all of them in detail, but I'll list a few of them:

—Reducing crew size. We are reducing the number of workers in highway crews by 273, and the $5.5 million from those salaries will go directly to maintaining the roads. We are also doubling the number of prison inmates working on the roads from 1,000 to 2,000.

—Reducing the amount of equipment. The department has eliminated over 4,000 pieces of equipment. We have also instituted stringent new procedures for acquiring equipment, so we make absolutely sure we need something before we buy it.

—Reducing the number of employees in the department. We have eliminated 1,100 positions at a savings of $14.5 million a year.

So we have the main tools we need to do a basic, minimum job of resurfacing—along with a *few* construction projects that are essential for economic development—but we haven't got a single dime to waste. We've got to make sure we spend every single dollar as wisely as we know how, and we've got to be ingenious about finding new ways to save. That's going to be one of your main jobs.

We want you to help us be more responsible and responsive to the taxpayers. They've told us, in effect, "We want you to have the tools you need to protect our roads, but we want to be sure you are working as efficiently as possible." Our legislators said that was the message they got from the people back home, and that's why I wrote Executive Order No. 65 to establish your councils:

"Each council will examine the work program, policies, methods, and operations of each Department of Transportation county maintenance unit.

"Each council will make recommendations to the governor and Board of Transportation on cutting costs and improving efficiency in those units. The department will implement those recommendations that are appropriate.

"Each council will act as a channel for citizens to express concerns, complaints, comments, and suggestions regarding highway work." [1]

Now many of you are in business yourselves. I'd bet all of you have a good bit of common sense. All of you were picked because you are key people in your communities, you have a wide range of contacts, and people feel good about talking to you. We want you to be our eyes and ears in the field, to listen to suggestions, to hear complaints and concerns, and to funnel those to your board member, who is the chairman of your council.

Now that's one of the keys to the effective operation of these councils: work through your board member, not your division or district engineers. This is the second-largest department in state government, with almost 13,000 employees scattered over the entire state, and we can't work effectively if we don't go through the right channels. If we tangle our lines of communication or promise something we can't deliver, we'll have a bigger mess than we started with.

It will not be your job to set transportation policy, or to decide which maintenance projects come first, or which construction projects are first on the list. That role belongs by law to the Board of Transportation. In fact, the board is now reviewing the entire Seven-Year Plan, and you are going to hear some screaming and hollering when the revised plan comes out, because some mighty popular projects are going to be left off or pushed back.

You'll probably have some people who want you to help them get jobs with the Transportation Department, and I'll be sure you have Joe Pell's phone number so you can tell them to call him in Raleigh.[2] You'll probably have Mrs. Jones calling you to get her road scraped and Mrs. Smith wanting some fresh tar put on her road, and you'll be tempted to call the local engineer's office and ask them to get right on over there—but don't yield to that temptation. Do go through your board member.

You'll get a lot of questions about why we do certain things a certain way in the department. You may, for example, get a question about why we put up the signs saying "Your Good Roads Program at work." The answer to that is, we had numerous inquiries from people who wanted to know where their additional gas-tax money was being spent. These signs point that out. You should also know that these signs are reusable and will be repainted and recycled for other highway needs.

I know you'll be under some pressure in your communities to get immediate solutions to problems, and I want you to help us find the right ways to address those problems as quickly as possible. Your board member will be your leader and guide in this.

We want to forge a closer working relationship with our citizens, and the quality of that relationship in large measure will depend on you. We are counting on you to help us do a more efficient job, to help explain the workings of this department to people, and to be our liaison with the citizens and the board. You'll have to learn a lot about how the department and state government work, and you'll have to learn right much about the highway system.

You'll be having regional meetings soon with your board members and engineers, and you'll get a much more detailed briefing then about such things as our policies and procedures for working inmates on the roads, our maintenance policy, and the process of scheduling and funding maintenance projects. You'll get detailed charts and descriptions of the structure of the department—who reports to whom, and what their responsibilities are.

You'll receive a briefing book at your regional meeting, or you may have already received it from your board member, that will outline all those issues and others. You'll find out that we have a lot of rules and regulations to work under—for instance, you won't be able to ride around in a state car with your division or district engineer. That may sound petty, but it's a law that was designed to prevent abuse of state property—which belongs to the taxpayers. All of us who serve the taxpayers have a special responsibility to be sure that we do not abuse, whether intentionally or not, any privileges of our positions.

Now, if it sounds like I'm asking a lot of you, it's because I am. We are not yet out of the woods with our Good Roads Program. If we do not get the additional funds from the legislature for the next two years, we will have *no* money to match federal aid after 1983. That means *no money* will be available in North Carolina for construction of the many primary highways that your local people have worked for for years, and we will lose that federal money our people have paid in federal highway taxes.

Whether or not we get additional funds from the legislature will depend in part on how good a job we do with the money they have already appropriated. In fact, some of them have said to me, "Governor, if you all show us you can manage the $158 million we gave you this year, we'll get the rest for you next year." Your legislators will serve ex officio on your councils, so they'll be working closely with you.

We are taking on this task of improving our highway system at a time when the federal government is pulling back from so much involvement in state affairs. Washington is pulling back mainly in terms of dollars; this is true not only in social service programs but in transportation programs too. We have heard recently a proposal out of Washington to leave unfinished certain portions of the interstate system, which would greatly impede our efforts to bring good jobs to all the parts of our state that need them.

The burden is increasingly on the states to set and meet their own goals, to come up with their own money, and to accept the responsibility for the wise use of that money. I feel very good about North Carolina's ability to meet those challenges. We have always had a balanced budget, and we have always had relatively efficient government. We have set goals of good jobs, top-flight education, a good quality of life, and fair opportunities for everyone. This is the North Carolina way.

Governor Kerr Scott got the people out of the mud when I was a boy and left us the legacy of the greatest state-maintained highway system in the world. It's up to us now to preserve that legacy. I'm proud to have you as our partners on this great transportation team. Never before have we had so many good people helping us on one project. Never has our potential been greater. I firmly believe we in North Carolina can show the nation that the states do have the will, the creativity, the muscle, and the brains to forge their own futures. Our future in North Carolina looks bright, and it's because people like you are willing to work hard together.

------

[1]Governor Hunt announced at a press conference May 21, 1981, the formation of County Transportation Efficiency councils; for the complete text of Executive Order No. 65, see *N.C. Session Laws, 1981*, 1768-1769.

[2]Joseph Andrew Pell, Jr. (1915-   ), senior assistant to Governor Hunt; president, North Carolina State School Board Association, 1960-1962, and of the Southeastern School Board Association, 1962-1964. Joseph Andrew Pell, Jr., to Jan-Michael Poff, October 25, 1983; also previously identified in Mitchell, *Addresses of Hunt*, I, 202n.

STATEMENT ON DOROTHEA DIX WOOD-FIRED BOILER

RALEIGH, OCTOBER 26, 1981

[The Dorothea Dix wood-fired boiler system was only one example of the Hunt administration's search for methods to free state government from the supply and cost fluctuations of foreign energy sources. While announcing on June 10, 1981, Peat Methanol Associates' plan to erect a $250 million peat-to-methanol conversion facility in Washington County, the governor mentioned the Transportation Department's modification of nineteen state vehicles to test the feasibility of methanol as a gasoline substitute.

Plans for the PMA plant were abandoned after Synthetic Fuels Corporation refused to increase the level of "federal loan guarantees and methanol price supports" established for the project in 1982. *News and Observer*, February 21, 1984.]

I want you to know that I am proud that the state's first major institutional wood-energy system is right here at Dorothea Dix Hospital. All of you, from North Carolina State University, Human Resources, and Administration, have worked long and hard to make this project a reality, but it is worth it. This wood-fired boiler will pay back its total cost of $1 million in less than three years and will pay back its extra cost over an oil or gas system in less than two years. Even more important, it will be an example to the public and to private industry of efficient use of alternative energy sources.

We're committed to finding ways to make ourselves energy independent. This is a sound step in that direction. Energy management is a real key to our progress, as a state, in the future. I hope dozens of industries in North Carolina will come to look at this plant and see how this principle can be adopted for their uses.

One of the best things about this plant is that it is using what used to be trash wood, wood that lumberyards had to throw away. Now we have found a way of using all parts of the tree when it is cut, and wood is a renewable resource which North Carolina has in abundance. The Dix boiler will consume 15,000 tons of chips a year. The production of these chips will increase forestry employment and revenue, and it will also triple the productivity of forestry in our state.

This wood-fired boiler will use 30,000 pounds of wood per hour. It is versatile. It can burn green, whole-tree wood chips, no. 6 fuel oil, and natural gas. Although other methods of developing fuel from wood-mill residues have been used in smaller areas, this will be the first North Carolina energy system to use whole-tree chips.

This boiler replaces one that produced 95 million pounds of steam last year—78 percent of that from October through April. This boiler has just begun its first test of being in service full time, and we fully expect it to perform at top levels. We estimate that this first year the boiler will consume 9,600 tons of chips between now and April. That will replace approximately 69 million cubic feet of no. 6 fuel oil. Now natural gas costs about $5.00 per thousand cubic feet, no. 6 fuel oil costs 80 cents a gallon, and wood chips cost $15.85 per ton, so we expect to have the cost of this conversion recouped by mid-1984.

I want to thank the plant staff of Dorothea Dix Hospital for their full cooperation. I also want to thank the wood coordinating group that developed this project. My father was the leader of that group.

This is not just an energy-saving project. It is also a good example of how efficient and innovative government can be when groups and agencies work together. From this we will learn more about using wood energy on a large scale, we'll be creating jobs for North Carolinians, we'll be using our own resources, and we'll be a leader in energy independence. This is a great example of the North Carolina way of doing things—with creativity, ingenuity, cooperation, and determination. I congratulate all of you who had a part in this, and I look forward to our brief tour of the plant.

AREA MENTAL HEALTH DIRECTORS

RALEIGH, NOVEMBER 2, 1981

[The name of the first of four plaintiffs listed in a class-action lawsuit brought against the state in federal court on October 3, 1979—Willie M.— came to designate all North Carolinians less than eighteen years old who, usually the products of an insecure home environment, "suffer from serious emotional, mental or neurological handicaps . . . accompanied by behavior which is characterized as violent or assaultive. . . ." Such children did not respond to conventional therapy in state institutions, and the suit was filed for the plaintiffs so that they and others similarly afflicted might obtain specialized attention leading to societal assimilation. Legal proceedings climaxed in September, 1980, when the defendants, including the governor and the heads of various state agencies, boards, and facilities, acceded to a consent decree ordering the state "to provide treatment, education, training and care for each member of the (Willie M.) class, such services being individually suited to the needs of each" child and furnished "under the most normal (or least restrictive) conditions appropriate for that person." A year later the defendants assented to a schedule ensuring the availability by July, 1983, of a complete therapy program. *Charlotte Observer*, October 2, 1983; *News and Observer*, December 11, 1983; *Willie M., a minor; Jeanette M., a minor; Tom H., a minor; Timothy B., a minor, all by their next friend, Albert Singer, on behalf of themselves and all others similarly situated, Plaintiffs,* v. *James B. Hunt, Jr., et al., Defendants.* United States District Court for the Western District of North Carolina, Charlotte Division, Civil Action No. CC 79-0294, pp. 1-4; *Willie M., et al., Plaintiffs,* v. *James B. Hunt, Jr., et al., Defendants*: Notice of Settlement, Civil Action Suit No. CC 79-0294, p. 5. For a progress report on this nationally recognized treatment strategy, see Gary Macbeth, "North Carolina's Willie M. Program: A Current Perspective," *Popular Government,* 50 (Winter, 1985), 32-39.]

All of us are here today to make common cause in meeting a great challenge. That challenge is creating a new system of services for aggressive, emotionally disturbed children—the Willie M. children. The lives and future of those children, in a real way, rest in our hands. We can keep them from becoming permanently institutionalized or ending up in prison. I wanted to come here today to tell you that the governor of North Carolina is committed to seeing that these children get appropriate services as close as possible to their own home. The people in this room today, if we work together, can make that happen.

Now, we all know that the state has signed a consent order guaranteeing that services will be provided, but I think you ought to realize something: We didn't have to sign the consent decree. We could have fought this thing out in the courts. But instead the state voluntarily entered into the consent decree because we believed that we should assure that these children will get the help they need.

We've agreed to provide 100 percent state funds to put these programs in place statewide. At the same time we want to make sure that the money is going for appropriate services for these children and that the programs can spend the dollars as soon as they are allocated. Doing that is going to take some help from you. When counties are ready to accept the money—in other words, when children are identified and assessed and program plans are in place—I will go to the legislature and ask for money for those programs in the zones that have shown they are ready.

As tight as dollars are right now, and as many cuts as we are experiencing in needed human services programs, I think that it is only right to wait to ask for the dollars when they are needed. But I can promise you that when the programs are ready, I will ask for the money. Right now we expect that another nine zones will be

ready by next June. We have estimated that to fund these zones we
will need to ask for an additional $8.1 million in the June session of
the legislature.

We have already gone to the legislature twice this year to request
money for the Willie M. programs. The first session the legislature
granted $1.5 million for Mental Health, $239,000 for Public Instruction, and $139,000 for Youth Services. We had requested $7.5 million for the first year of the biennium, but the legislature decided
to provide funds as zones became ready to receive them and to put
programs into place.

When we returned in the October session, proving readiness in
another zone, the legislature appropriated an additional $2.3 million
for Mental Health and $262,000 for Public Instruction. In addition
to these funds, administrative fees, attorneys' fees, and consultant
fees for evaluations have totaled over $200,000 out of funds already
appropriated to the Department of Human Resources.

Let me just say this: I expect counties that have already been
funded to have their programs in place and children being served
before the legislature returns. But before we get to the step of asking
the legislature for more money, we need to finish the evaluations of
all those children who were nominated by September 1. Those
evaluations must be finished by December 15 of this year. We've
provided state staff to help, but obviously for this job to be done,
you—the people who work the closest with these children, who
know their homes and families—have to help to get these evaluations finished.

But even more importantly, I think the Willie M. children will
give all of us a tremendous opportunity to establish the close
working ties between state and local agencies and among local
agencies that we have wanted to develop. We need to develop these
relationships to assure that the best programs are created and put
into use as quickly as possible. This case presents us with a chance
for Mental Health, Mental Retardation, Social Services, Public
Health, Youth Services, the Administrative Office of the Courts, and
the public school system to pull together and prove just how effective
programs for people can be when the needs of the individual are the
primary motive for us to work together rather than the needs of any
one agency. In fact, the whole concept we are working to implement
was one that you helped to develop. In every meeting in which the
needs of these children were discussed, the importance of agencies
working together was emphasized.

I want you to know that I believe in that. I know that we in North
Carolina are rich with people like you—dedicated professionals
who understand and care about the needs of all of the children in
North Carolina. I also know that when you pull together to provide
these children with the services they need, North Carolina will be
able to show the rest of the nation how possible it is to treat and save

the Willie M. children—those who have always been described as uniquely difficult to treat. I know that with your dedication and the strongest support possible from my office and from the Department of Human Resources we can and will make a difference in these children's lives.

DEPARTMENT OF TRANSPORTATION
EQUAL EMPLOYMENT OPPORTUNITY
AND AFFIRMATIVE ACTION CONFERENCE

RALEIGH, NOVEMBER 4, 1981

Thank you, Mr. Secretary, you are absolutely right. I am here today because I strongly believe in what you're doing. My administration continues to have the kind of commitment to equal opportunity that requires my personal attention and that of my cabinet secretaries. That in turn means your personal attention is also required. As Secretary Roberson said, there are a lot of reasons that justify reaching our affirmative action goals, but the most important is the fact that it is the right thing to do.

We are making progress, for example, in areas such as contracts with minority businesses. In 1977-1978 we awarded only $1.2 million in contracts to minority-owned businesses. In 1978-1979 that figure rose to $2.8 million. We slipped to only $2.5 million in 1979-1980, but in 1980-1981 we jumped to $10.4 million in contracts awarded to minority firms.

That big increase in the total contracts awarded to minority and female firms in 1980-1981 is primarily due to the participation by minorities and women in our MBE-WBE Internship Training Program.[1] We established goals based on funding availability and on the availability of minority-owned and female-owned firms to do the work. The overall goals in our MBE-WBE Program this past year were 3.6 percent MBE and .5 percent WBE, and we exceeded both goals. We are hoping that if funds are available for projects, our achievements for 1981-1982 will surpass 1980-1981.

As you all know, however, construction funds for highway improvements are becoming more and more limited. So we hope we can work even harder with minority firms in our contract maintenance projects. This year we will also concentrate on upgrading the skills of those minority businessmen who have already been identified and who have participated in our training programs.

We shouldn't kid ourselves, though, that it's going to be easy to achieve our goals of minority and female participation at a time when the whole highway industry is tightening up, but it's not impossible to continue making progress. In spite of a decrease of

2,139 employees in the total highway construction industry, minority participation by job categories was higher in 1980-1981 than the year before. We are pleased that most of the highway contractors are committed to affirmative action. They've been very willing to attend affirmative-action workshops and seminars conducted through our Supportive Services Program, and those workshops and seminars will be continued in the coming year.

One way we are working with contractors is in on-the-job training. Contractors teach minorities and females to improve their skills. This is done by assigning training slots to those projects that can afford them and that are located where minorities and females are available for work. The goal here is to improve participation by 6 percent for minorities and 2 percent for females. This kind of effort helps everybody: the contractors get good employees, people get jobs who wouldn't have had them, and we achieve our goals of equal opportunity.

As you very well know, we have cut back on positions here in the Department of Transportation. So it might be easy to use that as an excuse for not reaching our goals. But I see that as a challenge to make the extra effort to find those qualified minority applicants and hire them whenever we have an opening, and DOT has shown that it can be done. For example, we started four and a half years ago with 1,275 minorities, or about 9.8 percent of the work force, and 393 women in nontraditional jobs for about 3 percent of the work force. We have increased those numbers to 1,690 for minorities (14.08 percent) and 486 (3.98 percent) for women as of October 1, 1981. We can consider this pretty good progress under the circumstances, but we need to keep working hard at it.

As we look ahead, I ask you to keep this in mind: By the end of the fiscal year we would need to add about 738 minority employees to reach our goal of 20.7 percent. Those figures are projected with anticipated reductions in force for the department. You have set these hiring, training, and promotional goals, and we must work hard to meet them. For example, we need to place particular emphasis on getting women into our field jobs—as machine operators, surveyors, and truck drivers.

But hiring is just the beginning. We now need to turn our attention to keeping these people on the payroll. We have an investment in them for our time and effort in recruiting and training them to do their jobs. They should be trained and promoted even more. When you look at your work force, you can see that there are only a very few females and minorities in supervisory and management positions. Let's work to improve our representation in these kinds of jobs.

We just simply have to make sure that promotions are fairly and equitably made. One management tool you should use to do this is WPPR, or Work Planning and Performance Review. Not only does

WPPR stimulate productivity; it can also help ensure fairness in determining merit raises and promotions for those who deserve them.

With more than 13,000 employees, your department is one of the larger state government agencies. You have the opportunity to make a great impact on all of state government and a great impression on the people of North Carolina. You're already a good example, with achievements in terms of cost savings to the taxpayer, your citizen involvement programs, your national recognition in the FHWA [Federal Highway Administration] highway design competition, and, of course, your past accomplishments in the area of equal employment opportunity. That's one of the reasons we fought so hard in the legislature to give you the revenues to implement the Good Roads Program. I knew we could count on you to deliver on the commitments we've made to the legislature and to the people.

I'm also continuing to count on you to deliver on the commitments my administration has made in terms of equal opportunity and affirmative action. The secretary's appointment of Bill Oats as our new assistant secretary for civil rights is an example of our commitment to equal employment opportunity by this department and our administration. His participation on the secretary's management team will be a key element in the continued success and for even greater future accomplishments by this department.[2]

North Carolina already has a national reputation as the "Good Roads State." I'm depending on you to help us build another reputation, a reputation for fairness—fairness for all of our people; a reputation for making sure everybody in North Carolina has the opportunity to benefit from the better life we all have worked so hard to provide. I appreciate your past achievements and look forward to your future accomplishments as an example for the rest of state government and, indeed, for the state itself.

---

[1]The Minority Business Enterprise-Women's Business Enterprise Internship Training Program, begun in 1976, was designed to assist novice firms in overcoming a lack of experience in obtaining and executing highway construction contracts. The program matched a "prime contractor" with a "minority or female contractor," the former providing the latter with field experience in areas such as project estimating and bidding; job planning and cost accounting; equipment leasing and purchasing; and inventory and project quality control. William R. Oats, Jr., to Jan-Michael Poff, September 4, 1984.

[2]William R. Oats, Jr. (1947-   ), native of Selma; resident of Greenville; B.A., Fayetteville State University, 1969; M.P.A., University of Baltimore, 1978. Personnel officer, city of Baltimore, 1972-1974; equal opportunity director, University of Maryland at Baltimore, 1974-1979; Baltimore district equal employment opportunity officer, Internal Revenue Service, 1979-1981; assistant secretary for civil rights, state Transportation Department, since 1981. William R. Oats, Jr., to Jan-Michael Poff, September 4, 1984.

STATEMENT ON NORTH CAROLINA
BIOTECHNOLOGY CENTER

RALEIGH, NOVEMBER 5, 1981

[When created in 1981, the North Carolina Biotechnology Center was the nation's first state-sponsored initiative in the field of genetic research and development. Three years later, the governor announced that the center was to become a non-profit, independent corporation. Such a status would bestow "the increased flexibility it needs to respond rapidly to opportunities that arise in academic and industrial biotechnology," according to Hunt. "News Release from the Governor's Office," December 12, 1984.]

It is with great anticipation and excitement that I announce today the establishment of the North Carolina Biotechnology Center. The purpose of the center, to be located in the Research Triangle Park, will be to explore ways to put North Carolina in the forefront of the greatest advancement in the biological sciences since the invention of the microscope.

Biotechnology, sometimes referred to as "gene splicing" or "genetic engineering," involves altering the genetic codes that regulate the functions of living cells. In other words, a gene within a cell can be altered in such a way as to change the characteristics of that cell.

In the past few years we have seen astonishing advances in this field, and in the next few years we anticipate revolutionary advances in such fields as medicine, energy, agriculture, and forestry. Biotechnology will be used in the production of interferon for use in the treatment of cancer patients, and it will result in the development of better quality insulin, hormones, vaccines, and antitoxins. We will see the development of self-fertilizing crops that will be resistant to drought, disease, and insects. There will be improved strains of livestock, and enzymes that will extract valuable minerals from rock. The field is still very new, but already it is apparent that the possibilities are endless.

North Carolina is in a position to assume a pioneering role in biotechnology. Beginning in February of 1980, the North Carolina Board of Science and Technology began exploring the potential for research and development here. It was reported to us by key industrial, academic, and governmental leaders throughout the country that our research institutions, the existence of the Research Triangle Park, and a proven track record of cooperation between the public and private sectors make this state a uniquely attractive place for biotechnology research and development.

The center is being established as a first, interim step toward attracting to North Carolina what will one day be a burgeoning new industry. President Friday, President Sanford, and I developed plans for the center, and its staff will answer directly to the three of us. The center's job will be to pull together government, private industry, and the universities where research into biotechnology is being conducted. It is conservatively estimated that research institutions here have already received $10 million from various sources to finance this kind of research.

Initially, the center will have a staff of three people and a budget of $115,000 contributed by the Board of Science and Technology and the Department of Commerce. We are indeed fortunate that Dr. Leon Golberg, the retired president of the Chemical Industry Institute of Toxicology, has consented to become director of the center.[1] Dr. Golberg is an internationally renowned scientist who has held important positions of leadership with government, industry, and the academic community in the United States, England, and South Africa. The assistant director will be Dr. Laura Meagher, who received her Ph.D. in zoology at Duke University.[2]

Under the leadership of this outstanding team, the North Carolina Biotechnology Center will spend the next six months to a year exploring all the ramifications of this field. We will be looking into the latest developments in research, contacting the firms that will be translating this research into practical application, looking for possible sources of venture capital, and promoting the development of an outstanding community of molecular biologists within North Carolina. Within a year or so, Dr. Golberg, Dr. Meagher, President Friday, President Sanford, and others involved in this venture will make recommendations to me regarding what our long-term strategy should be.

Our state stands to benefit enormously from what we are beginning here today. In a few years all of this research will give birth to a clean, high-paying industry that will contribute greatly to the economic development of North Carolina. But just as important is the application of biotechnology to everyday life. For example, biotechnology is going to have a profound impact on agriculture and forestry, two of the most important segments of North Carolina's economy and way of life.

I want to emphasize to you that the North Carolina Biotechnology Center is not the biological equivalent of the Microelectronics Center of North Carolina—at least not yet. The primary distinction is that biotechnology has not yet moved into large-scale industrial production. But that will happen soon, and it will foster tremendous changes in the way we live. We must begin now to plan and prepare ourselves for this exciting future. The creation of the North Carolina Biotechnology Center is an important step in that direction.

[1] Leon Golberg (1915-   ), native of Limassol, Cyprus; resident of Raleigh; B.Sc. (Hons.), 1936, M.Sc., 1937, D.Sc., 1946, University of Witwatersrand; D.Phil., Oxford University, 1939; M.A., Cambridge University, 1948; M.B., B.Chir., University College Medical School, London, 1951; winner of numerous scientific honors; specialist in mechanisms of toxic action of environmental chemicals; metabolism, pharmacokinetics, and carcinogenesis. Medical research director, Benger Research Laboratories, Ltd., 1955-1961; director, British Industrial Biological Research Assn., 1961-1967; scientific director, Institute of Comparative and Human Toxicology, and research professor of pathology, Albany Medical College, 1967-1976; president, Chemical Industry Institute of Toxicology, Research Triangle Park, 1976-1981; director, North Carolina Biotechnology Center, 1981-1982; professor in community/ occupational medicine, Duke University, since 1981. Leon Golberg to Jan-Michael Poff, October 4, 1983.

[2] Laura Reinertsen Meagher, native of Chicago; resident of Durham; B.A., Middlebury College, 1973; Ph.D., Duke University, 1979. Consultant, North Carolina Board of Science and Technology, 1980; visiting assistant professor, North Carolina State University, 1980-1981; research analyst, Governor's Office, 1981; visiting scientist, Plant Breeding Institute, Cambridge, England, 1982-1983; assistant director, 1981-1982, acting administrator, January-October, 1984, and vice-president, since November, 1984, of North Carolina Biotechnology Center, Inc. Laura Reinertsen Meagher to Jan-Michael Poff, November 14, 1984.

NORTH CAROLINA LEAGUE OF MUNICIPALITIES

CHARLOTTE, NOVEMBER 10, 1981

[Warning on September 3, 1981, that "deeper cuts may be in the offing," the governor announced that a "preliminary analysis" of the revised federal budget demonstrated that "North Carolina, in the remaining nine months of the state fiscal year, will lose $120.82 million in federal funds. That figure will increase to $173.63 million next fiscal year." At a news conference the following week, Hunt expressed concern that construction of I-85 between Greensboro and Lexington, I-40 connecting Benson and Hillsborough, and U.S. 52 from Lexington to Winston-Salem was threatened by limited federal highway appropriations; furthermore, the possible eradication by the Reagan administration of "a special discretionary account in the U.S. Department of Transportation" could prevent completion of I-40 between Wilmington and Benson. Twelve million dollars were scheduled to be eliminated from highway safety improvement expenditures, and diminished funding for water-sewer construction and renovation reduced from seventy-eight to forty-three the number of such projects in North Carolina receiving federal support. Those facing abandonment included undertakings in Concord, Mayodan, Marshall, Washington, Knightdale, and Garner.

Hunt spoke before members of the North Carolina League of Municipalities and outlined examples of state-local initiatives that, he hoped, would begin to compensate for cuts in federal community development spending.]

I am honored to address the Seventy-second Annual Convention of the North Carolina League of Municipalities. Whenever I speak to meetings of local government officials, it always seems appropriate to say "thank you," and this occasion is no different.

My administration has dedicated itself to moving North Carolina forward—and we have had some gratifying successes—but I just wonder how successful we would have been without the help of the men and women in this room. You have been at the forefront of our efforts to improve our economy, to make our public schools better, to mount a successful fight against crime, and a host of other progressive initiatives. You have looked after the interests of your communities and at the same time you have realized that effective local government depends on looking at our state as a whole.

In North Carolina, state and local governments have historically worked together for the benefit of all our people. That is due in large part to the exceptional caliber of leadership exhibited by the League of Municipalities. We are all proud that one of your most distinguished leaders, Ferd Harrison, will be moving into the presidency of your national association later this year.[1] That is particularly heartening at a time when Richard Conder of Rockingham is serving as president of the National Association of Counties.[2]

For North Carolina to hold these two national posts at the same time is a remarkable achievement and a tribute to the strength of local government in our state. That kind of strength is going to be needed more than ever before in the years to come. That is because of the dramatic change in the federal government's posture toward state and local government.

Everybody in this room supports a balanced federal budget. That's because everybody in this room operates on a balanced budget and always has. I don't know how soon, if ever, the administration in Washington is going to achieve that goal, but I know state and local governments are bearing a huge share of the consequences of the administration's attempts to do it.

Grants to cities and states represent 14.2 percent of the entire federal budget, yet those grants are the target of one third of the administration's budget cuts. Funds for these programs have been slashed by 14 percent for fiscal 1982—25 percent after inflation—and the administration's new program to contain the deficit could mean an additional reduction of 12 percent. The cuts are being made in programs that make our economy stronger and make our people stronger, programs like education, skill training, highways, and water and sewer.

This shift in the burden is coming at a time when the ability of states and cities to generate new sources of revenue is shrinking. So what's going to happen to the roads, the bridges, the water systems, the sewer systems that communities depend upon for their very existence? How are communities going to grow and prosper when North Carolina is losing $56 million over the next two years in

federal highway funds? How are communities going to attract
industry and provide jobs in the face of losing $90 million a year in
water-sewer funds?

Those are tough questions, but a lot of weeping and wailing isn't
going to answer them. Our response must be positive and forward
looking—and courageous. Together, we must continue to make
investments in our people and in our future. In that spirit I urge
your continued support for the $300 million clean water bond issue
that must be approved by the people.[3] Without these bonds, our communities can't protect their environments and build their economies.
I hope you will support these bonds as if the very survival of your
cities and towns depended on it, because it very well might.

In view of the loss of federal highway funds, the Good Roads
Program that you were so instrumental in helping enact takes on
even greater importance. I will urge the General Assembly to take
the steps necessary to put into our Highway Fund the amount of
money the Moore commission said would be required.

You are to be commended for your active involvement in the
planning process for implementation of the Community Development Block Grant. I am committed to strong participation by local
government in that process and in the program itself. I will be
working closely with the league and the County Commissioners
Association in conducting a series of meetings across the state to
get your ideas on how a state-administered program can best meet
the needs of your communities. The Department of Natural Resources and Community Development has already conferred with
the Local Government Advocacy Council, and a technical advisory
committee composed by city and county managers and community
development directors has been appointed to work with them on the
block grant program.

In view of the diminished role of the federal government in state
and local affairs, I want to repeat my commitment to examine
thoroughly the issue of local government financing. We need to be
thinking about how we can work together in this area. The Property
Tax System Study Committee has begun its work and will report its
recommendations to the next full session of the General Assembly. I
hope those recommendations will be a departure point for some real
progress in this area.

The work of the Local Government Advocacy Council will be
particularly important with regard to local government financing.
With that in mind, I am determined to see the role of that agency
strengthened, because it is your voice in state government, and it
should be loud and clear. I am asking Paul Essex,[4] my special
assistant for intergovernmental relations, to work with your leadership on ways in which the council's work, and that of the Office of
Local Government Advocacy, can have a greater impact on state
policy.

The initiatives I have talked about won't solve all of our problems, but they indicate that we are not going to throw up our hands in despair because our relationship with Washington has changed. This change presents some awesome challenges but also some exciting opportunities. State and local governments literally have the chance to become laboratories for democracy. That is why I made sure that local government was strongly represented in our North Carolina 2000 program—an effort to determine where our state and our communities are, and where they will be twenty years from now.

We must begin now to make the decisions that will ensure a more prosperous, a more healthy, a more stable place to live, work, and play. I hope you will support the work of the Commission on the Future of North Carolina and the North Carolina 2000 committees in your counties. I take this effort seriously, because I believe we can shape our future. I believe we can mold it, change it, make it better. We can be innovative. We can be imaginative. We don't have to be reactionary.

Time and again, the men and women in this room have responded to great challenges. That is because you are great men and women. Now we face the greatest set of challenges ever, and you will respond again. And you will have my full and complete support.

---

[1] Ferd L. Harrison (1926-   ), native of Scotland Neck; B.B.A., Wake Forest College (now University), 1952; U.S. Army, 1944-1946. Mayor, Scotland Neck, 1958 to present; president, North Carolina League of Municipalities, 1970-1971, and of the National League of Cities, 1983. Chairman, Region L Council of Governments, 1975-1977, of the Small Cities Advisory Council, National League of Cities, 1979, and of the Halifax Development Commission, since 1981. Member, President's Advisory Commission on Federalism, 1981-1982, and of the Advisory Commission on Intergovernmental Relations, since 1983. Ferd L. Harrison to Jan-Michael Poff, October 21, 1983.

[2] J. Richard Conder (1930-   ), native of Hamlet; resident of Rockingham; B.S., East Carolina College (now University); Louisiana State University Graduate School of Banking, 1968; U.S. Air Force, 1951-1955. Vice-president, First Union National Bank, since 1974; Richmond County commissioner, since 1962; president, North Carolina Association of County Commissioners, 1972-1973, and of the National Association of Counties, 1981-1982. J. Richard Conder to Jan-Michael Poff, November 1, 1983.

[3] See "Statement on Clean Water Bond Referendum," May 7, 1982, below.

[4] J. Paul Essex, Jr. (1936-   ), native of Newark, New Jersey; resident of Raleigh; B.S., North Carolina State University, 1959; U.S. Army, 1959-1962. Chief copy editor, News and Observer Publishing Co., 1962-1971; communications director, Jim Hunt for Lieutenant Governor campaign, 1972; administrative assistant, Office of the Lieutenant Governor, 1972-1976; appointed special assistant to the governor for intergovernmental relations, 1977. J. Paul Essex, Jr., to Jan-Michael Poff, October 6, 1983.

NORTH CAROLINA COUNCIL ON
ECONOMIC EDUCATION

GREENSBORO, NOVEMBER 30, 1981

As honorary chairman of this council, it is my pleasure to be with you today and to express my appreciation to you. This council is composed of people from all corners of North Carolina's economy, coming together and working together on behalf of economic education for our people.

The importance of economic education was brought home to me again over the past two weeks, while I led an economic-development mission to Japan, Korea, and Taiwan. I was reminded again of how important it is that people have an understanding of our economy and how it works.

This council has done an outstanding job of promoting that understanding. It has worked with the state Department of Public Instruction to strengthen economic education in the schools. Thousands of teachers have been trained in the use of new economic programs as a result, and this council has done the best job of in-service training for teachers of any state in the nation. Our colleges and universities, businesses and foundations, and local community organizations all have been cooperating in this effort.

The council has reached beyond the schools and for the past three years sponsored an annual conference for ministers. These have been highly successful, and I am glad to see that program will be expanded.

Now, I am always bragging on North Carolina, and for good reason. But this is one area—economic education—where I believe we truly do lead the rest of the nation. That is something in which the members of this council can take a great deal of personal pride. I want you to know that you have the strong support of this governor.

The two things at the top of my "to do" list as governor are better jobs and better schools, and the two go hand in hand. I have emphasized making sure that our young people have the skills they need—reading, writing, and math—to be successful in the world. They need to understand how business works, how our total economy works, and most important, that profit isn't a dirty word. They need to understand that profits are what make our nation's standard of living and way of life what it is.

That is why, as lieutenant governor, I supported a bill requiring free enterprise education in our schools. That is why I have established a position for a governor's business liaison with the public schools.

We have seen real progress in our schools. We now have eight regional coordinators in economic education. They have worked with 12,000 teachers and administrators, and their goal is to provide training and materials in economic education to every single elementary schoolteacher and every social studies teacher in the secondary schools. Our university system has seven centers for economic education that help train teachers in this field.

We know this type of education works, because we have tested fifth graders for their knowledge of economics. Those who have had this special economic education score significantly higher than those who have not.

As I said before, my economic-development tour of the Orient made me realize again how important this matter of economic education is. My friends, we live in a competitive world. If the United States is going to remain a world leader, we must regain our economic and technological leadership.

The Japanese understand this. They make sure their young people learn what business is all about and why it is important. We have to ask ourselves whether we are doing well enough to stay competitive with them.

Our people need to understand what it takes to get the economy moving. It isn't just something that happens in Washington—it happens in Raleigh and in our own communities.

Economic growth doesn't come free. You have to do certain things to make it happen. We can't have good growth, for example, without adequate water and sewer facilities, and our people need to understand that. They need to know why we think we need to pass a $300 million water and sewer bond issue.

We can't have good growth without good roads, and our people need to understand that.

They need to understand that good growth means good public investments—in water and sewer, in roads, in job training.

They need to understand that good growth means good incentives for business—in tax and regulatory policies, for example.

This council has done an outstanding job of promoting that understanding, but let us not deceive ourselves: We still have a long way to go. Our nation cannot afford to be economically illiterate. We cannot afford simpleminded or uninformed approaches to economic issues. Our people face critical economic decisions in the years to come. We must rebuild our economic strength and regain our international leadership.

We cannot build a better economic future on a foundation of ignorance and lack of understanding. The job begins in our schools, with our children. You have started that job. I congratulate you, I wish you the best in the years to come, and I promise to give you my full support in that effort.

NORTH CAROLINA WHITE HOUSE CONFERENCE ON CHILDREN AND YOUTH

RALEIGH, DECEMBER 2, 1981

[Hunt made remarks similar to those presented below at the Frank Porter Graham Child Development Center, October 10, and before the Governor's Round Table on Children and Youth, December 2, 1981. On the latter occasion he announced his intention "to establish a special award for the chamber of commerce or company that has made the most significant contribution to improving the lives of children in 1981."]

This is a very significant day for the children of North Carolina.

Every ten years, since 1909, it has been traditional for the White House to convene a conference in Washington to discuss the problems and needs of children and young people. There will be no conference in Washington this year. Instead, the federal Department of Health and Human Services has made funds available for this and similar state meetings across the country.

That is perhaps illustrative of the changing nature of the federal system—of the diminishing role of the federal government in a wide range of programs, and the transfer of responsibility to state government, local government, and the private sector. This fundamental shift of responsibility comes at a time when state and local revenues are tight, when sources of new revenues are shrinking. I honestly don't know how other states are going to respond to this dilemma, but I can tell you this: North Carolina cannot, must not, will not turn its back on its children.

The challenge is great. In order to meet the needs of children and youth in the next decade and beyond, we will have to be imaginative, innovative, courageous. We will need the involvement of the private sector as never before.

But if we throw up our hands in despair in the face of federal cutbacks, we will have jeopardized the tremendous progress we have made, and we will have betrayed future generations. Let us consider for a moment how the lives of children and their families have been improved in North Carolina in recent years:

—The child poverty rate declined between 1970 and 1980, and median family income increased.

—We have attracted to North Carolina billions of dollars in new industrial investment, and hundreds of thousands of new jobs. And what better thing can you do for a child than give a mother and father an opportunity for a better job?

—We have reduced the number of children inappropriately placed in foster care by placing many of them with relatives or loving adoptive families. In fact, we have 20 percent fewer children subsidized by the state in foster care than we did in 1977.

—We have reduced the infant mortality rate—from 24 deaths per thousand live births in 1977 to 14.4 per thousand in 1980. We have a new state program for tracking high-risk newborns. We do a better job of neonatal care, and we have nutritional programs for pregnant women and newborn babies.

—We have a law, passed by the General Assembly this year, which guarantees prenatal care and hospital delivery for every poor woman in her first pregnancy.[1]

—We have high immunization rates, more handicapped children enjoying educational opportunities, more day-care services for working parents.

But I think the most dramatic accomplishments have come in the field of public education. Between 1970 and 1980 we have seen a 56 percent increase in the number of high school graduates. And last year, for the first time ever, our students performed at or above the national average in every subject area and at every grade level tested.

All right, that's the good news. Those are some examples of how far we've come. Now let's think a little bit about how far we have to go:

—Can we be satisfied as long as some children still grow up in poverty?

—Can we be satisfied as long as some children are institutionalized and without a family?

—Can we be satisfied with an infant mortality rate that is still too high? As long as it is still not safe for some babies to be born in North Carolina?

—Can we be satisfied as long as some children are on the streets, addicted to drugs, and headed for a life of crime and incarceration?

—Can we be satisfied when one of every three students who enter the ninth grade drops out before graduating, landing a menial job if they're lucky and becoming a part of the prison population if they're not?

No, ladies and gentlemen, we cannot be satisfied as long as a single child is poor, or sick, or underfed, or uneducated, or emotionally disturbed, or unloved.

The challenge is mind boggling, some would say insurmountable. Federal funds to attack the very problems I have enumerated have been cut back. State and local government cannot begin to compensate for the loss in terms of dollars spent. Nor can the private sector do it alone. Nor can citizen volunteers do it alone.

So what do we do? Wave around the crying towel? Talk about what a shame it is and go on about our business? No.

What we must do—indeed what God put us on this earth to do— is roll up our sleeves, forge a partnership among government, the private sector, and caring individuals. That's what we're here for today, to build that partnership and never let it dissolve.

As chief executive of my state, I know that government at this level can be imaginative. I know we can be innovative. I know we can tap the genius of our people. I know we don't have to be reactionary. I know that we can be a laboratory of democracy and that we can show Washington a thing or two. One of the things we will do is make a better life for our children and their families.

You must take that message to your local communities and apply it there. You must involve local business firms. You must organize local volunteer groups to, just as one example, match up every youngster headed for a life of crime with a caring, loving adult partner.

North Carolina's future depends on its commitment to its children. It is impossible to forge a healthy society if you don't raise up healthy children. If a society is to flourish intellectually, its children must be educated. If it is to flourish economically, it must invest in its young people.

A poet once wrote that "the child is the father of the man." [2] That simply means that our children are our future.

I see this conference as a turning point for our children and our future. I charge you to immerse yourselves in all of these problems and to begin talking about some solutions. Don't be intellectually confined by the traditional ways of doing things, because a new day is dawning. Have the guts to hash out new and different ideas.

You are a wonderful, dedicated group of people. That's why you're here today. On behalf of the people of North Carolina, and on behalf of the children of North Carolina, I thank you from the bottom of my heart for your determination to help get this job done.

---

[1] "An Act to Provide Funds for Prenatal Care for Eligible Pregnant Women" was ratified October 10. *N.C. Session Laws, 1981*, c. 1101.

[2] "The Child is the father of the Man" appears in William Wordsworth, *My Heart Leaps Up When I Behold* [1802]; see Bartlett, *Familiar Quotations*, 511.

REPORT ON TRADE AND INDUSTRY MISSION TO JAPAN, KOREA, AND TAIWAN

Raleigh, December 3, 1981

[Hunt also reported on his Far Eastern trade mission of November 15-25, 1981, at a December 3 news conference.]

This year, after our second economic-development mission to the Far East, North Carolina is firmly established as a real partner in the Pacific business community. We have solidified relationships begun on that earlier mission in 1979; we have reacquainted ourselves personally with government and business leaders; we have boosted the economic momentum that began with our successful mission to Japan and the People's Republic of China.

Japanese companies now have about $6 billion in plant investments in the United States—a $2 billion increase since 1979—that is estimated to rise to $20 billion in the next four years. North Carolina has made itself a leading contender for those jobs and investments.

Today North Carolina has twenty Japanese firms doing business in the state. Eight of them are manufacturers. Japanese firms are very actively, albeit cautiously, investigating the southeast United States for new plant locations. They are coming to view us, with plenty of land, productive workers, a good business climate, and the lowest construction costs in the U.S., as a vital part of their future.

The Japanese know that last year North Carolina was number one in the nation in the number of foreign investments announced. The fact that Ajinomoto, one of Japan's largest and most respected corporations, has located a $37 million plant in Raleigh is well known throughout the corporate boardrooms of Japan.

Japanese firms already located here are beginning to carry the word back home about their productive and profitable experiences here in North Carolina. At nearly every one of the ten corporations and five shipping companies we personally visited, corporate executives had already heard about our state. We were very cordially received in every case, and while it is too soon now to talk in concrete terms about plant announcements, I am certain that our visits will pay off in more jobs in the coming years. We believe at least one large Japanese plant may announce its plans to locate in North Carolina in the coming weeks. Two other companies, a seafood-processing plant and a poultry-processing plant, are looking very favorably at North Carolina and are doing further market research.

Japan continues to be North Carolina's single largest foreign buyer of flue-cured tobacco, and this week a Japanese tobacco container ship representing five shipping lines called for the first time at the port of Wilmington.

Since my earlier trip, we have established a North Carolina economic-development office in Tokyo and the first state-funded Japan Center in the U.S., located at North Carolina State University, to foster cultural understanding and communication. The center made videotapes narrated in Japanese about life in North Carolina and distributed them to a number of corporations on this trip. Center fellows are now studying in Japan and will return soon to share what they have learned.

The Japanese are coming to know North Carolina better and to agree that it is a good place to do business. They were impressed that we brought a team of our top leaders, including Lieutenant Governor James C. Green, Secretary of Natural Resources and

Community Development Joe Grimsley, Cultural Resources secretary Sara Hodgkins, and our ports director, Admiral Bill Greene.[1] We were accompanied by about twenty North Carolina business leaders who had the opportunity to learn firsthand about the Japanese way of doing business.

In South Korea we were assured by President Chun[2] himself that his country, which bought no U.S. tobacco this year, will resume purchases of North Carolina tobacco. In Taiwan we were told that purchases of our tobacco would be increased in the future. (Purchases are up this year 30 percent over last year, which was a poor crop year.)

In Taiwan we also discussed ways for North Carolina businesses to expand their exports to Taiwan; that country is one of the world's largest importers. There is great potential there for purchase of our other agricultural products, such as soybeans, and for industrial products as well.

In all three countries we made very good contacts on behalf of our ports, and I believe our ports' business will increase significantly as a result.

It is clear to me and also, I believe, to the leaders of the other southeastern states who are competing with us for new investment that a state's economic success depends, in great part, on success in the world market. No longer is it sufficient to look within the borders of the United States and our traditional trading partners in Europe for economic opportunity. Across the Pacific is a wealth of investment capital, technological research and development, and managerial expertise that we can tap. The states can work with other countries in economic partnership in a way that the federal government is unable to do. And in the process of building brighter economic futures for our citizens, the states can also help to strengthen in a more personal way the ties of democracy, free enterprise, and mutual understanding that enhance our relationships with other countries.

In this report to the people of North Carolina I want to share what we have learned about Japan, South Korea, and Taiwan and what it means to our future. I hope more North Carolinians will take an opportunity to learn more about these countries, with whom we share so many interests.

JAPAN

Economic Prospects

—We are very hopeful that one of Japan's largest manufacturers of pharmaceuticals will announce a multi-million-dollar location in North Carolina in the coming weeks. Officials told us they had an option to purchase land and were finalizing their study of the permitting process.

—A seafood-processing plant is interested in Wanchese Harbor as a location for a facility that would use mainly croakers bought from North Carolina fishermen. That company has recently located a plant in California.

—A poultry-processing company, a joint venture between two large companies, has decided that piedmont North Carolina is the best place for their new plant, if further market studies and economic conditions prove favorable.

—We visited a company that manufactures automobile parts for Nissan (Datsun). Nissan recently located an automobile manufacturing plant in Tennessee.

—We called on Japan's largest consumer electronics corporation, which is considering locating a plant in the United States, and made our first call on another large electrical firm.

—We called on the Toyoda company, which is the parent company of Toyota. Toyoda now has a sales and service office in Charlotte for its automatic textile loom business.

—A company that has developed new processes for strengthening structural steel requested a meeting with us. The company has been involved in many of Japan's major highway and office building construction projects.

—We were luncheon hosts for a plastic injection molding firm that has been looking at piedmont North Carolina locations for its new plant.

—We were hosts for a dinner in Osaka for all North Carolina businesses in that area. One company that manufactures electrical machinery indicated interest at the dinner in a location in North Carolina this coming year.

Our delegation hosted a breakfast for about thirty-five officials of Japanese steamship lines and officials of Japan Tobacco and Salt, the government tobacco monopoly. I personally visited the executives of all five steamship companies at their home offices and told them of our improvements at the ports of Wilmington and Morehead. Those companies included Japan Line, K-Line, Mitsui O.S.K. Line, N.Y.K. Line, and Y.S. Line. This year over 112,000 hogsheads of tobacco are expected to be exported through North Carolina's ports to Japan, a 20 percent increase from last year. I told the shipping companies that North Carolina would do everything possible to assure that they have the type of service they need at our ports.

Our delegation attended the two-day meeting of the Southeast U.S.-Japan Association in Tokyo, where we talked with dozens of business and government leaders. We told them of our new Microelectronics Center and of our recently announced Biotechnology Center.

General Observations

The single most outstanding characteristic of the Japanese corporation is its close cooperation with government. The relationship is amicable and cooperative, not adversarial. It is the rule, rather than the exception, that government and business leaders attend meetings and social functions together to share common knowledge and interests.

The second characteristic that distinguishes Japanese companies is their "family" relationship with their workers. Companies provide lifetime employment to their employees and provide services and benefits, including health care, recreation, and educational opportunities. In return, workers are generally expected to stay with one company. As a result, younger workers generally must wait longer to rise through the ranks to higher positions, and the age of the average executive is higher than it is in America. Unemployment in that country of 117 million is only about 1.2 million, but the increasing number of older citizens is putting pressure on both the government social service system and on businesses to adapt to the economic needs of the elderly, especially those able to work.

The Japanese management style is different from the American, in that decision making about such things as quality control and production levels is a team effort involving workers from all segments of the factory. As a result, a design engineer is likely to have a closer working relationship with a line worker than might be the case in an American plant. Some American companies are beginning to adapt versions of this management style, such as Westinghouse in Raleigh, which is using the "quality circle."

Japanese companies are very cautious about beginning new ventures and conduct meticulous studies before deciding on new plant locations. One company that we feel will decide to locate in North Carolina first became interested in our state at the Osaka Chamber of Commerce meeting two years ago. They are very close to making a decision and, in Japanese terms, have reached that stage in a very short time.

Once a company does decide to locate a new plant, it will likely be a fairly small operation, until the managers are satisfied with its progress. Quality is far more important to the Japanese than quantity of output. Japanese productivity in recent years has increased at a rate of about 4 percent a year.

SOUTH KOREA

Economic Prospects

Korean President Chun Doo Hwan told me himself that his country would resume its purchases of our tobacco. Korea bought

$32 million worth of North Carolina leaf in 1980 but has made no purchases in 1981.

In separate meetings I discussed tobacco purchases with President Chun, Foreign Minister S. M. Lho, and Tobacco Monopoly administrator Kim Hung Ki, and I also urged them to ship any future purchases through our North Carolina ports, instead of through Baltimore, where Korean ships customarily call.[3]

Korea is struggling to make a comeback now, following a deep recession last year, and economic prospects in that country should be brighter in the months and years ahead. Except for last year, economic growth in recent years has been about 10 percent a year.

General Observations

Korea is still very much a rural country and is working to build up its economic infrastructure. Small-scale machinery is being used in the rice fields, but farming is still a family affair. In the rural areas a government-sponsored movement called the *Saemaul Indong*, which means "new village," is bringing clean water, sanitation, and wider roads and bridges to the rural area. The *Saemaul* movement is a self-help, cooperative type of program incorporating many of the features of the American 4-H and adult community development programs. The *Saemaul* movement is also featured in factories in the cities and encourages such things as energy conservation, good health care, and physical exercise. We were briefed on the *Saemaul* movement by Chun Kyung Hwan,[4] brother to the president and secretary-general of the *Saemaul Indong*.

There is a great deal of housing construction going on, but the cities are very crowded and housing is scarce and expensive.

We toured the Demilitarized Zone and the Panmunjom Peace Village, about an hour's drive north of Seoul, and were very impressed by the fitness of South Korea's troops. Their memories of the Communist incursions thirty years ago are still very strong, and the road to Seoul is fortified with tank walls and iron gates.

Korean officials were very interested in our rural health clinic program and our scientific research going on at the Research Triangle. Korea is building a "Science City" near Taejon, patterned after RTI. I invited President Chun to send people to study both programs in North Carolina.

We concluded our visit to South Korea with lunch and a visit with the speaker and key leaders of their national Congress.

TAIWAN

Economic Prospects

The Taiwan Tobacco and Wine Monopoly told us that they would increase their purchases of our tobacco. Yueh-ai Wu, director of the monopoly, told us, "We have confidence in our expanding business, so the purchase of your tobacco will increase in the future."[5] Wu said tests of a new American-style cigarette in Taiwan have been successful. About 65 percent of the American tobacco purchased by Taiwan is from North Carolina. Monopoly officials also indicated they would continue to use North Carolina ports to ship their purchases.

Monopoly officials did indicate some concern about "nesting"— that is, the practice of hiding poor quality tobacco in a pile of higher-quality tobacco when it is sold at the warehouse. I thanked them for their frankness and told them I would take that matter up with the Flue-Cured Tobacco Stabilization Corporation, the Farm Bureau, and other state agriculture leaders.[6]

We also met with H. K. Shao,[7] director general of the Taiwan Board of Foreign Trade, and discussed ways for North Carolina companies to expand their exports to Taiwan. Taiwan is one of the world's largest importers, and last year bought $4 billion worth of goods from the U.S., including machinery, electrical equipment, farm products, and transportation equipment. We invited their trade and purchasing mission for next year to visit our state. They indicated that they would.

I would encourage all North Carolina businesses interested in the export trade to contact our Export Office in the Department of Commerce. Individual salesmanship is the only way we can significantly increase our exports to Taiwan.

I also met with the chairman of the board of Yang Ming Marine Transport Corporation, which provides shipping service to North Carolina's ports. Last week there were over 700 containers at the port of Wilmington awaiting shipment to Taiwan, and about 500 of them were filled with tobacco.

While we were there we also met with Edward K. Yung,[8] vice-minister of foreign affairs, who hosted a luncheon for our delegation and local business leaders.

General Observations

Taiwan, like so many other countries, including the U.S., is looking for new markets and trying to improve its balance of trade with Japan. Taiwan's economy is bustling, and the country is undertaking an energy expansion program during this decade that will require the purchase of millions of dollars in goods. Like Korea, Taiwan feels the presence of Communist China just 100 miles away and is concerned about the effects of possible unification with the mainland on its free enterprise economy.

---

[1]Joseph Wayne Grimsley (1936-   ), natural resources and community development secretary, 1981-1983. Previously identified in Mitchell, *Addresses of Hunt*, I,

73n; see also *North Carolina Manual, 1983,* 715, and "News Release from the Governor's Office," December 7, 1983.

William M. A. Greene (1920-   ), native of Linville; resident of Morehead City; attended Brevard College, Naval War College, and Industrial College of the Armed Forces; B.A., East Carolina Teachers' College (now East Carolina University); M.A., George Washington University; U.S. Navy, 1943-1973. Retired rear admiral; marine industrial wholesale company general manager, 1974-1977; executive director, North Carolina State Ports Authority, since 1977. William M. A. Greene to Jan-Michael Poff, December 14, 1983.

[2]Chun Doo Hwan (1931-   ), native of Hapch'on, Kyongsangnam-do Province, Korea; entered Korean Military Academy, 1951. Former commanding general, Defense Security Command; president, Republic of Korea, since 1980. Park Johng Seh, attaché, Korean Information Office, Embassy of Korea, to Jan-Michael Poff, November 29, 1984, hereinafter cited as Park correspondence.

[3]Lho Shin Yong (1930-   ), received law degree from Seoul University, 1955. Director, Planning and Management Office, 1967, vice-minister, 1974, and minister, 1980, Ministry of Foreign Affairs, Republic of Korea; consulate general in Los Angeles, 1969-1972, and New Delhi, 1972; ambassador to India, 1973, and Geneva, 1976; director, Agency for National Security, since 1982. Park correspondence.

Kim Hung Ki (1932-   ), was graduated from Seoul National University, 1957. Counselor for economics, Embassy of Korea, Washington, D.C., 1973; director, Investment Promotion Bureau, 1976, Foreign Capitals Management Bureau, 1977, and of the Office of Statistics, 1979, and vice-minister, since 1983, of Korea's Economic Planning Board; assistant minister for management, Ministry of National Defense, 1980; administrator, Tobacco and Ginseng Monopoly Administration, 1981; vice-minister, Ministry of Finance, 1982. Park correspondence.

[4]Chun Kyung Hwan (1942-   ), resident of Seoul; was graduated from army adjutant school, 1964, and Yeung Nam University College of Commerce, 1966; retired lieutenant colonel, Army of the Republic of Korea, 1968. Director, Korea Amateur Sports Assn., since 1980; secretary general, *Saemaul Indong,* since 1981; member, Seoul Asian Games Organizing Committee, since 1982; chief director, Korea Leader Rearing Scholarship Foundation, since 1983. Park correspondence.

[5]Wu Yueh-ai (1930?-   ), educated at Taiwan Provincial Junior College of Police Administration. Chief, Chiayi and Nantou County Government Financial Section; director, Pingtung, Taichung, and Kaohsiung county tax offices; deputy director, Taiwan Provincial Government Tax Bureau; director, Koahsiung Municipal Government Tax Bureau; director, Taiwan Tobacco and Wine Monopoly Bureau, since 1980. Sharon E. Denitto, General Affairs Section, Taipei Office, American Institute in Taiwan, to Jan-Michael Poff, December 28, 1984, hereinafter cited as Denitto correspondence.

[6]See "North Carolina Farm Bureau," Raleigh, December 7, 1981, below.

[7]Shao Hsioh-kwen (1917-   ), native of Chekiang, China; resident of Taipei; B.A., Nanking University. Branch chief, Chinese National Relief and Rehabilitation Administration, 1946-1948; senior specialist and deputy director, Supply Division, CUSA, 1949-1962; director, Program and General Administration divisions, CIECD, 1963-1965; economic counselor, Republic of China embassy, Vietnam, 1966-1968; deputy director general, 1968-1977, and director general, 1977-1981, Taiwan Board of Foreign Trade; administrative vice-minister of foreign affairs, Taiwan, since 1981. Denitto correspondence.

[8]Kuan Yung [Edward] (1925-   ), native of Tsingtao City, China; B.A., Fujen University; post-graduate studies, University of Houston. Vice-consul, Republic of China consulate in Houston, 1952-1956, and Vancouver, 1956-1960; consul in Vancouver, 1960-1961; section chief, Department of American Affairs, 1961-1965, deputy director, 1965-1967, and director, 1972-1976, North American Affairs department, Ministry of Foreign Affairs; adviser to Chinese United Nations delegation, 1965-1971; ambassador to Lesotho, 1967-1972, and to South Africa, 1976-1979; administrative vice-minister of foreign affairs, 1976, and since 1979. Denitto correspondence.

NORTH CAROLINA FARM BUREAU

Raleigh, December 7, 1981

Today we are witnessing one of the great ironies of history.

In 1981 the farmers of North Carolina and the United States have produced the most abundant supplies of food and fiber that any nation has ever known. We've enjoyed a good growing season, and farmers have made the most of it. It has been one of those rare years with no major crop failures or shortages in the entire country.

Production this year included more than 2 billion bushels of wheat, more than 2 billion bushels of soybeans, more than 8 billion bushels of corn, and more than 15 million bales of cotton. We have adequate supplies of tobacco for domestic and export needs and abundant supplies of pork, beef, milk, eggs, chicken, turkey, fruits, vegetables, and just about anything else you can name.

Our farmers are highly efficient and highly productive. Not only do they provide well for 220 million consumers in this country, they also export the output from two of every five acres of U.S. cropland. American agricultural exports currently are running at about $45 billion a year—an unprecedented achievement.

That's the good news.

The irony is that American farmers are having a difficult time. Their expenses this year—high interest rates and all the rest—have been enormously high. The very abundance they have produced has depressed prices in the marketplace.

It is one of the great ironies of history that our farm people, who have done such a good job, are being rewarded so meagerly. Farmers have prepared the feast, but in return they are getting only crumbs from the banquet table.

In Washington over the past several months, as you know, Congress has been involved in drafting new legislation for farm programs which expire this year. The task has not been easy, especially in view of the budgetary restraints imposed at the urging of the Reagan administration. Even this late in the year we still don't know exactly what the new Farm Bill of 1981 will contain. I am afraid, however, that the provisions of this legislation will in many instances be woefully inadequate to give our farmers even minimum levels of price protection in these difficult and uncertain times.

Over the past few months there has been a strong effort to destroy the peanut program and the tobacco program. Even now the future of the peanut program is uncertain. About the only sure thing about it is that the level of price support, if any, will be inadequate.

As for the tobacco program, it has been saved—but only for the time being. Opponents have served notice that they expect changes to be made. Some features of the tobacco program are objectionable to some members of Congress who would like to be able to vote for it. If there are things in the program that are unfair, or things that are fiscally unsound, we must seek to modify or eliminate them. Perhaps we need to seek ways to deescalate the controversy. Perhaps we should look for points on which we are willing to be flexible. As long as we retain the basic structure of the program— grower control of supply through an allotment and quota system in return for price support—it may be possible for us to accept modifications of some less important features.

We risk a great deal when we allow debate over the program to be cast in all-or-nothing terms. If we should lose such a debate, the consequences would be disastrous. Public hearings by Congress or USDA officials are likely to be called in early 1982 regarding means to strengthen tobacco programs.[1] As Congressman Charlie Rose[2] has indicated, input is especially needed on two questions:

—How can we operate the tobacco program without undue budget exposure?

—How can we ease tensions about the holding of allotments by nonfarming corporations and nonproducing individuals?

Let everyone understand clearly, however, that we cannot compromise, we will not compromise, on the guts of this program. We firmly believe that the only sound way to run a tobacco program is to permit growers, by their approval of quotas every three years, to maintain control of supply at a reasonable level in relation to demand. Supply control is basic, and this part of the program is nonnegotiable.

There are many thoughtful people in North Carolina who have good ideas to address such questions as how to operate the tobacco programs without undue budget exposure and how to ease tensions about nongrowers holding allotments. It is time now that public discussions be opened to deal with the future of an industry so vital to North Carolina.

For example, rapid growth areas of the state will face serious water shortages by the year 2000. Agriculture will be affected by our limited water resources in the future. Modern irrigation systems, as you well know, require enormous quantities of water.

We are losing 36,000 acres of prime North Carolina farmland each year to residential, commercial, and industrial development. If trends continue, by the year 2000 we will lose nearly 700,000 acres of prime farmland to development. On December 17 at the McKimmon Center here in Raleigh, I am holding a conference on the retention of prime farmland, and I sincerely hope this conference will come up with some ideas for addressing this problem.[3]

An even more serious threat to the future of agriculture is the loss of topsoil from 54,739 acres of good farming land each year as a result of erosion. We must come up with better land-management practices.

Working together, we can come up with the answers to many of our problems. We need the support of strong, viable, growing organizations like the North Carolina Farm Bureau.

As you perhaps know, recently I was in Asia, not only to seek new industry for North Carolina but also to promote the sale of North Carolina tobacco and other farm products. Unfortunately, there were some embarrassing moments. For example, officials of the Tobacco and Wine Monopoly in Taiwan complained to me that they had found nested tobacco in some of their North Carolina purchases. This practice, of course, is illegal. Only a very small portion of our tobacco is nested, but that small portion hurts the quality reputation of all North Carolina tobacco.

We must put a stop to the practice of nesting. There has been some talk about the Farm Bureau organizing a committee on each market to deal with the nesting problem locally. You might want to consider this idea further. We must not only come to grips with the nesting problem but go far beyond that and do everything possible to produce quality, sell quality, and promote the image of our tobacco as the very highest quality leaf in the entire world. Our future as tobacco growers and exporters depends on quality.

To you, the members of the North Carolina Farm Bureau and to your leaders, I extend a heartfelt "thank you" for your efforts and your support in trying to develop a better North Carolina for all of us. May each of you, and your families, be blessed richly at this holiday season.

---

[1] See "Testimony before Joint House-Senate Flue-Cured Tobacco Hearing," February 12, 1982, below.

[2] Charles Grandison (Charlie) Rose III (1939-   ), U.S. representative from North Carolina's Seventh Congressional District since 1973; chairman, Tobacco and Peanuts Subcommittee of the House Agricultural Committee. Previously identified in Mitchell, *Addresses of Hunt*, I, 375n; see also *North Carolina Manual, 1983*, 175.

[3] See "Governor's Conference on Retention of Prime and Important Farm and Forest Land," December 17, 1981, below.

GOVERNOR'S WASTE MANAGEMENT BOARD

RALEIGH, DECEMBER 9, 1981

[This address is comparable to one delivered before the Governor's Task Force on Waste Management, February 18, 1981.]

In the years I have served as governor, I have addressed scores of boards and commissions, charging them with widely varying responsibilities. All of them, in their own way, are important. But there is no way I can overstate to you the importance I place on the Governor's Waste Management Board.

The work you do in the coming months and years is going to determine in large measure whether North Carolina continues to develop economically, whether we are able to provide more good jobs for our people, and whether we protect our water, land, and air. Specifically, it will be your responsibility to plan and oversee the safe management of hazardous and low-level radioactive wastes generated within the borders of this state. That is your responsibility by law, and it is your responsibility to the people of North Carolina.

As you know, you have been given a hard job. On the one hand, we must continue to attract new, high-paying industry to North Carolina, the kinds of industries that provide our people with good jobs and produce the things we need. We must make it possible for those industries to safely dispose of the wastes that are a by-product of economic progress. At the same time, we must protect the health and safety of our people. We must protect our air, land, and water. Those two goals are not inconsistent, and they are of equal importance. If we do this job right, we can have economic progress while protecting the quality of our environment.

Please remember that you are not in this alone. The Waste Management Act of 1981, which created this board, assumes that you will bring together the leadership of the private sector, state and local government, and concerned interest groups.[1] As you formulate policies for waste management in North Carolina, all the genius we can muster will be at your disposal.

You will be called upon from time to time to balance competing interests and differences of opinion. But just about everybody agrees that we cannot ignore the problem of hazardous wastes and that we can no longer depend upon other states to take care of these wastes for us. That is our job now. For example, when a waste management facility is proposed for North Carolina, you must ensure that lines of communication are kept open. You must serve as the link between agencies of government, the private sector, and the public. You must ensure that correct information gets to the people involved. If that is done, a decision on a site and permit will be based on the right information, not on the fear and hysteria that results from misinformation.

I want you to place particular importance on exploring alternatives to land disposal of industrial wastes, to look to new technologies that will make it possible to reduce and treat wastes at the point of generation. I want you to study the possibilities of surface storage of wastes until new technologies are developed. Your job is not being made any easier by federal cuts that will slice deeply into programs that have served as safeguards to the environment. But we can't let what happens in Washington adversely affect our environment, our quality of life, or our economic progress. I'm counting on you to develop a plan that will meet our needs in these areas today and assure a clean, safe, and prosperous state for future generations of North Carolinians.

Each and every one of you has my profound gratitude for your willingness to take on this challenge, your willingness to contribute your time, your energy, and your intelligence to the people of North Carolina. I am confident that you will take this challenge as seriously as I do and that you will develop a system of waste management that will serve as a model for the nation.

---

[1] "An Act to Provide for the Management of Hazardous and Low-Level Radioactive Waste in North Carolina" was ratified June 26, 1981. *N.C. Session Laws, 1981,* c. 704. This legislation "put North Carolina ahead of any other state in dealing with waste management," Hunt stated on October 28, 1981, after announcing the appointment of Claud (Buck) O'Shields, of Wilmington, as chairman of the Governor's Waste Management Board. Establishment of the board was one of nineteen recommendations tendered in *Report of the Governor's Task Force on Waste Management* ([Raleigh]: State of North Carolina, February, 1981).

GOVERNOR'S CONFERENCE ON RETENTION OF PRIME AND IMPORTANT FARM AND FOREST LAND

RALEIGH, DECEMBER 17, 1981

[The governor's message to the Soil and Water Conservation Board of Supervisors, May 19, 1981, included many of the points mentioned below.]

I want to thank the various sponsoring organizations for holding this conference. This is the first time all of these organizations have gotten together under one roof to discuss the preservation of prime farm and forest land.

The problem we face is not difficult to understand. Simply stated, prime and important farm and forest land is not being conserved.[1] It is rapidly being converted to other uses: commercial and industrial development, transportation, housing, and so on. This issue has long been of concern to my father, who was a soil conservationist. But I think it really hit home to me for the first time about seven years ago, when I stood with my daughter, who was nine years old at the time, and watched construction work on Interstate 95. That road was cutting a swath through our farm. Rachel said to me, "Daddy, is there going to be any farmland left?"

Countless other farmers have stood and watched that scene for so many years, and it will happen again. In fact, if present trends continue, we will lose between 700,000 and a million acres of prime farmland in North Carolina between now and the year 2000. Consider the related problem of soil erosion. Erosion from construction sites, farmland, roadsides, surface mines, and cutover forest land claims 80 million tons of soil a year.

We are a growing, vibrant state. In the last five years alone, we have attracted almost $9 billion in new industrial development and almost 150,000 new jobs. This kind of economic growth should continue. The microelectronics industry alone will put North Carolina on the leading edge of what is fast becoming a new industrial revolution.

Jobs in microelectronics, and in the support industries that grow up around it, will raise our people's standard of living. Economic growth will bring more people to North Carolina from other states. About 5.9 million people live in North Carolina today; if present trends continue, our population will increase by almost 2 million people by the year 2000.

That kind of development puts pressure on farm and forest land. People have to have places to work, places to live, places to spend their leisure time, and roads to get them to where they work and shop. So it boils down to a very basic question: Can we continue to sustain rapid economic growth, can we continue to provide better paying jobs for our people, and at the same time conserve our prime and important farm and forest land that provides us with food, fiber, and energy? I don't see this as an "either/or" proposition.

As we seek economic growth, we must never lose sight of the fact that without the land and what it produces there can be no economic growth. It is the land that makes this country unique and enables it to be the great place that it is. In his book *People of Plenty*, the great historian David Potter theorized that America would never have developed as a democratic society had it not been for the availability of land. It allowed our population to disperse widely and for people to grow and produce what they needed. That resulted in prosperity, and dictatorships don't flourish where there is prosperity.[2]

Potter was right on the mark, in my opinion. The land has fed us, clothed us, given us shelter, and kept us warm. As a result, our families, our schools, our religious and political institutions are by tradition and of necessity tied to the land. If we lose the land, the foundations of our democratic society are uprooted and cannot survive.

For that reason, I am convinced that we must develop a statewide strategy for the preservation of our forests and our farmland. That is going to take a massive cooperative effort involving local and state government, the business and industrial community, and the organizations represented in this room today. This conference is an important step in the right direction. It brings together experts who see the issue from a lot of different angles.

I think state government in particular has to take a leadership role through its example. When government contemplates an action like building a road or a school or seeks to recruit a major new industry, the potential impact on forest and farmland should be taken into account. In the near future I intend to announce some initiatives in this area.

It is our land, as David Potter wrote, that has made us a people of plenty. But if we are not wise stewards of the land, if the continued quest for greater prosperity is not gone about with care, we could one day become a people of poverty. It is the land that has given our well-being as a nation and made it possible for us to inherit the great traditions of those who came before us. Similarly, our land is our future. We must preserve it for coming generations of North Carolinians. I think we can do this job and in doing it set a bold example for America to follow.

---

[1] H.B. 1066, "A Bill to be Entitled an Act to Encourage the Preservation of Prime and Locally Important Agricultural and Forestry Lands," was introduced May 20, 1981, and died after referral to the House Committee on Agriculture. *N.C. House Journal, 1981*, 609.

[2] David Morris Potter, *People of Plenty: Economic Abundance and the American Character* (Chicago: University of Chicago Press, 1954).

David Morris Potter (1910-1971), native of Augusta, Georgia; A.B., Emory University, 1932; M.A., 1933, Ph.D., 1940, Yale University; M.A. Oxford University, 1947; honorary degrees. Historian; faculty member, Yale University, 1942-1961, and at Stanford University, 1961-1971; author; editor. *Who Was Who in America, 1969-1973*, 579.

STATEMENT ON HIGHWAY CONSTRUCTION

RALEIGH, DECEMBER 17, 1981

[The state Board of Transportation announced its revised ten-year highway improvement program on December 18, 1981. The new plan canceled 95 of 279 projects scheduled for completion during the ensuing decade, along with 372 others awaiting placement on the construction agenda; in all, nearly $2 billion in projects were eliminated. Governor Hunt presaged the board's intentions and explained the reasons prompting the cutbacks in his press statement of December 17.]

Tomorrow morning the state Board of Transportation will meet in Raleigh to adopt a new highway construction program. I can safely predict that there will be much anguish and gnashing of teeth when people see what is in—and what is not in—that program.

This will be a new highway plan, based on new realities. The old days of major new road construction are gone and may never return. This is a new day, and it is important that all of us understand why that is and what it means for the future.

For years now highway costs have been rising while the money to pay for them has been drying up. It costs twice as much to build a new road today as it did just four years ago, and gasoline tax revenues are declining as people drive smaller cars. This new plan is a product of that trend. It is also the product of actions taken by the General Assembly this year.

First of all, and most important, North Carolina's highway program is now primarily a *maintenance* program. Almost half of our state highway money will go to keeping up the roads we already have, not building new ones. This is how I promised we would spend our money when I asked the General Assembly for an additional $180 million a year for highways. The legislature responded by appropriating about two thirds of that amount and by promising to provide an additional $20 million this spring.

That will enable us to come close to, but not achieve, what Governor Dan Moore's study commission concluded should be a minimum maintenance program. Under the new program we will be able to resurface 2,900 miles this year, compared to 387 miles last year. But keep in mind that the Moore commission said we should try to resurface 3,600 miles for each of the next five years so we could catch up on the backlog of unmet maintenance needs.

The plan that the board approves tomorrow will severely cut back highway construction in North Carolina. Last year we had $121 million for primary highway construction. This year we will spend less than half of that, about $51.4 million. Even if more state money were available, we could not spend more than that on construction. The legislature this year required the Department of Transportation to stop spending money on primary construction beyond what is required to match federal aid. After this coming year the money from our 1977 highway bond issue will run out. That means we will then have no money whatsoever to match federal aid after July, 1983.

All this means a lot of road projects have had to be cut back, cut out, and put off. Fewer new roads will be built. Those we build will have fewer lanes, with fewer interchanges and more narrow rights-of-way.

This has been a very difficult process for the Board of Transportation. It hasn't been fun being a board member this year. My instructions to the members were to stretch what money we have as far as it can go and to be fair to all parts of our state. I instructed them to use economic development as the main yardstick for measuring road needs. Roads and jobs go hand in hand, and we should build roads to support balanced growth across our state.

Once this new plan has been adopted, I expect you will hear a lot of screaming and hollering around the state. Some people will be unhappy. Some won't see their pet projects in the plan. But the people of North Carolina need to understand that we have carried

through the commitments I made when I called for the Good Roads
Program. We have cut back. The Department of Transportation is
leaner. We will be building fewer roads and buying less land for
them. We will put our emphasis on maintenance.

I believe we will be meeting our state's most essential transportation needs. We will be keeping our roads safe and in good
repair. We will be building roads where jobs are most needed. North
Carolina will remain competitive with other states, which are
having the same highway-funding problems, in the race for jobs
and economic growth.

This has been a yearlong process, beginning with the Moore
commission's completion of its study almost exactly a year ago. We
have pulled in our belts and fit our program to the new budget
realities. I commend the Board of Transportation for completing
this difficult assignment.

ACADEMIA, INDUSTRY AND GOVERNMENT: THE
ORGANIZATIONAL FRONTIER OF SCIENCE TODAY

WASHINGTON, D.C., JANUARY 4, 1982

[This address, presented at the annual meeting of the American Asso-
ciation for the Advancement of Science, is similar to another delivered
February 21, 1981, at the Conference on Technological Innovation for
Economic Prosperity, also held in the nation's capital.]

I. INTRODUCTION

Dr. Berendzen,[1] members and guests of the American Association
for the Advancement of Science: It is a distinct honor and privilege
to appear before you tonight. The 134-year history of this organization is a record of outstanding leadership and achievement. I am
always stimulated, in particular, by the penetrating editorials of
William Carey and Philip Abelson, as they appear in *Science*.[2] I
look forward also to what your president, Allan Bromley,[3] will say
as he speaks of the "other frontiers" of science later this week.

As a governor, I feel very keenly the need to stimulate vigorous
dialogue between scientists and engineers on the one hand and
political and industrial leaders on the other. I believe that we simply
cannot achieve the goals we set for ourselves, in North Carolina and
in this nation, without that dialogue.

Nearly twenty years ago James R. Killian, then chairman of MIT,
addressed a conference of state governors held in Miami. He began
as follows:

Much has been spoken and written in the last decade and a half about science and government, and the discourse has dealt almost exclusively with the *federal* government. . . . At MIT, I occasionally give a graduate seminar on science and public policy, and I must admit that state governments are hardly mentioned, an omission marking similar seminars in other universities and most of the books published on the subject.

Dr. Killian goes on to say that the governors' conference he was addressing was a "start in redressing this neglect" of science in state governments.[4]

Unfortunately, state governors have not made the progress expected twenty years ago—but neither has the federal government nor the private sector. The glaring fact is that, in the United States today, we are not realizing the full creative potential of science and technology. It is upon our failure to do so, and upon the steps we must take to realize this potential, that I concentrate my remarks tonight.

To me the creative potential of science—that is, the potential benefit to society—is achieved through technological innovation. I believe, however, that a serious crisis is now emerging in the United States because we have not mastered the processes of innovation, as have Japan and a few other nations.

II. THE EMERGING INNOVATION CRISIS

Before spelling out the nature and significance of this emerging crisis, let me describe what I mean by technological innovation.

Meaning and Importance of Innovation

I view technological innovation as consisting of two interrelated parts: *technical* and *organizational* innovation.

Technical innovation is developed through use of physics, chemistry, biology, and other natural sciences, plus mathematics and engineering. Such knowledge makes it possible to produce new or better physical or biological products, or produce them more efficiently.

Organizational innovation is accomplished through the use of economics, political science, sociology, and other social and behavioral sciences. The objective is to change the organization and operation of units of society. Organizational innovation can occur on a large scale, such as at the national level. Or it can be on a small scale, such as in an office or an industrial firm.

Now with these concepts in mind, let me call your attention to an observation made by Professor Don Price of Harvard University, as he surveyed the World War II period: "The most significant discovery or development" for science and technology to come from the war effort "was not the technical secrets that were involved in radar or the atomic bomb"; he said, "it was the administrative system and set of operating policies that produced such technological feats." [5]

In other words, the organizational innovations developed on a national scale during and following World War II were as important, if not more important, than the technical innovations of radar and atomic weaponry. But each is dependent upon the other. We cannot reap the benefits of science without both.

I suggest also that proper study of technological innovation, as I have defined it, is as challenging as genetic engineering or cellular biology. Forms of scientific and engineering knowledge, like genetic codes, influence the behavior of components of society; and, like the cellular structures of higher organisms, the interactive behavior of these components gives form and character to society.

The importance of technological innovation arises from the fact that no modern society can function as such today without making effective use of scientific knowledge. Our military strength, as Price has noted, depends upon it. But of greater significance to the emerging crisis today is the dependence of economic productivity upon our ability to innovate, both technically and organizationally. The problem, as I see it, is that we still have essentially the same organizational structure for science and technology that was designed in World War II and the Korean War. Even establishment of the National Science Foundation in the early 1950s was influenced by the war experience, and the burst of federal support for science that followed Sputnik in the late 1950s was inspired more by national security concerns than by the altruistic potential of science for all humanity.

Federal expenditures now dominate all research and development in the U.S.—$42 billion out of a total of $69 billion. Within the federal outlays, defense-related expenditures are by far the most dominant category—$24 billion out of $42 billion. [6] Thus, in several respects, it may be said that science and technology have ridden the coattails of defense and space since World War II.

The unique aspect of military and space research is that provision is made for technological innovation by actually producing and using weapons systems, rockets, tanks, ships, and guns. The Department of Defense and NASA organize to use the results of research in fulfilling these federal objectives. Whereas, for fundamental non-military research, little provision is made for effective utilization of results—the critical fault of our present system.

Evidence of the Emerging Crisis

A very great deal has been accomplished over the last thirty to forty years by our prevailing structure of science and technology. We have won wars. We have more Nobel laureates than any other nation. We have shared our technology through foreign assistance, and for a time we were the marvel of the world with respect to scientific achievement and technological advancement. Now, however, certain deficiencies are becoming apparent. I will list just a few:

1. *Economic productivity.* Output per man-hour in the U.S. has leveled off in recent years; in some it has declined. A recession now prevails, inflation continues, and unemployment is rising. What is more, we are now deliberately seeking to control inflation by slowing down economic growth, rather than by measures designed to increase productivity.

Fundamental research accomplishments no longer percolate through our economy with sufficient rapidity and effectiveness to substantially increase productivity. Japan, for example, drawing heavily upon our own research, is exceeding our ability to transform such fundamental knowledge into useful products with worldwide market potential.

2. *Education.* U.S. education, especially at the elementary and secondary levels, is significantly less rigorous than that of several other nations at the present time. For example, five million students graduate from secondary institutes in the USSR each year having had two years of rigorous instruction in calculus. By comparison, of all our high school graduates each year, little more than 100,000 complete but one year of calculus.[7]

Our work force as a whole is not keeping pace with the needs of a highly technical society. Critical shortages exist, not only of well-trained engineers but of engineering faculty. Shortages are emerging in relation to other areas as well, such as biotechnology. Financial support for universities, the status of scientific equipment and research facilities, and the opportunities for young faculty—all these and other measures of the vitality of our academic institutions are discouraging, as you well know.[8]

3. *Environmental Management.* The latest *New York Times*/CBS News Poll reports that "a large majority of the American public supports continued strong protection of the environment even if it requires economic sacrifice."[9] Clearly, we have the scientific capability to properly manage land, water, and air resources and to minimize the dangers associated with toxic, hazardous, and low-level radioactive waste. But we have not yet devised the organizational means to generate and use such knowledge adequately and effectively.

Views of the American Public

The American public views the present situation much as I have outlined, according to the pollster, Louis Harris.[10] Americans want inflation curbed, government expenditures cut, economic productivity increased, our technological capability greatly enhanced, and America's standing in the world restored. They feel that government performance has been costly and often ineffective, that industry has concentrated upon minor short-run gains at the expense of major long-run breakthroughs, that the scientific capacity of our universities is ten years out of date, and that things should begin to turn around by the end of 1982 if the policies of the Reagan administration and American business are going to prove effective.

Harris concludes that reliance by the Reagan administration upon free market forces will not right the economy, that the private sector may not be up to the task, and that American patience will be stretched to the breaking point within a year. Resolution of the crisis of confidence will not be through reversion to New Deal economics. Instead, a redefinition of the role of government will be essential.

I concur with Harris's conclusion. A redefinition of the role of government is needed *now*, however, and will likely be even more in order in the months ahead.

III. Innovation and the Role of Government

The emerging crisis presents a challenge to our ability to innovate comparable to that which we faced in World War II. The overriding question now, as then, is how to organize our remarkable scientific and engineering capability. Now it should be for peace; then it was for war.

The situation both then and now demonstrates the central importance of science and technology to this or any society. It follows, therefore, that those who devise the organizational means to resolve this emerging crisis—who successfully redefine the role of government in relation to academia, industry, and the general public—will also reap the rewards of economic and political support inherent in the fundamental desires of Americans throughout this country. I fully anticipate that the American Association for the Advancement of Science, as exemplified by this audience, will be in the forefront of these endeavors.

Leadership and Style

In redefining the role of government in relation to research institutions, industry, and the general public, I contend that *the center of gravity for technological innovation must shift from the federal government to state governments*. This will require greater differentiation between the role of the federal government and the roles of state and local governments. The style of government at each level will need to be catalytic, fostering the creative spirit of technological innovation throughout society, and not just down from the top.

The Federal Role

Before outlining the state role, I should note that the federal government must play an important supportive role. Elements of support should include: (1) maintaining a favorable economic environment by controlling inflation and ensuring adequate flows of capital at reasonable interest rates; (2) providing tax and other incentives designed to encourage investment in research and development; (3) strongly supporting basic research relevant to all states; and (4) assisting groups of states in combining together to pursue common research and development interests.

The point to be stressed is this: Measures such as these comprise the role of the federal government in fostering a broad-based program of technological innovation across this country. It is not to "administer" innovation through the same style of federal leadership that is followed in devising a new weapons system or in putting a man on the moon.

The Role of State and Local Governments

Turning now to the state government role, much is spoken these days of a partnership of government, academia, and industry. I believe that such a partnership is essential, and that the best way to organize it is through *state* government leadership.

Remember that, of the 184 research universities of this nation, 119 are public institutions, most of which are supported by state governments. Many of the remaining private institutions receive some form of state support. Virtually all university research is conducted by these 184 institutions, and they exist in every state. State governments are committed to higher education but, for the most part, they have not learned how to foster and utilize in a catalytic fashion the tremendous research capacity of our academic institutions. This must be remedied. Academia is where we train our scientists, engineers, and technicians. It is where scientific exploration takes place that makes technological innovation possible.

Remember also that elementary and secondary educational systems are the responsibility of state and local governments. Science and mathematics instruction at these levels of education needs extensive and striking improvement. Regardless of action by the federal government, *significant* improvements will be achieved only if state and local governments take the lead in doing so.

Remember too that industrial firms, farms, banks, wholesale and retail outlets, transportation systems, and all other forms of economic activity exist and function within state boundaries and relate closely to state and local governments. These units of government are the prime points of contact with respect to locational issues, labor relations, environmental management, provision of capital (both human and material), living conditions for employees, and other facets of economic activity that entail industry-government interaction.

Remember, in addition, that *people* live within state and local government jurisdictions. I include people as an absolutely essential partner in technological innovation because the entire system must work in their interest. We cannot regard people as simply another abstract factor of production called labor—a factor that is used and discarded at will, and for which the system has no overall responsibility. Our children, our youth, our people in their most productive years, and our senior citizens are all indispensable participants. People can relate to state and local governments easier than to a distant federal agency. Therefore, if state and local governments play a more significant role in technological change, that change is likely to be more responsive to the desires of people, particularly if the partnership reaches out to include them.

Examples of State Leadership

To illustrate how a state government can forge the partnership relations of which I speak, let me share some of the experience of North Carolina and a few other states.

First, certain state level organizational arrangements are essential. The North Carolina Board of Science and Technology is the unit that maps much of the strategy by which we are proceeding, building upon the work of our universities and the influence of our Research Triangle Park. As governor, I chair this fifteen-member board; the remaining members are scientists from our public and private research institutions and officials from state and local government.

I also have other groups that advise me and help develop the essential working relationships. One, for example, is a council of business leaders from across North Carolina. Our North Carolina Department of Commerce works closely with this group and other institutions, firms, and individuals within and outside North Carolina. As a consequence, new industrial investment in North Carolina has averaged approximately $2 billion per year for the past five years. Our unemployment rate is running about two percentage points *below* the national rate as the current recession unfolds.

Some twenty states now have organizational arrangements resembling that of North Carolina. Another ten are beginning to initiate such arrangements. The remaining twenty appear to be less active at present but are exploring possibilities.[11]

Next, in North Carolina we are investing in people, particularly young people. In our elementary and secondary schools, we have introduced competency testing, raised teacher pay and improved their training, reduced class size, and taken other measures to improve education in general. Significant improvements in national test scores are one indication that these changes are having an effect.

In addition, we have established the North Carolina School of Science and Mathematics. This is a residential high school for students with very high aptitudes for science and mathematics. The purpose of the school is twofold: (1) to train and inspire those students in residence to become future leaders of science, and (2) through outreach programs, to help upgrade science and mathematics instruction in all elementary and secondary schools of the state.

Now in its second year, 300 students are enrolled. No more than 900 will be in residence when it reaches full capacity, with about 15 percent from out-of-state. I should add that about an equal number of girls and boys are enrolled, that the distribution of students by race is proportionate to that in the state, and that students are drawn from small rural schools as well as from large city schools.

It is too early to gauge effects, but in its first year with 150 students enrolled, this school had the second largest number of National Merit Scholarship finalists of any school in the nation.

My last example consists of our Microelectronics Center and our Biotechnology Center. The Microelectronics Center of North Carolina is designed to enable six of our leading research institutions in North Carolina to have access to very sophisticated microelectronics research equipment on a sustained basis. This will make it possible for these institutions to remain on the frontier of research and education in this field. Such equipment is extremely expensive and becomes obsolete quickly. We established the center in order that these institutions may share this equipment. Otherwise we could not afford to equip each at this level of sophistication.

Further growth of microelectronics firms, and of firms that use microelectronics products, is expected in North Carolina as a consequence of the availability of highly trained engineers and other professionals, plus the advantage of being near vigorous research activity.

Our North Carolina Biotechnology Center is beginning on a relatively small scale but represents a long-run commitment to this field. We recognize that many financial, patent, and other issues must be explored carefully as we develop closer working relations between industry and our research institutions and industry and government. Our intent is for North Carolina to become a national leader in biotechnology research and development. Our key research institutions, working closely with the center and with our Department of Commerce, are planning major developments in research programs, faculty, and facilities in order to achieve this goal.

Other states are beginning to take action in relation to fields of exploration such as microelectronics and biotechnology. California has initiated a program of financial support to research and development in microelectronics. The states of Minnesota and Michigan are taking significant action also. Florida is providing significant funding for biotechnology. There are many more examples. The important point is that the nature and extent of state government activity is increasing steadily.

You may ask whether state governments are able and willing to provide financial support to such activity. Let me assert emphatically that I believe that any legislature will provide strong support for research and development *if* you demonstrate that the state will indeed benefit from the research. I do *not* subscribe to the belief that total support for research and development is fixed, and that if we increase expenditures for technology we take it away from basic research.

I make this assertion in spite of the fact that total appropriations by all fifty states for directed research is now less than $500 million per year. This is little more than one per cent of total current annual research and development expenditures by the federal government.

The North Carolina legislature, however, recently appropriated $24.4 million for our Microelectronics Center. Why? Because the members of the legislature saw the connection between the center and better jobs for our citizens.

Our legislature also is providing nearly $20 million per year for agricultural research and development, four times the federal expenditure for agricultural research in our state. Why? Because members of our legislature know that we cannot increase agricultural production without such research. The dollars we spend on agricultural research result in *increased* production on our farms. Translated into return on investment in research, each such dollar earns between 35 and 70 cents per year in increased productivity, a very good rate of return on investment indeed.[12] Farmers know this and farmers vote. Legislators know that farmers vote.

A broad-based program of technological innovation will be, among other things, that process by which citizens see and feel the benefits of research. If states deliberately ensure that the results of research are used for the benefit of citizens, legislators will provide the support. Citizens will insist that they do so. Congress also will help.

IV. Guiding Principles

I close now with the suggestion that technological innovation be construed as more than an end in itself. The larger purpose of innovation may be expressed as "meeting the needs and desires of people." Determination of needs and desires is a function of the values and beliefs of people, and of political and economic processes.

The emerging crisis I have described is a reflection of such concerns and desires. Government—and particularly state government in partnership with academia, industry, and people—has a clear responsibility in resolving this crisis.

Any partnership, however, runs the danger of becoming a collusive arrangement whereby one or more partners "rip off" other members, or whereby all partners conspire to take unfair advantage of those outside the partnership. Therefore, principles of integrity and purpose must be agreed upon explicitly. Provision for debate, negotiation, and periodic review are essential.

To forge the partnership required, and to establish durable operating principles, each state will likely find it necessary to reach beyond the domain of science and involve those versed in other relevant fields of knowledge and experience.

Let me put this reasoning in philosophic terms: When we forge and implement an important policy decision affecting much of society, we integrate forms of knowledge, factual evidence, values, and beliefs. Good or bad, a policy decision is what it is. But I operate under the assumption that our policy decisions are *better* decisions when we make full and effective use of scientific knowledge; this is why I feel so strongly about the importance of our scientific and engineering community, and why I welcomed the opportunity to meet with you tonight. It is also evident, however, that integrity, purpose, ethical and aesthetic values, and other considerations are essential in policy formation. Alfred North Whitehead stated the matter succinctly in noting that "when you understand all about the sun and all about the atmosphere and all about the rotation of the earth, you may still miss the radiance of the sunset." [13]

A lot has been said and written about what the Reagan administration calls the "New Federalism." Like it or not, the relationship between the federal government and states is undergoing a radical shift, a shift that has far-reaching implications for the advancement of science. This is the organizational frontier of science today. In light of these new realities, it is more important than ever that state governments take a leadership role. Again I say, those of you who, for the benefit of humanity, devise the organizational and technical means by which we master the processes of technological innovation will also reap the rewards of political and economic support inherent in the fundamental desires of the American people.

---

[1]Richard Earl Berendzen (1938-   ), native of Walters, Oklahoma; resident of Washington, D.C.; B.S., Massachusetts Institute of Technology, 1961; M.A., 1967, Ph.D., 1968, Harvard University. Staff scientist, 1959-1962; Boston University faculty member, 1965-1973; astronomy professor, 1971-1973, physics professor, 1974-1976, university provost, 1976-1979, and president, since 1980, American University; author. *Who's Who in America, 1982-1983*, I, 242.

[2]William Daniel Carey (1916-   ), native of New York City; A.B., 1940, M.A., 1941, Columbia University; M.P.A., Harvard University, 1942. Staff member, 1942-1960, and assistant director, 1960-1969, U.S. Bureau of the Budget; vice-president, Arthur D. Little, Inc., 1969-1974; American Association for the Advancement of Science executive officer, publisher of *Science* magazine, since 1975. *Who's Who in America, 1982-1983*, I, 508.

Philip Abelson (1913-   ), native of Tacoma, Washington; resident of Washington, D.C.; B.S., 1933, M.S., 1935, Washington State College (now University); Ph.D., University of California, 1939. Naval Research Laboratory physicist, 1941-1945; biophysics section chairman, Department of Terrestrial Magnetism, 1946-1953, geophysics lab director, 1953-1971, and president, 1971-1978, Carnegie Institute; author; editor, *Science* magazine, since 1972. *Who's Who In America, 1982-1983*, I, 5.

[3]David Allan Bromley (1926-   ), native of Westmeath, Ontario; resident of New Haven, Connecticut; B.Sc., 1948, M.Sc., 1950, Queen's University, Kingston, Ontario; Ph.D., University of Rochester, 1952. Operating engineer, Hydro Electric Power Commission of Ontario, 1947-1948; physics instructor and later assistant professor, University of Rochester, 1952-1955; senior research officer and section head, Atomic Energy Canada, Ltd., 1955-1960; faculty member, since 1960, and physics department chairman, 1970-1977, Yale University; president, American Association for the Advancement of Science, since 1981. *Who's Who in America, 1982-1983*, I, 399.

[4]James R. Killian, Jr. (1904-   ), native of Blacksburg, South Carolina; attended Trinity College (now Duke University), 1921-1923; B.S., Massachusetts Institute of Technology, 1926. Assistant managing editor, 1926-1927, managing editor, 1927-1930, and editor, 1930-1939, *Technology Review*; executive assistant to the president, 1939-1943, executive vice-president, 1943-1945, vice-president, 1945-1948, and president, 1948-1959, Massachusetts Institute of Technology. *Who's Who in America, 1982-1983*, I, 1803.

[5]Don K. Price (1910-   ), native of Middlesboro, Kentucky; resident of Cambridge, Massachusetts; A.B., Vanderbilt University; B.A., Oxford University (Rhodes scholarship, 1932), 1934. Reporter, editor, author; staff member, U.S. Bureau of the Budget, 1945-1946; deputy chairman, Research and Development Board, U.S. Department of Defense, 1952-1953; associate director, 1953-1954, and vice-president, 1954-1958, of the Ford Foundation; professor of government, 1958-1980, and professor emeritus, since 1980, Harvard University; president, American Association for the Advancement of Science, 1967. *Who's Who in America, 1982-1983*, II, 2706. Quotation from Price's testimony of July 7, 1970, as recorded in U.S. Congress, House Committee on Science and Astronautics, *National Science Policy: H. Con. Res. 666*, 91st Cong., 2nd sess., July 7, 8, 21, 22, 23, 28, 29; August 4, 5, 11, 12, 13; September 15, 16, 17, 1970 (Washington: Government Printing Office, 1970), No. 23, 5.

[6]Willis H. Shapley, Albert H. Teich, and Gail J. Breslow, *Research and Development, AAAS Report VI: New Directions for R&D* . . . (Washington, D.C.: American Association for the Advancement of Science, 1981), 17, 87.

[7]Izaak Wirszup to D. D. Aufenkamp and Joseph I. Lipson, December 14, 1979. Parts of this letter-report to the National Science Foundation appeared in Izaak Wirszup, "The Soviet Challenge," and "On Mathematics in the U.S.S.R.: A Conversation with Izaak Wirszup," *Educational Leadership*, 38 (February, 1981), 355, 358-360, 361-363. Izaak Wirszup to Jan-Michael Poff, September 4, 1985.

Izaak Wirszup (1915-   ), native of Wilno, Poland; resident of Chicago, Illinois; Magister of Philosophy in mathematics, University of Wilno, 1939; Ph.D., University of Chicago, 1955. Faculty member, since 1949, and mathematics professor, since 1965, University of Chicago; author; editor; consultant. *Who's Who in America, 1982-1983*, II, 3608.

[8]Willis H. Shapley, Albert H. Teich, Gail J. Breslow, and Charles V. Kidd, *Research and Development: AAAS Report V* . . . *FY 1981: Industry, Universities, State & Local Governments* (Washington, D.C.: American Association for the Advancement of Science, 1980), 88-90.

[9]*New York* (N.Y.) *Times*, October 4, 1981.

[10]Louis Harris, "The Crisis of '82," address presented at the Yale Political Union, Yale University, New Haven, Connecticut, September 10, 1981. Louis Smith Harris (1921-   ), native of New Haven; A.B., University of North Carolina at Chapel Hill, 1942. Public opinion analyst, proprietor of Louis Harris and Associates, Inc., since 1956. Alumni Office of the General Alumni Association (comp. and ed.), *The University of North Carolina at Chapel Hill Alumni Directory* (Chapel Hill: Alumni Office, University of North Carolina, 1975 edition, 1976), 487, hereinafter cited as *UNC Alumni Directory*; *Who's Who in America, 1982-1983*, I, 1414.

[11]See *State Activities to Encourage Technological Innovation: An Update* (Sacramento, Calif.: California Commission on Industrial Innovation, 1982), and its forerunner, *State Activities to Encourage Technological Innovation*, prepared for the National Governors' Association, August, 1981. A record of state progress in fostering technological growth is also maintained by the State Science, Engineering, and Technology Program, National Science Foundation, Washington, D.C.

[12]Robert E. Evenson, Paul E. Waggoner, and Vernon W. Ruttan, "Economic Benefits from Research: An Example from Agriculture," *Science*, 205 (September 14, 1979), 1103.

[13]See Alfred North Whitehead, *Science and the Modern World* (New York: Free Press, 1967), 199. Alfred North Whitehead (1861-1947), native of Ramsgate, England; B.A., 1884, M.A., 1887, D.Sc., 1905, Trinity College, Cambridge University. Faculty member, mathematician, Trinity College, 1885-1911, and at University College and the Imperial College of Science and Technology, University of London, 1911-1924; philosophy professor, 1924-1936, and professor emeritus, 1936-1947, Harvard University; author. *Who Was Who in America, 1943-1950*, 573.

STATEMENT ON STATE AGENCY CUTBACKS

RALEIGH, JANUARY 7, 1982

[Unemployment rates for the United States and North Carolina stood at 8.3 percent and 6.8 percent, respectively, at the end of 1981. As 1982 drew to a close and economic forecasters attempted to predict an end to the recession, 9 percent of the state's labor force was searching for work while, nationwide, with more than 11 million Americans idled, the jobless segment of the population climbed to 10.5 percent—0.4 percent short of the level established in 1941 during the Great Depression. Fifteen percent of the country's inhabitants lived below the poverty level, the worst record in seventeen years. Johnstown, Pennsylvania, with 22.7 percent, and Flint, Michigan, at 22 percent, were the two U.S. metropolitan areas with the highest unemployment rates; Raleigh-Durham, at 4.3 percent, and Stamford, Connecticut, with 4 percent, boasted the two lowest. Midway into 1983, as the national economy moved toward a more complete recovery, North Carolina's jobless rate slipped to 8.6 percent and that of the nation fell to 9.4 percent. "Where Jobs Were Scarcest in 1982," *U.S. News & World Report*, February 28, 1983, 8; "11 Million Jobless, and Worst is Yet to Come," *U.S. News and World Report*, October 18, 1982, 71; "What Recession Did to People's Incomes," *U.S. News & World Report*, August 25, 1983, 8; and "As Jobless Rates Dip in the States," *U.S. News & World Report*, September 26, 1983, 17.]

The nation's economic recession is making itself felt in North Carolina. More people are out of work, and the state revenue picture is very uncertain. No one knows how long this recession will last, or how deep it will be, but we do know that we are in for rough sledding the next few months. As a result, under my constitutional authority as director of the budget, I am taking a series of actions to ensure that we maintain a balanced budget in North Carolina.

I have directed the State Budget Office to reduce quarterly allotments of operating funds for state agencies to 95 percent of the authorized amount. This means that all agencies of state government will have to cut back their spending on such items as equipment and supplies, travel, hiring, printing, maintenance, and repairs.

In addition, we are granting fewer exceptions to the freeze on hiring. We will fill vacancies for only the most essential positions. Travel will be severely restricted, especially travel to meetings, conferences, and conventions. Agencies will be directed to reduce spending on materials and supplies.

An additional action that we are considering is a temporary delay in implementing the new ninth salary step for state employees. We have many outstanding employees who deserve this additional merit raise, and I want them to get it as soon as possible. But we are now looking at the timing of it, along with all of these other steps, to ensure that we have enough funds to balance our budget this year. Action to balance the budget cannot wait until the end of the year. By then, the money is spent. We must use caution and prudence now.

Although we are better off than most states around the country, we have already seen warning signs in our tax collections. While general fund revenues for the first six months of the current fiscal year are very close to our original projections, an analysis of key tax categories seems to indicate a worsening economy. For example, sales tax collections appear headed below our projections for the year, and preliminary figures show an increase of only about 5 percent for the big shopping month of December, well below the annual projection of 8.5 percent. Corporate income tax collections actually declined about 4.5 percent for the first six months from last year. Even though individual income tax collections are up by more than 14 percent for the six-month period, these revenues are principally those that have been withheld by employers. It is quite likely that refunds in the next six months will be considerably higher than they were last year.

Until fairly recently, we had expected an economic upturn early in 1982. Most economists now believe that such an upturn will not occur until this spring or summer at the earliest. North Carolina's unemployment rate now stands at 6.2 percent. That is below the national rate of 7.9 percent, but it represents an increase of joblessness. In fact, unemployment rose in 90 of 100 counties from October to November, and eight counties have double-digit unemployment rates.

These conditions and the probability that they will worsen clearly dictate that we take the series of steps that I have outlined. I will continue to consult with the Council of State and my cabinet on further actions that may be necessary.

STATEMENT ON INDUSTRIAL DEVELOPMENT

RALEIGH, JANUARY 13, 1982

Confronted by the deepest recession to hit this nation in seven years, and the highest interest rates in decades, North Carolina enjoyed remarkable industrial growth during 1981. The figures I am announcing today prove once again that our state, despite a lagging national economy, is one of the premier locations for industrial development and job opportunities.

During 1981, industry announced plans to create more than 32,000 jobs. That's the second highest total since 1966, exceeded only by the 37,000 jobs we announced in 1979. Investment announced by industry during the year was more than $2.1 billion, the third highest in our history. Only the $2.4 billion announced in 1979 and the $2.2 billion announced in 1980 were higher. In the five years since this administration took office, we have announced 155,000 jobs and $9.6 billion of investment in new and expanded industry. That's more jobs than in the previous seven years combined and more investment than in the previous fifteen years combined.

Of vital significance are the types of jobs being created and the type of investment occurring. More than one of every three jobs announced in 1981 fell into the categories of electrical and electronics, machinery, fabricated metal products, and transportation equipment. Those types of companies pay well above the average manufacturing wage in our state.

But it should be pointed out that expansion of traditional industries played a major role in keeping North Carolina moving forward during a time of recession. For example, the textile industry has undertaken a major campaign to modernize and increase productivity, and the industry announced more than $400 million of investment last year. In recent years, no other traditional industry in America has acted more boldly to capture a major share of the world market.

Economic growth is occurring throughout our state. Companies like Penn Elastic; Merck, Sharp and Dohme; Eli Lilly; Reliance Electric; and Wheelabrator-Frye announced new plants in Jamesville, Wilson, Creedmoor, Shelby, and Asheville. Volvo-White Truck

Corporation will locate its headquarters in Greensboro, and the largest division of Kennametal, Inc., moved its headquarters to Raleigh in 1981.

Secretary Faircloth and the Industrial Development staff in the Commerce Department did a magnificent job last year under very difficult conditions. I also want to thank all of the local industrial developers and civic and business leaders who helped attract new industry and encouraged existing industry to expand. They did the job through aggressive recruitment and by keeping their communities good places to live, work, and educate children. The companies themselves are to be commended for making these commitments during uncertain times.

Many companies have worked hard to seek out new business overseas. North Carolina exports are playing an increasingly prominent role in our economy, as illustrated by new tonnage records at our state ports.

Industrial development, with the jobs it provides and the related construction, service, and commercial jobs that result from it, will continue to be a high priority in the remaining years of this administration. It fuels our economy and pays for our public services, and it gives our people the opportunity for better, more prosperous lives. We must also continue to provide the educational opportunities, research facilities, roads, water supplies, and sewage facilities that are required for industrial growth. We must develop our economy in such a way that it does not jeopardize the clean, healthy environment that we enjoy in North Carolina.

STATEMENT ON EMPLOYMENT SECURITY OFFICE CLOSINGS

RALEIGH, JANUARY 28, 1982

[Predicting in September, 1981, that the national unemployment rate for the coming year would average only 7.2 percent, the Reagan administration cut $264 million in job placement service funds from the 1982 federal budget. The reduction threatened to close state employment offices across the country; Hunt warned that forty-eight of them might cease operating in North Carolina unless the measures he described at his January 28 press conference were adopted. However, the national jobless rate climbed to 8.9 percent by February, 1982, and the president, confessing to a miscalculation in his economic forecast of the previous autumn, asked Congress for $2.3 billion in pay and other benefits for the unemployed. The U.S. House and Senate approved, on February 8 and 9, the full amount Reagan requested, thus ensuring that all of the state's Employment Security Commission bureaus would remain open for the remainder of the fiscal year. ESC chairman Glenn Jernigan attributed the re-funding to "a ground swell support" from North Carolina business and government leaders "when the projected office closings were announced." *Charlotte Observer,* February 3, 11, 1982; see also *Congressional Quarterly Almanac, 1982,* 230-231.]

North Carolina's unemployment rate has risen to 6.8 percent, and more people have filed for unemployment insurance than at any time since the 1975 recession. That is why I am deeply concerned that federal budget cutbacks may force the Employment Security Commission [ESC], to close as many as forty-eight of its eighty-five local and branch offices in North Carolina. With the national economy in a recession and people being laid off every day, this is the wrong time to stop helping people find work.

When I learned last week what these federal cuts could mean, I told Glenn Jernigan,[1] our new Employment Security Commission chairman, that it is imperative that we keep open as many offices as possible. He and his staff have developed an emergency, stopgap plan that will delay closing our ESC offices for two months and give us time to work on a permanent solution.

Under this plan, the ESC will draw on money in a special contingency account to keep all offices open through March 31. This will still, however, require laying off 230 ESC employees who have been working to get people jobs. Between now and March 31, we will do two things:

—Try to get local people, particularly in business and industry, to help us get free office space and to contribute financial support to keep these offices open permanently. I have been pleased by the response we have had so far.

—We will also work with our congressional delegation and with other states to determine whether Congress will take action to keep these offices open and to help people find jobs.

The threatened cutbacks result from a continuing resolution passed by Congress in December. That resolution, which expires March 31, cuts the ESC budget for personnel and for office space by 12 percent, retroactive to last October 1. Because the cuts are retroactive, they must be much deeper than 12 percent. The ESC had already absorbed a 17 percent cutback as of October 1. Counting both cuts, the ESC will have lost almost 600 people.

These letters from business and industry leaders in our state demonstrate that the ESC is an indispensable part of our economic development program:[2]

—A Wilson manufacturer writes that his plant "has utilized the Wilson Employment Security Commission office as an exclusive source for applicant referral for production positions since the plant began operation in the spring of 1978."[3]

—The American Legion of North Carolina calls the impact of the cuts "devastating."[4]

—The Ashe County manager says the ESC office there has found jobs for more than 700 people in recent months.[5]
—The Edenton office has placed more than 1,650 people in jobs.[6]
These people and many more like them who are involved in economic development know that it isn't good business to cut back job services at a time when people need jobs.

---

[1] Glenn Reginald Jernigan (1939-   ), native of LaGrange; resident of Fayetteville; A.A., Campbell College, 1959; B.A., East Carolina University, 1961. President, Glenn Jernigan Realty and Investments, Inc.; member, state House, 1971-1975, and Senate, 1975-1981; chairman, State Employment Security Commission, 1981-1985. Glenn R. Jernigan to Jan-Michael Poff, December 18, 1984; *News and Observer*, January 23, 1985.

[2] Copies of the testimonial letters from which Hunt quotes, below, were attached to the press copy of this statement.

[3] George T. Clayton, industrial relations manager, Kerr Glass Manufacturing Corp., to the Honorable James B. Hunt, Jr., January 25, 1982.

[4] E. C. Toppin, department commander, American Legion Department of North Carolina, to the Honorable William H. Hendon [U.S. representative from North Carolina's Eleventh Congressional District], January 22, 1982.

[5] Richard C. Miller, Ashe County manager, to Glenn Jernigan, January 22, 1982.

[6] C. B. Smith, president, Albemarle Area Development Assn., to Hon. Glen [*sic*] Jernigan, January 22, 1982.

STATE BOARD OF ELECTIONS SEMINAR

WINSTON-SALEM, JANUARY 29, 1982

[Hunt signed a proclamation on April 8, designating 1982 as "Citizen Awareness Year" and signifying his approval of the State Board of Elections campaign to register 1.7 million new voters. Addressing the Council of Presidents of Youth Organizations, May 19, 1983, the governor encouraged the leaders of all student groups to begin registering their members to vote and offered the services of the state's Youth Involvement Office to assist in the endeavor. He also solicited support for Senate bills 109 and 157. "An Act to Provide for the Appointment of Special Library Registration Deputies to Register Voters in All Public Libraries," S.B. 109, was ratified June 23. "An Act to Authorize High School Employees Designated by the School Board and Appointed by the County Board of Elections to Register Voters," S.B. 157, was ratified July 8. *N.C. Session Laws, 1983*, cc. 588 and 707, respectively.]

This seminar today can be a historic occasion: It can mark the beginning of an unprecedented effort by a state to reach out to its citizens and get them involved in *their* government.

North Carolina has one of the finest election systems in the nation. Its integrity is unquestioned. Its efficiency is unequaled. That is because of each and every one of you. We take pride in that.

But we cannot take pride in our voter registration record. Of the twenty-five largest states in the nation, North Carolina ranks twenty-second in the percentage of voting-age citizens registered to vote. Only 59 percent of voting-age citizens are registered. In one fourth of our counties, less than 55 percent are registered.

What those percentages mean is that the number of North Carolinians of voting age who are not registered to vote exceeds 1.7 million people. Registration among minority citizens lags even farther behind. Our state ranks dead last among the southern states in minority registration.

Those figures are not low because our people are uninterested in their government or because they do not want to vote. Many people say it is too difficult, they don't know how to register, or where to register. The mobile nature of modern society compounds that problem. Many people do not register because they are handicapped and cannot leave their homes. Many elderly people have the same problem.

Our job is to make it easier for all of them to register. The registration process must become more active. It must reach out to people and show them how easy it is to register. That is what we are beginning today, and I congratulate the State Board of Elections for undertaking this challenge.

Now, some people will object. They will say people have all the opportunities to register that they need and that we should not "cater" to them. I believe that argument is elitist and narrow minded. Voting is a right belonging to every citizen, not a privilege.

So often those who are not registered are the elderly, the ill, the handicapped, the poor, the uneducated. They are citizens, too, and this is their government. They are precisely the people who most need to be brought into our political and governmental mainstream. For the greater the participation in the election process, the more representative and just government will be.

It is toward that goal that our State Board of Elections is striving. Under Bob Spearman's leadership, the board is mounting an unprecedented cooperative effort to get our people registered to vote.[1] The board will be seeking the cooperation of Democrats and Republicans and independents alike, of civic organizations, business groups, and citizen committees.

At the request of the state board, I am proclaiming 1982 as "Citizen Awareness Year" to help this effort. The board will set registration goals, put public service announcements on radio and TV, and encourage local boards to supply registrars on certain days at specific locations. Utility companies and local governments will mail out registration information with their monthly bills.

I hope you will join this great effort. I hope you will be innovative and aggressive in examining procedures that may make it harder for people to register. We must remove restrictions on the number of special registrars and on their authority to register voters. We must remove geographic restrictions on precinct registrars within counties. We must expand the use of libraries and schools as registration places. I want the board to investigate possible legislative action that will help meet our goal.

We can meet this challenge. North Carolina has a tradition of meeting challenges. Our challenge is to remove any obstacles that remain to registration. Our challenge is to raise our registration figure to the levels of other states. Our challenge is to assure that all North Carolinians have a chance to participate fully and freely in our elections.

Thomas Jefferson once wrote, "Men by their constitutions are naturally divided into two groups, (1) those who fear and distrust the people and wish to draw all powers from them into the hands of the higher classes; (2) those who identify themselves with the people, have confidence in them, cherish and consider them the most honest and safe depository of the public interest." [2] I cast my lot with the second group. Let us join together today to see that every North Carolinian has the opportunity to exercise that most precious freedom: the right to vote.

---

[1] Robert W. Spearman (1943-   ), native of Durham; resident of Raleigh; A.B., University of North Carolina at Chapel Hill, 1965; first class honors, Oxford University (Rhodes scholarship), 1967; LL.B., Yale University, 1970. Attorney; law clerk to Mr. Justice Hugo L. Black, United States Supreme Court, 1970-1971; member, National Democratic Party platform drafting commission, 1972; director, North Carolina Center for Public Policy Research, since 1976; member, North Carolina State Democratic Executive Committee, since 1977; chairman, State Board of Elections, 1981-1985. Robert W. Spearman to Jan-Michael Poff, February 8, 1985.

[2] Compare Hunt's rendition of Jefferson's remarks with the actual quotation: "Men by their constitutions are naturally divided into two parties: (1) Those who fear and distrust the people, and wish to draw all powers from them into the hands of the higher classes. (2) Those who identify themselves with the people, have confidence in them, cherish and consider them as the most honest and safe, although not the most wise depository of the public interests. In every country these two parties exist; and in every one where they are free to think, speak, and write, they will declare themselves." Letter to Henry Lee [August 10, 1824], quoted in Bartlett, *Familiar Quotations*, 473.

JAPANESE CONFERENCE
"DOING BUSINESS WITH JAPAN"

RALEIGH, FEBRUARY 2, 1982

I am delighted to join you at this seminar on "Doing Business with Japan." I want to thank International Trade Center director Dave Thomas for helping us expand the horizons of North Carolina businessmen. This partnership between business and the universities is one I've pushed throughout my administration.

As you know, I have a strong personal interest in Japan. Twice now I have had the pleasure of leading a group of distinguished North Carolinians to Japan. In November of last year we visited with companies in Tokyo, Odawara, Nagoya, and Osaka.

Among the things we discussed with those officials is that North Carolina is the first state in the country to invest public funds in the establishment of a Japan Center. The center's director, John Sylvester,[1] accompanied me throughout that trip.

Japan is already very important to the economy of our state. Japan is the largest overseas customer for our tobacco and soybeans. We also export to Japan products including wood chips, electronic equipment, and various machinery parts. In fact, figures to be released from the U.S. Commerce Department today indicate that from 1978 to 1980, North Carolina had a 90 percent increase in exports—moving up from thirteenth in the nation to eleventh—and we have the potential to do even better.

Japanese industrial investment in North Carolina has increased significantly in recent years. In January I announced that Takeda Chemicals will build a $10 million manufacturing complex that will likely grow to $100 million over the next several years in New Hanover and Pender counties. With Takeda we will have Japanese manufacturing plants in North Carolina all the way from Asheville to Wilmington.

We will have over twenty Japanese companies located in North Carolina, and nine of them are manufacturers. With the Takeda announcement, we have $60 million in industrial investment that has come in the last three years, and that will probably grow to over $160 million.

We will continue to work to expand our contacts with Japan on both sides of the economic ledger—reverse investment and exports.

In both cases the task is challenging, and different from many of the business dealings we are used to in other parts of the world. Japanese companies are most deliberate in their decisions and require an immense volume of information before they make decisions. For example, Takeda even knew that Wilmington had two oriental food stores.

The payoff of extra efforts will be significant. For a variety of reasons the Japanese are increasingly interested in investing in the United States. Nationwide their investment had reached $4 billion by 1979 and is expected to increase to $20 billion by 1985.

On the export side, there is no question the Japanese have tended to overly protect their own economy and to take too little an active role in furthering the broad interests of the free world.

The United States is properly pushing them to do more, and I believe the Japanese are responding. They have grown more confident of the basic strengths of their economy. They are most understanding of the need for Japan to do more as a citizen of the free world.

Their leaders are a responsible group. They know they must do more as world citizens. They understand that they must buy more American products to help rectify a trade imbalance that was close to $20 billion last year. In fact, it's very possible that within the next two or three years we may see a tremendous breakthrough in the opening up of the Japanese market.

For North Carolina companies to take advantage of that breakthrough, they must start now. They really should have started before this. North Carolina companies must strive to sell products tailored correctly for the Japanese markets. The Japanese have complained about the reluctance of American manufacturers to make those types of adaptations, and I think to a certain extent the criticism may be justified.

Perhaps more than anything, the Japanese have been experts at marketing their products in the U.S. They have anticipated what the American marketplace wants and have built the right "mousetrap" to capture a major share of that market.

At the state level our Department of Commerce will be happy to help you learn about the Japanese market. Walter Johnson of that staff speaks fluent Japanese.[2] Gordon McRoberts and the export staff can tell you about the ins and outs of exporting. To further that assistance, I am happy to announce today that North Carolina's state ports will soon have a full time representative in the Far East. A Japanese businessman, Mr. Ichiro Iwao, will have primary responsibility to generate cargo and trade throughout the Far East for our North Carolina ports of Wilmington and Morehead City.[3] He also will give us close contacts with companies involved in international trade in Japan. Mr. Iwao was with Japan Line for thirty years and knows both the American and Japanese sides of shipping.

We also need help on the federal level. I endorse the need for the establishment of a legal framework to allow American companies to create large trading companies of the sort that Japan has used so well to further its worldwide trade.

Finally, I would say that my major impression of my trips to Japan was the vitality of the country's economy. The Japanese consumers have money and like American products. They want, however, products of high quality that are appropriate for Japanese needs.

Working together we can take better advantage of those needs. I am pleased you have come here today to continue this learning and working process. I wish you good fortune, and I appreciate this opportunity to meet with you today.

[1]John Sylvester, Jr. (1930-   ), native of Newport, Rhode Island; resident of Raleigh; B.A., Williams College, 1952; B.S., Georgetown University, 1955; fellow, Woodrow Wilson School of Public and International Affairs, Princeton University, 1972-1973. Foreign Service officer, U.S. Department of State, holding various posts in Japan, 1955-1965, 1973-1976, Washington, D.C., 1965-1968, and South Vietnam, 1968-1972; director, North Carolina Japan Center, since 1981. John Sylvester, Jr., to Jan-Michael Poff, July 31, 1985.

[2]Walter R. Johnson III (1941-   ), native of Winston-Salem; resident of Cary; B.S., 1970, M.A., 1972, Sophia University; U.S. Air Force, 1959-1964. General controller, head of curriculum and instruction, Kanda Institute of Foreign Languages, 1972-1978; director of Japan Operations, state Department of Commerce, since 1978. Walter R. Johnson III to Jan-Michael Poff, February 18, 1985.

[3]Ichiro Iwao (1922-   ), native of Los Angeles, California; resident of Tokyo, Japan; graduated from Kobe College of Commerce, 1944; Japanese navy, 1944-1945. Chicago representative, 1968, chief representative, San Francisco, 1969-1970, general manager, Osaka, 1970-1973, and general manager, Petroleum Department and Office of the President, 1974-1982, Japan Line, Ltd.; director, Marketing and Trade Development—Asia, North Carolina State Ports Authority, since 1982. Ichiro Iwao to Jan-Michael Poff, March 14, 1985.

DINNER HONORING MARSE GRANT

RALEIGH, FEBRUARY 2, 1982

It is an honor for me to be here tonight and share my impressions of this man we all call friend. I have known Marse Grant[1] for many years. It is difficult for me to describe the profound appreciation I have for him, but I will give it a try.

He has been a wise and faithful counselor to many of us. How many people have been given a boost up the ladder of life by Marse? How many hopes have been ignited and visions raised? How many who were discouraged have been lifted up? How many who were broken have been healed? How many have been asked to reach deep within themselves and be all that God intended for them to be? Marse has been a mentor, a wise and faithful counselor, to me and countless others.

He is a first-rate journalist. Through *Charity and Children* and the *Biblical Recorder*, we have learned about ourselves and the world at large. The written word informed us about our friends, inspired us to be our best, and equipped us for service in God's kingdom.

Marse Grant has challenged us. He has never lacked for courage. He has never succumbed to what the Bible refers to as "tickling their ears."[2] He has challenged our consciences on many occasions on a variety of issues, from race relations to the abuse of alcohol.

Marse had only been on the job a month when the Greensboro sit-in took place. His response in the *Biblical Recorder* in his editorial "Dime Store Headlines" was: "God loves all people. To think that

He prefers one over another because of the color of skin is inconsistent with the teachings of the Bible. We have enough confidence in the Christian people of this state to believe that they will quietly lead the way to a solution to this and other problems that may arise in this sensitive area of human relations. If the Christian influence is not felt, the situation could become dangerous at any minute."[3]

In all his writings, editorials, and speeches, he called us to be the best we could be. He exposed our reluctance to practice all of Jesus' teachings. He questioned our commitments on many ethical issues and asked us to be more than we thought possible. He troubled us even as Jesus troubled the religious establishment of his day. North Carolina is the better because this man had the courage and integrity to confront us with the entire Gospel.

The secular press is absolutely right when it refers to Marse Grant as "Mr. Baptist." He has lived and has written according to the greatest writing of all, God's holy word. When Baptists embarrassed themselves, he said, "Well, that is how some of us are but there is also another side to us." When Baptists led the way for others, he said, "Walk humbly with thy God." For more than thirty-two years, he has invested his life in the Baptist faith. He is nothing more or less than a loyal member of those people called Baptists.

No man is an island and Marian Grant has helped Marse be more than he could ever have been alone. This woman who has walked through forty years of marriage with Marse has marked his life—providing comfort, insight, and strength. She has been a full partner in this ministry which we honor here tonight.[4]

My life is different, and I think better, because of him. Dear friend, thank you for being who you are and for doing what you do. I pray, for you and Marian, God's best gifts.

---

[1]J. Marse Grant (1920-   ), native of High Point; resident of Raleigh; was graduated from High Point College in 1941; honorary degrees. Editor, *Charity and Children*, until 1960; *Biblical Recorder* editor, 1960-1982, and editor emeritus; charter member, Good Neighbor Council (now North Carolina Human Relations Council); member, Task Force on Domestic Violence, North Carolina Commission on the Holocaust, and Governor's Task Force on Drunken Drivers; author, *Whiskey at the Wheel: The Scandal of Driving and Drinking*; newspaper columnist. J. Marse Grant to Jan-Michael Poff, February 15, 1985.

[2]2 Timothy 4:3.

[3]"Dime Store Headlines," *Biblical Recorder*, February 27, 1960. On February 1, 1960, Ezell Blair, Franklin McCain, Joseph McNeil, and David Richmond seated themselves at F. W. Woolworth Company's "whites only" lunch counter, in Greensboro, and asked for service. Although the request of the four North Carolina A&T students was refused, the "sit-in" they began touched off a series of similar protests in other states over he next two weeks. Woolworth's and two other Greensboro department stores desegregated their lunch counters by the following July. Thomas C. Parramore, *Express Lanes and Country Roads: The Way We Lived in North Carolina, 1920-1970* (Chapel Hill: University of North Carolina Press, 1983), 90.

[4]Marian Gibbs Grant, native of Commerce, Georgia; resident of Raleigh; educated

in Greensboro public schools. President and treasurer, Grant Tours, Inc.; chairwoman of Advocacy Council for the Mentally Ill and Developmentally Disabled, and of Governor's Advocacy Council for Persons with Disabilities; first woman recording secretary, Baptist State Convention of North Carolina. Marian Gibbs Grant to Jan-Michael Poff, February 15, 1985.

TESTIMONY BEFORE JOINT U.S. HOUSE-SENATE FLUE-CURED TOBACCO HEARING

RALEIGH, FEBRUARY 12, 1982

Mr. Chairman,[1] Members of the Senate Committee on Agriculture, Nutrition and Forestry, and Members of the House Agriculture Subcommittee on Tobacco and Peanuts:

As governor of North Carolina, the nation's number-one state in tobacco production and manufacture, I want to thank you for holding this and other hearings on ways to improve and strengthen the tobacco program. I welcome this distinguished group of leaders in agricultural legislation to North Carolina and assure you that I am deeply interested in your mission here. We appreciate the leadership of our North Carolina leaders, Senator Helms and Congressman Rose, as chairmen of these committees so crucial to the people of our state.

The tobacco program has been eminently successful over a period of more than forty years. It has kept many small farmers in business and has added hundreds of millions of dollars to the agricultural economy of this and other tobacco producing states. But now certain features of the program have "gotten out of kilter," so to speak, and modifications are needed. Congress has mandated that the program must be operated at no net cost to taxpayers (except for administrative costs), and this will necessitate administrative and legislative changes. I believe that a vast majority of our growers realize the seriousness of the problems that have arisen in connection with the tobacco program in recent years. I think most growers are ready now, as perhaps never before, to accept needed and desirable changes.

I support the no-cost position of the Congress. We must balance the federal budget, and tobacco farmers are willing to accept their share of the responsibility for this task. In fact, growers are so tired of hearing the program referred to inaccurately as a subsidy program that I believe they will welcome the opportunity to make absolutely certain that the price support program operates on the basis of no net cost to the taxpayer. A consensus appears to be developing among growers in favor of a checkoff to be collected when the producer markets his tobacco. Such a checkoff, if authorized, should be large enough to provide adequate reserve funds to take care of price support losses.

There is pressure for change in the quota and allotment system. A substantial majority of allotment holders no longer grow tobacco; instead, they lease out their quota for production on other farms. The leasing rates charged actual producers have risen until they now account for 20 to 25 percent of the average market price received for tobacco. The situation has evoked much criticism, not only in tobacco areas but also from our friends in Congress who are from nontobacco areas.

There is danger of getting away from the historical view that the quota "belongs to the land and not the man." A big step away from this principle was taken back in the 1960s when lease and transfer was authorized. The more we separate the quota from the land, the more problems we create in regard to both the integrity and the public image of the program.

Despite its shortcomings, lease and transfer provides flexibility for bona fide tobacco growers who need to expand their production in order to take advantage of mechanization. Perhaps some of the abuses in lease and transfer can be eliminated by discontinuing fall leasing.

Consideration is now being given to a provision permitting sale of allotments within each county. We should recognize that the better-financed and large land-based farmers are going to be in better position to bid for allotments offered for sale. Many of our young farmers must rent and have limited equity.

I support property rights, and a tobacco allotment is property. If any nonfarming corporation or any nontobacco-growing landowner is to be compelled to give up an allotment, I would urge that due process and opportunity for adequate compensation be provided. The rights of all parties, including tenant farmers, must be protected.

As for price, there is no doubt that adjustments are needed in support or loan rates by grades. Our medium and better grades are of premium quality and can command premium prices on world markets. However, our lower grades are priced noncompetitively. Tobacco of similar quality is available in many foreign countries at much lower prices.

There is merit, I believe, in authorizing the U.S. secretary of agriculture, with the required help of a producer advisory committee, to adjust price supports by grades in order to hold down increases on grades which are in excess supply, are not in demand, and appear likely to cause losses in the loan program. Price support on the good-quality, ripe, flavorful grades should rise in accordance with inflation and market demand. Support levels on the lower stalk and filler grades should be discounted to find their worth on the domestic or export market. Some grade standards may need to be revised to separate out those grades resulting from misuse or excessive use of nitrogen, MH,[2] or chemical ripening agents.

The tobacco program, and especially the schedule of grade loan rates, must encourage the production of the highest possible quality. Our growers have the resources to continue producing the world's finest quality leaf. They have access to varieties, cultural and chemical practices, soil and climatic conditions, a long heritage, and management skills to do the job. We must make sure that the program is so structured as to reward those who produce quality.

We must strive to be quality/price competitive in world markets. Since our medium and better grades are of premium quality, we expect premium prices for those grades. If our lower grades are discounted, we may be able to increase export sales. However, we must keep in mind that *net income* is the thing that keeps farmers in business. An increase in sales or even gross cash receipts would be futile if it did not boost the *net* returns of growers.

The problems that are paramount at this time concern primarily flue-cured producers. Any program changes made, however, should be for the best interests of all types of tobacco if the producers desire the program.

Before closing I should like to repeat a long-standing concern which I feel in regard to tobacco imports. Neither the U.S. Customs Service nor the U.S. International Trade Commission has provided any real assistance to us in coping with the increasing threat posed by U.S. manufacturers' and dealers' purchases of "offshore" or foreign-grown tobacco. No matter how tight you close the front door to your house, it isn't going to stay warm in winter if the back door is left wide open. Likewise, we cannot maintain stable tobacco supplies and prices in this country if American manufacturers and dealers continue to bring in large quantities of cheap foreign tobacco. We have only to look at the U.S. auto industry to see the havoc that can be wrought by unrestricted cheap imports.

Few commodities were profitable to North Carolina farmers in 1981. Tobacco was profitable, but only because there was a quota control and price support program. We need to continue the tobacco program, and we must do so in separate, permanent-type legislation rather than as part of the omnibus farm bill which must be renewed every four years.

This, I think, is a golden moment in the history of the tobacco program. Farmers see the need for adjustments in the program to keep pace with changing conditions. We are grateful that Congress has provided an opportunity for us to work together toward a stronger, more viable tobacco program for the years ahead. We shall be counting on your support as we work together to develop a program that will be fair and equitable to all parties, a program that will encourage the production and marketing of quality leaf, a program that will make our tobacco quality/price competitive in world markets, and a program that can be operated at no net cost to taxpayers.

[1]Jesse Alexander Helms, Jr. (1921-   ), native of Monroe; resident of Raleigh; attended Wingate (Junior) College and Wake Forest College (now University); U.S. Naval Reserve, 1942-1945. *Raleigh Times* city editor, 1941-1942; news and program director, WRAL Radio, 1948-1951; administrative assistant to U.S. senators Willis Smith and Alton Lennon, of North Carolina, 1951-1953; executive director, North Carolina Bankers Association, 1953-1960; Raleigh city councilman, 1957-1961; editorialist, WRAL Television, and past executive vice-president, vice-chairman of the board, and assistant chief executive officer, Capitol Broadcasting Co., 1960-1972; U.S. senator from North Carolina since 1973, and chairman of the Senate Committee on Agriculture. *North Carolina Manual, 1983*, 155; "To the Right, March!" *Time*, September 14, 1981, 24-35; *Who's Who in America, 1982-1983*, I, 1473.

[2]Maleic hydrazide is a chemical used for tobacco plant sucker control. Carlton Blalock to Jan-Michael Poff, October 9, 1984.

MEETING WITH NORTH CAROLINA LEAGUE OF MUNICIPALITIES AND NORTH CAROLINA ASSOCIATION OF COUNTY COMMISSIONERS

RALEIGH, FEBRUARY 19, 1982

[President Reagan outlined his ideas for a "New Federalism," a plan to control the size of U.S. government by swapping certain programs between state and federal levels of administration, in his "State of the Union Address," January 26, and his "Budget Message to Congress," February 9, 1982. However, White House officials were unable to convince organizations like the National Governors' Association of the efficacy of the proposal for the reapportionment of responsibility and consequently forwarded no legislation to Congress, in 1982, to initiate such a shift. *Congressional Quarterly Almanac, 1982*, 18, 5-E, 12-E.]

I asked to meet with you today because there has never been a time when it was more important for leaders of state government and leaders of local government to enter into a dialogue. I am not here just to talk to you. I want to listen.

I am leaving for Washington tomorrow, to attend the annual meeting of the National Governors' Association. We will spend three days talking about President Reagan's proposal for a "New Federalism." But it won't be enough to just talk about state and federal government. We need to talk about what New Federalism means for federal, state, and local governments.

I sincerely hope that the fundamental importance of this issue will not be lost in the politics of the moment. I certainly don't agree with the president on everything, but I am glad that he has brought to the attention of the entire nation this issue of federalism—the issue of, in effect, "which level of government does what best?"

Over the last fifty years, the role of the federal government has grown enormously. One observer said recently that state governments had, in some ways, become nothing more than "branch offices" of the federal government. That is an overstatement, but it makes the point that now is the time for us to engage in a constructive national debate on the future of our federal system. That debate can determine the shape of our system of government for decades to come.

For years, I have been saying that the states should take on more responsibilities. I think the states can be laboratories for democracy. I think North Carolina has shown the way with its progress in economic development, protection against crime, human development, protection of our natural resources, and wise stewardship of the taxpayers' dollar.

I do have serious reservations about the specific swap of responsibilities that the president has proposed. The nation's governors have long held the position—and I agree with it—that income security programs like Medicaid, food stamps, and AFDC should be federal responsibilities.

The swap President Reagan has proposed—giving states AFDC and food stamps and Washington taking Medicaid—wouldn't be an even trade. North Carolina would lose $200 million on the deal. Needless to say, I don't think that is a good deal.

In the long run, the cost would be even higher. Our State Budget Office has prepared an analysis of the president's program that, between now and 1991, [indicates] the total price tag for the state of North Carolina would be $1 billion. To keep services at their present level, in other words, you and I would have to raise taxes by $1 billion over the next ten years. But I am glad to see that the president has indicated his willingness to consult with the governors, and I think we governors need to consult with you county commissioners and mayors and town council members.

Let me raise a caution flag here. We cannot let this debate over federalism take our eye off the ball. The most important thing we have to do in this country today is get the economy healthy again. New Federalism is important, but it doesn't put a single person back to work. It doesn't reduce that federal deficit by one dollar. It doesn't add one decimal point to our nation's productivity.

Economic growth and good jobs are the number-one concerns of many of you, just as they are to me. I am concerned that the president's program does not do enough to promote growth and create jobs. I would be interested in any comments you have on that.

So now I want to hear from you. What questions and concerns from local government do you want me to have in mind as I talk with other governors and with administration officials and members of Congress in Washington?

What do you think of the swap the president has proposed?

What would be the outlook for your property taxes if we accepted that swap?

What do you think the various levels of government do best?

What do you think of the governors' position that income-security programs should be a federal responsibility?

What programs do you think local and state governments should run?

And, most important, how should we all work together to help the people in your cities and towns and counties get good jobs?

WOMEN'S NATIONAL DEMOCRATIC CLUB

WASHINGTON, D.C., FEBRUARY 22, 1982

At a time when so much attention has been focused on the 100th anniversary of the birth of Franklin Delano Roosevelt, it's especially significant to me to be here in this club that has such strong connections to Eleanor Roosevelt.[1] I understand she used to do her radio broadcasts from here and remained a staunch supporter of this club's programs over the years. The legacy that Franklin and Eleanor Roosevelt left this country was one of fairness and equity. They led us through a political revolution fifty years ago that brought government down affirmatively on the side of jobs and economic opportunity for everyone.

We are now engaged in a revolution that may be just as fundamental. I know Ronald Reagan likes to compare himself to FDR, but I say to you that a president with a program like Ronald Reagan's has no right to compare himself to Franklin Delano Roosevelt.

Throughout all the revolutionary and evolutionary changes our country has undergone in the last sixty years, your club has been a forum for discussion of the issues and action on the issues. You have always been among the most influential leaders in this country. We are greatly indebted to you for your hard work and loyalty to the Democratic party, and I know personally how crucial the support and political savvy of women can be to a campaign. If it hadn't been for Carolyn,[2] and for Jane Patterson and Betty McCain,[3] and all the other women who raised money, and made speeches, and won votes for me, I'd be in Wilson County today farming and practicing law.

Today the Democratic party has the potential to tap even more support from the women of this country. A recent poll commissioned by the Democratic National Committee [DNC] shows just how strongly women support our party. Fifty-five percent of women polled identified themselves as Democrats. For working women that is 59 percent.

If women controlled the legislatures of this nation, equal rights would not be a debatable issue. I know of your long-standing commitment to the Equal Rights Amendment, and I know circumstances are not as we would wish. But I do believe ERA has a chance this year, and I am firmly committed to do all I can to get it passed in North Carolina. I know how tough it is, but I am prepared to press ahead. I also do not flinch at the prospect of starting all over again, because I know this cause is right.

Why do women support Democrats so strongly—working women in particular? In part I believe it is because of our historic commitment to fairness and to equal rights, but it's also because of economic issues. Over 50 percent of the women in this country work outside the home. In my state that's 55 percent.

Of course women are looking for peace in the world, and safe streets at home, and for a clean environment in which to raise their children. But I believe that more than ever before, women are vitally interested in the economic health of this country. They are looking for lower interest rates, so they can buy a car or a house, or start a business. They are looking for an expanding economy which will mean more opportunities for getting a raise or a promotion. They want better job training, and day care. They are looking for a fair shake in the workplace, and for an equal chance to provide for themselves and for their families.

I believe we lost the 1980 elections in part because we let the Republicans take the economic issues away from us. At their convention in 1980 they talked about "jobs, jobs, jobs."

That was their program when they were running, but what is it today? Ten million people out of work and looking for jobs. And do you know what the Republican response was to those people? They tried to close down unemployment offices all over this country. That's not what the American people voted for, and we Democrats must not let the Republicans take the jobs issue away from us ever again.

This nation needs a Democratic alternative, and the Democratic party needs a strategy for winning in 1982 and 1984. Essential to that, I think, is making some changes in the way we nominate presidential candidates.

I had the honor of chairing our party's Commission on Presidential Nomination. We have recommended changes that I believe will help us nominate our strongest candidate. But let me say that my first commitment in this process was to maintaining equal division and affirmative action. That was a given, and that was not a position I arrived at recently. Twelve years ago I chaired the state party commission that carried out the McGovern commission's guidelines for increased involvement by young people, women, and minorities.[4]

I believe our most important recommendation is that the Democratic party bring greater numbers of its elected officials and party leaders back into the national convention as unpledged delegates. They are a great resource to our party, and we need them if we're going to win. As your testimony last November said, "The convention and the party must have the benefit of the political experience, political sensitivity, and national and international perspective of these officials to be successful in choosing a presidential candidate who can win the election and govern the nation."[5] One of the key leaders responsible for our compromise on the elected officials issue was Representative Geraldine Ferraro of New York. She was its author and floor manager, and I cannot praise her work too highly.[6]

We recommended that 14 percent of the convention, about 550 delegates, be set aside as unpledged slots for members of Congress, governors, mayors of large cities, and key party leaders. We recommended that another 10 percent be set aside for elected officials and party leaders as committed delegates, without the requirement of candidate approval. A high priority for these seats would go to state legislators, which is where you are most likely to find women. We made other recommendations that would improve the process:

—Shortening the primary/caucus season by five weeks, so that it begins late in February, not the middle of January.

—Loosening the binding restrictions on delegates and giving the convention more flexibility so it can be more deliberative and respond to changing political circumstances.

Not everyone will agree with all of our recommendations. I understand, for example, that some of you have a concern about the so-called "loophole primaries."[7] But this is an excellent overall package, and we need your help to get it through the DNC. I think everyone can take pride in how our commission worked.

But winning the White House and regaining a majority in both houses of Congress require more than writing new rules. They require a restoration of the Democratic party to its rightful place in the mainstream of American society. They require a Democratic alternative that speaks to the working people of this country, men and women who are concerned about jobs and economic opportunities—for themselves and their families.

I do not see the Republican program offering them hope. It does not offer investments in economic strength. Instead, it offers retreat and retrenchment in the very things that mean economic growth—water and sewer projects, highways, airports, skill training, vocational education, industrial revenue bonds, and community development.

The Republican program does not offer investments in our human capital. Instead, it offers retreat and retrenchment in education, student loans, and health care.

What the Republican program does offer is an irresponsible fiscal policy that shortchanges economic growth and gives us record budget deficits that soak up investment capital and choke off recovery.

It is not enough to just criticize President Reagan. The American people want a positive alternative, and I sense that alternative emerging from our party. Yes, we speak with many voices. Our diversity and our debates and our differences are the "big-D" Democratic way of doing things. But, as I talk with Democrats across this nation, I hear a chorus of voices speaking the same language.

We are calling for a national strategy that will get the economy moving again.

We are calling for fostering high technology, science, research and development, and the growth industries of the future—computers, communications, and microelectronics.

We are calling for better public education and job-skill training.

We are calling for strengthening the foundations of our economy—water and sewer projects, highways, and airports.

We are calling for support of the greatest source of new jobs—small businesses and ambitious entrepreneurs, particularly minorities and women.

We are calling, in other words, for a strategy that will mean jobs, not longer unemployment lines; economic recovery, not stagnation; hope, not hopelessness.

We must not fail to give the people of this country a chance to make that choice.

It is up to us to offer a choice. It is up to us to write rules that will help us nominate a strong presidential candidate. It is up to us to develop a program in the American mainstream. It is up to us to build solid relationships between our presidential and congressional candidates. It is up to us to talk sense to the American people. It is up to us to win in 1982 and in 1984 and to offer this nation a new course.

I believe the people of this country want the opportunity that the American writer from North Carolina, Thomas Wolfe, spoke of when he said, "To every man his chance, to every man, regardless of his birth, his shining golden opportunity—to every man the right to live, to work, to be himself, and to become whatever thing his manhood and his vision can combine to make him—this, seeker, is the promise of America." [8]

---

[1] Anna Eleanor Roosevelt (1884-1962), native of New York City; educated in private schools. Educational, social, and political activist; author; assistant director, Office of Civilian Defense, 1941-1942; U.S. United Nations representative, 1945-1952, 1961-1962; chairwoman, UNESCO Human Rights Commission, 1946; wife of President Franklin Delano Roosevelt. *Who Was Who in America, 1961-1968*, 809; *World Book Encyclopedia*, 1982 ed., s.v. "Roosevelt, Eleanor."

[2] Carolyn Leonard Hunt (1937-   ), native of Mingo, Iowa; resident of Rock Ridge; attended Iowa State University; A.B., University of North Carolina at Chapel Hill, 1964. Married James Baxter Hunt, Jr., 1958; schoolteacher in Katmandu, Nepal,

1964-1966; first lady of North Carolina, 1977-1985, and organizer, N.C. Friendship Force program. *News and Observer,* December 26, 1982; *Spectator* (Raleigh), December 16, 1982; *UNC Alumni Directory,* 567; *Winston-Salem Journal,* January 6, 1977.

[3]Betty Ray McCain (1931-   ), Democratic Women of North Carolina president, 1971-1972, and chairwoman, North Carolina Democratic Executive Committee, 1976-1979; member, Democratic National Committee, and of its Rules Committee, since 1980. Betty Ray McCain to Jan-Michael Poff, October 25, 1983; also previously identified in Mitchell, *Addresses of Hunt,* I, 307n.

[4]For more information on the McGovern Commission, see "American Assembly on the Future of American Political Parties," April 16, 1982, footnote 7, below.

[5]Neither the source nor accuracy of this quotation could be verified.

[6]Geraldine A. Ferraro (1935-   ), native of Newburgh, New York; resident of Forest Hills, New York; was graduated from Marymount College in 1956; J.D., Fordham University, 1960. Practicing attorney, 1961-1974; chief, Special Victims Bureau and Confidential Unit, New York District Attorney's Office, 1974-1978; elected to U.S. House of Representatives from New York's Ninth Congressional District, 1978, and returned in subsequent elections; unsuccessful Democratic candidate for U.S. vice-president, 1984. Barone and Ujifusa, *Almanac of American Politics, 1984,* 806; *News and Observer,* November 7, 1984.

[7]Direct-election primaries, in which voters select party convention delegates by name, frequently generate "winner-take-all" outcomes. The reason, according to political scientist David Eugene Price, is that people casting ballots "favoring a given presidential candidate were likely to vote for all . . . of the delegates pledged to that preference." Such an arrangement circumvented the 1972 Democratic national convention's order that runners-up be awarded a proportionate share of the delegates. The "loophole primary," as the direct-election process was known to its critics, was prohibited in 1978 by the Winograd Commission of the Democratic National Committee; it was restored four years later by the Hunt Commission. Price, *Bringing Back the Parties* (Washington, D.C.: Congressional Quarterly Press, 1984), 151; see also David Eugene Price to Jan-Michael Poff, October 7, 1985.

[8]Thomas Clayton Wolfe (1900-1938), native of Asheville; A.B., University of North Carolina at Chapel Hill, 1920; A.M., Harvard University, 1922. Novelist, short-story writer; author of *Look Homeward, Angel* (1929), *You Can't Go Home Again* (1940), and others. *Who Was Who in America, 1897-1942,* 1372. Quotation previously identified in Mitchell, *Addresses of Hunt,* I, 164n.

TESTIMONY BEFORE U.S. HOUSE COMMITTEE ON SCIENCE AND TECHNOLOGY, SUBCOMMITTEE ON SCIENCE, RESEARCH, AND TECHNOLOGY

WASHINGTON, D.C., FEBRUARY 23, 1982

Mr. Chairman:[1]

I am pleased to have the opportunity to testify today at this hearing. The future of science and technology in this nation, and of the National Science Foundation in particular, is of great importance to the state of North Carolina and to the United States.

Each member of this committee is aware that our nation is confronted with severe economic problems. I believe that one of the major causes of our difficulties is our failure to translate adequately the knowledge gained through research into products and services essential to our economic growth. The United States has provided, and has the potential to continue to provide, the fundamental scientific knowledge essential to sweeping technological changes. But Japan, as an example of a growing number of nations, is exceeding our ability to transform results of our research into superior products.

In my judgment, the National Science Foundation should be concerned with the entire process of research and development. I believe the record clearly demonstrates that the National Science Board, the foundation itself, OMB [Office of Management and Budget], and the Office of Science and Technology Policy (OSTP) have been preoccupied with the basic research aspects of the process and ignored or downplayed the remainder.

The National Science Foundation sought, in its latest reorganization, to overcome the shortcomings of which I speak, but we are still far behind Japan and perhaps a few other nations in effectively using the results of research for the benefit of our people. Thus, as a nation, we must pursue fundamental forms of scientific exploration *and* develop the necessary institutional arrangements, private sector financial support, and other means essential to effective use of scientific research results.

I do not believe that it is feasible for the federal government to implement directly all the measures required to ensure effective use of research results. A partnership of government, academia, and industry is necessary, and state and local governments should play much more important roles in this partnership than in the past.

There is much, however, that agencies of the federal government can do. For example, they should maintain a favorable economic environment by controlling inflation and ensuring adequate flows of capital at reasonable interest rates. They should devise incentives designed to encourage investment in research and development. They should support basic research relevant to all states and assist groups of states in pursuing common research and development interests.

We have concluded in North Carolina that state government should help support institutions, agencies, and firms in making sure that our research capacity is used effectively. The unit that helps plan our strategy is the North Carolina Board of Science and Technology. Several departments and agencies of state government assist in the process, including our Department of Commerce.

We are taking deliberate steps to improve the quality of education in our elementary and secondary schools. To put us on the cutting edge of two important fields of technological change, we have established a Biotechnology Center and a Microelectronics Center, investing more than $24 million of state funds. We have created a Waste Management Board and enacted legislation to ensure that we are properly managing toxic, hazardous, and low-level radio-active waste.

We have been able to move faster than many states. Even so, the support of the National Science Foundation, through its State Science, Engineering, and Technology (SSET) Program, has been of great assistance to us in recent years. Unfortunately, it is being cut out of the NSF budget in the current fiscal year.

The SSET program is small but of critical importance to states. It can become a strong influence in causing state governments to fulfill their roles in making technological innovation effective. Somewhere in the federal government it is absolutely essential that leadership be exercised in fostering the type of activity such as is taking place in North Carolina, and in a few other states.

Now let me conclude by suggesting that the leadership responsibilities I envision for the federal government could be exercised to a significant degree by the National Science Board, the National Science Foundation, the president's science advisor and his associated Office of Science and Technology Policy. To do so, however, will require much rethinking on the part of each as to their collective role in fostering action by state and local governments and the private sector, such as is beginning to occur in North Carolina. We can no longer assume that research utilization will take place automatically by some trickle-down theory.

The proposed NSF budget clearly falls short of fostering the kind of activity that must take place at the national level if we are to do a better job of translating research into better products and services. If NSF is not going to be given the means to carry out this function, I think Congress should give serious consideration to Representative George Brown's proposal for establishing a National Technology Foundation.[2]

In any case, pure research must not take place in a vacuum. If it does, the United States will relinquish its position as the world's leader in technology, and our ability to rebuild our economy will be seriously weakened.

[1]Douglas Walgren (1940-   ), native of Rochester, New York; resident of Pittsburgh; B.A., Dartmouth College, 1963; LL.B., Stanford University, 1966. Attorney; elected U.S. representative from Pennsylvania's Eighteenth Congressional District, 1976; chairman, Subcommittee on Science, Research, and Technology, of the House Committee on Science and Technology; Democrat. Barone and Ujifusa, *Almanac of American Politics, 1984*, 1038.

[2]George E. Brown, Jr. (1920-   ), native of Holtville, resident of Colton, California; B.A., University of California-Los Angeles, 1946; served in U.S. Army during World War II. Mayor, Monterey Park, California, 1954-1958; personnel, engineering, and management consultant for the city of Los Angeles, 1957-1961; member, California legislature, 1959-1962, and of the U.S. House of Representatives, 1962-1970; reelected from California's Thirty-sixth Congressional District, 1972, and returned in subsequent elections; Democrat. Barone and Ujifusa, *Almanac of American Politics, 1984*, 159.

The worst drought in forty-seven years gripped the South in 1983. Governor Hunt, shown here inspecting stunted and withered corn with a Granville County farmer, formally lobbied President Reagan for ten months before the federal government, in June, 1984, declared all North Carolina counties eligible for FmHA disaster loan assistance.

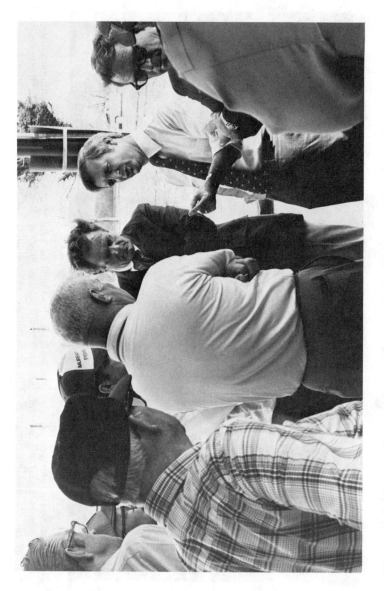

Hunt meets in Edenton with commercial fishermen to discuss the devastating effect of vast colonies of blue-green algae upon aquatic life in the Chowan River and Albemarle Sound. John Gilliam Wood, chairman of the state Board of Natural Resources and Community Development, listens on the governor's right.

STATEMENT ON THE ECONOMY

RALEIGH, FEBRUARY 25, 1982

I believe the nation's governors made good progress this week in our discussions with the Reagan administration and members of Congress on New Federalism, but the bad economic news that hit North Carolina this week emphasizes that the nation's first order of business must be getting out of the recession and stimulating economic growth. Our state's unemployment rate reached 9.1 percent in January, the highest since the 1975 recession. That means 263,700 North Carolinians are looking for jobs.

The recession has also caused a serious slump in our state tax revenues, and they are lagging behind our projections last year. This shows that the projected economic recovery is far behind schedule. Our nation's economic house is on fire. We need action to bring down interest rates and put our people back to work.

The unemployment rate and the revenue drop, I believe, demonstrate that the Reagan administration's economic recovery program is not working. This is not the time to be running up huge deficits and abandoning economic-development programs. From our conversations in Washington it is clear to me that Congress, including some of the leading Republicans, is not satisfied with the administration's program and will be giving it tough scrutiny. That is welcome news. We governors, Democrats and Republicans alike, remain committed to progress on New Federalism this year, and we will work hard for that. But the economy must come first.

STATEMENT ON JOB TRAINING

RALEIGH, MARCH 3, 1982

To get a good job today, you need a skill. Higher skills mean higher wages. It's as simple as that. So I am today signing an executive order that I believe will help people in North Carolina get the training they need to get a good job.[1]

This order will help us answer the most important question anyone can ask: What skill do I need to learn to get a job that pays well and offers a good future? If we can't tell a young person looking for a first job or an adult looking for a new one what kind of jobs will be available in years to come and what skills they will need, we have failed. It won't matter how much money we spend on training or how good our instructional equipment is. Our state's skill training program can be no better than the labor market information on which it is based.

This executive order designates the Employment Security Commission as the government agency that will have the responsibility for collecting, coordinating, and providing reliable and complete labor market information. An assistant director of the ESC will be appointed to be in charge of that function.

Government collects a lot of this information already, but too often it is incomplete, uncoordinated, and ineffectively used. The first step in correcting that, I believe, is to clearly fix the responsibility for compiling the information that all other agencies of government will use. The people who are given that responsibility must also have the tools they need to carry it out. So, in addition to designating ESC as the lead agency, I am also creating an oversight committee that will assist the commission in these duties. The committee will be chaired by a representative of private industry, and its membership will include people from all the government agencies that collect or use labor market information.

We need the involvement of private industry in this process to help assure that we are training people for the right jobs. This approach to labor market information, as a matter of fact, was strongly suggested by my Council on Management and Development, an advisory group of corporate leaders in our state. Not only will this approach save money in the collection and use of information, it will help us make the best possible use of every dollar that we put into training programs and equipment.

This executive order is the second major step we have taken in the development of a comprehensive skill training program. Last May, I announced that our system of technical colleges will serve as the "presumptive deliverer" of skill training in North Carolina—that is, they will do the training unless there is good reason for it to be done elsewhere. Our community and technical colleges will be among the primary users of this labor market information. It will tell them, as well as public school guidance counselors, what skills we should be teaching our young people.

Computers and modern technology are, in many ways, revolutionizing industry today. That is true not only in industries like microelectronics, but in textiles and other traditional industries that are critically important to North Carolina's economy. Our people must have the skills those industries need if North Carolina is going to stay competitive. Technological innovation can help us meet the challenge of foreign competition, but technology is useless without skilled people. That is why skill training is so important, and a good training policy must begin with good labor market information.

---

[1] Executive Order No. 77, "Governor's Oversight Committee for Official Labor Market Information," was signed March 3, 1982. *N.C. Session Laws, 1981, Regular and Extra Sessions, 1982*, 335-338.

STATEMENT ANNOUNCING
SAM RAGAN AS POET LAUREATE

RALEIGH, MARCH 11, 1982

One of my official duties as governor is the appointment of North Carolina's poet laureate. It is a duty I consider a tribute to those whose minds and hearts have made North Carolina the State of the Arts. It is a distinct honor for me to announce this morning the appointment of Sam Ragan[1] as this state's new poet laureate.

In 1935 the General Assembly called upon the governor to make this designation. Since then, two poets have held the office: Arthur Talmage Abernethy of Burke County, appointed by Governor R. Gregg Cherry; and James Larkin Pearson of Wilkes County, who was appointed by Governor William Umstead and who held the post until his death last year.[2]

Several months ago, I asked Sara Hodgkins, secretary of cultural resources, to form a committee to recommend candidates to succeed Mr. Pearson. The committee, chaired by Richard Walser[3] of North Carolina State University, and the state Arts Council did an excellent job of reviewing the credentials of a number of deserving candidates. My choice is a familiar name and a familiar face to many of you. He is a poet of the first rank and one of North Carolina's most distinguished and respected journalists.

After graduating from Atlantic Christian College in 1936, Sam Ragan began his newspaper career as editor of the *Plain Dealer* in Robbins. From 1941 until 1968, he worked at the *News and Observer*, where he held the positions of managing editor and executive editor. In 1968, he bought the *Pilot*, the newspaper in Southern Pines which he and his wife Marjorie[4] publish. In addition to being a distinguished man of letters, Sam Ragan has been a dedicated public servant. He was the first secretary of the North Carolina Department of Art, Culture, and History, now the Department of Cultural Resources.

He has published three books of poetry: *The Tree in the Far Pasture*, *To the Water's Edge*, and *Journey into Morning*, which was published last year and has been nominated for a Pulitzer Prize.[5] Through his works, he reminds us again and again that the poet's task is to capture the beauty of our world in words we can all understand. He once wrote:

> We begin with the word,
> We hold, we see, we hear, we feel.
> These are the fragments,
> We put them together and fasten them down
> With the strong glue of words.[6]

I introduce to you now a man who has been a friend and mentor to many of you in this room, North Carolina's new poet laureate, Sam Ragan of Southern Pines.

---

[1]Samuel Talmadge Ragan (1915-   ), editor and publisher of the Southern Pines *Pilot* since 1969. Previously identified in Mitchell, *Addresses of Hunt*, I, 570n.

[2]Arthur Talmage Abernethy (1872-1956), native of Rutherford College; was graduated from Rutherford College; M.A., Trinity College (now Duke University); Ph.D., Johns Hopkins University; Newspaper editor, columnist, feature writer, and drama critic; author; minister; North Carolina poet laureate, 1948-1958. Williams S. Powell (ed.), *Dictionary of North Carolina Biography* (Chapel Hill: University of North Carolina Press, projected multivolume series, 1979—), I, 4, hereinafter cited as Powell, *DNCB*.

Robert Gregg Cherry (1891-1957), native of Catawba Junction, South Carolina; A.B., 1912, attended law school, 1913-1914, Trinity College (now Duke University); U.S. Army, 1917-1919. Attorney; mayor of Gastonia, 1919-1923; member, state House, 1931-1939 (speaker, 1937-1938), and Senate, 1941-1943; governor, 1945-1949. Cheney, *North Carolina Government*, 423, 507, 508, 510, 511, 512, 515, 517; Powell, *DNCB*, I, 361-362.

James Larkin Pearson (1879-1981), native of Moravian Falls; educated in Wilkes County. Author, publisher; North Carolina poet laureate, 1953-1981. William S. Powell, *North Carolina Lives: The Tar Heel Who's Who* (Hopkinsville, Kentucky: Historical Record Association, 1962), 957-958; *Winston-Salem Journal*, August 28, 1981.

William Bradley Umstead (1895-1954), native of Mangum Township, Durham County; A.B., University of North Carolina at Chapel Hill, 1916; law student at Trinity College (now Duke University), 1919-1921; U.S. Army, 1917-1919. Kinston High School teacher, 1916-1917; attorney; U.S. representative from North Carolina's Sixth Congressional District, 1933-1938; U.S. senator, 1946-1948; governor, 1953-1954. *North Carolina Manual, 1953*, 369; *University of North Carolina Alumni Review*, XLII (October, 1954), 60.

[3]Richard Gaither Walser (1908-   ), native of Lexington; resident of Raleigh; A.B., 1929, M.A., 1933, University of North Carolina at Chapel Hill; U.S. Naval Reserve, 1942-1946, awarded Bronze Star. English professor, 1946-1970, and professor emeritus, since 1971, North Carolina State University; author, editor. Richard Gaither Walser to Jan-Michael Poff, March 7, 1985.

[4]Marjorie Usher Ragan (1917-   ), native of Laurel Hill; resident of Southern Pines; A.B., University of North Carolina at Chapel Hill, 1937. Associate editor, the *Pilot* since 1969. Marjorie Usher Ragan to Jan-Michael Poff, March 7, 1985.

[5]See Sam Ragan, *The Tree in the Far Pasture* (Winston-Salem: John F. Blair, Publisher, 1964); *To the Water's Edge* (Durham: Moore Publishing Company, 1971); and *Journey into Morning: Poems by Sam Ragan* (Laurinburg: St. Andrews Press, 1981), hereinafter cited as Ragan, *Journey into Morning*.

[6]"On Writing a Poem," Ragan, *Journey into Morning*, 14.

GOVERNOR'S TASK FORCE
ON DRUNKEN DRIVERS

Raleigh, March 19, 1982

["Drunken driving is a crime, and as such it causes economic loss, human misery, and death. If we are to protect our citizens, those who drive drunk must face a greater certainty of arrest, prosecution, conviction, and punishment," Hunt declared February 11, 1982, in his announcement of the creation of the Governor's Task Force on Drunken Drivers. Executive Order No. 75, signed the same day, established the task force. *N.C. Session Laws, 1981, Regular and Extra Sessions, 1982,* 331-333.]

I want to thank each and every one of you for your willingness to serve on this task force. There is a very simple reason why all of you are here: Drunken drivers are killing and maiming themselves and innocent people on the streets and highways of North Carolina.

This is a problem of national proportions. All over this country there has been an increasing awareness of, and indignation toward, the drunken driver. In many instances this indignation has been constructively channeled into citizen action; Mothers against Drunk Driving is one example. It would be irresponsible for government to fail to respond to this nationwide outpouring of concern and anger. In appointing the Governor's Task Force on Drunken Drivers, I have tried to bring together a group of caring and knowledgeable people who will ask the right questions and come forward with workable recommendations.

Let me try to briefly illustrate the problem. In 1980, 1,516 people lost their lives on our highways. At least 414 of those deaths are known to have been caused by drunken driving, and drunken driving was the suspected cause of another 567 fatalities. This terrible carnage has occured despite the fact that more than 82,000 arrests for driving under the influence were made in North Carolina during that same year—more than in any other state except for Texas and California.

But while the arrest rate has been high, the conviction rate has steadily declined. Since 1977, for example, the conviction rate for DUI has declined by 7 percent, while the acceptance of pleas to such lesser offenses as driving after drinking and careless and reckless driving has increased by 28 percent. Overall, the DUI conviction rate since 1977 has dropped from 60 percent to 53 percent.

Your mandate is a broad and demanding one. I am asking you to analyze the nature and scope of the problem of drunken driving, how well we are responding to it, and how we can do a better job of keeping drunken drivers off the road. I commend to you as a starting point for your deliberations the recently completed Governor's Crime Commission report on driving under the influence in North Carolina. It contains some intriguing recommendations that are worthy of your study.[1]

I charge you to gather as much information as you can about how other states are approaching this problem, and I want you to actively solicit the ideas and opinions of North Carolinians from all walks of life. You will be holding a series of public hearings across the state and giving as many people as possible an opportunity to be heard. I expect a report from you by December 1 of this year—earlier if possible. I want that report to include specific recommendations about any changes we need to make, whether they be statutory or administrative.[2]

I can't stress to you enough the importance of maximum public involvement. If we are to effectively address this issue, our people must feel they have had a chance to be heard. They must feel that they have a stake in what we are doing.

I am giving you a very demanding assignment. But each of you was appointed because I felt like you were up to the task, that you cared enough to devote the time that would be required. I am deeply grateful to all of you for the contribution you are going to make to our people. What comes out of your deliberations and your study can literally save lives. That is the most important thing any human being can do for another.

---

[1]See *Driving under the Influence: A Report from the Governor's Crime Commission* ([Raleigh: The Commission], February, 1982).

[2]*Driving while Impaired: An Executive Response . . . Recommendations of the Governor's Task Force on Drunken Drivers, Executive Summary Report* ([Raleigh: The Task Force], November, 1982), 6-24.

AMERICAN ISRAEL PUBLIC AFFAIRS COMMITTEE WORKSHOP ON POLITICS

GREENSBORO, MARCH 20, 1982

It is my pleasure to welcome this workshop to Greensboro and to North Carolina. We read and hear a lot today about NCPAC [National Conservative Political Action Committee] and all the other far right-wing political action committees. I am glad our nation has an effective PAC working on the other side of the political fence.

At your workshop tomorrow, you will be learning the nuts and bolts of political involvement. I would submit to you that nothing is more important to the future of our nation today than for good, caring, religious people to become active in politics. You have got to do it if we are going to save this nation and preserve our freedoms for generations to come.

I have very serious concerns about the direction some would have this nation take. I do believe it is a time to restrain spending and to restore the federal government to its proper role, but now is not the time to turn our backs on hope and progress—as some in Washington would have us do. I am a governor, for instance, who cares deeply about education, about how well our children are prepared for the competitive world we will leave them. That is why the very severe cuts that are proposed in education, particularly in college student loans, deeply concern me.

More than that, I am concerned by the tone some people take. I am concerned about the lack of equity and fairness that we see. Our society cannot survive if people are set against each other, if certain groups feel that they are shut out. If that happens, we cannot know who will be next.

I am concerned about the voices of intolerance and prejudice that we hear coming from the far right, from those who presume to judge the "morality" of the rest of us. That is not the heritage of this nation.

All of us must resolve to preserve our true heritage, one of a free and open society, one of pluralism and cultural traditions. I know how important that is to the Jewish community. I have heard it from Arthur Cassell, Ruth Cook, Ted Kaplan, and Howard Kramer.[1]

That is why I have established the North Carolina Council on the Holocaust, so that none of our citizens will ever forget.

That is why I have established a visiting scholar program between North Carolina and Israel, to promote scholarship and educational exchange. I visited Israel myself in 1978, and I was tremendously impressed by the incredible advances that young nation has made.

For moral and strategic reasons, I believe it is imperative that America continue to be Israel's strong ally. We must never pretend that the threat to Israel's existence has faded. Today, that threat is greater than ever. We must help keep Israel strong enough to survive. I was deeply concerned earlier this year, during the debate over the AWACS sale to Saudi Arabia, when leaders of the Reagan administration raised the threat of anti-Semitism erupting if the sale were defeated.[2] That is not responsible, and that is dangerous politics to play.

That is why this committee and all of you have an important responsibility. Throughout its history, North Carolina has been fertile ground for religious tolerance and diversity and proper separation of church and state. We must not let that fertile ground turn barren. We must not forsake the wisdom of our founding fathers. Hillel wrote in "Wisdom of the Fathers": "If I am not for myself, who is for me? But if I am for myself alone, what am I? And if not now, when?"[3]

---

[1]Ruth E. Cook (1929-   ), native of Berlin, Germany; resident of Raleigh; attended New York University. Former executive director, State Council for Social Legislation; state House member from Wake County, 1975-1983; appointed by Governor Hunt to serve eight-year term on N.C. Public Utilities Commission, beginning 1983. News and Observer, June 26, 1983; North Carolina Manual, 1983, 330.

Ian Theodore (Ted) Kaplan (1946-   ), native of Greensboro; resident of Forsyth County; attended Guilford College. Vice-president, Kaplan School Supply Corp.; state House member from Forsyth, 1977-1981. *North Carolina Manual, 1981,* 334.

Howard Kramer (1946-   ), native of Alexandria, Louisiana; resident of Raleigh; B.S., University of Wisconsin, 1966; J.D., University of North Carolina at Chapel Hill, 1969. Assistant vice-president, Savings Bank Life Insurance Fund, 1970-1972; associate attorney general, 1972-1974, special assistant to the attorney general, 1974-1975, and chief deputy attorney general, 1975-1979, state of North Carolina; attorney in private practice since 1979. Howard Kramer to Jan-Michael Poff, August 13, 1985.

[2]AWACS, or Airborne Warning and Control System, is a surveillance and command post aircraft, perhaps the most unique feature of which is an external, rotating, thirty-foot radar dome capable of tracking 400 planes simultaneously. On October 28, 1981, after having been warned by Reagan administration officials that obstruction of the sale of such equipment to Saudi Arabia could ignite a public opinion backlash against Israel's American Jewish supporters, the U.S. Senate approved the deal. "AWACS: He Does It Again," *Time,* November 9, 1981, 14; "One More Time for 'AWACS Diplomacy,'" *U.S. News & World Report,* February 28, 1983.

Steven L. Spiegel believed that the sale of AWACS to Saudi Arabia was enhanced by a growing American perception of the Middle East in which the "wealth and leadership" of moderate Saudis could be instrumental in ensuring peace in the region; that the security of the Persian Gulf states was vital for the protection of indigenous oil fields and Western economic and industrial interests; and that "the major impediment to a policy based on the foregoing propositions is the Jews of the United States. . . ." However, he contends, "The fact that the AWACS proposal could be offered in the first place was a monument to the American Jews' *lack* of control over U.S. policy." Spiegel, "The Middle East: A Consensus of Error," *Commentary,* 73 (March, 1982), 15, 23; see also Murray Friedman, "AWACS and the Jewish Community," *Commentary,* 73 (April, 1982), 29-33, and Steven Emerson, "The Petrodollar Connection," *New Republic,* February 17, 1982, 18-25.

[3]Pirkei Avot 1:14. Hillel the Elder (1 B.C.) "was an extraordinarily gifted [Jewish] scholar and teacher who held an extremely important and powerful position in the overlapping, confusing labyrinth of the religious and secular Judean power structure." Martin P. Beifield, Jr., Rabbi, Temple Beth Or, to Jan-Michael Poff, December 12, 1985. See also *Encyclopedia Judaica,* s.v. "Hillel (the Elder)."

YOUTH-CONDUCTED HEARING
ON VOLUNTEERISM

RALEIGH, MARCH 31, 1982

I speak to you today as a supporter of volunteerism, a lifelong supporter of student volunteerism, and as a supporter of academic credit for student volunteer work. I believe that volunteerism is not just a good thing to do—it is something that needs to be done by all our citizens—and young people do not need to wait until graduation to begin contributing to the world outside the school.

Traditional volunteer work is usually done by the church or some community agency, but volunteerism takes on new seriousness with the school's active support. Experience has shown that students work most effectively in their communities and receive the most educational benefits when the school serves as coordinator. With student volunteerism, our motto can be "learning to serve and serving to learn." Here are the main reasons why I believe that academic credit for volunteer work is important, particularly at this time:

—Volunteering is a good way to explore career interests. If you think you'd like to be a nurse or medical technician, you can work at the local hospital. If you think you'd like a career in law enforcement, you can be an intern with the police department. And maybe volunteering will open new doors to careers you've never ever thought about.

—With the high rate of youth unemployment, volunteerism provides young people with the opportunity to gain work experience. When you apply for that all-important first job, one of the first questions you'll be asked is, "What experience do you have?" Many employers are now looking at volunteerism as worthwhile contributions on your résumé.

—Budget cutbacks are affecting many important social programs. Youth volunteerism can fill many of those gaps in service.

—It is important for young people to feel that they are part of their community and to take responsibility for how the community functions. Youth should be contributing members of society today, not just future contributors.

—Volunteerism is an excellent way for young people to develop their leadership potential and refine their communication skills. Most of this state's leaders and this nation's leaders were active, striving youth who made their marks in areas such as Boy Scouts, Future Farmers, and others.

—Community involvement can help make high school studies relevant and meaningful. We all learn better by doing.

The notion of academic credit for student volunteer work is not foreign to North Carolina. Some effort is being made in that area, but we need to encourage more. The North Carolina School of Science and Mathematics requires that each student serve an internship in order to satisfy graduation requirements. I understand that testimony to be given later today will discuss that program in detail.

I see basically two options for academic credit for volunteer work. The first is to offer field courses, in which volunteer activity would be incorporated into a course. For example, a student would complete 20 hours of volunteer work in the community as a part of a civics course. Another example would be a peer tutoring program, perhaps as a part of an advanced studies class in math, science, or almost any subject.

The second of the two options would be special courses which hold no classes and require no, or little, academic work. A student could receive one or more hours of academic credit for volunteering after school. It would have to be specified how often and how long the student would volunteer.

Student volunteerism is limitless. A group may be formed for drug abuse education. Students may serve internships as volunteer hospital aides or public library aides. They may work side by side with social service workers or in charitable organizations like the Heart Fund or Cancer Society, or involve themselves in roadside cleanups.

There are many ways in which to serve, and the youth of this state are a tremendous, virtually untapped resource. As John F. Kennedy once said: "It is time for a new generation of leadership, to cope with new problems and new opportunities. For there is a new world to be won." [1]

This group has my full support. I join with you in encouraging the state's school systems to seek effective, meaningful ways to bring about increased student volunteerism.

There is real and needed work that is waiting. There are enthusiastic and eager young people ready to get the job done, and the schools are the ideal place to bring the two together.

---

[1] The remarks, which Hunt quoted accurately, are from a televised speech Kennedy made July 4, 1960. Bartlett, *Familiar Quotations*, 1072.

STATEMENT ON ALTERNATIVE HEALTH CARE PROGRAMS

RALEIGH, APRIL 14, 1982

I am announcing today the establishment of the North Carolina Foundation for Alternative Health Care Programs. The foundation will explore all available options for meeting the health care needs of our people, particularly state employees and Medicaid recipients. We must place a higher priority on preventive care and controlling costs.

In a time when the cost of medical care continues to rise at an alarming rate, it is absolutely essential that we look for innovative ways of providing the best possible care in an economical way. Between 1965 and 1979, the annual cost of medical care in the United States increased from $212 per capita to $942 per capita. Even after adjusting those figures for inflation, the cost doubled during that period.

In North Carolina, the cost of medical care rose by 70 percent from 1974 to 1979, and Medicaid costs increased by 22 percent from 1979 to 1980. In 1981, the cost of health insurance for state employees increased 30 percent over the previous year.

Hospital costs in North Carolina rose more than 18 percent last year, and that followed a 20 percent increase the previous year. The cost of a physical examination is between $85 and $120. Having a baby can cost $1,500 for the hospital and another $1,300 for the physician.

In 1978, the General Assembly created the North Carolina Commission on Prepaid Health Plans to examine the feasibility of the prepayment concept. After two years of study, the commission concluded that prepaid health care is a realistic alternative and recommended the establishment of a nonprofit corporation to help develop alternative plans of this kind.[1] Under a prepaid plan, health care providers are paid in advance for the estimated cost of a patient's medical care over a certain period of time. That protects the patient from unexpected costs resulting from illness or injury, and it gives the provider an incentive to provide preventive care and to refrain from unnecessary services.

I am asking this foundation to look at this and other alternatives in the hope that state employees and our taxpayers can save money on health care costs. Such alternatives would not replace our current health insurance system, but simply would make more options available on a voluntary basis. The foundation will also work with business and industry in formulating alternative programs of their own. Approximately $1 million has been donated by private foundations to support this effort. I particularly want to thank the John A. Hartford Foundation of New York and the Henry J. Kaiser Family Foundation of California for their help.

James Bernstein, chief of the Office of Rural Health Services in the North Carolina Department of Human Resources, will be executive director of the foundation.[2] A distinguished group of business, medical, and professional people will serve as foundation directors. I am confident that under this kind of leadership, we in North Carolina can develop means for saving our taxpayers' money, holding down the cost of health care to individuals, and providing our people with the kind of care they need and deserve.

---

[1]"An Act to Establish a Commission to Plan the Development of an Optional Prepaid Health Plan in the Research Triangle Area, and to Make an Appropriation, so as to Implement the Recommendations of the Legislative Commission on Medical Cost Containment" was ratified June 16, 1978. *N.C. Session Laws, 1977, Second Session, 1978,* c. 1291. The group's findings and recommendations are listed in *North Carolina Commission on Prepaid Health Plans: Final Report* (Raleigh: [The Commission], 3 volumes, 1980), I, 5-36.

[2]James D. Bernstein (1942-   ), resident of Chapel Hill; B.A., Johns Hopkins University, 1964; M.H.A., University of Michigan, 1968; Peace Corps volunteer, 1964-1966. Research associate, Health Services Center, University of North Carolina at Chapel Hill, since 1970; chief, Office of Rural Health Services, state Human Resources Department, since 1973; director, Winthrop Rockefeller Foundation, 1977-1983; adjunct assistant professor, Duke University medical school, since 1978; adjunct associate professor, UNC medical school, since 1979; president, North Carolina Foundation for Alternative Health Programs, Inc., since 1982; consultant. James D. Bernstein to Jan-Michael Poff, February 26, 1985.

AMERICAN ASSEMBLY ON THE FUTURE
OF AMERICAN POLITICAL PARTIES

HARRIMAN, N.Y., APRIL 16, 1982

I am especially pleased to have the opportunity to be a part of the sixty-second American Assembly and to discuss with you "The Future of American Political Parties." I found the invitation irresistible, partly because of the persuasive powers of my friend Joel Fleishman[1] and the high quality I know one can anticipate for any conference he has a hand in organizing. What was also especially attractive was the opportunity, after eight months of intense involvement in the writing of the Democratic party's rules for 1984—a real nuts-and-bolts job if there ever was one—to take a broader look at where the parties are going and at the conditions of party renewal.

The topic you have chosen is on a great many people's minds. It was certainly on our minds as we examined the presidential nomination process and recast the rules governing that process. Of course we Democrats have had special reasons for soul searching during the past eighteen months, but there is enough evidence of decline in the health of our parties to concern people of all political persuasions. There are some encouraging signs as well, which several of the papers prepared for this conference explore in detail. My own conviction is that the future is potentially bright for our party system, but I am not inclined to take its durability and health for granted. I would like to share with you tonight some thoughts as to why party renewal is a task worthy of our effort and concern, and then to reflect briefly on the relationship of party reform to such renewal.

First, we need the party as a guide to consistent and rational electoral choice. The public opinion pollsters still get a generally positive reaction when they ask people whether it is best to vote for the person rather than the party, but many thoughtful people are becoming critical of this bit of conventional wisdom. It has become clear that all too often the alternative to following the party cue is a vote based on superficial personality traits, or on the issue that is hot at the moment, or on the mere fact of incumbency or name familiarity. Voting "for the person," moreover, has brought a disconcerting kind of volatility to our politics—wide swings from election to election—as different issues and personalities come into prominence; and large disparities in voting, up and down the ballot, as people split their tickets with abandon.

Party labels in this country, of course, have generally given only an approximate guide to what a candidate would do once in office. But they give a generally reliable indication of where a candidate stands on a *range* of issues and of the kind of people he or she is likely to bring into government. For these reasons a party vote, even if reflexively cast, is often more "rational" than one based on charisma or issue appeal, communicated as these often are through 30-second television spots.

Secondly, the party is a valuable mediating institution between citizens and their government. The kind of tangible presence the party once was in many wards and precincts is not likely to be re-created—the advent of civil service, the welfare state, television, and many other fixtures of modern life have seen to that. But as the politics of personal contact is increasingly displaced by remote-control campaigns and faceless government, it is critically important to preserve the party as a contact point among citizens and between citizens and public officials.

In North Carolina we have just held our yearly round of precinct meetings and county conventions. I would not want to romanticize these exercises in grass-roots democracy, but I would not want to underestimate their importance either. Often they serve a kind of town meeting function, enabling citizens to express themselves not only on the burning issues of the day but also on the need for new road signs or for altered community development priorities or for improved bus service.

The party organization can thus become a vehicle for specific concerns close to home. But the party is critically different from most interest groups and from groups dedicated to the pursuit of a single policy goal. The party forces a kind of *broadening* on individuals and groups, whereby they must learn to listen to and accommodate others whose views and interests differ from their own. It opens a window on the wider world, tempering the local and the particular with an awareness of broader issues and purposes.

The party, in other words, is a mediating institution of great importance, engaging diverse groups and individuals, providing a vehicle for expressing their interests and for working together, and linking the local community to what often seem to be remote centers of power. I share the concern that many are expressing nowadays about the erosion of such mediating institutions and organizations in our communities. As governor, I have worked hard to kindle enthusiasm and encourage participation in a broad range of volunteer and service organizations. My interest in revitalized political parties—not just at the national level, but right down to the counties and the precincts—is rooted in similar concerns.

Thirdly, our parties remain a vital key to effective governance. The framers of our state and federal constitutions generally did a better job of checking and balancing power than they did of ensuring that government could pull itself together for the achievement of positive purposes. This latter task required them to organize political parties, often in spite of themselves. Most of the founders shared an apprehensiveness, expressed by George Washington in his farewell address, of "the baneful effects of the spirit of party."[2] But as Austin Ranney remarks about Jefferson and Madison, when they actually tried to govern "they were faced with a fact, not a theory." The fact was that the only way they could defeat Hamilton's schemes was to unify the anti-Hamiltonian forces in Congress and to increase their numbers by contesting elections.[3] Jefferson and Madison carried out these organizational tasks quite successfully, and today we honor these two antiparty theorists as the founders of the Democratic party!

Like any governor whose party holds a majority in the legislature, I have a particular stake in strengthening the party as a link between the branches of government and have had numerous occasions to wish that link were stronger. As the only governor in the nation whose constitution deprives him of a veto, it has been absolutely essential for me to work with and through the party leadership. This was particularly true in the two most visible and politically difficult battles of my administration, the passage of a constitutional amendment to permit a governor to succeed himself, and the increase in the tax on gasoline. Here we were not merely drawing on the party loyalties of the members themselves but were working through the state and county party organizations to build a vocal and active base of pressure and support.

Our government needs that kind of capacity for teamwork. Regardless of any differences I might have with the content of the Reagan administration's program, I have to admire the kind of party discipline the Republicans displayed in Congress in putting its key elements into place. Our record on the Democratic side, of course, is more mixed. The party unity scores of our House and Senate members have declined over the past few decades. While recent years have seen a narrowing of the gap between the northern and southern wings of the party, one analyst has concluded that only about one fifth of the party's northern and western members could be counted on to support the leadership on a full range of issues in the late 1970s.

There have been some encouraging developments as well. The House Rules Committee now generally acts as an arm of the leadership, and committee assignments have been placed where they should be, firmly within party control. Speaker O'Neill[4] has developed an expanded whip system and has experimented with task forces to handle bills that otherwise would be parceled out to scattered committees. Still, the past administration was marked by policy-making frustrations which often could be traced to the lack of party cohesion. Our party has rightly been sobered by that experience, and the issues of the eighties are likely to be even more difficult to resolve.

Lester Thurow convincingly argues that many of our most important policy dilemmas—inflation, economic development, energy supplies and costs, environmental protection, taxation—have "zero-sum" features; that is, they require tough choices between conflicting goals, and they require sacrifices on the part of some to advance the general good. Interestingly enough, Thurow points to the weakening of our parties as a major reason for our inability to deal realistically and coherently with these problems: "Every politician with his or her own platform is the American way," he says, "but it is not a way that is going to be able to solve America's economic problems."[5] It is no longer tolerable for each special interest to exercise veto power, or for each committee and subcommittee to fence off its piece of policy turf. This, in the end, is the most compelling reason for strengthening what Jim Sundquist calls the "web of party"; without it we are threatened with the loss of our capacity to govern.[6]

At all of these levels—in the realm of electoral choice, in the life of our communities, and as we attempt to organize responsive and effective governments—we need healthy parties. Organized above and beyond our constitutional structure, always slightly suspect and often maligned, our parties are in reality critically important instruments of democracy. We have good reason to be concerned, then, when we find half of the new generation of voters declaring themselves "independents," or when we find "independent expenditures" and PACs dominating the campaign scene, or when we find legislators disdainful of their party's interests. We have good reason to devote a great deal of thought and energy to bringing the party back.

It would be a mistake, however, merely to adopt a reactive posture with respect to these trends, or to cling to an image of the party system that is rooted in the past. I am not ready to declare face-to-face work in the precincts, a strong system of caucuses and conventions, or even party patronage obsolete. At the same time, it is clear that revitalized parties must adapt positively to television and other new communication technologies, must recognize the values of efficiency and professionalism in government, must provide a receptive forum for new groups and issues, and must have a stronger national component than did the old party system.

Revitalized parties, then, will take new forms and assume new functions. We must be realistic about the prospects for change. The demographic and sociological and technological developments that have undermined the parties' traditional roles must be adapted to; they are not going to be reversed. It is important to recognize this, but it is also important to recognize the things that *can* be done. It does make a difference, for example, how we design our campaign finance laws, whether they promote a central role for parties or encourage their neglect. It does make a difference how those of us running for office conduct our campaigns; on grounds of both self-interest and the public interest I think the trend in recent years toward highly individualistic, Lone Ranger-type campaigns is in need of a searching reexamination.

This brings me, finally, to a few thoughts about party reform. I referred earlier to the antiparty views of the founders, an ambivalence toward parties that has continued to characterize American political thought. The tradition of party reform has partaken fully of that ambivalence. Reform has come in three phases. The first saw the removal of presidential nominations from the congressional caucus in the 1820s and the calling of the first national nominating conventions before the 1832 election. The second period of reform, spurred by the progressive movement and concentrated around the turn of the century, had as its hallmark the direct primary. The third period is still with us; the reform impulse reached its zenith in the Democratic party after the tumultuous 1968 convention and has found somewhat less intense expression in the GOP as well. In all of these instances, party reformers have regarded party structures and processes as barriers to democracy standing between the people and their government. What they often missed was how parties could actually *facilitate* accountability and responsiveness in government—and how the changes reformers made could weaken parties in ways that went beyond their original intent.

Our Commission on Presidential Nomination is the fourth in a series of Democratic rules-writing bodies that began with the landmark McGovern-Fraser commission in 1969.[7] We fully appreciated and embraced the efforts of this generation of reformers to establish procedural openness and fairness and broadened participation in party affairs. We recognized, however, that our present nomination system has weakened the party in critical ways. Primaries have proliferated—the extent to which rules changes are responsible for this is, of course, hotly debated—removing decision-making power from party caucuses and conventions. The Democratic National Convention has almost become what one critic called a "rubber stamp electoral college."[8] And to an alarming extent elected officials, particularly the party's congressional wing, have ceased to play an active convention role.

I like Jim Sundquist's phrase: to "nudge" the party system toward change. That is all a single rules-writing commission can hope to do. I believe we nudged the Democratic party in some positive directions. We added some 550 slots to be filled by party and elected officials, who would come to the convention as unpledged delegates; about 175 of these would be chosen by the House and Senate Democratic caucuses, the rest by state parties. We removed the 1980 rule which bound all delegates to vote for their pledged preference on the first ballot. We retained the ban on the "open" primary. We shortened the primary/caucus season by some five weeks, and we relaxed strict proportional representation requirements for the allocation of delegates.

There are areas where I wish we could have nudged a bit further. I would have preferred a larger number of unpledged delegates—to give state parties more flexibility and to permit a more diverse demographic mix—and I would have preferred to give candidate organizations less control over who could run for delegate and participate in the selection of delegates. But the compromises we made were reasonable ones, and I expect the new rules to have a cumulative party-strengthening effect. The addition of unpledged delegates and removal of the "binding" rule should give the convention more flexibility and authority and make participation in the process more significant and more attractive. The effects of shortening the season and of modifying proportional representation will depend on the nature of the field of candidates, but these changes should generally reduce the fragmentation of the process and facilitate party unity. The addition of elected officials should give the convention a broader representative cast, restore an element of peer review to the nomination process, give congressional Democrats a stronger stake in the nominee and the platform, and provide incentives for the kind of coalition-building within the party we need if our candidates are to campaign and to govern effectively.

That the Democratic party was able to make these changes is one of many encouraging signs, I think, of the durability and resilience of our country's party system. I am also encouraged by the calling of conferences such as this one—coming as it does in the wake of the Duke Forum, the work of the Kennedy School and the Miller Center, the Sloan Foundation study, and other similar efforts. Just as "reform" has shed much of its traditional ambivalence and taken a marked party-building turn, so are a broad range of thoughtful people giving renewed attention and concern to the future of our parties. There is reason to hope that a new ethos may arise that gives to parties a new prominence and legitimacy as instruments of democratic governance. It is important that we join together in this process of discussion and public education—that we reflect critically on the current state of our public life and think creatively about how, through revitalized parties, we can increase the responsiveness and competence of government. I welcome the chance to join with you in that task.

---

[1]Joel Lawrence Fleishman (1934-   ), native of Fayetteville; resident of Chapel Hill; A.B., 1955, M.A., 1959, J.D., 1959, University of North Carolina at Chapel Hill; U.S. Naval Reserve, 1955-1956. Assistant to director, Walter E. Meyer Research Institute of Law, 1960-1961; legal assistant to Governor Terry Sanford, 1961-1965; associate provost of Urban Studies and Programs, 1967-1969, and political science lecturer, 1969-1971, Yale University; director, Institute of Policy Sciences, since 1971, professor of law and policy sciences, since 1974, and vice-chancellor, since 1978, Duke University; author. *Who's Who in America, 1982-1983*, I, 1062.

[2]George Washington, Farewell Address [September 17, 1796], quoted in Bartlett, *Familiar Quotations*, 461.

[3]See Austin Ranney, *Curing the Mischiefs of Faction: Party Reform in America* (Berkeley: University of California Press, 1975), 24.

[4]Thomas P. (Tip) O'Neill, Jr. (1912-   ), native, resident of Cambridge, Massachusetts; A.B., Boston College, 1936. Insurance business; member, Massachusetts House of Representatives, 1936-1952; member, U.S. House from Massachusetts's Eighth Congressional District, since 1953, and speaker since 1976. Barone and Ujifusa, *Almanac of American Politics, 1984*, 558-559.

[5]Lester Carl Thurow (1938-   ), native of Livingston, Montana; B.A., Williams College, 1960; M.A., Oxford University, 1964. Staff member, President's Council of Economic Advisors, 1964-1965; assistant professor of economics, Harvard University, 1965-1968; faculty member, since 1968, and currently professor of economics and management, Massachusetts Institute of Technology; author. *Who's Who in America, 1982-1983*, II, 3336. Quotation from Thurow, *The Zero-Sum Society: Distribution and the Possibilities for Economic Change* (New York: Basic Books, Inc., Publishers, 1980), 214.

[6]James Lloyd Sundquist (1915-   ), native of West Point, Utah; resident of Arlington, Virginia; attended Weber College, 1934, and Northwestern University, 1934-1935; B.S., University of Utah, 1939; M.S., Syracuse University, 1941. Former newspaper reporter, budget analyst, and statistics officer; management control director, U.S. Army, Berlin, 1947-1949; assistant to the chairman, Democratic National Committee, 1953-1954; assistant secretary to the governor of New York, 1955-1956; assistant to U.S. senator Ramsey Clark, 1957-1962; deputy undersecretary, U.S. Department of Agriculture, 1963-1965; Brookings Institute senior fellow, since 1965; platform committee secretary, National Democratic Convention, 1960, 1968; editor; author. *Who's Who in America, 1982-1983*, II, 3260. Quotation could not be verified.

[7]The purpose of the Commission on Party Structure and Delegate Selection was to define "in specific language how the state parties would implement the [1968 national] convention's mandate 'to give all Democratic voters . . . a full, meaningful, and timely opportunity' to participate in the delegate selection process." It was frequently referred to as the McGovern-Fraser commission, named for George McGovern, U.S. senator from South Dakota, and Congressman Donald Fraser of Minnesota. Fraser succeeded McGovern as chairman after the latter resigned to campaign for the 1972 Democratic presidential nomination. John G. Stewart, *One Last Chance: The Democratic Party, 1971-1976* (New York: Praeger Publishers, 1974), 52.

[8]The critic could not be identified.

DURHAM TECHNICAL INSTITUTE DISCUSSION ON BUSINESS AND INDUSTRY TRAINING

RESEARCH TRIANGLE PARK, APRIL 20, 1982

I am pleased to be in one of my favorite places in all of North Carolina. It is here, in the Research Triangle Park, that much of our future lies. I am convinced that the good jobs of the future — those jobs that mean better pay and better lives for our people — are in microelectronics, computers, electronics, pharmaceuticals, biotechnology, and other sophisticated, high-technology industries.

I believe that you and your companies hold the key to this future for many North Carolinians. You are innovators. You break new ground daily in research. You are trendsetters with an international reputation for productivity and creativity. My challenge to you today is to break new ground in education and job training. We need a dramatic breakthrough.

We face a future being revolutionized by changing technology, brought about in great part by companies such as your own. How we train our young people, how we train their parents and others whose skills the new technology makes obsolete, depends upon you. What you do today will determine in great part the quality of workers you hire tomorrow.

Last year more than one out of every three new jobs announced were in the categories of electronics and electrical production, machinery, fabricated metal products, and transportation equipment. These types of companies pay well above the average manufacturing wage in our state, but how can our citizens learn the new technologies required by these jobs if they can't read or write? How can they begin preparing for a career in chemical technology or electronics engineering technology when they have no understanding of what these fields are all about? I believe that a considerable share of the responsibility for ensuring that this does not happen, for ensuring that our people are prepared for a future that is oriented toward the new technologies, lies with you, the leaders in our state and nation of these new industries.

Our community college system is the best in the nation. A little more than a year ago NBC television singled out the system for national attention as the example of an educational system that works.

Durham Technical Institute is a leader in providing industry with the kind of customized training programs it needs, and this school is at the forefront in making programs available to people when they need them. When you close down for the day, Durham Tech opens its doors to students who must get training and education in off-duty hours, in the evening, and on weekends. I am proud of the efforts this school has made in meeting the needs of the microelectronics industry for skilled technicians. When General Electric begins its new industrial training program this spring with Durham Tech, it will find a tailor-made training program.

Our community college system is first rate. The facilities are in place. The leadership is there. The training expertise is there. The commitment is there, and your company's future employees are there.

Our community college system in North Carolina is just that—a system of community-based institutions—and you are the community. If you don't take an active role in the life of your technical school, you and I and all North Carolinians will bear the consequences of out-of-date skills.

As you know, our community college system is in need of up-to-date training equipment. I am determined that they will have, in the short run, the money they need to provide you with the kind of skilled workers you need. But the problem of replacing obsolete equipment is not going to be solved in the long run by a one-shot dose of dollars. We need a better solution for the future.

Business and industry in this state have donated more than $4.5 million worth of equipment, supplies, and materials to our community college system. On behalf of Carl Horn and myself, I want to thank you for your response to our appeal for donations.

This $4.5 million does not even begin to take into account the gifts your companies give to an individual technical school. It does not reflect arrangements that some companies have made which give our Department of Community Colleges first refusal, after branch offices, on surplus equipment. I urge you to continue to give training equipment to our system. We have obtained a ruling from our state Department of Revenue that allows a deduction, not only for donations of equipment, but for the loan of such equipment. And we are working at the federal level to establish similar rulings.

One of the most critical training issues we face in North Carolina is the need to keep our instructors current. We also are losing instructors to industry, to higher salaries and more attractive benefits. It is becoming more and more difficult to replace those who leave. Help us find creative ways to solve our problems. How can we keep our instructors up to date? How can we continue to make teaching attractive to others?

We have a tradition in our state of supporting our colleges and universities. We establish chair professorships and endowments. Today I challenge you to do the same for our faculty and students at technical schools.

Last December I went to Winston-Salem to announce Wachovia Bank and Trust Company's endowment of a technical scholarship program for our community college system. It is a landmark gift and one that needs repeating by others.

Lend one of your top technicians or engineers to Durham Technical Institute for six months or a year. Establish an adjunct professorship.

Look at what our state's oldest and largest manufacturing employer, the textile industry, is doing to help itself as it begins to undergo modernization. With the cooperation of one of our technical schools, a number of textile companies, and the North Carolina Textile Manufacturers Association, a partnership has been struck that I think could be a model for how we conduct our training programs in this state. These companies are providing training equipment and making training areas in their plants available to technical students enrolled in the textile manufacturing program. They are also going to offer students incentives—higher beginning wages, preferential hiring, and scholarships. The textile companies and the technical school have faced head-on the problem of how to keep instructors current by offering instructors on-the-job training through internships and vacation jobs.

Finally, we need to give people better information about where the jobs will be and what skills they will need to get these jobs. We have made some progress in attracting students to those areas in which there is a critical need for workers, and with some special funding from the General Assembly, many of our schools have been able to set up programs for training in a number of areas. Last year, for example, twenty-seven schools offered electronic engineering technology. This year thirty-five schools have this program. Last year 2,300 students enrolled in the electronic engineering technology program. This year that number was up by one third.

I am optimistic about the future. If you know the community college system in our state as well as I do, you know we have reason for confidence.

I want our people to be able to enjoy the benefits of top rankings in per capita income and wages. That challenge is still with us. We have made some progress, but we have a long way to go. I hope you'll join with me in helping to lead our people into a brighter, more prosperous future. I thank you for your past support, and for your continued commitment to a better North Carolina.

TESTIMONY BEFORE U.S. HOUSE COMMITTEE ON WAYS AND MEANS, SUBCOMMITTEE ON PUBLIC ASSISTANCE AND UNEMPLOYMENT COMPENSATION

WASHINGTON, D.C., APRIL 21, 1982

[The essential elements of the governor's testimony before the House Public Assistance Subcommittee were repeated in his remarks at the North Carolina Social Services Association annual conference, May 27, and the Southeastern Child Welfare League, June 2, 1982. The Reagan administration's proposed cuts in entitlement programs, to which Hunt referred below, and congressional action thereon, are summarized in *Congressional Quarterly Almanac, 1982,* 476-478; progress on the president's block grants system is covered on pages 536-539 of the *Almanac.*]

Mr. Chairman,[1] I am James B. Hunt, Jr., governor of North Carolina and chairman of the Human Resources Committee of the National Governors' Association. I am pleased to have the opportunity to appear before you today to discuss the position of the National Governors' Association on the proposals contained in the president's FY 83 budget. In order to have time for questions, I will speak briefly and will submit the full text of my remarks for the record.

Governors recognize the critical nature of the economic problems that confront the nation. States support proposals to manage programs more effectively and to establish priorities for limited resources, but we cannot continue to bear a disproportionate share of this burden. Remember, states and local governments are already doing more with less. The administration has stressed that it has not reduced the total level of government spending but instead has reduced the rate of growth. While this may be true in general, it is not the case for needs-tested programs or for programs of assistance to state and local governments.

The chart before you shows the level of federal aid to state and local governments over the past six years. It shows in constant dollars that federal aid has dropped from $68.4 billion in FY 77 to a proposed level of $49.9 billion in FY 83. In this fiscal year, 1982, the budget authority for state aid programs dropped dramatically from about $106 billion in FY 81 to $78 billion.

Dramatic cuts have come in funding for needs-tested income assistance programs as well. The change is particularly stark in the AFDC program, where the president proposed a drop from $8 billion in FY 81 to $6.6 billion in FY 83. Similar real dollar reductions have been proposed in other programs such as Title XX, Child Welfare Services, and Low-Income Energy Assistance.

For the most part, we supported the first round of budget reductions. We believed that if given the authority to make administrative changes, we could absorb reductions of some 10 percent and still do the job. We were given cuts, however, that in many cases exceeded 25 percent. We did not get the administrative flexibility we sought in many instances, and we now need time to adjust to the cuts before we consider new and heavier cuts in these same programs.

I think there is a general recognition that some reductions have been needed. But we can't turn back to doing things the way we did then. We're not going to return to the days of sending people to the poor house or the county home. We have learned that there are better ways of meeting human needs, and we must find ways to continue to meet those needs.

This job cannot be done overnight. It's going to take time. I urge you to give us time to design new alternatives for meeting human needs.

We have suggested to the administration, and shared with your staff, suggestions as to specific program improvements that may help reduce program expenditures without shifting costs to the states. While most of these changes are in the Medicare and Medicaid program, I would be pleased to supply copies to this committee to suggest areas for more productive exploration.

In addition, the National Governors' Association, in a letter to the president on December 4 of last year and in action at its winter meeting earlier this year, has suggested the need to examine defense spending, non-needs-tested entitlements, and tax expenditures as other means of reducing the deficit. I urge your continued support for such initiatives, and I hope that you will join with the governors in calling for a freeze on further cuts in block grants and state and local assistance and the continuation of the needs-tested entitlements at least at their current levels.

Now, I would like to turn to some of the specific proposals before your committee, beginning with the proposal to create a child welfare block grant. Governors have long supported the additional flexibility inherent in the block grant concept, but we are concerned with two aspects of this proposal: First, the level of funding reflects a cut of 27 percent, but there is no evidence to suggest that problems which are to be addressed by this grant have seen a similar reduction. Second, the adoption assistance and foster care programs were created originally and are now funded as entitlement programs, and including them in this block grant would be contrary to that concept.

Another new block grant proposal would combine the low-income energy assistance program with the emergency assistance program for AFDC families. Block grant flexibility to meet emergency needs through a single effort is important, but the proposed cut of over $600 million will undermine the effectiveness of both programs.

Governors generally support the need to tighten rules which permit recipients to earn limited income and not lose AFDC benefits. We support legislation that would give states flexibility to develop incentives that would encourage recipients to continue to assume responsibility for their support beyond the four-month period mandated under present legislation.

We believe it is critical to maintain a strong incentive to work in the AFDC program itself since other changes in the Medicaid and food stamp programs further reduce the rewards of work. It should be a fundamental principle of any welfare program that those who work are better off than those who do not. Some independent analyses suggest that we have modified the programs to the extent that this may no longer be the case.

The final areas in AFDC concern proposals to penalize states for AFDC errors in excess of 3 percent and to place a cap on administrative reimbursement at 95 percent of the FY 82 level. We feel that these proposals are mutually exclusive. We want to reduce errors, but it is obvious to governors that the changes in AFDC procedures last year on top of proposals for FY 83 suggest more, and not less, administrative costs.

There is no question that our goal in this program, and in all assistance programs, should be the lowest error rate possible, but with the complexity of the federal regulations and the frequency of changes enacted by Congress, it is unrealistic to expect that states can reach even a 3 percent error level within the near future. Even the Supplemental Security Income (SSI) program has consistently had an error rate of 5 percent or more despite the best efforts of the Social Security Administration to reduce it, and welfare experts generally agree that the SSI program is substantially less error prone than the AFDC program. As governors we are prepared to do our part in further error reduction. At the same time, the federal government must accept the responsibility for sharing in the legitimate costs of this system until it can be simplified to the point where it can be administered with fewer errors.

In closing, I would like to make brief reference to the federalism proposals which we understand may be submitted to Congress in the near future. The governors are strong advocates of an improved federal system. We urge the Congress to give careful attention to the president's proposal.

However, unlike the president, we believe that the federal government should retain a major role in the financing and administration of all income security programs. Only at the national level is it possible to equalize among the states the impact of poverty and to offset the costs of economic crises that are far beyond the control of any individual state.

For these reasons we urge cautious examination of any proposal that would turn back the financing of income security programs to the states. We believe that alternative federalism approaches are available—for example, the position adopted at the recent NGA winter meeting—and would be pleased to work with the Congress on such approaches. For your information, I would like to provide copies of the association's positions on income security and federalism for the record.

Mr. Chairman, the actions of this committee will play a critical role in the congressional response to the FY 83 budget. I hope that my comments and the materials that we will supply for the record will be of assistance. I appreciate the opportunity to testify on behalf of the governors and would be glad to respond to any questions, now or in the future.

---

[1] Harold E. Ford (1945-   ), native, resident of Memphis, Tennessee; B.S., Tennessee State University, 1967; L.F.D., L.E.D., John Gupton College, 1969. Mortician, 1969-1975; member, Tennessee state House, 1971-1974; U.S. representative from Tennessee's Ninth Congressional District since 1975, and chairman, Subcommittee on Public Assistance and Unemployment Compensation of the House Committee on Ways and Means. Barone and Ujifusa, *Almanac of American Politics, 1984*, 1113.

STATEMENT ON SPEEDY TRIAL ACT

RALEIGH, APRIL 22, 1982

[Statistics compiled by the Administrative Office of the Courts and released in 1982 indicated a marked decrease in the number of court cases, between the 1979-1980 and 1980-1981 fiscal years, dismissed for failure to come before a judge within the 120-day period established by the Speedy Trial Act. According to a newspaper article carried by United Press International in April, 1982, proponents of the measure interpreted the findings as proof of its effectiveness and that the state's judicial system once again was functioning smoothly. However, the act's critics argued that an increase in the median age of felony cases demonstrated that the courts were still overburdened; furthermore, they contended that the AOC figures masked an untold number of legal disputes that were either declared exempt from the law or resolved by plea bargain by trial lawyers and district attorneys hard pressed to meet a rigid timetable for processing cases. *News and Observer*, April 19, 1982. The governor's response to the UPI article and opponents of the act appears below.]

I have read with interest recent news articles focusing on the Speedy Trial Act. I would like to take this opportunity to express my view that this law is working very well in North Carolina. Studies by the Administrative Office of the Courts and the Institute of Government show that the law is doing precisely what it was intended to do. Cases are being brought to trial sooner, and those found guilty of crimes are being punished more swiftly.

I pushed for legislative approval of the Speedy Trial Act in 1977 because it was clear that if we were going to prevent crime, something had to be done about procedural delays that were causing cases to languish. This situation undermined the principle of swift and certain punishment, and it was unfair to victims, witnesses, jurors, court personnel, and criminal defendants. Something needed to be done to make the system work in a way that would deter crime and correct a serious erosion of public confidence in our courts.

Some of our judges and district attorneys had initial misgivings, but they nonetheless were determined to help make the Speedy Trial Act work.

The annual report of the Administrative Office of the Courts, which is to be released in a few weeks, shows a steady decline in the amount of time required to dispose of a criminal case. During the fiscal year ending June 30, 1979, it took an average of 128 days to dispose of a case. During the 1979-1980 fiscal year, that figure dropped to 103 days. And during the 1980-1981 fiscal year, the average time for disposition decreased to 100 days. We put teeth in the law by requiring that cases be dismissed if not brought to trial on time. In 1980-1981, only sixty-six cases were dismissed for failure to come to trial within the required 120 days. That is less than two tenths of one percent of the total number of cases, and it represents a dramatic decrease from the 120 cases dismissed the previous year.[1]

A study soon to be released by the Institute of Government tracked all felony cases arising during a three-month period in twelve North Carolina counties in 1979. It was found that 75 percent of the cases were completed within ninety days of indictment, and more than half were completed in sixty days or less.[2]

These figures demonstrate that our district attorneys, judges, and clerks are doing an excellent job of managing the case loads and swiftly moving cases through the system. Wade Barber of Pittsboro,[3] the president of the state district attorneys' association, is here with me today, and I want to publicly thank Wade and his colleagues for all they have done to make this law work. The Speedy Trial Act represents a bold step forward in the administration of justice and the fight against crime. Those who would violate the law are now on notice that they will be punished swiftly for their criminal acts.

---

[1] *North Carolina Courts, 1980-1981. Annual Report of the Administrative Office of the Courts* ([Raleigh: Administrative Office of the Courts, 1982]), 100-107, 141-158. For more detailed statistical information on the period 1979-1980, see also *Annual Report, 1978-1979*, 102-109, 148-155, and *1979-1980*, 106-113, 153-160.

[2] Stevens H. Clarke and others, *Felony Prosecution and Sentencing in North Carolina: A Report to the Governor's Crime Commission and the National Institute of Justice* (Chapel Hill: Institute of Government, University of North Carolina at Chapel Hill, May, 1982), 45.

[3] Wade Barber, Jr. (1944-　　　), native of Durham County; resident of Chatham County; B.A., Davidson College, 1967; J.D., University of North Carolina at Chapel Hill, 1970; U.S. Army Reserve, 1968-1976. Mecklenburg Legal Aide Society attorney, 1970-1971, opened Model Cities Office; attorney in private practice, 1971-1977, and since 1984; district attorney for Judicial District 15B (Chatham and Orange counties), 1977-1984; president, North Carolina District Attorneys Association, 1981-1982; member of numerous boards and commissions. Wade Barber, Jr., to Jan-Michael Poff, August 8, 1985.

GOVERNOR'S CONFERENCE ON TRAVEL AND TOURISM

GREENSBORO, APRIL 26, 1982

[Tourists spent a record-breaking $3.4 billion in North Carolina during 1983, Hunt revealed at his January 26, 1984, press conference. The figure was 11 percent higher than that posted in 1982, and 240 percent above the 1975 level. Increases in promotional budgets and aggressive marketing by both the state and private enterprise, coupled with the lure of North

Carolina's natural, recreational, and cultural attractions, were instrumental for success, the governor felt. "Important and unique about this industry," he explained to the Governor's Conference on Travel and Tourism, held April 9, 1984, "is the fact that (visitors') initial expenditures turn over approximately three and a half times before they leave the state. That translates into a total economic impact of more than $10 billion to the North Carolina economy by the travel industry."

Hunt delivered a speech similar to that reproduced below to the Governor's Advisory Committee on Travel and Tourism on January 19, 1982.]

I am delighted to be here and to reaffirm a partnership that is absolutely essential to the continued economic progress of this state.

You, the leaders of North Carolina's growing and vital travel industry, are a strong and progressive force. You protect and defend the interests of your industry, but at the same time you are concerned about the well-being of all of our people. That is why I turned to you last year and asked for your help with the Good Roads Program. Because you came through, the economic future of this state is more secure. Every citizen of North Carolina owes you a debt of gratitude for that.

The theme of this year's conference is an appropriate one: "Opportunity '82." That reflects this administration's philosophy toward the travel industry. We have tried to seize those opportunities that make the industry even more viable.

For example, as a result of the excellent advertising program by McKinney, Silver, and Rockett, the Division of Travel and Tourism processed almost 360,000 inquiries last year—an all-time high. Last month, we received more than 84,000 cards and letters—also a record—and two of every three people who write actually plan to visit North Carolina.

Our Canadian Days program was a success again this year, largely because so many of you took part and made our Canadian visitors feel welcome.[1]

Last night, you saw our new travel film, *North Carolina: A Special Kind of Splendor*. It is the first travel film we have produced in more than a decade, and it is a superb piece of work. We are grateful to Charles Kuralt and Andy Griffith for their help with that project.[2] We have contacted a distributor who has guaranteed that 50 million people will see the film during the next five years. I believe those people will like what they see.

We'll be opening a new Welcome Center on I-77 in Surry County next week; construction has begun on another center along I-26 in Polk County, and we are planning yet another center for I-77 in Mecklenburg. Last year, almost 3.6 million people visited our five existing centers.

The 1982 World's Fair in Knoxville presents us with a great opportunity, and we are capitalizing on it. Our state will have a marvelous exhibit that will help attract visitors to North Carolina for years to come.

I can't tell you how excited I am about the upcoming celebration of the 400th anniversary of the birth of English America. It will give North Carolinians a new sense of pride in their heritage, and visitors from out of state will develop a greater appreciation of our history and their own.

Throughout 1982 and beyond, we will continue to seek out new opportunities. The Division of Travel and Tourism has launched an aggressive new effort to promote our state as a site for national and regional meetings. This Four Seasons complex is compelling evidence that we can handle those kinds of functions.[3]

So there are a lot of reasons to be optimistic about the future of this great industry. To be sure, not all the news is good. We are in a recession and no one knows when recovery will come. We are also faced with a diminishing level of federal support, as illustrated by a Reagan administration proposal that the U.S. Travel and Tourism Administration appropriation be cut by a third.[4]

Be that as it may, *this* administration will continue to support, and invest in, this state's third largest industry. We can't afford not to. We're talking about $2.7 billion in annual expenditures by tourists and jobs for 142,000 North Carolinians.

I believe it is important that visible support for this industry come from the very top. That is why I readily agreed to be cochairman of the committee to save the Cape Hatteras Lighthouse. Hugh Morton[5] is right in his argument that this very important symbol of our heritage must be preserved.

Finally, I want to thank each and every one of you for helping to make North Carolina a better place to live, work, and play. You have helped to make this state a place where people can come with their families and enjoy themselves, where they can be in a setting of stunning natural beauty and warm hospitality. That is the kind of place North Carolina is and always has been. What our great partnership means is the preservation of that tradition and that quality of life. With our roots in the past, and with our eyes on the future, North Carolina will continue to be a place of beauty, a place of warm hospitality, a place of opportunity and promise. The leaders of the travel industry have helped make this state the kind of place it is, and you are in a very real sense entrusted with keeping it that way for future generations.

---

[1] Fifteen North Carolina localities participated in the second annual Canadian Days celebration, February 15-March 31, 1982. In announcing the promotional campaign on January 19, Hunt noted that cooperating travel facilities would offer discounts, travel packages, and monetary exchange resources to visiting Canadians, and that in 1981 the program drew over 5,000 tourists to the state.

[2] Charles Bishop Kuralt (1934-   ), native of Wilmington; A.B., University of

North Carolina at Chapel Hill, 1955. *Charlotte News* reporter, columnist, 1955-1957; writer, 1957-1959, and correspondent, since 1959, for CBS News; author. *Who's Who in America, 1982-1983*, I, 1894.

   Andrew Samuel (Andy) Griffith (1926-   ), native of Mount Airy; A.B., University of North Carolina at Chapel Hill, 1949. Actor; star of "Andy Griffith Show," 1960-1969. *UNC Alumni Directory*, 450; *Who's Who in America, 1982-1983*, I, 1313.

   [3] The grand opening of the Holiday Inn-Four Seasons complex, a 522-room, $18 million hotel and convention center built in Greensboro, was celebrated April 26, 1982. Hunt presented prepared remarks during the ceremony.

   [4] Although the House Committee on Appropriations was prepared to provide only about $5 million—approximately two thirds the 1982 expenditure—for the U.S. Travel and Tourism Administration's 1983 budget, Congress passed a stopgap funding bill on October 1, 1982, which included $7.6 million for the agency in the new fiscal year. *Congressional Quarterly Almanac, 1982*, 248, 335-336.

   [5] Hugh MacRae Morton (1921-   ), chairman, Governor's Advisory Committee on Travel and Tourism. Previously identified in Mitchell, *Addresses of Hunt*, I, 733, 735n.

NATIONAL CONFERENCE ON STATE ACTION TO IMPROVE CHILD HEALTH

WASHINGTON, D.C., MAY 6, 1982

All of us here today are indebted to the Bush Foundation and to Jim Gallagher[1] of the Frank Porter Graham Child Development Center in North Carolina for making this conference possible. This is a gathering of people who care about children and who have worked for better health for children—as expert witnesses testifying on their behalf, as researchers studying their needs, as monitors evaluating government-sponsored programs and, most of all, as advocates for children.

All of you know that, since the election of 1980, the political climate in this nation has changed. Those of you who served on the Select Panel for the Promotion of Child Health know it very well. This nation is engaged in a debate about the role of government, the role of the family, the role of the community, and the role of the private sector; a debate about the role of the federal government and the role of state and local governments; a debate about the size and scope and shape of child health programs; in truth, a debate about the future health of our children and our nation.

First and foremost today, we must demand that this nation maintain its commitment to the health of our children. Then we must develop creative strategies and politically practical plans that will help us meet that challenge.

I want to talk today about taking action. The times do not allow us the luxuries of generalities, rhetoric, and simply bemoaning the loss of federal dollars. I want to talk to you about what North Carolina is doing. I want to talk to you about how aggressive, innovative state leadership can fill the gaps Washington has left.

I suggest that our strategy should be based on a set of four actions: getting good information about our problems, taking innovative government initiatives to address them, saving administrative costs and, most important of all, mobilizing the private sector and caring human beings on behalf of our children.

The first action I suggested is an assessment of problems and needs. You have in your packet the single-page fact sheet we produced in North Carolina. On that one page, we can see where every one of our state's 100 counties ranks in seven important areas: infant mortality, motor vehicle fatalities, the number of children living in poverty, the number living in AFDC families, the number of working women with children, the school dropout rate, and the rate of juvenile justice cases—seven key indicators of the health and welfare of our children.

So those are the needs. To see how well we are meeting them, North Carolina has adopted a "children's budget," because as Marian Wright Edelman says, "policy is budget." [2] That children's budget cuts across the line items in health, mental health, justice, economic development—the entire state budget—to show what we are spending on children.

These are tremendously valuable tools. But let me say this: It is essential that the federal government continue to carry out its responsibility of supporting the information gathering, data collection, and research here. We cannot afford the high price that ignorance will exact.

The second action I suggested is taking public initiatives to meet those needs. In North Carolina, for example, we have attacked infant mortality by beginning early identification and tracking of high-risk infants, by establishing a regionalized perinatal system, by expanding the WIC—Women, Infants, and Children—nutrition program to 95 of our 100 counties, and by extending Medicaid coverage to women in their first pregnancy. North Carolina has attacked the problem of deaths and injuries from accidents by passing a law requiring parents to use child safety seats on youngsters two years old and younger. [3] I believe those initiatives show that North Carolinians are willing to make investments in their children despite the cynicism and negativism abroad in many circles today.

The third action I suggested is saving money in administration and using it on services. North Carolina has lost 20 percent of the federal funds for maternal and child health services, but we held the reductions in spending on services to 8.8 percent. How did we do it? Through administrative reform, an overhaul of standards, and the elimination of duplication.

This leads me to the fourth and most important action: mobilizing the private sector. In my opinion, that is where the action must be in the coming decades and that is the challenge all of us here today must meet. We cannot afford to simply replace federal tax dollars with state tax dollars, and we cannot give business a bill for filling those gaps. But there are creative ways the private sector—businesses, churches and synagogues, civic groups, and individuals—can help children and families. And I am not just talking about what they *can* do. I am talking about what they *are* doing already. Let me give you just three examples:

—A private foundation has given the General Baptist State Convention in North Carolina funds to train natural leaders in the black community who can help pregnant women do a few simple but important things, like good nutrition and exercise, that will mean a healthy baby.

—The Independent Insurance Agents in our state donated $10,000 to buy child safety seats that can be loaned to parents who cannot afford them, and the American Automobile Association is helping to pool requests for the seats and order them in volume at a discount.

—And many employers in North Carolina are offering innovative health benefit packages to their employees. They go beyond hospitalization insurance and offer prevention programs and services such as marital and family counseling, drug and alcohol abuse services, and day care benefits. We in state and local governments would do well to copy them.

Those three examples of what the private sector *is* doing show us what we *can* do, if we have the will, the intelligence, and the imagination. That is the challenge to you leaders here today.

Let me conclude with this: We live in a competitive world. My state competes with yours for industry and jobs. Our nation competes for wealth and respect in the world. Our ability to compete—through the rest of this century and into the twenty-first century—depends on our children. If they grow up healthy, strong, smart, and with a sense of values, our nation will grow healthy, strong, smart, and with a sense of values. If our children fall behind, our nation falls behind, and all the political and economic debate about supply-side tax cuts, federal budgets, regulations, interest rates, deflation, recessions, and all the rest will be nothing more than noise.

The future of this nation is not being set so much by the debates in Washington, or in Raleigh, North Carolina, or in Gary, Indiana. The future is being set in the minds and bodies of our children. If we fail them, our nation fails. If we lift them up, our nation will be lifted up. So I would commend to you the advice of a great governor of North Carolina, Charles Brantley Aycock, who said this at the turn of the century: "It undoubtedly appears cheaper to neglect the aged, the feeble, the infirm, the defective, to forget the children of this generation, but the man who does it is cursed of God and the state that permits it is certain of destruction." So, he said, "I would have the strong to bear the burdens of the weak and to lift them up and make them strong, teaching men and women everywhere that real strength consists not in serving ourselves, but in doing for others." [4]

---

[1] James J. Gallagher (1926-   ), native of Pittsburgh; resident of Chapel Hill; B.S., University of Pittsburgh, 1948; M.A., 1950, Ph.D., 1951, Pennsylvania State University; U.S. Navy, 1943-1945. Assistant professor, University of Illinois, 1954-1968; associate commissioner of education and chief of the Bureau of Education for the Handicapped, 1967-1969, and deputy assistant secretary for planning, research, and evaluation, 1969-1970, U.S. Office of Education; director, Frank Porter Graham Child Development Center, and Kenan professor of education, University of North Carolina at Chapel Hill, since 1970. Ruth Kirkendall, administrative assistant to James J. Gallagher, to Jan-Michael Poff, September 29, 1983.

[2] Marian Wright Edelman (1939-   ), native of Bennettsville, South Carolina; B.A., Spellman College, 1960; LL.B., Yale University, 1963. Attorney; staff lawyer, New York City office, 1963-1964, and Jackson, Mississippi office, 1964-1968, NAACP Legal Defense and Education Fund, Inc.; congressional and federal liaison, Poor People's Campaign, 1968; partner, Washington Research Project, Southern Center for Public Policy, 1968-1973; president, Children's Defense Fund, since 1973. *Who's Who in America, 1982-1983,* I, 919. The quotation Hunt attributes to Edelman could not be verified.

[3] "An Act to Require Passenger Restraint Systems for Children under Four Years of Age," *N.C. Session Laws, 1981,* c. 804, was ratified July 3. It was effective from July 1, 1982, through June 30, 1985.

[4] See "Address before the Democratic State Convention at Greensboro, June 23, 1904," in Connor and Poe, *Life and Speeches of Aycock,* 256, 266-267.

STATEMENT ON CLEAN WATER BOND REFERENDUM

RALEIGH, MAY 7, 1982

The 1981 General Assembly authorized a statewide referendum on issuing $300 million in industrial clean water bonds.[1] I have decided that, because of the continuing recession and economic uncertainty, it would not be wise to schedule that referendum at the time of the spring primary.

These bonds would finance water and sewer improvements in cities, towns, and communities all across North Carolina, and they are absolutely essential to economic growth and to environmental protection. For that reason, I believe they should be voted on in as near-normal economic times as possible. Clearly, now is not such a time:

—The hundred-billion-dollar deficits proposed by President Reagan are keeping interest rates high and retarding economic recovery.

—Our state budget revenues reflect the sluggishness in the economy.

—Unemployment has reached 9.7 percent in North Carolina, the first time we have been above the national unemployment rate since the 1974-1975 recession.

I will make a decision later on whether to schedule the referendum this November. That decision will depend, again, on the condition of the economy.[2]

In our state today, 149 municipalities cannot add a new industry or new house to their water-sewer system. Of those, eighty-one communities need to build new waste-water facilities in the next four years, but, without the state bonds, over half of them cannot afford those improvements.

The recession is also making our state budget situation very difficult. Revenue collections from January through April this year are only 5.6 percent above the same period for 1981. We are already facing a shortfall of $55 to $60 million in revenue collections this year. Because we have a freeze on hiring and stringent restrictions on travel, and by other means have cut spending by about $150 million this year, we will be able to balance the budget. But meeting our needs in the coming budget year will be a very tough job.

---

[1] "An Act to Authorize the Issuance of Three Hundred Million Dollars in Bonds of the State to Provide Funds for Environmental Improvement through Grants to Units of Government for Construction and Improvement of Wastewater Treatment Works, Wastewater Collection Systems, and Water Supply Systems," c. 993, was ratified October 9. *N.C. Session Laws, 1981.* It was amended under c. 1282, "An Act to Modify Current Operations and Capital Improvements Appropriations for North Carolina State Government for the Fiscal Year 1982-83, and to Make Other Changes in the Budget Operation of the State," s. 54, ratified June 22, 1982. *N.C. Session Laws, 1981, Regular and Extra Sessions, 1982.* The legislation directed the governor to call a referendum, to be held on the statewide primary or general election days in 1982, "or the date in 1983 that elections are conducted in those municipalities which have the nonpartisan simple plurality method of election," to determine the future of the clean water bond issue.

[2] Citing a continued poor economic outlook for the state, the governor announced in August, 1982, that the bond referendum would not be scheduled for the November general elections. Leigh Wilson, executive director of the North Carolina League of Municipalities, agreed with Hunt's decision, saying, "This is a difficult time to propose a major bond issue and have any reasonable expectations of voter approval." *Durham Morning Herald,* August 3, 1982. The General Assembly later replaced the bond issue with a local option tax increase. See "An Act to Authorize Counties to Levy One-half Percent Sales and Use Taxes and to Designate How Part of the Revenue from These Taxes Shall be Used, to Allow Certain Cities to Spend Sales Tax Revenue on Housing, and to Authorize Various Transient Occupancy Taxes," c. 908, s. 3, ratified July 21, 1983. *N.C. Session Laws, 1983.*

GROUNDBREAKING FOR MICROELECTRONICS CENTER OF NORTH CAROLINA

RESEARCH TRIANGLE PARK, MAY 13, 1982

[The Microelectronics Center of North Carolina (MCNC) board of directors selected Donald S. Beilman as its first president, Hunt announced in a press conference held on July 2, 1982. Beilman was appointed vice-president and general manager of General Electric's Advanced Micro-electronics Operations in 1979.

Speaking at the center's dedication on June 12, 1984, the governor said the facility's creation provided "solid evidence of our conviction that we must act boldly in today's complex world to influence our own destiny." MCNC was "uniquely qualified," he asserted, "to bridge the gap between university research and industrial application." Hunt also envisioned that, in time, microelectronics programs at universities in other states would join with their North Carolina counterparts, already involved with MCNC, to speed the "transfer of research into technology for the benefit of American companies . . . who must compete with the concentrated leadership programs in other countries."]

In the years ahead, all of us here today can look back on this ceremony and say that we were present at one of the landmark events in the history of North Carolina. This Microelectronics Center is the heart of North Carolina's efforts to harness the economic power of microelectronics for the economic future of our state's people. It is an investment that is already paying dividends:

—On March 1, General Electric announced that the Research Triangle Park would be the location for the headquarters of its new Semiconductor Division.

—On March 23, Analog Devices' Computer Labs Division established a $3 million microelectronics-related manufacturing plant in Greensboro.

—On April 20, Verbatim Corporation broke ground for a $14 million plant to produce computer magnetic storage products.

—And yesterday, Texas Instruments, one of the world's largest and most renowned manufacturers of microelectronics components and products, purchased land near Apex and Asheville for future expansion of its operations. That is a development of tremendous importance for North Carolina. It demonstrates, to all of us and to all the nation, that we are well on our way to becoming the East Coast capital of high-technology industry. A lot of people worked hard to bring Texas Instruments to North Carolina. I met with their officials twice, and I even made a secret trip to their corporate headquarters.

All of this—these exciting industrial announcements and the establishment of this Microelectronics Center—is the result of the dedicated work of a lot of people: George Herbert of the Research Triangle Institute; Sherwood Smith and all the members of the Center's Board of Directors; John A. Williams, Jr., of my staff; Senator Kenneth Royall; Representative Al Adams; Bill Friday; Terry Sanford; Larry Blake and our entire community college system, particularly including President Phail Wynn and Durham Technical Institute; and Secretary of Commerce Lauch Faircloth and the tremendous men and women in out state's Department of Commerce.[1] This center is an investment that is already attracting jobs and capital investment to North Carolina, in the face of a national economic recession that has put one of every ten North Carolinians out of work.

This center puts North Carolina ahead of the pack in competing for economic growth in the future. This is the fastest-growing industry in the world. World demand for integrated circuits is growing more than 20 percent a year. Production totaled $8 billion in 1980; it is expected to be $20 billion by 1985 and $40 billion by the end of this decade. It is literally a second Industrial Revolution, and this center puts North Carolina on the leading edge of the world's economic and technological future.

It is a future that belongs to trained hands and intelligent minds. It is a future of high-speed communications systems linking the most distant corners of the world in mere seconds. It is a future of specialized computers that will revolutionize our life-styles—from automobiles to home entertainment to education. It is a future of industrial robots that can dramatically increase the productivity of our labor force. What steel was to industry in the past, the silicon chip will be in the future. What muscles were in the past, brains will be in the future.

This center represents North Carolina's determination to develop the trained hands and minds that future will require. We will need to teach not just the three R's, but also the three C's: computers, calculating, and communications. We will need to make our children as familiar with the computer terminal as they are with pencil and paper. We will need better instruction in math and science. Our nation will need more scientists and engineers. Fewer than 6 percent of our college graduates are engineers. In Japan, the figure is 20 percent; in West Germany, 37 percent.

We are in a race for the future. Our nation is being challenged by other nations for the economic and technological leadership of the world. It is a race for prosperity and economic security for our people. It is a race that belongs, not to the swift, but to the smart.

This center will put North Carolina ahead in that race. It demonstrates that North Carolina has the vision to see the future and the courage to meet its challenges. With this groundbreaking, North Carolina opens a door and steps into the frontier of the future.

[1]Sherwood H. Smith, Jr. (1934-   ), native of Jacksonville, Florida; resident of Raleigh; A.B., 1956, J.D., 1960, University of North Carolina at Chapel Hill. Attorney practicing in Charlotte and Raleigh, 1960-1965; associate general counsel, 1971-1974, executive vice-president for administration, 1974-1976, president and chief administrative officer, 1976-1980, and chairman, president, and chief executive officer, since 1980, of Carolina Power and Light Co. *News and Observer*, January 2, 1977; Sherwood H. Smith, Jr., to Jan-Michael Poff, February 15, 1985.

John A. Williams, Jr., executive assistant to Governor Hunt, 1977-1985. Previously identified in Mitchell, *Addresses of Hunt*, I, 202n.

Allen Adams (1932-   ), native of Greensboro; resident of Raleigh; attended Boston University, 1948-1949; A.B., 1952, J.D., 1954, University of North Carolina at Chapel Hill; U.S. Naval Reserve. Attorney; elected to state House from Wake County in 1974, and was returned in subsequent elections; retired from office in 1984. *North Carolina Manual, 1983*, 300.

Phail Wynn, Jr. (1947-   ), native of Wewoka, Oklahoma; B.S., University of Oklahoma, 1969; M.Ed., 1974, D. Ed., 1977, North Carolina State University; U.S. Army, 1969-1975. Assistant to the president, 1977-1979, vice-president for support services, 1979-1980, and president, since 1980, of Durham Technical Institute. Phail Wynn, Jr., to Jan-Michael Poff, June 21, 1985.

GOVERNOR'S ADVISORY COUNCIL ON MILITARY AFFAIRS

RALEIGH, MAY 13, 1982

[The title of the speech and a textual reference notwithstanding, Hunt delivered the following address to the Governor's Advisory Commission— not Council—on Military Affairs. Executive Order Number 80, signed April 30, 1982, established the commission.]

It is fitting that we meet in these Senate chambers of the Capitol of North Carolina today. They echo with the acts of North Carolinians who met here to work for the good of the citizens of this great state. That is what we are here today to do—work for the good of the military citizens of North Carolina.

I have asked you to serve on the Governor's Advisory Council on Military Affairs to study ways North Carolina can improve relations among the military installations in the state and the communities they are located near, and how the state can improve the welfare of the military families who serve at these bases, or who have chosen to retire here. North Carolina serves a vital role in maintaining a strong national defense. Military installations in North Carolina—Fort Bragg in Fayetteville, Seymour Johnson Air Force Base in Goldsboro, Camp Lejeune Marine Base in Jacksonville, and others—are among the largest and most essential in the nation. Military families are an integral part of our communities, and citizens of this state are proud of the important presence of these vital military installations and the families that serve at them.

Not enough people realize how important the armed forces are to North Carolina's economy. Tobacco, textiles, and furniture generally are thought of as basic industries in our state. I would add the military to that list. The payroll of the United States armed forces represents the largest in North Carolina—$1.7 billion in 1980. Add to that the $713 million in prime military contracts let in North Carolina in 1980, and it becomes obvious that the military greatly benefits our state's economy.

The military provides jobs—good-paying jobs—for many of our people. One of the main goals of my administration has been to improve job opportunities in North Carolina. The military employs about 85,000 men and women in active service and another 13,000 civilians in this state. Our state and local governments operate more efficiently because of military-trained personnel. Many of our administrative posts are filled with highly qualified, retired military people.

All North Carolinians owe you a great debt of gratitude, and that is why we are here today—to start finding ways North Carolina can pay back a little of that debt.

We are not coming empty-handed, however. By state law, war veterans receive preference when applying for state jobs.[1] North Carolina provides scholarships for children of certain deceased, disabled, or POW/MIA veterans. These scholarships can provide free tuition, a room and board allowance, and exemption from certain fees in our university and community college/technical institute system, or up to $1,200 per year at a private college.[2] The North Carolina Division of Veterans Affairs offers assistance to veterans and their dependents with claims for federal, state, and local benefits.

But I want this group to look into ways the state can do more. One area you might take a look at is whether the state can waive the residency requirement for dependents of military personnel based in North Carolina to attend our university system.[3] We are one of seventeen states in the nation that does not allow this now.

Overall, I am asking you to include the following in your responsibilities:

—Providing a forum for discussing issues concerning major military installations in the state.

—Setting goals and objectives to bring about better cooperation and understanding among the military components, the communities, state and local governments, and the general public.

—Studying information related to supporting and strengthening the military.

—Reviewing proposed military affairs legislation.

—Advising me on measures and activities which would support and enhance defense installations and military families within the state.

North Carolina is a state of good neighbors. Our communities want to be neighbors with the military families that work to defend us. Help show us the way to accomplish that goal.

----

[1]G.S. 128-15, 15.1 ensures preferred hiring of veterans applying for state jobs. Hunt reaffirmed his administration's commitment to enforcing the statute in remarks to the Veterans' Employment Representatives Conference on November 2, 1983. Expressing displeasure that the law was "*still* not being followed in some state government offices," he urged conferees to contact Dudley Robbins, chairman of the governor's Jobs for Veterans committee, as soon as legal violations occurred.

[2]See G.S. 165-22 for scholarship authorization.

[3]"An Act to Modify Current Operations and Capital Improvements Appropriations for North Carolina State Government for the 1984-1985 Fiscal Year and to Make Other Changes in the Budget Operation of the State," c. 1034, was ratified June 19, 1984. Sections 99 and 100 allow in-state tuition rates for military personnel stationed in North Carolina, and their dependents, who attend a state college, university, technical school, or community college. *N.C. Session Laws, 1983, Regular and Extra Sessions, 1984.*

GOVERNOR'S CONFERENCE ON SCHOOL DROPOUTS

RALEIGH, MAY 18, 1982

["Last year, 12,129 people entered the North Carolina prison system, and more than 9,000 of them had less than a high school education," Hunt told reporters on May 14, 1982. In an appearance at the Western North Carolina Conference on School Dropouts, on October 26, 1982, he noted that the annual number of state youth leaving school without graduating fell from 30,000, in 1977, to 25,000 for the 1981-1982 academic year. The governor credited the reduction to the success of local initiatives and his administration's programs; however, he also acknowledged "that 25,000 dropouts is still 25,000 too many."]

We have worked hard in recent years to open doors to opportunity for North Carolinians. We have been successful in attracting to this state new, better-paying jobs. We have improved our schools and made them more accountable. We have strengthened our skills- training programs and provided day-care options for working parents. Through these initiatives and numerous others, we have tried to create a climate in which people can take full advantage of the capabilities God gave them.

The reason we are here today is to push open the door to opportunity a little wider. Despite all the progress we have made, there still hangs around our neck a millstone—a weight that keeps us from reaching our economic, intellectual, and social potential. One of every three students entering the ninth grade in this state doesn't graduate from high school. This is not a problem unique to

North Carolina. We share this burden with other southern states. For every eight high school dropouts, three come from the South.

It is certainly no coincidence that, despite all you read and hear about the economic strength of the Sunbelt, we remain the poorest region in the country. Research shows a correlation between the number of years of education a person receives and such things as income, employment, health, and the likelihood of needing public assistance. So each of us bears part of the burden for every student who drops out of school, and we all have an interest in doing something about it. It won't be easy, but I believe we can turn it around.

An effective, statewide strategy to reduce the dropout rate must contain some essential elements:

—We must identify potential dropouts earlier.

—Once these youngsters are identified, we must intensify our guidance and remediation efforts, and these efforts must be designed for each individual student.

—We need to establish job centers and increase the work and service opportunities for our students.

—We need to diversify the curriculum so as to offer these youngsters the kinds of courses that will interest them and make them want to stay in school.

—And we must keep track of the ones who do drop out.

Our Annual Testing Program can help us identify the potential dropout. Through these test scores and by observing patterns of behavior, I believe we can identify a lot of these youngsters before they begin the seventh grade.

Then comes the hard part: developing an individualized program of guidance, counseling, and instruction that will make that child realize the importance of staying in school and make him want to stay in school. You can't just sit them down and tell them they shouldn't drop out, because you're dealing with kids who are carrying a lot of negative baggage. A lot of them don't believe anybody cares. A lot have been abused and neglected. Some have been in trouble with the law. A lot of them live in poverty.

Breaking through that wall of despair, suspicion, and low self-esteem takes a lot of one-on-one counseling. It takes help from mental health and social service agencies. It takes volunteer programs like Big Brother/Sister and Adopt-a-School. It takes positive reinforcement from peer groups. It's going to take more in-school suspension programs.

Our strategy must also include linking these students to the world of work. Right now, there are only eight job centers in the entire state. I want to add 100 during the next year, and by the fall of 1984, I want to have a job center in every high school in North Carolina. These centers would provide employment counseling and placement services and would serve as clearinghouses for employers. They would attract potential dropouts to special vocational and work-study programs. If these job centers are to function effectively, we will need to establish extended-day programs in all of our high schools.[1]

We must fine tune the school curriculum or at least make better use of the existing curriculum. No single instructional program can be applied to all potential dropouts, because they are all different. Putting together an individualized tutoring and instructional program for each student is absolutely essential. This will necessarily require remedial work in the basic skills. A youngster who doesn't read, write, or handle math isn't going to be motivated to stay in school.

Despite all of our efforts, some are still going to drop out. That is why we must track these youngsters and look for opportunities for them to get that diploma. I will be looking to our community college system to do this tracking and to provide the opportunities for these people to graduate.

There are two important things to remember about the general strategy I have outlined for you. To begin with, it requires the close cooperation of different agencies and organizations, both at the state and local level. The help of every single agency and group with an interest in children must be brought to bear.

Secondly, we must put this strategy into effect without substantial additional funding. Federal support for education is being cut, and state and local budgets are strained to the limit. That doesn't mean we can't do it. It just means we have to do it with better use of existing resources and with a great deal of volunteer help.

I don't think anybody in this room will be satisfied until every child is able to complete a high school education, until every young person has the tools to get and hold a good job. Let us resolve today to push open that door of opportunity that much wider. Charles McIver,[2] the great nineteenth-century educator, recognized what was at stake: "People, not rocks and rivers and imaginary boundary lines, make a state. And the state is great just in proportion as its people are educated."[3]

---

[1] The number of job placement centers had increased from eight to seventy-seven by autumn, 1982, and eighty-three school districts reported having extended-day programs, according to Hunt's October 26, 1982, address at the Western North Carolina Conference on School Dropouts.

[2] Charles Duncan McIver (1860-1906), proponent of higher education for women and first president of the State Normal and Industrial School (now University of North Carolina at Greensboro). Previously identified in Mitchell, *Addresses of Hunt*, I, 610n.

[3] "The future will recognize that people—not trees, and rocks and rivers, and imaginary boundary lines—make a state, and that the state is great, intelligent, wealthy and powerful, or is small, ignorant, poverty-stricken and weak, just in proportion as its people are educated, or as they are untrained and raw like the

natural material around them." Speech by Charles Duncan McIver to eleventh annual session of the Southern Educational Association, Columbia, South Carolina, December 26, 1901, Charles Duncan McIver Papers, University Archives, Jackson Library, University of North Carolina at Greensboro. James A. Rogerson, assistant, University Archives, University of North Carolina at Greensboro, to Jan-Michael Poff, December 30, 1985. The condensed version Hunt quotes, above, is from a plaque on the base of the statue of McIver located in the southeast quadrant of Union Square, Raleigh.

UNIVERSITY-INDUSTRY-GOVERNMENT INTERACTIONS: THE IMPORTANCE OF GUIDING PRINCIPLES

CHAPEL HILL, JUNE 4, 1982

[This address was delivered at the second convocation of Kenan professors at the University of North Carolina.]

I. INTRODUCTION

Chancellor Fordham,[1] distinguished Kenan Professors, and guests: You do me great honor to ask that I speak before perhaps the most impressive group of intellectual leaders in this or any other nation. I am reminded of John Kennedy's observation that a group he was addressing represented the most unique concentration of intellectual leadership ever assembled at the White House for dinner, with the possible exception of those occasions when Thomas Jefferson dined alone.[2]

But what is more, to request that I address the topic you have chosen for this second convocation of Kenan professors—that is, federal-state-industry interactions and university governance— elevates the role of governor to an intellectual level that far exceeds what the framers of the Constitution of North Carolina may have had in mind. Our governors have always been limited in powers, if not in capabilities. It would appear also that the committee planning this conference may be seeking to provide a subtle hint to President Friday regarding his unique qualifications for continued involvement in government, university, and industry affairs. Nevertheless, I accept the challenge, but I do so with considerable humility.

I am acutely aware of the extreme importance and timeliness of the topic you have chosen. At the annual meeting of the American Association for the Advancement of Science [AAAS] last January, I contended that the issues that confront academia, industry, and government comprise the organizational frontier of science today. This evening, I seek to deal with the same university-industry-government interactions that were my concern in January. But since Kenan professors are quite wisely chosen from several academic fields, I will present a view of society and these interactions that may be of interest to humanists and others, as well as to scientists. The intent is to further develop the view expressed in January, rather than to restate it.

II. INTERACTIONS, SOCIETY, and DECISION MAKING

Without question, a partnership of universities, industries, government, and people, acting in the public interest, can be a tremendous constructive force within any society. The assumption underlying such a partnership, however, is that it will indeed function in the public interest. Thomas Bender, in a *New York Times* review of Derek Bok's recent book, *Beyond the Ivory Tower*, notes that institutions of higher learning in America have periodically renegotiated their relationships to the larger society. But, Bender observes, present-day universities are powerful, integral parts of society; not relatively small, isolated autonomous institutions. He concludes that when confronting the messy problems of social responsibility, Bok's argument for neutrality in university governance is seriously deficient with respect to moral and intellectual judgment. Bender contends that Bok's managerial approach to governance, with its emphasis upon research, may simply place the university in the position of merely responding to the effective market demands of society when, instead, it should be exercising moral and intellectual leadership.[3]

Bender's charge is serious. It strikes at the core of federal-state-industry-university relationships and university governance. As a proponent of partnership relations, I am committed to the proposition that these relationships can result in constructive measures in North Carolina, in the United States, and in the world. But they can do so only if the partnership functions in accordance with moral and intellectual standards, what I call "guiding principles."

The basis of my conviction is the fact that universities, industry, labor, government, and other major organizational components are all now powerful, integral parts of our society. None can withdraw like Isaiah, calling society to task for its transgressions.[4] Instead, each must exercise the moral and intellectual judgment of which Bender speaks, through a process of debate and consensus-building that gives rise to explicit principles by which the partnership may be guided for the benefit of our entire society.

Society and Decision Making

We can view society as an organism, which changes its structure through decision making, just as a living organism grows and changes in response to its environment and its genetic code. The structure consists of government units; economic firms; educational, religious, and other institutions; families; communities; and so on. It is important to visualize this structure carefully and not be misled by the abstractions arising from specialized scientific analysis. The manager of an individual firm, for example, may deal strictly with economic variables in deciding how much of each product to produce this year. But in doing so everything else is not held constant, as economic theory dictates, if his firm is also lobbying heavily in Washington for a special tax break.

People relate to the structure of society through decision making. Like genes and genetic codes, they make those decisions that define the structure itself as well as those that carry forward the functions of each entity defined. A healthy society is one in which participation is widespread, complete in that all citizens are caught up in meaningful forms of decision making. A sense of justice prevails; the integrity of government, of institutions, of economic firms, and of other units of society is maintained and respected.

By contrast, an unhealthy society is one in which many people cannot participate—perhaps because decision making is concentrated in a few hands, perhaps because of organizational voids, perhaps because there are too many people to be involved under any circumstance or perhaps because, as in many less developed nations, there is no feasible way to provide for the meaningful participation of all people. When participation by many is seriously limited for whatever reason, then fear, injustice, selfishness, violence, and distrust emerge—among individuals, within nations, and among nations. Justice, order, and integrity are violated. Society deteriorates. Within a city, the result is riots or crime. Within a nation, it is civil war. Among nations, it is total war.

Decisions that draw heavily upon scientific knowledge have seriously affected how we view the role of people in relation to society.[5] Development and elaboration of Newtonian physics, for example, gave science a distinctly deterministic orientation. So successful was the Newtonian interpretation of natural phenomena that it was construed by many as representing the infinite and divine power of God in governing the universe. Determine the laws of nature and you determine what must occur by the will of God. When related to society, many natural laws were construed by some as rigid laws of human behavior to which people must conform.

More recent scientific advances, however, have undermined this deterministic orientation. I am told, for example, that when an atomic physicist makes a specific observation regarding the components of atoms, he no longer is held to be the completely objective, impersonal observer we thought him to be. What he actually observes depends upon his choice of equipment, how he designed his experiment, and other things. Thus, the difference between the potential results and actual results depends in part upon the observer and what he does. In short, there is an interaction between the observer and the observed, even in physical science.[6]

I do not want to divert us into a philosophic discussion this evening, but many now argue that the meaning of human existence cannot be fully described and understood in scientific terms. To me this means that we cannot look to some precise law of science or nature to predict the outcome of decisions that people make as they function within society. Governors, university presidents, industrial leaders, and others in key decision-making positions learn this lesson quickly, or they do not long continue in such roles.

Technological Innovation

I do not imply from this interpretation of decision making that we exclude or downplay scientific theories and empirical evidence as we formulate and execute decisions. Instead, I believe that we do and should take scientific knowledge into account through technological innovation. In my AAAS address last January, I noted that technological innovation is the process by which we utilize the power of science. In addition, I differentiated between technical innovation and organizational innovation, contending that technical innovation is made possible by physical and biological science, and organizational innovation by social and behavioral science. A few years ago, Don Price of Harvard University made a similar assertion with respect to the World War II period when he observed that the organizational innovations that altered the administrative system—developed on a national scale during and following World War II—were as important, if not more important, than the technical innovations of radar and atomic weaponry.[7] Technical and organizational innovations are interdependent. We cannot reap the benefits of science without both. Together, they comprise technological innovation or change, but both must be related to a frame of reference that extends beyond the realm of science.

III. Guiding Principles and the Structure of Society

This leads me to the matter of guiding principles in the university-industry-government relationship.

Science and the Wisdom of Choice

Scientific knowledge gives humanity the power to make changes in the nature and purpose of society and in the scope and meaning of human existence. Science, in other words, expands our potential, our range of possible choices. But it does not necessarily provide us with the wisdom to make the right choice. We can develop that wisdom and understanding only through fields of knowledge and experience known as the arts and the humanities. If we are to transform the potential of science into actuality, we must integrate scientific knowledge with the wisdom of philosophic reflection; the lessons of historical insight; the vision of poetic imagination; the beauty of art, architecture, and nature; the humor of literature; the inspiration of religious faith; and the pain and suffering of inescapable tragedy. Only through those forms of human expression and experience can we guide and control the power of science.

I believe, then, that our guiding principles are inherent in such concepts as justice, order, integrity, compassion, and faith. They provide the wisdom of choice upon which a complex society depends, but they are not rigid coefficients providing eternal, changeless answers. As the potential power of science changes and increases, society's interpretations of these principles must change, also.

Change in the Organization

These guiding principles are integrated with scientific knowledge through the process of technological innovation, and the result at any point in time is the prevailing organizational structure of society. This is our means for fusing knowledge and experience in formulating and implementing decisions—right or wrong, good or bad. It is how those of us in government, industry, and universities make the difficult decisions upon which people's lives depend. It is my conviction that this structure works best, that we make better decisions, when we integrate scientific knowledge with the wisdom and inspiration of the arts and humanities, as well as with the values, beliefs, and experiences of people. And our ability to achieve that integration is greatly enhanced by the interaction between government, university, and industry, through that process of debate and consensus.

IV. ISSUES AND INTERACTIONS

This process of decision making takes place at several levels of society: local, state and national, and international. I will consider each in turn.

Local Levels of Society

It is my fundamental belief that it is easier to see our problems, and to address them, at the local level. Society is built from the bottom up, and it is best changed from the bottom up. For example, we can try to strengthen public education by proposing a new national strategy at the federal level. But I believe it is far more effective to bring parents and citizens into their local schools to see the needs and to work for changes at local and state levels. That is the approach we have taken in North Carolina.

We can try to make our neighborhoods and homes safer from

crime by enacting legislation in Congress, or we can demonstrate to people how they can protect themselves and their neighbors by being more alert to potential criminal activity. Which do you think works best and most quickly?

My point is simply that it is at the local level—the base of society where the most effective and meaningful changes are made—where people participate most effectively in decisions to change, or not to change. To try to order or impose changes from outside ignores the need for people to participate in decisions. That influence from outside must work as a catalyst, stimulating and guiding, but not forcing and imposing.

The State Level

At the state level, those conditions that prove effective at local levels become the basis for broader policy and program decisions encompassing many local communities. But at the state level we must first understand how people at local levels can bring about change consistent with guiding principles. This is why, for example, we place emphasis in North Carolina upon a *Community* Watch instead of a *state* police force. It is why we have a *state* School of Science and Mathematics operating at the *high school* level, with the mission of helping improve science and mathematics in all local schools as well as helping develop leading scientists of tomorrow. It is why we have, in addition to the three great research universities of the Triangle area, a statewide public university system, a statewide network of private colleges and universities, and a *community* college system. It is why, in placing so much emphasis upon balanced growth, we ensure that all local communities participate in and benefit from economic development. It is why our environmental concerns are with the beauty and productivity of our natural resources as perceived and desired at local levels, and not just with the regulatory perspective at state and federal levels.

In my address to the American Association for the Advancement of Science last January, I contended that the center of gravity for technological innovation should shift from the federal government to state governments and it should work through the partnership of university, government, industry, and people. At the state level, this partnership, following our guiding principles, is best able to adopt technical and organizational innovations that help us achieve a healthy society and avoid the poverty, violence, distrust, and other characteristics of an unhealthy society.

As we decide how and for what purpose the power of science should be used, we decide a great deal about human existence, in North Carolina and in other states.

We are not foreordained to use the power of science to destroy the beauty and productivity of our natural resources. Deliberately or otherwise, we will decide the quality of our environment ourselves.

It will not be through the unfolding of events beyond our control that our population will consist of a small portion of very rich and powerful people, leaving the rest in poverty. Such a situation could only result through the decisions we make. Children will be handicapped for the rest of their lives by improper diets, poor education, and inadequate parental care, not because that is their destiny; it will be due to our failure to realize that the future depends upon their ability.

The features of an unhealthy society will come to prevail in North Carolina and elsewhere not because such conditions are bound to happen sooner or later, but only because of the decisions we make or fail to make.

National and International Levels

The final illustration of my view pertains to national and international levels of world society. Many domestic aspects of national policy in the United States can be examined in relation to the process of technological innovation now challenging all states, but within the remaining time available I must limit myself to global aspects. It is at the global level that the potential of nuclear warfare is now with us; that population disparities are clearly evident; and that the effects of resource exploitation and ecological imbalance are accumulating.

It is at the global level also that we find the most flagrant misuse of the power of science. I refer, of course, to nuclear weapons and the armament race. No form of human activity represents such an acute pathological distortion of human potential, and no form of human activity is so completely dependent upon advances in science. Furthermore, no other single form of human activity has the real potential of destroying the whole of civilization; no other deliberate use of the power of science forecloses so many alternative uses of this power for creative purposes.

Barbara Tuchman, in a recent article in *New York Times Magazine*, makes two arguments that bear on this subject.[8] The first is that the causes of quarrels among nations must be eliminated before disarmament can take place. Nations do not distrust each other because they are armed; they become armed because they distrust each other. The second point, she says, is that we cannot count on governments as such to achieve meaningful arms reduction. As a historian she finds nothing in the history of nations to suggest otherwise.

If Barbara Tuchman is correct in these assertions, what recourse do we have? I suggest that the answer lies in university-industry-government interaction at subnational levels within and among nations of the world, interaction dedicated to creative rather than destructive uses of science. I am convinced that there are alternatives to the armament race and that they lie in forms of technological innovation directed toward the needs and concerns of local people in every nation. We have demonstrated, through our World War II and subsequent experience, that it is possible to harness science for unprecedented warfare. But it is also within our power to design a world society capable of striking an ecological balance between population and environment consistent with such guiding principles as justice, integrity, and compassion.

To be against the armament race, although highly important, is not enough. The causes of international distrust must be addressed also. I need not remind you of the creative uses of science that have taken place in Japan since World War II. They have been of far greater mutual benefit than the uses made of science during and before the war.

The report of the Independent Commission on International Development Issues, chaired by Willy Brandt, former chancellor of West Germany, stated the choices rather clearly in 1978:

> We are well aware of the fact that the concept of global responsibility for economic and social development is comparatively new—in state-to-state terms it does not go back much more than one generation. . . .

* * *

> The relationship between armament and development is . . . only dawning on people. The annual [world] military bill is now approaching $450 billion U.S. dollars [in 1978], while official development aid accounts for only five percent of this figure.[9]

The report points out that the price of one modern tank will provide 1,000 classrooms for 30,000 children. One jet fighter is equivalent to 40,000 village pharmacies. One-half of one percent of one year's world military expenditure would pay for all the farm equipment needed to increase food production and approach self-sufficiency in food deficient, low income countries by 1990. These comparisons of four years ago would be even more striking in view of projected arms spending today.

V. UNIVERSITY GOVERNANCE

I close now with three observations regarding university governance, plus a suggestion with respect to Kenan professors. The first observation is that the system of technological innovation that we devised in World War II, and that still prevails for the most part, is geared to federal interests, federal goals, and federal objectives. The administrative aspects of this system also are being emulated in university governance. Senator Moynihan pointed this out in an article in *Harper's* a year and a half ago.[10] University research programs are heavily dependent upon federal support, and their structures and priorities reflect this dependence. More than half of federal research and development expenditures flow through the Defense Department.

My second observation is that a serious deficiency exists in our ability as a society to deliberately utilize the power of science to build a healthy society. Our destructive uses have been perfected to an excessively high degree, as exemplified by the armament race. Our programs of technical assistance to less developed countries, however, are far less impressive. And domestically—in spite of our power and our achievements in basic science—conditions of poverty, of central city decay, of unemployment, and other serious problems remain unresolved.

Third, somehow it appears that the deterministic orientation of science still prevails within universities, with its differentiation and specialization; with its dispassionate search for truth in isolation from the values, beliefs, and aspirations of people; with its separation from the arts and the humanities. I do not speak disparagingly of this orientation of science. Major accomplishments are the result of these methods. But if the frontier of science is the frontier of the potential power of change possessed by humanity, and if the wisdom of choice is to be found in concepts such as justice, order, compassion, beauty, and faith, then more integrative pursuits must be fostered by university governance.

Kenan Professors

Kenan professorships, it seems, provide recipients with a greater degree of security and independence than is otherwise possible for many professors. I know of no greater challenge to the human intellect than the issues I have sought to put before you this evening, and I urge you to address them seriously. But I do not believe that those of us in government, industry, and other components of society should ask you to confront these issues alone, and that is why I have addressed them here.

Through debate and consensus—within this nation and with our counterparts in other nations—we must define essential guiding principles and we must visualize the forms of technological innovation that pertain to the *creative* potential of science, as opposed to its *destructive* potential. Through the decisions we make in accordance with this vision, we will transform with wisdom and imagination the potential of science into the actuality of a creative world society.

---

[1]Christopher Columbus Fordham III (1926-   ), chancellor of the University of North Carolina at Chapel Hill since 1981. Previously identified in Mitchell, *Addresses of Hunt,* I, 80n.

[2]"I think this is the most extraordinary collection of talent, of human knowledge, that has ever been gathered together at the White House, with the possible exception

of when Thomas Jefferson dined alone." Address by John F. Kennedy at White House dinner and reception honoring Nobel Prize winners, April, 1962, quoted in Bartlett, *Familiar Quotations*, 1074.

[3]Thomas Bender, review of *Beyond the Ivory Tower*, by Derek Bok, *New York Times Book Review*, LXXXVII (May 23, 1982), 14-15, 20. Bender, author of *Toward an Urban Vision* and *Community and Social Change in America*, is Samuel Rudin Professor in Humanities at New York University. Bok is president of Harvard University.

[4]When King Ahaz of Judah (735-715 B.C.) ignored Isaiah's message from God and sought assistance from the king of Assyria against the Syro-Ephraimite alliance, the prophet refrained from making further public pronouncements. His "withdrawal" is believed to have lasted from 734 until Hezekiah succeeded Ahaz in 715 B.C. R. B. Y. Scott and G. G. D. Kilpatrick, "The Book of Isaiah," in George Arthur Buttrick and others (eds.), *The Interpreter's Bible: The Holy Scriptures in the King James and Revised Standard Versions* ... (New York: Abingdon Press, 12 volumes, 1956), V, 161, 227; see also Isaiah 8:16-18.

[5]The following paragraph is a summary of Ivor Leclerc, *The Nature of Physical Existence* (London: George Allen & Unwin, Ltd., 1972), 41-97.

[6]See Werner Heisenberg, *Physics and Philosophy* (New York: Harper & Brothers, Publishers, 1958), 54-55.

[7]See "Academia, Industry, and Government: The Organizational Frontier of Science Today," January 4, 1982, footnote 5, above.

[8]Barbara Tuchman, "The Alternative to Arms Control," *New York Times Magazine*, April 18, 1982, 44. Barbara Wertheim Tuchman (1912-   ), native of New York City; resident of Cos Cob, Connecticut; B.A., Radcliffe College, 1933. Staff writer, correspondent; author; won Pulitzer Prize for *The Guns of August* (1962) and *Stilwell and the American Experience in China* (1971). *Who's Who is America, 1982-1983*, II, 3374.

[9]Willy Brandt, chairman, *North-South: A Programme for Survival. Report of the Commission on International Development Issues* (Cambridge, Massachusetts: MIT Press, 1980), 8, 13-14. Willy Brandt (Herbert Ernst Karl Frahm, 1913-   ), native of Lübeck, Germany; was graduated from Lübeck Johanneum, 1932; attended University of Oslo. Correspondent for Scandinavian newspapers, 1933-1945; representative from West Berlin in the Bundestag, 1949-1957, 1961-1969, and as president of the Bundesrat, 1957-1958; chief editor, *Berliner Stadtblatt*, 1950-1951; mayor of West Berlin, 1957-1966; chairman, Berlin Social Democratic party organization, 1958-1964; vice-chancellor and minister of foreign affairs, 1966-1969, and chancellor, 1969-1974, Federal Republic of Germany; recipient, Nobel Prize for Peace, 1971. Arthur S. Banks and William Overstreet (eds.), *Political Handbook of the World: 1980 — Governments, Regional Issues, and Intergovernmental Organizations as of January 1, 1980* (New York: Published for the Center for Social Analysis of the State University of New York at Binghamton and for the Council on Foreign Relations, by McGraw Hill Book Company, 1980), 186, 190; Charles Moritz and others (eds.), *Current Biography Yearbook, 1973* (New York: H. W. Wilson Company, 1974), 55-59; *World Book Encyclopedia*, 1982 ed., s.v. "Brandt, Willy."

[10]Daniel Patrick Moynihan, "State vs. Academe," *Harper's*, December, 1980, 31-40. Daniel Patrick Moynihan (1927-   ), native of Tulsa, Oklahoma; resident of New York City; attended City College of New York, 1943; B.A., 1948, M.A., 1949, Ph.D., 1961, Tufts University. University professor; U.S. assistant labor secretary, 1963-1965; assistant to the president for urban affairs, 1969-1970; U.S. ambassador to India, 1973-1974, and to the United Nations, 1975-1976; U.S. senator from New York since 1976. Barone and Ujifusa, *Almanac of American Politics, 1984*, 785.

EQUAL RIGHTS AMENDMENT RALLY

RALEIGH, JUNE 6, 1982

[A Louis Harris poll conducted in April, 1982, indicated that 61 percent of more than 800 North Carolinians surveyed approved the ratification of the proposed Equal Rights Amendment to the United States Constitution. However, neither the Harris organization's findings, which Hunt revealed at a May 16 press conference, nor the intensive lobbying activities of women's rights groups, convinced state senators to endorse the ERA bills introduced before them on June 4. Thus, the North Carolina General Assembly became one of fifteen state legislatures, two thirds of which were southern, that refused to sanction the ERA; the national deadline for ratification of the measure expired June 30, 1982, three states short of the thirty-eight necessary for its adoption. Nevertheless, efforts were begun in the U.S. House and Senate, on June 24 and July 14, respectively, to add an identical amendment to the federal Constitution. See *Congressional Quarterly Almanac, 1982*, 377-378; *News and Observer*, May 21 and June 5, 1982; and "State of the State Address," January 15, 1981, footnote 22, above.

Hunt spoke in favor of ERA ratification at the Conference on Leadership Development for Women, March 11, 1982, where he also mentioned that his administration had worked effectively for passage of the Domestic Violence Act of 1979, the equal distribution of marital property act, and stricter sexual assault statutes. He delivered a speech similar to the one reprinted below at the North Carolinians United for ERA program on July 1.]

The people of North Carolina believe in the Equal Rights Amendment. They believe the time has come in this state and this nation to add to our Constitution some simple words of protection for women and men: "Equality of rights under the law shall not be denied or abridged by the United States or by any state on account of sex."

I know North Carolina is for ERA because I see you here today. I know North Carolina is for ERA because I have been out among our people in all parts of the state, and they have told me they are for it. And I know North Carolinians are for ERA in greater numbers than ever before. The Harris poll showed that in every part of the state, a strong majority of men and women, young and old, black and white, of all religions and both political parties, believe it is time to write into our Constitution equality for all people.

I believe the reason North Carolina is so strongly for the Equal Rights Amendment is because we know how badly it is needed to protect women and families. Over 55 percent of the women in North Carolina work outside the home. That's higher than the national average. Those women get paid less and promoted less. North Carolina working women get paid, on the average, 61 cents for every dollar a man gets. Women with college degrees generally make less than men with eighth-grade educations. That's wrong.

And that kind of treatment in the workplace discriminates not only against women—it discriminates against families who depend on those working wives and mothers.

I understand the concerns of many people who say they oppose ERA because they are genuinely concerned about what's happening to families. They want to keep the strong relationships between home, family, and church, and they're concerned about the stresses that modern life puts on family members. I share their concerns. I know you do, too. But I don't believe ERA is part of the problem. I believe ERA is part of the solution.

I believe the Equal Rights Amendment will strengthen, not hurt families, because I believe it will make women stronger. ERA will give women a better chance on the job, in the courtroom, and at the bank. It will mean women will be treated more fairly in Social Security and retirement plans. The Equal Rights Amendment will give women of all ages a better chance to succeed in life, whether they choose to marry or not, whether they become divorced or widowed, whether they live in Alaska or Alabama. And I believe that when you treat everyone in a family fairly and equally, then the family is stronger.

I don't have to tell you that we have a tough uphill battle ahead for ERA. It has been a long fight, and we will have to fight even longer. You have worked hard, and I have, and so have many others who could not be here today. But we're not in this fight because it's easy. We're here because it's right, and I believe we will ultimately prevail. I believe the Equal Rights Amendment will be added to the Constitution, and I believe we will ratify it in North Carolina.

I wish we could have made more headway in the legislature here this session. I do not believe that the action that was taken in the Senate reflects the will of the people, and we must work even harder to show them what the will of the people is. We are looking at every alternative available to us for the rest of this session.

As long as this General Assembly is in session, we will not cease our efforts. And on July 1, if the Equal Rights Amendment has not been ratified in this country, we will start the fight all over again in the halls of Congress. We must make it clear that this issue will not go away.

We must fight on every front. We must organize and mobilize to be active in the primary and general elections this year, both in legislative races and Congressional races. We must help those who are for us with our contributions of time, energy, and money. We must not let those who oppose us get the upper hand. They may be able to outspend us, but after what I've seen in the past few weeks, I know they can never outwork us.

I hope, too, that this effort will cause more women to run for political office and to be active in their parties. I hope you will show this state and this nation that a woman's place *is* in the House—

and in the Senate, in the Congress, in the courthouse, in the mayor's office, and someday, in the White House.

As a Democrat, I am proud that ERA has been in our platform every time, and I would hope that every Democrat would take that policy statement very seriously. I have tremendous pride in the women in my cabinet—Jane Patterson, Sara Hodgkins, and Sarah Morrow, and in the men in my cabinet who have worked so hard on this issue. I want to thank all of you, and all the organizations you represent, for the great work you have done. It's not hard to be for an issue like this with people like you working together.

I hope you will go away from this rally renewed in spirit. I hope you will go back home more determined than ever to see that justice and equality for all becomes a reality. I hope you will make true the words of Susan B. Anthony: "There will never be another season of silence until women have the same rights as men have on this green earth." The cause of fairness and equality will not go away. ERA will not go away.

NORTH CAROLINA TEXTILES 2000:
A SYMPOSIUM

RALEIGH, JUNE 10, 1982

["I pushed hard as lieutenant governor for the fuel adjustment clause because fuel prices were fluctuating wildly," Hunt told a meeting of the North Carolina Rural Electric Cooperatives on March 31, 1982. "It made sense to pass on these increases automatically, because the utilities had no control over them. The fuel clause also reduced the frequency of rate cases, but that law did not anticipate the current shifts in the types of fuel being used. It was clearly not the intent of the fuel clause to force people to pay higher rates when a nuclear plant shuts down and coal has to be utilized." On June 10 the governor complained to members of the North Carolina Merchants Association that "rate increases have become too automatic" and blamed rising electricity costs on the "poor performance of nuclear plants" operating at less than full capacity. He added, "The Utilities Commission today does not have the power to examine poor plant performance and decide whether stockholders, instead of taxpayers, should be forced to pay for it. That is what I want to change. . . ." The governor announced at a press conference, held the same day, his backing of a bill before the General Assembly that would substitute annual fuel cost hearings for those held thrice yearly; provide the Utilities Commission sufficient authority to inspect the management practices and operations of the state's electric power generating companies; and support "adequate public hearings, investigation, and cross-examination in the fuel clause proceedings." Hunt also urged support for the proposed legislation in his speech, reprinted below, before the Textiles 2000 symposium. For further information on the fuel adjustment clause and legislative action, see *News and Observer*, March 21, 26, April 1, 18, and June 18, 20, 1982.]

I want to commend each and every one of you, and especially
Arthur Jackson and Charles Dunn, for having the foresight to plan
and conduct this symposium.[1]

I think there is a popular and widespread misconception that the
textile industry hasn't changed much over the years and isn't likely
to change much in the future. But let's examine that for a moment.
The first cotton mill in this state was established in Lincolnton
about 150 years ago. That's not a terribly long time, and in that time
we have seen the emergence of a $13 billion industry that provides
more jobs than any other industry in North Carolina.

When I walk into a new textile mill today, I see electronically
controlled looms and spinning machines. This new technology
represents tremendous change from just ten years ago, and I predict
to you today that this industry will go through more changes
between now and the year 2000 than it has in the last century and a
half.

That is so because this planet, this nation, and this state are
changing at an ever accelerating rate. In North Carolina, we will
have two million more people by the beginning of the next century
than we have today. That fact alone has momentous implications
for jobs, housing, water and food supply, and health care.

You understand that. That is why you are here today—to get
about the difficult business of preparing your industry for the
future.

That's what the North Carolina 2000 project is all about—not
waiting for events to overtake us, but making those decisions today
that will give us the kind of future we want for ourselves and for
succeeding generations.

This administration and the textile industry have joined forces in
planning for the future. The international market, for example,
holds tremendous potential for the textile industry and for North
Carolina's economy as a whole. But you have only begun to realize
that potential. To assist you in the expansion of international trade,
Secretary of Commerce Lauch Faircloth has started a special
program in his department's International Division to increase
textile exports from North Carolina. A similar project for the furniture industry has proven highly successful, and I am committed to
providing the same kind of support for our state's largest provider of
jobs.

We are working together to develop adequate skills training
programs for the changes that are coming in textile jobs. Our
community colleges and technical institutes have undertaken a
major effort to tailor their training programs to the industry's
needs. Much more needs to be done, and we will continue to
strengthen those programs.

In the next twenty years, as technology changes, the textile industry will become far more dependent than ever before on basic research and development. That will require a growing partnership of state government, the universities, and the textile industry.

If the textile industry and other sectors of this state's economy are to prosper in the years to come, if we are going to keep expanding job opportunities for our people, we must have a reliable and affordable supply of energy. Accordingly, I am working very closely right now with the leaders of the textile industry to convince the General Assembly to significantly modify the fuel adjustment clause for utility rates.

The fuel clause is being abused right now. When a nuclear generating facility goes out of service, the increased cost of switching to an alternate fuel is almost automatically passed on to the smallest household and the largest textile plant. When a utility seeks to recover those fuel costs, we must be able to take a hard look at such factors as plant performance.

The utilities rightfully contend that they must recover their legitimate costs. All we are asking is that we have a process that determines which costs are in fact legitimate. That will require an adversary proceeding and public hearings. Only in that way can the Utilities Commission make a fair and intelligent decision based on the facts.

We have introduced legislation in the General Assembly to accomplish these objectives, but it's going to be a tough fight and we need to stick together. I urge everyone in this room to contact legislators and impress upon them the crucial importance of this bill. I want them to know that the governor, the textile industry, and the consumers of this state are united on this issue. That's an alliance they cannot ignore.

I believe this kind of alliance can be an enduring one. When you get right down to it, we're not just talking about the economic interests of the textile industry, or the legislative track record of an administration. We're talking about strengthening the climate for good jobs and economic progress. That depends on fairness in setting utility rates. It means skills training. It means day care for working mothers and health screening programs.

It means investing in human capital. Despite all the changes to come by the beginning of the next century, one fact will remain unchanged: This state's greatest resource, and all of its hopes, are its people. I hope that thought will stay with you throughout this symposium. As we fix our eye on the future, we must never forget that our people are our future—not machines, but the people we must train to operate them.

The fact that you are holding this symposium shows that you are a visionary group of people. You are setting a superb example for other sectors of our economy. I thank you for what you are doing, and I pledge my continuing support as you help to mold and shape the kind of future that will make North Carolina a better place to live and work.

---

[1] Arthur L. Jackson (1927-   ), native of Kings Mountain; resident of Lookout Mountain, Tennessee; B.S., North Carolina State College (now University), 1948; attended Westminster College (Fulton, Missouri), and Yale University; served in U.S. Navy air corps. Retired as executive vice-president, Fieldcrest Mills, Inc., 1983; executive vice-president, Dixie Yarns, Inc., 1983-1985; consultant. Arthur L. Jackson to Jan-Michael Poff, June 7, 1985.

Charles Jerome Dunn, Jr. (1934-   ), executive vice-president, North Carolina Textile Manufacturers Association. Previously identified in Mitchell, *Addresses of Hunt*, I, 722n.

[2] See "An Act To Amend Chapter 62 of the General Statutes to Provide For Utilities Commission Consideration of Annual Fuel Adjustment to Electric Utility Rates Established Pursuant to G.S. 62-133," ratified June 17, 1982. *N.C. Session Laws, 1981, Second and Extra Sessions, 1982*, c. 1197.

STATEMENT ON ANNUAL TESTING PROGRAM

RALEIGH, JUNE 30, 1982

Last year, when we received the report of how North Carolina students performed on the annual tests administered during 1981, I remarked that those test scores were the best news we had received in North Carolina since I became governor. For the first time, our students scored above the national average in all subject areas and at all grade levels tested.

I am delighted to report to you today that the news this year is even better. Once again, students in the first, second, third, sixth, and ninth grades have exceeded the national average in all subject areas.

More important, our students did even better than last year. On the average, they improved a full school month over last year, and that was apparent in all of the eight educational regions across the state.

The 1982 annual *Report of Student Performance* reveals that the average North Carolina student did better when grouped by sex, ethnic origin, handicap, region, and educational level of parents. In comparison with the national norm, North Carolina has a higher proportion of students at or above the ninety-sixth percentile in academic achievement. Seven percent of our students scored at this level, compared to 4 percent nationally.[1]

Early in this administration, we pushed for legislative enactment of initiatives designed to make our schools better and more accountable. These included the Annual Testing Program, the Competency Testing Program, and the Primary Reading Program.

The results of this comprehensive approach speak for themselves. It has been a team effort—supported by the Department of Public Instruction, the State Board of Education, the Annual Testing Commission, and most of all, our teachers, parents, and the youngsters themselves.

Teachers are doing a better job of teaching and the kids are doing a better job of learning. Because of that, these students are better equipping themselves for what awaits them after they leave school. They will be in a better position to find a good job, and our state will be stronger economically. That is what public education is supposed to be all about.

We have a long way to go before we have the kind of educational system we want. We must reduce dropouts; we must further reduce class size; we must increase teachers' salaries; we must find ways to finance school construction and maintenance; and we must improve instruction in science and mathematics. But since the inception of these programs in 1978, we have taken a big step in the direction of educational excellence. The annual testing scores are the latest evidence of that.

---

[1] *Report of Student Performance: Update from Spring 1978 to Spring 1982. North Carolina Annual Testing Program, Basic Skills.* (Raleigh: Division of Research, North Carolina Department of Public Instruction, [1982]), 5-56, also contains a summary of 1981 results.

STATEMENT ON INFANT MORTALITY

Raleigh, July 8, 1982

A high rate of infant mortality has historically been one of North Carolina's most serious health problems. This administration has undertaken an all-out effort to make this state a safer place for children to be born.

I am deeply gratified to announce today that North Carolina's infant mortality rate has declined by 25.6 percent since 1976. Eight percent of that decline occurred between 1980 and 1981. In 1976, the mortality rate was 17.8 per 1,000 live births. Today, the rate is 13.2 per 1,000 live births. Had that dramatic reduction not occurred, 1,166 more children would not have lived until their first birthday.

The decline in infant mortality is attributable to improved care of pregnant women and infants. In the last five years, the state has placed an unprecedented emphasis on programs for mothers and newborn children. We have worked to ensure that services are available everywhere in North Carolina, so that women get proper prenatal care; so that mothers who have a high risk of difficult delivery get the best possible medical attention; and so that critically ill newborns have the benefit of advanced medical technology.

We have established a regionalized perinatal program, and we have significantly improved the collaboration among our major medical centers, family physicians, and local health departments in order to give patients the full benefit of available medical services. We have worked to identify high-risk mothers and get them into treatment programs as early as possible. High-risk infants are also being identified early and treated quickly in an effort to prevent any medical problems from becoming life threatening or crippling.

Through Medicaid, the Crippled Children's Program, and the Perinatal Program, we are providing sophisticated medical treatment to premature infants born to low-income families. Studies of three-year-olds indicate that 75 percent of those who were seriously premature are now normal children. This is a great improvement over the days when prematurity was a frequent precursor of mental retardation.

We have for too long had one of the worst records in the nation in infant mortality. We won't know until December how the latest statistics will affect our ranking among the states.[1] But because we have faced up to this problem, young lives are being saved in North Carolina.

We are not satisfied with the present statistics, even though they represent a substantial improvement. We must continue to work to reduce our infant mortality rate, and our goal is to make North Carolina the safest and healthiest place anywhere for children to be born and grow up.

---

[1]The state's infant mortality rate dropped from fifth highest in the nation, in 1980, to eighth highest in 1981. However, in 1982 only the District of Columbia, South Carolina, Alabama, and Mississippi registered more deaths per 1,000 live births than North Carolina. *Indicators of Children's Needs in North Carolina* (Raleigh: Office of Policy and Planning, North Carolina Department of Administration, January, 1985), 12; *NCHS* [National Center for Health Statistics] *Monthly Vital Statistics Report*, 32 (September 21, 1984), 11.

SUPERINTENDENTS' SUMMER CONFERENCE

WILMINGTON, JULY 9, 1982

[The governor made the same speech on July 13, 1982, at the Principals' Summer Conference.]

We meet in a time of unprecedented challenge to public education in America. You know that the public schools have lost more than just dollars from Washington; they have lost vital moral support from the national administration.

You don't hear our nation's leadership in the White House speak up for children, for public schools, and for school people. When the Reagan administration has an encouraging word for education, you can bet they're talking about *private* schools, not public schools. I think that's wrong, and it ought to be changed![1]

I wish the Reagan administration could hear what a Republican president named Dwight Eisenhower said twenty-five years ago: "If the United States is to maintain its position of leadership and if we are further to enhance the quality of our society, we must see to it that today's young people are prepared to contribute the maximum to our future strength and progress, and that they achieve the highest possible excellence in the schools."[2] Dwight Eisenhower was right, and Ronald Reagan ought to pay attention to what he said!

Thanks to you, North Carolina is leading the way and showing what can be done—with our kindergarten program, our Primary Reading Program, our Community Schools Program, our Adopt-a-School programs, and our annual test and competency test. We have taken those steps. We have made that progress, and we have made those investments despite limited budgetary resources—and that picture has grown even darker. The national recession means we will have even fewer resources available. Fewer dollars are available from Washington.

You and I and all the friends of public education face a tremendous challenge—the challenge, against all these odds, of achieving excellence in public education. But we can do it. We can do it by having excellent teachers and administrators, by having good and fair performance evaluation, by having a good quality assurance program, and by having good training. Most of all, we can do it by paying a decent salary to the people who are responsible for teaching our children, and that must be the first priority for the money we have.

We can achieve excellence by strengthening the curriculum—the basic skills, writing, social studies, science, geometry, and algebra —and by adding those skills to our testing program.

We can achieve excellence by providing better school buildings and equipment, and I have at work today an excellent Governor's Task Force on Financing Public School Facilities that includes some of North Carolina's top business leaders.[3]

We can achieve excellence by continuing to bring volunteers into the classrooms and increasing community support for the schools.

We can achieve excellence by continuing to strengthen education for special populations—like the handicapped and the gifted and talented.

Most of all, we can achieve excellence by helping more young people stay in school and graduate, instead of dropping out. You know the plan I have outlined for attacking our dropout problem. It doesn't call for a lot of new dollars, but it calls for a lot of hard work and cooperation, for early identification of potential dropouts, for counseling and special curriculum, for in-school suspension programs and for extended-day programs, for individual student education plans, for job placement centers, for tracking students who slip through the cracks, and for the public schools and our community college system working together to help dropouts. We cannot achieve true excellence if 30 percent of our young people drop out before they graduate. This will be the real measure of our success.

I want us to begin to recognize true excellence in education. Beginning next spring, I want to begin officially recognizing what I would call Schools of Excellence. I will ask the State Board of Education to develop criteria for these awards, and those schools that are chosen will be able to fly a special flag over their building marking that achievement.

We simply need more people standing up for public education and recognizing what the schools *can* do and *are* doing. Next month, I will become chairman of the Education Commission of the States, one of the premier education organizations in this nation. I will use that forum to promote one major theme: that 1983 should be "The Year of the Public School" in America.[4] I want to get every governor, every mayor, and every board of county commissioners to make that proclamation, to set up special activities, and to focus on the importance of public education.

Our goal, as a nation, should be excellence in education. A strong national defense, a healthy national economy, a position of respect and leadership in the world—all these require excellence in education. A nation rises or falls on the quality of its public schools. The nation that shortchanges the education of its children robs its own future.

The United States is in a race—a race that belongs not to the swift, but to the smart; not an arms race, but a brains race. North Carolina competes with other states for industry, for better jobs, for opportunities, for a better life for people. So does our nation compete with other nations. We cannot afford to become an economic colony of Japan and West Germany.

I read not long ago that the average IQ of Japanese children is ten points higher than our children. We must recognize that the future belongs to the nation with the smartest kids. Our generation must resolve to make this next generation the best educated in the world.

When he addressed our Dropout Conference, Dr. Ernest Boyer said: "It is in my judgment absolutely urgent that we understand that there is no nation without the young, there is no future without education."[5] We must reawaken this nation to that realization. We must take the lead and carry this crusade to every corner of North Carolina.

We must have leadership that stands up for education, not tears it down; leadership that speaks up for the schools, not stays silent. As a state and as a nation, we must have a new commitment to excellence in education. I ask you to join me in that crusade.

---

[1] In his address to the National Catholic Educational Association on April 15, 1982, President Reagan announced a plan to offer income tax credits to parents who send their children to private primary and secondary schools. Although Reagan envisioned the proposal as a means of assisting lower- and middle-class families to offset the financial burden incurred when faced with private school costs and state and local school taxes, opponents argued that such a measure would benefit only the wealthy and, furthermore, subsidize a system of racially segregated education. The program, which would have cost the federal government nearly $3 billion in lost income tax revenue over the next five years, was made public at a time when the Reagan administration was calling for a freeze in public education spending as one method of checking the growing federal budget deficit. The president's plan was defeated in November, 1983. *Congressional Quarterly Almanac, 1982*, 489-490, and *Congressional Quarterly Almanac, 1983*, 395.

[2] Dwight David Eisenhower (1890-1969), native of Denison, Texas; B.S., United States Military Academy, 1915; U.S. Army, 1915-1948. Appointed commanding general, Allied powers, European theater of operations, 1943; commander, U.S. forces of occupation in Germany, 1945; U.S. Army chief of staff, 1945-1948; Columbia University president, 1948-1952; thirty-fourth U.S. president, 1953-1957, 1957-1961. *Who Was Who in America, 1969-1973*, 211. Neither the source nor accuracy of the quotation Hunt attributes to Eisenhower could be verified.

[3] Executive Order No. 81, signed June 3, 1982, established the Governor's Task Force on Financing Public School Facilities. *N.C. Session Laws, 1981, Regular and Extra Sessions, 1982*, 353-354.

[4] Hunt read a proclamation on August 27, 1982, at a school friends luncheon in Winston-Salem, recognizing 1982-1983 as the "Year of the Public Schools" in North Carolina.

[5] Ernest Leroy Boyer (1928-   ), native of Dayton, Ohio; resident of McLean, Virginia; A.B., Greenville College, 1950; M.A., 1955, Ph.D., 1957, University of Southern California, and recipient of numerous honorary degrees. Educator; U.S. commissioner of education, 1977-1979; president, Carnegie Foundation for the Advancement of Teaching, since 1979. *Who's Who in America, 1982-1983*, I, 355. The Governor's Statewide Conference on School Dropouts was held May 18, 1982.

STATEMENT ON NORTH CAROLINA 2000 SURVEY RESULTS

RALEIGH, JULY 22, 1982

I am happy to be here today with William Friday, president of the University of North Carolina and chairman of the Commission on the Future. We are announcing the results of two recent surveys of North Carolinians about the future of this state. Although the surveys were done differently, the results show remarkable agreement on what we should be doing now to prepare for our future.

Both surveys are part of the North Carolina 2000 project. They were done to get citizens thinking about an agenda for our future and to get a sense of their priorities. The Commission on the Future and local North Carolina 2000 committees will consider the results in formulating their recommendations.

The North Carolina 2000 questionnaire was widely distributed early this spring through libraries, schools, banks, civic clubs, and by local North Carolina 2000 committees. Many newspapers reprinted the questionnaire as a public service. It asked citizens to choose the ten most important qualities for North Carolina to have in the future and which ones needed the most improvement. We received 112,000 replies, which shows that people care enough about their state to volunteer their answers and send them in.

Citizens said the most important area for improvement was the availability of jobs. At the same time, they said they do not want us to backslide in maintaining farmland and agriculture. They do not want the quality of the environment to deteriorate.

People said improved education was the next most important priority, and that we should at the very least maintain it at its present level of quality. The availability and cost of housing ranked third on the list of improvements needed, which I believe reflects the current problem with high interest rates.

People also said we need to improve in such areas as protection from crime, fairness of taxes, efficiency in state and local government, help for the needy, farmland and agriculture, environmental quality, water supply, and roads.

While this survey was not scientific, it gave me the same kind of readings I get from going out and meeting people, and it got 112,000 people thinking more about the kind of state they want North Carolina to be in the year 2000. We have returned this data to the local North Carolina 2000 committees for their consideration. It is vitally important that local leaders have feedback from their citizens as they make decisions about schools, industries, taxes, and other issues.

The Commission on the Future participated in a scientific survey designed to get more detailed information. It was conducted by the Office of State Budget and it involved twenty-five-minute telephone interviews with 804 randomly selected adults. This survey generally supported the findings of the North Carolina 2000 questionnaire. The number-one goal was, again, quality education for our children. Ranking just below that were preservation of natural resources, protection from crime, fair taxes, and good jobs.

When we asked people what they thought would be the most serious problem facing North Carolina in the next twenty years, almost half named problems related to the economy. Citizens also put a very high priority on environmental protection. When people were given a hypothetical choice between two government programs, one that cost more but was less environmentally harmful, and one that cost less, but was more harmful, 83 percent chose the more costly, but less harmful option. Almost half of those surveyed thought we now have a good balance between industrial development and environmental protection. This survey will also be considered by the Commission on the Future, and by the local North Carolina 2000 committees.

NATIONAL ASSOCIATION OF STATE PERSONNEL EXECUTIVES

ATLANTA JULY 23, 1982

[Much of the information presented below was included in Hunt's addresses to the PRO '81 Conference, Nashville, Tennessee, January 16, 1981, and the Governor's Commission on Governmental Productivity, Raleigh, May 6 and 7, 1981.]

State personnel executives and governors have some great challenges ahead. We are called upon to be more productive in a time of declining national productivity, to do more with less. We have fewer resources for rewarding good employees, and it is becoming harder to compete with the private sector for the highly skilled employees our computerized age demands.

I look to the personnel executive to help deal with the management of human resources. We spend most of our dollars on salaries and fringe benefits, so your advice and expertise are increasingly valuable. In North Carolina we are proud of Harold Webb and are pleased that you have recognized his talents by electing him as president of your association.[1] We feel that his leadership will contribute to the growth and achievements of your association.

It is a challenge to us as public administrators to help our employees reach the goals the people have elected us to meet. We must be progressive, innovative, and responsive. We can no longer simply add staff when the job gets bigger. We need to increase development of existing human resources, to encourage technological innovation, and to streamline our procedures. We must find new ways to reward achievers.

In North Carolina we have examined our total management system. We have reorganized our Office of State Personnel to assess what its goals should be, to allocate resources consistent with those goals, and to increase productivity. We are establishing standards for personnel operation and an auditing system for those standards. I'd like to share with you some of the other things we are doing in our state in employee development, productivity, employee recognition, and in employer-employee relations:

—I have sent all my cabinet officers to the executive managers program at the School of Business Administration at the University of North Carolina. We have developed our own Government Executives Institute and have trained nearly 300 government executives in the latest management techniques, including cost-benefit analysis, affirmative action compliance, and labor-management relations.

—We have implemented a public management program for middle-level executives, with eleven short courses of three days each, over a period of two and a half years. All courses are work related, and we are working with our university system and the National Consortium of States for graduate credit and national certification.

—I have asked all my cabinet departments to appoint an assistant secretary for productivity, to give our strong emphasis on productivity the importance it deserves within the system. Their job is to make their department more productive.[2]

—We have established a Work Planning and Performance Review system, which provides for each employee and supervisor to agree on a plan of work for the employee and for a review of performance. This makes sure both agree on what is to be done, and it is used as a tool for awarding merit increases.

—We have a Productivity Commission, the first of its kind in any state government, which involves local government and private industry in identifying productivity problems and offering solutions.

—Our Employee Suggestion System has saved us over a million dollars and has rewarded employees as well. Since it has been implemented, the suggestion system has resulted in seventy-three employees getting $58,000 in cash awards. Employees may receive 25 percent of the savings their suggestion brings, up to $5,000. Non-cash awards, such as time off, were given to 195 employees.

—For rewarding units of employees, we have an incentive pay system which also provides for employees to receive a portion of their savings, up to 25 percent. We have five major departments participating, including thirty-five divisions or units. In the four years of its operation it has saved the taxpayers over a million dollars. This also is the only program of its kind in the nation.

—But it's not always possible or appropriate to reward employees with dollars, so I established the Governor's Award for Excellence. Through a tough recommendation and selection process, this year we recognized four employees from across the state for outstanding service.[3]

—In order to provide more take-home dollars for employees, we have deferred taxes on the retirement contribution for each employee. We have also surveyed state employees to see whether there is a need for state government to help ensure the availability of good day care near major state offices. I believe that it is in the area of benefits that state government will be more likely to be competitive with private industry.

—Through our Troubled Employee Program, we try to find out why an employee's attendance, attitude, or productivity has fallen. We encourage the employee to seek proper counseling. We have a Work Options Program, which allows employees and managers to modify the work schedule together. This allows flexibility in the employee's schedule, and allows job sharing and other innovations, while getting the job done for the taxpayers.

—We have tapped a reservoir of talent for state government through the Retired Senior Executives Program, where we recruit top executives who are retired in the state, and we put them on various projects in line with their expertise. So far we have had twenty-one executives working on ten projects, at almost no cost to the state. A side benefit of this program is that state employees are exposed to new business techniques, and the executive gains an appreciation of the work of government.

—In my Department of Administration, which is the business arm of state government and where many of these efforts I've described are housed, we are embarking on a "Work Smarter" campaign. That will include all these programs that are going on and will put special emphasis on motivating and rewarding employees and getting them to constantly think of ways to "work smarter," not just harder. It will be developed with the advice and consultation of private industry and will try to bring to state government the kind of partnership between employer and employee that is found in countries like Japan, where teamwork is basic.

I believe that state governments are real laboratories for making democracy work. I think the burden is on us more than ever to prove that government can work, that it doesn't have to be inefficient or fat. We have kept the rate of growth in government in North Carolina lower than it has been in this century, but the population is growing, and needs are growing.

We have some tremendous challenges ahead of us, and the greatest of those is to keep the people's confidence in government. To do that, we must be more resourceful, more productive, more responsible and responsive. As David Kearns, president of Xerox Corporation, said at our last statewide productivity conference: "The wealth of this nation is not in the ground. It's in our minds ... and that's a renewable resource. Our real wealth is the power to generate new ideas. In that sense, we can create new wealth ... and we have." [4]

---

[1] Harold Hudson Webb (1925-   ), appointed state personnel director, 1977. Previously identified in Mitchell, *Addresses of Hunt*, I, 141n.

[2] Executive Order No. 62, signed March 25, 1981, established the position of assistant secretary of productivity and the Governor's Management Council. *N.C. Sessions Laws, 1981*, 1760-1762.

[3] The Governor's Award for Excellence was established by Executive Order No. 53, dated October 8, 1980. *N.C. Session Laws, 1981*, 1735-1736.

[4] David Todd Kearns (1930-   ), native of Rochester, New York; B.S., University of Rochester, 1952; U.S. Naval Reserve, 1952-1954. Employed by IBM Corp., 1954-1971, eventually attaining the post of vice-president, Marketing Operations, Data Processing Division; joined Xerox Corp. in 1971 and became its president and chief executive officer six years later. *Who's Who in America, 1982-1983*, I, 1762. The remarks Hunt attributes to Kearns could not be verified.

DINNER FOR CONGRESSMAN CHARLIE ROSE

FAYETTEVILLE, AUGUST 24, 1982

It is a distinct pleasure to have the opportunity to welcome a man who is a cherished, personal friend of mine and who has been a steadfast friend of North Carolina.

President Carter's loyalty to North Carolina is something Charlie Rose and I have thought about a lot in the past year. Congressman Rose and I have been working very hard to convince people of the wisdom of the tobacco price support program and of the very serious consequences of increasing the tax on cigarettes. Thanks to the leadership and statesmanship of people like Congressman Rose, our tobacco program remains intact. And because the Republican administration has saddled this country with an enormous deficit, the cigarette tax increase was enacted.

How much easier our job would have been these past months had Jimmy Carter still been president.[1] During his term of office, everybody knew—on Capitol Hill and in Fayetteville, North Carolina—that tobacco had a friend in the White House. He knew the problems confronting North Carolina tobacco farmers because he knows what it's like to try to make a living off the land.

Prior to January of 1981, there was no talk about raising the tax on cigarettes, because the Carter administration wasn't frantically searching around for ways to reduce a record federal deficit. We were moving in a sober, orderly fashion toward a balanced budget. We got closer to that goal than we had been in many years, and closer than we are likely to get for many years to come.

I get very angry when I hear President Reagan say he inherited the economic problems of this nation from the Carter administration, because that just isn't so. Among the things he inherited were a reduced deficit, declining unemployment, a growing gross national product, increased industrial production, and rising capacity utilization. The country was in a period of economic recovery.

He also inherited a rational energy policy that has since been dismantled. That energy policy, based on conservation and reduced dependence on foreign oil, is the reason why the price of gasoline is lower at the pump today.

You don't hear much talk out of Washington today about protecting our environment, an issue which poll after poll shows to be a vitally important priority to the people of this country. Clean air and clean water were at the top of the agenda in the Carter administration. So was public education—the idea that if you are going to compete in the international economic arena, you had to make those investments in public education, you had to have the smartest kids in the world.

Every day we all read the grim news coming out of the Middle East. I often stop and think about how much worse the situation in that troubled part of the world would be today if it weren't for this man who is with us tonight. How much worse might it be if Jimmy Carter had not gone to Camp David, sat down with the leaders of Israel and Egypt, and engineered one of the greatest foreign policy achievements in the history of the world? The world remains a dangerous place. But because he did that it is a less dangerous place than it otherwise would have been.

Today, at home and abroad, there is a good deal of confusion about just what the present administration stands for, what its ideals are, what its values are. Under President Carter, America stood for equal rights at home and human rights abroad, for a clean environment, for fiscal responsibility, for energy independence, and for good schools.

He turned America in the direction of those ideals, and he paid a heavy political price for not resorting to quick-fix solutions. Because of that, the history books will treat him as a man of courage and as one who reminded Americans of what this country is supposed to be all about. It is in that spirit that I introduce to you the former president of the United States, Jimmy Carter.

---

¹James Earl (Jimmy) Carter, Jr. (1924-   ), native of Plains, Georgia; B.S., United States Naval Academy, 1946; U.S. Navy, 1946-1954. Farmer; member, Georgia state Senate, 1962-1966; governor of Georgia, 1971-1975; chairman, National Democratic Campaign Committee, 1974; U.S. president, 1977-1981. *North Carolina Manual, 1979*, 229; *1981*, 148.

DEDICATION OF R. J. REYNOLDS AVIARY, NORTH CAROLINA ZOOLOGICAL PARK

ASHEBORO, AUGUST 26, 1982

This is truly a great day for the North Carolina Zoological Park and for all the people of this state. We are taking another giant step toward making this zoo the best public zoological facility for research, education, and tourism in the nation.

I have followed the development of our zoo since before I became lieutenant governor. I remember coming here to see the tortoises, the zoo's first arrivals, nearly a decade ago. Many of us were on these grounds just two summers ago to dedicate and open the Africa section, of which this unique aviary is an important part. All of you here today have played a special role in the creation and development of our zoo and this $1.5 million addition we are unveiling today, and we thank you for helping us make this dream a reality.

I want to emphasize that this aviary, and this entire zoo, is a direct result of a great public-private partnership we have developed in this state. The North Carolina Zoological Society, through the leadership of Bill Henderson[1] and his current and past board members, has led the way for the private sector to contribute so much to this public facility.

David Stedman, president of the North Carolina Citizens Association, was one of the key local leaders who raised nearly $500,000 in development funds and pushed the state to locate the park in Randolph County. He also joined Bill Henderson and then zoo director Bill Hoff in 1976 to appeal to R. J. Reynolds to make this major contribution to the zoo's development.[2]

We have received many contributions from businesses and corporations over the years, but R. J. Reynolds is the first company to provide major funding for a particular structure. Tylee,[3] I hope you will convey to your corporate leadership and your board the deep gratitude all of us feel for the tremendous contribution Reynolds has made.

The Lance Corporation of Charlotte also deserves special recognition for providing the funds for this colorful flamingo habitat.

I hope other corporations, businesses, and foundations will take note of what R. J. Reynolds and others have provided. There are unlimited possibilities here, and I encourage more private firms to become involved with our zoo.

In partnership with these private efforts, the people of North Carolina and Randolph County have contributed greatly through the Randolph County board of commissioners and our North Carolina General Assembly. The major budget contributions made by state and local government have played a vital role in making this a reality. I want to personally thank Senator Russell Walker[4] for his great leadership in this effort. He has really been a mover and shaker in helping us bring about this great zoo.

All these public and private efforts have really paid off. Nearly a half million people are visiting the zoo each year. Now that we have opened this aviary and will be completing Africa in the next few years, more and more people will come. Already, this zoo is paying big dividends to the travel and tourism industry in this area. In 1981 alone, Randolph County received nearly $11 million in tourist-generated income. Tourism is the third largest industry in this state and one of the fastest-growing sectors of our economy. The travel industry has stayed strong despite a national recession, and it is vitally important to North Carolina's economy.

This zoo is also a tremendous educational experience for the thousands of schoolchildren who visit each year. The zoo staff has made great efforts to develop an exciting educational program for them. And, of course, the natural habitat concept is so important here, and I am pleased this aviary carries through that concept.

Now, where do we go from here? The African Plains, which will be stocked with antelope and other plains animals, is now in the final construction stage and should open next year; in 1984, the 40,000 square-foot, football-field size African Pavilion will be finished. That pavilion will complete the Africa section. Major new funding will be needed to begin the North America Continent section and to have it partially constructed by the end of this decade.

Once again a public-private partnership will be necessary to continue development of this zoo and to ensure that it becomes what its planners and developers envisioned many years ago. I firmly believe that the North Carolina Zoological Park can become the best zoo in the nation, and possibly in the world. I want North Carolina to be known as a state whose citizens, government, and businesses worked together to create something unique that will last for generations, and that will be an integral part of our state's economy and quality of life. I thank each of you for helping us work toward that goal.

---

[1] William R. Henderson (1922-   ), native of Kannapolis; resident of Raleigh; B.S., High Point College, 1943; graduate student at Duke University and University of North Carolina at Chapel Hill; U.S. Marine Corps, 1943-1946. President, North Carolina Jaycees, 1953-1954; director, state Commerce Division, 1956-1962, and of the Business Development Corporation of North Carolina, 1956-1982; board chairman, 1968-1974, and trustee, 1974-1985, North Carolina Zoological Society; president, W. R. Henderson and Associates since 1962 and board chairman, Sir Walter Realty. William R. Henderson to Jan-Michael Poff, March 12, 1985.

[2] William David Stedman (1921-   ), native of Asheboro; A.B., Duke University, 1942; degree in industrial administration, Harvard University, 1943; M.A., Georgetown University, 1961; U.S. Naval Reserve. President, board chairman, Stedman Corporation. News and Observer, March 5, 1978; We the People of North Carolina, June, 1972, 8, 10, 13, 46.

William Hoff (1926-   ), native of Chicago; attended Ripon College, Northwestern University, and Roosevelt University; U.S. Army, 1944-1946. Draftsman, Chicago Park District, 1946-1951; general curator, Lincoln Park Zoo, 1961-1967; executive director, Cincinnati Zoo, 1961-1967; executive director, 1968-1970, and director, 1970-1973, St. Louis Zoo; director, North Carolina Zoological Park, 1973-1978. News and Observer, May 26, 1974; Robert L. Fry, director, North Carolina Zoological Park, to Jan-Michael Poff, February 25, 1985.

[3] J. Tylee Wilson is identified in "Governor's Business Council on the Arts and Humanities," April 9, 1981, footnote 1, above.

[4] Russell Grady Walker (1918-   ), native of Conetoe; resident of Randolph County; was graduated from High Point High School and the U.S. Army Air Force pilot training school; U.S. Army Air Force, 1941-1946; U.S. Air Force Reserve, 1947-1955. Retired supermarket executive; state senator from the Sixteenth District since 1975; former state Democratic party chairman. Duke Policy News, 11 (March, 1983), 1; North Carolina Manual, 1983, 251.

TESTIMONY BEFORE U.S. HOUSE COMMITTEE ON EDUCATION AND LABOR

RALEIGH, SEPTEMBER 1, 1982

[During 1982, the governor stressed the importance of joining together government, the schools, and business in an "alliance for education." Speeches covering the topic, in varying degrees of detail, included those delivered at the Education Commission of the States meeting in Portland, Oregon, on August 20; at the Conference on the Status of Pre-College Science and Mathematics Education, September 11; to the Executive Committee of the Council of State Governments, November 19; to the National Conference of State Legislatures, December 9, and at a news conference, in which he announced the appointment of the National Task Force on Education for Economic Growth, also on December 9. All of the above-mentioned messages were similar in content to his testimony, below, before the House Committee on Education and Labor.

Hunt told Education Commission of the States members gathered in Portland that his mission, as ECS chairman, would be "to mobilize the friends of education across the United States; to focus the attention of our people on the schools, in every state, city, county, and school district; to build an alliance with all national education organizations; to get the people of this country into their schools, to see what they need, and to see how they can do a better job."]

Chairman Perkins, Congressman Andrews:[1]

I deeply appreciate this opportunity to appear before you. I speak today as governor of a state that has a deep and historic commitment to public education. Additionally, I am testifying as the chairman of the Education Commission of the States, as chairman of the Education Subcommittee of the National Governors' Association [NGA] Committee on Human Resources, and as chairman of the NGA Task Force on Technological Innovation. So, while I am wearing a lot of different hats today, they all have to do with the very critical challenges confronting public education in this country today.

This hearing is taking place against the backdrop of a diminishing federal role in public education. That role is diminishing not only in terms of the dollars spent on educational programs, but also in terms of Washington's advocacy of the role of education in modern society. I would be remiss if I did not pause at this point and pay tribute to you, Chairman Perkins, and you, Congressman Andrews, for your unceasing efforts on behalf of education. I'm sure the people of Kentucky are well aware of Congressman Perkins's support of our schools. We are indeed fortunate in North Carolina to be represented by Ike Andrews, who understands that a nation is only as strong as its educational system. Our children have benefited enormously from his presence in Congress.

I referred a moment ago to the declining federal role in education. I am not here today to enumerate a list of specific federal programs for which funding should be continued or increased. I do want to emphasize to you, however, that when you in the Congress make decisions about these different programs, you should do so with some important realities in mind.

The future security and economic strength of this nation are dependent in large part on our commitment to education. Simply stated, we are in a war. Not a military confrontation, but a high-stakes struggle with countries like Japan and Germany for the economic leadership of the world. The nation that does the best job of educating its children, the nation that does the best job of training its people to work in the high-technology jobs of the future, is going to prevail. The victory will go not to the strong but to the smart. We must assemble an army—an army of technicians, engineers, scientists, and mathematicians. Anyone who doubts the seriousness of the challenge need only look at the tremendous strides the Japanese are making in the field of microelectronics.

State and local governments across this country are demonstrating that they are willing to do their part in meeting this challenge. In North Carolina, we have upgraded our public schools through such initiatives as new testing programs, a Primary Reading Program, reduced class size, improved education in basic skills, a quality assurance program for teachers, dropout prevention projects, and the mobilization of thousands of adult volunteer tutors in the classrooms. We are actively exploring ways in which we can increase the number of engineering graduates from our universities, and our system of community colleges and technical institutes is committed to providing the skills training that our people must have to work in the new, higher-paying jobs that are coming to North Carolina. These initiatives are showing results, and none of them were mandated by the federal government.

I have proclaimed 1982-1983 as the "Year of the Public School" in North Carolina—not as a public relations gesture, but as a means for getting more people involved in the school system, getting them to think about how the schools can do a better job. We want to involve people as individual volunteers, and we want increased participation by business. A number of firms in North Carolina have been generous with their money for education programs, but we want their minds as well. Business can offer a wealth of expertise in such areas as curriculum planning and administrative skills.

The Education Commission of the States can make an enormous contribution in this area. As chairman, I am going to make it my top priority to make that organization the voice of education in America. By doing that, ECS can involve business in the educational process on a national scale. We can help drive home the point to the business community that the future of private enterprise depends on trained minds and skilled hands.

If we are to succeed in this struggle, if we are to develop a strong economy based on high technology, it is absolutely essential that we improve the state of math and science education in America. During the coming year, the NGA Task Force on Technological Innovation and the NGA Subcommittee on Education will undertake a survey of math-science education in the United States. We will do a state-by-state analysis in an attempt to determine the state of the art in math-science training. We can share information, for example, about the North Carolina School of Science and Mathematics, and perhaps inspire other states to establish similar programs. Likewise, states like California, Texas, Oregon and so on can make available information about their own innovative programs.

The point I seek to make is this: State and local government is responding to the declining federal role in education by assuming the leadership role that Washington has abdicated. We are seizing the initiative because we at this level of government know how important education is. We are doing things that can provide the federal government with some important and beneficial lessons.

Despite all of that, state governments, local governments, citizen volunteers, and the business community can't do it alone. The federal government still has a role to play in the education of America's children. When a particular piece of legislation pertaining to education comes before this committee, I strongly urge you to judge it on the basis of whether or not it will make us stronger in our efforts to compete in the international economic arena. Will it help equip our children with the kinds of skills that make America stronger?

There are certain areas in which the federal government has a fundamental obligation. I am referring to the education of the children of migrants, handicapped youngsters, military dependents, and the severely disadvantaged. Moreover, the federal government is best equipped to foster and administer basic educational research, which of course involves some funding for model programs. Initiatives like public kindergarten and Head Start are the product of the kind of research I am talking about. Yes, the federal government still has a role to play in the process; because these fundamental responsibilities are still present, the U.S. Department of Education should not be dismantled.

I am fully aware that when I say these things to people of the stature and foresight of Carl Perkins and Ike Andrews, I am preaching to the choir. Your records of leadership bear that out. But when you go back to Washington and discuss these matters with your colleagues, I hope you will report to them that we at the state and local level are ready to forge the strongest partnership for education in our history. We know the nation with the smartest kids is going to be the economic leader of the world.

The federal government must participate in this partnership or it will not succeed. If we abandon education, we abandon our children. And if we abandon our children, we sell out our future. Education, Mr. Chairman and Congressman Andrews, is the highway that leads us into the sunshine of a bright new day. I thank you for the opportunity to speak to you today, and I will now be happy to respond to your questions.

---

[1]Carl D. Perkins (1912-   ), native, resident, of Hindman, Kentucky; attended Caney Junior College and Lees Junior College; LL.B., University of Louisville, 1935; served in U.S. Army during World War II. Attorney, 1935-1948; member, Kentucky House of Representatives, 1940; attorney for Knott County, 1941-1948; elected to Congress in 1948 and returned in subsequent elections; chairman, House Committee on Education and Labor, and of the Elementary, Secondary, and Vocational Education Subcommittee; Democrat. Barone and Ujifusa, *Almanac of American Politics, 1984,* 469.

Ike Franklin Andrews (1925-   ), member, U.S. House of Representatives from North Carolina's Fourth Congressional District, 1973-1985, and chairman, Human Resources Subcommittee, House Committee on Education and Labor; Democrat. Previously identified in Mitchell, *Addresses of Hunt,* I, 555n; see also *News and Observer,* November 7, 1984.

NORTH CAROLINA
CRIME AND JUSTICE CONFERENCE

RALEIGH, SEPTEMBER 15, 1982

[Presiding over a September 15, 1982, news conference, Hunt called on the Governor's Crime Commission to propose "legislation that would make fraudulent evasion of income tax and mishandling of withheld state taxes felony offenses." He also sought a bill that would make "willful failure to file a state income-tax return . . . a two-year misdemeanor."]

I am delighted to keynote the first meeting of this kind ever held in North Carolina. Never before have representatives of all the elements of the criminal justice system—judges, prosecutors, probation officers, clerks, law enforcement officers, court counselors —gotten together under one roof.

If we are truly going to have a "system" as opposed to a loose organization of parts, we have to work in concert. Having a statewide meeting to bring it all together and focus attention on the system is a wonderful idea, but I urge you to take this concept home with you. For example, in Mecklenburg County, under the leadership of Judge Frank Snepp, a Criminal Justice Coordinating Council is actively functioning.[1] Judge Gil Burnett is using the same approach in New Hanover County,[2] and Alamance County is starting a similar program. The councils ensure communication and cooperation within the system, and that is urgently needed if we are going to fight crime in a systematic way.

I thank you for being here and I thank you for what you are doing. You are working your heads off and you don't get paid a lot of money for it. Yet you are making it work. I especially want to thank all of you judges, DAs, clerks, and police officers who are making speedy trials and fair sentencing a reality in North Carolina. We have got to see to it that a person contemplating a crime is fairly certain that he or she will be apprehended, tried, convicted, and punished swiftly and severely. That kind of certainty is the only real deterrent we have.

I salute our volunteers in Community Watch and Crimestoppers and the law enforcement people who work with them. These programs are growing rapidly and they are getting results. Thousands of crimes are being prevented, and hundreds of others are being solved.

Thanks to the volunteers and the professionals who work with them, we are making progress in diverting young people away from lives of crime. We are establishing new local programs, patterned after Volunteers to the Court in Guilford County, Bertie-Hertford Volunteers to the Court, Buncombe Alternatives, Partners, and others. We've got a long way to go before we have such a program established in every county, but the Governor's One-on-One Program is committed to do just that, at the rate of one new county each month. These will work with the community-based alternatives that are already in place and doing such a terrific job.

We wouldn't be here today, and we wouldn't have made as much progress as we have in pulling all the pieces together, were it not for the excellent work of the Governor's Crime Commission, which convened here in Raleigh this morning. The commission has correctly advocated the philosophy that we are all in this fight against crime together. We will win or lose together. We need to plan together if we are to succeed.

The members of the commission have been the architects of my legislative initiatives to combat crime, and they are working now on the crime package we will take to the General Assembly in January. One of the initiatives they are now focusing on is a long-overdue toughening of our laws dealing with tax cheaters and evaders in North Carolina. These people are stealing out of the pockets of those citizens who pay their fair share. I am going to ask the legislature to make the laws dealing with these crimes tougher, and we are going to back it up with adequate enforcement capability. I hold tax cheaters in no higher regard than I do the bid riggers. Cheating is cheating and stealing is stealing.

We've cleaned up bid rigging in North Carolina, a practice that had been going on for half a century. And I don't believe we'll have a repeat performance, because we have a tough new law that makes a bid rigger a felon, subject to a presumptive sentence of three years and a possible sentence of ten years.

During the remaining two years of this administration, there will be no letup in our efforts to fight crime. Next year, I will again go before the General Assembly to deliver a special message on crime. I will at that time outline a package of legislative proposals. We will want to consolidate a lot of things we have started. We will continue to focus maximum public attention on the need to work one-on-one with young people. That kind of volunteer effort represents our greatest hope of significantly reducing the crime rate in future years.

I want the criminal justice system to focus greater emphasis on the victims of crime. A victim is not a mere witness in an investigation and trial. We're talking about a person who has been robbed or raped or assaulted. We can help victims and at the same time deter crime with greater use of restitution. I am very proud of North Carolina's national leadership in this area. Nearly $12 million in restitution orders will be issued by our courts this year. You judges and DAs and clerks are doing a great job in this area, but we need to use restitution even more.

I am proud of the work being done by witness coordinators in several of our judicial districts. The work they do in assisting victims and witnesses as their cases work their way through the courts demonstrates to people that the system does care about them. We must expand this program.

Our Rape Victim Assistance Program is now in place and working well. It seems to me that if we are going to encourage victims to report rapes, require them to undergo a physical examination, and expose them to the prospect of having their character attacked on cross-examination, the least we can do is reimburse that poor victim for the cost of the examination. To date, our Rape Victim Assistance Fund has paid out $38,000 for examinations in fifteen months' time.

And speaking of victims, let's think for a minute about the victims of drunken driving. I wish you could see some of my mail. How do you reply to a parent whose three-year-old child was run over by a drinking driver? How do you try to explain to that parent why that person never went to jail and is now licensed to drive again?

Drunken drivers kill 26,000 Americans a year. In two years, they kill more Americans than died in Vietnam.

You police officers know what I'm talking about. When you arrest somebody for drinking while driving, you are oftentimes tied up for several hours with procedural work when you could be out on patrol. Sometimes, you have to knock on the door and tell a wife or a parent or a husband that the unthinkable has happened.

The drunken driver is not just the nice fellow who lives up the street and belongs to the country club and takes one too many every now and then. He's a criminal. When this agreeable fellow who lives a couple of houses away kills somebody, his victim is just as dead as the clerk who was shot in an armed robbery. The victim's family is just as bereaved. It's no consolation to that family that the man who killed their loved one is a nice guy most of the time.

I'm going to the legislature next year with very, very tough legislation. Those who would drink and drive are going to know that they are letting themselves in for some very unpleasant consequences. This slaughter has got to stop, and I'm going to need your help in the General Assembly.

I am proud of all of you because you are demonstrating that we at the state and local level have the imagination and the foresight and the toughness to deal with crime. But while this is where the action is, the federal government has a role to play. I commend President Reagan for the proposals he announced in recent days. He is showing leadership in the fight against crime and for that he deserves our gratitude and our support.[3]

You have a lot of work remaining during this conference and a lot more speakers to hear from. Thank you for coming, and thank you for the contributions you are making to the creation of a safer North Carolina.

---

[1]Frank W. Snepp, Jr. (1919-   ), native of Memphis, Tennessee; resident of Charlotte; A.B., Columbia University, 1940; attended Columbia University law school, 1940-1941; J.D., Duke University, 1948; U.S. Marine Corps, 1941-1945. State representative from Mecklenburg County, 1957, 1959; resident superior court judge, Twenty-sixth Judicial District, since 1967, and senior superior court judge since 1969; member of numerous commissions. Frank W. Snepp, Jr., to Jan-Michael Poff, June 17, 1985.

[2]Gilbert Henry Burnett (1925-   ), native of Burgaw; resident of Wilmington; attended University of North Carolina at Chapel Hill; was graduated from Wake Forest law school; served in U.S. Army Air Force during World War II. Elected district court judge, Fifth Judicial District, in 1968; senior chief district court judge since 1970. Gilbert Henry Burnett to Jan-Michael Poff, June 17, 1985.

[3]See President Reagan's "Message on Crime Legislation," September 13, 1982, in *Congressional Quarterly Almanac, 1982*, 28E-29E.

STATEMENT ON
WARREN COUNTY PCB LANDFILL

RALEIGH, SEPTEMBER 23, 1982

[The state transported approximately 40,000 cubic yards of soil contaminated with carcinogenic PCB—polychlorinated biphenyl—to a 20-acre landfill in the Afton area of Warren County between September 14 and November 8, 1982. During that time, North Carolina highway patrolmen expended better than 36,000 man-hours on duty at the specially constructed waste-storage facility and arrested 523 protesters, some of them from out of state, for attempting to block trucks from hauling in the tainted dirt. County residents opposed the landfill's location as a health and environmental hazard, and cries of racial discrimination were also heard. Some protesters felt that sparsely populated Warren was chosen for the landfill because it had relatively little political clout and was predominantly black. However, Governor Hunt contended that the site, including a 120-acre buffer zone, was selected because it was the least densely inhabited and most geologically feasible tract available to the state; it was also located in a county where "a substantial amount" of the toxic PCB-laden oil had been dumped.

PCB-impregnated oil, used as a coolant in electrical transformers, had been evacuated along 243 miles of North Carolina roadways in the summer of 1978. Robert E. "Buck" Ward, president of Ward Transformer Co. of Raleigh, and three New Yorkers were convicted, as a result of the dumping, of violating state and federal regulations. Manufacture of PCB was outlawed by the U.S. government in 1979. *Chapel Hill Newspaper,* November 23, 1982; *Charlotte Observer,* October 6, 1982; *Fayetteville Observer,* September 16, 1982; *News and Observer,* May 27, September 21, October 13, 1982; "No Dumping," *Time,* November 1, 1982, 29. See also Mitchell, *Addresses of Hunt,* I, 348-351, for background information on the PCB dumping and the landfill site selection problem.]

There has been a great deal of controversy over the PCB landfill in Warren County, and I think everyone should keep some important facts in mind. The dumping [of PCBs] occurred more than four years ago. Since then, the state and the federal government have explored every alternative for disposing of this material. The Environmental Protection Agency has ruled out in-place treatment. This is the only alternative available to the state.

We have looked at about 100 possible locations for a disposal site. The site in Warren County is the only one that met all the safety requirements and that could be obtained by the state. The federal courts have thoroughly reviewed this matter.[1]

All of us can understand the apprehensions people feel when any landfill is placed in their community. But we can assure the residents of Warren County that this landfill will be safe and will present no danger to them or to their families, now or in the future, and that no other material will be stored there in the future.

Obviously, this is an emotional issue. Our society is having to learn to deal with hazardous waste issues, and it is tough. It is unfortunate that we have had to station more than seventy highway patrolmen in Warren County to handle these protests. All of us would prefer to have those patrolmen on our state's roads and highways. But the responsibility of the state of North Carolina is to do what is right and what protects the health of our people—those who live in Warren County as well as those who live in the thirteen other counties where the material was dumped. The state will meet that responsibility.

---

[1]In November, 1981, a federal court rejected a lawsuit filed by Warren County residents and officials hoping to block construction of the landfill. An appeal before

the Fourth U.S. Circuit Court of Appeals was dropped on May 26, 1982, after the plaintiffs and the state arrived at an agreement concerning the site of the PCB storage facility and its future. *News and Observer*, May 27, 1982.

NORTH CAROLINA EDUCATION POLICY SEMINAR: EDUCATION FOR A HIGH-TECHNOLOGY ECONOMY

RESEARCH TRIANGLE PARK, SEPTEMBER 29, 1982

[Hunt's prepared remarks to the inaugural meeting of the Governor's Task Force on Science and Technology, September 23, 1982, likewise focused on the need to improve elementary and secondary mathematics and science education.]

I. Opening Remarks
   A.   As chairman of Education Commission of the States and as governor, I welcome all of you to this special State Education Policy Seminar on Education for a High-Technology Economy.
   B.   *Purpose of Session.*   We have put together this special Education Policy Seminar to provide a forum through which we can examine the serious problems North Carolina and the country are facing in the quality and quantity of elementary and secondary science and mathematics education, and to outline the steps that must be taken by all of us to address the problem. Perhaps the best way to demonstrate the need for our continued attention to science and mathematics education is to reflect for a moment on previous spurts of activity in this area.

October 4, 1982, will mark the twenty-fifth anniversary of the launching of Sputnik. The country's international prestige and preeminence had been threatened. The nation placed the highest priority, symbolized by the goal to land a man on the moon, on remaining the leader. The federal government led the way. Activities began with bursts of enthusiasm, money, and commitment, all of which waned considerably by the late 1960s and early 1970s. Assessments of those initiatives indicate that, while they led to increases in the quantity and quality of scientists and engineers, they were less successful in improving the understanding of science among most other students. In addition, the current deficiencies in science and mathematics education, which we will hear about shortly, are evidence that these previous programs alone were not able to bring about *lasting* changes in the system.

Today, the nation is threatened by the unraveling of the threads of its economic fabric. It is not a contest of symbolic events, but of survival in the international market system. Winning, likewise, will not come from single events; there will be no quick fixes. Lester

Thurow, the economist from MIT, has said that, "The economy is not going to thrive unless there is a major effort to upgrade the American labor force from the top to the bottom." This requires a collaborative, continuing spirit that pervades all sectors of society, not simply a top-down approach by the federal government in response to crises.

Improvements in science and mathematics education and technical training are essential ingredients in this effort. Achieving these improvements, however, requires a different perspective than that of twenty-five years ago. First, the goal now goes beyond international preeminence in science and technology to economic health and national security. Strengthening scientific and engineering resources are not ends in themselves, but are means for reaching these goals. Education and training programs, therefore, must prepare all our citizens to be full and active participants in an economic and social structure that will be highly influenced by science and technology.

Second, science and mathematics programs require constant nurturing. Steps taken in response to the Sputnik challenge—curricula changes, teacher training, and equipment purchases—are not necessarily appropriate today, nor will today's materials and practices meet all the needs of the twenty-first century.

Finally, regardless of action by the federal government, significant improvements in science and mathematics education will be achieved and sustained only if state and local governments—the units responsible for elementary and secondary education—take the lead in doing so. And we are here today, in my view, to examine how best to assume our leadership responsibilities, yours and mine.

C. *Outline of Procedure.*

[II-IV. Panelists' Remarks]
[Following the governor's overview of the format of the seminar were presentations on science and mathematics education by Roy Forbes, associate director, Education Commission of the States; Dr. Michael Usdan, president, Institute for Educational Leadership, Washington, D.C.; and Dr. George P. Williams, Jr., Wake Forest University physics professor and chairman, Governor's Task Force on Science and Technology.]

V. Critical Components of a State/Local Program
Roy Forbes has given us a succinct and disturbing description of the scope and magnitude of our deficiencies in pre-college education in science and mathematics throughout the United States. Dr. Usdan has outlined vividly why—from the standpoint of government, of industry, and of our position in international affairs —we must rectify this situation as quickly and as thoroughly as we possibly can. Dr. Williams has outlined some important steps we can take. These panelists have made it very clear that a comprehen-

sive approach is required rather than a patch job. Let me outline what I mean by a comprehensive approach.

A. *Where the Decisions Must Be Made.* First, let us consider where the decisions must be made. Clearly, whatever we do, the end result must be significant improvement in the interest and proficiency of pre-college students in science and mathematics. This means that *decisions made at the school level* are of critical importance. Which teachers are hired and retained, their qualifications for teaching science and mathematics, the course content, requirements for graduation, understanding and interest of students and parents in science and mathematics courses—all such choices mean the difference between good, rigorous training in science and mathematics and average or poor training.

The next level of decision making is the local government, local business and industry, and local community level. It is at this level that local community spirit, interest, and involvement in the school are strong or weak. It is here that parents, community leaders, and business and industrial firms consider the school as a distinct asset, to be improved and utilized for the benefit of all—or as another tax burden to bear, another public expense that should be minimized.

The third level is the state level. Here we find the policies, the standards, the guidelines, the support, the vision, and leadership— all the things that can mean the difference between a state with good schools and one with poor schools. Finally, there is the *federal level of decision making*, with various programs and forms of financial support intended to improve *pre-college* education throughout the country.

B. *Issues To Be Faced.* There are certain issues that must be faced, certain goals that must be established and be pursued if we are to improve education in science and mathematics in North Carolina and, indeed, throughout the United States. Let me list these briefly:

1. In the elementary grades, students must learn to read, to write, and to do elementary arithmetic. If these basic forms of instruction are not effective, then secondary education in any subject will be seriously handicapped.

2. At the middle and secondary levels, teachers of science and mathematics must be properly qualified through training and experience. In North Carolina, 30 to 40 percent of all teachers of science and mathematics are neither trained nor experienced. In some courses and grade levels the percentage is even higher.

In dealing with this issue we must provide effective incentives to attract and hold outstanding teachers of science and mathematics at both elementary and secondary levels. Various incentives can be provided. These include: (1) time for proper laboratory and instructional preparation; (2) grants to enable teachers to attend summer school and thereby upgrade their qualifications in science and mathematics; (3) provision of adequate facilities and equipment for both laboratory and classroom instruction; and (4) increase in the pay of teachers when possible. I know that increasing the pay to a level that will permit schools to compete effectively with industry and other forms of employment will be expensive. But higher salaries alone will not result necessarily in improved instruction in science and mathematics. Other steps must be taken also to ensure that the teachers of these subjects are highly qualified and given the time to teach effectively.

3. The content of science and mathematics courses must be rigorous and up to date, and minimum requirements for graduation from high school must be raised. We have far too many high school students graduating with very few courses in science and mathematics. And of those courses taken, the knowledge gained is far less than desirable. Raising the minimum requirements for graduation must also be accompanied by more rigorous requirements for admission to universities and colleges.

4. The community within which each school exists must take an active interest in the entire school, and insist upon rigorous instruction in science and mathematics. Without this interest and support, qualified teachers will not be recruited and retained, students will neither understand nor desire to become proficient in science or mathematics, and political and economic support required to overcome existing deficiencies will be difficult to mobilize.

5. In our colleges and universities, training programs for teachers must be examined closely. If they are not now turning out new teachers who know their subjects well, particularly science and mathematics subjects, or if they are not providing effective courses for present teachers who desire to improve their qualifications, then corrective measures must be taken. You may wish to add to this list of issues to be addressed or goals to be pursued. It is my conviction, however, that no one or two things—such as just increasing teacher pay, or just tightening up teacher certification requirements—will result in major improvements in science and mathematics instruction.

C. *Brief Responses To Panelists.*   I know that many significant actions are already taking place. To open this meeting for discussion, I'm going to call on a few people to give us brief comments on what they know about science and math education in North Carolina and what they think our course of action should be.

[Commentators were Dr. Delma Blinson, Greenville School System superintendent; Dr. Barbara Tapscott, representing Burlington City Schools; state House member Lura Tally; and Dr. Barbara Parramore, of North Carolina State University.]

VI. Conclusions, Recommendations, and Action Plan

A. *Observations and Questions.* It is evident from the remarks of our panelists and our discussion that there are serious deficiencies in K through 12 education in science and mathematics. It is also evident that it is in the interest of the students, in the interest of business and industry, and in the interest of federal, state, and local governments that we take vigorous and effective action to overcome these deficiencies. Clearly, from the remarks made here today, we know that various steps are being taken already but we need to do a great deal more. But let me pose the following questions to help us decide what we want to do next:

1. Are we doing enough in North Carolina? If not, what more should each of us do to foster the changes needed in the schools?
2. What should be the role of state government, of local governments, and of the private sector in finding solutions?
3. How can we effectively involve the business community of North Carolina in helping us find solutions to this particular education problem—to help overcome present deficiencies in science and mathematics education in our schools? Should a task force, for example, help develop a plan of action for working with the private sector? (Mention intent to name the ECS Task Force on Education for a High-Technology Economy and a state counterpart.)

B. *Conclusion.*

[Hunt's extemporaneous remarks included a summary of the seminar and words of thanks to the participants.]

NORTH CAROLINA SOYBEAN FESTIVAL

ELIZABETH CITY, OCTOBER 8, 1982

[The relationship between agricultural exports and state and national farm economies also received emphasis in the governor's speeches to the North Carolina Soybean Producers Association, January 16, and the Cooperative Council of North Carolina, January 27, 1981; the Tobacco Associates' thirty-fifth annual meeting, March 19, 1982; in the Tobacco Day, U.S.A., announcement, November 18, and an address to the Woodlot Owners' Forum, November 29, 1983; and the North Carolina Farm Bureau annual convention, December 3, 1984.

Although the press copy of the remarks to be delivered at the North Carolina Soybean Festival was dated October 7, Hunt's schedule indicates the speech was presented the following day.]

It is great to be here today at this Albemarle 4-H Livestock Building, which was financed by our North Carolina General Assembly through the great leadership of your state representative,

Vernon James.[1] It is most appropriate for the Soybean Festival to be held here in Elizabeth City, where a marker will be placed on U.S. 17 with this inscription: "Commercial processing of domestic soybeans in the United States began in 1915 at a plant which was located two miles north."[2]

Of course, what most people don't realize is that the first soybean to be grown in America was grown right here in Elizabeth City. Soybeans are a major part of agriculture in this Albemarle region. In 1980 the farm receipts from soybeans were about $60 million in the ten counties in Region R, nearly 30 percent of farm income here.[3] When you include the value of soybeans to local merchants and service industries, soybeans are worth more than $120 million to this area.

About 40 percent of the U.S. production of soybeans is exported, and the 25 million metric tons exported this year will represent 80 percent of the world's exports of soybeans.

Of course, as we all know, these are not the best of times for farmers, and that includes soybean farmers. Soybean production in North Carolina and in the nation is forecast at record-high levels this year. As a result of this abundant harvest, our national recession, the strengthening of the U.S. dollar in international exchange, and the economic stagnation in other nations, soybean prices are the lowest they have been in ten years.

Soybean prices have been particularly hurt because of their increased use in meat production. When people are out of work or are not getting cost-of-living pay raises, as many are not this year, people turn to extenders like cereals, potatoes, and other less costly items, and buy less high-value foods like meat, eggs, and vegetables.

The eye of the economic storm is over us. As one economist put it, the economic viability of a number of farmers now hangs in the balance. That's one way of saying that many farmers are going to go broke unless conditions improve. Considering the views of the current national administration, it appears that we will not return to the supply management programs that were in effect for basic farm commodities from the 1930s until 1973. So what, then, can we do to improve and stabilize farm income in the years ahead?

—First, we can encourage farmers to develop strong commodity associations to see that their interests are represented and to promote better adjustment of production in line with expected demand.

—Second, we can vigorously promote export markets for U.S. farm commodities.

—Third, Congress and federal officials must keep in mind the importance of a strong, viable agricultural industry. The goal should be to provide an atmosphere in which farmers can earn reasonable, adequate returns for their investment, labor, and management.

—Fourth, ways must be found to cope with emergency situations.

—Fifth, if farmers must operate in a system oriented to the free market, the transition can be eased by more widespread participation in the farmer-owned grain reserve program, thus smoothing the peaks and valleys in grain supplies and prices.

I pledge to you today to continue to work for our farmers, to try and find ways of decreasing the burden on farmers today. Agriculture is king in North Carolina, and I assure you that as governor, I will do all I can to see that it stays that way.

---

[1]Vernon Grant James (1910-   ), native of Pasquotank County; attended North Carolina State College (now University), 1930-1931. Farmer; president, manager, James Brothers, Inc.; member, state House of Representatives, 1945, 1947, was reelected in 1972, and returned in subsequent elections. *North Carolina Manual, 1983*, 368.

[2]The commemorative marker to which Hunt referred, No. A70, was erected at the corner of Ehringhaus and McMorine streets, in Elizabeth City, December, 1982. Information from the files of the North Carolina Highway Historical Marker Program, Division of Archives and History, Department of Cultural Resources, Raleigh.

[3]Region R of the North Carolina Council of Governments includes Camden, Chowan, Currituck, Dare, Gates, Hyde, Pasquotank, Perquimans, Tyrrell, and Washington counties. John L. Cheney, Jr. (comp.), *Directory of the State and County Officials of North Carolina, 1984* (Raleigh: North Carolina Department of the Secretary of State, n.d.), 68.

VANCE-AYCOCK DINNER

ASHEVILLE, OCTOBER 23, 1982

[The 1982 election year saw Governor Hunt campaign successfully on behalf of North Carolina's incumbent Democratic congressmen as well as a number of party candidates hoping to become freshman representatives. Speaking in Morehead City November 17 at a meeting of Carteret County Democrats, Hunt dismissed as "an exaggeration" the assertions of the state's news media that the results of the November 2 balloting were "a great personal victory for me." Instead, he maintained that "the real winners were . . . people like you all across this state. I'm talking about county and precinct organization" and "caring, committed Democrats who gave their votes, their time, their energy, and their money to our party's candidates." He also noted, in a reference to the financial clout and campaign tactics of the Republican party and the Congressional Club, that "issues still decide elections in North Carolina," and that voters "want their elected officials to steer a moderate course, not follow the path of extremism."

Hunt delivered a brief version of his earlier speeches, supporting various state Democratic congressional candidates, on October 23 at the Vance-Aycock Dinner. Senator Alan Cranston, whom the governor introduced to those attending the banquet, was only one of the prospective hopefuls for the 1984 Democratic presidential nomination who visited North Carolina in 1982. Others whom Hunt welcomed to state party functions included John Glenn, featured speaker at the Jefferson-Jackson Dinner, April 24, Raleigh; Fritz Hollings, who addressed the Young Democrats of North Carolina, June 5, in Charlotte; and former Florida governor Reubin Askew, who appeared in Hendersonville, September 24, at the annual convention of the Democratic Women of North Carolina.]

You can really feel the enthusiasm in this room. Democrats across North Carolina are ready to do battle and ensure a big victory on November 2. Let's don't deceive ourselves. It will take every ounce of courage, energy, and determination we can muster.

Election day is a week from Tuesday. The remaining days will determine whether our people and our issues can prevail over their money. The answer to that question is important for North Carolina and important for America.

Are we going to allow the Republicans and the Congressional Club to buy seats in the Congress and the General Assembly? If we allow that, we have done a disservice to people—people who are out of work or who are afraid they'll be laid off next, people who depend on Social Security, children who need a good education. The greatest thing that could happen on November 2 would be for North Carolinians to go to the polls and deliver this message to the Tom Ellises [1] of the world: Elective office in North Carolina is not for sale. Dirty campaigns based on the Big Lie are no longer tolerated here.

In these last days we must combat their tactics by driving home the facts—that Democrats like Jamie Clarke and Ike Andrews and Robin Britt and Bill Hefner and Charlie Whitley and Charlie Rose and all the rest of our candidates are the people who can cast the votes to get this economy back on track. [2] These are people who believe in fairness, in a balanced budget, in protecting Social Security, in education. These people will literally force the president of the United States to do something he hasn't done up to now, and that is to be fair.

Our speaker tonight is a man who has fought for fairness on the floor of the United States Senate. He is one of the most distinguished men serving in Congress. He is a learned, thoughtful man who has made fairness and integrity the hallmarks of his marvelous career in public life.

When he was first elected to the Senate in 1968, he overcame the very kind of opposition that I have been talking about. He has been reelected twice now, and he is in his third term as Senate Democratic whip. It has been said that he is testing the waters for a possible presidential candidacy. It would be more accurate to say that he is at least waist deep in that water. It is my profound pleasure to introduce to you one of the brightest stars in American political life: United States senator Alan Cranston of California. [3]

[1]Thomas F. Ellis (1920-   ), practicing attorney and chairman, National Congressional Club. Previously identified in Mitchell, *Addresses of Hunt*, I, 613n.

[2]James McClure Clarke (1917-   ), native of Manchester, Vermont; resident of Buncombe County; A.B., Princeton University, 1939; U.S. Naval Reserve, 1942-1945. Farmer, orchard operator; secretary, James G. McClure Educational and Development Fund, since 1956; associate editor, *Ashville Citizen-Times*, 1960-1969; assistant to the president, Warren Wilson College, 1969-1981; member of state House, 1977-1981, and Senate, 1981-1982; elected to U.S. House from North Carolina's Eleventh Congressional District, 1982. *North Carolina Manual, 1983*, 181.

C. Robin Britt (1942-   ), native of San Antonio, Texas; resident of Guilford County; received undergraduate degree, 1963, and law degree, 1973, from University of North Carolina at Chapel Hill; U.S. Naval Reserve. Attorney; chairman, Guilford County Democratic party, 1971-1981; delegate, Democratic National Convention, 1980; elected to U.S. House from North Carolina's Sixth Congressional District, 1982. *North Carolina Manual, 1983*, 171.

Charles Orville Whitley (1927-   ), native of Siler City; resident of Wayne County; B.A., 1948, LL.B., 1950, Wake Forest University; M.A., George Washington University, 1974; U.S. Army, 1944-1946, U.S. Army Reserve, 1946-1950. Mount Olive town attorney, 1951-1956; administrative assistant to Rep. David N. Henderson, 1961-1976; elected to U.S. House from North Carolina's Third Congressional District, 1976, and returned in subsequent elections. *North Carolina Manual, 1983*, 165.

[3]Alan Cranston (1914-   ), native of Palo Alto, California; resident of Los Angeles; attended Pomona College, 1932-1933, and the University of Mexico; B.A., Stanford University, 1936; served in U.S. Army during World War II. International News Service foreign correspondent, 1936-1938; Common Council for American Unity lobbyist, 1939; realtor, 1947-1967; California state comptroller, 1958-1966; elected to U.S. Senate in 1968 and returned in subsequent elections; unsuccessful candidate for Democratic presidential nomination, 1984. Barone and Ujifusa, *Almanac of American Politics, 1984*, 78.

DEDICATION OF *ELIZABETH II* KEEL AND FRAME

MANTEO, NOVEMBER 17, 1982

This is a great day. It is a day which gives us a rare chance to look back at the rich heritage of our state's past. But it is also a day which gives us the chance to look forward to the unfinished tasks of the future.

What we're going to do in a few minutes is a simple task. We're going to take a few tacks, a hammer, and a plaque made of copper from the dome of the State Capitol in Raleigh, and we're going to put the plaque in the unfinished frame of the *Elizabeth II*. The task won't take long, but it will represent a commitment from us and from the state of North Carolina. It will represent a commitment to finish the ship itself, and to make sure that the celebration of the beginning of America as we know it will be one of the most significant events in our state in our lifetime.

I believe the commemoration of America's 400th anniversary is indeed that important, and I am personally committed to its success. Why does it matter so much?

Look first at the dollars and cents side. This celebration of North

Carolina's unique past is in fact a solid investment in our future. Many of you are from the northeast. You know how much tourism means here. You have known for years the potential the 400th anniversary has for strengthening that vital industry here, and indeed across the state. But potential doesn't equal success without careful planning and solid programs. That's why we're putting so much effort into the 400th anniversary now.

Part of the effort is going into events and festivals which will take place between the summer of 1984 and the summer of 1987. They will draw hundreds of thousands of visitors and millions of dollars. But the biggest part of the effort will be to ensure that the benefits of the 400th anniversary don't stop dead when the official commemoration is over. The *Elizabeth II* and its visitor center will remain; the refurbished Manteo waterfront will remain; the beautiful Roanoke Corridor will remain; projects sponsored by 400th anniversary committees in all 100 counties will remain. Because we have remembered events of 400 years ago, the North Carolina of the future will be a better and more prosperous place.

That's the economic good news of America's 400th anniversary, but dollars and cents aren't the only returns we'll collect from this investment. There's also the sense of pride that comes with knowing and appreciating our heritage.

I think it's particularly fitting that the part of our heritage which we dedicate today is a ship—and a sailing ship, at that. There's something about the image of a sailing ship that fires the imagination and strengthens the spirit. Remember how we felt when we watched the tall ships six years ago? I think it's time to rekindle that feeling, and I'm proud that North Carolina has the chance to light the flame.

In my second "Inaugural Address," I said the time had come for North Carolina to sail against the wind, to set a course of hope and courage against trends of pessimism and negativism that seemed to be blowing so strong. Sailing against the wind is a task which suits our spirit as a state and as a people.

Look at the small, fragile frame of this ship *Elizabeth II*, and think about the sturdy spirits of the men and women who rode ships very much like this to our shores four centuries ago. They came with tremendous courage in their hearts and a vision of a new land and a new freedom in their minds.

Perhaps they left us only a little on the land to remind us that they were once here, but they gave to their countrymen the courage to try again and to succeed twenty years later. They have given us an example of courage and dedication in the face of incredible hardship. Today, we make our promise to them and to their memory that we will celebrate their accomplishment. We make our promise to all the people of North Carolina as well, that the celebration itself will be a shining achievement.

STATEMENT ON ENERGY CONSERVATION

RALEIGH, NOVEMBER 18, 1982

["Our state's energy conservation programs saved North Carolinians the
equivalent of more than $600 million worth of oil in 1980 alone," Hunt told
participants attending the Energy Management Exposition, September 16,
1981. Speaking at the North Carolina Solar Energy Association's Carolina
Sun Conference, November 12, 1982, the governor outlined some of the
measures his administration supported to encourage the use of alternative
sources of energy: tax credits and incentives for the installation of active
solar energy systems to attract photovoltaics manufacturers to North
Carolina; a solar design service and other programs offered by the Energy
Division of the state Commerce Department; a solar vocational education
program cosponsored by the Alternative Energy Corporation and the state
Department of Public Instruction; and the creation of a Solar Law Task
Force "to investigate ways of speeding the commercialization of solar
techniques by removing state and local legal barriers."]

This nation responded to the energy crisis of the 1970s by making
a strong commitment to conservation, energy efficiency, and the
development of alternative sources of energy. Under Democratic
and Republican leadership, we made dramatic progress, both in
terms of technology and in making people aware of the dangers of
depending too much on foreign oil.

The energy crisis has dropped off the front pages, but an aggressive energy strategy is just as vital to our national security and
economic strength today as it was in the 1970s. The predictions that
this may be one of the coldest winters in many years should remind
us of that.

I believe this nation has lost ground since 1981. The current
administration in Washington has put energy on the back burner,
and I believe that this is a serious mistake that could undermine
America's strength and security in the years ahead. I want to make
it clear today that North Carolina is not backing away from its
commitment to a strategy of energy efficiency and development. We
have one of the most aggressive energy programs in the nation, and
it has been recognized as such by outside observers.

A centerpiece of our commitment to innovation is the Alternative
Energy Corporation, and I believe it is absolutely essential that
North Carolina continue to support that program. The corporation
was created by the Utilities Commission and funded by a special
rate charge to electric utility companies. Its specific mission is to
help curb the growing demand for electricity and reduce the need for
expensive new generating plants.

At a cost of about 45 cents a year to the average North Carolinian,
the Alternative Energy Corporation is already producing some

dramatic examples of how the public and private sector can now use alternatives that were only on the drawing board a few years ago. The AEC is supporting energy management training of local school and community college officials. Participants are already saving thousands of dollars a year—in one case, enough to pay the salary of an additional teacher—and the program could ultimately save up to $9 million in electric bills.

The AEC is working with industries to identify manufacturing plants with good potential for cogeneration, which uses excess heat from industrial boilers to generate electricity. We believe that cogeneration projects could, in the long run, eliminate the need for one medium-to-large electric generating station.

The Showcase of Solar Homes, a program cosponsored by AEC and the state Energy Division, has opened more than 100 moderately priced, solar homes to the public. Other projects include:

—An energy management training program for local governments.

—Technical assistance and financial support for the more than 15,000 nonprofit agencies in North Carolina that do not qualify for energy tax-credit incentives.

—A study of ways in which the demand for electricity in North Carolina's 41,000 tobacco curing barns could be reduced, without affecting leaf quality.

In the years to come, these and other innovative programs are going to put our state in a stronger position to provide our people with good jobs and expanded opportunities. I do not expect the federal government's indifference in this area to change any time soon, but that won't prevent North Carolina from making a significant contribution to energy conservation and development.

BOARD FOR NEED-BASED MEDICAL LOANS

RALEIGH, DECEMBER 1, 1982

I want to welcome you as new members of a very important board. Thank you for your willingness to serve our state during a time when economic conditions challenge us to find new ways of dealing with limited resources, but still meet the needs of our people.

As you may know, this medical loan program has been in existence for many years. Now, for the first time, it has its own governing board. It also has a mandate that all loans should be granted on the basis of need.[1] During much of its recent history, loans have been made mainly to the financially needy applicant due to the rising costs of training and the ever-increasing demand for the loans. However, the main emphasis for the program until the

1982 legislation was to place qualified health professionals in areas and programs experiencing personnel shortages.

We can be proud of our medical loan program in North Carolina. The program has been a model for other states and federal programs. At a time when default rates on student loans have become a serious national issue, the Medical Student Loan Program has a default rate of less than one percent. Blacks and Indians are practicing to fulfill their loan obligations as dentists and physicians at a rate comparable to the ratio of each in our population, or 22 percent—unlike the general statewide practice rate of less than 5 percent for each.

Today, our medical loan program has a staff of five and an annual appropriation of $1.25 million, of which $1.13 million goes for the loan fund. The program has invested in the training of 1,300 North Carolinians. As members of the governing board, I suggest you look at:

—Interest rates and how they affect the needy in borrowing money for an education and how they affect the service repayment component of the program.

—Creative ways to ensure that more North Carolinians serve in areas with critical shortages of doctors.

—Health disciplines not now covered by the program, and those now supported which should perhaps be removed.

—A fair system of appeal so an administrative decision may be challenged without going directly to the courts.

—Opening up teaching as an option for all fields. We are not only unable to provide better salaries for faculty in our training programs, we must also look at ways we can bring diversification to our instructional staffs.

—The suitability of current loan amounts to adequately help financially needy applicants during times of escalating educational costs.

—Opening up the opportunity for practices in other than the now-defined "primary care" specialties to fulfill the loan obligation. I am aware of at least one case—that of a black anesthesiologist practicing at L. Richardson Memorial Hospital in Greensboro, the first since 1927. The area served by the hospital is considered underprivileged by any standards. This raises the question: Should each case be considered on individual merit?

This is just a glimpse at the important role that you have accepted. Judging from your past achievements and leadership roles, I know you will be effective in providing sound direction for this program. With your help, we can ensure that qualified young people, regardless of their financial situation, have the opportunity to become doctors and provide needed medical service to people across this state. With your help, we can work to provide a healthy future for the people of North Carolina.

[1]"An Act to Establish a Board to Administer Need-Based Loans to Students in the Health Professions" was ratified June 23, 1982. *N.C. Session Laws, 1981, Regular and Extra Sessions, 1982*, c. 1388.

STATEMENT ON HAZARDOUS-WASTE LANDFILLS

RALEIGH, DECEMBER 2, 1982

North Carolina has worked very hard to develop a waste-management program that will support economic growth and protect the health of our people and the quality of our environment. In 1981 the General Assembly enacted the comprehensive Waste Management Act, and we established the Waste Management Board. Those steps made North Carolina a national leader in this area.

The Waste Management Board has been working since then under the leadership of Buck O'Shields to develop a total plan for disposing of hazardous waste—a plan that emphasizes the prevention and reduction of waste material and minimizes the need for landfills. Yesterday, the board recommended that the state delay granting any permits for hazardous-waste landfills. The board asked for the delay so its members and state regulatory agencies can have more time to study the new federal regulations on landfills and to determine whether they offer adequate protection. I believe the board's recommendation is timely and wise.

I am directing the Department of Human Resources not to grant any permits for hazardous-waste landfills until the Waste Management Board has completed its review of the new federal regulations. I agree with the board that the public should know more about the regulations and have an opportunity to comment on them, and I am pleased to see that the board is planning a series of public meetings in February for that purpose.

Landfills alone are *not* the answer to society's waste-management problems. This state's policy is that landfills should be used only as a last resort—after all other alternatives have been exhausted and after the material to be buried has been reduced to the smallest amount possible. But we must have adequate regulations for landfills when they are the only alternative. They can be made safe and secure, as the state has demonstrated with the PCB landfill in Warren County. The safety features there far exceed the new federal requirements.

The Waste Management Board and the Department of Human Resources are not satisfied that the new regulations are adequate. That is why the state will grant no permits until review of those regulations is completed.

In closing, let me also say that I was gratified by the board's endorsement of the "Pollution Prevention Pays" concept. Under that program, the state will work with industries and other waste generators to demonstrate that the prevention, recycling, and reduction of waste not only protects the environment, but also saves money. That program will have my strong support.

STATEMENT ON FLUE-CURED
TOBACCO REFERENDUM

RALEIGH, DECEMBER 8, 1982

[Growers of flue-cured tobacco in North and South Carolina, Alabama, Georgia, Florida, and Virginia voted overwhelmingly, on December 16, 1982, to extend the crop's federal price support program for another three years. Prior to the referendum, John H. Cyrus, tobacco affairs director for the state Department of Agriculture, warned that three factors could adversely influence the outcome of the balloting and thereby jeopardize the future of the system. They were: rising fees for farmers who leased tobacco allotments; the 10 percent cut in the 1983 quota; and the 100 percent increase in the assessment, required to maintain the program at no net cost to taxpayers, which was levied on each 100 pounds of tobacco sold. *News and Observer*, December 17 and 18, 1982. Hunt endorsed the program's continuation in the following statement.]

A week from tomorrow, tobacco farmers in North Carolina and five other states will be making some very crucial decisions about the future of the tobacco program. On Thursday, December 16, the growers of flue-cured leaf will vote on whether or not to continue the tobacco marketing quota program for the next three years. They will also decide whether to continue an assessment program that provides funds to develop and promote world markets through Tobacco Associates. Voting will take place in the sixty-seven North Carolina counties where flue-cured tobacco is grown. If both programs are to be continued, they must get the support of two thirds of those voting in the six states.

This is not a routine vote. It is vitally important that the two programs get overwhelming support. Failure to continue the quota program would seriously weaken this state's economy. It would mean an end to production controls, a sharp decline in the price paid to the farmer, and would effectively shut the small farmer out of growing tobacco. Raising tobacco would be left in the hands of big corporate enterprises, not the small family farms we have now.

Under the present system, flue-cured crops have been worth about $1 billion a year to North Carolina farmers. Ending the quota program would substantially reduce the cash value of the crop.

The promotional program is becoming more important every year. About 50 percent of the flue-cured tobacco that farmers offer at auction now goes into export, and additional quantities are shipped abroad in cigarettes and other manufactured goods. This means that about six out of every ten acres of leaf that are produced end up on the export market. But foreign competition is becoming more intense. Retention of the promotional program will enable us to maintain and expand our exports.

This referendum will be one of the most important in the history of our tobacco program, because of the significant changes it has undergone recently. We were able to save the program in Congress because of the willingness of our farmers to agree that there should be no net cost to the taxpayers. But opponents of tobacco, in Congress and elsewhere, have not given up. They will look for future opportunities to attack it.

Opponents will watch the December 16 voting very closely. That is why an overwhelming vote of confidence is so vital. With their votes, tobacco farmers have an opportunity to demonstrate to Congress and the nation that the tobacco program has the solid support of the people who count most, those who earn a living by growing tobacco.

STATEMENT ON FAIR SENTENCING ACT

RALEIGH, DECEMBER 16, 1982

Fair sentencing has been in effect in North Carolina since July 1, 1981. I strongly supported passage of the Fair Sentencing Act because of the wide disparity in the sentences being handed down in our courts for similar types of felony crimes. Our courts were not dispensing swift and certain punishment, and that was undermining public confidence in the system.

Professor Stevens Clarke[1] of the Institute of Government in Chapel Hill is now doing a study of how the Fair Sentencing Act is working after one year. His preliminary findings show a dramatic reduction in the disparity of sentences. That means that law is doing what it is supposed to do: bringing about more certainty in sentencing. I strongly believe swift and sure punishment is the best weapon against crime. This study demonstrates that the Fair Sentencing Act is helping North Carolina in the fight against crime.

As you know, the act sets forth presumptive sentences for different categories of felonies. The judge must either impose the presumptive sentence following conviction or specify in writing why that was not done. Professor Clarke has analyzed court, police, and correctional data from twelve representative counties and 2,500 felony defendants. His preliminary findings show that the idea of swift and certain punishment is being met. For example, a typical group of defendants convicted of felonious breaking and entering under the Fair Sentencing Act received sentences ranging from thirty-three to forty-five months. During the last year under the old law, a typical group of defendants convicted of the same crime got sentences ranging from ten months to fifty-nine months.

The study also shows no major change in the severity of sentences. A related study by the Department of Correction indicates that the Fair Sentencing Act will not cause the prison population to rise faster than it was expected to rise under the old law.[2]

Fair sentencing has not caused longer trials or fewer guilty pleas. The time from arrest to trial has decreased significantly. The percentage of cases decided by guilty pleas has remained about the same. There is a greater reliance on formal, written plea bargains that are open to public scrutiny.

By March of next year, when this study is expected to be completed, its findings will be based on data from almost all felony cases arising in all 100 counties. I am confident the final report will show that North Carolina's courts are now dispensing swift and certain punishments to convicted felons.[3]

Our judges, district attorneys, law enforcement officers, and other court officials are to be commended for making the Fair Sentencing Act work. This kind of certainty is our most effective deterrent to crime.

-----

[1]Stevens H. Clarke (1937-   ), resident of Chapel Hill; A.B., Harvard University; LL.B., Columbia University, 1966. Computer programmer-analyst for Sperry Rand Corp. and International Business Machines Corp.; criminal justice, legal, and legislative consultant; faculty member, Institute of Government, University of North Carolina at Chapel Hill, since 1971; director, North Carolina Sentencing Study, 1983-1984; editor, *Popular Government*, since 1980; author. Stevens H. Clarke to Jan-Michael Poff, March 7, 1985.

[2]The Department of Correction study that Hunt mentioned was intended for intradepartmental use and therefore not published. Kenneth L. Parker, Management Information and Research, Department of Correction, to Jan-Michael Poff, August 15, 1985.

[3]Stevens H. Clarke and others, *North Carolina's Determinate Sentencing Legislation: An Evaluation of the First Year's Experience* (Chapel Hill: Institute of Government, University of North Carolina, 1983). The report was condensed in Clarke, "North Carolina's determinate sentencing legislation," *Judicature*, 68 (October-November, 1984), 140-152.

STATEMENT ON DOROTHEA DIX HOSPITAL

RALEIGH, JANUARY 6, 1983

[On February 10, 1983, Hunt commented to members of the Commission for Mental Health, Mental Retardation, and Substance Abuse Services, on his administration's collaboration with the U.S. Housing and Urban Development Agency and the North Carolina Association of Retarded

Citizens to provide federal construction funds to erect local group homes for the mentally handicapped. He also noted that the proposed Medicaid waiver, allowing state government more flexibility in the way it allocated the program's financial resources, had "received preliminary approval." Much of the remainder of the speech was nearly identical to the remarks reprinted below.

Citing a decrease in the state's prison population, the governor announced, on June 4, 1984, that the section of Dorothea Dix Hospital previously scheduled to house convicts—as originally mentioned at his January 6, 1983, press conference—would be used, instead, to provide space necessary for emotionally disturbed children. The hospital's Adolescent Treatment Unit "cannot be expanded unless it is left at its present location on the west campus," Hunt said, "and it cannot be left on the west campus if a minimum security prison is built there." The unit was to be enlarged under a $350,000 appropriation from the General Assembly. "News Release from the Governor's Office," June 4, July 26, 1984.]

During the past several weeks, I have been giving careful consideration to the future of Dorothea Dix Hospital. I have met several times with Dr. Sarah Morrow, secretary of the Department of Human Resources, and Dr. Gene Douglas,[1] director of the Division of Mental Health, to review their recommendations. I have met with and listened to leaders of city and county government, members of the Wake County legislative delegation, representatives of the employees at Dix, residents of the neighborhoods around Dix, and families and friends of patients who are served by the hospital.

I have decided that Dix Hospital should not be closed.

Dix is one of the nation's leading mental hospitals, with a long tradition of humane and progressive care. It is meeting an important need in our state. But, as Dr. Morrow and Dr. Douglas have pointed out, the state of North Carolina must make better use of the hospital property. Too much of it sits empty and idle. In tight economic and budget times, we cannot afford to squander valuable resources that can be used to meet the great needs of our people. We must meet that responsibility to the taxpayers.

I have asked Dr. Morrow to consolidate the mental health activities on the east side of the property. The savings from that consolidation will go to community programs.

I also believe we have before us a rare opportunity to make creative use of the rest of the hospital property—use that will be consistent with the tradition and mission of Dix Hospital, with the needs of North Carolina, and with the character of the surrounding community.

I am directing the Departments of Human Resources and Correction to work together to develop an innovative, shared-use program on the hospital property that will concentrate on special populations in our correctional system. Those include inmates who suffer from mental illness and who are retarded. They include nonviolent offenders, young people who can be rehabilitated, and female inmates. All would be minimum custody.

I believe we should take advantage of the excellent psychiatric facilities and personnel at Dorothea Dix to offer diagnostic and treatment services to such inmates. This will help us relieve overcrowding and meet the special needs of inmates who are not hardened, dangerous criminals.

The first consideration in planning this program must be security, and I will instruct the departments to keep that uppermost in their minds.

I am also instructing the Departments of Human Resources and Administration to work with the city of Raleigh to determine whether some of the hospital property can and should be made available for private development, especially medium- to high-density housing that would be compatible with the existing neighborhood. I believe this will help strengthen downtown Raleigh and prevent urban sprawl from developing in the area beyond the new southern beltline. What happens to the hospital property is extremely important to the future of Raleigh, as well as to our state as a whole. Accordingly, these plans must be developed in a careful and comprehensive way.

Making more efficient use of the hospital property, I believe, will free up funds that can be used to improve community mental-health programs in our state. North Carolina has committed itself to supporting community treatment. Some patients require institutional care. Many more can be treated with much greater success in the communities where they live, near their families and friends. Last year, more than 114,000 people in North Carolina received mental health services in their home communities.

The federal government has drastically reduced its support for these community programs. In North Carolina, they will lose an additional $3.8 million in federal funds this coming fiscal year and, by 1985-1986, that loss will increase to almost $5 million. The state must be imaginative and innovative in finding ways to continue its strong support of community programs. This will require tough management decisions at Dix and the three other state mental hospitals.

It is clear that Wake County's mental health program has benefited for many years from the location of Dix. It is imperative that Wake County gradually take on greater responsibility for the support of mental health treatment, when community treatment is appropriate, as other counties have done.

This new mission for Dix will require much of the employees there and of the surrounding community. I have been impressed by the caring, compassionate people who work at Dix, and I believe they will be willing to help inmates who can be helped. I have also been impressed by the tremendous support that exists in the community for Dix Hospital. I sincerely hope that these friends of Dix will respond, as volunteers and in other ways, to the new patients that Dix will be serving.

---

[1]A. Eugene Douglas (1934-   ), native of Greensboro; resident of Lumberton; M.D., University of North Carolina at Chapel Hill, 1959; U.S. Navy, 1963-1965. Area director, 1965-1978, and medical director, 1978-1982, and since 1985, Southeastern Regional Mental Health Center; director, Division of Mental Health, Mental Retardation, and Substance Abuse Services, Department of Human Resources, 1982-1985. A. Eugene Douglas to Jan-Michael Poff, August 27, 1985.

STATEWIDE TELEVISION ADDRESS ON DRUNKEN DRIVERS

RALEIGH, JANUARY 24, 1983

[A more condensed version of this speech was delivered before the Governor's Conference on Drunken Drivers, November 16, 1982.]

Good evening. Before I finish speaking to you tonight, somewhere in the United States a drunk driver will kill somebody. It might be your son or daughter, your husband or wife, your mother or father. It might be a friend, or a neighbor down the street.

It happens in this nation every twenty minutes. Every twenty minutes, somebody dies at the hands of a person who has been drinking and driving. It is a tragedy that has grown like an epidemic. It does not distinguish between rich or poor, young or old, male or female.

Each year, drunk drivers kill 25,000 Americans. That means that, in just two years, as many Americans will die on our highways as died during the entire Vietnam war. In 1981, almost 800 people in North Carolina died in alcohol-related accidents. That was more than two people every day. Many of them are young people. More than 5,000 teenagers died on our nation's highways last year because somebody was drinking and driving. Traffic accidents are the number-one cause of death for young people between sixteen and nineteen years old.

The people of North Carolina are outraged about this, and so am I. They are demanding action to get the drinking driver off the road, and the time for action has come. We are all tired of reading stories in the newspaper like this one: A man who has been convicted of drunk driving four times and has permanently lost his license goes out on the road anyway, drunk again, slams into another car, and puts a father and his seventeen-year-old son in the hospital in critical condition. Or this one: Two people go to court the same day on a drunk driving charge, and the one with a blood alcohol level almost three times higher than the other gets off with a lighter sentence.

Many of you have written me about how you feel. These are just a few of the letters I have received:

[Reads letters.]

Earlier this month, I met with almost 800 church leaders from throughout North Carolina to talk about drunk driving. They represented different denominations, different faiths, different philosophies, but they had one thing in common: They have been to the homes and the hospitals. They have seen the broken, twisted bodies, and they have tried to offer some comfort to a family shattered by tragedy. They—and people who belong to groups like Mothers against Drunken Driving and Students against Driving Drunk—have seen it and suffered through it firsthand. They know what a tragedy it is. And they know that we need to do more than just arrest more drunk drivers.

Our State Highway Patrol and our local law enforcement officers are doing a good job of arresting them [drunken drivers] today. North Carolina is the tenth most populous state but, last year, only two other states arrested more people for drunk driving than our officers did. There are more drunk-driving arrests per capita in North Carolina than in any other state.

What we have to do is see that, once a drunk driver is arrested, he gets what he has coming to him: punishment that is swift, sure, and severe. We have to show him that he had better not get on the road in the first place if he's had something to drink. Most important of all, we have to change our attitudes, as individuals and as a society, about drinking and driving. It is not okay, or fun, or a big joke. It can kill somebody. It is a crime, and it is going to be punished in North Carolina. We have a plan that will do that. I want to tell you about that plan tonight, and I want to ask for your support.

This war against drunk driving didn't originate with government. It is a grass-roots movement, one that came from the people of North Carolina and many other states across the nation. It came from people like those who wrote the letters I read.

It came from people like Marlyn Sugg of Albemarle, whose eleven-year-old son, Mark, was killed by a drunk driver. Like any parent would be, she was shattered by the death of her son. She was also driven to do something, to see that other families did not suffer the same tragedy. So she formed the North Carolina chapter of Mothers against Drunken Driving. She started reading and learning more about drunk driving. She started talking to other families who had lost a loved one at the hands of a drunk driver. She started sitting in courtrooms and seeing what happened when drunk drivers came to trial, and what she saw made her mad.

She saw drunk drivers who had been arrested three, four, five times getting off, walking away with just a fine, and getting right back behind the wheel. It was Marlyn Sugg and the others like her who made all of us wake up to what was happening, and North Carolina has responded to them.

Last February, I appointed the Governor's Task Force on Drunken Drivers. The chairman was Jack Stevens of Asheville, a former legislator who is one of North Carolina's most respected lawyers. The members included leaders from law enforcement, the courts, business, churches, alcohol treatment groups, and, most important, private citizens who want to get the drunk driver off the road. They held public hearings all across the state—in Asheville, Boone, Charlotte, Winston-Salem, Raleigh, Fayetteville, Greenville, and Wilmington. They wanted to hear from the people of North Carolina.

What they heard was the outrage and cries of families who had lost loved ones. They heard from ministers. They heard from emergency room doctors. They heard from former alcoholics. They heard from thousands of citizens who know personally the tragedy of drunken driving.

The message they heard was loud and clear: The way our system deals with the drunk driver makes that crime almost a form of socially accepted murder. People told how the drunk driver who had killed a member of their family or a friend had gotten very little or no jail time, was now free, and again had a license to drive—and maybe, to kill again. Former alcoholics and convicted drunk drivers told the task force that the only way to change their behavior was to give them a slap in the face, not give them a break or feel sorry for them.

The central theme in all the task force heard was this: North Carolina must make our laws against drunk driving tougher and more mandatory. We should have one law for everybody, no matter who they are, no matter what they do, no matter who they know, no matter how well-off they are. So the task force carefully developed a plan—a tough, comprehensive plan to get the drunk driver off the road and protect innocent people against him.

I have adopted their plan. It has been introduced in the North Carolina General Assembly this month as House Bill 1 and Senate Bill 1, the first bill to go into the legislature. It is called the "Safe Roads Act of 1983." I think it is the most important business before the legislature this year. Passing it will be my number-one goal in the legislature, and we need your help to get it passed into law.[1]

The Safe Roads Act has four goals:

—First, to make it more likely that the drunk driver will be arrested.

—Second, to see that he is punished swiftly and with certainty.

—Third, to make his punishment severe, and

—Fourth, to increase public awareness that this is how North Carolina is going to deal with the drunk driver.

To achieve these four goals, the Safe Roads Act would make a series of sweeping changes in our laws. Let me tell you what those changes would be.

The most important change of all would be to create a new offense, called "driving while impaired," that would be easier to prove in court and would eliminate plea bargaining. It would mean that the drunk driver could no longer walk out of the courtroom with a slap on the wrist and a smile on his face. The problem with the law we have today is that it is too easy to get a plea bargain—to get the charge of driving under the influence reduced down to a charge of driving with a blood alcohol level of 0.10, or careless and reckless driving after drinking.

The new "driving while impaired" law would do away with those lesser charges. All the prosecutor would have to do is prove one of two things:

—That the driver's blood alcohol level was 0.10, or more, or

—That his physical or mental faculties were impaired by alcohol, drugs, or any other substance.

Under the law we are proposing, once either of those two things is proven, the driver would be guilty of driving while impaired. The way the law is today, even if one of those two things is proven in court, the drunk driver can still get off with a reduced charge.

The Safe Roads Act would put a stop to that. It would change the law so that the most serious offense, the kind you and I hear about and just get angry, would land a drunk driver straight in jail. A jail sentence would be mandatory if he had done any one of the following things:

—If he had a previous drunk driving offense during the past ten years,

—If he was speeding to avoid being arrested,

—If he was speeding thirty miles an hour over the posted limit,

—If he was driving while his license was revoked for a drunk-driving offense, or,

—If he caused an accident that seriously injured another person.

If any one of those five factors applied, the drunk driver would be guilty of a new offense, called "grossly aggravated drunk driving." He would have to go to jail for at least seven days and it could be up to one year, and he would have to pay a fine of up to $1,000. If any two of those factors applied, he would go to jail for at least fourteen days and up to two years and he would have to pay a fine of up to $2,000.

That is not all. Even if none of those grossly aggravating factors applied, the Safe Roads Act would still set very strict guidelines for what kind of sentence the judge could give a drunk driver. The judge would have to base the sentence on the following factors:

—Was the offender seriously impaired?

—Was he driving recklessly?

—Did he refuse to take the breathalyzer test?

—Did he have any previous traffic record?

—Was he abusive to the arresting officer?

There would be no plea bargaining. There would be no shopping around for an easy judge. There would be no hiring a good lawyer and getting off easy.

Even if it's not a grossly aggravated situation, every person convicted of drunk driving would be required to either go to jail, do several days of community service work, or lose their license for one to three months—plus pay a fine. And there would be no limited driving permits until the sentence was completed.

In short, every person convicted as a drunk driver would lose their driver's license for some period of time, in addition to their other punishment. The message would be clear: If you drink and drive, you are going to get the book thrown at you. And if it's a serious offense, you are going to jail. Period. That is deterrence. That is the best way to protect ourselves against the drunk driver: by keeping him off the road in the first place.

If we give our courts this tough and effective tool against the drunk driver, we need to be sure it is being used the way it's intended. So the Safe Roads Act would require the state, every six months, to publish a report card showing how each county, each district attorney, and each judge handle drunk-driving cases. I believe you want to know what is happening to drunk drivers in your courts. That is something every citizen of North Carolina has a right to know.

The Safe Roads Act would make other important changes in our law. It would put sharp restrictions on the limited driving privileges. These can be given only to first offenders who are not guilty of a grossly aggravated offense. A drunk driver could no longer walk out of court with a limited permit. He would have to come back after the sentence was served and apply for limited driving privileges. Those who work or go to school during regular weekday hours would be restricted to driving during those hours only, Monday through Friday.

The Safe Roads Act would give the magistrate down at the courthouse the power to take away the license, for ten days, of a drunk driver who blew 0.10, right on the spot. Some people think that is too tough. I don't.

A judge could even impound the car of somebody who was caught driving while his license was suspended or revoked for a prior drunk-driving offense. If taking away his license doesn't stop him, taking away his car will. And if somebody refuses to take a breathalyzer test, thinking he can get off that way, he will automatically lose his license for a full year.

But we need to recognize that, for some people, it doesn't matter whether you take away their license or their car. They are "problem drinkers," and they are a threat to the rest of us. So the Safe Roads Act would require that anybody who blows 0.20 or who is arrested for a second impaired-driving offense would have to get professional treatment for alcoholism. To get that drunk, they would have had to drink twelve mixed drinks or twelve beers in two hours. That is a serious drinking problem, and that person needs help.

The act would give the magistrate the authority to detain a drunk driver for up to twenty-four hours, so he can't hurt himself or somebody else, and the act specifically includes community service restitution as an alternative punishment where a jail sentence is not appropriate. I would hope that in such cases judges would sentence drunk drivers to cleaning up roadsides, building parks, and helping people with needs in their communities. Maybe it would do some of them good to have to work in a hospital where they could see firsthand what driving and drinking does to the victims.

People need to understand that they have a responsibility for their own actions, and that must be an important part of this campaign against drunk driving. That is the philosophy behind one controversial part of this bill, what is called the "dram shop" statute.

What that means, very simply, is, that if a bar serves a drink to a minor or to a person who is already drunk, that bar could be sued if that person causes an accident. It is already a crime to sell to a minor or a drunk, but this would hit where it hurts most: in the pocketbook. It is a crucial part of the bill, since it would clearly save lives by encouraging establishments to be much more careful about who they serve.

The Safe Roads Act would make it illegal for the driver to have an open beer or bottle of wine in a car. It's already illegal for the driver to have an open bottle of liquor; the same should apply to beer and wine.

We should put more officers on the road looking for drunk drivers. We should give them more training in detecting the drunk driver and more training in giving breathalyzer tests for drunkenness. We should make it easier to get those results put into evidence in a trial, and we should provide more assistance to witnesses in drunk-driving trials.

These changes are aimed at every single person who drives and drinks. But there is one group that deserves special attention, whose lives and safety we especially cherish: our teenagers.

All of us know how difficult those adolescent years can be, physically and emotionally. It's tough learning to handle the responsibilities that come with age—like learning to drive safely— and teenagers are even less able than adults to handle both drinking and driving. That is why the Safe Roads Act pays particular attention to young drivers.

I support the recommendation that the minimum age for drinking beer and wine be raised from eighteen to nineteen. Frankly, perhaps it should be higher than that. I would not oppose raising it to twenty-one. But our primary goal must be to get drinking out of the high schools, where an eighteen-year-old buys beer and gives it to a seventeen-year-old, who gives it to a sixteen-year-old and on down the line.

I think raising the age to nineteen will be adequate also because the Safe Roads Act has so many other very tough and very effective provisions against teenagers who drive and drink. For example, if any young person sixteen or seventeen years old is caught driving with any amount of alcohol or drugs in their blood, they would lose their license until they turn eighteen. Period. No exceptions. And they would get a fine of up to $100 or up to sixty days in jail.

The most important thing we must do is educate our teenagers about the dangers of drinking and driving. How many of you have heard the tragic stories? A carload of young people on their way home from a game or a dance, somebody loses control of the car, and their families are grieving. Then it comes out: The driver had been drinking.

It is a shame that our society—in our advertising, our TV shows, our movies—makes drinking look like something glamorous and sophisticated. It's not; and we ought to be ashamed of that.

From the time our children are in kindergarten to the time they graduate, we ought to be teaching them what alcohol can do to them. Driver education courses should show them what can happen if they drink and drive, and we adults ought to be setting a better example. We have to do more than change laws. We've got to change minds and hearts and attitudes. We have got to get away from the attitude that it is okay to drink and drive. It is not okay. It kills people. It destroys families.

I think newspapers ought to make a practice of running the names and addresses of drunk-driving cases in the courts. I am happy to know that the North Carolina Association of Broadcasters is planning to launch an intensive public-service advertising campaign against drunk driving on all of our state's radio and television stations, and I appreciate those stations making this time available tonight.

All of us have a responsibility in making our roads safer. We can make a dramatic beginning by passing the Safe Roads Act during this session of the legislature. You have heard tonight what it would do:

—Mandatory jail terms for serious drunk-driving offenses.
—Strict guidelines for sentencing in all drunk-driving cases.
—All drunk drivers lose their licenses for some period of time.
—Strong action to keep the drunk driver off the road.
—Tough steps to keep teenagers from drinking and driving.
—New laws to keep bars from serving minors and drunks.

The Safe Roads Act is a good bill. It has a lot of support from the people of North Carolina, but there will be a lot of lobbyists working in Raleigh to kill that bill, to water it down, to protect some special group. The members of the General Assembly will be hearing from the lobbyists. They need to hear from you, too.

Many of them have already signed the bill and promised to support it. It is being sponsored in the Senate by Senators Henson Barnes of Wayne County and Aaron Plyler of Union County.[2] In the House, it is sponsored by Representatives Martin Lancaster of Wayne County, George Miller of Durham, and Charles Evans of Dare County.[3] I am going to be working as hard as I can to help them get it passed, in full and as quickly as possible. They need your help, too. I hope you will help them.

And I hope you will do something more: When you see somebody leaving a party or a restaurant, car keys in hand, and you know they have had too much to drink, stop them. Give them a ride home. Keep them from killing themselves, or somebody else. If you see a car weaving down the road, call the police or the sheriff or the Highway Patrol.

Let me read you a letter I received from a couple, the parents of a son who was a fine baseball player in college. They were having breakfast at home one Saturday morning when the phone rang. The wife answered the phone.

In his letter, the father wrote, "I could tell immediately by my wife's reaction that it was bad news. Her voice turned immediately from a cheerful tone to an anxious one, and my heart came to my throat when I heard her chokingly say, 'I don't want to hear this.' Then in anguish I heard her say the words that will be in my mind forever: 'Scott is dead? Not Scotty.'"

The man went on to explain in the letter that his son had been killed in a collision with a drinking driver who had swerved onto the wrong side of the road and hit him head on.

He wrote, "I ask you, please, help get the drunk driver off the roads so other parents will be spared that dreadful Saturday morning phone call."

Nothing we do will ever bring back Scott or the other children, or mothers, or fathers, who lost their lives because of drunk drivers, but we can heed that plea from Scott's father. We can spare ourselves, our families, and our friends from that terrible phone call. We can start tonight, and we can do it together. Please call or write your senators and representatives and tell them how you feel about the Safe Roads Act of 1983.

Thank you, and good night.

---

[1] See "Special Message on Crime," January 25, 1983, footnote 6, above.

[2] Henson Perrymoore Barnes (1934-   ), native of Bladen County; resident of

Wayne County; A.A., Wilmington College (now University of North Carolina at Wilmington), 1958; A.B., 1959, J.D., 1961, University of North Carolina at Chapel Hill; U.S. Army, 1953-1956. Attorney; farm owner; member, state House, 1975-1976; state senator since 1977 and chairman, Senate Judiciary III Committee; Democrat. *North Carolina Manual, 1983*, 214.

Aaron W. Plyler (1926-   ), from Monroe; state House member since 1975. Previously identified in Mitchell, *Addresses of Hunt*, I, 496n.

[3]H. Martin Lancaster (1943-   ), native, resident of Wayne County; A.B., 1965, J.D., 1967, University of North Carolina at Chapel Hill; U.S. Navy, 1967-1970; U.S. Air Force Reserve, 1971-1982; U.S. Naval Reserve, since 1982. Attorney; member, state House, since 1979; chairman, House Judiciary III Committee; Democrat. *North Carolina Manual, 1983*, 377.

George W. Miller, Jr. (1930-   ), state House member, since 1971, and chairman of House Judiciary I Committee. Previously identified in Mitchell, *Addresses of Hunt*, I, 232n.

Charles Douglas Evans (1944-   ), native of Manteo; resident of Dare County; A.B., 1967, J.D., 1972, University of North Carolina at Chapel Hill; U.S. Army Reserve, 1967-1975. Attorney; commissioner, 1973-1978, and mayor, 1975-1978, town of Nags Head; state House member since 1979; chairman, House Banks and Thrift Institutions Committee; Democrat. *North Carolina Manual, 1983*, 342.

FARMING IN EASTERN NORTH CAROLINA IN THE YEAR 2000

RALEIGH, FEBRUARY 8, 1983

Thank you for being here today. I consider this one of the most important conferences that I have attended during my six years as governor. We are here today to talk about *change*—change as it affects the $3 billion agricultural business of eastern North Carolina.

We cannot say for certain what the future will bring, but we do know that the future belongs to those who prepare for it. We are entering a period that could be called the "Information Revolution"—an age of computers and cables and satellites and word processors and related technologies. Likewise, the agricultural industry is becoming more technically oriented—with more and more new technologies becoming a part of farming in our state.

As we consider the future of our state, and especially the future of agriculture in eastern North Carolina, there are some priorities I think we need to keep in mind.

Our highest priority must be people development. By that I mean education—the education and training of our people for the kinds of jobs likely to be available in the future. With agriculture becoming more and more complex each year and with more and more new technologies, only the well-educated, the well-trained, will be able to compete as farm operators in the future. So it is critical that we train our young people and help them prepare for these changes on the farm.

As we look toward the twenty-first century, we know that agricultural research and education will need our full support. Farm surpluses today may be followed by shortages of farm products within two decades, especially if we slacken our efforts in agricultural research, teaching, and extension work. It is through those efforts that we help our farmers apply technology and, as a result, produce the abundance that we enjoy today.

We must also keep in mind the importance of resource development as we look to the future. I am referring here to our natural resources—land, air, and water. These resources, as you know, are subject to many threats, including erosion, pollution, and misuse or abuse.

We can sum up our responsibilities with regard to our natural resources in a single word: conservation. Conservation doesn't mean hiding our resources, or letting them wither from lack of use. Conservation means using our land and air and water and other resources wisely and passing on a resource inheritance to our children that will give them opportunities equal to our own.

Conservation means *protecting* resources from any and all threats. It means following, as much as possible, policies to guard our most productive farmland from needless encroachment by nonagricultural interests. Each time the productive topsoil from another acre of land washes away, or another body of water becomes hopelessly polluted, every resident of our state becomes poorer. Each such loss also further limits the opportunities that our future will bring. So educating and training our young people and protecting and conserving our natural resources are crucial to preparing for the future.

With regard to the future of particular crops, I believe that tobacco will continue to be an important cash crop in eastern North Carolina in the years ahead. I am not sure, though, that the tobacco quota and support program will help our farmers as much in the future as it has in the past. Unfortunately, a degree of dissension within the ranks of tobacco producing and buying interests has developed in North Carolina and other flue-cured states, and Congress does not seem to be as supportive of the program.

I deeply hope we can hold on to the program and improve it, but that won't be easy. I do however, expect tobacco to continue to make a substantial contribution to the farm income of eastern North Carolina in 2000 and beyond.

We also have made great strides in agricultural diversification in eastern North Carolina, especially in hogs, poultry, and fruits and vegetables. An area that needs increased attention in connection with these enterprises is marketing.

Since more than half of our land is in trees, we can expect farm forestry to become increasingly important, especially if landowners are encouraged to manage their resources for greatest profit.

The demand for North Carolina agricultural products in the future will grow, and if we plan well for the future, we can make that future brighter and more prosperous. At this gathering today we have some of the finest minds, the greatest brainpower in this wonderful state in which we live. You know and understand the problems we will be confronting in the years ahead, and you can help guide us as we seek the most effective solutions and answers to those problems.

Let us do well what we have set out to do. Even as we make plans to look back 400 years to the first attempt by the English to establish a colony in the New World on the coast of our state, let us look to the future with determination and courage and vision. While preserving the best from the past, we have always looked to the future and planned for the future.

We need determination to do the most with what we have. We need courage to be realistic and face the facts, no matter how unpleasant they may be at times. We need vision to realize that the people of this state are people of great character who can and will respond when confronted with challenges. Let's continue to work together to make agriculture one of the most prosperous industries in the state and ensure that future farmers in North Carolina can have successful careers in agriculture.

TESTIMONY BEFORE U.S. HOUSE COMMITTEE ON MERCHANT MARINE AND FISHERIES, SUBCOMMITTEE ON OCEANOGRAPHY

WASHINGTON, D.C., MARCH 1, 1983

Good morning. I appreciate the opportunity to appear before the committee. We are indeed fortunate in North Carolina to have Congressman Walter B. Jones representing our First Congressional District, which includes half of our entire coastal area. We very much appreciate his dedicated work and able leadership on coastal and marine matters.[1]

I am here to express the views of the state of North Carolina on H.R. 5, a bill to establish an ocean and coastal resource management and development block grant program. North Carolina strongly supports this bill. I urge your early and favorable consideration of it.[2]

Ocean and coastal resources are vitally important to the state of North Carolina. Our rivers, sounds, wetlands, and beaches are the lifeblood of our coastal area. They support a vibrant commercial and sport fishing industry. Our beaches are nationally renowned recreation areas. We have the nation's first national seashore at

Cape Hatteras and have now added a second at Cape Lookout. These resources are a national treasure.

These resources have important economic value to the state and nation as well. For example, the dockside value of commercial fishing landings in North Carolina exceeds $70 million a year. Some $200 million a year is generated by sport fishing. Recreation and tourism provide the vast majority of jobs and income for many communities along our 320 miles of oceanfront.

Without doubt, we in North Carolina have been truly blessed with coastal resources unsurpassed in beauty and abundance. However, we recognize potential threats to the beauty and productivity of our coastal area. Growth can bring tremendous benefits in terms of jobs, new energy sources, and a better quality of life for our citizens. If these forces are not carefully managed, however, they will weaken and destroy our resources. Uncontrolled growth can turn our natural blessings into a tragedy of our own creation. Here are just three examples:

First, improper decisions on waste-water disposal and land use can destroy the clean waters and marshes essential to the fishing industry. Almost 320,000 acres of productive shellfish waters in North Carolina are now closed to harvesting because of water quality problems.

Second, cluttered, high-density development in hazardous beach-front areas can result in loss of life and property. Such unwise development can lead to increased public costs for disaster relief, erosion control, and provision of public services like roads and sewer lines. With half of our coast having erosion rates of over two feet per year, in addition to the more dramatic danger of storms and hurricanes, such losses can be catastrophic. Unmanaged development can also block the access to and use of public beaches that is so important for tourism and our enjoyment of the beach.

Third, accelerated exploration and production of offshore oil and gas resources, without careful management, bring risks to our fisheries, beaches, and cultural resources. We face seven OCS [outer continental shelf] lease sales off North Carolina in the Department of the Interior's current five-year plan, and the next offering alone, Lease Sale 78, has twenty times the acreage offered in the last lease sale.[3]

North Carolina is not alone in facing these issues. Most coastal states have similar pressures and management needs. Because of the magnitude of these threats, it is critically important for the entire nation that we establish and maintain an effective ocean and coastal resource management program.

I believe that our nation has accomplished a great deal over the past ten years to effectively address these important concerns. In many respects, I think North Carolina can serve as a model for responsible ocean and coastal resource management. We have established in North Carolina a coastal management program widely regarded as one of the best in the nation. This program is an excellent example of the creative federal, state, and local partnership necessary for successful natural resource management.

At the federal level, the Coastal Zone Management Act of 1972 provided important incentives for state action. These incentives included financial assistance and the promise of federal consistency with state programs. The law also established baseline standards to encourage and secure a national management effort. The federal government could not prepare and implement the kind of detailed management we have, but it could and did make the financial and technical resources available to allow us to take the necessary action.[4]

At the state level, we have indeed taken action. We passed a Coastal Area Management Act in 1974.[5] It was then, and remains, perhaps the most visible and actively debated piece of environmental legislation in the state's history. It is also perhaps the most successful.

We are protecting key environmental areas and managing development in hazard areas. We recently enacted a new beach access program and appropriated a million dollars for its implementation.[6] We are now in the process of establishing an estuarine sanctuary system and developing policies on rebuilding after major storms. We are clearly committed to good resource management.

At the local level, more than seventy of our coastal local governments have adopted detailed land-use plans, with extensive public participation, to guide growth and development. Federal financial resources and a state framework were critical, but it has been the interest and dedication of local officials and citizens that have made this work.

We have established similar working partnerships in other areas of ocean and coastal resource management. We have developed a sound program for identifying, evaluating, and resolving the complex issues associated with coastal energy development. With essential federal support, we are participating in a timely and responsible fashion in the review of OCS lease sales and exploration plans and, should either of the two drilling expeditions scheduled for this year prove productive, development plans as well. By anticipating, studying, and resolving concerns early in the resource development process, state and local concerns can be addressed without undue delay to responsible offshore energy development. We are also assessing the onshore impacts of offshore energy development and the impacts of energy transport, peat mining, and oil refineries. Again, the work reflects effective federal, state, and local cooperation.

We have established good, cooperative fisheries research and management programs. This work is essential to identification and protection of prime nursery areas, to effective fishery stock management, and equitable treatment of our fishermen.

Our participation in the National Sea Grant College program is yet another effective partnership. This has provided us with vital research, education, leadership development, and technical assistance. Through this program, we have, for example, been able to design better septic tank systems for areas with poor coastal soils, promoted use of more effective and less environmentally damaging erosion control methods, and we have learned how to better manage and use fishery stocks.

Working together in these ways, all three levels of government have met their responsibilities. None of the accomplishments would have been possible by any one level of government working alone. We had to have the support of all levels of government to make it work. Collectively we are resolving difficult issues of having coastal growth without sacrificing environmental quality. It is in the national interest that these and other vital resource management partnerships continue. The threats to our nation's coasts and oceans are growing, not diminishing.

We have established a workable framework for good resource management. We have learned a great deal and can be proud of our significant accomplishments, but much remains to be done. We cannot sustain our beautiful and productive coastal resources by wishful thinking or resting on past deeds. We must act to meet our stewardship responsibilities, responsibilities shared by our national, state, and local governments.

We are making a serious effort at the state level to assume a greater share of the financial responsibility for these programs. Even though the budget is as tight in my state capital as it is here in Washington, I am asking our legislature for significant increases in funding for these programs. However, even if we are able to secure the doubling of funds for coastal management I am requesting for next year, which will be almost doubled yet again the following year, we will still have to operate our program on 65 percent of the resources we had two years ago. And this will provide no funds to continue our work on coastal energy impact, research and education, and fisheries management programs. Many of our local governments are also increasing their expenditures on these programs.

These programs are so important, however, that we must make this effort—even now in these tight times. It is an investment we cannot defer. It is extremely important, then, that the federal government take immediate action to maintain its share of the responsibility. Our seas and fisheries, our enjoyment of beaches, our need for energy—these know no state boundaries. These are national issues that generate the need for good resource management, and the benefits that result are national in scope.

Yet in the face of these pressing national needs, the administration is recommending no funding for coastal zone management, coastal energy impact, or Sea Grant College programs. Such action would have the federal government turn its back on years of hard work and investment. The new block grant program proposed in H.R. 5 will, however, make an important contribution to maintaining our partnership in the vital area of ocean and coastal resource management, and it therefore has our strong support.

The funds provided through H.R. 5 will allow us to continue to address these critical issues in the most efficient and cost-effective manner possible: an active federal, state, local management partnership. H.R. 5 allows us to target a modest portion—only 10 percent of our increase in revenues from the exploitation of non-renewable coastal and ocean resources—to assure good management of our coastal environment. It is important that a realistic base year be chosen for calculating the funds so as to assure adequate resources for these important programs. This bill also encourages states to share these revenues with local governments, which has been an essential part of our success in North Carolina. These are good provisions that have our support.

The approach embodied in H.R. 5 has broad support. It has been endorsed by the Coastal States Organization, the National Governors' Association and just recently, on my motion, was again approved by the Southern Governors' Association. We need the bill.

The future of our oceans and coasts depends upon our responsible stewardship. We need this bill to effectively carry out these responsibilities. I urge you to support it. Thank you.

---

[1] Walter Beaman Jones (1913-   ), native of Fayetteville; resident of Farmville; B.S., North Carolina State College (now University), 1934. Office equipment dealer; commissioner and mayor pro tem, 1947-1949, and mayor and recorder's court judge, town of Farmville, 1949-1953; member, state House, 1955-1959, and Senate, 1965; U.S. representative from North Carolina's First Congressional District since 1967, and chairman, House Merchant Marine and Fisheries Committee; Democrat. *North Carolina Manual, 1983*, 161.

[2] The Reagan administration opposed H.R. 5, the ocean and coastal resources management bill, contending that such legislation, if enacted, would absorb money intended for the general treasury and thus contribute to the growing federal budget deficit. However, the U.S. House endorsed it on September 14, 1983, by a 301-95 margin. As approved, the plan would distribute funds to thirty-one states and five territories as support for ocean and coastal resource projects. *Congressional Quarterly Almanac, 1983*, 359, 94-H.

[3] For more information on South Atlantic Lease Sale 78, see "Statement on Offshore Oil and Gas Exploration," April 20, 1983, below.

[4] "An Act to Establish a National Policy and Develop a National Program for the Management, Beneficial Use, Protection, and Development of the Nation's Coastal Zones, and for Other Purposes," 86 Stat. 1280-1289, was approved October 27, 1972.

[5] "An Act to Appropriate Funds to Implement the Coastal Area Management Act of 1974," c. 1232, was ratified April 10, 1974, and became effective with the passage of

"An Act Relating to Management of the Coastal Area of North Carolina," c. 1284, ratified April 11. *N.C. Session Laws, 1973, Second Session, 1974.*

⁶"An Act to Establish a Program to Purchase and Maintain Coastal Lands Subject to Natural Hazards for Beach Access and Use," c. 925, was ratified July 10, 1981. *N.C. Session Laws, 1981.*

TESTIMONY SUBMITTED TO U.S. HOUSE COMMITTEE ON PUBLIC WORKS AND TRANSPORTATION, SUBCOMMITTEE ON ECONOMIC DEVELOPMENT

WASHINGTON, D.C., MARCH 1, 1983

I regret that I cannot be with you in person today, for over the years I have been a strong supporter of ARC's [Appalachian Regional Commission] comprehensive development programs. In 1978 I served as states' cochairman. But today, I want to tell you of my special interest in education as an essential part of our overall Appalachian development program. In my state I support and participate in a wide range of educational efforts: volunteerism in the schools, increasing student mastery of basic skills, innovative training programs including solar and computer technology, involving business and business people in working partnerships with the schools, and establishing the new school of science and technology for high school-age students.

When I was states' cochairman of the ARC, I convened a conference of Appalachian citizens devoted to "Raising a New Generation in Appalachia." As the current chairman of the Education Commission of the States (ECS) I have appointed a National Task Force on Economic Growth of approximately thirty national leaders, including eleven governors and eleven chief executive officers of corporations, to focus primarily on strategies for improving the quality of high school graduates—especially in those skills required for economic growth.

Only seventeen years ago, the government's first major report on Appalachia painted a grim picture of education conditions in the region.[1] Education in Appalachia had a different look than the one most Americans knew:

—Facilities were small and hardly better than the housing in the surrounding communities.

—One out of every three students completed high school.

—Access to higher education was so remote a dream that only one in ten entered college, and one in twenty completed college.

—Vocational training was available to less than 25 percent of eleventh- and twelfth-grade students.

Underlying the statistics on low education attainment levels was a limited labor market requiring few skills and making completion of high school often seem unnecessary.

Anyone who knew the region then and now would find the changes nothing short of phenomenal. In barely two decades, special efforts—predominantly governmental—stimulated growth and development unequaled since the initial settlement of the region. Today:

—Three out of every four youths complete high school.

—There are over 280 institutions of higher education in the region; now one out of every five persons has gone to college, and one out of every ten persons has completed college.

—There is in place a region-wide network of post-secondary and secondary vocational facilities that offers training to approximately one-half million persons, including over 50 percent of the region's eleventh and twelfth graders.

This progress is even more dramatic for Appalachian North Carolina, where now one out of every four persons has gone to college, one out of every nine has completed college, and 53 percent of the eleventh and twelfth graders are enrolled in vocational education training programs.

These changes were possible because of state and local initiatives to improve education using state and local funds of over $25,000,000 and over $30,000,000 of available ARC funds. ARC funds in my state have helped:

—Construct seventy-seven secondary and post-secondary facilities of both vocational and higher education.

—Add new vocational training programs.

—Establish two model regional education centers serving local school districts which were so successful they were established in the rest of the state.

—Initiate basic skills for both youths and adults, computer literacy, and teacher improvement projects.

Because of our past investments, the educational prospects are much brighter for the 4,048,110 young Appalachians now in public and private schools in the region's 1,038 school districts, including approximately 239,000 students in thirty-four school districts in Appalachian North Carolina. But the problems of the past have persistent effects on the region's ability to adapt to profound changes in the economy and job markets. Of the 12 million adults over twenty-five, one in four has no better than an eighth grade education, and less than 60 percent have completed high school.

These figures illustrate the need to combine continued basic skills education with the specialized training programs necessary to prepare the Appalachian work force for the future. The technological revolution that was predicted for the 1960s is materializing in the 1980s. The pace of this technological change is accelerating, and the existing work force is ill-prepared to make the necessary changes.

The report of the Appalachian governors two years ago foresaw the need to train or retrain millions of workers because of the impact of foreign competition and new technologies on Appalachia's traditional industries.[2] The commission's Jobs and Private Investment program includes a focus on upgrading manpower for new and emerging regional jobs. The program would help the states address three of the most critical areas of training: customized training to fill jobs of specific employers; updating vocational programs and equipment to meet job needs; and establishing basic skills programs for adults and vocational students.

"Economic growth in the modern world depends to a large degree on educational excellence," so stated the 1964 Report of the President's Appalachian Regional Commission.[3] This is even more true in 1983. The commission's program in education will help provide a basic tool for economic progress: a skilled work force.

I applaud your introduction of H.R. 10. It will enable us to continue this and other essential activities of the Appalachian Regional Commission. It will still leave us with an unfinished agenda, but it will close the gap significantly, and it will bring us closer to attaining our ultimate objective: an Appalachia fully in the mainstream of the American economy.[4]

---

[1] *Appalachia: A Report by the President's Appalachian Regional Commission, 1964* (Washington, D.C.: U.S. Government Printing Office, [1964]), 8-12, hereinafter cited as *Appalachia: A Report.*

[2] For a synopsis of the 1981 report to Congress, see "Appalachian Governors Propose Finish-up Program for ARC," *Appalachia*, November-December, 1981/January-February, 1982, 1-7.

[3] *Appalachia: A Report*, 8.

[4] The U.S. House passed H.R. 10, the National Development Investment Act, on July 12, 1983. *Congressional Quarterly, 1983*, 230.

REGIONAL FORUM ON THE FUTURE OF RESEARCH TRIANGLE PARK

DURHAM, MARCH 10, 1983

[Development of Research Triangle Park and the surrounding area was also the topic of an address, delivered on October 27, 1983, at the Horizons Unlimited Decision Conference.]

Thank you for inviting me to participate in this forum on the future of the Research Triangle. I don't have a lot of ready answers, but I know what general direction I would like to see growth in this area take. The Project 2000 effort undertaken by the counties in this region is an excellent example of the long-range vision we need.

My own ideas are grounded in my belief that this area will be a major microelectronics center in the future. The Research Triangle area is a natural for the development of this industry. We have such strong universities to provide education and research. We have companies conducting research in related fields. Recent industry expansion in the area shows the commitment of industry—IBM, General Electric, Hewlett Packard, have all expanded their facilities.

High-technology industries, which rely on advanced technology in their manufacturing process, will want to locate near the microelectronics industry. By doing so, they can be near the companies that are developing the equipment they are using. Shipping costs will be reduced. Machine downtime can be reduced. Feedback on machine operations will occur more frequently. Companies developing software packages will also want to locate near the research and development activities as well as near the high-tech industries.

This anticipated development has great implications for the Research Triangle area. We can expect more industry, more demands for skilled workers, and the associated demands for housing, water and sewer, and highways. Can we respond to these demands in an orderly fashion while preserving the heritage of the park? Yes, but only if we take some important steps.

The visual image of the park is one of its trademarks. In order to maintain this image and carry it beyond the park's boundaries, I would offer some suggestions. First and foremost, the units of government in this area must work in harmony. This means some standardization of ordinances as they apply to the area surrounding the park, especially between Raleigh and Durham.

Second, we should consider maintaining the parklike atmosphere by placing limits on the percentage of land that can be covered with buildings. We must plan for the anticipated demands for water, sewer, and housing. We should decide where we want residential development and then steer it there. Likewise with commercial and industrial development.

The capacity of our existing capital facilities, our infrastructure, may prove to be a limiting factor. Can we serve more people with existing water and sewer facilities; can our public schools hold more students; are our roads sufficient?

Another development which could affect the growth of this area is the establishment of a foreign trade zone. This zone will be very beneficial to manufacturers in the Research Triangle area who use foreign parts or labor or sell to foreign markets. This zone will make North Carolina products more competitive and will increase the attractiveness of the Research Triangle area.[1]

You have a real challenge before you. You must decide now what you want this area to be like ten years and twenty years from now. These are tight times financially for all of us. The typical response might be to accept whatever offers we get, regardless of the environmental consequences. We must guard against development which does not meet our needs.

Looking around the room, seeing the leadership of the area here, I am convinced you are up to meeting this challenge. The future of the Research Triangle area will depend on a strong working partnership among business and governmental leaders. We must keep in mind that every decision we make about the future development of Research Triangle Park and the surrounding area will in some way affect every citizen of North Carolina.

We must be careful stewards of Research Triangle's heritage and yet we must be prepared for revolutionary changes in the economy of this state and this nation. I don't believe those ideals are inconsistent—not if we plan wisely.

This forum is a very significant step in ensuring the kind of healthy and prosperous future we all want to have. I commend you on your leadership and your vision, and I pledge to you my assistance and support as we begin making the decisions that will shape that future.

---

[1] On November 8, 1983, the U.S. Department of Commerce approved the establishment of Foreign Trade Zone 93 in the Research Triangle Park vicinity; it was opened officially in the spring of 1984. Such zones permit the duty-free importation and storage of goods. If components brought into a foreign trade zone are used in a finished product, which is then shipped out of the country, no tariffs are assessed. However, if the completed item is destined for the U.S. domestic market, customs duties are imposed. *Durham Morning Herald*, November 9, 1983, April 1, 1984.

NORTH CAROLINA CAMPAIGN FUND DINNER

ATLANTA, GEORGIA, MARCH 12, 1983

[When the North Carolina Campaign Fund was established in 1982, its main objectives included thwarting U.S. senator Jesse Helms's 1984 reelection bid and diminishing his national political influence. While the organization financially assisted state Democratic congressional candidates, some of whom faced stiff competition from Congressional Club-backed opponents, NCCF was recognized as a fund-raising apparatus for the governor's yet-unannounced Senate campaign. However, Hunt's name was not mentioned in the fund's advertising or direct-mail solicitations. Primarily as a result of Federal Election Commission restrictions on independent political action groups, NCCF was disbanded in July, 1983, after having met only one fifth of its goal to raise $5 million. The fund's most noteworthy accomplishment, according to director John Bennett, was the compilation of a 38,000-name mailing list to be offered to the Democratic contender for Helms's seat.

NCCF's fund-raising activities were not limited to North Carolina. Hunt spoke on behalf of the organization at a dinner in Atlanta on March 12. Governors Joe Frank Harris, of Georgia; Dick Riley, of South Carolina; Bob Graham, of Florida; Chuck Robb, of Virginia; and Harry Hughes, of Maryland, were honorary cochairmen of the event. *Durham Morning Herald*, February 18, July 2, August 7, 14, 1983; Snider, *Helms and Hunt*, 92.]

This past December, the North Carolina Campaign Fund held a fund raiser that was the largest and most successful in the history of North Carolina. Tonight, Richardson Preyer [1] and the Campaign Fund bring their cause to the South as a whole. They have come here tonight because North Carolina needs your help; North Carolina wants to lead, and it is time for the South to lead this nation again.

All of us are here tonight because we are united in a common cause—not for party, but for people; not for politics, but for principles. We want to set this nation on the right course again, a course that will restore vitality to our economy, full and equal opportunities to our people, and balance and common sense to Washington. We are tired of the politics of negativism and division. We are tired of politics that puts ideology above people. We are tired of politics that serves wealthy special interests at the expense of the public interest.

We in North Carolina are ready to strike a blow in 1984 that will be felt across this nation. We are ready to do our part to restore to Washington the kind of leadership this nation needs today:

—Leadership that gives our people jobs and hope, not unemployment and fear.

—Leadership that builds up public education, not tears it down.

—Leadership that preserves Social Security and Medicare, not destroys them.

—Leadership that protects our environment, not gives us James Watt.[2]

—Leadership that believes in being fair to *all* of our people and in bringing us together, not tearing us apart.

—Leadership that appeals to the best in us, not the worst.

—We in North Carolina are ready, most of all, to send the Congressional Club and that whole crowd across this country a message they will never forget! And we need your help!

The South can lead this nation again. Bert Lance [3] is right when he says the South is the key to the election of 1984. The White House will be won or lost in the South. The arithmetic in the Electoral College dictates it. And even more important, the South, today, stands squarely in the mainstream of American public opinion.

To win the White House next year, our party must nominate a candidate who is in that mainstream. He must be free of single-issue pressure groups. He must believe in full and equal opportunities for all of our people, in jobs, in education, in health care,

and in providing a secure economic future. He must believe in fiscal
responsibility. He must believe in a strong national defense. And
I'm not afraid to say that Jimmy Carter was moving our party and
our nation in that direction, and it was the right direction!

Our national party has adopted a set of rules that will help us
nominate a candidate in the mainstream, rules that will give elected
officials and party leaders a key role in the nominating process—
rules that will, more than anything else, help us win the White
House in 1984 and govern effectively in the four years after that.

The White House is important, but North Carolina has an
important race in 1984, too, and we can win it if we have your help!
The Democrats of North Carolina showed last November what we
can do. We showed that a united campaign, a positive campaign,
talking to people about the issues, can beat the Congressional Club
and its millions of dollars. That is the kind of campaign we must
have in 1984: one that offers a positive and constructive program for
this nation's future, one that talks sense to people.

But we need your help. We cannot raise the kind of money in
North Carolina that the Congressional Club rakes in from special
interests across this country. We need your help to get our issues and
our message before the voters. That is the help Richardson Preyer
and the North Carolina Campaign Fund are asking you for.

I thank you for responding to them tonight. I thank you for your
help. But tonight is only a beginning. A long, hard road lies ahead.

We can meet the challenge. It will be worth the effort. We can do
our part. Twenty years ago, President Kennedy said: "A party is of
no use unless it fulfills some national purpose. Our country is not yet
at the top of the hill, but on the side of the hill. Someday America
will reach the summit. And I hope they will then say that we have
done our part." Thank you.

---

[1]Lunsford Richardson Preyer (1919-   ), North Carolina congressman, 1969-
1981, and North Carolina Campaign Fund chairman, 1982-1983. Previously identified in Mitchell, *Addresses of Hunt,* I, 375n; see also *Durham Morning Herald,* July
2, 1983.

[2]James Gaius Watt (1938-   ), native of Lusk, Wyoming; B.S., 1960, J.D., 1962,
University of Wyoming. Legal assistant to U.S. senator Milward L. Simpson of
Wyoming, 1962-1966; deputy assistant secretary for water and power development,
U.S. Interior Department, 1969-1972; director, Bureau of Outdoor Recreation, 1972-
1975; vice-chairman, Federal Power Commission, 1975-1977; president, chief legal
officer, Mountain States Legal Defense Foundation, 1977-1980; U.S. interior secretary, 1981-1983. "Watt's Out, Clark's In—What's Next?" *Wilderness,* 47 (Winter,
1983), 39-40; *Who's Who in America, 1982-1983,* II, 3489.

[3]Thomas Bertram (Bert) Lance (1931-   ), native of Gainesville, Georgia; resident
of Calhoun, Georgia; attended Emory University, 1948-1950, and University of
Georgia, 1951; was graduated from Rutgers University banking graduate school,
1963. Executive vice-president, 1958-1963, president and chief executive officer, 1963-
1974, and board chairman, 1974-1977, and since 1981, Calhoun First National Bank;
Georgia highway director, 1970-1973; director, federal Office of Management and

Budget, 1977; Georgia Democratic state chairman, 1982-1985. *News and Observer*, July 7 and 12, 1985; *Who's Who in America, 1982-1983*, II, 1912.

COMMISSION ON THE FUTURE OF NORTH CAROLINA

RALEIGH, MARCH 15, 1983

When we initiated the North Carolina 2000 project in June of 1981, we began a vast undertaking. Because of the sheer magnitude of trying to get a handle on where we are and where we are going to be as a state in the next century, this project was greeted with cynicism in some corners.

I knew that if this job was to be done right, if it was going to have the kind of credibility that it must have, I would have to assemble the very best, most energetic, and most creative minds in North Carolina to lead this effort. Bill Friday, Elizabeth Koontz, and all of you answered the call. You are the people who have helped to bring this state to where it is now—and where we are now is on the threshold of a bright, healthy, and prosperous future.

We can't leave that to chance. The basic ingredients for a truly glittering future are all present, but we must take those ingredients —our productive work force, our good educational system, our excellent business climate, the boundless energy and determination of our people—and direct them toward ensuring the kind of future we want to have.

Because of the thousands of hours that you, collectively, have put into this task, I have been presented today with a roadmap to the twenty-first century.[1] This is not a pie-in-the-sky document. It is the product of our idealism, but it addresses real trends, real problems, and real options. It addresses such things as the quality of math and science instruction, crime prevention, economic development, management of hazardous wastes, raising healthy children, and seeing to it that senior citizens live healthy, productive lives.

I told you at the first meeting of the Commission on the Future that your work product would not gather dust on a shelf, and it will not. From this day forward, your report becomes a living, breathing element in the decision-making process. I will begin by directing state agencies to evaluate the report within the context of their programs and priorities. Tomorrow, I will go before the State Goals and Policy Board and charge them with the responsibility for monitoring the progress of your recommendations.[2]

The public dialogue that has been generated by your work and that of the local 2000 committees has been invaluable. That process must continue. Accordingly, a copy of this document will be placed in every public library in this state—and I will ask all local

governing bodies to devote at least one meeting to a discussion of
the issues you have raised. Further, we will involve the private
sector, representatives of various interest groups, state legislators,
and others.

The discussion and debate you have brought about must continue.
This report must be the fire that keeps the pot boiling. To paraphrase John Gardner, North Carolina is not a finished product—it
is constantly being built and rebuilt, adjusted and repaired, fine
tuned.[3] We must make sure that the rebuilding process carries us
toward the goals we all share: good schools, good jobs, safe neighborhoods, a clean environment, and the preservation of a free and just
society.

You have given to me today a blueprint for accomplishing all of
that, a blueprint that will be periodically updated as events and
trends dictate. You are the architects. Because of what you have
done, I think we will one day look back upon this meeting as a
historic step in the building of a North Carolina where the human
mind and body and spirit can grow and flourish.

Thank you for what you have done. You have helped prepare us to
step into the future with hope, courage, and the determination to
fashion a better world for ourselves and for our children.

[1] See Hunt's message to a joint session of the General Assembly, April 27, 1983,
"Presentation of the North Carolina 2000 Report," footnote 2, above.

[2] The governor instructed the State Goals and Policy Board, on March 16, to begin
an immediate investigation into three of the potential problem areas identified in the
commission's report: hazardous substances and wastes, health care policies and
costs, and technical assistance to small businesses.

[3] The John W. Gardner quotation to which the governor referred is identified in
Mitchell, *Addresses of Hunt*, I, 182n.

NORTH CAROLINA STUDENT LEGISLATURE

RALEIGH, MARCH 23, 1983

This is one of those appearances I look forward to every year—a
chance to speak to the future leaders of North Carolina. As student
legislators you share a unique opportunity. You learn the ins and
outs of legislating; you learn the language of parliamentary procedure; and you learn about the art that permeates the entire
process—politics.

As student legislators, you become involved. I can't stress enough
how important that is. By joining in the activities of this group, you
plug into the issues facing North Carolina and the nation. You link
up with students with similar interests from across the state. The
work you accomplish in these historic chambers sends a signal to

the legislators, to the people, and to me. It says, "This is how the students of North Carolina feel about the issues."

Instead of talking to you about specific issues, however, I want to talk to you today in broader terms—about attitudes, about what government should be doing, and how we should be using government.

There is a very fundamental debate going on in the United States today, as fundamental in some ways as the debate almost 200 years ago that shaped our Constitution and our form of government. The debate centers on this question: What is the role of government? How much should it try to do? And, within that overall picture, what should be the role of each level of government—the federal, the state, and the local?

Whether you agree with him on everything or not, and I don't, Ronald Reagan helped start this debate and that is a healthy development. He has changed his views about the role of government. When he was inaugurated, the president said, "Government *is* the problem." But, when he gave his "State of the Union" speech this year, he acknowledged that government has a responsibility to help people who need help.[1]

Clearly, government *can* be a problem. It can tax too much, spend too much, regulate too much, waste too much, and try to do too much. Government can also do too little.

What we must have is a balance—a balance between a government that spends too much and a government that cuts too much; between a government that does too much to stifle and control business and economic growth and a government that does too little to protect citizens and the environment.

Government can be a problem, but government can also be a solution. We not only *can* do something about which it is, we have a *responsibility* to do something.

Government has a responsibility to stimulate economic growth and help people get good jobs.

Government has a responsibility to see that every young person in this nation gets a decent education.

Government has a responsibility to see that every person—young and old, black and white, male and female—has a full and fair chance to succeed in life.

Government has a responsibility to protect the air and water from degradation and exploitation, and that means not selling off treasures like our national forests here in North Carolina.[2]

Finally, government has a responsibility to lead us and to bring us together.

I firmly believe that there are, ultimately, two types of leaders in the world: those who set people against each other, who play on suspicion and division to divide people for their own ends, and those who try to bring people together, to reach a compromise, to reconcile differing and competing interests, to work toward a common goal.

I try to be that second type. That is what I believe in. It isn't always as easy as standing up and denouncing somebody else, or taking an extreme view to start a controversy and get attention, but I think it's the right way. We are all in this together. The government belongs to all of us, and what happens to this state and this nation belongs to us.

That is the process you are engaged in this week—hearing different points of view, reconciling different interests, trying to move toward a common goal. I think that is the right way, and I am glad to see you doing it, because that bodes well for our future.

North Carolina has a special role to play in this nation. We held out on the Constitution until the Bill of Rights was adopted. Today, 200 years later, we can make a difference again. We can give this nation new leadership. We can help set it straight. Let us ask ourselves, today, what kind of leadership we want North Carolina to give our nation.

---

[1] President Reagan's January 20, 1981, inaugural address was reprinted in *Congressional Quarterly Almanac, 1981*, 11E-13E. His "State of the Union" message of January 25, 1983, can be found in *Congressional Quarterly Almanac, 1983*, 3E-7E.

[2] Hunt might have been reacting to a 1981 draft of a U.S. Forest Service regional planning report that called for a huge increase in timber sale targets for the Nantahala and Pisgah national forests. *News and Observer*, July 12, 1984.

GOVERNMENT EXECUTIVES INSTITUTE MANAGEMENT FORUM

RALEIGH, MARCH 25, 1983

I am very pleased to see at this forum members of my cabinet, the Council of State, and the Governor's Management Council. We'd like to send a clear message to you and others that we care about management and our managers. We hope you'll do likewise with those you manage.

I'm very proud of our Government Executives Institute [GEI] and you graduates. You represent the top management cadre of North Carolina government. I strongly support your continuing development, and I applaud this pilot series of GEI Management Forums.

The subject of this first forum, "Management and Transition," is and should be a vital concern to all of us. We bear and share the responsibility for managing the *business* of government—the largest business, by the way, in this state. We are and should be accountable for good management, now and in the transitional period ahead.

We've been faced with the challenge of doing more with the same, or even less. I think we have met the challenge. It hasn't been easy, and it may not get any easier.

We have established a management agenda, set forth management themes—productivity and accountability, partnerships, and pride in government—and developed a number of management initiatives. Such actions are relatively timeless. They could apply to any administration and at any stage. But administrations do change. For some of us, the meter is running. The challenges of transition lay before us. In many ways, they are unique and demand very special attention.

Pictures of the future sometimes are painted in nautical images. Elected officials, including myself, tend to be lofty: "sailing against the wind" or "staying the course." Seasoned transition-watchers tend to be more practical: "don't rock the boat," "jumping ship," and "lame duck."

The "lame duck" image has the governor no longer governing and managers no longer managing. Those with visions of either future political office or retaining their job in another administration avoid "rocking the boat." Boat rockers grow impatient with such a scenario and may "jump ship" well before the journey is scheduled to end. And those jockeying for positions in a new administration may jump to the ship they think will come in first.

Politics as usual? The norm for transition? I hope not. I intend to keep governing for the rest of my term. I hope you intend to keep managing. We need to do both. Whether we like it or not, we're already in "transition." I've given my final "State of the State" message. This is my last long session of the General Assembly. The media are feasting on political speculations and motivations.

Pressures mount from outside and inside state government. The external pressures are largely political: campaigns being rumored or launched, supporters being marshaled, appointments being sought, issues being discussed, people becoming distracted from the task at hand. The internal pressures are largely managerial: how to minimize distractions, how to get the job done, how to keep the system from deteriorating, how to leave a legacy on which future administrations can build.

These pressures bring special challenges, and those challenges require special approaches. I have three approaches to suggest:

1. *Consolidate*—that is, get done what we're doing now and deeply root what we've started;

2. *Move forward*—that is, continue to think about and talk about what should be done, do what we can, and help plan what might be done by others; and

3. *Manage*—that is, stay in charge and lead the state through the balance of our "contract" with the people of North Carolina.

Consolidation means using what we've got—holding down our

spending, cutting out waste, living within our means—while still trying to be responsive to our mandates. It means that we resist changing everything, we limit our legislative agenda, and we don't reorganize anymore. To consolidate also means deeply rooting our various initiatives and programs. We must improve the effectiveness and workability of what's already under way, get our programs in good shape, and make sure they stay there.

That doesn't mean we stand still. It requires us to *move forward*. We don't lower our goals. We've got to do the job completely and successfully, with strength and integrity. We must know what we intend to do—our game plan, if you will—and do it well. In the words of Kerr Scott, we must "plough out to the end of the furrow."[1]

We must also think farther ahead as we move forward. We must be large minded and focus on the big things. We must help North Carolina focus on what needs to be done in the rest of this century. We must figure out how we can creatively blend our current agenda with recommendations of the Commission on the Future of North Carolina. We should work with others, including potential candidates, to help shape and elevate the issues representing the agenda for North Carolina's future.

While consolidating and moving forward, we must *manage*. As good government is good politics, good government requires good management. Individually, each of us must run a good, tight ship, avoid overreaching, use good judgment, be disciplined, do and say the right things. We must be extra vigilant ethically, maintaining the highest standards of conduct and avoiding even the appearance of conflicts of interest. My general advice to each of you is to do right, be open and honest, correct any mistakes, and get on with it.

Collectively, we should work as a management team. We should help reduce surprises. We must keep working on our relationships. We must help our employees feel better about themselves, their work, and their public service. Public service is our business. We must put the public's interest first, in every way we can. We must make more visible to the public what we're doing and how we're doing it. We must serve those to whom we answer.

Mackenzie King, the late Canadian economist and prime minister, put public service and management in humbling perspective over sixty years ago. He said, "Labor can do nothing without capital, capital nothing without labor, and neither labor nor capital can do anything without the guiding genius of management; and management, however wise its genius may be, can do nothing without the privileges which the community affords."[2]

Our community—be it a town or city, a county, or the state of North Carolina—has afforded us the privilege of governing and managing. We must continue to do so to the full extent of our talents and our contract with the people. Thank you.

[1] "Plowing to the end of the row" and "catching up with my hauling" were two phrases Governor Scott used frequently; they became something of a personal trademark. Corbitt, *Addresses of Scott*, xix.

[2] William Lyon Mackenzie King (1874-1950), native of Berlin (now Kitchener), Ontario; B.S., 1895, LL.B., 1896, M.A., 1897, University of Toronto; A.M., 1898, Ph.D., 1909, Harvard University; numerous honorary degrees. Deputy labor minister, and editor, *Labour Gazette*, 1900-1908; member of Canadian parliament, 1908-1948; prime minister of Canada, 1921-1926, 1926-1930, 1935-1948; author. *Who Was Who in America, 1951-1960*, 478; *World Book Encyclopedia*, 1982 ed., s.v. "Prime Minister of Canada." Hunt borrowed an excerpt from King's Canadian Club speech, Montreal, March 17, 1919, as quoted in Bartlett, *Familiar Quotations*, 931.

STATEMENT ON
DRUNKEN DRIVING LEGISLATION

RALEIGH, MARCH 31, 1983

We are now within days of passing the nation's toughest law against drunk driving. All that remains is for a legislative conference committee to work out differences between the House and Senate versions of the Safe Roads Act. I am confident that that will be done promptly.

Both versions of the bill contain those elements that are essential to having the toughest law in the country. An analysis by the Department of Crime Control and Public Safety shows that no state has taken as comprehensive an approach as North Carolina. For example:

—The provision for an immediate, automatic, ten-day suspension of the driver's license of any person who registers a .10 on the breathalyzer is a swift and certain loss of driving privilege. No other state has this provision.

—Our bill has the most severe penalties for first offenders convicted of grossly aggravated drunk driving. If a single, grossly aggravating factor is present, a seven-day jail term is mandatory. If two such factors are present, a fourteen-day jail term is mandatory.

—We are the only state in the country that will require anyone who registers a .20 on the breathalyzer to undergo professional treatment. These people are typically repeat offenders and problem drinkers, and they are the most dangerous class of drunk drivers.

Our proposed law meets or exceeds three of the four requirements for receiving major federal grants for enforcement. The three requirements we meet or exceed are mandatory jail terms for repeat offenders, a blood alcohol content of .10 being sufficient evidence for conviction of impaired driving, and increased enforcement and public education. In order to receive supplementary federal grants, states will be required to meet eight of twenty-one additional criteria within three years. Representative Lancaster has concluded that we will meet fifteen of those requirements immediately.

An official of the Department of Transportation has said that our bill is the best and toughest he has seen, and I am confident we will be eligible for federal funds.[1] When you consider these unique features of our bill—along with such factors as the elimination of plea bargaining, the increase in the drinking age, and the automatic revocation of the driver's license of anyone under eighteen who drives with any amount of alcohol or drugs in his body—there emerges a very clear understanding that we are fighting drunk driving with more weapons and on more fronts than any other state.

I want to express my gratitude to Jack Stevens and his fellow members of the Governor's Task Force on Drunken Drivers for putting together the report on which this legislation is based. I asked Senator Henson Barnes and Representative Martin Lancaster to come out of the trenches long enough to be with me here today. These two outstanding legislators have spent countless hours guiding the Safe Roads Act through committee and to overwhelming passage on the floor. Every citizen of North Carolina owes them a debt of gratitude.

---

[1] Raymond A. Peck, Jr., a U.S. Department of Transportation administrator, tendered his assessment of North Carolina's anti-drunk driving bill on March 24, 1983. Four state legislators met with Peck and other officials to discuss the proposed act's compliance with federal guidelines. *Raleigh Times*, March 25, 1983.

NORTH CAROLINA MUSEUM OF ART OPENING

RALEIGH, APRIL 5, 1983

I stand here this afternoon with a deep feeling of excitement, a thrill of pride in what we have accomplished together. I also have the sense that maybe we've all been here before! Almost two years ago, we gathered here to dedicate this new building. Many of the faces I saw that afternoon I see today. Then we came together to admire and to dedicate a building—a fine building, but basically an empty one. That day, we walked on uncarpeted floors and looked at unfinished walls and talked about the promise of the future.

At last the future has become the present. Today we stand not just in a building, but in an art museum—the new North Carolina Museum of Art—ready to take its place among the great museums of this country and the world. Look around you now, and marvel at the monuments to mankind's creative spirit and unique vision through five thousand years. What is it that we have in North

Carolina that has brought us to this day of pride and accomplishment? I think the answer lies in those same qualities of creativity and vision, this time applied not to the fashioning of beautiful objects, but to the delicate art of leadership.

I'm not going to try to list every person and every organization whose leadership has contributed to the success of the North Carolina Museum of Art. The currents of creative vision run strong and deep through decades of our state's history, encompassing generations of leadership. They include artists, members of the North Carolina Art Society, and other citizens who began the push for a state museum; members of the General Assembly who responded first with money for a collection, then with support for the original museum, and finally with the foresight to provide for the design and construction of a new and fitting home. They include every governor for the past several decades, and leaders of our state's businesses and industries.

People of the highest caliber have pledged their commitment to the North Carolina Museum of Art—and, of course, I mean the people who are here today. If I asked each of you your reasons, I imagine I would hear seven or eight hundred different ones. The business leaders among you might say, "A great art museum makes North Carolina an attractive environment for our employees." Educators might say, "A fine art museum teaches in a way we can't in the classroom." You legislators might join me in saying, "We need a museum to provide the best of everything for our citizens."

But I think deep down, we all share an understanding of a few simple truths about art, art museums, and their rightful place in our state. We understand that a healthy, vital society creates art as an expression of its own vigor. We understand that a sensible society provides places where art is preserved, enjoyed, and encouraged, and we understand that the development of great art and great art museums depends upon vigorous protection of artistic freedom.

The protection of freedom is perhaps the ultimate test of creative leadership in any issue in our state and, indeed, in our nation. How many times have we all had to remind ourselves to step back a minute and resist the impulse to impose what we think is right on others who may have very different ideas? How many times have we been tempted to put our own priorities first and sweep other ideas aside? The temptation is there for all of us, but it is perhaps strongest for those who hold political and financial power.

This museum is not a showcase for a single artistic style or a particular political viewpoint. It is a statement to North Carolina's citizens and to the world that this state, her leaders, and her people understand the priceless qualities that art of every style, from every age, brings. Education, spiritual enrichment, essential balance for an existence too often tilted toward the harsh realities of survival— these are the gifts of art. These are the reasons you and I and generations of leaders who preceded us have supported the North Carolina Museum of Art.

I said a few moments ago that I wouldn't try to single out individuals who've made that commitment through the long history of this museum. But I find today, as I found two years ago, that I must acknowledge the extraordinary leadership of one person, one man whose sparkling creativity and deep love for his state gave us so much of what we value today. Robert Lee Humber of Pitt County had his own reasons for devoting many years of his life to the cause of a truly fine North Carolina Museum of Art. Five days before he died in 1970, he expressed them with unparalleled eloquence. He wrote, "I hope we can erect in Raleigh a Museum that will embody the spirit of our people, serve their cultural needs and become a center of international influence in the appreciation of art." [1]

I know there are members of Mr. Humber's family here today. I'm sure that Mr. Humber's vivid spirit is with us, too. I take great pleasure and enormous pride in being able to say to them, and to you, "At last we have it!" A museum to embody North Carolina's spirit of generosity, her drive for excellence, her deep appreciation for those who have come before and those yet to come. A museum to serve all our needs. A museum to share with our friends throughout the nation and the world. Ladies and gentlemen, welcome to the new North Carolina Museum of Art and to a new world of vision and creativity!

---

[1] Robert Lee Humber (1898-1970), state senator from Pitt County, 1959-1963. Previously identified in Mitchell, *Addresses of Hunt*, I, 800n. Quotation from letter from Humber to Ola Maie Foushee appeared in *Chapel Hill Newspaper*, November 18, 1970.

TESTIMONY BEFORE U.S. HOUSE COMMITTEE ON SMALL BUSINESS

RALEIGH, APRIL 11, 1983

I want to thank the House Small Business Committee for selecting North Carolina as a site for one of its hearings on small business. You've come to the right place for a number of reasons.

First, small business is the lifeblood of our economy. We have nearly 100,000 [small] businesses in North Carolina, each employing fewer than 20 persons. That represents nearly 90 percent of the businesses in our state. In fact, the average firm in North Carolina employs under 17 people.

Second, recognizing the importance of those companies to our economy, our administration has set out on a broad front to provide assistance to small business. In 1980 we established the Small

Business Advocacy Council.[1] Through a series of statewide hearings, that council focused attention on the importance and needs of small business. That increased participation of small business in government helped convince the General Assembly to create House and Senate small business committees for the first time.

We created the state's first Business Assistance Division, which provides technical, financial, and managerial advice to small businesses. Part of that division is the Minority Business Development Agency headed by Assistant Secretary of Commerce Lew Myers.[2] Among the many accomplishments of that agency is publication of the nation's finest minority business directory. I have brought the newest version of that directory with me today for your information.

Other activities have included organizing a series of meetings between chief executive officers of major corporations to meet with their counterparts in minority-owned firms. Those meetings have resulted in hundreds of thousands of dollars in sales. We have held buyer-supplier conferences between small businesses and large corporations. We have appointed blacks, Indians, and women to boards and commissions that deal directly with economic development.

But we are not satisfied with the progress that has been made. We are supporting state legislation that would enable local government to create its own outreach programs to encourage purchase of goods and services from small and minority businesses. We are continuing to increase funding for the state's Minority Business Development Agency, and I have recently asked our State Goals and Policy Board to undertake an intensive study of the needs of small business in the state and to make recommendations for further assistance—particularly in the area of financing.

Congressman Mitchell,[3] I share your concern that many small businesses in this country never get started because of financing. The continual double-digit interest rates make start-up of a new business more risky than usual for normal financial outlets. People interested in starting a small business are caught almost in a Catch-22 situation: They can get a loan if they have a proven track record, but they can't develop a track record unless they can get a loan to get started. With great courage and hard work and ingenuity, some minority business men and women in North Carolina have managed to break out of that cycle. Some of them are here today and I would urge you to pay special attention to their comments, based on firsthand experience.

This is not a problem that will be solved by any one level of government. The private sector will continue to be a key player. But looking at the changes under way in our country—with large companies accounting for fewer jobs—it's essential to our future that we act to strengthen the position of small businesses in our state and this country.

[1] Executive Order No. 51, signed May 16, 1980, created the North Carolina Small Business Advocacy Council. *N.C. Session Laws, 1979, Second Session, 1980,* 307-309. It was amended by Executive Order No. 87, of November 8, 1982. *N.C. Session Laws, 1983,* 1410.

[2] Lewis H. Myers (1946-   ), resident of Durham; B.A., Franklin and Marshall College, 1968; M.B.A., University of North Carolina at Chapel Hill, 1974. Executive director, Harvard Project Upward Bound, Harvard University, 1969-1971; community affairs director, 1971-1973, and associate director, 1973-1976, Soul City Foundation; assistant vice-president, and later, vice-president for corporate and institutional development, 1976-1978, and vice-president and director of marketing, 1978-1979, Soul City Company; private economic, industrial, and community development consultant, 1979-1980; Minority Business Development Agency director, 1980-1981, and assistant secretary, since 1982, state Commerce Department. Lewis H. Myers to Jan-Michael Poff, August 28, 1985.

[3] Parren J. Mitchell (1922-   ), native, resident of Baltimore, Maryland; B.A., Morgan State College, 1950; M.A., University of Maryland, 1952; served in U.S. Army during World War II. Morgan State College professor and assistant director, Urban Studies Institute; executive secretary, Maryland Commission on Interracial Problems and Relations, 1963-1965; executive director, Baltimore Community Action Agency, 1965-1968; first elected to U.S. House from Maryland's Seventh Congressional District in 1970 and returned in subsequent elections; chairman, House Committee on Small Business; Democrat. Barone and Ujifusa, *Almanac of American Politics, 1984,* 527.

STATEMENT ON OFFSHORE OIL AND GAS EXPLORATION

RALEIGH, APRIL 20, 1983

[Unless certain areas were exempted from the U.S. Interior Department's July, 1983, sale of offshore oil and natural gas drilling leases, the Hunt administration warned, North Carolina would begin legal proceedings to block the entire offering — 5,718 tracts, stretching from the Outer Banks to Florida. At the heart of the dispute lay 151 parcels, covering 1,359 square miles of ocean bottom and ranging fifteen to thirty miles from the North Carolina shore; the governor outlined his objections to the inclusion of this territory, in the federal sale, in his statement of April 20. Less than a month later, on May 13, Washington officials announced that the tracts in question would be deleted if North Carolina dropped its proposed lawsuit. James A. Summers, then deputy secretary of natural resources and community development, acknowledged the state's tentative approval of the arrangement, noting that final judgment awaited a written copy of the agreement and its review by the attorney general's staff. In 1981 North Carolina sued to halt the sale of six tracts twelve miles off the Outer Banks, but the action was terminated after buyers failed to show interest in them. *Fayetteville Observer,* July 25, 1982; *News and Observer,* May 14, 1983.]

A proposed federal offshore lease sale for oil and gas exploration includes 151 tracts that pose an unacceptable risk to our environment. I will inform Secretary of the Interior James Watt this week that the state of North Carolina is prepared to go to court to force the deletion of these tracts from the sale.

In its final environmental impact statement and notice of sale for South Atlantic Lease Sale 78, the Department of the Interior disregarded my administration's recommendations that the tracts be deleted. These recommendations were based on the need to protect North Carolina's fishing interests, our tourism industry, and the site of the U.S.S. *Monitor* Marine Sanctuary. My administration has consistently supported an accelerated offshore leasing program as a means of reducing our dependence upon foreign energy sources, but that program should take into account the natural, cultural, and social integrity of our coast.

Exploration of these tracts presents an excessive risk of an oil spill reaching our coast and resulting in disastrous consequences for tourism and the fishing industry. Oceanographic experts have indicated that Interior's environmental impact statement seriously underestimates this risk. Further, the questionable potential for discovery of oil and gas on these tracts does not justify endangering a national treasure, the U.S.S. *Monitor*. The people of North Carolina are willing to do their share for energy independence, but that does not mean they are ready to throw caution to the wind and unnecessarily endanger the resources that make economic security possible.

We will continue to work with Secretary Watt in the hope that this matter can be resolved in a way that is consistent with the protection of our environment. If that is not successful, we will pursue all available legal remedies to stop this sale.

SOUTHERN CORRECTIONAL
CENTER DEDICATION

TROY, MAY 20, 1983

[Hunt restated, below, positions expressed in remarks at the dedication of Central Prison, September 9, 1982, and of Eastern Correctional Center, April 18, 1983.]

I am honored to be with you today to dedicate Southern Correctional Center. This dedication ceremony marks the completion of a $110 million expansion program for North Carolina's correctional system that was started over six years ago. We have moved forward; we have made progress, and with this dedication ceremony today we are affirming our determination to keep North Carolina a safe, secure, and beautiful place.

Just last month I dedicated this facility's twin institution, Eastern Correctional Center in Greene County, and I want you to know that good, old-fashioned southern hospitality was shown to us. As we waited to leave, those huge gates finally rolled back, and the armed guards stepped aside to let us out. One of them smiled at me and said, "I hope you come back to see us real soon."

This institution has been built on a foundation of cooperation and understanding by all of you here today—members of the General Assembly, Montgomery County commissioners and public officials, district and superior court judges, mayors, law enforcement officials, and concerned, involved citizens everywhere. I particularly want to thank our legislators who had the vision and courage to respond to our state's need for additional prison space.

I think North Carolina's taxpayers got their money's worth. By duplicating the design for the Southern and Eastern Correctional centers, we saved $380,000 in architectural and engineering fees. By using wood-burning boilers instead of oil furnaces, fuel savings will be close to $55,000 each year at these institutions. The annual payroll here will mean $3.5 million for Montgomery County's economy.

Both of these correctional centers will play an important role in North Carolina's war against crime. They will help relieve our overcrowding problem. We have 17,000 inmates in a system designed for 15,283—and that is a serious problem—but we cannot allow that problem to make us lose sight of the fact that prison is a place to punish lawbreakers. We need and must have safe and secure prisons.

But our prisons must also be a place where criminals can learn to become useful and productive citizens. Under the guidance of Superintendent Michael Bumgarner,[1] this center will teach inmates a useful skill, a trade they can use to rebuild their lives. They'll work with Montgomery Technical College and with programs operated within the prison to help them complete their high school degrees.

Some prisoners can and should be rehabilitated and reformed. For some, however, the only answer is a prison cell. Let me make it clear that we in North Carolina are prepared to build all the prisons we need to fight crime and protect our people.

But we cannot afford to build more prisons than we need. That is why we must use alternative forms of punishment where they will work. We need a strong program of community correction.

Building prisons is important, but it is not the only answer to crime. We must try to turn people—particularly young people— away from the road that eventually leads to prison. We need more one-on-one programs where an adult provides friendship, help, and leadership for a young person. But in the end, if our best efforts sometimes fail, we need punishment that is swift, sure, and severe. That is the best deterrent to crime.

I hope all of you here today will rededicate yourselves to preventing crime and making this state a safe and secure place. We have got to work together to turn young people away from crime. We must instill respect for the law. We must work to build a society where order and respect and kindness rise above the confusion and chaos that can ruin lives. It is not just a job for the sheriff, or the police, or the judges, or the prisons. It is a job for each and every one of us.

To those of you who have dedicated your lives to that job, to making us all safe, let me express my sincere thanks. To Secretary Jim Woodard, Rae McNamara,[2] Superintendent Bumgarner, and all the staff here, I want to express my thanks and good wishes. North Carolina is proud of you and grateful to you. And, as your governor, I am proud to dedicate this facility. I hope it stands for a safer North Carolina for all of us.

---

[1] Michael E. Bumgarner (1947-), native of Charlotte; resident of Montgomery County; A.B., Davidson College, 1970; Master of Urban Administration, University of North Carolina at Charlotte, 1983; U.S. Army Reserve, 1970-1977. Correctional programs supervisor, 1972-1973, and case analyst supervisor, 1973-1974, South Piedmont Area Diagnostic Center; program director III, 1974-1979, South Piedmont Area Office; assistant superintendent for programs, 1979-1982, and superintendent IV, since 1982, Piedmont Correctional Center. Michael E. Bumgarner to Jan-Michael Poff, November 27, 1985.

[2] Rae H. McNamara (1939-), native of Beaufort; resident of Raleigh; B.A., Duke University; M.Ed., North Carolina State University. Former schoolteacher, state government personnel analyst; staff member, Commission on Correctional Programs, 1975-1977; parole commissioner, 1977-1981; director, Division of Prisons, Department of Correction, 1981-1985. Rae H. McNamara to Jan-Michael Poff, October 5, 1983; News and Observer, March 14, 1985.

STATEMENT ON INTERSTATE 40

WILMINGTON, MAY 24, 1983

[The *Wilmington Morning Star* and Governor Hunt found themselves at odds over the source of construction funds for the I-40 connector between Wilmington and Benson. The newspaper supported a plan under which the project was eligible for 95 percent federal funding. Hunt, however, preferred an alternative financial avenue; his opposition to the 95 percent plan drew criticism from the *Morning Star*, which speculated that the governor considered completion of I-40 a low-priority matter. In response to those charges, Hunt explained his position in the following statement—and in a letter, which appeared in the April 30, 1983, issue of the *Morning Star*. *Wilmington Morning Star*, April 21, 22, 30, May 6, 25, 26, 1983.]

I am delighted to be in Wilmington today, because it gives me the opportunity to tell the people of southeastern North Carolina firsthand of my administration's commitment to extend I-40 from Benson to Wilmington. I have said repeatedly that if this region—

and indeed all of North Carolina—is to realize its tremendous economic potential, this project must be completed.

I feel it necessary to restate that commitment today because, frankly, the editorial page of the *Wilmington Star-News* and other parties have misinformed the people of this area about this issue. The fact is that I-40 has remained on schedule during a time when the Board of Transportation has scaled down other projects to the tune of $1.2 billion. Here is how the I-40 project has fared since we began work in 1978:

—All of the right of way has been acquired for the entire 91.4 miles from Benson to Wilmington.

—Since November of 1978, $97.7 million has been authorized for the project, including $32.6 million in state funds. This commitment represents 43 percent of the estimated cost of the entire project.

—Contracts for grading, structures, and paving for the 31-mile section from N.C. 132 at Wilmington to U.S. 117 south of Wallace have been awarded, and that work is scheduled to be completed by May of 1986.

This project has received the heaviest funding and the most accelerated scheduling of any project in North Carolina during my administration. In fact, no highway has been built in this short a time, with so much money, in the past quarter century. Given all of the resources that have gone into this effort, my administration is not about to retreat from the commitment to build a modern, east-west system of highways to link the port of Wilmington to the interstate system through the piedmont and the mountains.

Now, a great deal of debate has been generated about the state/federal funding formula for I-40. It is true that this project is eligible for 95 percent federal funding, as compared to the normal 75 percent. It has been suggested that opting for 95 percent federal money would result in a savings to the state.[1] But that savings would come at the expense of every other highway project in the state. I-40 is the only project eligible for funding under the 95-5 formula.

To adopt the 95-5 formula, then, would result in the appropriation of fewer state dollars for our highway program. While it would accelerate work on I-40, it would unfairly delay other vitally needed projects—such as U.S. 17, U.S. 74, and U.S. 117. These pressing transportation needs can be met in a fair and equitable way only if the General Assembly provides the funds necessary to fully match our share of federal highway aid.[2] Additionally, the Federal Highway Administration is expected to make available still more federal funds in August to qualifying states; to qualify, North Carolina must provide the state matching funds. This money would allow us to move further ahead with I-40 and other important priorities.

It was suggested by one editorial writer here that my administration has "betrayed" southeastern North Carolina with respect to

I-40.[3] The history of this project demonstrates that this is not true. Everyone here, including me, is anxious to know how much money we can put into I-40 in the immediate future. It would be premature and irresponsible for me to speculate on that before the General Assembly acts to appropriate matching funds. You may rest assured, however, that my recommendation to the Board of Transportation later this year will reflect my determination to proceed with I-40 as fast as possible.

---

[1] State Representative Harry Payne, a Democrat from New Hanover County who supported the 95 percent federal funding plan, estimated that the savings to North Carolina would amount to $14 million over two years. *Wilmington Morning Star*, May 6, 26, 1983.

[2] A reserve to match federal highway funds was established by *N.C. Session Laws, 1983*, c. 761, s. 8a. Section 8a was repealed under c. 1034, s. 201, *N.C. Session Laws, 1983, Second Session, 1984.*

[3] *Wilmington Morning Star*, April 30, 1983.

JOINT MEETING, SEMICONDUCTOR RESEARCH CORPORATION AND SEMICONDUCTOR INDUSTRY ASSOCIATION

RESEARCH TRIANGLE PARK, MAY 26, 1983

[From 1981 to 1985, the Hunt administration worked diligently to attract microelectronics firms to the state, with some notable successes having been announced in 1983: GTE Communications Systems Division, E. I. du Pont de Nemours and Co., and Sumitomo Electric Industries, of Osaka, Japan, unveiled plans to establish research and development facilities in Research Triangle Park, and Mitsubishi Electric Co. confirmed its intention to build a $29 million microchip production plant in northern Durham County. In 1984 the state added such microelectronics heavyweights as Wang Laboratories, Inc., Semicon, Inc., and West Germany's Dynamit Nobel AG to its growing list of high-technology newcomers. Significantly, the annual American survey conducted by Britain's *Electronics Location File* indicated that, by 1984, North Carolina had risen to fifth place—from tenth position a year earlier—in nationwide esteem as a location for new electronics manufacturing and commercial operations. "News Release from the Governor's Office," August 13, 1984.

However, one juicy, high-tech plum eluded the state's grasp. By the spring of 1983, Microelectronics and Computer Technology Corp., or MCC, had narrowed its consideration of possible headquarters sites to four choices: Research Triangle Park, Atlanta, San Diego, and Austin. Suspense ended on May 13 when Bobby Ray Inman, president of the heavily recruited, eleven-company consortium established to design and research software and componentry for future generations of computers, declared that Texas's capital was to become MCC's home. Although it was widely recognized that the corporation, once operational, would entice other high-technology research, development, and manufacturing concerns to relocate nearby, bringing hundreds of jobs, North Carolina nevertheless could not afford to match the inducements the Lone Star state used to lure MCC to Austin: a $15 million pledge to Texas universities for computer science training, relocation assistance for MCC employees, the use of private aircraft, a 200,000 square-foot research facility, and a multi-million-dollar, low-interest loan subsidy package. *Durham Morning Herald*, May 18, 21, 24, 1983.]

I know many of you are joining us here straight from a meeting in Texas yesterday, and I want to welcome you to North Carolina. I hope you enjoy your visit here and get to see our beautiful state, and I hope you will return often. We have a number of our state officials here for your meeting, and they will be glad to answer any questions you have or help you in any way we can to make your visit here both enjoyable and profitable to you. I understand George Herbert and others from the Research Triangle community have invited you to a reception later this afternoon at the National Humanities Center here in the park. This is something we are very proud of. It was located here after a national site selection process— and one where we obviously were successful. It's something we are very proud of, and I think you will enjoy seeing the building and learning a little about the program it holds.

I do want to talk a little this morning about another site selection process—one you are all familiar with, and one where we were not so successful—and that is with MCC. Some of you here in the room were involved in the site selection for this exciting program, and I want to say at the outset that I was very impressed with the selection process itself and the professional way in which it was conducted. All of you can be proud of the industry leaders involved in this and proud of Bob Inman[1] for his outstanding contributions.

I would be less than candid if I did not say we were disappointed by the outcome. We wanted those folks here. There's no question about that. We worked very hard to structure a good representation to them, and I want to touch on this in just a minute.

But let me say at the outset that all of the people here agree that our participation in this nationwide competition was a very enriching experience for us and one that, we believe, will benefit us tremendously. We now are much more aware of our strengths and our commitment to build a national center of excellence here in North Carolina that will benefit the entire semiconductor industry. You will hear later on this afternoon from Don Beilman, president of the Microelectronics Center of North Carolina, about the $40 million center that is the focal point of our efforts. We are aware of areas in which we need to do more work and we are taking steps to strengthen our program, particularly in the computer science area. Within a few months, seven new faculty positions will be filled at our state universities and five new positions at Duke University, which is a partner in our efforts here.

I think one of the things we gained out of the search process was a better understanding of your needs, a new height of awareness of your goals, and how we might best work together to meet those goals—and I think I speak for our state officials, our university leaders, members of our General Assembly, and our local officials when I say this. All of us emerged from this process even more firmly committed to a strong North Carolina program of excellence.

Finally, let me mention one thing about the proposal we made to MCC, and I think it is important for everyone to understand this: Our proposal was structured to draw on the strengths of our existing program in microelectronics and on our plans for the future. We have a long history in our state of not offering subsidies to industries to locate here, and in the case of MCC, we made a decision early on that we would not deviate from that policy which, by and large, has served us well. We did not offer this consortium a single thing that is not available to any company represented in this room today, and I hope all of you understand and appreciate that.

Obviously we wanted MCC here. We think we have a lot to offer: a good program, a good living and working environment, and in the case of MCC, that it would find a lot of support for its efforts here. We are enormously proud that we were one of the final four sites to be considered, and we certainly wish MCC well in its new location. But I did want you to know that the plans we have made—our goals, our promises, our commitment, our partnership with industry —all of this will continue here as we build a national center of excellence for the semiconductor industry.

The work that we are doing, and that you are doing through the Semiconductor Research Corporation [SRC], is of enormous importance. It addresses one of the most crucial challenges facing our country today. It is a challenge in which every single American has a stake—Americans who need a good job, and American businesses who need markets for their products and services. It is a challenge that will determine the future vitality of the American economy and of our society. It is the challenge we face to maintain America's technological advantage in the world marketplace.

The semiconductor industry is already intimately familiar with this challenge. For several years your companies have dealt with stiff competition from semiconductor manufacturers in other countries. SRC represents one of the most important strategies you have devised for outthinking and outperforming your foreign competition.

North Carolina is proud that SRC's headquarters is here. We're proud to be part of SRC's work that will benefit semiconductor manufacturers throughout the country. Through the Semiconductor Research Corporation, your industry is providing direct support for basic research at colleges and universities throughout our nation. I am very aware that you have signed contracts for nearly $400,000 in research with our schools here in North Carolina; and I was delighted to learn that a $550,000 research contract was signed just yesterday by SRC and the Microelectronics Center of North Carolina, which acted on behalf of its five constituent research universities. This will be a strong part of our partnership efforts with industry.

You've cut out duplication, you've used faculty expertise instead of maintaining your own large research staffs, and you've started solving problems. SRC is truly a leader and North Carolina is proud to be your partner, and we want to be a partner of whom you can be proud.

I firmly believe state and local governments have an essential role to play in helping industry meet overseas competition. To begin with, government must understand and address the needs of industry. That means fair taxation; we must remain tax competitive, and we must maintain regulatory policies that promote a good business climate—and I believe that's what we've done in North Carolina.

At my press conference this week, I was delighted to announce that North Carolina is on the way to one of its best years ever in industrial growth. We've just had our best first quarter in history by attracting almost a half billion dollars worth of new and expanded industries. Our first quarter investment total was $490.9 million, over 40 percent higher than the same period last year. Combining that quarter with investments announced in April, our total industrial growth so far this year has been $624 million. For the first four months of last year, the total was $481 million; the total for last year was $1.3 billion.

Since January, 1977, North Carolina has attracted $11.5 billion in industrial development and created 185,000 new manufacturing jobs. The economy here is bullish; it's improving, and we are going to make it even better. We're going to make it better because we are committed to excellence in education. We are committed to making our schools educate for economic growth and jobs for the twenty-first century.

I think here in North Carolina we have provided optimistic, positive answers to some of the problems troubling American education:

—We've adopted annual testing programs and implemented a Primary Reading Program, and our children are now above the national average in reading and mathematics.

—We have established the nation's only tuition-free residential high school for talented math and science students, and last year the North Carolina School of Science and Mathematics graduated the second-largest number of National Merit Scholars in the country.

—And we have established strong ties to the business community, both in our state and nationally through the Task Force on Education for Economic Growth, which I chair along with Frank Cary of IBM and Governor Pete du Pont of Delaware,[2] to devise new strategies to meet our education and economic growth needs.

The answers to overseas competition are right here. They're not in Washington—not with federal cutbacks in education and reductions in basic and applied research. If we are optimistic and positive about our partnership between business and government, then we will meet the competition head-on and we will win.

We have a partnership here in North Carolina between business, government, and education. Our Microelectronics Center is a shining example of that partnership spirit. The new contract SRC and the Microelectronics Center have signed is another demonstration that the partnership spirit is alive and well here in the park. It pays off for both education and business.

There is a wave of a change sweeping over the world. But I think that if we work together—North Carolina, the Semiconductor Research Corporation, and all of our businesses and schools—we can ride that wave to a new day.

---

[1] Bobby Ray Inman (1931-   ), native of Rhonesboro, Texas; B.A., University of Texas, 1950; was graduated from National War College, 1972; U.S. Navy, 1952-1981. Navy admiral; Naval Intelligence director, 1974-1976; Defense Intelligence Agency vice-director, 1976-1977; National Security Agency director, 1977-1981; Central Intelligence Agency deputy director, 1981-1982; appointed director of MCC, 1982. "MCC Moves out of the Idea Stage," *Science*, June 17, 1983, 1256; *Who's Who in America, 1982-1983*, I, 1633.

[2] Frank Taylor Cary (1920-   ), has held various positions with International Business Machines since 1948; president, since 1971, and board chairman and chief executive officer, since 1973, of IBM. *Who's Who in America, 1982-1983*, I, 532; also previously identified in Mitchell, *Addresses of Hunt*, I, 491n.

Pierre S. (Pete) du Pont IV (1935-   ), native, resident of Wilmington, Delaware; B.S.E., Princeton University, 1956; LL.B., Harvard University, 1963; U.S. Navy, 1957-1960. Business executive, Photo Products Division, E. I. du Pont and Co., 1963-1970; member, Delaware House, 1968-1970; member, U.S. House, 1971-1977; governor of Delaware, 1977-1981, 1981-1985; Republican. Barone and Ujifusa, *Almanac of American Politics, 1984*, 224.

AFFIRMATIVE ACTION CONFERENCE

RALEIGH, JUNE 2, 1983

I have come here today to reaffirm the state of North Carolina's obligation and responsibility to lead this nation in providing equal opportunity for all our citizens. I know all of you are here because you have dedicated your careers and your lives to the goals of affirmative action and equal opportunity. You are committed to building something better, something more perfect and more equal for those who will follow us. That is my goal as governor of this state. That is our vision together.

Affirmative action programs grew out of the great civil rights wave that swept this nation in the 1960s. Those programs were designed not to win victories at the expense of others, but to win victories for all of us. Those programs, and all of you, were committed to a spirit that would raise all of us up to a new plateau.

But now we see Washington trying to turn back the clock to another era. What is this nation to think when we are confronted with a wholesale firing of three Civil Rights Commission members whose philosophies were not in tune with that of the current administration?[1] Let me say here today that North Carolina will not retreat.

This nation should stand for basic human rights and simple human dignity, and that commitment should not flutter up and down like a political flag in the wind. We cannot and we will not be a land of true opportunity until we are known as the land of equal opportunity, equal for all. Good intentions will not lift up this land and all our people. Real accomplishments and affirmative action programs that work will lift us up to new heights.

The purpose and intent of affirmative action is clear. As a people, we have made a decision to address the basic inequities that exist in this land. Time, effort, vision, and *commitment* will carry us forward. And until that great day when there is equal opportunity for all, affirmative action programs and laws will ensure equal access for men and women, blacks and whites, Indians, the handicapped—all our citizens.

Over the past five years, North Carolina has made progress in reducing the underrepresentation of women and minorities in state government. In 1977 minorities made up 20.2 percent of state government's total work force. Today they number 24.3 percent. In 1977 women were 38.5 percent of our work force. Today they compose 40.5 percent of our workers.

That is progress, and I think we should all be pleased. But we should not be satisfied, because hiring is just the beginning. State government has a special responsibility to keep women and minorities in the work force and help them progress as they grow in their jobs. Women represent 49.5 percent, and minorities represent 14.3 percent, of North Carolina's professional employees. But women represent only 17.1 percent of our state's officials and administrators, and minorities represent only 7.9 percent. There's plenty of room for improvement in both of these occupational categories.

Our state's managers have used the Work Planning and Performance Review program as their primary management tool to ensure fairness as they make decisions on promotions. We've made progress in a tight economy, but we are not satisfied.

As governor of this state, I want to reaffirm state government's commitment to the affirmative action policy established by our State Personnel Commission. I am ordering additional steps to make sure that policy is followed. I am asking the North Carolina Human Relations Council to advise both the Office of State Personnel and me in the implementation of a strong and effective state affirmative action policy. I am also asking the Office of State Personnel to submit semiannual reports to me on our affirmative action progress.

There is still more we can do. Through our schools, community colleges, and universities, we must encourage women and minorities to obtain the training and skills they will need in the new occupations of the twenty-first century. We must tear down the barriers that have confined women and minorities, Indians, the elderly, and the handicapped to traditional jobs—or no job at all—and we must build up our schools, our math, science, and vocational training programs that will prepare all our workers for a new century. The schooling, training, and job-preparedness of all Americans in the 1980s will be directly linked to American productivity and economic success in the twenty-first century. If we waste the talents and abilities of any one group, if we confine anyone's skills, then we will have wasted our national strength.

I wish all of you good luck. I wish you the strength of your convictions, and I hope you will remember something Martin Luther King wrote from a Birmingham jail cell in 1963: "Injustice anywhere," he wrote, "is a threat to justice everywhere." [2]

Let us work together for justice everywhere.

---

[1] President Reagan removed three of the six members of the Commission on Civil Rights in mid-1983, replacing them with persons opposed to busing and racial quotas. "In Trouble with Blacks," *Time*, June 6, 1983, 28.

[2] Martin Luther King, Jr.'s letter from Birmingham jail quoted in Bartlett, *Familiar Quotations*, 1082.

STATEWIDE CONFERENCE
ON SCHOOL DISCIPLINE

RALEIGH, JUNE 16, 1983

[Hunt credited the preventative programs established during his administration with reducing the state's high school dropout rate from 31.2 percent in 1977 to 28.2 percent in 1983. Speaking before the Governor's Eastern North Carolina Conference on School Dropouts on March 8, 1983, Governor Hunt expressed the hope that the number of students leaving without graduating could be cut to 10 percent by 1990.]

We have gathered here today for an exciting and compelling reason: to seek new answers and new solutions that will improve school discipline and strengthen the classroom learning environment in schools throughout North Carolina.

We've all heard so much lately about what's wrong in our nation's schools. Lagging salaries, inadequate facilities, weak curricula, classrooms isolated from the community's expertise and help—all of these problems are real. Yet there are good things happening in the schools, particularly in North Carolina. There are shining examples of excellence. Our achievement test scores are up. Our children are learning more. The list of good things, of positive accomplishments, is a long one.

To have the kind of quality education we must have, our classrooms must have a climate that encourages learning and performance. Excellence in education can flourish only in an atmosphere of rigor, standards, and high expectations. That atmosphere fosters a respect for learning, a respect for the teacher, a respect for the school, a respect for other people and, most of all, self-respect. And that respect is the beginning of the answer to many of the education problems our nation faces.

School discipline means self-discipline. It means a sense of individual responsibility, a code of behavior, and a sense of right and wrong.

North Carolina has achieved a long list of firsts in education. Today, we add another: the pilot project of the Statewide Interagency School Discipline Program. I want to take a moment to thank and congratulate each one of the communities and school systems which participated in this project: the city of Washington; Wilmington-New Hanover County; and Northampton, Sampson, Columbus, Union, Iredell, Alamance, and Buncombe counties. I also want to thank the Governor's Crime Commission, the Department of Public Instruction, and the Interagency Committee. Through open minds, cooperation, and creativity, all of you have built a working school discipline model for North Carolina and the entire country. And we are proud of you.

The message you brought to us is that discipline is not just the school's concern—it is everyone's concern and responsibility. It's not just one person's job. It's a community job. Do the parents keep track of their children's activities both in and out of school? That's an important determinant of behavior. Do the agencies and institutions of the community, in partnership with the schools, support those students who are becoming discipline problems?

Academic performance is also a key factor in discipline. Perhaps the most critical element here is expectation, what others expect of the student and what the student expects of himself or herself. For the student who loses his perspective, that tragic circle of low expectations and academic disappointment is followed by misbehavior and failure. That tragedy must be stopped. We must rebuild for that student a new learning discipline and self-respect. We must rebuild a curriculum broad and flexible enough to challenge the student and offer a measure of success. Most importantly, we must reduce class size and improve the quality of the student-teacher relationship.

From our Statewide Interagency School Discipline Program we have found that community partnerships are the key in rebuilding that disciplined learning environment. That partnership starts with a strong tone set by the principal. That is the key to everything. Trust between students and teachers in a stable environment is vital, and you must establish deep ties between the schools and the community. Everyone has a job—superintendents, school boards, county commissioners, law enforcement officials, judges, court counselors, and representatives of community agencies. In Union County, for example, the local mental health center and schools have joined forces to help students who are involved with drugs. The center has given fifteen hours per week of a counselor's time to work with students facing severe family strife.

I think we've all come to the conclusion that all the answers are not in Washington. But that's Washington, D.C. In *our* city of Washington, the high school dropout rate has been cut by 25 percent. They had an 18 percent reduction in absenteeism and cut high school suspensions from ninety-four to forty-six this year. They accomplished all of that because they went the extra mile. They brought in area ministers to counsel students who were constantly in trouble. For the parents of students with the most severe discipline problems, the schools held a workshop; they offered volunteer baby-sitting and a free ride to the workshops. The parents, many of whom had given up hope, came to find new answers.

The good news and success stories poured out of every community. The new guidebook for implementing a discipline program, which you have received today, will outline many strategies and ideas for you. The scope of our problem is nowhere near what is taking place in other states, but that does not reduce our level of concern. We want North Carolina education to be synonymous with excellence in education. *We* will set the standard for excellence.

School discipline and the improvement of our classroom learning environment must be a priority for all of us, and I am counting on the Governor's Crime Commission, the Department of Public Instruction, and our Interagency Committee to help expand our school discipline program to communities all across North Carolina. The self-discipline and self-respect that we seek to build will not be accomplished overnight. What we are building is a value system.

But we must start now. I wish all of you good luck and Godspeed as you begin to form these new partnerships in learning for your community.

GOVERNOR'S CONFERENCE ON ALCOHOL LAW ENFORCEMENT

RALEIGH, JUNE 23, 1983

I am proud to be here with all of you, the people who make North Carolina a safer place to live. I want you to know that you are appreciated and respected, and I am counting on your leadership in several new initiatives that will make North Carolina roads and highways safer—particularly for our young people.

North Carolina has shown the nation that we mean business when we say the drunk driver has no place on our roads. We have taken a bold and historic step with the passage of the Safe Roads Act. Now that we have the nation's toughest drunk driving law, we must back up that law in three ways: strict enforcement, swift and sure punishment by our courts, and—most importantly—the support and cooperation of all North Carolinians.

Today we will review with you our strategy to implement the new Safe Roads Act. You will hear from Crime Control and Public Safety deputy secretary Bob Melott,[1] Alcoholic Law Enforcement Division director Don Murray,[2] Bill Powell of our Alcoholic Board of Control,[3] and representatives of the Raleigh and Greensboro police departments. You will receive a thorough briefing on the provisions of the Safe Roads Act. We will discuss how state and local law enforcement agencies can cooperate, and you will hear about the very tough sanctions our Alcoholic Board of Control will be handing out.

But you will also hear something else. You will hear about our response to a crime that has reached epidemic proportions in North Carolina: the crime of selling alcohol to minors. As a result of several undercover operations, we have documented the scope of this problem. The scores are in, and they are outrageous.

In Greensboro, the score was 95 out of 110. An undercover, underage agent bought beer in 95 out of 110 stores, and some even sold to her after she produced an I.D. which showed she was only 16 years old. In Raleigh, 51 stores out of 54 sold illegally to an underage agent. Just last week, the Roxboro Police Department announced the results of its undercover operation: 28 out of 41 businesses sold illegally.

This is intolerable. An overwhelming majority of businesses in each one of these undercover operations just thumbed their noses at the law. For the price of a three-dollar six-pack, they broke the law and sent an underage young person out the door and onto the highway with alcohol. I hope the message that will go out from here today is loud and clear: North Carolina will not tolerate that type of behavior. It is unacceptable, it is illegal, and it will be stopped.

In response to this blatant flouting of the law, our Alcoholic Board of Control will suspend the ABC permit of first-time violators for a minimum of thirty days. Three days of that suspension will be active and the remaining twenty-seven days suspended for one year. And for repeat offenders, the penalties get even tougher.

I have directed our Alcoholic Law Enforcement [ALE] Division to expand its undercover operations in the area of illegal sales to minors. We are going to get very tough. Every business that sells alcohol to a young person better make sure that the buyer is of legal age, because the next time they sell to a young person that buyer could be an undercover agent.

We will be tough, but we will also be fair. To clarify our procedures and prevent any abuses, a detailed directive has been sent to all ALE offices. This crackdown is not an attempt to harass, handcuff, or punish responsible businesses. It is meant to save lives.

ALE will fully cooperate with our sheriffs, local police, district attorneys, and community agencies. We know that we will never be able to police every dark highway or irresponsible business in this state. But with your help, we can build a cooperative partnership among all law enforcement agencies. We can also build a spirit of voluntary compliance among North Carolina businesses and communities.

I think that spirit is growing stronger every day. Stories are already coming back to me that more and more businesses are carefully checking I.D.s. They are training their checkout people and providing them with firm instructions about selling alcohol to young people: Be legal or be gone. I want to congratulate the 7-Eleven and Fast Fare stores for setting an excellent example with their advertising campaigns and self-policing efforts. They are willing to go that extra mile to make sure they are not selling alcohol to a minor.

I hope every North Carolina retail establishment will get behind the Safe Roads Act and help us make this a statewide community project, a project that will bring us closer together and literally save young lives. Many of you probably read about the four teenagers who died last February in that horrible automobile accident. Three of them were seventeen years old, and one was sixteen. They breezed into a store, bought some beer, and off they went. Four sets of parents received early Saturday morning telephone calls. The newspapers reprinted one parent's reaction to that telephone call: "Oh God," the father said, "it was terrible."

Life is too precious to be thrown away like that. But with your help and cooperation, we can put a stop to those early morning telephone calls. We can make North Carolina roads the nation's safest roads.

---

[1] Robert Arthur Melott (1936-   ), native of Steubenville, Ohio; resident of Raleigh; B.S., United States Military Academy, 1958; J.D., University of North Carolina at Chapel Hill, 1965; U.S. Army, 1958-1961. Federal Bureau of Investigation special agent, 1961-1963; attorney in private practice, since 1965; assistant dean, 1967-1972, and executive director, 1971-1974, North Carolina Law Center; faculty member, University of North Carolina law school, 1967-1975; deputy secretary, Crime Control and Public Safety Department, 1980-1985; state special attorney general, since 1985. Robert Arthur Melott to Jan-Michael Poff, August 27, 1985.

[2] Donald M. Murray (1929-   ), native of Buffalo, New York; resident of Raleigh; B.S., Canisius College, 1955; U.S. Army, 1952-1954. Federal Bureau of Investigation senior agent, 1955-1979; Alcohol Law Enforcement Division director, Crime Control and Public Safety Department, since 1980. Donald M. Murray to Jan-Michael Poff, August 28, 1985.

[3] William O. Powell (1951-   ), native, resident of Oxford; A.A., Chowan College, 1976; B.S.B.A., East Carolina University, 1978; U.S. Army, 1971-1974; has served in North Carolina National Guard since 1980. Deputy administrator, North Carolina Alcoholic Beverage Control Commission, 1979-1985; administrative coordinator, Empire Distributors, since 1985. William O. Powell to Jan-Michael Poff, August 29, 1985.

STATEMENT ON HAZARDOUS WASTES

RALEIGH, JUNE 30, 1983

As the General Assembly moves into the final weeks of this session, two bills remain that are critically important to the growth of our economy and the protection of our environment.

These bills would:

—Encourage alternatives to hazardous-waste landfills and set tough restrictions on any landfills that must be built.[1]

—Enter North Carolina into a southeastern regional approach to handling low-level radioactive waste.[2]

North Carolina cannot afford to be without the protections of the waste-management bill. Our state's policy is to encourage the use of recycling and reduction of waste material. Landfills must be a last resort. If the legislature does not pass this bill, North Carolina's only protection against unsafe landfills will be the woefully inadequate federal regulations—regulations that allow a truck to back up to a landfill and dump in liquid chemicals.

If we fail to enact the low-level radioactive waste bill, we will jeopardize the future of research and medical facilities in our state, as well as manufacturing and utility companies. Hazardous and low-level radioactive wastes are unpleasant but unavoidable effects of a modern industrial and research-oriented society. We can handle them in a responsible way—a way that protects both the health and safety of our people and the vitality of our economy.

These two bills embody that responsible approach, and they should be enacted during this legislative session.

These matters are totally different from the question of high-level radioactive waste disposal, which is completely a federal government responsibility. The prime sites for disposal of high level wastes are the salt domes in the south central and western part of the United States. I am surprised that any sites in North Carolina are even being considered for high-level nuclear wastes.[3] The salt dome formations in other parts of the country have been clearly identified by experts for several years now as the most promising sites for that type of waste.

---

[1] H.B. 559, "A Bill to be Entitled an Act to Prohibit the Use of Landfilling for Certain Cases of Hazardous Wastes and Other Solid Wastes," introduced March 29, 1983, by Representative William E. Clark of Cumberland County, languished in a conference committee when the General Assembly adjourned later in the year. *Durham Morning Herald,* July 1, 1983; *N.C. House Journal, 1983,* 253, 678, 1042, 1059, 1092, 1094. However, "An Act to Create the North Carolina Hazardous Waste Commission," *N.C. Session Laws, 1983, Second Session, 1984,* c. 973, was ratified on June 26, 1984. Hunt called it "one of the unfinished items from last year's legislative session" and praised the state's lawmakers for having "enacted legislation that will put additional teeth into our . . . efforts to manage hazardous wastes." "News Release from the Governor's Office," June 26, 1984.

[2] "An Act to Approve the Southeast Interstate Low-level Radioactive Waste Management Compact," c. 714, was ratified July 11. *N.C. Session Laws, 1983.*

[3] A federal Department of Energy spokesman indicated on June 29, 1983, that geological characteristics qualified twenty underground sites, in eleven North Carolina counties, for inclusion among other East Coast locations being considered as possible storage dumps for spent nuclear fuel. Experts disagreed whether or not the proposed areas were earthquake prone; nevertheless, on December 11, 1984, the Energy Department disclosed that ten more sites in North Carolina had been added to the original list, expanding the number of potentially affected counties to fifty-two. The same day, the governor issued a prepared statement in which he decried the choice of any location in the state for the disposal of high-level nuclear waste and asserted that Washington's conclusions were based on faulty data. "My administration has repeatedly advised the Department of Energy of this, and we have sought meetings with federal officials in an attempt to share our documentation with them. These requests have been ignored," Hunt said. "Simply put, our geological information is better and more up to date than theirs." *Durham Sun,* June 29, July 8, 1983, December 12, 1984; "News Release from the Governor's Office," December 11, 1984.

STATEMENT ON 1983 GENERAL ASSEMBLY

RALEIGH, JULY 14, 1983

We are now very close to the end of what has been a long, tough, but productive legislative session. I am particularly proud of what I believe will be remembered as the two crowning achievements of the

1983 General Assembly: America's toughest law against drunk driving and a budget that will strengthen North Carolina's drive toward economic progress and a high-technology future.

The complete rewrite of this state's laws relating to alcohol and driving was a difficult and controversial task. But the elimination of plea bargaining, an increase in the drinking age, and immediate ten-day suspension of a driver's license for registering a .10 on the breathalyzer, and other far-reaching changes are absolutely essential to having a real impact on this problem. The grass-roots movement against drunk driving is national in scope, but no state has taken as comprehensive an approach as North Carolina. The Safe Roads Act of 1983 provides for swift, certain, and severe punishment of those who would drink and drive. It will save hundreds of innocent lives.

The budget for the new biennium provides the kinds of investments in education and skills training that are essential to economic growth. Accordingly, appropriations for the community college system include funding for new faculty and increased enrollment, new equipment, and a new industry training program.[1] The university system will receive funding for a new computer science building at UNC-Chapel Hill, for microelectronics programs at UNC-Chapel Hill and North Carolina State University, and for new engineering buildings at North Carolina A&T and UNC-Charlotte.[2]

In the area of public education, funds will be appropriated to hire additional mathematics, science, and computer teachers. There will be an increase in the per-student expenditure for instructional supplies, and a new vocational education program for grades seven and eight.[3]

The 5 percent salary increase for public schoolteachers and state employees is not enough, but it is the best we could do with the money available.[4] Next year, if we have the kind of continued economic recovery we expect, we will provide these people with the kind of raise they need and deserve.

Significant progress has also been made this session in such areas as environmental protection, the fight against crime, and overall management of state government.

The goals I outlined in my "State of the State Address" back in January have almost all been met. I wish to thank the members of the General Assembly for helping to strengthen North Carolina's historical commitment to healthier, safer, and more prosperous lives for our citizens.

------

[1] N.C. Session Laws, 1983, c. 761, ss. 95-106.

[2] "An Act to Make Appropriations to Provide Capital Improvements for State Departments, Institutions, and Agencies," c. 757, was ratified July 14, 1983, and made effective retroactive to July 1. Sections 3.1 and 12 provided funding for University of North Carolina System building projects. N.C. Session Laws, 1983.

[3]Instructional supplies expenditures were increased under c. 761, s. 89, *N.C. Session Laws, 1983.* "An Act for a Program for Basic and Vocational Skills at Grades Seven and Eight" was ratified May 20, 1983. *N.C. Session Laws, 1983,* c. 340.

[4]*N.C. Session Laws, 1983,* c. 761, s. 193.

STATEMENT ON PUBLIC ASSISTANCE PROGRAMS

RALEIGH, JULY 19, 1983

[Presiding over hearings on the reauthorization of the federal food stamp program in March, 1982, U.S. Senate Agriculture Committee chairman Jesse A. Helms criticized North Carolina's record of distributing benefits as one of the nation's worst. Although Helms refrained from mentioning the governor personally, some thought his remarks were aimed at the state's Democratic administration. R. Brent Hackney, Hunt's deputy press secretary, called the senator's comments "a significant overstatement" but also acknowledged that the governor had been aware of the lapses in efficiency and was taking corrective action. According to U.S. General Accounting Office statistics, North Carolina had a 15.8 percent error rate in issuing food stamps—versus the national average of 13.3 percent. Only ten other states handled the program less successfully. *News and Observer,* March 30, 1982.

Hunt was able to announce, by July, 1983, a marked improvement in North Carolina's direction of certain federal entitlement projects (see below). He later noted, at a December, 1984, meeting of the State Computer Commission, that automation of certain administrative procedures resulted in North Carolina having one of the lowest rates of error for disbursement of public assistance program benefits in the country.]

I'm proud to announce today that North Carolina is making great progress in reducing errors in our two major public assistance programs. During the latest six-month reporting period, ending in April, 1983, the error rate for our AFDC, or Aid to Families with Dependent Children, program was only 2.3 percent. Although the final statistics have not been released yet, we have been assured that this is one of the lowest AFDC error rates in the country.

Our food stamp error rate also has improved dramatically. In April of 1981, our error rate was over 14 percent. During the most recent six-month reporting period, ending in April of this year, the error rate had dropped by more than 50 percent. Our error rate now stands at 6.5 percent.

I won't be satisfied until we reduce the error rate in our public assistance programs to zero, but we are making tremendous strides in guaranteeing that only those North Carolinians who need help are receiving it. The Department of Human Resources' Division of Social Services and our county departments of social services have done a fine job of working together to bring these error rates down during the past two years, and we're going to continue making progress—by better screening applicants, by better training our county social services workers, by continuing to update the state's computer system so that we can handle applications quickly and more accurately, and by working to simplify reporting forms to reduce unnecessary errors and red tape. We must continue to provide services to needy people so that they will have a chance for a good life, and we must continue to improve and refine our system of payments so that our tax dollars are used wisely.

OPENING SESSION, EDUCATION COMMISSION OF THE STATES

DENVER, COLORADO, JULY 21, 1983

[The idea of cooperation among the schools, government, and business as a key factor in improving public education in the United States provided the nucleus for a number of Hunt's 1982 speeches (see "Testimony before U.S. House Committee on Education and Labor," September 1, 1982, above). The governor continued to focus on that relationship, in 1983, in addresses before the Advanced Leadership Program Services Seminar, March 18; Durham Chamber of Commerce Business/Education Conference, March 30; NCNB Management Awareness Series Conference, June 13; Education Commission of the States, July 20; National Governors' Association, July 31; Southern Regional Education Board Legislative Workshop, August 17; American Council on Education, Commission on Higher Education and the Adult Learner, October 26; and in his statements to the press on June 22 and 23.]

I am delighted to join with my cochairmen, Frank Cary and Governor Pete du Pont, in bringing before the Education Commission of the States a report that does not bemoan what is *wrong* with education in America but proclaims what can be made *right*.

For six months this year the Task Force on Education for Economic Growth tested American education. What we found convinced us that our nation faces a real emergency. But I can report to this commission that every single member of our task force responded with hope and optimism.

We agreed that this emergency does not call for despair or hand wringing or blame. It calls for action, and *Action for Excellence* is the title of our report and our call to America.[1]

Looking around this morning, you can see the faces of many task force members. They come from government and business, education and labor. They represent universities, high schools, state legislatures, and scientists. This group represents the diversity of American society and American institutions, and it was in their diversity that our task force discovered strength and answers to the problems facing American education today.

This task force submits to you today a report that does not call on one single institution or group in society to revitalize American education. Instead, we call on all America—government, business, educators, labor, students, parents, and concerned citizens everywhere—to join in a new social contract dedicated to excellence in education. That precept is the foundation of our philosophy: We are all part of the problem. Together, we can all be the solution.

It is our strong conviction that America must rededicate its schools to the principles of accountability, rigor, hard work, discipline, performance, high standards, and high expectations. Of all these principles, high standards and high expectations may be the most important. It is clear that if we want our nation to flourish, and flourish for all our citizens, we must raise our standards and our expectations of American education.

As everyone in this room knows, there is much that is excellent in America's public schools. Our task force has been encouraged by examples of excellence from Charlotte to Arkansas, from Houston to Colorado. Those success stories prove that, whatever the problems and the challenges we face, there is a foundation of support for education—excellent education—in this nation. Americans *believe* in education; they *believe* in the power and potential of an educated mind, and, as you will see this morning, the fundamental belief of our task force is that education is the key to economic growth in this nation.

Today, America stands in danger of losing its economic and technological leadership in the world. We stand on that precipice because all our students are not learning the fundamental skills, the new basics, they need in a modern economy. This task force believes that American strength and security in the world and our prosperity as a nation depend on the values, knowledge, and ingenuity we instill in our young people. Our very future as a world leader, dedicated to peace and prosperity for all nations and all people, will depend on how we answer this challenge.

Our report reflects our belief that only deep and lasting change in our public schools will make a difference. In the small group sessions later this morning, you will be reviewing our recommendations, but I want to share with you some of our strongest beliefs.

We believe we must substantially raise the level of pay for all teachers. You get what you pay for. If this nation wants extraordinary teachers, we must offer extraordinary rewards for teaching. Teachers must also be rewarded not solely for seniority, but most of all for superiority. They must have incentives to achieve excellence, and teachers must participate in developing those incentives. Furthermore, our teachers must be given the support, the resources, and the leadership that will enable them to be the most effective educators in the world—nothing less. We can expect excellence only when we invest in an environment that promotes excellence.

We believe that our schools must become the heart of every community, a focal point of attention, excellence, and community commitment. We believe that parents and business people must become involved as genuine partners with our schools—to help determine what is taught, to ensure that it is learned, and to demand action for excellence in their own communities. While we believe state and local governments must take the primary responsibility, we also believe that the federal government must provide leadership and support to strengthen education.

Our chief recommendation is that each governor join with legislators, state and local boards of education, educators, business, labor, and communities to create a state task force and develop their own state "action plan" to improve education.

These beliefs reflect out conviction that American education will never be made excellent until it is revitalized with the collective support and strength that has made our country strong. That strength rests with teachers and parents, state school officers, and PTAs. It rests with governors, chancellors, principals, school board members, and budget officers. It rests with business, labor, and legislative leaders, as well as with the young people whose future we cherish.

Each one of you holds the future of American education within your grasp, and while your individual influence is considerable, your collective strength is immeasurable. It is to *all of you* that the Task Force on Education for Economic Growth directs its reports. As leaders, as educators, as concerned citizens, we call on you for action for excellence.

---

[1] Task Force on Education for Economic Growth, *Action for Excellence: A Comprehensive Plan to Improve Our Nation's Schools* ([Denver]: Education Commission of the States, June, 1983).

CHAIRMAN'S BANQUET, EDUCATION COMMISSION OF THE STATES

DENVER, COLORADO, JULY 22, 1983

[The following message is similar to one presented at the North Carolina Association of Educators Leadership Conference, July 29, 1983.]

To all of you, let me begin tonight by thanking you for allowing me the high honor of serving as your chairman. Let me say, too, that the Education Commission of the States is fortunate to have as its new chairman a man of the drive and vision of Governor Pete du Pont.

To Governor du Pont, let me say that you may never again find yourself working with as dedicated and brilliant a group of men and women in this nation. To Bob Andringa,[1] to Roy Forbes, and to the staff of this commission, let me express my deep appreciation for the long hours and the hard work. To Betty Owen[2] of my staff, let me simply say thank you for all you have meant to me as governor and as chairman of this commission.

For education and for this commission, this has been a year that none of us could have anticipated. For too long, the education issue slept quietly in the national consciousness. But, suddenly, the giant has awakened; education has leaped onto the front pages and the network news as an issue of paramount national importance. I think it's about time.

This commission has helped put education out front on our nation's agenda for action. Now, we have before us a historic opportunity to make deep and lasting changes in American education. The time for action is here, and this commission must seize the moment. The tide is running with us, and we must determine whether it will be a riptide of indecision or a powerful, sweeping tide that can carry America to new heights. *You* are the leaders who bear this responsibility for our nation.

Over the past year, many groups have studied our schools and reported their findings. None has the experience, the knowledge, and the clout of the Education Commission of the States. *You* are the decision-makers in the states, the cities, the counties, and the communities across this nation. You know what is right and what is wrong in the classrooms. You know what must be done, and you know how to get it done.

Last year, as I became your chairman, I declared that our goal would be to become a catalyst for change in education. This year, our goal must be to mobilize America for that change.

During this conference, we have talked about the critical role education must play in the economic growth of our nation. We have explored how excellence in education is vital to the strength and prosperity of America. We have dramatized how the challenge of technology must be met in the classroom.

Our Task Force on Education for Economic Growth has presented this nation with a blueprint of *Action for Excellence*, but our job has only begun. We must be the flag-bearers in this crusade for education. We must stride out front, answer the tough questions, confront the doubters, and convince this nation that change may be difficult, demanding, and painful, but it will be worth it.

We must talk sense to the American people. We must make it plain that, for America to be number one, education must be number one in America.

We must have the courage to speak difficult truths.

To the taxpayers, we must say that excellence costs money. We get what we pay for, and we must guarantee them results for what they pay for.

To teachers, we must say that we want better performance. They must be paid not just for seniority, but most of all for superiority. And, in return, we are willing to pay them more.

To students, we must say that they need to learn more and that we will expect more.

To parents, we must say that they must become more involved in the education of their children. They can't just leave it up to somebody else.

To business, we must say that if they want better employees and better profits, they better get involved in what the schools teach and how they teach it.

To Congress and to legislatures and to local governments, we must say that they are going to have to find more resources for the schools. It may mean tax increases, it may mean first call on current revenues—whatever it means, it is a price we must pay.

To governors, it means that we must get out front, take some political risks, do some educating of our own, and make it clear that the schools and our children come first.

And, to the president, our message must be this: Mr. President, we welcome you to the cause of education. You are right to make it a front-page issue. We have been trying to do that for years. But this job requires a deep and lasting commitment from the White House. Education is primarily a state and local responsibility, but this cause will fail without national leadership.

I believe that Americans will respond to this call. They are listening—with experienced ears. They rightly reject simplistic answers that seem to say, "Just give us the money and trust us; everything will turn out all right." But they pay attention to common sense and to facts. They are willing to contribute—not just their money, but their time and energy, as volunteers, as active parents, and as advisers and advocates for the schools. They know that sacrifices lie ahead, but they are willing to sacrifice for the cause of their children's education. We must provide the leadership that summons individual Americans to citizenship, to the pursuit of something deep and lasting: a better education for this generation and for all the generations to come.

We in America are still searching, still striving. We are a nation of pioneers. We drove westward, and we dared to leap into space, but we are not satisfied that this nation is yet all that it can be. North Carolina's Thomas Wolfe once wrote:

I think the true discovery of America is before us. I think the true fulfillment of our spirit, of our people, of our mighty and immortal land, is yet to come. I think the true discovery of our own democracy is still before us. And I think that all these things are as certain as morning, as inevitable as noon. I think I speak for most men living when I say that our America is here, is now, and beckons on before us, and that this glorious assurance is not only our living hope, but our dream to be accomplished.[3]

As your chairman, I have witnessed your faith in a dream yet to be accomplished—the dream of excellence in education and all that dream promises for our nation. Because your faith is strong, that dream lives and offers hope for America. Because I know you, I, like Thomas Wolfe, am as certain as morning that we will discover the America that stretches out before us.

---

[1] Robert Charles Andringa (1940-   ), native of Grand Rapids, Michigan; B.A., 1963, M.A., 1964, Ph.D., 1967, Michigan State University; U.S. Army Reserve, 1967-1969. Minority staff director, U.S. House Committee on Education and Labor, 1969-1977; campaign manager, Al Quie for governor of Minnesota, 1977-1978; policy research director, Office of the Governor of Minnesota, 1978-1980; executive director, Education Commission of the States, 1980-1984; president, since 1984, Discovery Network, Inc. *Who's Who in the West, 20th Edition, 1985-1986* (Chicago: Marquis Who's Who, Inc., 1985), 15.

[2] Betty Combs Owen (1935-   ), native of Hazard, Kentucky; resident of Cary; B.A., University of Kentucky, 1957; M.P.H., University of North Carolina at Chapel Hill, 1962. English teacher, San Diego school district, 1957-1959, Louisville/Jefferson County schools, 1959-1960, and Charlotte/Mecklenburg County schools, 1974-1975; health education consultant, Kentucky Department of Health, 1960-1962; private consultant in education, health, and public policy, 1964-1977; senior policy analyst, state Department of Administration, and senior policy adviser to Governor Hunt for education, health, and human and cultural resources, 1977-1985; representative and adviser, Education Commission of the States' National Task Force on Education for Economic Growth, and contributor to *Action for Excellence* (1983); chief of staff, North Carolina Commission on Education for Economic Growth, 1984. Betty Combs Owen to Jan-Michael Poff, October 31, 1985.

[3] Quotation previously identified in Mitchell, *Addresses of Hunt*, I, 12n.

ELECTRONICS LUNCHEON

Los Angeles, July 27, 1983

[Many of the same points were addressed in Hunt's press statement of July 28 and in his remarks to a meeting of British motor industry executives, held in London, on November 14, 1983.]

I am delighted that the North Carolina economic development team could meet with you and tell you what we are doing to make North Carolina a technological greenhouse for new research, development, and manufacturing. In fact, we believe North Carolina is doing more than any other state in the country to prepare for a new, high-technology future.

We understand a basic fact of life in North Carolina: You get what you pay for, and you get what you work for. We're determined to make our schools, our community colleges, and our university system excellent, and we're prepared to put our money behind our convictions. In our state's budget, which was passed last week, we invested $71 million for high-technology research, education, and training programs for the next two years.[1]

North Carolina has always been an education state. Our universities are known for a great deal more than basketball, and you're never more than a thirty-minute drive from a community college or technical institute. We have, over the past few years, strengthened our math, science, and vocational education programs. We've placed special emphasis on reading, writing, and math in our elementary grades. We have established the nation's first tuition-free residential high school for students gifted in science and math.

But this year we redoubled our commitment to train and plan and educate for a new twenty-first century economy that has already arrived. We secured $1 million for each year of the biennium to hire 100 new math, science, and computer teachers. Every high school in the state will now have a lead science or math teacher for an extra six weeks in the summer.

Our legislature funded summer institutes to upgrade the skills of seventh- and eighth-grade science and math teachers, and it provided one hundred $1,000 scholarships to high school science and math teachers to sharpen their skills.

We spent $4.4 million to provide our teachers with a duty-free period to prepare for their classes.

For our state's fifty-eight community and technical colleges, our new budget includes $14.4 million for new training equipment. We're investing almost $20 million to hire new faculty and increase enrollment, some of which will come from tuition increases. We have invested $4.5 million in our community college system's new industry training program and $3.3 million for new high-technology training programs at several campuses around the state.

At the university level, we are building new engineering buildings at the University of North Carolina at Charlotte and North Carolina A&T in Greensboro. We will be spending over $9 million to plan for and build a new computer science building at the University of North Carolina at Chapel Hill. We're spending more money to strengthen our microelectronics programs at Carolina and N.C. State in Raleigh, and more than $11 million has been set aside for teaching and research improvements in engineering and science departments throughout our university system.

Our new budget provides $17.2 million for our state's Microelectronics Center. This appropriation brings North Carolina's total commitment to the center to more than $40 million. This fall, the Microelectronics Center will complete construction of a new research and development facility at North Carolina's Research Triangle Park. This new building will include all of the equipment necessary for the design, fabrication, and testing of new integrated circuits. And if you give Don Beilman one minute he can tell you everything you always wanted to know about how our Microelectronics Center is involved with the engineering, science, and computer schools at five of our universities.

This year our legislature passed a bill called the New Technology Jobs Act. The act creates a North Carolina Innovation Research Fund which provides grants to individuals for up to $50,000 for the research stage of product development. It also creates the North Carolina Technological Development Authority, a body that will award grants up to $200,000 to local community partnerships— business, financial, and academic partnerships—to create incubator facilities.[2]

All of these millions of dollars that we have invested in education and training represent our commitment to you. North Carolina is a state where the relationship between education and economic growth is understood and appreciated. We want jobs, and we want economic growth. We're prepared to invest and work for those jobs and for the quality of life that has made North Carolina famous.

We're writing a success story in North Carolina. IBM, General Electric, ITT, Northern Telecom, and Bendix Automation Group are part of that story—and there are many more. We are lean, and we are hungry. We're ready to work with you.

---

[1] *N.C. Session Laws, 1983*, c. 761.
[2] "An Act to Create the New Technology Jobs Act," c. 899, was ratified July 21. *N.C. Session Laws, 1983*.

NORTH CAROLINA SHERIFFS ASSOCIATION

ASHEVILLE, AUGUST 9, 1983

I am delighted to be here tonight, in the safest room in North Carolina. I am also standing in close proximity to the greatest concentration of political power in this state. I'm only kidding—I know folks like Ottis Jones and Raymond Goodman and Tom Morrissey don't have time for politics, but they would have a fair amount of clout if they ever decided to get involved in that sort of thing.[1]

The main reason I'm glad to be here is that I am among friends— the people who have always been there on those many occasions that I have asked for your help. You were there when we were working to get a speedy trial law and a fair sentencing law. You were right beside me when we were working for mandatory jail terms for armed robbers. You were there when we were pushing legislation to require long prison sentences for drug smugglers, and when we were getting a law to put the head shops out of business. You supported our successful efforts to pay the medical expenses of rape victims.

You were there, years ago, when Community Watch was only a good idea. We worked together on what has turned out to be one of the most successful grass-roots campaigns in this state's history. Largely as a result of Community Watch, the statewide crime rate in your jurisdictions dropped by almost 4 percent last year.

Thanks to your dedicated efforts to protect our people, North Carolina is becoming a safer place to live and work and raise a family. Here's the proof: The total crime rate in North Carolina increased in 1982 by only 1.6 percent. In suburban counties, rape was down 8 percent; robbery was down 8 percent; burglary was down 5 percent. In rural counties, rape was down 10 percent; robbery was down 1 percent; burglaries were down by 6 percent. On behalf of the people of North Carolina, I want to express to you my heartfelt gratitude for that.

While I am thanking you, I want you to know how deeply grateful I am that you were by my side during that long, tough fight to enact America's toughest law against drunk driving. Come October 1, the free ride across the center line is over. Some criminals—and that's just what they are—are going to get the shock of their lives when they blow a .10 and leave the courthouse on foot. That's just the beginning of what's going to happen to them. A lot of them are going to end up checking into your hotels for a while.

As governor, I'll have perhaps one more opportunity to address your annual meeting. But this is no lame-duck administration, especially when it comes to fighting crime. I'll be asking for your help again, starting tonight.

We need your help, for example, in our statewide crackdown on the sale of alcohol to minors. Recent undercover operations have shown that a lot of people are thumbing their noses at the law.

I'll need your help in the community service alternatives program in drunken driving cases. The legislature appropriated $2 million to provide a program coordinator in each judicial district.[2] Alma Nesbitt of the Governor's Crime Commission will be here tomorrow to review the program for you and answer any questions.[3]

I'll be needing your help as this administration sets its sights on our next target in the fight against crime: illegal drugs. As I said earlier, we have made some progress in this area with the enactment of severe and mandatory sentences for drug smugglers, but I'm not going to sugarcoat this situation. Last year our State Bureau of Investigation confiscated $129 million worth of domestically grown marijuana. That might account for 7 or 8 percent of the market here. We believe that marijuana alone is a billion-dollar-a-year business in this state. That makes it one of North Carolina's largest industries, and I'm not going to tolerate that.

The use of cocaine is up. The use of heroin is increasing. Not too long ago, the SBI busted an illegal lab where quaaludes were being processed in a concrete mixer.

During the remainder of my term of office, I will be working with the SBI, the Department of Crime Control and Public Safety, and local law enforcement agencies to launch an all-out assault on drug trafficking. Some recommendations are now being prepared for my review, and I'll be seeking your advice on those recommendations after they reach my desk. We're going to do something about this problem. I want you to remember that, if you don't remember anything else I've said here.

There's one matter we need to deal with right away with respect to drug enforcement. I am referring to the newly enacted law that could frustrate your efforts to use informants in criminal cases— especially drug cases.[4] It would be nice if most crimes were solved purely by the kind of razzle-dazzle detective work you see on television, but the police chief from Murfreesboro[5] told me in a meeting many of you attended last week that he could count on the fingers of one hand the number of cases he had solved that way.

The fact is that many, if not most, crimes are solved with the help of informants. You, along with the state's district attorneys and police chiefs, have asked me to call a special session of the General Assembly to seek repeal or modification of this law.

I am giving that strong consideration. What I need you to do over the next couple of weeks is contact your legislators. They need to know how you feel about this matter, because they'll listen to you. And, by contacting them, you can give me some feedback about how many votes in that legislature we could count on in the event a special session is called.

So the fight against crime in North Carolina continues. I want these last several years—and the next year and a half, and beyond—to be remembered as the time North Carolina revitalized its economy, created a climate for the best public school system in the world, and turned the corner in the fight against crime. With your continued help, the history books will describe these exciting years in just that way. Thank you, again, for all you have done to make North Carolina a free, safe, and secure place.

---

[1] Ottis F. Jones, (1931-   ), native of Erwin; resident of Fayetteville; completed law enforcement training under auspices of Federal Bureau of Investigation, State Bureau of Investigation, and the Institute of Government, University of North Carolina at Chapel Hill; served nine years in North Carolina National Guard. Rose in rank from deputy sheriff to chief deputy, 1953-1972, Cumberland County Sheriff's Department; first elected sheriff of Cumberland County in 1972 and returned in subsequent elections; past president, 1981-1982, and executive board chairman, 1983, North Carolina Sheriffs' Association; chairman, North Carolina Sheriffs' Training and Standards Commission. Ottis F. Jones to Jan-Michael Poff, September 18, 1985.

Raymond W. Goodman (1915-   ), native, resident of Rockingham; attended
Richmond County public schools and completed continuing education course work;
honorably discharged from U.S. Navy in 1937. Founder, in 1941, and president, R. W.
Goodman Co., Inc., department store; executive vice-president, W. H. Parker Insurance Agency, Inc.; executive vice-president, treasurer, Privett Furniture Co., Inc.;
president, treasurer, Richmond Yarns, Inc.; executive committee member, United
Carolina Bank (formerly Richmond County Bank); Richmond County sheriff since
1950. Raymond W. Goodman to Jan-Michael Poff, August 29, 1985.

   Thomas H. Morrissey (1927-   ), native of Cambridge, Massachusetts; resident of
Arden; attended U.S. Army Finance School, U.S. Army Intelligence School, Indiana
University, University of California at San Francisco, and University of Alaska;
U.S. Army Intelligence Corps special agent, 1945-1965. Sales manager, 1968-1970,
Product Engineering, Asheville; Buncombe County sheriff since 1970; past president,
North Carolina Sheriffs' Association; member of numerous civic and professional
boards. Thomas H. Morrissey to Jan-Michael Poff, August 28, 1985.

   [2]See "An Act to Make Appropriations for Current Operations of State Departments, Institutions, and Agencies, and for Other Purposes," ratified July 15. N.C.
Session Laws, 1983, c. 761, s. 154.

   [3]Alma W. (Nesbitt) Brown, resident of Raleigh; attended University of North
Carolina at Chapel Hill, 1969-1971; National Center for Paralegal Training, 1979;
B.A., Columbia Pacific University, 1985. Community development specialist for the
Governor's Crime Commission, 1981-1982; community service supervisor, 1982-1983,
and deputy director, since 1984, Division of Victim and Justice Services, state Crime
Control and Public Safety Department. Alma W. Brown to Jan-Michael Poff, August
27, 1985.

   [4]See "Statement on the Discovery Law," August 17, 1983, footnote 1, below.
   [5]Robert Ed Harris (1943-   ), resident of Murfreesboro; attended Chowan College,
1962-1964, and FBI National Academy, 1978; North Carolina National Guard, 1966-
1972. Served with Murfreesboro Police Department since 1968, appointed chief of
police in 1979. Robert Ed Harris to Jan-Michael Poff, August 29, 1985.

STATEMENT ON DISCOVERY LAW

RALEIGH, AUGUST 17, 1983

I have had extensive discussions this week with leaders of the
General Assembly regarding the new discovery law on criminal
evidence.[1] It is my opinion, as I have said before, that changes are
needed in the new law and that a special session of the legislature
will be required to make those changes. I will not make a decision to
call a special session until the special House committee chaired by
Representative Al Adams has had time to complete its review of
this matter. That committee is doing an excellent job, and the more
time we spend studying and considering this issue before a special
session, the less time the legislature will have to meet and the less
cost there will be to the taxpayers. I would hope that a special
session would not last more than one day.

It is important to clarify exactly why the new law needs to be
changed. Some reports have not been completely accurate. The law
applies only to statements a defendant has made, not to things a
witness has observed as, for example, in a Community Watch

program. Before this new law went into effect July 14, defendants in a criminal trial had a right to:

—Any exculpatory statements available to the prosecution—that is, any statements made by the defendant that would tend to establish his innocence.

—Any statements made to law enforcement officers by the defendant that the prosecution intended to use in the trial.

The legislature changed the law to require that the state give the defendant in writing the substance of *any* statement he made to *any* person. It no longer has to be made to law enforcement officers, and it does not matter whether the state intends to use it against the defendant in the trial. This law concerns law enforcement officers and district attorneys in two areas:

—An informant who gives a tip that leads to an arrest in a serious case, like a drug trafficking case, cannot be *guaranteed* confidentiality.

—Many cases are initiated because a family member, a neighbor, or a close friend tells the police about what he heard someone say. Those people may no longer be willing to give that kind of information if the defendant must be told who turned him in.

These are valid concerns. We cannot afford to take away the tools of our law enforcement officers. On the other hand, a defendant must be in a position to properly prepare for his defense. The key questions in resolving this conflict are what information should be made available to a defendant and when.

I am not certain now precisely how this important legal issue should be resolved. I will continue to work with the House committee and with parties on both sides of the issue to develop an approach that will protect the defendants' right to a fair trial and at the same time serve to protect the people of North Carolina against crime. I am confident we can reach a fair and responsible solution for consideration by the General Assembly.

---

[1]"An Act to Provide Fair Discovery to Defendants in Criminal Prosecutions" was ratified July 14. *N.C. Session Laws, 1983*, c. 759.

STATEMENT ANNOUNCING
SPECIAL LEGISLATIVE SESSION

RALEIGH, AUGUST 24, 1983

I will convene a special session of the General Assembly at 10:00 A.M. this Friday to make urgently needed changes in the new criminal discovery law.[1]

The discovery law must be changed to protect the identity

of confidential informants in criminal cases. Law enforcement agencies simply cannot protect our people without the use of informants, and informants are not going to talk if they think their identity will be disclosed. After many hours of discussions with legislators, prosecutors, law enforcement officers, and trial lawyers, I am convinced that we can protect these sources of information without infringing on the legitimate rights of the accused. I will urge the special session to change the law so that prosecutors can keep confidential oral statements made by defendants to informants when those statements are not to be used at trial.[2]

Now, some district attorneys have expressed concerns to me that the discovery process might be a burden to administer. If the State Budget Office finds that the law causes such hardships, I will use my power as director of the budget to see that adequate administrative resources are provided to do the job and protect our people.

I will also ask the legislature to plug a gaping loophole in the law prohibiting the sale of alcoholic beverages to underaged persons. The law was changed to require a prosecutor to prove that a person "knowingly" sold alcohol to a minor. That means that beginning October 1, businesses could sell alcohol to minors with impunity. All they will have to do is not ask for identification. Then it could not be proven in court that they knowingly violated the law. This places an impossible burden on prosecutors and would instantly dismantle our program of using minors as undercover agents to detect violations. The General Assembly can easily correct the problem by deleting the word "knowingly" from the law.[3]

I believe the General Assembly can deal with this short but urgent agenda in a single day.

Finally, I want to thank the members of the special subcommittees appointed by Lieutenant Governor Green and Speaker Ramsey to study the discovery law, and the district attorneys, law enforcement officers, trial attorneys, and others. Their deliberations and advice have been invaluable.

---

[1] See "Statement on the Discovery Law," August 17, 1983, footnote 1, above.

[2] "An Act to Clarify Criminal Discovery of Oral Statements of the Defendant," which amended c. 759 of the 1983 *Session Laws*, was ratified August 26. *N.C. Session Laws, 1983, Extra Session, 1983*, c. 6.

[3] "An Act to Strengthen Laws Regulating Sales of Alcoholic Beverages" was ratified August 26. *N.C. Session Laws, 1983, Extra Session, 1983*, c. 5.

Highway Patrol officers receive words of praise from their commander in chief.

Governor Hunt congratulates Public Service Award recipient Hugh M. Morton, chairman of the Governor's Advisory Council on Travel and Tourism, at the twentieth-annual North Carolina Awards presentation held November 3, 1983. Morton was best known as developer of Grandfather Mountain and for his role in mustering state support for such projects as bringing the USS *North Carolina* to Wilmington and the establishment of the North Carolina Zoological Park. The North Carolina Awards are the highest honor given by the state recognizing contributions from individuals; five are given each year.

STATEMENT ON NORTH CAROLINA COMMISSION ON EDUCATION FOR ECONOMIC GROWTH

RALEIGH, OCTOBER 13, 1983

[Hunt told reporters on June 23, 1983, that he would "soon appoint a North Carolina task force that closely parallels the structure and purpose" of the ECS Commission on Education for Economic Growth. He also indicated his belief that the state's improving economy would result in an increase in incoming revenues and that "the public schools should have first call on those resources" in 1984.

The North Carolina Commission on Education for Economic Growth was created by Executive Order No. 98, signed October 13. *N.C. Session Laws, 1983*, 1448-1450.]

The time has come for North Carolina to take a fresh approach to education, and I am today beginning a massive statewide effort to chart a course of action, mobilize public support, and forge a consensus for deep and lasting change in our state's public schools. I am appointing fifty leading citizens—including business executives, educators, legislators, local and state government leaders, parents, and students—to the North Carolina Commission on Education for Economic Growth.

Over the next five months, this commission, which I will chair, will listen to our people, take a hard look at what is happening in our schools, propose a specific plan of action, and, most important of all, build a coalition among the friends of public education that will be strong, deeply rooted, and unified. Some of the proposals we develop will require legislative action. Others will call for action by business, by parents, by citizens, by students, and by educators.

What makes North Carolina's approach unique will be our focus on education for economic growth—not education just for the sake of education, but for the sake of our nation, our economy, and our future. This emphasis on education for economic growth can be the rallying point for public support. It can be the cause that enlists the active and enthusiastic support of business for our public schools in the same way business has supported higher education in North Carolina.

We must act with a sense of urgency if our nation and our children are to compete in this world. A silent war is being waged in our classrooms today, a war that will surely determine whether our nation retains its leadership in the world and whether this generation will have a better life than ours.

This commission will work on a tight timetable. It will hold its first meeting a week from today in Raleigh. It will hold regional hearings in Raleigh, Asheville, Greenville, and Charlotte this fall and winter. In February we will hold a daylong meeting to hammer out our course of action. In March, we will release our final report.[1]

The commission will be backed up by two structures:

—An advisory panel composed of representatives of statewide organizations concerned about education—such as the NCAE, the School Boards Association, the North Carolina Citizens for Business and Industry, the North Carolina Association of School Administrators, and the PTA.

—An informal network of "Friends for Improving Public Education" that will provide information on the commission's work and solicit advice from anyone in North Carolina who is interested and wants to contribute to this work.

This overall structure is designed to bring into this process thousands of concerned North Carolinians. We need to translate their concern into commitment and constructive action. It will not be enough to propose a laundry list of recommendations. The commission must build public support for them and mobilize the friends of education to see that changes are made.

North Carolina has already taken giant steps in education, steps other states are striving to copy: a Primary Reading Program, testing programs, tougher requirements for graduation, a quality assurance program, the North Carolina School of Science and Mathematics. Some key issues we must address now include:

—How to pay teachers in a way that will attract and keep the best.

—How to make the curriculum more rigorous.

—How to make classroom time more productive.

—How to make homework more valuable.

—How to strengthen the management of schools.

—How to reduce the dropout rate.

—Most important of all, how to prepare today's students for tomorrow's world. That is our ultimate goal, and I believe this commission can be the means to that end.

---

[1] See "Special Address on Education," June 7, 1984, footnote 4, above, for source of recommendations.

MARY REYNOLDS BABCOCK FOUNDATION

CHAPEL HILL, OCTOBER 19, 1983

I'm delighted to be with all of you and welcome you to North Carolina, but I warn you that I came here today to do more listening than talking.

I share your concern about youth unemployment and those young people who are falling through the cracks of our educational system, but I hope George Autry[1] has told you that North Carolina is more than concerned. We are doing something about it.

Since I came into office in 1977, we have pursued a four-part strategy to attack youth unemployment problems.

Our dropout prevention programs are aimed at keeping students in school. We're promoting remediation, one-on-one, and in-school suspension programs. We'll spend $4 million this year in 173 high schools that have established Job Placement/Dropout Prevention centers to serve about 7,000 students.

Our dropout rate fell from 29 percent in the 1981-1982 school year to 26.8 percent last year. Although 4,400 more students stayed in school, 26.8 percent means that over 22,000 students felt that school was not the answer for them.

I hope an Extended Day Program is part of the answer for them. We'll spend $1.5 million next year to serve about 1,000 dropouts in our Extended Day Program. Staff in twenty-nine high schools will actively recruit dropouts back into school and provide them with special help and counseling.

Our Job Readiness Training Program focuses on helping disadvantaged students who are about to graduate but have no plans beyond graduation night.[2] I know several foundations here funded that program. I hope we have some news for you soon about how this program ties together local school systems and local businesses. MDC [North Carolina Manpower Development Corp.] and George Autry redesigned this program based on the successful Human Resources Development Motivation Program in our community college system.

To me, a big part of the answer for youth employment problems is in the classroom. Our Primary Reading Program and our teachers' aides programs have shown tremendous results, and those results are being translated into steadily climbing national test scores at all grade levels. Competency and achievement tests are also part of our classroom focus.

As chairman of the Education Commission of the States and its Task Force on Education for Economic Growth, I tried to promote the notion that a solid education is the first answer to the problems of youth employment. Our schools need to be as excellent as they can be, and that means we must motivate every student—particularly the financially disadvantaged or unenthusiastic student. They need the basic skills necessary to make it in today's job market. If they can learn the basics, if we can encourage them to stay in school despite all the pressures, then we have taken the first step toward breaking the cycle of structural unemployment that haunts their lives.

We must—we absolutely must—make sure that no one is left behind as the fever for educational reform takes hold. We cannot develop one educational system for philosopher-kings and one for everyone else. We need one system that is flexible enough to lift up every student.

I know some young people are falling through the cracks right now. What do we do with our dropouts, and graduates from last year, who are not adequately prepared for today's—and tomorrow's—job market?

Here in North Carolina, I think our community colleges and technical institutes are going to help us answer those questions. No one is ever more than a thirty-minute drive from those schools, and they can help a student complete his or her high school degree and then move on to skills-training programs.

I also think the new federal Job Training Partnership Act will help. In North Carolina we will spend over $15 million during the next twelve months to make this new program work. Those dollars will go to youth job training programs which will be planned and monitored by our Private Industry councils in the community.

I know there is more we need to do to coordinate our programs, our departments, and especially to encourage business to provide leadership. Our new state Commission on Education for Economic Growth is going to come up with a plan to build a strong and permanent business/education partnership in every North Carolina community.

You need to watch what we do. I hope you'll review our Job Readiness Training programs and our dropout programs. We need your advice. A little money wouldn't be bad, either. Foundations can influence broad social policy in this country. You can touch people's lives. I want you to know that North Carolina is going to work with you in every way possible. We want to build something permanent and lasting in this state for *all* North Carolinians.

---

[1]George B. Autry (1937-   ), resident of Chapel Hill; A.B., 1958, J.D., 1961, Duke University; attended George Washington University Graduate School of Public Law. Attorney; former chief counsel, Subcommittee on Revision and Codification, U.S. Senate Judiciary Committee; became president, North Carolina Manpower Development Corp., in 1967. *News and Observer*, April 27, 1975.

[2]The Job Readiness Training Program's purpose was "to prepare public high school seniors for the transition from school to jobs or to skills-training in the community college system." It was designed as a subsequent step for former participants in the Basic and Vocational Skills Program. *N.C. Session Laws, 1983, Second Session, 1984*, c. 1034, s. 18.

STATEMENT ON TEXTILE INDUSTRY

CHARLOTTE, OCTOBER 20, 1983

[This speech is nearly identical to one delivered in Belmont on October 25, 1983.]

"Crafted with Pride in U.S.A." is the slogan selected by the American Fiber, Textile, Apparel Coalition [AFTAC] as the center-piece of its new campaign encouraging our nation's consumers to "buy American" when they shop for textile products. The coalition's membership includes trade associations and labor unions from a wide array of industries closely related to our country's textile manufacturing complex.

The success of AFTAC's buy-American campaign is critically important to North Carolina. The textile industry is our state's largest manufacturing employer. The more than 1,300 textile plants now operating in North Carolina distribute payrolls totaling more than $2.87 billion a year and account for more than a quarter of all Tar Heel manufacturing shipments. Textile manufacturers, together with our state's apparel and fiber producers, employ more than 300,000 North Carolinians.

No other state employs more workers in textile manufacturing or is so closely tied to the economic fortunes of the American textile industry. Because of these close ties, we in North Carolina already know about the heavy impact overseas competition is having on America's textile industry.

Over the last few decades, overseas textile manufacturers subsi-dized by foreign governments and paying wages that would be illegal in this country have dramatically increased their share of the American textile market.

Between 1977 and 1982 textile and apparel imports to the United States nearly doubled, increasing at an average annual rate of more than 15 percent, while total United States consumption of textile and apparel products grew at a rate of only 2 to 3 percent annually. As a result, foreign textile manufacturers now control over $10 billion worth of American textile and apparel sales, and experts estimate this share will grow to more than $12 billion by the end of this year.

In an effort to compete with this unfair foreign competition, American textile manufacturers have invested an average of more than $1.3 billion in modernization programs annually during the last decade. Automation and other process improvements have dramatically increased both productivity and quality in American textile manufacturing operations. The textile industry has also rightly sought help from our federal government, but our nation has failed to win the kind of comprehensive trade agreements needed to adequately limit textile imports.

Textile and apparel agreements signed within the last year with Taiwan, South Korea, the People's Republic of China, and other Asian nations limit import growth in less than forty textile product categories. An equal number of categories remain uncapped. Experts estimate these and other loopholes in the new agreements leave room for substantial increases in textile imports over the next five years.[1]

Until more comprehensive agreements can be reached, our nation's textile industry must rely on the American people to hold the line against unfair foreign competition. As governor of North Carolina, I urge all our state's citizens—and consumers across the nation—to help preserve American textile jobs and investment by buying quality, American-made textile products in the months and years ahead.

---

[1] Reacting to reports of record high textile imports in January and February, 1984, Hunt wrote to President Reagan on April 6, accusing "some of our competitors" of "disregarding the intent, if not the letter, of the Multi-Fiber Agreement. . . ." Hunt further insisted that competitors "are taking advantage of loopholes in the bilateral trade agreements; and that our response is often only after market disruption has occurred." He concluded, "I suggest, Mr. President, a reaffirmation of your 1980 statement that import growth should not be greater than domestic market growth" and a "stronger, more unified response to the import problem by all administrative departments and agencies involved with international trade." "News Release from the Governor's Office," [April] 6, 1984.

In his September 24 announcement that Al Calloway had been appointed the state Commerce Department's special representative for textiles, the governor noted that imports were 44 percent higher for the first seven months of 1984 than they had been for the same period in 1983, and that the 1983 level had been 70 percent higher than that established four years earlier. It was Calloway's job, as "the industry's personal contact in state government," to devise plans for textile research and employee training and to work for the enactment of stricter regulations on textile importation. "News Release from the Governor's Office," September 24, 1984.

STATEMENT SUBMITTED TO U.S. SENATE COMMITTEE ON LABOR AND HUMAN RESOURCES

WASHINGTON, D.C., OCTOBER 20, 1983

Chairman Hatch, Senator Kennedy, members of the committee:

I want to commend this committee for addressing itself to one of the most significant health-care issues confronting this country today. Rapid advances in medicine are moving organ transplant surgery out of the realm of experimentation and research and into accepted medical practice. The medical community, insurance carriers, and national policy makers must move quickly to explore and confront the implications of these medical advances. It is obvious that Congress must establish a national policy in this area.

I wholeheartedly support the creation of the proposed National Task Force on Organ Procurement and Transplant Reimbursement. I stand ready to work for enactment of S. 1728.[1]

The plight of little Joshua Brooks has brought this home dramatically to North Carolinians.[2] Josh's parents, Rick and June, are with you today and are far more able than I to tell you of the difficulties they have encountered in trying to arrange for liver transplant surgery.

The Brooks case has shown us that three very serious obstacles stand between a liver transplant candidate and the chance for prolonged life. Most important, there is no national computer network to quickly match available organs with a recipient. Secondly, there is no reliable system for rapid, standby transportation of organs and recipients to those hospitals where the surgery is to be performed. Finally, there is no consensus within the insurance industry as to whether transplant surgery is covered under major medical policies.

I am very proud of what North Carolina has done with respect to the insurance question. Our state recently adopted a self-insurance plan to cover state employees and teachers. However, when the plan was established by our legislature, transplant surgery was neither included nor excluded.

Josh Brooks's father is a public schoolteacher, and when this case arose the board of trustees overseeing our health insurance plan had to make a policy decision in this area. At my urging, the board decided a few weeks ago that liver transplants and certain other categories of transplants would be funded by our plan. If a liver becomes available for Josh Brooks, surgery at the University of Minnesota Hospital will be paid for.

I believe other states and private carriers will, in time, follow our lead. The simple fact of the matter is that, with the development of such drugs as cyclosporine,[3] several types of transplant surgery will very soon be universally accepted. As that occurs, the cost of surgery and drugs will go down.

Let me emphasize again that a national approach to these issues is required, and the federal government must take the lead. I was disturbed by the recent statement by an administration official who opposed a national transplant network. The official indicated that the volunteer blood donor program proved that the private sector could handle the problem.

The analogy is terribly flawed. Blood can be stored for a long period of time. But if a kidney becomes available for little Joshua Brooks, the organ and the child must be at the hospital within about six hours. Our response must be instantaneous.

I am grateful to this committee for hearing today from Joshua Brooks's parents. Their courage has been an inspiration to North Carolinians. I hope their story will make a contribution toward a national response to a very critical issue.

---

[1] S. 1728 was never enacted; however, S. 2048 was. See PL 98-507, "An Act for the Establishment of the Task Force on Organ Transplantation and the Organ Procurement and Transplantation Network, to Authorize Financial Assistance for Organ Procurement, and for Other Purposes," signed October 19, 1984. 98 Stat. 2339-2348.

[2] Joshua Brooks's fight for life captured nationwide attention. The nine-month-old Laurinburg infant, suffering from biliary artesia, underwent liver transplant surgery

at University of Minnesota Hospital on November 11, 1983. He died of multiple organ failure fifteen days later. *News and Observer*, November 27, 1983.

   [3] Cyclosporine is used to counteract the human body's rejection of transplanted organs. "Cyclosporine: The Breakthrough Drug," *Newsweek*, August 29, 1983, 41.

STATEMENT ON INDUSTRIAL MISSION TO EUROPE

CHARLOTTE, OCTOBER 25, 1983

[The governor issued a statement, much like the one reprinted below, following his opening of the U.S. exhibit at the Interkama trade fair on November 9.]

I am today announcing my plans to lead a major industrial recruitment mission to Europe November 7 through 15.

This mission will be an important follow-up to a similar mission led by our state secretary of commerce, C. C. Hope, Jr., [1] early this summer. That mission found that North Carolina enjoys a wide reputation as one of America's leading centers for new economic growth and development—particularly in fields related to high technology.

With the slow but continuing improvement in the American economy in recent months, we believe that many of Europe's leading firms will soon be considering expansion plans for this country. The mission I will lead in November will reinforce North Carolina's excellent position in the competition for these new investments.

Our state is already enjoying a banner year in the field of foreign investment. In the first nine months of 1983, new and expanding foreign-owned firms in North Carolina announced more than $277 million of investments. Those investments resulted in the creation of more than 3,400 jobs. That investment total makes 1983 the best foreign investment year in North Carolina history and brings foreign investment in our state since 1977 to more than $1 billion. Few other states in America can rival this impressive record in overseas industrial recruitment.

Much of our success in recruiting overseas is a result of the sound economic development programs that have also benefited North Carolina's existing businesses, communities, and educational institutions.

In my upcoming mission to Europe, for example, I will be putting special emphasis on the new $71 million high-technology funding package approved this summer by our General Assembly. The package includes new funding for a variety of projects, including a new engineering building for UNC-Charlotte, support for high-technology small businesses, and a complete upgrading of our state community college system's skills training equipment.

While in Europe, I will visit top officials of leading Swiss, French, German, and British manufacturing firms. I will also open the U.S. exhibit of the Interkama Industrial Fair in Düsseldorf, West Germany, on November 9, and address a meeting of top British automotive industry executives November 14.

I'm making this announcement here today because of Charlotte's keen interest in international investment and trade. There are 138 foreign-owned firms in Charlotte—that amounts to more than one third of all foreign-owned business in North Carolina. We worked hard with Charlotte to establish a foreign trade zone here to help those businesses.

International investment and trade are a big part of Charlotte's life. We saw that interest reflected in your recent Octoberfest celebration. With this recruitment mission, we hope to bring even more international businesses—and good jobs—to Charlotte and to all of North Carolina.

---

[1]Clarence Caldwell Hope, Jr. (1920-   ), native of Charlotte; received two-year degree from Mars Hill College; was graduated from Wake Forest College (now University), 1943; pursued graduate studies at Harvard University business school and at Rutgers University. Vice-chairman, First Union National Bank; senior executive, First Union Corp.; president, American Bankers Assn., 1980; state commerce secretary, 1983-1985. "C. C. Hope, Jr., of First Union National Bank," *We the People of North Carolina*, October, 1979, 13-14, 16, 63-65; *News and Observer*, April 13, 1980.

GOVERNOR'S CONFERENCE ON PREVENTION OF CRIMES AGAINST WOMEN AND CHILDREN

MURPHY, OCTOBER 31, 1983

[The following speech is similar to one delivered in Kinston, August 15, 1983.]

Today, you have heard from our experts: Secretary Heman R. Clark, Major Don Truelove of the Orange County Sheriff's Department, and Ellen Scouten, assistant district attorney for Orange and Chatham counties, and many others.[1] They have brought before you a bleak side of human nature: spouse abuse, domestic violence, sexual assault—it all adds up to a very ugly picture. I know these are not easy topics to discuss. We should be fighting unemployment, poverty, inflation, and ignorance—those are easy subjects. But for too many people, the battleground lines have been drawn within the family circle.

You've heard all the numbers—one out of every seven homicides in North Carolina is a spouse killing a spouse. Those murders are the climax of a relationship which has endured years of abuse and violence. One spouse, usually the wife, has been repeatedly beaten and abused until she explodes and retaliates—or is beaten one last, fatal time. I am constantly astounded to hear that domestic violence is believed to be the most unreported crime in the country, with only one in ten assaulted women reporting abuse. Across this state, mental health professionals and counselors report that domestic violence cases are at an all-time high.

In addition to the family's plight, there is extreme risk for those who intervene. Approximately one fourth of the assaults on law enforcement officers take place while they are responding to domestic disturbance calls.

If there are children in the family, they are witness to this tragedy. Violence begets violence. And in children who are abused, or witness abuse, are sown the seeds of a new generation of victims and abusers.

Then there is the specter of rape and sexual assault. Our Police Information Network reports an almost unbelievable statistic: In North Carolina, a rape is committed every eight hours. In 1982 there were more than 1,300 rapes reported in this state. That's probably only about half of the rapes that actually occur. Since 1976 reported rapes in North Carolina have increased by over 60 percent —and that makes rape the fastest-growing violent crime across the country and right here in our home state.

We're faced with a confusing picture because statistics tell us that about 50 percent of all rape victims know their assailant before the attack. Because of this fact, some people may think a "real crime" has not taken place. They are very wrong. A rape is a crime— period. It is a cold, hard, calculated act that has nothing to do with passion. It is a violent act.

So far, I have only painted half of the picture for you. The other half is the progress North Carolina has made against these crimes over the past few years. In 1980 the Governor's Task Force on Domestic Violence was established—and many of its members are here today. Because of their hard work, and the work of many others, the General Assembly appropriated $210,000 in 1982 to fund local domestic violence programs.[2] And this year the General Assembly approved our request for $500,000 to fund domestic violence programs over the next two years.

We have also taken steps against rape and sexual assault. In 1979 we rewrote the laws on rape and sexual assault. We now have the rape victim shield law. The Council on the Status of Women's Sexual Assault Task Force has worked very hard to support our Rape Victim Assistance Program, which was expanded this year to include counseling and ambulance service costs.[3] For the last two years the Sexual Assault Task Force landed federal funds to help local rape crisis centers.

We've seen great progress made by centers such as REACH of Clay, Cherokee, and Graham counties and RESPECT of Macon County. Centers such as these provide community education to more than 20,000 people each year, and more than 3,000 women have been trained by our Crime Prevention Division to avoid becoming a rape or spouse abuse victim. But we must do more. If we are going to put a stop to these crimes, we must organize a partnership between government and the community. Out here in the west, *you* are the experts and opinion leaders. So today we are asking for *your* leadership and *your* commitment.

RESPECT and REACH and other programs which help victims of domestic abuse and sexual assault need your help. We need a cooperative effort from the grass roots up that includes law enforcement, medical and mental health personnel, district attorneys, church and civic groups. Each county needs a streamlined procedure — from law enforcement to psychological counseling — that will support the victim with the strength and compassion of the local community. State government can't solve this problem, and Washington, D.C., doesn't have the answer. The answer is in your heart. Today I am asking you take that commitment home with you and put it to work to make North Carolina a safer state for everyone.

---

[1] Heman Robinson Clark (1915-   ), native of Elizabethtown; A.B., Davidson College, 1937; LL.B., University of North Carolina at Chapel Hill, 1941; U.S. Army, 1942-1945. Attorney; crime control and public safety secretary, 1982-1985. *North Carolina Manual, 1983,* 651.

Don Truelove (1951-   ), native of Person County; resident of Orange County; A.A., Durham Technical Institute, 1971; was graduated from National Training Institute, 1974, and FBI National Academy, 1985. Former patrol officer, investigator, and lieutenant of investigations, Chapel Hill Police Department; Orange County Sheriff's Department major of operations. Don Truelove to Jan-Michael Poff, August 23, 1985.

Ellen Bradshaw Scouten (1943-   ), resident of Chatham County; A.B., 1964, J.D., 1978, University of North Carolina at Chapel Hill. Assistant district attorney, Judicial District 15B (Chatham and Orange counties), 1978-1984; assistant attorney general, Special Prosecutions Division, state Department of Justice, since 1984. Ellen B. Scouten to Jan-Michael Poff, November 14, 1985.

[2] Executive Order No. 55, signed October 27, 1980, established the Governor's Task Force on Domestic Violence. *N.C. Session Laws, 1981,* 1738-1739. "An Act to Appropriate Funds for Spouse Abuse Programs," *N.C. Session Laws, 1981, Regular and Extra Sessions, 1982,* c. 1346, was ratified June 23, 1982.

[3] "An Act to Clarify the Rape Victim Assistance Program by Specifying that Ambulance Service and Mental Health Counseling Costs are Covered and to Provide Approved Kits for the Collection of Medical Evidence in Rape Cases" was ratified on July 11, 1983. *N.C. Session Laws, 1983,* c. 715.

MEETING ON ROANOKE RIVER BASIN

ROANOKE RAPIDS, NOVEMBER 2, 1983

[The U.S. Army Corps of Engineers granted a permit to Virginia Beach, in January, 1984, allowing the construction of an 85-mile-long pipeline to Lake Gaston. Scheduled for completion in 1993, the $175 million project would daily drain 60 million gallons of water from the vicinity of Pea Hill Creek, in Brunswick County, Virginia, to meet the needs of tidewater cities and towns. The Hunt administration, and residents of southside Virginia and neighboring North Carolina counties, objected to the pipeline, citing potential economic and environmental danger to Lake Gaston, Kerr Lake, and contiguous rural areas. *News and Observer*, September 7, 1984, April 5, 1985.

Speaking in Roanoke Rapids, Governor Hunt summarized his opposition to the Lake Gaston pipeline and emphasized cooperation between the citizens in the Old Dominion and the Tar Heel state in combating the project. See also his February 8, 1984, testimony before the Subcommittee on Water Resources, U.S. House Public Works and Transportation Committee, below.]

We are all here today because of our shared concern for the future of the Roanoke River basin. More specifically, we are here because the city of Virginia Beach proposes to unilaterally divert 60 million gallons of water per day from the Roanoke basin. That is more water than is presently used by any city in either North Carolina *or* Virginia.

Despite the magnitude of this project, despite the very disturbing implications of it, the Army Corps of Engineers wants to let it happen without even conducting an in-depth study of the environmental and economic consequences. They would let it happen despite the glaring lack of effective controls on future water levels for Kerr Lake, Lake Gaston, and the Roanoke River. They would let it happen despite the availability of sources of water within the commonwealth of Virginia.

I am here today to assure you that as long as North Carolina has any legal means of preventing it from happening, not one drop of water will be taken. Not one drop of water will be taken from the Roanoke basin for an ill-planned, long-distance solution to a local problem. Literally within moments of the issuance of a permit for this project, Attorney General Rufus Edmisten and I will file suit in the appropriate court. And we are prepared to stay in court for as long as it takes.

A whole host of very serious issues have been given cavalier treatment in this matter: What about the future water levels of Kerr Lake? What about the recreation sites on Kerr Lake, which attracted 1.5 million visitors in the past year? What about the $650,000 invested by private businesses in the past year in marina facilities on Kerr Lake, and the $300,000 in investment planned for the future? What about the striped bass fishery on the Roanoke River that is already on the decline? What about the anticipated reduced flow of the Roanoke downstream from the Roanoke Rapids Dam? The city of Virginia Beach and Corps of Engineers may not care about these questions, but you and I care.

I believe this region has a bright economic future, a future that depends on adequate water resources. We are not being narrow-minded or provincial. We bear no ill will toward the commonwealth of Virginia or the cities and towns of tidewater Virginia. We simply call upon the communities involved to cooperate with each other toward taking advantage of more accessible sources of water.

We are prepared to raise all of these issues in detail at the November 14 public hearing, here in Roanoke Rapids. There will be representatives from several state agencies here after this meeting today to assist any of you in preparing your presentations for the public hearing. Also ready to assist you is Congressman Tim Valentine.[1] He could not be here today because of a series of very important roll-call votes in Congress. But, as you know, his position and mine are one and the same. He is represented here today by A. B. Swindell of his staff.

Attorney General Rufus Edmisten will represent the state of North Carolina at the November 14 hearing, and I am happy to report that Virginia's former attorney general, Andrew Miller,[2] now practicing law in Washington, has been retained to assist us in this dispute. Andy Miller isn't the only Virginian who questions the wisdom of the Lake Gaston pipeline. Congressman Dan Daniel,[3] members of the Virginia General Assembly, and many local government officials north of the border are opposed.

We met here today not as obstructionists but as reasonable people who share a deep concern and bright hopes for the future of this region. Our words about that future would ring awfully hollow if we were not prepared to fight the uncontrolled and ill-advised diversion of water from the Roanoke basin. I appreciate the opportunity to join with you today in this effort.

---

[1] Itimous Thaddeus (Tim) Valentine, Jr. (1926-   ), native of Rocky Mount, Nash County; A.B., Citadel, 1948; LL.B., University of North Carolina at Chapel Hill, 1952. Attorney; legal adviser, 1965, and legislative counsel, 1967, to Governor Dan K. Moore; chairman, state Democratic Executive Committee, 1966-1968; U.S. representative from North Carolina's Second Congressional District since 1983 and reelected in 1984. *North Carolina Manual, 1983,* 163.

[2] Andrew Pickens Miller (1932-   ), native of Fairfax, Virginia; resident of Alexandria, Virginia; A.B., Princeton University, 1954; LL.B., University of Virginia, 1960; U.S. Army, 1955-1957. Practicing attorney, 1960-1969, and since 1977; Virginia attorney general, 1970-1977; Democrat. *Who's Who in America, 1982-1983,* II, 2308.

[3] W. C. (Dan) Daniel (1914-   ), native of Chatham, Virginia; resident of Danville, Virginia. Resigned as assistant to the board chairman, Dan River Mills, Inc., in

1968; member, Virginia House of Delegates, 1959-1968; first elected to U.S. House from Virginia's Fifth Congressional District in 1968 and returned in subsequent elections; Democrat. Barone and Ujifusa, *Almanac of American Politics, 1984*, 1218.

STATEWIDE CONFERENCE ON SCIENCE AND TECHNOLOGY

RALEIGH, NOVEMBER 2, 1983

[Hunt frequently recounted, before business, education, civic, and scientific groups his guidelines for sustaining economic growth. Speeches addressing this topic, similar in content to the one reprinted below, were delivered at the Wilson County Leadership Conference, in Raleigh, June 7; the Governor's Economic Development Conference, Raleigh, October 19; the Charlotte Downtown Rotary Club, October 25; a news conference and the N.C. League of Municipalities, October 31; and the Winston-Salem Rotary Club, December 13, 1983.]

This Governor's Task Force on Science and Technology has drawn on a broad spectrum of North Carolina: business and labor, state and local government, the public schools, higher education, and community leaders. The task force members and their staff have dedicated the last fifteen months to this report.[1] Today, all of you—leaders in this state—have come here to review their work and, in a frank and open way, tell me as governor and all North Carolina how we can achieve the goals of educational excellence, quality research, and economic prosperity.

North Carolina is making progress. Over the last decade, we have broadened, diversified, and strengthened our economy. We have become a leader in technology. We have strengthened education, health care, transportation, and environmental management. Now, the task force recognizes that new challenges are before us:

—Challenges in the form of advancing technologies, which can both create new jobs and eliminate existing jobs.

—Challenges in the form of international competition, which opens new channels of trade but also threatens to cut off those who fail to compete.

—Challenges that shift from the federal government to states and communities the responsibility and the opportunity to promote creativity and excellence in education and economic development.

The task force offers a strategy for our response to these challenges. It calls on business, education, and government at every level to work as partners to make the critical investments we need to grow and prosper socially and economically:

—Investments in new technologies, technologies that put people *to* work, not out of work. Research, innovation, and technology made American farms the most productive in the world; they can do the same for American factories.

—Investments in job training, in our fifty-eight community colleges, and the other resources that can train new workers and retrain those who lose a job and need new skills.

—Investments in education, not just for the sake of education, but for the sake of economic growth.

—Investments in the infrastructure, so that roads and water and waste-water systems can support economic growth.

—Investments in protecting our natural resources and wisely managing their use.

—Investments in healthy people—in children, the handicapped, and the elderly—so that they can use their energies and talents.

The challenge to you and me, as leaders, is to mobilize all of society's resources to make those investments. It used to be that we looked to Washington for leadership and answers. Now, we should be looking to Raleigh and to your hometown, to our universities, and our public schools. Most of all, we should be looking to business—to the boardrooms, to the shop floors, to the research labs.

As governor, I see a special role for state government: as the catalyst that brings together business, education, and government, that helps to translate technology into economic growth and jobs:

—Jobs in the textile, furniture, apparel, and agriculture-related industries, where technology can cut costs and increase productivity.

—Jobs in the new, high-technology industries that North Carolina is attracting—from microelectronics to medicine.

—Jobs in the hundreds of small businesses that turn new ideas into new products and services.

This means developing new ways of working together and accomplishing our goals. Just as we look to technology to help create jobs, we must look to innovative leadership to help create dynamic and productive partnerships among business, education, and government. Just as we turn to science to foster economic growth, we must turn to the vision and inspiration of the arts and humanities to see that the human spirit rises to its fullest potential.

That requires not just looking at our economy, but at society as a whole. It requires a new vision of society—one that sets as its ultimate goal the full development and growth of every single individual as a responsible, valuable, and participating member of society. It used to be that society made progress by conquering new frontiers of land. Now the new frontiers are the frontiers of innovation—in business and industry, in schools and universities, in the halls of government. If we work as partners—guided by principles of justice, integrity, and equality—we can cross new frontiers and meet new challenges.

It all comes down to reaching out and touching people where they live and where they work. That is where the changes count. If we do that, we can set off tiny ripples of individual success and well-being that can become great waves of social and economic prosperity.

---

[1]The report to which Hunt refers is *New Challenges for a New Era: Progress through Innovation, Education, and Research in North Carolina. Final Report of the Governor's Task Force on Science and Technology* (Raleigh, North Carolina: N.C. Board of Science and Technology, Office of the Governor, 4 vols. [draft], November, 1983). The final version was released in 1984.

TESTIMONY SUBMITTED TO U.S. DEPARTMENT OF COMMERCE IMPORT ADMINISTRATION

WASHINGTON, D.C., NOVEMBER 14, 1983

[Members of both houses of Congress and the American Textile Manufacturers Association demanded that countervailing duties be imposed upon textile imports from the People's Republic of China. Supporters of the measure contended that the country's dual exchange rate amounted to an illegal subsidy that supported its textile industry at the expense of American jobs. Conversely, U.S. commercial and agriculture interests, as well as some Reagan administration officials, feared Beijing would revoke its $2 billion grain contract and cancel orders for aircraft and high-technology equipment if duties were enacted. Import limits were approved, and in 1983 communist China canceled its U.S. grain purchases. "Putting a Chill on Trade with China," *Business Week*, November 21, 1983, 117; "Skirting Quotas," *Fortune*, September 17, 1984, 6.]

I want to thank the department for permitting me to submit this statement for the record of its special conference on countervailing duties. The issues that you are considering are of the greatest concern to me and to the people of North Carolina. Only long-standing, pressing commitments prevented me from coming to Washington to express my views to you personally.

According to your notice, you are focusing on two issues. The first is whether the countervailing duty law applies to countries that do not have a free-market economy. Frankly, I do not think that there is any room for controversy here. When the law speaks in clear, unambiguous language—as the countervailing duty [CVD] law does—the government has no choice but to enforce it according to its terms. That means the department must apply the countervailing duty law to subsidized exports from *any* country, including both free-market and state-controlled economy countries. Quite simply, that is what the statute requires.[1]

I can understand the concerns that motivate others to urge the department to accord China special treatment. However, that would be a terrible precedent. It is one of the great principles of our legal system that our law is applied equally to all, and that enforcement is not abandoned when it becomes inconvenient or unpopular. This principle should be a cornerstone of our developing relations with China. In time, I am sure they will learn to appreciate its considerable value in assuring fairness to all parties.

Further, our relations with China cannot be purchased at the price of domestic jobs and the destruction of the U.S. textile and apparel industries. In the past few years, we have lost thousands of textile jobs in North Carolina and throughout the South. Many of these jobs were lost to subsidized and dumped imports—oftentimes, imports from China.

What we need now is more vigorous enforcement of our trade, not loopholes. The administration simply cannot ignore its responsibility to enforce the laws *fully and fairly*—and to protect American industries and jobs—in order to appease the Chinese.

On the first issue, therefore, the law is clear and it is your obligation to enforce it. The second issue to be considered here is whether a dual exchange rate in nonconvertible currency that applies to the entire trade sector can confer a countervailable subsidy on exports. The answer has to be, "Yes, it can." Although I have an advanced degree in economics, I do not consider myself to be an expert in exchange rate practices. However, I have no doubt that I could construct a dual exchange rate system, complete with auxiliary tax rebates and direct import subsidies, that everyone would agree conferred a countervailable subsidy on exports.

The real question the department has to consider here is whether the Chinese system confers a countervailable subsidy on textile and apparel exports to the United States. And the place to consider that question is not in this conference, which deals with the issue in abstract terms, but in the China CVD case, where it is presented in a meaningful, factual context.

When the department scrutinizes the Chinese system, as it must in the China CVD case, the countervailing duty law itself, and its past administrative and judicial interpretations, will be your guide. Thus, however the Chinese system operates, if it is intended to subsidize exports and actually has the effect of subsidizing exports, it must be declared a countervailable subsidy under the law.

Under those circumstances, the department has a clear legal obligation to the people of the U.S. textile and apparel industries—including many of my own constituents—to impose an appropriate offsetting duty.

We expect that you will proceed quickly with the China CVD case and that your decision there will reflect the scrupulous, evenhanded, vigorous enforcement of the law that is required to vindicate its purpose and protect U.S. industries from unfair foreign competition. We will be looking to you for just such action. Thank you for your attention.

[1] For countervailing duties procedures and determinations, see 19 CFR Ch. III (4-1-85 edition), *Code of Federal Regulations* (Washington, D.C.: U.S. Government Printing Office, 1985), s. 355.

COMMUNITY COLLEGE CONFERENCE ON HIGH TECHNOLOGY

RALEIGH, NOVEMBER 21, 1983

Governor Scott,[1] I deeply appreciate your kind introduction, but I think it is more appropriate right now for me to pay tribute to you and the leadership you are giving to the community college system. Bob Scott understands as well as anybody in this state that this system is where the action is and where it is going to be for a long time to come. He summed it up very well not too long ago, when I heard him describe the system as now having an "identity in education that is unique."

As you know, I recently returned from an industrial recruitment mission to Europe. Those European business executives who knew anything about North Carolina mentioned to me, almost without fail, the reputation our state's workers have for productivity. That reminded me of what a great job that all of you, under the leadership of President Scott, are doing to build and strengthen North Carolina's economy.

Mr. President, you and the community college system have come together at a very fortunate time in our state's history. From my perspective, as a governor who places the highest priority on education and economic development, I see the community college system coming of age.

If North Carolina is to compete successfully for new jobs, and to take a place on the leading edge of the technological revolution, we must be able to tell prospective firms that we will provide them with the trained workers they need. Thanks to all of you, we were able to do just that.

Over the next two decades, we are going to see tremendous numbers of adults reentering the classroom. They will be searching for new skills and new futures. They will be looking to you for help. Technological innovation is reshaping our economy and our day-to-day lives. North Carolina's hands and minds must be trained differently now.

You have the very difficult challenge of making possible practically every announcement of a new industry coming to North Carolina.

Why North Carolina? I'll tell you what industry says: They say they pick North Carolina because our community colleges can deliver the flexible, high-quality job training that is essential in a rapidly changing economy.

The list of new partnerships grows ever longer: Asplundh and Vance-Granville Community College, Bendix and Gaston College, Central Piedmont and Verbatim, Durham Tech and Mitsubishi and Sumitomo.

Since 1977 you have helped bring $12 billion in industrial investment and 200,000 manufacturing jobs to North Carolina. That is all the proof anybody needs that our investment in this system is paying off.

The programs that are being established around the state are very exciting. I'm talking about the robotics curriculum at Catawba Valley Technical College and the industrial management and maintenance programs that Forsyth Tech will be offering to twenty-year employees of Western Electric. Our cooperative Skills Training centers are zeroing in on the needs of existing industries that are ready to expand and modernize.

These are some of the reasons why the General Assembly this year was willing to invest $28 million in new equipment, $19.6 million for new enrollment, and $12.6 million for new industries.

Your next great challenge will be in small business development. We already know that community colleges and technical institutes are the most important contact for someone interested in starting or expanding a small business.

You are touching lives as no other agency of government can. Looking at it from a broader vantage point, you are an essential element in meeting the greatest challenge facing America: the challenge to our economic and technological leadership of the world.

That challenge is not merely theoretical. It is real, as evidenced by what has happened in recent years in the steel, auto, and textile industries. Technological innovation brought us to our position of world leadership, and that is what will preserve it for us if we are up to the challenge. The outcome of this struggle will determine whether we in North Carolina and across America will be able to provide ourselves with the ingredients of a good standard of living.

As the foundation of North Carolina's economy, you are the key to its future. I believe you are up to the challenge. I believe you have come of age, and that's why I believe North Carolina's greatest days lie ahead.

---

[1] Robert Walter Scott (1929-   ), lieutenant governor, 1965-1969, and governor, 1969-1973, of North Carolina; president, North Carolina Department of Community Colleges, since 1983. Previously identified in Mitchell, *Addresses of Hunt*, I, 275n; see also *North Carolina Manual, 1983*, 631.

ELIZABETH II LAUNCHING

MANTEO, NOVEMBER 22, 1983

We have come here this morning to mark an important moment in the building of our ship, our symbol of the unique link that binds the shores of Roanoke Island to the British Isles. This launching marks the end of the *Elizabeth II*'s construction on land, where her timber was cut and shaped and fitted by skilled hands. But it is the beginning of *Elizabeth II*'s adventure in her element—the water that brought the Roanoke voyagers to this first encounter with a new continent.

We can, and we will, celebrate those days of almost 400 years ago in many ways before this commemoration ends in 1987. In song, in drama, in books and stories, we will rejoice in our heritage—and I promise all of you here today that, whatever the obstacles, this ship will sail our sounds![1] But I think it's proper that we celebrate most visibly with this ship, this symbol we are building to remind us of what we are all about.

The men and women who sailed on ships like this to our shores were builders. They built a fort. They built houses. They built a town they called the Cittie of Raleigh. But, most important of all, they built in their own hearts, and in the hearts and minds of the countrymen who came after them, a dream of freedom in a new land. They brought with them the dream of a new order built upon the foundation of law and language from their homeland and infused it with the energy of the new.

Today, their houses and town are gone. The remains of those structures are hidden somewhere on this island, or nearby—and I think we'll find them before this anniversary celebration is over—but we don't have to search far for the dream that was built on this shore. It's here, all around us, in the reality of a nation that grew strong from English beginnings.

It was a dream of democracy that would reach out and welcome other cultures and other people to a new nation. Yes, they knew hunger and disease and poverty; they knew hardship and sacrifice. But they also knew that something bound them together. It was the value of a job well done. It was the joy in extending a hand to lift up your brothers and sisters. It was the belief in a new start, a new land, a new freedom. Strong families and proud communities grew up here. They made their beliefs American articles of faith, and in turn, they were all made stronger by their democratic union.

Even as this ship we build is not yet finished, even as it awaits final touches and testing, so too is the dream it represents still in progress. For all our sakes, I hope we never finish building the dream that has driven North Carolina and America over four centuries. For I believe it is the work of building itself that propels us confidently into the future.

From this place where toil and courage and determination launched our country's history 400 years ago, we know we are still young. Our dreams are young, our faith is strong, and our visions are still fresh. And this ship will sail on those strong, fresh winds.

---

[1] The governor was referring to the six-foot depth of some areas of Manteo's harbor, versus the eight-foot draw of the *Elizabeth II*, and the necessity of dredging a deeper shipping channel. For details, see *News and Observer*, January 5, 1985.

STATEMENT ON OFFICE
OF BUSINESS DEVELOPMENT

SALISBURY, DECEMBER 5, 1983

A few months ago, several of our state's largest and most innovative corporations joined together to form a special task force on business development. Working in cooperation with state government, these companies laid the groundwork for a unique new public-private partnership designed to help match investors to development opportunities in North Carolina cities and towns.

It is my pleasure to announce today that the state Department of Commerce is establishing a new Office of Business Development to follow through on this important new initiative. The office will be supported by grants from the Z. Smith Reynolds Foundation and members of the business development task force, including Carolina Telephone and Telegraph Company, Carolina Power and Light Company, NCNB National Bank of North Carolina, Virginia Electric Power Company, and United Carolina Bank.

In January of next year, the office will begin business recruitment pilot programs in Salisbury, Asheville, and Tarboro. Each community will establish a team of local business and government leaders to supervise the program in their area. Advertising programs and other promotional tools perfected by our state's industrial recruitment program will be used to attract commercial and other investors. By working to attract service, retail, and other commercial businesses, this development program will build on the great downtown revitalization progress these pilot communities have already made under our state's innovative "Main Street" approach. The result will be increased retail sales, further support for downtown revitalization, and hundreds of new jobs for the people of these areas.

I want to commend our secretary of commerce, C. C. Hope, for his fine work in launching this new initiative. Under his direction, the Department of Commerce has moved rapidly to plan and implement a variety of new economic development programs. Today's announcement is just the first of these initiatives to be made public. I believe the effort we are beginning today has the potential to bring cities and towns across North Carolina the same kind of strong economic growth that our industrial development program has brought to our state in general.

NORTH CAROLINA FARM BUREAU FEDERATION

ASHEVILLE, DECEMBER 5, 1983

[Hunt's addresses before the state Future Farmers of America convention, June 16, 1982; Cooperative Council of North Carolina, January 19, 1983; Southern Farm Show, February 1, 1984; Farm Bureau Women's Leadership Conference, March 15, 1984; and the North Carolina Farm Bureau annual convention, December 3, 1984, also dealt with a number of the issues discussed below.]

It is a pleasure for me to be with you and have a part in this Forty-eighth Annual Convention of the North Carolina Farm Bureau Federation. As I near the end of my tenure as governor, I want to commend the tens of thousands of Farm Bureau members all across North Carolina for their great efforts to build better communities, strengthen agriculture, and develop a better state. In particular, I am grateful for the leadership of your distinguished president, John Sledge,[1] and your other officers and board members. Without the efforts of the total Farm Bureau "family"—a family that is quite large, well over 200,000 members—this would be a poorer state today in many ways.

We've worked together to promote economic growth, to improve our educational system at all levels, to strengthen our criminal justice system, to preserve our best agricultural land for farming, and in general to promote the wise use and conservation of our many natural resources. I am grateful for your help.

Of special importance, you and I have worked together successfully for a sound fiscal policy for this state. For seven years in a row, we have had a balanced state budget without any general increase in taxes except the gasoline tax which was critical for our highway system. To balance seven budgets in a row, we have had to take some hard steps such as limiting the growth in the number of state employees, in some instances reducing the number of employees, and holding back on salary increases. We've had to hold back on development of new programs or expansion of old ones.

Along with most of our citizens, I have become increasingly concerned about the utter failure of Washington to balance the federal budget. We have expressed our concern in a call for a constitutional convention to require a balanced federal budget. In fiscal 1982 the deficit was $110 billion, and in fiscal '83 it soared to an all-time high of $210 billion. The projection for fiscal 1984 is for a deficit of $180 billion. Stated another way, the federal deficit amounted to only 1.7 percent of the gross national product in 1978 and 2.2 percent in 1980. By 1982, however, the deficit had risen to 4 percent of GNP, and for fiscal 1983 it was projected at 6.5 percent of GNP.

The deficit situation today is alarming. It is threatening our future. The effects are being felt today and will be felt by our children and grandchildren for years to come. We simply must come to grips with this problem and bite the bullet at the federal level as we have already done in North Carolina.

American agriculture has had, and continues to have, particularly tough times. The great American dream of prosperity for all is a hollow mockery as far as most of our farmers are concerned. The truth is, many, many farmers are nearer to bankruptcy today than they are to prosperity. Why? Not just because of the 1983 summer drought, even though that was quite severe and caused very heavy losses.

A major reason for the financial disaster on our farms is that this nation's overall monetary and fiscal policies over the past three years have been made without adequate consideration of the effects on agriculture. Instead of a "sound" American dollar, we have a "high" dollar which has dealt a body blow to agriculture. Huge deficits and a mounting burden of federal debt have kept interest rates high. This has had the effect of increasing the value of our dollar relative to the world's other major currencies. In fact, when measured against all major currencies, the dollar today is 40 percent higher than at the beginning of 1980.

This means our products, farm and nonfarm, are 40 percent *less competitive* in world markets. As you know so very well, export sales are tremendously important to American farmers. We need foreign markets in order to stay in the farming business—to utilize our productive capacity and keep farm income at satisfactory levels—and the entire nation needs the very positive contribution that agriculture makes to our balance of payments. Is it any wonder that our farm exports have fallen sharply, from $43 billion in 1980 to about $34 billion this marketing year? At the same time, our imports have increased. Other countries around the world are subsidizing their exports in order to build markets for the future.

The troubles of many U.S. farmers can be attributed directly to the PIK or payment-in-kind program, which was hastily conceived and poorly administered.[2] PIK worked at cross purposes, favoring grain producers at the expense of livestock and poultry producers.

Yet this program will cost the government between $10 billion and $21 billion, depending upon the bookkeeping system used.

PIK will also prove costly to consumers. Because of higher feed prices, production costs have increased three to four cents a dozen for eggs; two to three cents a pound for broilers; one to two cents a pound for turkeys; three to four cents a pound for pork; and ten to twenty cents a pound for feeder calves. These increases likely will show up in higher food prices in retail stores.

We have finally got ninety-six counties eligible for emergency assistance. I have worked hard for emergency assistance for drought-stricken farmers, and I have continually insisted that our livestock and poultry farmers should have access to the emergency livestock feeding program. The needs are so great, yet so little has been done to help farmers who suffered heavy losses as a result of this summer's blistering heat and drought.[3]

We need assistance through Farmers Home Administration, but the farmer who needs FmHA credit also needs supervised credit. FmHA assistance should not be to bail out mismanagers or bring additional production into an already oversupplied market. Worthy young farmers need help, as do limited resource farmers. All farmers should manage their affairs so as to protect their equity. [However,] there is a point beyond which new extensions of credit, no matter how easy the terms, are simply not in the best interest of the borrower.

Adding to the woes of agriculture, an assessment program was imposed on dairy farmers, *and* the federal excise tax on cigarettes was doubled, from eight cents to sixteen cents a pack.[4] Many states and cities also raised their cigarette taxes. These higher taxes imposed on cigarettes have cost the tobacco farmers of North Carolina tens of millions of dollars.

Recently I saw a news article from the North Carolina Agricultural Extension Service in which the specialist in charge of economics and business was offering farm families tips on strategies for survival.[5] These were not tips on how to prosper, but simply on how to survive. Another article from the extension service gave basic information on federal laws on bankruptcy.[6] These are two indications of the very serious problems confronting our farm people in North Carolina and elsewhere.

What can be done to improve the agricultural situation in North Carolina and the nation? I propose several steps:

First—and you are working toward that end at this convention— we must continue to formulate sound policies to present to our policy makers.

Second, we must focus on *net* income and be aggressive. We must make every reasonable effort to expand agricultural exports, even if some slight subsidy is needed. Otherwise, we must devise and develop ways by which commodity growers, with the aid of the government, may effectively manage production and supplies.

Third, we must promote agriculture not only as a basic industry but also as a substantial part of our national economy. If we want economic growth in this country, we must see that agriculture gets fair treatment and opportunities for full development of its potential.

Fourth, we need to do more to promote wise use and conservation of our soil, our water, and other resources. The federal government simply must reassert its leadership role in this area. The father of the soil conservation movement in this country was a native North Carolinian, the late Hugh Hammond Bennett.[7] Dr. Bennett taught us that all of civilization is dependent upon a few inches of precious, priceless topsoil, along with adequate water. Yet today, erosion of farmland is taking place at a frightening rate. Unless we can reverse current trends, the losses to farmers and our entire society will be catastrophic.

Finally, it is time for us to start rebuilding—in Washington and all across the nation—a coalition of forces that will work for the best interests of agriculture and our nation's farm families. No matter how worthy our goals or how pressing our needs, we can hope to achieve them only with the help and support of a broad range of leaders, organizations, and people, both farm and nonfarm. That is the objective toward which we should be working constantly, day in and day out.

Building and holding together a coalition is not easy. It requires a lot of nurturing, coaxing, and compromise. There is no place for the politics of extremism, for, as we have seen many times, extremism is divisive and destructive. It is not the foundation for building any kind of effective coalition to help agriculture or any other cause.

I am optimistic about the future of agriculture. It will always be our nation's basic industry. Wherever I am, whatever I am doing, your membership and interests will be close to my heart.

I do believe we have work to do. Some people will claim that all of agriculture's problems are being solved and properly managed right now. I say we have an unfinished agenda. We need to develop the programs and policies that will make agriculture more than just a passable way to earn a living. We need for agriculture to be profitable.

Not many governors or congressmen in this country grew up milking cows and cropping tobacco. Not many of these officials have their home on a farm. Not many have a son or daughter living on the family farm and depending on its success and profitability for their livelihood. These things can make quite a difference in your perspective, feelings, and attitude about the problems of agriculture and farm people. Despite our immediate problems, I have faith that the most ingenious of all Americans—our farmers—can deal with

those problems if given a fair chance and reasonable help. I intend
to do all in my power to see that you get that.

[1] John William Sledge (1924-1985), president, North Carolina Farm Bureau Federation, 1974-1985. Previously identified in Mitchell, *Addresses of Hunt*, I, 742n; see also
News and Observer, April 24, 1985.

[2] PIK was envisioned as a means for the United States government to reduce the
costs of storing surplus cotton, corn, rice, and wheat, while alleviating the over-
abundance of these commodities that had forced prices down. Farmers participating
in the program agreed to curtail production of specific crops; in turn, they were
awarded up to 95 percent of their normal annual yield of these products from those
already in government warehouses. The plan was not entirely successful. "A Bumper
Crop of Blunders in Reagan's Farm Program," *Business Week*, December 12, 1983,
62; "Carving Out a New Dust Bowl," *Time*, June 27, 1983, 27; "Getting PIK-ed to
Pieces," *Time*, April 18, 1983, 75; "How PIK is Poisoning Farm Policy," *Business
Week*, August 8, 1983, 62.

[3] The governor finally was able to announce in June, 1984, that "adverse weather
conditions" beginning March 1, 1983, and ending March 29, 1984, qualified all of the
state's counties for Farmers Home Administration disaster loan assistance. "News
Release from the Governor's Office," June 21, 1984.

[4] Although Congress empowered U.S. agriculture secretary John Block to enact a
50-cent-per-hundredweight tax on raw milk in 1982, lawsuits from outraged dairy
farmers prevented it from taking effect until the following year. The measure was
designed to curb milk production. "Plugging a Leak in Dairy Supports," *Business
Week*, May 9, 1983, 145.

The federal excise tax on cigarettes was doubled as part of a $98.3 billion revenue-
increase package, which Congress approved in mid-August, 1982. It was scheduled to
revert to 8 cents per pack in 1985. However, the U.S. House passed a budget deficit
reduction bill on the last day of October, 1985, that would have kept the levy at 16
cents. *Durham Morning Herald*, August 20, 1982; *News and Observer*, November 1,
1985.

[5] Press Release, "Farmers Offered Strategy Tips for Survival," October 18, 1983,
Department of Agricultural Communications, North Carolina State University.

[6] Press Release, "Bankruptcy is Answer for Some Families," October 19, 1983,
Department of Agricultural Communications, North Carolina State University.

[7] Hugh Hammond Bennett (1881-1960), native of Wadesboro; B.S., University of
North Carolina at Chapel Hill, 1903. Soil conservationist; Soil Erosion Service
director, U.S. Interior Department, 1933-1935; Soil Conservation Service director,
U.S. Agriculture Department, 19351951; author. Powell, *DNCB*, I, 137-138.

EMPLOYMENT SECURITY COMMISSION
LOCAL MANAGERS CONFERENCE

RALEIGH, DECEMBER 7, 1983

On behalf of all the North Carolinians you helped put to work
this year, I want to thank you. This year, all of you—our Employment Security Commission team—helped to give the greatest
Christmas gift anyone could ever receive: a good job.

Lately, North Carolina's Employment Security Commission has
set several records that will be tough to beat. But I know you had to

fight for everything you gained. One of those fights was to keep as many as forty-eight local offices open. Those offices are our grassroots link with our work force, and to make a cut there would be the same as cutting thousands of North Carolinians out of their chance at a job.

This year, the results of your hard work have been very impressive:

—Your placement staff productivity ranked North Carolina number one in the nation for the first nine months of this past fiscal year, and number two nationally for the entire fiscal year. This is the highest ranking in ESC history.

—You found jobs for more than 20,000 veterans—and that resulted in a placement rate of more than 38 percent, in addition to a 10 percent increase in the placement of disabled veterans. This means you put more veterans to work this year than ever before in ESC history.

—As a result of more than 57,000 placement transactions, you found work for more than 15,000 migrant farm workers.

—Your partnership with our state's more than 103,000 employers put more than 124,000 people back in the North Carolina work force last year—another record-setting accomplishment.

One of the things all this tells me is that Chairman Glenn Jernigan did not take lightly the challenge I gave him. Two years ago, I stated very emphatically that I wanted our Employment Security Commission to be a place where you come to *get a job*, not just a check. Now, two years later, we can say with confidence that the North Carolina Employment Security Commission is truly a job service office, *not* an unemployment office.

Many people have been justifiably concerned about the North Carolina Unemployment Insurance Fund. Today, I would like to point out that at a time when twenty-nine states have unemployment insurance funds that are bankrupt, North Carolina paid out more than $522 million over the last fiscal year, including extended benefits and federal supplemental compensation. Weekly benefit checks averaged $107 for more than 292,000 jobless workers. During the same period of time, ESC tax auditors collected $228 million.

The strength of North Carolina's Unemployment Insurance Fund, even after an extended recession, ranks us fifth in the nation in terms of solvency. I think that ranking is a proud testament to your hard work and to North Carolina's fiscal integrity. Thanks to the 1983 General Assembly, we have replenished our fund and protected its solvency for years to come.[1] And thanks to your diligence in controlling fraud, our courts are sending out a very real warning to those who would abuse our system. I understand that from January, 1982, to October, 1983, ESC tried 1,506 cases of fraud, and the courts found 1,505 guilty.

North Carolina's economy has made tremendous progress since

1977. Investments in new and expanding industry have grown by more than $12 billion, creating over 200,000 new manufacturing jobs. For every one of those manufacturing jobs, we estimate that two additional jobs were created in service-related industries.

That diversification by design has helped strengthen North Carolina's economy, but we now live in an age where technology is changing our economic base almost daily. ESC's job is to respond to those changes as quickly as possible, and I've heard that you have taken up that challenge. In Wilmington and Rockingham County, for example, I understand our Dislocated Worker Program, as part of the federal Job Training Partnership Act, has the potential to be a national model.[2] I've heard that you're working with our community college system and the business community to provide job counseling, training, and new work opportunities to dislocated workers in those two communities.

Those workers need a variety of services. Some simply need a referral. Some will require extensive job retraining and perhaps relocation. What it all comes down to is that they need individualized services, and that's the challenge to ESC professionals—to help design a job training and retraining program that fits the individual.

To plan for the job futures of those individuals, I hope Executive Order 77, which designated ESC as our lead agency for labor market information, will be helpful. Now we will have a coordinated effort to link government, education, and our business community with reliable, uniform, and comprehensive labor market information.

It's vital that we begin now to coordinate our planning and job training efforts.

Fewer people are entering the labor market, and our labor force is, on average, growing older. Our current labor force will constitute more than 80 percent of our work force in 1990, and more than 70 percent of our work force by the year 2000.

So we need to invest right now in job training, retraining, and skills programs that work. Those programs—and the workers they train today—will determine the strength and security of our economy into the next century.

My purpose in being with you today is to commend you as members of North Carolina's Employment Security team. Local office managers, professionals and support staff, commission members—you are all a part of North Carolina's future. As state employees, you have met the challenge to render service to your fellow North Carolinians; during tough times, you have rendered that service in a professional, responsible manner. In the years to come, we will continue to need your help and guidance as we build for North Carolina a competitive, world-class economy. With your record of service and accomplishment, I am confident we can keep North Carolina and North Carolinians working toward progress.

[1]"An Act to Assure Unemployment Insurance Trust Fund Solvency and Compliance with Federal Law," c. 585, was ratified June 22 and became effective August 1, 1983. *N.C. Session Laws, 1983.*

[2]PL 97-300, "An Act to Provide for a Job Training Program, and for Other Purposes," 96 Stat. 1322-1399, also known as the "Job Training Partnership Act," was signed into law on October 13, 1982. See Title III, "Employment and Training Assistance for Dislocated Workers," 96 Stat. 1364-1367.

STATEMENT ON MELVILLE
CORPORATION PLANT CLOSINGS

ASHEVILLE, DECEMBER 15, 1983

[Asked to explain the president's directive ending the "orderly marketing agreement" limiting the number of shoes imported into the United States from South Korea and Taiwan, White House spokesman David Gergen replied that Reagan was "'committed to removing as many barriers as possible in the context of free and fair trade,'" and that the action should be considered "'as an expression of faith in the competitive ability of the American shoe industry.'" Business analysts were less sanguine in their assessment of the possible effects of revoking the four-year-old pact, however, pointing out that it had held shoe exports from the two Asian countries to 22 percent of the U.S. market. With the agreement's abolition it was expected that the total would increase significantly and, as a result, 36,000 Americans would find themselves unemployed. "Reagan Drops the Other Shoe," *Newsweek*, July 13, 1981, 59.]

I am delighted to be on the campus of this great university,[1] which today will be the site of a second in a series of four regional hearings by the Commission on Education for Economic Growth. As chairman of the commission, I look forward to hearing from educators, business leaders, parents, and interested citizens concerning what we need to do in North Carolina to make our schools better. My own remarks for the hearing have been handed to you in advance, and I will be happy to answer your questions about them after I have made my statement. At this point, however, I want to make some comments about a terrible blow that has been dealt to the economy of western North Carolina.

The recent announcement by the Melville Corporation that it is shutting down its shoe-manufacturing plants in Hot Springs, Sparta, Boone, and Wilkesboro means almost 2,000 workers are facing unemployment. It would be bad enough if these closings were due only to domestic economic conditions, but the fact of the matter is that this did not have to happen. It is happening because the Reagan administration has left the American footwear industry to the mercy of unfair foreign competition.

An orderly marketing agreement negotiated by the Carter administration in 1977 limited shoe imports to about 50 percent of the

American domestic market. The Reagan administration could have renewed that agreement for another three years in 1981, and the U.S. International Trade Commission recommended such an extension. Instead, the administration allowed the agreement to expire. Since the middle of 1981, this country has been flooded by imported footwear. Imports are up 17 percent this year alone.

Before the most recent announcement of plant closings, 455 Carolinians employed in the shoe-manufacturing industry had already been affected in 1983 by closings and layoffs. The previous year, another 620 workers were affected by closings and layoffs. Today, there are about 3,900 people employed in thirteen shoe-manufacturing plants in North Carolina. By the time the Melville Corporation has completed its shutdown in mid-1984, the footwear industry in North Carolina will have been cut in half.

North Carolina workers are the most productive in America, and our industries will more than hold their own against fair competition. But a 17 percent increase in imports in one year—bringing the total foreign share of the market to 65 percent—is plainly unfair. State government is limited in its ability to deal with this problem, but we are doing what we can. Secretary of Commerce C. C. Hope has contacted officials of the Melville Corporation and let them know that we want to work with them to locate other manufacturing operations at the plants they are vacating.

There clearly must be a national response to the unfair and unnecessary pressure confronting this industry. I urge the administration to immediately take steps that will result in foreign trade agreements that will allow the American footwear industry to vigorously compete in a fair marketplace.

---

[1] University of North Carolina at Asheville.

NORTH CAROLINA ASSOCIATION
OF SOIL AND WATER CONSERVATION DISTRICTS

CHARLOTTE, JANUARY 9, 1984

It is an honor to join you today for the Forty-first Annual Meeting of the North Carolina Association of Soil and Water Conservation Districts. Charlie Patton, [1] I thank you for the leadership you have given to this association. Your commitment to the cause of conservation will bear dividends for years to come. I also want to commend the Soil and Water Conservation Commission and its chairman, Bob Bowers.[2] This commission provides excellent leadership for soil and water conservation programs in North Carolina by working closely with our Department of Natural Resources and Community Development.

Many of you know my father was a soil conservationist, and you know we practiced what he preached. In the early 1950s, he advertised to buy the most eroded farm within fifty miles of Raleigh. Under his guidance, my FFA [Future Farmers of America] chapter reclaimed the farm. Since those early days, I have had great respect for soil and water supervisors. I know how much North Carolina needs your experience.

That's why I recently invited you to take on an expanded role in protecting our prime farmlands in North Carolina. As a result of our joint efforts I issued an executive order on August 23, 1983, which directs that whenever state funds are proposed for land acquisitions, development projects, or other activities, the projects must be evaluated for their impact on prime farmland and forest land.[3] Your local Boards of Soil and Water Conservation Supervisors will determine if there is a significant impact on prime land. We designed the program this way because you are in the best position to make judgments on land use at the local level.

Today I am inviting you to take on a still larger role in the management of our natural resources, particularly in protecting our nutrient-sensitive waters.

We are entering a new era of change and growth. As we look toward the year 2000, we expect the population of our state to increase by almost a million people. We're witnessing the revitalization of our traditional industries as well as a high technology boom that will carry us into a new century. Travel and tourism will continue to expand because of the climate, terrain, and natural beauty of our state. We welcome good growth in North Carolina and the prospect for more and better jobs and expanded opportunities for our people. But with growth we can expect more pressures on North Carolina's natural resources.

We have devoted a great deal of time and effort recently to an intensive look at one of our most precious and fundamental resources: water. This effort has been led by Joe Grimsley, former secretary of Natural Resources and Community Development, and is now being carried forward by Secretary Jim Summers.[4] These are some of our concerns:

—First, the age-old problem of erosion still haunts us. Not only does this have a dramatic effect on the productive potential of the land, but it becomes sediment in our state's waters. In fact, sediment—just plain dirt—is the largest polluter, by volume, of surface water in North Carolina.

—Second, we are concerned about our "nutrient-sensitive" waters—those that have excessive amounts of certain elements, especially phosphorous, entering our waters and producing undesirable growth of algae. Three bodies of water have already been declared "nutrient sensitive" by the Environmental Management Commission: the Falls and Jordan lakes and the Chowan River.

—Third, we are very concerned over toxic chemicals in our waters. There are tens of thousands of chemical compounds in use today with about 2,000 new chemicals being produced yearly. Recent attention has focused on one of these chemicals, called biocides, used as a germ killer in a number of manufacturing operations.

These are just a few of our concerns about the quality of North Carolina's water. How well we respond will determine the future quality of life in this state. That's why I want to share with you our strategy on water quality and ask for your guidance, your support, and your participation.

We are taking the unprecedented step of preparing a Nutrient Sensitive Watershed Budget for the Chowan River and Falls and Jordan watersheds. This budget will include a significant increase in state support for cost-sharing programs to maintain soil productivity, reduce erosion, and keep nutrients and pesticides from getting into our streams and lakes. The budget will provide increased technical assistance to farmers to help make these cost-sharing funds work for the individual landowner. In addition, the budget will address similar needs in forestry management practices and erosion control from developing areas.[5] I will be asking the legislature to appropriate funds to help you do your job better and protect the quality of our water.

Many other efforts are under way. We have developed an action plan for the Falls and Jordan areas. We have developed a system of classifying our groundwater for better protection. We are working on an innovative approach to pollution control called Pollution Prevention Pays. The idea is to find and promote ways to reduce, prevent, recycle, or eliminate wastes and turn wastes into useful resources.

I know that some of your districts are already tackling these issues; for others of you, they may not have arrived yet, but they will. These are complex issues and there are few, if any, simple answers. Your districts will be called on to interact with government agencies and more and varied organizations and interest groups than ever before. We want your leadership and the benefits of your collective experience in soil and water conservation.

You have the opportunity before you to protect and preserve our water and soil resources for future generations. You have a rich conservation heritage. You have a proven track record. You are caring and innovative, and deep down you believe, as I do, that we have a special responsibility to nurture and protect this land of freedom and plenty. It is a tribute to you that this year you are launching a major statewide effort to build public awareness of the importance of soil and water to our lives. Charlie Patton and

Garland Strickland, you have both been leading forces behind this effort, and I ask you to join me here as I make a special proclamation.[6]

---

[1]Charles R. Patton (1913-), native of Franklin; resident of Asheville; B.S., North Carolina State College (now University), 1935. Retired from U.S. Soil Conservation Service, 1973, after having held various posts in North Carolina and Tennessee; elected supervisor, 1976, Buncombe County Soil and Water Conservation District; president, North Carolina State Association of Soil and Water Conservation Districts, 1983. Charles R. Patton to Jan-Michael Poff, February 24, 1986.

[2]Robert J. Bowers (1926-), native, resident of Sanford; attended Elon College; B.S., North Carolina State College (now University), 1952; U.S. Navy, 1944-1946; state commander, Veterans of Foreign Wars, 1962-1963. Supervisor, Lee County Soil and Water Conservation District, since 1957; member, North Carolina Sedimentation Control Commission, 1978-1985; chairman, state Soil and Water Conservation Commission, 1978-1985; state vice-president, North Carolina Tobacco Growers Assn., since 1983. Robert J. Bowers to Jan-Michael Poff, February 19, 1986.

[3]See Executive Order No. 96, "Conservation of Prime Agricultural and Forest Lands," *N.C. Session Laws, 1983*, 1440-1445.

[4]James A. Summers (1928-), native of Salisbury; resident of Cary; B.A., Duke University, 1949; U.S. Naval Reserve. Mayor of Salisbury, 1975-1979; deputy secretary, 1981-1984, and secretary, 1984-1985, Department of Natural Resources and Community Development; became Cary town manager in February, 1985. James A. Summers to Jan-Michael Poff, March 16, 1986.

[5]See "Special Address on Education," June 7, 1984, footnote 24, above.

[6]Garland E. Strickland (1915-), native of Nash County; educated in Nash County schools. Nash County Soil and Water Conservation District supervisor for forty years; state treasurer, for thirty years, and president, in 1984, of North Carolina Association of Soil and Water Conservation District Supervisors; member, state Soil and Water Conservation Commission, 1983-1985. Garland E. Strickland to Jan-Michael Poff, April 1, 1986.

The proclamation Hunt issued designated 1984 as the "Year of Soil and Water Conservation" in North Carolina. Proclamation of January 9, 1984, Governors Papers, James B. Hunt, Jr., Archives, Division of Archives and History, Raleigh.

MECKLENBURG COUNTY HEALTH CARE COST MANAGEMENT COUNCIL

CHARLOTTE, JANUARY 9, 1984

[The rising cost of health care was also the topic of the governor's speech before the winter meeting of the North Carolina Hospital Association, January 20, 1983.]

We are here to talk about one of the most serious issues facing us today: the cost of health care. The questions we need to answer are not whether rising costs will change our health care system, but how they will change it, and what we can do to help shape those changes.

In 1982 one out of every ten dollars spent in this country was spent on health care. At the same time, the Consumer Price Index went up 3.9 percent for all items together—but the health care component shot up 11 percent. As business people, you know we cannot afford to have this country's third largest industry growing at more than twice the rate of the rest of the economy.

Rising health care costs affect just about every area of our lives. They threaten business. They destroy the financial security of our citizens. Health care costs eat up budgets at every level of government. Medicaid costs alone make up over 9 percent of our state budget; back in 1970 that figure was only 5 percent. The state cannot bear this increasing load, and neither can business. A 1982 survey found that health insurance costs for many companies in North Carolina went up that year by over 25 percent.

We have to slow this trend down. Here in North Carolina, we have the opportunity to be a model for the nation in our cost containment efforts. One of the reasons that's true is because a lot of outstanding people are working on this problem right now.

This council is a remarkable group of dedicated people. The leadership of Dr. John Foust and Wayne Godwin has already brought you a long way.[1] The spirit of the council, and the cooperation between all its members, is just what we need. That kind of partnership can move mountains.

The North Carolina Foundation for Alternative Health Programs has also been working diligently on this issue. It has been a big help to this council and to other groups, too. It works closely with other state agencies that pay for health care for the needy. The foundation is performing the critical role of catalyst by opening new doors in alternative health care plans.

Our legislature is also taking a hard look at ways to stop these rising costs. Senator Craig Lawing and Dr. Jim Black have devoted so much of their time to this issue. Their Medical Cost Containment committee is now studying possible solutions and hopes to have a report ready for the 1984 General Assembly session.[2]

We need to find those solutions and we don't have much time. Already the federal government has introduced sweeping changes in Medicare reimbursement to hospitals. We don't know now what the long-run effect of the diagnosis-related groupings will be, but we *do* know it will be felt by everyone. The day is probably not far off when other insurers will turn to this type of plan.

So time is not on our side. We need to take action now. Government regulation of hospital costs has been tried in a few states; so has the competition model of bringing down charges. But there are problems with both those systems. Today, many people are calling for an "all-payer" system where everyone shares equally in hospital costs.

I believe that we in North Carolina must find our own way. We must develop our own system, one that best suits the people of this state. It must, above all, be a system that assures us of quality care. We can never allow reduced costs to equal reduced quality of care.

This council and the foundation are on the right road. I commend all of you for your initiative and commitment, but you cannot solve the problem alone. We all must work together on controlling the cost of health care, because the outcome will affect us all.

The answers won't come easily. There is much to be considered and many areas of cost to be studied. For example, I believe one very important area is long-term care. We need to find better ways of coordinating services for long-term patients so that they can go back home as quickly as possible. The savings could be tremendous. In November 1983, for instance, the Medicaid payment per person for nursing home care was $1,069. But for in-home care, the payment was only $323. We need to expand and improve the coordination of services, so that patients can go home without any interruption of care.

We must put a priority on prevention. If we are going to make a significant change in health care costs we must help people stay well. For many North Carolinians the way they live is the biggest threat to their health. We need to provide a strong educational and preventive care program for them.

We already have some excellent ones. For instance, our Division of Aging has a program called AHOY, or Add Health to Our Years. It teaches senior citizens how to keep both mentally and physically alert. As you know, health care for the elderly is a big factor in rising costs. That makes programs like this all the more important.

Now those are just a few of the many issues that concern me and that concern you. Time is short, but I have great faith in this council. You have a big responsibility. But, working together, I believe you will find some important answers as you help shape the future of health care in North Carolina.

I'm delighted that Dr. Walter McClure could be here today. He is president of the Center for Policy Studies in Minneapolis, a research organization devoted to improved delivery and financing of health care. During the past ten years, he has been a leader in developing answers to the problems of rising health care costs. He has been a consultant to the U.S. Department of Health and Human Services as well as to various congressional committees, and to medical, hospital, business, and labor organizations. In fact, he was a speaker last month at the National Governors' Association meeting on health care costs.

Before joining the Center of Policy Studies, Dr. McClure was vice-president of InterStudy, a private health policy research organization. It may interest you to know that he trained in theoretical nuclear physics. He says that he left physics to go into health policy research for reasons having to do with "relevance." It is my privilege to introduce to you a man searching for relevant answers, Dr. Walter McClure.

---

[1]John W. Foust (1930-   ), native of Lexington; resident of Charlotte; B.S., 1952, M.D., 1955, University of North Carolina at Chapel Hill; U.S. Air Force, 1957-1959. Instructor, 1961-1963, clinical instructor, 1965-1969, of otolaryngology, University of North Carolina School of Medicine; surgeon, private practice in otolaryngology since 1963; vice-president, 1984, 1985, and cofounder, Mecklenburg County Health Care Cost Management Council; president, North Carolina Medical Society, 1986. John W. Foust to Jan-Michael Poff, May 1, 1986.

Richard Wayne Godwin, (1941-   ), native of New Orleans; resident of Charlotte; B.S., Rensselaer Polytechnic Institute, 1963; Ph.D., Duke University, 1966. President, Celanese Fibers Co., 1982-1984; vice-president, Celanese Specialty Operations, 1985; president, BASF Structural Materials, Inc., since June, 1985. Richard Wayne Godwin to Jan-Michael Poff, June 3, 1986.

[2]William Craig Lawing (1925-   ), native, resident of Mecklenburg County; attended University of Chattanooga and Repperts School of Auctioneering; U.S. Army Air Force, 1943-1946. President, Lawing, Inc., real estate, insurance, and auctioneering firm; member, state House, 1971-1976, and Senate, 1977-1980. *North Carolina Manual, 1979*, 289-290.

James Boyce Black (1935-   ), native of Charlotte; B.A., Lenoir Rhyne College, 1958; B.S., 1960, Doctor of Optometry, 1962, Southern College of Optometry; U.S. Navy, 1956-1957. Optometrist; first elected to state House in 1980 and returned in subsequent elections. *North Carolina Manual, 1983*, 311.

See *Final Report of the Legislative Commission on Medical Cost Containment* ([Raleigh: The Commission], July 17, 1985). "An Act to Create the Legislative Commission on Medical Cost Containment" was ratified on July 20, 1983. *N.C. Session Laws, 1983*, c. 875.

REGIONAL HEARING, NORTH CAROLINA COMMISSION ON EDUCATION FOR ECONOMIC GROWTH

CHARLOTTE, JANUARY 9, 1984

["Studies and expert recommendations are part of our work," said Hunt on November 23, 1983, as he announced research strategies utilized by the state Commission on Education for Economic Growth. But in order to "better understand and improve education in North Carolina," he continued, recommendations from concerned citizens were crucial. Therefore the governor stated that, during the ensuing seven weeks, the commission would hold four regional public hearings; the first was scheduled for November 28 in Raleigh. The governor's prepared comments at hearings in Asheville, December 15, 1983, and Greenville, January 5, 1984, were almost identical in content to the speech, below, delivered in Charlotte.]

We are here tonight because business, industry, and the citizens of North Carolina understand that the way to have strong, progressive economic growth is to have excellent schools and to give our young people a good education.

We know that foreign competition and new technologies challenge our economy as never before. North Carolina must meet that challenge by attracting new, exciting industries; by promoting research and development; by offering plentiful, well-protected natural resources; by supporting excellence in our public schools.

We are known all over America as a leader in attracting the best industries, the best jobs, but we must do more. Education is the catalyst that will bring our industries, our plentiful resources, and our hard-working people together for a strong economy.

We have already taken major steps in education in North Carolina. Our Primary Reading Program placed an aide in the classes of our first three grades. Special materials and testing were added. The results are outstanding: Reading achievement has risen above national averages; slower learners get the personal attention they need.

The time has come for us to redouble our efforts. From our hearings we know that the answer to our education problem in North Carolina is not just more money. First we need to do more with what we have.

The commission will address specific issues as we plan to improve the quality of education our young people receive. A key area is curriculum: We have heard that it is too soft. We have heard business leaders list the skills and attitudes that will be required for tomorrow's jobs—tomorrow's better jobs. We have heard educators speak of the noninstructional demands placed on instruction time. We have heard individuals speak of the need to include foreign language, health, music, fine arts, and other humanities as part of the curriculum.

We need to identify a core, a base curriculum, for each level of schooling. We need to clearly state what is expected of students, teachers, administrators, and parents. We need to provide schools with the opportunities to design and test instructional approaches based on the best research available on how students learn.

At the top of every list is the teacher. We need to attract and retain the best. We need to provide teachers with a working environment that promotes good teaching and effective learning. We need to provide teachers with opportunities for career growth and still let them be classroom teachers. We need to recognize and reward effective teachers. We need to help teachers build on their strengths and correct their weaknesses.

Career growth plans will require state and local leadership. Jay Robinson[1] and the Charlotte/Mecklenburg Schools are demonstrating that leadership here in Charlotte.

The Charlotte plan[2] has caught the attention of educators nationwide, and for good reason. It demonstrates a thoughtful, strong approach to a complex problem. We must look closely at your efforts as we encourage career growth for teachers throughout North Carolina.

We must also remove incompetent teachers. There is no room for teachers who do not strive to correct their weaknesses and build new strengths.

We need to make sure that the staff, the textbooks, the materials, the supplies, and the equipment required to implement the curriculum are available — available in all schools, no matter how small or large, no matter how urban or rural, no matter how economically poor or affluent.

But there should be no room for waste. We cannot afford to have equipment sit idle. We cannot afford to let facilities go unused when needs exist. We cannot afford to respond to every special interest request by adding nonessentials to the curriculum. We cannot afford to pay professional salaries for clerical activities. We cannot afford interruptions during instructional time. We cannot afford to manage inefficiently and ineffectively.

Another message that comes through clearly as we listen is that we must continue to be sensitive to the needs of special students. We must improve upon our efforts to serve the economically disadvantaged student. We need to better serve the gifted and talented student.

We need to deal more effectively with the habitually disruptive student. Providing services to these few students will benefit the many. Strong, but fair discipline is a key.

We need to identify and serve the potential dropout. Those students, who through their poor attendance and noninvolvement, are signaling that they require special help.

But again we need to be very clear about expectations. We need to be clear about what is expected of the student, the teacher, the administrator, and the parent. We cannot afford to make excuses for problems. We must take positive actions.

We need to serve young people with special needs, but we cannot afford to let those efforts prevent us from effectively serving the nonhandicapped students. We must do both.

One thing that comes through very clearly as we listen is the need for more accountability. Expectations and accomplishments must be compared, and when our accomplishments fall short of our expectations we must be willing to act. We need to be able to say to the taxpayer, "Your dollars are being well spent." As we listen, we hear people calling for real change. We are prepared to recommend real change. I look forward to your comments tonight on what changes must be made to make North Carolina's schools the best in the nation — the strongest in the world.

¹Jay M. Robinson (1928-   ), native of Mitchell County; B.S., Appalachian State University, 1950; M.A., University of North Carolina at Chapel Hill, 1957; Ed.D., Duke University, 1976; U.S. Army Air Force, 1946-1948. Assistant superintendent, 1964-1965, and superintendent, 1965-1977, Cabarrus County Schools; superintendent, 1977-1986, Charlotte-Mecklenburg Schools; appointed vice-president for public affairs, University of North Carolina system, 1986. Jay M. Robinson to Jan-Michael Poff, April 4, 1986; *News and Observer,* April 9, 1986.

²The Charlotte-Mecklenburg Schools Career Development Program was implemented in August, 1984, after four years of preparation. All new teachers participated in a four-step training and practice plan, of four to six years' duration, that emphasized staff development. The goal was to produce experienced, successful educators who could also be rewarded financially for their accomplishments. An anticipated teacher retirement rate of 70 percent, between 1980 and 1995, for the Charlotte-Mecklenburg system, and the declining quality of college graduates entering the teaching profession, were two factors that prompted the creation of the program. Enclosure, Jay M. Robinson to Jan-Michael Poff, April 4, 1986.

NORTH CAROLINA ASSOCIATION OF CHAMBER OF COMMERCE EXECUTIVES

RALEIGH, JANUARY 24, 1984

[The speech, below, to the North Carolina Association of Chamber of Commerce Executives, was almost identical to addresses presented in Mount Airy, January 10; Tabor City, January 19; Ahoskie, January 31; and Elizabethtown, June 12, 1984.]

As business and community leaders, you know that North Carolina's economy gives us reason for optimism in this new year. North Carolina is leading the national economy. Retail sales are up. Housing construction is up. Business investment is growing at a healthy rate.

We just completed our second best year ever in attracting new industry. During 1983, new and expanding industries announced more than $2.1 billion worth of industrial investment in North Carolina. Those dollars will translate into more than 30,200 new jobs, making 1983 the second best industrial growth year in North Carolina's history.

Over the last seven years, businesses have invested more than $13.1 billion in North Carolina, creating over 207,000 new jobs. And for every one of those manufacturing jobs, we estimate that two new jobs were created in service industries.

Here in the Research Triangle, we've had announcements of major new investments by such businesses as du Pont, Ciba-Geigy, Northern Telecom, Sumitomo, Mitsubishi, and Underwriter's Laboratories.

In western North Carolina, we've seen investments by Chase Brass and Copper in Shelby, Outboard Marine Corporation in Spruce Pine, and Hanes Printables in Morganton.

In Tobaccoville, R. J. Reynolds is building the largest tobacco manufacturing facility in the world.

From Goodyear Tire and Rubber in Asheboro, to Lenox China in Oxford, to Takeda in Wilmington, to Burlington Industries' state-of-the-art facility in Erwin, this economy is on the move. As chamber of commerce executives, as leaders in your communities, all of you have been at the heart of North Carolina's economic progress.

Today, we are on the road to recovery. North Carolina's budget is balanced. Our house is in order. We are making strong, steady economic progress. Our confidence is high because North Carolina has built a solid foundation for economic growth for years to come.

We have a healthy business climate. Business and government work together in a cooperative way, and state government knows that business, not government, creates jobs and growth.

We have a right-to-work law and the hardest-working, most productive people in the world.

We have a world-class university system, excellent private colleges and universities, and a top-notch community college system. We know our schools still are not as good as they should be, but North Carolina has led the nation in improving education in recent years.

North Carolina is leading this nation in building partnerships between business and education. All over this state, school doors are being opened to the resources and enthusiasm of North Carolina businesses. R. J. Reynolds, Weyerhaeuser, Burlington Industries, and many others—they are all involved in innovative programs with local schools. In communities all across the state, businesses are sponsoring science fairs and exchange programs. We're seeing new ventures, such as the Wilkes County Education Foundation, generate enthusiasm throughout the school and business community.

Here in North Carolina, we are determined to modernize our factories. We will boost our productivity. We will meet foreign competition. We will build an economy dedicated to long-term economic growth. We will do all this because we are committed to seeing our economy grow, but we will *succeed* because we understand the fundamental link between education and economic growth.

Another reason North Carolina succeeds is that we know how to live within our means and balance our budget. We have had a balanced budget every year I have been governor. Now we had to make some hard decisions, but the people of North Carolina expected us to show discipline during hard times, and that is what they got—discipline, and a determined belief that we were on the right track and things were going to get better.

We believe we have worked harder and smarter in state government. Productivity has increased through more training and improved supervision. We have substituted high technology for manual effort, as you have done in your businesses. When we were faced in 1982 with a certain shortfall in tax revenues of $195 million, we held back on salary increases. We resisted pressure to develop new programs and expand old ones.

When 10 percent of all North Carolinians did not have a job, much less a salary increase, we had to exercise some discipline. We held the growth in state government, excluding education, to just 1.7 percent in seven years, or less than 0.3 percent a year—almost no growth. And, except for a vitally important gas tax needed to maintain our roads, we have done all this in North Carolina without raising taxes. In fact,we have one of the lowest tax burdens in the nation, forty-first out of all states. Yet no state outranks us in our determination to maintain the roads that will bring good jobs to North Carolina.

All of these are things we have done to strengthen North Carolina's economy, and I think we need the same approach at the federal level to assure long-term economic growth in this nation. The most important thing we must do now is get interest rates down. For farmers, for young people just getting started, for families who want to buy a home, for small businesses, we must get control of interest rates. The way to do that is for Congress to bite the bullet the same way we have done in North Carolina. Our nation must become fiscally responsible, and we must put the brakes on a runaway budget and federal deficit. That's why I support a constitutional amendment to require Congress to balance the federal budget, and that is why our legislature made North Carolina one of the thirty-two states that have formally called for the amendment.

I think the nation could learn a lot from North Carolina; I am proud of what we have done here. We have built up a spirit and a way of life here that is very special. In our neighborhoods and communities we still respect the traditions, values, and beliefs that launched this nation. We believe in hard work and the value of a job well done. We believe in discipline. We are a state where tradition and technology prosper together.

As chamber of commerce executives, you have helped to build up this state of strong families and churches, good schools, hard-working businesses and farms. But as leaders in your communities, you are the spark that fires our commitment to build something excellent in North Carolina. You have faith in your communities and faith in North Carolina. Because I believe that faith is strong, because I believe in the strength of our neighborhoods and communities, I am an optimist about the future of North Carolina and this nation.

THE CONFERENCE BOARD, INC.: "BUSINESS AND THE PUBLIC SCHOOLS— A NEW PARTNERSHIP"

WASHINGTON, D.C., JANUARY 25, 1984

This meeting demonstrates the great concern that business and industry in America have for education in America. This concern is not just for students in colleges and universities and job training programs, those students who will be entering the job market next spring or next year—but also for children in the earliest grades of school, those people who will be our employees or perhaps our employers or our competitors in the twenty-first century.

That concern is demonstrated by more than your presence. Many of you here today already contribute leadership and resources to our public schools. You know the value of that investment in education.

I believe that the time has come in the United States for education and business to draw up a contract—a contract dedicated to achieving excellence in education, a contract dedicated to strengthening the relationship between business and education, a contract dedicated to the strength and prosperity of this nation.

As leaders in business, you know that the best prescription for the health of this nation is strong, sustained economic growth. You know the economic challenges we face through the rest of this century:

—Modernizing our older industries as well as fostering the growth of new technologies.

—Developing a trained and productive work force.

—Getting interest rates down and increasing capital investment.

—Meeting foreign competition and competing for overseas markets.

I believe that the secret to meeting each one of those challenges rests in this nation's system of education—not just in our colleges and universities, but also in our public elementary and secondary schools. That is where we must develop the human capital—the brainpower, the skills, the imagination—that will enable America to meet the challenge of technology, the challenge of competition, and the challenge of tomorrow.

For too long, education issues slept quietly in the national consciousness, but I can tell you from personal experience that the giant has awakened. There have been a lot of studies done of education this last year, but the National Task Force on Education for Economic Growth, which I chaired with Frank Cary of IBM and Governor Pete du Pont of Delaware, was the *first* to make clear the relationship that exists between good schools and good jobs, between education and economic growth.

As Garza Baldwin, a North Carolina businessman from Pisgah, said at a hearing at home: "A well-trained, intelligent, highly motivated work force is the most valuable resource any business can have." Period. That's as clear as you can get. And I am convinced that the best possible way to marshal public support and the resources, for deep and lasting change in the schools, is to make clear to people the link between good schools and good jobs.

This new contract—the partnership between business, education, and government—is the key to that deep and lasting change. As any sound contract must, the business/school partnership will benefit both participants. Both schools *and* business stand to gain.

I think North Carolina's experience demonstrates what this partnership can mean. In North Carolina over the last eight years, we have enacted a sweeping series of education reforms without greatly expanding our budget *or* raising taxes. We have emphasized the basics—reading, mathematics, and science—in elementary and secondary schools. We have bolstered teacher training. We have prepared more young people for careers in high-technology industries. We have used standardized tests as key measurements at benchmark years and competency testing to assure the citizens and business that we are getting our money's worth from our public schools.

What is rising in North Carolina is our commitment to excellence in education. North Carolina's schools are getting better, not worse. Our students are learning more, not less.

The response of the 1980s must differ from decades before in this nation. Our response must not be just more dollars for the same performance, not just higher salaries, but more dollars for greater performance—the kind of things successful industries have been doing for years.

Business and education partnerships are working all across North Carolina:

—R. J. Reynolds Industries makes an in-depth commitment of both human and financial resources in math/science education. RJR sponsors computer science programs for teachers and students, lends expert personnel, and assists in meaningful ways, like the local "Homework Hotline," which offers teacher assistance to students with homework problems.

—Weyerhaeuser Company provides students in our eastern counties with the opportunity to view its operations. The company gives employees time to tutor students and to lecture high school classes.

—Burlington Industries sponsors tutorial programs and special enrichment opportunities for its employees' children.

—Small businesses are active, too. The Foote Mineral Company in the Kings Mountain area contributes by providing financial and organizational resources to sponsor local school science fairs.

—Our School of Science and Mathematics, the nation's only public residential high school for outstanding students, receives over $7 million from business.

Just as schools benefit, so should business gain from these school partnerships. In fact, business and industry must gain if this business/education contract is to be both permanent and successful. To the business leaders here today, you should not hesitate to be hard bargainers in this education partnership. Demand productivity; demand efficiency; demand rigor; above all, demand excellence from your schools—but help to provide the resources to make the schools meet those expectations.

What is required of you is leadership and vision. The lessons we have learned in North Carolina are true for all business/education partnerships. Businesses that lend employees to schools, provide resources, or give other assistance find that:

—Employees are more excited about their work and more productive; morale soars.

—The standing of business rises in the community.

—Students exposed to the advantages businesses can offer become better students and, ultimately, better employees.

—As local schools improve, communities prosper and new industries and markets arrive.

Finally, I want to add that the skilled worker is just one goal of education. The knowledgeable citizen, the wise and humane leader —these, too, must be the products of our public schools. We all benefit from an intelligent, informed populace, one that understands the great role business plays in building this country; our schools must do a better job of telling the success stories of a free market system. The citizens of this nation have awakened to the need for better schools, but we rely on business to be a partner in providing the expertise, the resources, and perhaps most of all, the decisive, hard-charging demand for excellence.

Partnerships between business and education can determine whether the current enthusiasm for education is short-lived, as it was during the Sputnik era, or deep and lasting, as I believe it must be. "If history teaches us anything," President Kennedy once said, "it is that man, in his quest for knowledge and progress, is determined and cannot be deterred."

Today we are on the cutting edge of something enormously important. We can make history that will live beyond our years. We can build more than bricks and mortar. We can build a new attitude, a new spirit. Our quest for better schools is a quest for America and her future. Let us begin today.

NORTH CAROLINA PRESS ASSOCIATION

Chapel Hill, January 26, 1984

[The 1984 race for the U.S. Senate began heating up in 1983, as advertisements supporting Jesse Helms's reelection began appearing in the media. Reacting to his portrayal in his opponent's commercials, Hunt told Democrats gathered in Nags Head, on April 15, 1983, "We don't want a divided America, but we're already seeing the negative, divisive politics of the Congressional Club. Negative ads, untruths. Ugly pictures. You know, I've seen some of those pictures. Does anyone here have a good picture of me? Will you please send it to Senator Helms?" At a meeting of the North Carolina Press Association early in the new year, the governor responded to Helms's attacks on his record as the state's chief executive and challenged journalists to maintain their objectivity in the coming months (see below).

Hunt did not officially announce his candidacy for the Democratic Senate nomination until February 4, 1984; nevertheless, late in 1983 he pledged "to run a positive campaign. We will offer the voters a constructive choice. We will talk about the issues," said the governor on October 18 in Chapel Hill. "The issues are what I call the four E's: the economy, education, elderly, and the environment."

However, as the grueling contest for the Senate wore on, the Hunt campaign shifted its emphasis. The Congressional Club's ubiquitous, high-voltage advertising depicted the governor as a wishy-washy "Mondale liberal," denigrated his political record, and consequently eroded his popularity in the opinion polls. Frustrated by the apparent success of such tactics, the Hunt campaign retaliated with negative reprisals of its own. William C. Friday reflected on the sensational methods used by both camps in the Helms-Hunt race: "I think our state went through a very difficult experience," he told a Salisbury interviewer in December, 1984. "It bothered me . . . that this whole thing slid into character assassination and (an) almost obscene use of money and dragging on for months and months and months." He continued, "I move around a lot, in circles out of North Carolina, . . . and I know it didn't help North Carolina one bit." *News and Observer*, February 5, December 13, 1984, May 12, 1985. For a recounting of the campaign, see Snider, *Helms and Hunt*, previously identified in "Inaugural Address," January 10, 1981, footnote 2, above.]

This is the eighth year that I have addressed the awards ceremony of the North Carolina Press Association as governor. For those of you who have been here all eight times, that is the bad news. The good news is that this will be the *last* time. I have been coming here so long I feel like I ought to get one of these awards, but I understand that some of you have been coming a lot longer than I have—and you still don't have your award, either.

Actually, I look forward to this. Once a year, our roles are reversed, and I get to tell you how to do *your* job. The trouble is, you don't listen to me any better than I listen to you. The *Wilmington Star-News* continues to ignore my helpful advice about how they should write their editorials about I-40.[1] The people in my press office keep telling me that if I get out of politics, I could become an editor. Somehow, I don't think they mean that as a compliment.

Well, the reputation of your profession is safe. I do not plan to become a journalist. I have other plans for next year, and I want you all to be the first to know that I will be a candidate for the United States Senate in 1984. I am going to do my best to see that, even though this is my last year as governor, you are going to have Jim Hunt to kick around some more.

I am going to say a word about that campaign, but first I want to talk to you about something that is more important. Whatever happens to me in this election, I intend to shake hands next January with my successor, walk out of the Governor's Office, and be able to say to myself and my family: "I have done the very best job I could do. I have served the people of North Carolina well."

I will have been governor for eight years. I will have served as lieutenant governor four years. I want it to be said that those twelve years were good for North Carolina, that North Carolina became a better place. It is easy to find failings and shortcomings; they are many. But I firmly believe that North Carolina has come a long way, North Carolina is a better place today, and North Carolina is headed in the right direction.

When I ran for governor in 1976, I talked most about two things: helping kids learn to read and helping people get better jobs. Better jobs and better schools, a better chance in life for people—that is what it is all about. Whatever the critics and cynics may say, I think I have kept those promises to the people of North Carolina.

Yes, our schools have their problems. But they are getting better, not worse. Our kids are learning more, not less. And we are not finished yet. Some of the biggest changes in our public schools may very well come this year.

Yes, North Carolina is still a poor state, but we are no longer falling behind. We no longer have to say, "Thank God for Mississippi." We can compete with any state in any region for jobs and economic growth.

I came into office talking about jobs and schools; I will go out of office the same way. I will run on my record this year. Both Senator Helms and I have been in public office since 1973, and the voters will compare our records as they make up their minds. I will spell out, chapter and verse, what I will do if I am elected to the United States Senate. I will debate *all* the issues with Senator Helms, and I welcome your scrutiny.

I think this campaign will present an extraordinary challenge to you as professional journalists. You will have not only the responsibility of telling your readers what they need to know to cast an informed vote, but also the responsibility of reporting more than the mechanics and minutiae of the campaign; the responsibility of critically examining what candidates say, not just taking the easy way out and dismissing it all as "just more political rhetoric"; the responsibility of refusing to be intimidated by charges of "press bias"; and the responsibility of giving candidates a fair chance to respond to the charges made against them.

I know what kind of charges and attacks are coming. They have been on the air and in your pages for ten months. All I ask of you— and every candidate has a right to expect it—is a fair chance to present my case and answer my critics. If I have that I will be satisfied with the outcome of the election, whatever it is.

In return, I recognize that you have a responsibility to your readers to look me in the eye and ask me your questions. As long as I have been governor, my policy has been to give you that chance, and that will continue to be my policy. I may not always enjoy it, you understand, and I will not promise to give you the quote you want, but you are welcome to ask. In other words, if *you* want to know where Jim Hunt stands, all you have to do is ask me.[2]

---

[1]See "Statement on Interstate 40," May 24, 1983, above.

[2]Helms referred to Hunt as "the windshield-wiper candidate: 'first one way and then the other,'" according to William D. Snider. Helms's television advertising for ten months prior to the election primarily was based on the recurring theme, "Where do you stand, Jim?" Snider, *Helms and Hunt*, 113-114.

TESTIMONY BEFORE U.S. HOUSE COMMITTEE ON INTERIOR AND INSULAR AFFAIRS, SUBCOMMITTEE ON PUBLIC LANDS AND NATIONAL PARKS

WASHINGTON, D.C., JANUARY 27, 1984

[Although Congress approved the construction of twin jetties at Oregon Inlet in 1970, cost, project feasibility, and environmental objections prevented them from being built. H.R. 3082, introduced by Congressman Walter Jones, would have permitted the use of federal lands to anchor the controversial breakwaters, thus overruling Interior Department opposition to the plan and opening the way for its implementation. The bill passed the House on September 20, 1984, but was stalled in the Senate when Congress adjourned on October 12. *News and Observer*, March 1, September 21, October 13, 1984; "News Release from the Governor's Office," September 20, 1984.]

Mr. Chairman,[1] I very much appreciate the opportunity to appear before you today to speak on behalf of the stabilization of Oregon Inlet. I have worked alongside many other people over the years toward the realization of this critical project. As time has passed, the urgency of completing this project has become greater.

North Carolina state government stands united with our coastal local governments, with the fishing industry, and with our congressional delegation in urging the United States Congress to move ahead with the timely completion of this project, which was authorized in 1970 and for which construction funds already have been appropriated.

The Oregon Inlet project has been controversial. There has been much misinformation and misunderstanding of the project. We have determined our position on this project with great care. Our state Department of Natural Resources and Community Development convened in the spring of 1983 a panel of state and university experts to review the plan for the jetties and to evaluate it by engineering, economic, and environmental standards. I have personally consulted with knowledgeable persons on the design of the project. After this careful review, I am even more convinced that the project is sound and that it should move forward as soon as possible. Today I will discuss my conclusions on five major points.

First, dredging alone is not enough. The Corps of Engineers has been making a valiant effort to maintain a safe channel by dredging in recent years. At one point, all three of the Corps' sidecasting dredges were working simultaneously in Oregon Inlet. However, in December, 1982, one winter storm wiped out all the work done by the intensive dredging effort in a matter of days. The same thing happened the winter before when a storm produced such sudden and drastic shoaling of the channel that the United States Coast Guard had to close the inlet to navigation, with a very destructive effect on our fishing industry and on the economy of northeastern North Carolina.

Some individuals have urged the Corps of Engineers to use hopper dredges, which would remove sand from the area of the inlet rather than just shifting it to the side of the channel. Studies by the Corps of Engineers have shown that the hopper dredges will not be able to dump their loads of sand close enough to the shore for the sand to get back into the beach system. Intensive hopper dredging would mean the loss of large quantities of sand from the beach system and would greatly increase the erosion rate on the nearby beaches. This kind of dredging is not only inadequate for navigation reliability and safety, it is also unacceptable for environmental reasons.

The basic flaw with dredging is that a single winter storm can wipe out the accomplishments of several months of expensive dredging in a matter of a few days. In the last two winters, we have clearly seen that dredging alone cannot possibly maintain a reliable and safe channel during our winter fishing season.

Second, we are confident that the project is economically sound.

We know the value of the fishing industry and employment associated with fishing in northeastern North Carolina. We can see the enormous benefits that the project would bring by making our Wanchese Seafood Industrial Park viable.

The federal government places a much stricter standard of economic justification on projects like Oregon Inlet. These projects, unlike other types of government expenditures, require a formal benefit-cost analysis. When errors were discovered in the original economic analysis, the federal administration asked the Corps of Engineers to go back and restudy the benefits and costs. This work has been under way for over a year. The results have been promised for some time but not yet produced. We urge the administration to complete its economic reanalysis and make it public. We are confident that any objective review will confirm the strong economic benefits of this project.

Third, the construction of jetties at Oregon Inlet will not drastically increase erosion on nearby beaches. This committee needs to appreciate that any inlet blocks the natural movement of sand along the coast and tends to cause erosion on nearby beaches.

Right now with no jetties in place, the beach on Pea Island south of the inlet is presently eroding at an average of about seven feet each year over an extensive area. The jetty project is based on careful consideration of the movement of sand along the coast. We know that the jetties will block sand on the north side of the inlet. The project plan calls for this sand to be systematically transferred to the south side of the inlet to prevent an increase in erosion. Our support of the jetty construction is based on the commitment by the Corps of Engineers to carry out regular bypassing of sand around the inlet as needed.

Fourth, jetty construction will not permanently harm recreation. The shore along Oregon Inlet is extensively used by the public for surf fishing, sunbathing, walking, and just enjoyment of this beautiful part of our state. During the construction of the jetties, there will be some limit to access by dune buggies to the construction area. After the project has been constructed, fishermen and sunbathers, including those off-road vehicles, will still have access to the lands along the north side.

What is more, we know that jetties serve as attractors to many species of fish. Jetties have the same benefits as the artificial reefs that we build to improve fish habitat. The plan for the jetties calls for paved walkways along the top of each jetty to make them accessible to fishermen and will even increase the recreational use of this area.

Finally, I want to stress the value of this project in protecting the lives of our citizens. Altogether, eight lives have been lost in shipwrecks at the inlet. Three vessels have been lost in three years. The value of the project for saving lives goes much beyond the fishermen and recreational boaters who are trying to pass through Oregon Inlet. Admiral John D. Costello,[2] commander of the Fifth District of the Coast Guard, has testified that when Oregon Inlet is closed to navigation, his patrol boat has to travel 125 miles to respond to a distress call that could be only two or three miles off the inlet. This is not a matter to be considered lightly.

The Oregon Inlet Coast Guard station averages about 300 distress calls a year. Benefit-cost analysis can never adequately measure the value of saving a life. Our fishermen who make a living by going back and forth through Oregon Inlet face a level of danger that we would never accept on the highways and at the airports that we use for our own business.

I would also like to express the state of North Carolina's strong support for the provisions of this bill which are designed to protect our nation's valuable wetland resources. The preservation of wetlands in a natural state is imperative. Wetlands serve as vital habitat for migratory waterfowl. They provide the nursery areas essential in the life cycles of many of fish species, fish which provide the catch of vessels using Oregon Inlet. Natural wetlands reduce water pollution and aid in the productivity of our fisheries. They also store flood waters and protect shorelines from erosion.

We are fortunate to have several key wetland areas in North Carolina that have been preserved. We are continuing to identify and seek ways to preserve other valuable areas. However, such important initiatives will not be possible in the future without the enactment of this bill. We are particularly supportive of the new Wetland Conservation Fund, the Wetlands Loan Act repayment deletion, the increased flexibility for the Land and Water Conservation Fund program, and the expedited completion of the national wetlands inventory. We urge you to give careful thought to the necessity of charging new entrance fees for visitors to wildlife refuges.

I would like to thank the members of this committee for giving me the opportunity to make this statement. We have considered the Oregon Inlet project very carefully. Our firm conclusion is that the construction of jetties is the only way to provide a safe navigation channel through Oregon Inlet. The environmental effects of the project would be very minor. The economic benefits and the added safety for our fishermen and for those who call on the Coast Guard for assistance will be extremely great. I ask your support in passing H.R. 3082 and in moving this project ahead to construction as soon as possible.

---

[1]John F. Seiberling (1918-   ), native, resident of Akron, Ohio; B.A., Harvard University, 1941; LL.B., Columbia University, 1949; served in U.S. Army during World War II. Attorney, Goodyear Tire and Rubber Co., 1954-1970; elected to U.S. House from Ohio's Fourteenth Congressional District, 1970, and returned in subse-

quent elections; chairman, Public Lands and National Parks Subcommittee, U.S. House Committee on Interior and Insular Affairs; Democrat. Barone and Ujifusa, *Almanac of American Politics, 1984*, 940.

[2]John D. Costello (1930-   ), native of Englewood, New Jersey; resident of Portsmouth, Virginia; B.A., United States Coast Guard Academy, 1952; M.A., George Washington University, 1969; ensign, 1952, advanced through ranks to admiral, 1979, U.S. Coast Guard. Commander, Fifth Coast Guard District, since 1981. *Who's Who in America, 1982-1983*, I, 683.

GOVERNOR'S STATEWIDE CONFERENCE ON SMALL BUSINESS

RALEIGH, FEBRUARY 1, 1984

Before I begin, I want to thank Al Lineberry and the North Carolina Small Business Advocacy Council for the many days and hours of hard work they have put in on behalf of the small businesses of this state.

One of the biggest challenges facing any small business development effort is the great diversity of the businesses it must serve. More than 97 percent of all North Carolina businesses employ less than 100 people, and more than 80 percent of our state's companies employ twenty workers or less. No matter how you slice it, that is a lot of small companies, run by a lot of small businessmen and -women. Your ranks include barbers, mechanics, plumbers, programmers, merchants, manufacturers, and a wide variety of other trades and professions.

But despite the diversity of small business, there are common concerns shared by all small business persons. One of the most important is the well-being of our nation's economy.

As businessmen, you know that our nation's economy gives us good reason for optimism in 1984. Here in North Carolina the picture is particularly bright. Retail sales are up, housing starts are rising, and business investment is growing at a healthy rate.

North Carolina is leading our nation's economic recovery, and it is no accident. North Carolina's economy is strong because our state has fostered a healthy economic climate. Business and government work together in a cooperative way. Our tax burden is among the lowest in the nation—forty-first out of all states—and year after year we balance our state budget.

These principles have placed North Carolina ahead of the pack in economic growth. But if we are to stay on the road of economic recovery, we must have stability in our national economy. The keys to that stability are a balanced federal budget and reduced interest rates.

High interest rates can do more to choke off economic growth than anything else we can imagine. As small businessmen, you know that customers from almost anywhere will take one look at skyrocketing interest rates, turn around, and go home. High interest rates make it particularly difficult for small businesses to invest in new ideas, new technologies.

Here in North Carolina, we are taking steps to help our entrepreneurs overcome this handicap. Last year, our state's General Assembly approved $1 million for a new North Carolina Technological Development Authority. The authority will use its money to take equity positions in businesses testing or developing new technologies. For a share of the payoff, the authority will help entrepreneurs afford the cost of product development.

The Technological Development Authority is also charged with the task of establishing new "incubator facilities" to support and protect small businesses in their earliest stages of growth. The incubators will provide low-cost space for operations along with technical and managerial assistance to participating small businesses. Through these two programs, the North Carolina Technological Development Authority will work to cut the "infant mortality rate" among our state's budding small businesses.

Encouraging innovation is just one small part of the growing range of small business assistance programs now being offered by state government. These include assistance in getting federal Small Business Innovation Research grants; working to assure small businesses a fair opportunity to bid for state purchasing contracts; sponsoring an ongoing series of buyer-supplier conferences, including several sessions on state and federal government procurement opportunities; and offering special export assistance to small, high-technology businesses.

Those are just a few of the steps North Carolina is already taking to help its small businesses flourish; Al Lineberry mentioned other initiatives in his report earlier this morning. But there are still important challenges ahead—venture financing and other capitalization issues must be addressed, and there is a growing need for quality management training for small businessmen. Under the direction of Secretary C. C. Hope, our state Department of Commerce is leading an interagency effort to address those needs.

Secretary Hope is meeting with leaders of our state's top corporations and financial institutions to find better ways of matching entrepreneurs to sources of financial assistance. As a former president of the American Bankers' Association and a top executive of one of our state's leading banks, Secretary Hope is uniquely qualified to help our state meet this challenge.

In addition to help with financing, we in North Carolina need to help small businesses get better management training and assistance. As governor, I am today announcing my support for a new initiative in small business assistance proposed by our community college system in cooperation with the North Carolina Department of Commerce. This new program will build into our existing community college system a strong business assistance network. The program will identify key personnel at each community college to coordinate assistance services. It will provide courses, workshops, and other continuing education opportunities geared to the needs of our small wholesale, service, and manufacturing businesses. Ultimately, the program will make each of our community colleges a contact point where small businessmen gain access to professional advice, computerized data bases, or other sources of information.

To the small computer software producer in Sylva this business assistance network could mean a helpful course on long-range planning or quick access to advice from a retired senior business executive. To the small manufacturer in Kinston, this new program might mean a workshop in inventory control or use of reference materials on government purchasing practices and specifications.

Six of our community colleges are already offering some of these services. Next fall, we will expand these offerings to all of these schools and extend the program to several additional campuses. Within eight years the program will be available at all fifty-eight of our state community colleges.

North Carolina's community colleges are already providing some of the most extensive skills training programs in the nation to North Carolina's new and expanding industries. I believe that the best thing we can do for our small businesses today is put our community college system to work for them. This demonstrates our commitment to small business.

Small business forms the backbone of North Carolina's economy. The economic well-being of our people depends, in large measure, on the vitality and prosperity of small companies like those represented here today. I am proud of this administration's record in the area of small business. I thank those of you here today, and other small businessmen across North Carolina, for your continued and persistent efforts in this area. Together, we are making small business a big business in North Carolina.

TESTIMONY BEFORE U.S. HOUSE COMMITTEE ON PUBLIC WORKS AND TRANSPORTATION, SUBCOMMITTEE ON WATER RESOURCES

WASHINGTON, D.C., FEBRUARY 8, 1984

[North Carolina filed a lawsuit in U.S. District Court on January 12, 1984, blocking construction of the Lake Gaston pipeline and claiming that the U.S. Army Corps of Engineers ran afoul of several state and federal laws in approving the project. The state demanded that the permit be rescinded;

Virginia Beach responded with a countersuit intended to expedite the completion of the pipeline. *News and Observer*, January 13, 1984, April 5, 1985. The pipeline issue had not been resolved before Hunt left office.]

Mr. Chairman [1] and members of the committee:

Thank you very much for giving me this opportunity to appear before you to support the bill introduced by Congressman Walter Jones, and cosponsored by Congressmen Steve Neal,[2] Tim Valentine, Jim Martin,[3] and Dan Daniel, to require an environmental impact statement on the proposed diversion of water from Lake Gaston. The citizens of North Carolina are greatly concerned about this proposal to permanently divert 60 million gallons a day of water out of the Roanoke River basin. Our state agencies have done much detailed research on this proposal. We have carefully documented our concerns.[4]

We have shown that the diversion of this large amount of water from the Roanoke basin will affect lake levels at Kerr Lake. We are particularly concerned about the reduced lake levels that could occur during dry periods and could damage the use of the lake for recreation.

We have documented the effect of this proposal in reducing flows downstream from Roanoke Rapids in the Roanoke River. The project will reduce the amount of water available for striped bass spawning. The U.S. Fish and Wildlife Service has expressed its strong concern about this aspect of the project.

We have documented the effect of the project in reducing the flow of water in the Roanoke River during dry periods. This raises serious concerns about the effects on water quality, both in the Roanoke River and in the Albemarle Sound.

When the Norfolk District of the Corps of Engineers held its first scoping meeting on the permit application by the city of Virginia Beach, North Carolina outlined the need for careful environmental review of this project. We listed the items that should be studied before making a decision on the permit. The Corps of Engineers turned a deaf ear to this request.

The Norfolk District of the Corps of Engineers issued a very minimal environmental assessment on this major action. The Wilmington District of the Corps of Engineers concurred in this inadequate environmental review. During the comment period, we carefully documented our concerns about the environmental impacts of this project. I am submitting copies of our comments to your committee, for the record.

In evaluating a major water supply project, the first step is to evaluate alternative sources of water supply. The Corps of Engineers' environmental assessment is particularly weak in this area. We have repeatedly urged the corps to study the possibilities of regional water sharing and incremental additions to the existing regional supplies. The corps has continuously refused to give the alternative sources of water supply an objective review.

North Carolina has documented some increased needs for water supply in the North Carolina portion of the Roanoke basin. We have documented future water supply needs for electric power plant cooling, industrial and municipal use, and for agricultural irrigation. The Corps of Engineers' environmental assessment has not even made a minimal attempt to study the long-range need for water within the Roanoke basin and to place the proposed diversion in this context of all needs of the basin.

We are particularly concerned that the Norfolk District of the Corps of Engineers was scheduled to complete a draft of a water supply study for the southside Hampton Roads area in the same month that it issued the permit for the Virginia Beach project. The Corps of Engineers' study has been under way for many years. If done correctly, it should answer many of our questions about the pros and cons of the alternative water sources, and about the amount of water really needed in tidewater Virginia. We are distressed that the Corps of Engineers would issue a permit on a project of this size before releasing the results of this long-awaited study to the public.

Throughout this process, both the Norfolk District and the Wilmington District of the Corps of Engineers have given every impression of partiality and haste in reaching this critical decision. North Carolina's request for an environmental impact statement was ignored from the very beginning. The Norfolk District of the Corps of Engineers made its decision on granting the permit less than one working day after the close of the comment period. To us, this shows their lack of willingness to seriously consider comments by the state of North Carolina and by any other interested parties.

In my experience as governor of North Carolina, I have had to face many difficult and controversial decisions. I have learned by experience that the best approach in these difficult cases is to bring all the facts together for examination by the public. The National Environmental Policy Act created the environmental impact statement requirement just for this type of complex and controversial decision.[5] After the facts are gathered, and the proposal has received open review and comments from people affected by the proposal, the decision maker can make these major decisions in a very careful and considered way, with due regard for the long-range interests of all parties concerned.

In this present case, adequate study has not been given to the impacts of the project and to the alternative sources of water supply. Instead of a careful decision-making process, we have faced a hasty and careless approach by the Corps of Engineers with a total disregard for public concern. We are talking about the permanent commitment of enough water to serve a population of a half million persons. We are talking about the irreversible diversion of more water from the Roanoke basin than is presently used by any municipal water system in either North Carolina or Virginia. To keep public confidence in government, decisions of this import must be made with more fairness and more care.

We are asking the support of this committee and of Congress in providing a fair and objective environmental impact statement on this major project. We cannot condone the closed process that has taken place to date. Our request is that we examine the alternatives in the open process established by Congress under the National Environmental Policy Act. Thank you very much for giving me this opportunity to present our viewpoint.

---

[1] Robert A. Roe (1924-   ), native, resident of Wayne, New Jersey; attended Oregon State University and Washington State University; served in U.S. Army during World War II. Wayne Township committeeman, 1955-1956; Wayne mayor, 1956-1961; member, 1959-1963, and director, 1962-1963, Passaic County Board of Freeholders; commissioner, New Jersey Department of Conservation and Economic Development, 1963-1969; elected to U.S. House from New Jersey's Eighth Congressional District, 1969, and returned in subsequent elections; chairman, Subcommittee on Water Resources, U.S. House Committee on Public Works and Transportation; Democrat. Barone and Ujifusa, *Almanac of American Politics, 1984*, 747.

[2] Stephen Lybrook Neal (1934-   ), U.S. representative from North Carolina's Fifth Congressional District since 1975. Previously identified in Mitchell, *Addresses of Hunt*, I, 729n.

[3] James Grubbs Martin (1935-   ), native of Savannah, Georgia; resident of Raleigh; B.S., Davidson College, 1957; Ph.D., Princeton University, 1960. Associate professor of chemistry, Davidson College; Mecklenburg County commissioner, 1966-1972, and board chairman, 1967-1968, 1970-1971; president, North Carolina Association of County Commissioners, 1970-1971; U.S. representative from North Carolina's Ninth Congressional District, 1973-1984; elected governor, 1984. *North Carolina Manual, 1983*, 177.

[4] "News Release from the Governor's Office," December 29, 1983, included a thirty-five-page position paper, "Written Comments of the State of North Carolina on Proposed Lake Gaston Water Supply Diversion Project under Consideration by the Army Corps of Engineers." Copies of letters from Hunt to the corps' Norfolk and Wilmington district engineers, expressing concern over the permit-granting procedure followed for the project, were also appended.

[5] See PL 91-190, "An Act to Establish a National Policy for the Environment, to Provide for the Establishment of a Council on Environmental Quality, and for Other Purposes," approved January 1, 1970, and amendments. 83 Stat. 852-856.

GOVERNOR'S WASTE MANAGEMENT BOARD

RALEIGH, FEBRUARY 16, 1984

I appreciate this opportunity to be with you and to address three important issues related to the wise management of hazardous waste in North Carolina and the nation.

First, I have reviewed the technical committee report on hazardous waste management strategies for North Carolina.[1] I believe it is precisely the approach we should be taking toward the sage and proper management of industrial wastes.

Second, I want to make clear my commitment to the Pollution Prevention Pays strategy in North Carolina. It is not enough to treat waste; we have to prevent it.

Third, I think the federal government needs to adopt the same strategy as a national policy. I believe we should call on the United States Senate to pass legislation reauthorizing the Resource Conservation and Recovery Act and adopting that approach this year.

Members of the technical advisory committee deserve our thanks for the many hours of hard work and research that went into the preparation of this hazardous waste report. All of you board members have worked hard on it. Even though the final report is just now being issued, it has already accomplished something we've been working on for years. It has brought government, industry, environmental groups, and citizens together and in agreement with each other, something that rarely happens when you talk about hazardous waste. They all agree, as I do, that this report is the approach North Carolina should be taking.

It points out the need for an adequate number and variety of hazardous waste treatment, storage, and disposal facilities. We need high-temperature incinerators, resource recovery facilities, recyclers, and a long-term storage facility, and we need them now.

The next task of the Waste Management Board and the various groups involved in this matter is to put this report into action. We must continue to work together to create a favorable climate for waste treatment facilities to locate in North Carolina so that industries can have access to the types of facilities they need.

But bringing in waste treatment facilities is only one part of our total waste management strategy. Our first priority is to reduce the amount of waste generated in North Carolina. One way to do that is through recycling and recovery. But an even better way is through pollution prevention, something my administration and this board have been preaching since day one.

Our Pollution Prevention Pays policy is based on the belief that it is much wiser to invest money now in ways to eliminate pollution than spending huge sums of money later to clean up environmental problems after they occur. We now have a Pollution Prevention Pays work program that will help more industries save money while they protect public health and the environment. I am strongly committed to that program.

With the Pollution Prevention Pays program and this report on waste management strategies, North Carolina is leading the way toward the proper handling of hazardous waste. In fact, the United States Senate is currently considering a bill that would have the rest of the nation following North Carolina's lead. Senate Bill 757, which reauthorizes the Resource Conservation and Recovery Act of 1976, would establish Pollution Prevention Pays as a national policy.[2] This bill would require all hazardous waste generators to certify that they have a waste reduction program in place — something we in North Carolina already encourage. That is a good approach, although it must be done in a way that is fair to small businesses.

Pollution prevention is not the only area in which the federal government wants to follow our lead. This bill also addresses four issues which were acted on by our Health Services Commission last August. These are more stringent landfill liner requirements, a ban on the disposal of liquids on landfills, regular reporting by hazardous waste handlers, and the use of alternative disposal methods whenever possible. You know, it is heartening for me to see the U.S. Senate considering issues which have already been addressed and resolved here in North Carolina.

The Senate is scheduled to take up this bill on March 8 and 9. I hope that you, as a board, will endorse that general approach. And I might add that I hope North Carolina's two senators will vote in favor of a sound national policy on hazardous waste.[3]

Let me conclude by thanking all of you. You, better than anyone, know how controversial and emotional hazardous waste issues can be. You have led the way to developing a sound and workable approach to solving these problems. Because of you, North Carolina is leading the way in dealing with hazardous waste. I want you to know that I support you, and I believe we can make a giant step forward now.

---

[1] See *Hazardous Waste Management Strategies for North Carolina: Foundations for a Comprehensive Hazardous Waste Management Plan* (Raleigh, North Carolina: Governor's Waste Management Board, February 16, 1984, updated, June, 1984).

[2] The Resource Conservation and Recovery Act of 1976 (PL 94-580) was reauthorized by PL 98-616 (formerly H.R. 2867). H.R. 2867, which received certain provisions of S. 757 before passage by the U.S. Senate on July 25, 1984, was not signed into law until November 8 — over a month after having been approved by both houses of Congress. *Congressional Quarterly Almanac, 1984,* 305.

[3] Hunt also backed reauthorization of the federal "Superfund" program for cleaning up abandoned hazardous-waste dumps and sent telegrams to Senators Jesse Helms and John East in an attempt to enlist their support for the measure. A funding bill passed the U.S. House on August 10, 1984, but a similar proposal remained stalled in the Senate Finance Committee after mid-September. Superfund reauthorization failed to materialize from the second session of the Ninety-eighth Congress before it adjourned in 1984. *Congressional Quarterly Almanac, 1984,* 309-313; "News Release from the Governor's Office," September 29, 1984.

WOMEN'S NATIONAL DEMOCRATIC CLUB

WASHINGTON, D.C., FEBRUARY 24, 1984

[Earlier the same day, Hunt spoke before the North Carolina Democratic Club, in Washington, D.C. His speech to them, like the one reprinted below, centered on the 1984 Senate race.]

I had the honor of addressing you two years ago this week, in an election year when Steve Neal and our Democratic congressional candidates had tough Republican opponents who were handpicked and heavily financed by Senator Jesse Helms. You must have been good luck. We won nine out of ten contested races. So I am back again! Next February, with your help, I want to come back here as the new Democratic United States senator from North Carolina!

I deeply appreciate the tremendous help and support you are giving my campaign. I need your help. We are facing a very tough race in North Carolina. Senator Helms is the incumbent, and you know what that means. The Republican party nationally is pulling out all the stops to protect his seat, and so is NCPAC and Jerry Falwell[1] and that whole crowd. They have boasted that they will spend $15 million, $20 million, whatever it takes, to win this election. Already, in 1983 alone, his campaign spent more than $4 million against us. They have been running television and radio ads since last April Fool's Day, appropriately enough. They are on television at home today, and they will be on television every day from now until November 6.

They have closed the gap in the polls, as we knew they would. We never put any stock in that twenty-point lead we had last summer; it was like a basketball team leading by twenty points in the first quarter: There is a lot of time left. But that gap forced Senator Helms to start early to try to catch up. Today, ten months later and $4 million poorer, he is still behind—the latest polls show us with a four-point lead. But there are eight months left, and he has plenty of money where that came from.

We know the kind of campaign he will run—negative ads attacking me and my record, scurrilous leaflets, whisper campaigns, the appeals to prejudice. We are already seeing that. We have seen those campaigns work before in North Carolina, but it will not work this time!

It will not work, because we may be outspent, but we won't be outworked, and we won't be outvoted. It will not work, because the people of North Carolina deserve better representation. And we are going to offer them a clear choice and a new direction that will restore dignity and fairness and leadership to this Senate seat from North Carolina! That is how we are going to win in North Carolina, and that is what our party must offer to prevail across the nation this year.

We need a new approach to reach that disaffected voter, the new voter, the nonvoter—what I call the "low-inspiration voter." If we can give them a reason to vote on election day, if we can increase voter turnout by just a few percentage points, we will win this election and we will give this nation the leadership it needs.

In 1984 we must regain our credibility as a party—a party of ideas, a party that speaks for the hopes of the average man and woman in this country. They hear us preaching about budget deficits, but they know their history well enough to suspect that Democrats have not learned to say no. They want to feel optimistic about what the future holds for the country, for themselves, for their children. They may or may not feel that they are better off today than they were four years ago, but they are anxious about whether they and their children will be better off next year, five years, ten years, twenty years from now.

The comic Robin Williams[2] was on "Saturday Night Live" a couple of weeks ago, and he told a story that expresses that anxiety so well. He talked about his baby son and the two alternating dreams he has about that boy as an adult. In one dream, the boy is saying, "I humbly accept this Nobel Prize." In the other, he says, "Do you want some fries with that?"

Something is happening out there, and we had better be aware of it. We see it in the tremendous upsurge of voter registration. We see it in the tremendous increase of working women. We see more single-parent families and more families where both adults work. We see more adults losing the only job they ever knew. We see more older people living alone. Those people are searching for something in American political life, and I do not think they have found it yet. I do not believe the Republicans can answer their anxieties, but I do not believe we can win this election if the only choice they have is between the Republicans' past and our past.

The most powerful force in politics is an idea. We must offer the American people ideas, a vision, a new approach, a positive program for this nation's future. We must be the party of jobs and growth, that works for a healthy and competitive economy—a fair economy where tax cuts go to working families and the middle class, not just to loopholes and tax shelters for the rich.

We must be the party that works to see that equal rights and civil rights are treated as they should be: a moral imperative and the law of the land. We must be the party that works for a strong and vigorous and growing and confident America, an America that has enough room for every single person—young and old, man and woman, black and white—to achieve their dreams.

We must be the party that knows when to spend and when to cut, that knows how to say yes to the people's interest and no to the special interest. We must be the party that works for an America that has the military strength to defend freedom in the world and the moral course to put tough American negotiators across the table from the Soviets and find a way to save the world from nuclear war.

That is the choice and the direction that we must offer to the American people. If we offer that choice and that direction, we can do more than win this election. We can turn America around. We can lead a reawakening all across this nation. We can give Americans a new hope, a new spirit, and a new future.

---

[1]Jerry L. Falwell (1933-   ), native of Lynchburg, Virginia; B.A., Baptist Bible College, 1956. Founder, 1956, and senior pastor, Thomas Road Baptist Church, Lynchburg; founder, 1979, and president, Moral Majority, Inc.; director, National Association of Religious Broadcasters; author, *The Fundamentalist Phenomenon* (1981). *Who's Who in America, 1982-1983*, I, 996.

[2]Robin Williams (1952-   ), native of Chicago; attended Claremont Men's College and the Juilliard School. Actor, comedian; star of ABC-TV series "Mork and Mindy" and films *Popeye* and *The World According to Garp*; won Grammy award, 1979, for record album "Reality: What a Concept." *Who's Who in America, 1982-1983*, II, 3581.

TESTIMONY BEFORE U.S. HOUSE SELECT COMMITTEE ON AGING

WASHINGTON, D.C., FEBRUARY 28, 1984

[Prompted by a 1980 General Accounting Office report that indicated that the Social Security disability program had squandered $2 billion, the Reagan administration, in its efforts to control the federal budget deficit, began enforcing stricter medical review criteria for benefit recipients. Between March, 1981, and February, 1984, more than 350,000 Americans were removed from the disability rolls. However, critics argued that enactment of the revised procedures caused the termination of benefits to scores of individuals whose infirmities "had remained stable or worsened" since they initially were admitted to the program; they also affirmed that many of the judgments, made against persons unemployable for obvious, medical reasons, were founded on "flimsy and incomplete evidence. . . ." *Congressional Quarterly Almanac, 1984*, 160-161; *News and Observer*, February 5, 1984.

The day prior to his February 28 appearance before the House Select Committee on Aging, Hunt attended a meeting between members of the National Governors' Association and President Reagan. At the close of the conference, he handed the president a letter, which, he hoped, would persuade the president to order the Social Security Administration to abide by federal court decisions directing that disabled persons be able to demonstrate significant medical improvements before benefits could be rescinded. The governor wrote that, in North Carolina, "I know of at least 28 people who have died from medical conditions that the Social Security Administration ruled were not disabling. I am aware of a significant number of former recipients who have lost their homes, cars, and furniture, and were unable to pay for much-needed medication." Copy of letter from Hunt to President Reagan, February 27, 1984, attached to "News Release from the Governor's Office," February 27, 1984.

Congressional attempts to amend disability program medical review standards proved futile in 1983, as Hunt mentioned in his testimony, below. The House Ways and Means committee endorsed a bill, introduced on August 3 by Texas Representative J. J. Pickle, which would have revised the controversial regulations. H.R. 3755 was ultimately attached to H.R. 4170, a tax bill, which failed to reach the House floor. On November 17, reform-minded senators hoped to affix a measure, much like H.R. 3755, to a supplemental appropriations bill ccnference report. The proposal was tabled, 49-46.

H.R. 3755 passed both houses of Congress almost a year later and was signed, on October 9, by President Reagan. "The Social Security Reform Act of 1984," PL 98-460, required the Social Security Administration to demonstrate that a recipient's medical condition had improved, and that he or she was capable of returning to work, before benefits could be revoked. It also enabled those purged from the rolls to continue receiving program benefits while their cases were under appeal. *Congressional Quarterly Almanac, 1983*, 273, 274, 12-F, *1984*, 161.

Much of Hunt's testimony to the select committee was foreshadowed in his February 23, 1984, statement to the press.]

Mr. Chairman,[1] members of the committee:

Our Social Security disability program is deteriorating into a state of complete disarray. What has transpired in my state of North Carolina is a perfect example of the confusion and frustration generated by the federal government's refusal to recognize the law of the land, our federal court decisions.

After the Social Security Administration [SSA]'s accelerated review process had been operational for approximately two years, I became suddenly and painfully aware of a large population of North Carolinians, an estimated 15,000, who had been terminated from receiving benefits with absolutely no showing of improvement in their medical conditions. There is nothing in the law to support these terminations. SSA was completely ignoring statutes and legal precedent, and people that SSA determined were able to work were dying.

Consequently, on September 7, 1983, I declared a moratorium on terminating Social Security disability benefits pending congressional action to establish medical improvement standards.[2] At that time I was optimistic that the Pickle bill would be ratified. It never got out of the House.[3]

Then, in October, 1983, in the case of a man named Harley Dotson, the Fourth Circuit Court of Appeals held that the burden of proof is on SSA to demonstrate improvement in a recipient's medical condition before benefits can be terminated. Harley Dotson never saw a penny of those benefits because he died shortly after the opinion was handed down. In fact, he died of the very disease that the SSA found not disabling. A human life seems a high price to pay to get a medical improvement standard in North Carolina.[4]

Meanwhile, *Hyatt* v. *Heckler*, a class action, was filed in federal district court in our circuit to litigate the issue of nonacquiescence by SSA in three specific Fourth Circuit Court of Appeals decisions, Harley Dotson's case among them. In a bold but necessary step, the state of North Carolina intervened on behalf of that class against the federal government. I realize that the state had entered an agreement with the federal government to administer the federal disability program, but North Carolina never agreed to adhere to illegal federal administrative standards, ignoring federal court interpretations of those standards. On February 14, 1984, following a full trial on the merits, the federal district court, in *Hyatt* v. *Heckler*, ordered the SSA to follow the three Fourth Circuit decisions at issue.[5]

This *Hyatt* case has once again graphically demonstrated the human hardship caused by a bureaucracy run amok. One of the Fourth Circuit cases at issue in *Hyatt* held that SSA may not require end-organ damage as an exclusive precondition to the establishment of a disability from hypertension or diabetes. One of the three named plaintiffs in the class action, a man named Herman O. Caudle, was suffering from severe hypertension with accompanying complications.[6] In March of 1983 he was informed that his disability had ended. He immediately began pursuing the administrative appeals that were available to him. No severe impairment was found because he did not suffer any end-organ damage.

So, on October 21, 1983, Mr. Caudle filed a timely request with the Appeals Council for review of the ALJ [administrative law judge's] decision. Three days later his heart blew out. He was dead, apparently from the hypertension and other ailments which had disabled him for several years. His treating physician had attempted to hospitalize Mr. Caudle for intensive diagnostic procedures, but he refused hospitalization due to a lack of insurance coverage and the threatened loss of his disability benefits. Is this the kind of end-organ damage the SSA wants to see? What has happened to reason and common sense among officials of the Social Security Administration?

At the time I declared the moratorium in North Carolina, I was confident that reform legislation would be passed by the Congress. Senators Cohen and Levin and Representative Pickle had bills in each house that addressed key disability issues.[7] I regret that neither bill has been enacted.

In the last six months I have been very involved with two federal court cases in my circuit. In both cases a man has died. Therefore, the state had to litigate the issue of eligibility—and still the administration shows no signs of taking meaningful action to take corrective action.

Disability issues are being litigated all over the country. The resulting patchwork of federal court decisions has removed any vestige of uniformity in the Social Security disability program. Secretary Heckler[8] herself has recognized this in a directive she issued to the fifty states on January 24, 1984. Depending on the current status of litigation in that state, Ms. Heckler chose one of four different directives to send to that state. I was one of six governors instructed to keep a heretofore "illegal" moratorium in effect pending the outcome of litigation in my circuit. This demonstrates a crying need for the Congress to speak out and tell the secretary, tell the states, and most importantly, tell the disabled citizens of this country what they can expect from the Social Security disability program.

---

[1]Edward R. Roybal (1916-   ), native of Albuquerque, New Mexico; resident of Los Angeles; attended University of California-Los Angeles, and Southwestern University; served in U.S. Army during World War II. Member, 1949-1962, and president pro tem, 1961-1962, Los Angeles city council; elected to U.S. House from California's Twenty-fifth Congressional District, 1962, and returned in subsequent elections; chairman, U.S. House Select Committee on Aging; Democrat. Barone and Ujifusa, *Almanac of American Politics, 1984,* 136.

[2]Hunt was referring to Executive Order No. 97, *N.C. Session Laws, 1983,* 1446-1447. On July 20, 1983, the General Assembly created the Disability Review Commission, the purpose of which was to investigate state-supported methods of minimizing problems faced by North Carolinians who had their Social Security disability benefits revoked. See "An Act to Authorize a Review of the State's Disability Services," *N.C. Session Laws, 1983,* c. 880.

[3]H.R. 3755 was also known as "the Pickle bill." See headnote, above.

[4]See *News and Observer,* February 5, 1984.

[5]Hunt ordered the Department of Human Resources, late in 1983, to file a motion supporting the plaintiffs in *Hyatt* v. *Heckler,* then pending in the U.S. District Court in Charlotte. "News Release from the Governor's Office," December 6, 1983. For a summary of the case, see *Charlotte Observer,* February 15, 1984, and *News and Observer,* February 5, 15, 1984. The governor stated that Judge James B. McMillan's decision was "a victory . . . for all recipients of Social Security benefits," and that it "vindicat[ed] the moratorium that the state of North Carolina imposed against unjust terminations." "News Release from the Governor's Office," February 14, 1984.

[6]Herman O. Caudle, of Winston-Salem, was joined in the case by plaintiffs Patrick Hyatt and Mary Lovingood, both of Mecklenburg County. *News and Observer,* February 5, 15, 1984.

[7]William S. Cohen (1940-   ), native, resident of Bangor, Maine; B.A., 1962, LL.B., 1965, Boston University. Practicing attorney, 1965-1972; University of Maine instructor, 1968-1972; Bangor mayor, 1971-1972; elected to U.S. Senate in 1978; Republican. Barone and Ujifusa, *Almanac of American Politics, 1981,* 501.

Carl Levin (1933-   ), native, resident of Detroit; B.A., Swarthmore College, 1956; LL.B., Harvard University, 1959. Practicing attorney; assistant attorney general and civil rights commission general counsel, 1964-1967, and special assistant attorney general, 1968-1969, state of Michigan; member, 1968-1978, and president, 1973-1978, Detroit city council; elected to U.S. Senate in 1978; Democrat. Barone and Ujifusa, *Almanac of American Politics, 1984,* 574.

J. J. (Jake) Pickle (1913-   ), native of Big Spring, Texas; resident of Austin; B.A.,

University of Texas, 1938; served in U.S. Navy during World War II. Area director, National Youth Administration, 1938-1941; advertising and public relations executive; director, Texas state Democratic executive committee, 1957-1960; member, Texas Employment Commission, 1961-1963; elected to U.S. House from Texas's Tenth Congressional District, 1963, and returned in subsequent elections; chairman, Subcommittee on Social Security, U.S. House Committee on Ways and Means. Barone and Ujifusa, *Almanac of American Politics, 1984*, 1145. Proposed legislation to which Hunt referred is described in headnote, above.

[8]Margaret Mary Heckler (1931-   ), native of Flushing, New York; resident of Wellesley, Massachusetts; B.A., Albertus Magnus College, 1953; LL.B., Boston College, 1956; attended University of Leiden, Holland, 1952. Boston attorney, 1956-1966; U.S. representative from Massachusetts's Tenth Congressional District, 1967-1982; U.S. health and human resources secretary, 1983-1985. *News and Observer*, October 1, 1985; *Who's Who in America, 1982-1983*, I, 1458.

LOCAL ECONOMIC DEVELOPMENT CONFERENCE

ELIZABETH CITY, MARCH 9, 1984

[While he tailored certain aspects of the following address to particular audiences, Governor Hunt delivered essentially the same message in Asheville, February 21; Raleigh, March 1; Charlotte, March 20; Hickory, March 22; Winston-Salem, March 27; Wilson, March 29; and Jacksonville, April 10.]

I am here today with members of my cabinet not just to talk, but to listen. As representatives of your state government, we are here to reaffirm our commitment to work with you to build a vigorous and healthy economy in northeastern North Carolina and to protect the natural beauty and the good communities that make this part of our state so special.

North Carolina has made tremendous economic progress over the past few years, but in the short time between today and the dawn of a new century, we face challenges:

—Nearly 90 percent of all new jobs will be found outside manufacturing and agriculture. Many of those jobs will be in small businesses.

—Advances in technology and new industries will displace many people from the only jobs they ever knew. New jobs will require new skills.

—Competition for jobs will be fierce, and our people must learn the basic skills that will enable them to compete.

I know those challenges hit home for the sixteen counties represented here today. Unemployment is too high here, in double digits in seven of sixteen counties. We have young people moving away from home because they cannot find a job. That leaves four northeastern counties—Perquimans, Hyde, Tyrrell, and Chowan counties—with the highest percentage of elderly residents in the entire state. And they have special needs.

Per capita income is low, ranging from $5,256 in Hyde County to a high of only $7,634 in Washington County. Those families need education, health care, and more than anything else, good jobs.

Those are formidable problems, but you have made impressive progress in spite of them. Since 1977, the sixteen counties represented here have attracted over $1 billion in industrial investment, creating more than 6,800 new manufacturing jobs. The 400th Anniversary celebration will offer a tremendous boost to the businesses that thrive on travel and tourism. You have your Northeastern North Carolina Tomorrow planning effort. You have Elizabeth City State University, your community colleges and technical institutes, and your schools.

You have built a solid foundation for progress. Now is the time for us to join together—business, education, state, local, and federal governments—to set North Carolina on a course that will mean long-term economic growth in the 1980s, the 1990s, and the twenty-first century.

We have developed a comprehensive strategy for economic growth in North Carolina. Our strategy builds on investments in five critical areas: education, technology, skill training, environmental protection, and the infrastructure.

Very soon, the Commission on Education for Economic Growth, which I chair, will be proposing fundamental reforms in North Carolina's public schools—in the curriculum, in testing, in teacher pay, in building closer relationships with business. These changes are vital if we are going to prepare our young people for a modern economy and a new world.

North Carolina needs to help business and industry take advantage of technological advances. We are working on ways to give special attention to the needs of small businesses through our universities and our community college system.

State government also must help train both new workers and older workers who have been displaced from their jobs.

The protection of our natural resources, especially clean water, is a key to your economic future. I am determined that we will save Lake Gaston's water for northeastern North Carolina's future. We will also protect the quality of the Roanoke River basin, and I will ask the legislature this year for funds to protect the Chowan River.

We must continue to invest in the infrastructure of our communities—good roads, bridges, and airports.

To bring all of this together, we must have good working relationships between local, state, and federal government. Each level of government has a special job to do to help create growth and new jobs. It will not matter what we do here, for example, if the federal government does not get serious about reducing the enormous budget deficit that threatens our economic future.

The different levels of government must work together in a special way to help the farm economy, which is suffering a recession today. Agriculture is basic to the economy of northeastern North Carolina, and the potential for agricultural growth is probably greater here than anywhere else in the state. These sixteen counties have a fourth of our state's harvested cropland, and we can expect more growth in corn, soybeans, broilers, and swine.

No statewide strategy can meet the needs of all our counties and communities. As local leaders, you have to make the strategy fit your community's special needs. But if we work together, I believe we can develop an economic growth strategy that will bring new progress to northeastern North Carolina.

That is why we are here today—to talk about what we can do together. We are not going to solve all our problems today, but we can make a start—a start that will mean a better life for our children and grandchildren, for generations of North Carolinians.

NATIONAL WILDLIFE FEDERATION

ATLANTA, MARCH 17, 1984

It is a great pleasure to speak before the 48th Annual Meeting of the National Wildlife Federation. I am honored to share this same platform with your distinguished guests: the governor of Georgia, the secretary of the interior, and the administrator of EPA.[1] But I am truly overwhelmed by the opportunity to serve as warm-up for this evening's address by one of the great statesmen of our time, Kermit the Frog.[2]

In truth, Kermit and I are here for the same reason: to pay homage, each in his own way, to the four million members of this organization who have led the fight to conserve our precious natural resources for almost half a century.

The great success of this organization, I know, is directly due to the fact that your executive vice-president is a North Carolinian. Dr. Jay Hair is one of America's most dynamic and dedicated leaders in the cause of conservation, and he is one of North Carolina's most important contributions to that cause.[3] He is also my good friend and trusted adviser, and I thank him for his leadership and for the honor of being with him today. I also salute the members here today from the North Carolina Wildlife Federation. We have worked closely together on many issues, including appointments to our state Wildlife Resources Commission and the income tax checkoff [for] wildlife protection programs.[4]

All of you deserve the thanks of all Americans for all you have done to conserve our nation's natural resources. It has not been easy. Those who want to use resources wisely and productively are seldom appreciated in their own time. Those who reject extremism are seldom seen on the evening news. Those who tackle the special interests are seldom invited to ride in the back seat of the limousine. Nevertheless, you persisted. And today, you are squarely in the mainstream of a grass-roots movement that is remaking the political, social, and spiritual life of our country.

Conservationism transcends normal politics. To be sure, it has its practical sides: coalitions, compromises, bipartisanship. But it is also an ethos, a way of seeing the world differently, a way of relating to the world differently, and a way of caring for the world differently. As such, it is changing the way we think, work, and play.

The National Wildlife Federation was present at the creation of this new ethos, and today, as the largest conservation organization in the world, you are carrying the message into new terrain. You are talking to environmental extremists and showing them how to win through moderation. You are talking to business leaders and showing them how to profit through conservation. You are talking to government leaders and showing them how to manage through collaboration. You are talking to all Americans and showing them that economic growth and resource conservation can exist side-by-side—that this is not a zero-sum game, that growth in the economy does not equal an irretrievable loss to the environment, that additional protections for the environment do not equal a slowdown in the economy.

We in North Carolina not only see environmental protection and economic growth as consistent, we see them as inextricably linked together. We believe economic growth requires the protection of our resource base, the productive use of our resources, and the preservation of those resources for recreation and the other benefits that make our communities good places to live.

Come see our hazy, blue mountains, our wide beaches, our productive forests, our family farms. Come see how we have harmonized a productive economy with a magnificent natural endowment. Strategic thinking enables us to enjoy the best of both worlds. In our experience, resource conservation pays. It pays in hard returns on the bottom line, and it pays in the intangibles that make living in North Carolina living the good life.

In my own life and in my own state, I have seen the transforming effects of conservationism. I am the son of a soil conservationist. My father once advertised in the newspaper to find the sorriest land in Wilson County. He found it, and he proved that it could be reclaimed and made productive.

I grew up on a farm that has been in my family for generations, and I still have my home there. I like to fish, feed our ducks, walk through the fields, and mow the pastures. That land is where my family has lived and made its living. It is our home, our past, and our future.

That heritage has served me well in the Governor's Office. As in many other growing southern states, North Carolina has grappled with tough problems related to resource conservation and environmental protection. We put into place one of the strongest coastal management programs in the country. Together, state and local governments are making sure that future generations will have free access to clean, uncluttered beaches; that our wetlands will remain a vibrant habitat for waterfowl; and that our coastal rivers and sounds remain productive for our fisheries.

After our people were jolted by the construction of a high-rise, ten-story condominium project atop a mountain at the edge of the Blue Ridge, we enacted a Mountain Ridge Protection Act in 1983 that prohibits construction on those ridges; allows local governments the freedom to further regulate mountain development; and is the first state law in the country to regulate a significant aspect of development *throughout* a state's mountain region.[5]

We passed legislation and established a tough state waste management policy aimed at minimizing the amount of waste generated and at working with industry, through a program called Pollution Prevention Pays, to demonstrate how to prevent waste and save money. Our policy concentrates on helping the private sector establish the waste-treatment facilities we need: incinerators and recycling centers, not landfills.

This year, I am preparing to submit to our legislature a "Clean Water Budget":

—Grants to promote best management practices on farms and forests to protect three nutrient-sensitive watersheds.

—Money to establish a statewide program to control toxics in our waters.

This has been the North Carolina approach, one that emphasizes cooperation, not confrontation; one that recognizes the interrelationship between economic growth and resource protection. We are proud of North Carolina's record. But we know that North Carolina alone, that no state alone, can do all that must be done to protect the land, the air, and the water for generations to come.

The federal government must take a strong and vigorous role. We must have strong national pollution standards, and we must have a strong financial commitment by the federal government. Unfortunately, the federal government has retreated from this commitment during the past four years. This should not be a partisan issue; America's commitment to resource protection and environmental protection was built over a period of fifteen years, in both Republican and Democratic administrations. It must be restored by bipartisan leadership and commitment.

Here, by way of example, are a few key issues that are beyond reach of a state's resources and that require strong federal involvement:

—Agriculture. Federal policy determines in large measure whether local agricultural practices are consistent with sound environmental principles. Incentives that drive farmers to plow fence to fence leave little room for wildlife habitat. A land retirement program that discourages the planting of grasses and legumes not only hurts wildlife; it also promotes soil erosion. And the federal government should provide incentives for farmers to use the best management practices to reduce stream pollution.

—Acid Rain. Rapidly accumulating evidence indicates that the forests throughout the eastern United States, including those in the western part of my state, are in decline, and man-made pollution is looked to as the chief suspect. It appears that acid rain is not limited to isolated areas of our country, and it knows no state boundaries. It is a national problem, and it deserves a national solution. Obviously we need to know a great deal more about it, and a vigorous national research effort needs to be pursued. But at the same time, we need to pursue a national program similar to the one endorsed by my fellow governors at our winter meeting last month. This calls for a two-phase, 10-million-ton reduction in sulfur dioxide emissions, and it is very close to the call of the National Wildlife Federation and the National Academy of Sciences that we strive for a 50 percent reduction in sulfate emissions this decade.

—Wetlands. Half a million acres of irreplaceable wetlands are lost each year. The effect on migratory fish, birds, and other wildlife is enormous. Yet states are virtually powerless to halt this trend without federal monies and authorities. We also need to halt all efforts to weaken Section 404 of the Clean Water Act, which protects natural resources, including endangered species, from the effects of reduced stream flows caused by water-diversion projects.[6]

—Toxics. We need new legislation to require more controls over toxics, and we need to maintain uniform national requirements for cleaning up waste water before it's dumped into public sewers. Finally, we need a serious commitment from EPA to monitor and disarm dangerous toxic dump sites where seepage into underground aquifers threatens our precious drinking water.

—Wildlife Refuges. We need to repudiate the administration's attitude toward wildlife refuges: the less the better. Before time runs out, we must create a nationwide system of sanctuaries for disappearing species. A similar spirit should guide our quest for wilderness areas.

—Coal and Oil. The federal government is moving too fast and recklessly on the leasing of coalfields and offshore oil reserves. We have some breathing room; we should use it to learn how to mitigate the worst effects of risky explorations and exploitations. I do support a program of oil and gas lease sales, but it must be an environmentally sound program—and it must recognize the continued role of the states in the process.

It is time to restore this nation's historic commitment to conservation. It is time to recognize that there is a connection between concern for wildlife and concern for human life, a connection between conservation and economic growth that can bring us the best of both.

Our friend Kermit the Frog has a theme song, and it is entitled— appropriately enough, on St. Patrick's Day—"It's Not Easy Being Green." Nor is it easy keeping this beautiful Earth green.

Let me conclude by thanking you for the extraordinary efforts of the National Wildlife Federation over the past half century. This nation's lovers and dreamers—those of us who love this land, those of us who dream of an even stronger and more beautiful America— thank you for it.

---

[1]Joe Frank Harris (1936-   ), native of Atco, Georgia; B.A., University of Georgia, 1958; U.S. Army, 1953-1964. Businessman; member, Georgia House, 1964-1980; elected governor of Georgia in 1982; Democrat. Barone and Ujifusa, *Almanac of American Politics, 1984*, 279.

William Patrick Clark (1931-   ), native of Oxnard, California; attended Stanford University, 1949-1951, and Loyola University law school, 1955; U.S. Army, 1951-1953. Rancher; attorney; chief of staff for California governor Ronald Reagan, 1966-1969; San Luis Obispo County superior court judge, 1969-1971; Los Angeles County appellate judge, 1971-1973; California supreme court justice, 1973-1981; deputy U.S. secretary of state, 1981-1982; National Security Adviser, 1982-1983; appointed Interior Department secretary in 1983; Republican. *Current Biography Yearbook, 1982* (New York: H. W. Wilson Company, 1983), 68-71; "Reagan Makes His Moves," *Time,* October 24, 1983, 16-19; *Who's Who in America, 1982-1983,* I, 594.

William Doyle Ruckelshaus (1932-   ), native of Indianapolis, Indiana; B.A., Princeton University, 1957; LL.B., Harvard University, 1960; U.S. Army, 1953-1955. Attorney; member, Indiana House, 1966-1969; U.S. Environmental Protection Agency administrator, 1970-1973, 1983-1984; Federal Bureau of Investigation acting director, 1973; senior vice-president, Weyerhaeuser Corp., 1975-1983. "EPA: Ruckelshaus Bows Out," *Newsweek,* December 10, 1984, 39; "How Do You Spell Relief," *Newsweek,* April 4, 1983, 22; *Who's Who in America, 1982-1983,* II, 2887.

[2]In 1955 college student Jim Henson cut some cloth from an old green coat belonging to his mother and created Kermit the Frog, the first of many puppetlike characters known as "The Muppets." That same year Kermit made his television debut on the Emmy award-winning "Sam and Friends" program, which originated in Washington, D.C. He eventually appeared as a guest on many variety shows and starred in two very successful television series, "Sesame Street" and "The Muppet Show." *News and Observer,* January 6, 1986.

[3]Jay D. Hair (1945-   ), native of Miami, Florida; resident of Cary; B.S., 1967, M.S., 1969, Clemson University; Ph.D., University of Alberta, 1975; U.S. Army, 1970-1971. Associate professor of zoology and forestry, North Carolina State University, 1977-1981; executive vice-president, National Wildlife Federation, since 1981; editor; author; *News and Observer,* July 19, 1981; *Who's Who in America, 1982-1983,* I, 1356-1357.

[4]"An Act to Establish the North Carolina Income Tax Refund Checkoff Program for the Management of Nongame and Endangered Species" was ratified July 20. *N.C. Session Laws, 1983,* c. 865.

⁵"An Act to Regulate the Height of Tall Buildings or Structures on Mountain Ridges" was ratified July 5. *N.C. Session Laws, 1983*, c. 676.

⁶H.R. 3282, reauthorizing the Clean Water Act, passed the U.S. House on June 26, 1984. The Senate version of the bill failed to clear the upper house, however. *Congressional Quarterly Almanac, 1984*, 15, 329-331.

CITIZENS CONFERENCE ON ACID RAIN

RALEIGH, MARCH 23, 1984

Just last Saturday, I addressed the annual meeting of the National Wildlife Federation in Atlanta and was honored to receive the federation's National Conservation Award. In my remarks, I paid tribute to this organization for leading the fight to conserve our nation's precious natural resources for almost half a century. This conference on acid rain is only the most recent example of that fight, and I thank the federation and Dr. Jay Hair for focusing North Carolina's attention on this problem.

When we talk about acid rain, we are talking about a threat to our vital natural resources—a threat to the long-term health of our lakes, rivers and streams, our groundwater, our soil, our agricultural crops, our wilderness and natural areas, and, ultimately, our economic well-being.

There is evidence suggesting that our forests in North Carolina are being affected by air pollution and associated acid rain. We have recorded rainfall that is much more acid than it should be. The *New York Times* recently ran an extensive story about trees dying and failing to reproduce at high elevations on North Carolina's highest peak, Mount Mitchell.¹ Acid rain may be to blame.

If acid rain is not brought under control, North Carolina could suffer devastating effects—to our environment and to our economy. The loss would be far greater than a few fish or a few trees. Our attractiveness to business and industry would decline. Our farm economy would suffer. The intangibles that make North Carolina a good place to live would be lost.

As governor of North Carolina, I believe our state has a great deal at stake. We are already making great strides. Since the early 1970s, we have set for ourselves tougher limits on sulfur dioxide emissions than most other states in the nation. Our utilities and industries are required to keep our air clean and are working hard to do so. Both Carolina Power and Light and Duke Power burn low-sulfur coal. Duke Power recently phased out eleven coal-fired plants except during emergency periods. If all states were doing as well, we would not be facing an acid rain dilemma today. But other states have not, and regional differences make this a difficult problem to resolve.

We talked a great deal about acid rain at the recent winter meeting of the National Governors' Association. Believe me, the debate was hot. And the regional accents were as thick and angry as I have ever heard them on any issue before the nation's governors. Finally, the governors agreed on a policy that calls for the thirty-one eastern states to participate in a two-phase program to reduce sulfur dioxide emissions by 10 million tons—which is similar to the magnitude of reduction sought by the National Wildlife Federation and the National Academy of Sciences.

Because of the regional differences and the interstate and inter-regional nature of the acid rain problem, I am convinced that the only solution to the problem is a national solution. But what has been sorely missing in the administration in Washington and in Congress has been the leadership to face up to the problem and take action. The Reagan administration has not responded, even though the new director[2] of the Environmental Protection Agency has argued in the president's cabinet for action and even though there have been calls for action from our own nation and from one of our strongest allies, Canada.

Furthermore, I believe that it is in North Carolina's best interest to push for a solution and to be part of the solution. Like other pollutants, acid rain does not respect state boundaries. Our emissions can find their way into other states and their emissions into ours. Under any solution North Carolinians will have to help foot the bill, directly or indirectly. But we stand ready to do our fair share to control acid rain, just as we expect all other states to do their part as well.

Unless the method of funding the program is very carefully constructed, we here in North Carolina may be called upon to pay more than our fair share of a national control program—not because we have done a bad job, but because we have done a good job and because emissions here are at such a low level that it may take very expensive measures to further reduce them. Further, if Midwestern power companies go to the same low-sulfur coal we use here in North Carolina, the higher demand for coal will force our utilities to pay a higher price. So any program developed by Congress must be equitable, it must minimize economic disruptions and job losses, and it must make allowances for past investments to control emissions.

There will be a cost involved. There is no question about that. But we must understand that failing to control acid rain could be even more costly—to our environment and to our economy in North Carolina. Our economic growth and our attractiveness depend on our beauty, our quality of life, our clean air and clean water, our beautiful coast and mountains, our fertile farms, our livable communities. Environmental protection and economic growth are not contradictory; they are complementary.

Certainly, we do not know everything there is to know about acid rain, and I support more research along the lines of what Dr. Cowling[3] is doing at North Carolina State University, but the need for more research is no excuse for failing to act now. We must face up to the problem now, just as we enacted the first coastal area management plan in the nation, just as we took steps last year to protect our mountain ridges against development, just as we established a Pollution Prevention Pays program, just as we adopted a tough program to prevent and manage toxic and hazardous wastes, just as we are protecting our groundwater, just as we are preparing a Clean Water Budget for the General Assembly to protect against toxics and against eutrophication in our rivers and lakes.

That is the North Carolina way—facing our environmental problems early and learning to prevent them from getting to the crisis stage. That is the way this nation should confront the problem of acid rain today, and North Carolina stands ready to lead the way.

---

[1] *New York Times*, February 26, 1984.

[2] William Doyle Ruckelshaus

[3] Dr. Ellis B. Cowling, an internationally respected expert on acid rain, was associate dean of forestry at North Carolina State University. *News and Observer*, December 4, 1984.

STATEMENT ON 1984 LEGISLATIVE SESSION

RALEIGH, MARCH 28, 1984

The June session of the General Assembly should be devoted primarily to education. Next week, my Commission on Education for Economic Growth will release its final report. We have already begun talking with the legislative leadership about the need for significant action this year.

While education is the most important issue before the legislature, I do hope the session will be able to address several critical matters regarding environmental protection in North Carolina—including management of toxic and hazardous wastes and a "Clean Water Budget" to protect North Carolina's waterways against pollution. My administration is working closely with the legislative study committees in these areas. The Waste Management Board has been actively seeking the type of integrated waste treatment facility that it has concluded North Carolina needs at this time. Our policy is to emphasize the incineration and reduction of waste materials, instead of long-term storage.

In addition, I hope the legislature will be able to consider two bills that passed the House in 1983: legislation providing for strict liability in handling waste materials[1] and legislation giving the state authority to clean up "orphan" dump sites and bill the owners for the cost. This would be similar to the federal "Superfund."[2]

In addition, I am planning to include in my budget request a modest but important recommendation for a Clean Water Budget. This would include funds for:

—Expansion of the state's Pollution Prevention Pays program, which works with industry to prevent waste products;

—Protecting three nutrient-sensitive watersheds—the Chowan River, and the Falls and Jordan lakes—against eutrophication;

—Providing additional equipment and people so the state can monitor toxic discharges into rivers, streams, and lakes;

—Funds to carry out several recommendations of the Governor's Coastal Water Management Task Force, which has put together a plan for balancing growth in agriculture and forestry in our coastal areas with preservation of our valuable natural resources. These recommendations include a resource inventory, research, demonstration projects, and education efforts. Today, I am releasing a status report on the recommendations of the task force to bring you up to date on this important work.[3]

---

[1] H.B. 738, "A Bill to be Entitled an Act to Provide for Strict Liability for Damages Resulting from Hazardous Wastes in North Carolina," was introduced in the state House on April 7, 1983; it passed its third reading and was sent to the Senate on July 12. *N.C. House Journal, 1983, Regular Session,* 314, 984. The Senate Special Ways and Means Committee reported unfavorably on H.B. 738 on June 25, 1984. Instead, it recommended a substitute, "A Bill to Authorize the Legislative Research Commission to Study the Issue of Strict Liability for Damages Resulting from Hazardous Wastes in North Carolina," which was subsequently incorporated into "An Act Authorizing Studies by the Legislative Research Commission, Authorizing Additional Studies, and Making Various Appropriations for Studies," ratified on July 7, 1984. *N.C. Senate Journal, 1983, Second Session, 1984,* 55, 89, 168-169, 182; *N.C. Session Laws, 1983, Second Session, 1984,* c. 1112, ss. 1, 2.

[2] Representatives Joe Hackney and Wilbur Bruce Etheridge introduced H.B. 1383, "A Bill to be Entitled an Act Concerning Inactive Hazardous Substance Disposal Sites," before the state House on June 30, 1983. It went to the Senate on July 8, 1983, where it met the approval of the Special Ways and Means Committee on June 21, 1984. H.B. 1383 was then referred to the Senate Appropriations Committee. *N.C. House Journal, 1983, Regular Session,* 871, 964; *N.C. Senate Journal, 1983, Second Session, 1984,* 55, 110.

[3] *Governor's Coastal Water Management Task Force: Status Report, February, 1984* ([Raleigh]: North Carolina Department of Natural Resources and Community Development, [1984]).

NOTES FOR BLACK JACK
FREE WILL BAPTIST CHURCH
FAMILY FESTIVAL

GREENVILLE, MARCH 28, 1984

[A transcript of a tape recording of Hunt's remarks at Black Jack Free Will Baptist Church appears as an appendix to this volume.]

INTRODUCTION

Although it has been said, "You can't go home again," [1] I do feel at home. You are my kind of people, and I can't think of anywhere else I had rather be. What I want to do is: (1) Be informal and share with you from my heart. Sort of a testimony. (2) Rather than giving a speech on government programs and family, I prefer to tell you what family means to me personally.

I. First, I believe that the family is the bedrock (seedbed) of society. No accident that the first institution God created was the home. The quality of all society depends upon the health and strength of the family. Thus, most important work a church or government can do is to help families be all that God created them to be.

Emphasis upon economy—help mothers and fathers get good jobs so that they can take care of their own children. Some families need help, and it is appropriate for churches and government to lend a helping hand. Turning our backs on needy families is contrary to the parable of the Good Samaritan. Emphasize work of compassion. (Can refer to any number of works here, i.e., food, clothing, shelter, medical care, needs of children, elderly, etc.)

II. Second, I believe that family is essential in passing on the right values to the next generation.

Relay race in track—handoff determines who wins or loses. From my Christian parents, I learned the importance of belief in Jesus Christ, church attendance, honesty, hard work, love, justice, discipline, love, faithfulness, compassion, and stewardship. The Bible says, "Train up a child in the way he should go, and when he is old, he will not depart from it." (Proverbs 22:6)

When faced with hard decisions, I often remember my parents' instructions. I remember biblical truths learned as a child. I am so proud of the Bible I received as a child from my church for memorizing scriptures. I remember what I heard last Sunday in Sunday School and worship. Dr. Pierce,[2] you and all these Sunday school teachers must never underestimate the contribution you are making by sharing God's truths each week. Those truths become our values upon which we base our actions.

Because some children do not have good home environments, schools should also teach broad, universal values. We need to teach right living as well as right learning. We need to teach honesty as well as history. We need to teach equality as well as English. We need to teach morality as well as math.

I firmly believe that God gave us families so that we can pass on those values which will make us good and godly. Every parent must set the right example because their children will soon be following in their footsteps.

III. A third reason I believe families are so important is that home is the place where we need to hear affectionate words. Words that build up our self-image and challenge us to have a productive future. Too many live in families where they are never hugged or even hear the words, "I love you." (Relate volunteer experience with youths.)

So many youths are told that they can't make it or be somebody. They hear words like "failures" and "losers." Tell someone something long enough and he will believe it. Expect nothing of a person and that is usually what he will become.

I am positive and optimistic about the future. There are too many negative people in the world. Too many prophets of gloom and doom. (This can be developed—obvious reference)

My parents told me that I could—even had an obligation to—make a contribution to society.

My parents were open and generous with their affection, and Carolyn and I are with each other and with our children.

And the greatest love of all was God's love for us—so much that He gave his only begotten Son. That love, that affection, that positive good news must be told over and over; and our future, with God's help, can become the abundant life which the Bible talks about. If churches, civic organizations, and government work together, the lives of all our citizens can be positive and abundant.

CONCLUSION

Let me conclude by reminding you that good families don't first happen—they are the result of hard work.

No way to repay the sacrifices my mother and father made for me.

Churches, government, and individuals need to make family relationships a high priority.

I have been accused of being a governor who takes my family life seriously. Perhaps the greatest accomplishment during my public service is that after twelve years of serving as lieutenant governor and governor, I have a wife of [twenty-six] years who loves me, supports me—and yes, even corrects me—and four absolutely super children. It has not been easy, but family is important to all of us. I make it a policy to make Sunday a day of worship and family time.

As governor, a number of my staff are assigned the duties of determining policies that are best for families of this state. I have placed great emphasis upon children and the elderly. As governor, I have tried to establish policies that will build up and strengthen families. Policies that will minister to broken and fragmented families. There are so many who hurt, and the burden of my heart is that we haven't been able to do it all. My prayer is that we have been successful in helping some.

I am not sure how history will remember me, but I hope it will be said of Jim Hunt: "He was a son who honored his mother and father. He was a husband and father who tried very hard."

Would you pray with me? (Then lead in a short prayer.)

---

[1]The governor was referring to the title of a Thomas Wolfe novel previously identified in Mitchell, *Addresses of Hunt*, I, 10n.

[2]Cedric D. Pierce, Jr. (1939-   ), native, resident of Wayne County; B.A., Wake Forest University, 1962; M.Ed., East Carolina University, 1974; D.D., Associated Missionary Society and Bible College, 1982; postgraduate study. Ordained minister in 1959; pastor of Shady Grove Free Will Baptist Church, Dunn, 1966-1968, 1973-1978, of Black Jack Free Will Baptist Church, Greenville, 1968-1971, 1978-1985, and of Pleasant Grove Free Will Baptist Church, Pikeville, since May 1, 1985; superintendent, Free Will Baptist Children's Home, 1971-1973; director, Extended Day School Program, Sampson County, 1973-1975; academic dean, professor, Carolina Bible Institute and Seminary, since 1976. Cedric D. Pierce, Jr., to Jan-Michael Poff, March 5, 1986.

LOCAL ECONOMIC DEVELOPMENT CONFERENCE

FAYETTEVILLE, APRIL 2, 1984

[A series of tornadoes, some of them packing winds in excess of 200 miles per hour, touched down along a 310-mile path stretching from Ware Shoals, South Carolina, to Bennetts Creek, North Carolina, on the evening of March 28, 1984. In North Carolina alone, fifteen of the twisters claimed forty-four lives, left better than 800 injured and 2,000 homeless, and caused an estimated $200 million in property damage. Hunt toured storm-ravaged parts of Pitt County late on the twenty-eighth, after having delivered a speech at Black Jack Free Will Baptist Church (see preceding address); he visited other major disaster sites the following day and later called for federal assistance for tornado victims. President Reagan responded on March 30 and declared Bertie, Duplin, Hertford, Pitt, Robeson, and Wayne counties to be disaster areas; Cumberland, Gates, Greene, Lenoir, Nash, Perquimans, Sampson, and Scotland were accorded the same status by April 4. All the while, private and corporate contributions of food, money, and other necessities, from across the state and nation, poured into damage-stricken localities to aid victims of one of the worst natural disasters in North Carolina history. *News and Observer*, March 29, 31,

April 1, 3, 5, May 9, August 5, 1984; "News Release from the Governor's Office," April 6, 1984; *Raleigh Times*, March 29, 1984.]

We have suffered a great loss in North Carolina. The economic loss will be in the millions of dollars, but the human loss cannot be counted; it cannot be measured. We had originally scheduled this conference to talk about North Carolina's economic future. I believe we are going to have to pull through the shock of this moment before we can begin to plan for the future.

I am convinced we are going to pull through. Surrounded by tragedy, by destruction and the loss of life, I have seen in this state a special kind of courage and spirit over the past few days. I have seen how North Carolina people can pull together. I have heard that many people are opening up their homes to the homeless. Churches, volunteer groups, and people from all over the country are pitching in to help. The National Guard and Red Cross chapters all over the state are working together. The Salvation Army, Civil Air Patrol, the North Carolina Highway Patrol, and local law enforcement agencies are all working together. Rescue squads, volunteer fire departments, and the men and women in charge of our public utilities have been working around the clock. I could not even begin to list all the organizations involved in this effort.

I have asked President Reagan to declare our damaged counties a disaster area, but we know no amount of money can replace the losses suffered here. We know this is a situation where people can do more than government.

For many of the counties here today, the losses will be counted in the millions. Others have not been hit so hard. But we know the entire economy of this region will be affected by the human and economic loss we have suffered. For you to travel here today, amid all this, tells me you are already thinking about how to rebuild after this tragedy.

At these economic development conferences, I have talked about North Carolina's economic development strategy. I have said that strategy builds on investments in five areas: education, technology, skill training, environmental protection, and the infrastructure.

For many of our people, those five areas seem very distant and academic. We have lost schools and businesses. People have lost their jobs and their homes. We have lost bridges and roads, and so much more. But we have not lost our faith in each other.

We will come back, and we will help each other rebuild. I have seen out here a cooperative spirit that will pull together the counties of eastern North Carolina, and all North Carolinians, like never before.

I declared yesterday, Sunday, a statewide day of prayer for those who suffered losses in this tragedy.[1] Today, I believe we can start putting those prayers to work. We can start planning how we, as

North Carolinians, can pull together to rebuild the lives, businesses, and future of those who have endured this tragedy. By making them strong again, we will have taken the first step toward building a North Carolina economy, and a North Carolina future, that includes all our people.

---

[1] Governor Hunt issued a proclamation on March 30 designating Sunday, April 1, as a day of prayer and ordered flags to be flown at half mast. He also announced the creation of the North Carolina Tornado Victims Housing Fund. "News Release from the Governor's Office," March 30, 1984.

NORTH CAROLINA CRIME
AND JUSTICE CONFERENCE

RALEIGH, APRIL 4, 1984

This may be my last opportunity as governor to address the members of the North Carolina criminal justice system. Of course, I hope it will not be the last time you invite me to speak as an elected official of North Carolina. Later tonight this conference will recognize outstanding achievement with the Criminal Justice Awards; now I want to recognize the entire North Carolina criminal justice system for outstanding achievement.

Since I became governor in 1977, I have seen this system come together and work together in a way that is unprecedented in our history. You have worked hard, you have worked together, and it has paid off. Because of your hard work, and because of the crime-fighting laws we have put on the books, the people of North Carolina have turned the tide in the war against crime. The figures show our progress:

—The new figures show the overall crime rate in North Carolina *down more than 7 percent in 1983 from 1982.*

—Violent crime is down 7.5 percent and property crime is down 7.2 percent. Murder, robbery, aggravated assault, breaking and entering, larceny, motor vehicle thefts, arson, assaults on law officers—all are down.

—North Carolina's crime rate is significantly lower than the national crime rate—18 percent lower in 1982.

—The increase in the violent crime rate for North Carolina was 56 percent less than the increase in the national rate between 1977 and 1982.

Those figures tell a story you know: North Carolina is becoming a safer place. We are getting the hardened criminal off the streets. We have restored the death penalty for heinous murders. We require a mandatory life sentence for aggravated rape and a mandatory seven years in prison for armed robbery. We have harsh penalties for drug trafficking, and we have driven the headshops out of business. And, today, we are running the drunk drivers off the roads.

The Speedy Trial Act and the Fair Sentencing Act that we passed have made justice swifter and more certain in North Carolina. A study by the Institute of Government shows that, under the Fair Sentencing Act:

—Sentences are more consistent and less arbitrary and capricious.

—A convicted felon's chance of getting active time has increased. At least 90 percent of them got either active prison terms or supervised probation.[1]

The act has not crowded our prisons, as some critics said it would. Seven years ago, some judges refused to send convicted criminals to overcrowded prison cells. Today, we have the cells we need, and, for the first time since 1973, our prison capacity exceeds prison population.

We must always remain ready to fine tune the Fair Sentencing Act whenever necessary to make sure the violent offender, the career criminal, the drug trafficker and the like get the long prison terms they deserve.

Fair Sentencing and Speedy Trials have worked, and they have worked well. Today, a criminal in North Carolina had better beware—because he cannot go judge-shopping and trial-hopping to beat a rap.

We have cracked down on the hardened criminal, but, at the same time, we have learned a better way of keeping the young, first-time offender from graduating into a career of crime. We now have sentencing alternatives for those who deserve a second chance. We have community-based programs to work with them. We counsel them through in-school suspension programs, instead of kicking them out the door. We have youthful offenders paying restitution to their victims instead of going to prison. Here, again, the figures show our progress. *Reports of juvenile crime declined 32 percent in North Carolina last year.* That is a remarkable record.

We have not forgotten the victims of crime, either. We have made restitution to victims a higher priority in court-ordered fines and fees. Last year, the courts ordered more than $10 million in restitution payments in the 83 counties for which we have figures. Victims were paid more than $4.5 million. We are now paying up to $500 in immediate medical expenses to victims of rape or sexual assault. In the first thirty months of the program, more than $117,000 has been paid to 1,141 victims.

On July 1 of this year, the new Crime Victims Compensation Act will go into effect to help pay victims of violent crimes for their losses.[2] We now have ten victim and witness coordinators working in courts across the state to save witnesses and victims countless hours waiting for trials and to help them seek restitution for their losses.

And, today, we are seeing the impact of what may be the crowning achievement of our war against crime: our war against the drunk driver. After the Safe Roads Act became law last October, *drunk-driving arrests in North Carolina declined by more than 1,000 a month.* For all of 1983, drunk-driving arrests declined by more than 13 percent. For the first two months of 1984, DWI arrests by the State Highway Patrol were down 20 percent from the same period last year.

The evidence is clear: We are scaring drunk drivers off the roads. We have put many convicted drunk drivers to work doing community service. As of February, almost 5,000 offenders had done more than 60,000 hours of community service work, and a lot of judges say we ought to extend that program to crimes besides drunk driving.

Alcohol is our leading substance abuse problem, but it is not our only problem. Marijuana and cocaine have pervaded our society, and we must protect our young people against this cancer. I have appointed a Governor's Task Force on Alcohol and Drug Abuse in the Schools to take the lead in tackling this problem.

I have asked the Governor's Crime Commission to make a special study of substance abuse and its impact on crime, and the commission will hold public hearings across the state on this problem. We must turn the same energies to the war on drugs as we did in the war on drunk drivers.

Seven years ago, I delivered the first "Special Message on Crime" to the North Carolina General Assembly. Then, and in each succeeding session of the legislature, I have come forward with a special package of legislation to protect our citizens against crime. The General Assembly has responded. The criminal justice system has responded. Our law enforcement officers have responded. Our citizens have responded, and the criminals have gotten the message.

We have done more than make North Carolina a safer place to live, as significant an accomplishment as that is. We have shown what a people working through their government can achieve. We have shown what a community, whether a small neighborhood or a state of six million people, can do. We have turned the tide against crime. Now, let us press the fight to an end.

---

[1]See "Statement on Fair Sentencing Act," December 16, 1982, above, footnote 3.

[2]"An Act Providing Compensation for Innocent Victims of Crime," was ratified July 20. *N.C. Session Laws, 1983,* c. 832.

Right: A proponent of the application of advanced technology to the learning process, the governor watches a student demonstrate his ability with a computer. Hunt was also a vigorous advocate of citizen involvement in education and served as a volunteer in Raleigh schools throughout his two terms in office. *Below:* Macon County schoolchildren press for autographs.

Speaking before an audience in the Raleigh Civic Center on April 5, 1984, Governor Hunt unveils the report of the North Carolina Commission on Education for Economic Growth. Hunt created the commission in 1983, and its recommendations for improvements in the state's primary and secondary schools continued to influence legislative debate on education after he left office. Commission members William C. Friday, left, president of the University of North Carolina, and C. Dixon Spangler, Jr., right, president of the State Board of Education and Friday's successor at UNC, flank the governor.

NORTH CAROLINA ASSOCIATION OF EDUCATORS ANNUAL CONVENTION

GREENSBORO, APRIL 13, 1984

[Explaining the NCAE's withholding of an expected January endorsement of a U.S. Senate candidate, the organization's president, Frances Cummings, stated: " 'I could hardly see how anyone could vote for Senator Helms based on his voting record on education. But at the same time, we are not pleased with Governor Hunt and we will look to him for change in June' " when the General Assembly was to conduct its short session. She continued: " 'The sentiment is the result of the salary freeze and the wonderful rhetoric but not delivering for the past couple of years.' " *News and Observer*, January 29, 1984.

Responding to the NCAE's decision, a *News and Observer* editorial admitted that the paper itself frequently had reprimanded the governor for his "insufficient boldness in pursuing educational priorities and for the drop in North Carolina's average teacher pay. But there can be no doubt about his commitment to improving public education." It concluded, "The NCAE can sulk about Hunt's imperfect report card if it likes, but its refusal to endorse betrays a lack of political sophistication. Does it want the public to think its endorsement 'purchased' in the 1984 legislative session?" *News and Observer*, February 1, 1984.

The NCAE announced its endorsement of Governor Hunt on July 27. A month earlier the General Assembly appropriated $250 million for teacher salaries, textbooks, classroom enrollment reductions, math-science equipment, and other educational needs. *News and Observer*, July 29, August 1, 1984.]

I believe North Carolina stands today on the threshold of a giant step forward in education—a giant step that will add dignity to your profession and impetus to the development of North Carolina as one of the most dynamic, fast-growing, and progressive states in this nation.

We brought together leading citizens of this state on the North Carolina Commission on Education for Economic Growth: legislators, business executives, local government leaders, educators, parents, and students. Together, we have begun a crusade—a crusade for excellence in education, a crusade for expanded opportunities for our children, a crusade for North Carolina's future.

When the General Assembly convenes in just two months, I will call on it to set a course that can make North Carolina's schools the best in the nation. The time for action has come. The time has come to build upon the foundation we have laid.

North Carolina has made enormous progress the last few years— the new businesses and industries, the hundreds of thousands of new jobs, the new homes, the rising standards of living. We have made our schools better, too, and you deserve credit for that. We have shown the taxpayers that we can have better schools without raising taxes, with reforms like the Primary Reading Program, the testing program, the North Carolina School of Science and Mathematics, just to name a few. Student achievement scores are higher than the national average at all levels.

Now we have more work to do. We have a future to build.

We can, and we must, build strong new public support for the schools—from the neighborhood school to the capital.

We can, and we must, strengthen the curriculum and ensure that students are learning what they need to learn.

We can, and we must, reduce class sizes in the critical years following the third grade.

We can, and we must, provide careers for teachers and educators that reward hard work and dedication. That means higher salaries —and it means career opportunities and a classroom environment that makes teaching a pleasure, not a burden.

Those are the steps that I am going to ask the legislature to take in June.

Now, let me say a final word about another critical decision this state will make in 1984: Who will represent North Carolina in the United States Senate.

This campaign is not just Jim Hunt against Jesse Helms. It is not just a battle of television commercials. This campaign is about which direction North Carolina and the nation will take the next six years. It is about whether we will live in the past or look to the future. It is about whether we will move forward or slide backward. It is about whether we will remove from office one of the most negative forces in American politics and replace it with a positive voice for progress.

For reasons that have been debated in countless news reports and editorials, NCAE-PACE [1] chose not to make an endorsement in the Senate race in the May primary. I have no quarrel with your right to make that decision.

But I will admit I was a bit surprised when I heard one of Senator Helms's ads on the radio one morning implying that you were endorsing him.[2] I understand that some of you were surprised too. And the public is confused about where the educators of North Carolina stand in this race.

I do not think that serves this state well. I do not think it is in the best interest of North Carolina to leave the impression that you are supporting a man who has fought for tuition tax credits that would destroy our public school system; who tried to force the federal government to continue allowing tax deductions for segregated schools; who voted against every attempt to form the Department of Education; who, time and time again, when the needs of public education are before the Senate of the United States, has voted no, no, no.

Now, I know you and I have had disagreements and differences. You did not like the salary freeze, and I know that is hurting me today. But I supported the freeze rather than raise taxes on the people of North Carolina when 10 percent of them were out of work in the worst recession we have had in forty years. I believe that was the right decision. And I believe it was the right decision to keep teachers on the payroll rather than dismiss several thousand so we could pay the rest more. I think that decision was humane, and it was correct.

I will be the first one to say that we have not been able to afford to do the things we would have liked to do in education the last three years, but North Carolina has weathered the recession better than most states. North Carolina is leading the recovery. North Carolina has one of the healthiest and fastest-growing economies in the nation. And, thanks to that economic growth, North Carolina can afford to take a giant step forward in education this year.

Eight years ago we began a partnership for North Carolina. We began a process of building up our schools, of treating teachers and school administrators decently and fairly, of giving the taxpayers reason to support their public schools. We have made a beginning. We have come a long way. We have far to go. The time for action has come. This is a year of decision. May God grant us the wisdom and the courage to do what is right.

---

[1] PACE is NCAE's political council. *News and Observer*, January 29, 1984.

[2] In February, "Teachers for Helms" began a $5,000 media attack discrediting the governor's record on education. The group, an organ of the senator's reelection campaign, consisted of only five members—two of them nonteachers. One of its radio advertisements, emphasizing a decline in college board scores among the state's high school students since 1972, the year Hunt was elected lieutenant governor, concluded with a reminder that he had not received NCAE's endorsement. *News and Observer*, February 10, 1984; Snider, *Helms and Hunt*, 119-120.

STATEMENT ON FARM FINANCE AMENDMENT

RALEIGH, APRIL 20, 1984

Today, I am joining with leaders in our farm industry to ask North Carolinians to vote on May 8 for the Farm Finance Amendment to the North Carolina Constitution.[1] This amendment would authorize a new state agency, the North Carolina Agricultural Financing Agency, to sell revenue bonds to finance capital growth in agriculture. It comes at a time when agriculture needs help before a very real recession drives a generation of family farmers off the land.

If the amendment passes, qualifying farmers could receive long-term loans for capital improvements, land, building, machinery, and equipment purchases. Farm cooperatives could use the funds to build agricultural processing facilities. These funds would not be used for operating capital. They are to help North Carolina farmers build, grow, and become more efficient.

With up to $200 million made available to lenders, farmers would be eligible for loans up to $500,000, and farmer-owned cooperatives could borrow up to $2 million.

We know huge federal deficits have a stranglehold on America's future. Those sky-high deficits are swallowing up more and more of our available credit—credit our farmers need if they are to maintain, improve, and modernize their operations.

This amendment, which will finance good farmers and well-managed farm operations, will offer the funds our farmers need to make North Carolina agriculture more productive and efficient. That is good news for all North Carolina families.

I want to emphasize that this is not a bail-out for farmers. It is a wise, prudent investment already being used, in various forms, by twenty-one other states.

The state's financial integrity would never be compromised under this program. Revenue bonds would be sold by the state to investors. That money would be available to lending institutions, such as our banks and savings and loan associations. They would loan the money, under strict guidelines established by the Agricultural Financing Agency, to eligible borrowers. Collateral will secure the loans, and insurance will guarantee repayment.

I want to congratulate Representative Bobby Etheridge for his hard work in guiding this idea—his idea—through the General Assembly. He put together a strong coalition of legislators dedicated to helping our farmers. Edmund Aycock, executive vice-president of the North Carolina Agribusiness Council, has done an outstanding job as chairman of the Committee for Agricultural Finance.[2]

A large number of our farm and commodity organizations have endorsed this amendment. It is supported by farm leaders such as John Sledge, president of the North Carolina Farm Bureau Federation; Jim Oliver,[3] master of the State Grange; and Commissioner of Agriculture Jim Graham.

We know that three times a day farmers are the most important people in North Carolina. Together, we hope all North Carolinians will return that support and vote for the Farm Finance Amendment on May 8.

---

[1]The Farm Finance Amendment was approved by 54.5 percent of the voters who turned out for the May 8 primary election. *Raleigh Times*, May 9, 1984.

[2]Bobby R. Etheridge (1941-   ), native of Sampson County; resident of Harnett County; B.S., Campbell College (now University), 1965; attended North Carolina State University; U.S. Army, 1965-1967. Vice-president, sales, Sorensen-Christian Industries; president, WLLN Radio Station; state House member since 1979; Democrat. *North Carolina Manual, 1983*, 340.

M. Edmund Aycock (1913-   ), native of Wayne County; resident of Raleigh; attended University of North Carolina at Chapel Hill, 1929-1930; B.S., North Carolina State College (now University), 1936. Assistant county farm agent for Vance, 1936-1937, and Johnston, 1937-1943, and Lenoir county farm agent, 1943-1946, North Carolina Agricultural Extension Service; farm manager, Z. V. Pate, Inc., 1946-1955; joined Wachovia Bank and Trust Co. in 1955 and retired, in 1978, as vice-president; Wake County commissioner since 1978; executive vice-president of North Carolina Agribusiness Council, Inc., since 1981. M. Edmund Aycock to Jan-Michael Poff, August 28, 1985.

[3]James R. Oliver (1932-   ), native, resident of Robeson County; B.S., North Carolina State College (now University), 1954; U.S. Army, 1954-1956. Farmer; electrical, heating, and air-conditioning contractor; elected state Grange master, 1982. *News and Observer*, February 13, 1983.

PRESENTATION OF ROANOKE
VOYAGES COMMEMORATIVE PLAQUE

PLYMOUTH, ENGLAND, APRIL 27, 1984

[Introduced by Plymouth's lord mayor, Derek Mitchell, and a trumpet fanfare by the Royal Marines, Governor Hunt unveiled a plaque on the city's waterfront commemorating the 400th anniversary of the Roanoke voyages. The ceremony, televised by satellite, was only one of a number of special English events in which Hunt participated during April 26-28, marking the celebration of Sir Walter Raleigh's efforts to colonize the New World. *News and Observer*, April 23, 28, 1984.]

Lord Mayor, Lady Mayoress, distinguished guests, my fellow North Carolinians—here and watching at home:

We stand here today at the edge of a proud nation, facing a powerful sea. Today, we know the city and the country at our backs, and we know the ocean and the land across it. We know how to make the connections by travel and by technology.

Four hundred years ago, a small band of brave men stood here. They knew that behind them was a city already rich in history and a nation bursting into full flower. And in front of them? They knew something about this ocean—its treachery, its sudden storms and deadly calms. They knew that on the other side was a vast land claimed then by another nation not counted among England's friends. They probably knew there was danger. They probably guessed there was death.

And yet they sailed from here, from Plymouth, 400 years ago today. They sailed west in small wooden ships, with courage in their hearts and the dream of discovery in their minds, on the first try at planting the law and language of England in fertile new soil.

We have come here today from that land across the ocean and from this city of ancient memory to remember them, and to honor the effort they began. In a moment, we will unveil a lasting memorial to those brave men. Let me share with you what it says:

"From Plymouth on 27 April 1584 Walter Ralegh sent Philip Amadas and Arthur Barlowe to North America to explore and prepare for English colonisation. On 13 July they claimed land in the name of Queen Elizabeth. Called Virginia in her honour, this area is now known as North Carolina. In 1585 a colony under Governor Ralph Lane settled there on Roanoke Island, remaining a year. In 1587 a second colony under Governor John White established the 'Cittie of Ralegh' at the same site. This settlement, known as Ralegh's 'lost colony' disappeared between 1587 and 1590.

"This plaque, unveiled by the Governor of North Carolina in the presence of the Lord Mayor of Plymouth on 27 April 1984, commemorates the 400th anniversary of Sir Walter Raleigh's colonies."

Today, we celebrate the beginning. In July, come with us—all of you—to Roanoke Island, North Carolina, where those brave men walked, and celebrate the blooming of the old world's dream of a new world of freedom and vision. Thank you.

1984 CONFERENCE ON INDUSTRIAL SCIENCE AND TECHNOLOGICAL INNOVATION

Raleigh, May 15, 1984

I want to commend the National Science Foundation for the vision and imagination of the Industrial Science and Technological Innovation Program. I am proud that North Carolina universities and businesses are involved, and that North Carolina State University has taken the lead in putting together an outstanding and extremely important conference.

The theme of this conference, "Converting United States Scientific Leadership into Technological Leadership," expresses a concern we all share in a nation powered by change and strengthened by knowledge. The United States leads the world in Nobel prizes and in other measures of fundamental scientific advance. But in converting basic scientific knowledge—knowledge originating in the United States—into innovative products and services, we are being overtaken by nations such as Japan and West Germany.

This conversion of basic knowledge into innovative products and services, the process of technological innovation, consists of two interrelated parts: technical innovation and organizational innovation. Understanding both the technical and organizational aspects of innovation is essential because of the critical, interrelated national objectives we must pursue in the United States. They include creating jobs for our people; increasing our economic productivity; overcoming international trade deficits; and balancing the federal budget.

In North Carolina, and throughout the country, we have an obligation to cause our economy to grow so that we have useful and rewarding jobs. Yet just any kind of growth will not do. It must be innovative, competitive, highly productive growth. Otherwise, we cannot compete effectively in either domestic or international markets. In today's world, this means that economic growth must be based on important advances in science and engineering.

The traditional sources of economic growth are gone; there is no unsettled frontier we can turn to as the basis for growth. We have no new, unexploited sources of oil or minerals in North Carolina or any state. We have no new, hidden, cheap sources of energy we can tap. In short, we must do a better job of using what we have, particularly our people and our natural resources. We will still face the classic dilemma of modernization. When we improve the economic productivity of workers in a textile mill through automation, for example, we reduce the number of jobs in that mill through organizational changes. Simultaneously then, we must cause some other part of our economy to grow in order to absorb workers who lose their textile jobs. It comes down to this: We must make our economy more productive. To do so depends, now and in the future, on the theme of this conference: converting scientific leadership into technological leadership.

Technical and organizational innovation is simple to describe but difficult to achieve. Any businessman who has started a new firm from scratch can tell you that. So can a banker who has helped finance a new firm or helped an existing firm reshape its operations in the face of stiff foreign or domestic competition. Our farmers in North Carolina know that if they do not keep up with technological change, they go out of business. Scientists, engineers, economists, business school faculty, and others in our universities who have been caught up in this process also know how tough the going is. And I am one governor, along with several other governors across the country, who knows how tough it is. We know because state governments have begun to assume a leadership role in deliberately fostering technological innovation.

We believe a partnership of government, industry, and universities is necessary in order to make the process work statewide. State governments are in the best position, in my judgment, to lead the development of this working partnership. Of the 184 research universities of this nation, 119 are public institutions, most of which are supported by state governments. Elementary and secondary educational systems are the responsibility of state and local governments. State and local governments are the prime points of contact with the many aspects of economic activity that entail industry-government cooperation. Moreover, people are essential in technological innovation, and people can more easily relate to state and local governments than to distant federal agencies.

In short, government, academic institutions, and the private sector must work in close harmony to pursue the processes of technological innovation, and this is most effectively done at state and local levels. Federal government can and must help with a supportive policy structure, but the action must take place at state and local levels of our society.

Time does not permit me to elaborate on all that we have done over the last seven and a half years to stimulate the conversion of scientific leadership into technological leadership in North Carolina. Our overriding goal has always been to create more and better jobs for our people, and we have not limited ourselves to the conventional notion of high technology. Instead, we prefer the term "new technology," meaning that we are concerned with technological innovation in new high-tech firms, in our traditional industries, in agriculture and forestry, in infrastructure development, in improving our public and private health services, and in other public and private organizational units—including improvements in our schools and our research and higher education institutions.

Recognizing that public and private research and development expenditures in North Carolina now total more than $600 million per year, we are now placing great emphasis on small business development. We can, and we must, utilize more of the results of this research and development in spin-off economic growth in the state. We have created our Microelectronics Center to lead the way in microelectronics research and to link our research institutions with industry. We have created our Biotechnology Center to do the same with that emerging field on the frontier of science, and plans are being developed to provide much additional support.

Our School of Science and Mathematics is helping set the pace for fundamental improvements in education.

We have established our Technological Development Authority under the New Technology Jobs Act passed by our legislature. This authority is helping local communities establish incubator facilities to hatch new firms and expand existing firms. It also is providing start-up capital to individual firms. And our private sector, I am told, has about completed arrangements for a North Carolina-based venture capital firm.

All fifty states now report activities similar to those taking place in North Carolina. The National Governors' Association Task Force on Technological Innovation, which I chair, recently completed a nationwide survey that makes it clear that states are now assuming leadership roles in fostering technological change. Nevertheless, states must continue to act in partnership with federal agencies, and the task force is now developing recommendations pertaining to federal policy. The recommendations will be presented at a special work session at the summer meeting of the Governors' Association, in July.

First, the task force will press for a much stronger federal research and development budget dealing with the *civilian* economy. This will be for research and development to support activities such as those you are concerned with in this conference. We will also insist on a stronger *state* voice—representing universities, private firms, and state and local governments—in setting that federal research and development agenda. Stronger support for state-based, university-industry cooperative research centers is an example of what could flow from this recommendation.

Our second recommendation illustrates why it is important to draw on state experience in setting research and development policy in Washington. Take the Small Business Innovation Research (SBIR) program, for example.[1] This program will put about $500 million of federal research and development money per year into the process of technological innovation. Industrial firms throughout the United States, however, must deal directly with distant federal agencies in determining federal priorities, in submitting proposals, and in working their way through three stages of funding.

In many respects, SBIR is a good program. We pursue it vigorously in North Carolina. I testified in support of federal legislation establishing it, but I do believe that the operation could be more efficient. Small, inexperienced firms have trouble working their way through the federal system. Moving from one stage of financing to another is time consuming. Firms can easily run short of cash while waiting for review and approval of the next stage.

To make the SBIR program effective, I suggest that we consider having *states* qualify for taking the management of proposal review and funding flow processes. States manage many federal programs that require close working relations between the administering agency and constituent clientele. The agricultural research and extension services are good examples of that relationship; so is the Community Development Block Grant program. Our Technological Development Authority, for example, is performing functions almost identical to those of the SBIR program. Several other states have similar agencies. Procedures could be established whereby this authority could act as the agent of federal agencies in requesting proposals from small business firms, in selecting qualified proposals, and in advancing funds and ensuring proper use.

My third NGA Task Force recommendation—and remember, I am only covering three of several—will deal with the steps that must be taken to balance the federal budget. Huge budget deficits weigh heavily upon our entire economy, yet it is through growth in the *civilian* economy that we will eliminate the deficits. The heart of the matter relates to the interplay between federal policies relating to military objectives versus those that affect the civilian economy. There appears to be an implicit assumption in Washington that pursuing military objectives and controlling inflation will automatically create sufficient funds and solve the shortcomings of our civilian economy.

In other policy statements, I have made my position clear regarding our defense posture. There should be no misunderstanding whatever: I support a strong, efficiently organized, highly effective military capability. Yet Frank Long, head of the Program on Science, Technology, and Society at Cornell University, cites a key aspect of the problem: Since 1980, in constant 1984 dollars, our total federal research and development budget increased 17 percent. Of this total, however, the national defense part *increased 65 percent*. But all other budgets—the "civilian economy" part, so to speak—declined by 30 percent. In only one nondefense component, that failure to properly support civilian research and development is undermining the future prosperity of our nation.[2]

The point is this: Important as proper defense is, we cannot allow our defense objectives to dominate our economy. If we are to create useful jobs for all occupational categories, if we are to have a highly competitive economy, if we are to increase our tax base and balance the budget, and if we are to pay for a strong defense rather than to buy it on credit, we must give equal attention to the strategy by which we increase the growth and effectiveness of civilian production. And here, successful state government experiences, such as the North Carolina experience, must be utilized to the fullest extent possible.

It is actually a question of proper perspective. As a nation, we must be concerned first with the fundamental strength and character of our society as a whole. Only when we have a strong, viable civilian economy; only when we have a well-educated, enlightened populace; and only when we have a society committed to those ideals and principles of justice and integrity upon which the advance of civilization depends—only then do we have the technical and economic ability to defend our society, and the will and reason to defend it. This is the orientation of our research and development effort in North Carolina, and it is the orientation pursued by many other states. It is, I believe, the proper orientation—the challenge of this conference—in converting scientific leadership into constructive technological leadership.

---

[1]PL 97-219, "An Act to Amend the Small Business Act to Strengthen the Role of the Small, Innovative Firms in Federally Funded Research and Development, and to

Utilize Federal Research and Development as a Base for Technological Innovation to Meet Agency Needs and to Contribute to the Growth and Strength of the Nation's Economy," was approved July 22, 1982. 96 Stat. 217-221.

[2] Franklin A. Long (1910-   ), native of Great Falls, Montana; resident of Ithaca, New York; B.A., 1931, M.A., 1932, University of Montana; Ph.D., University of California-Berkeley, 1935. Chemistry instructor, University of California-Berkeley, 1935-1936, and University of Chicago, 1936-1937; chemistry professor, 1937-1979, department chairman, 1950-1960, Program on Science, Technology, and Society director, 1969-1973, Peace Studies director, 1976-1979, and professor emeritus of chemistry and of science and society, since 1979, Cornell University; consultant, U.S. Arms Control and Disarmament Agency, 1963-1973, 1977-1979; author. Franklin A. Long to Jan-Michael Poff, November 18, 1985. The information Hunt cited can be found in Franklin A. Long, "Federal R&D Budget: Guns Versus Butter," *Science*, March 16, 1984, 1133.

GOVERNOR'S PRODUCTIVITY CONFERENCE

RALEIGH, MAY 16, 1984

[Hunt emphasized the necessity of improving governmental productivity in remarks to the sixty-one graduates of North Carolina's first Public Manager Program, on June 16, 1984.]

It is a pleasure to be with you today at the 1984 Productivity Conference. You certainly have some exciting speakers, workshops, and exhibits planned for this conference; I was particularly interested to note that Jeremy Main, a member of the board of editors of *Fortune* magazine, will be speaking to you tomorrow. Mr. Main, some of you may recall, wrote a series of articles for *Fortune* in 1981 entitled, "Why Government Works Dumb."[1] With all due respect to Mr. Main and his excellent series, let me assure you—we do *not* work dumb in North Carolina! As a matter of fact, as your conference theme indicates, we are working smarter now than we ever have before.

Improving the efficiency and effectiveness of state government has been one of my top priorities, and I am happy to say that we have a number of success stories—success stories like our Incentive Pay Program, which was started as a pilot program six years ago to give employees a chance to share in the savings generated by their work groups. Since its inception six years ago, the program has grown from 164 employees in two work groups to 2,277 employees in 41 work groups. The program now shows net annual savings of $1.2 million, with approximately $393,000 being shared by workers.

I'm also talking about success stories such as our Employee Suggestion System, which to date has saved the state $1.8 million by putting employees' suggestions to work; our Office Automation Pilot Project, which is helping state offices to be more productive;

our management training program, which includes the Government Executives Institute, the Public Managers Program, and the Supervisory Skills Program.

All of these have helped North Carolina to have a more productive state government. That means a government that is more responsive to the needs of our citizens, and a government that makes more efficient use of our tax dollars. That is something we can all appreciate, only a month past April 15.

But while North Carolina has made progress on the productivity front, the same cannot be said for the country as a whole. We have seen the growth rate of productivity in the United States decline from 3.2 percent from 1947 to 1966, to an all-time low of 0.8 percent from 1973 to 1979. You all may remember the oil crisis that occurred during that time.

But there appears to be some cause for optimism. The rate has shown a slight increase, to 2.1 percent, during the past three years. Nonetheless, countries such as Japan, France, and even Great Britain are ahead of us in productivity. What can be done to solve this problem that so threatens the economy of the United States? Several solutions have been offered, and I am happy to say that, once again, North Carolina is out in front in their implementation.

The first is increased use of machines and computers. We have seen the success of our office automation project. Computers and word processors are now routine parts of offices in the public and private sectors. Our Microelectronics Center and other such organizations in Research Triangle Park are leading the way in the research and development of new information technology.

Harvard economist Dale Jorgenson says that, "What we have to do is develop institutions that bring technology in the United States up to the best levels quickly." [2] In North Carolina we're helping prepare for the future by giving our young people a solid grounding in computer courses. Through our community colleges, our technical institutes, the public schools, and the North Carolina School of Science and Mathematics, we are making sure that the Age of Information is a Golden Age for North Carolina.

Participative management and quality of work life are also cited as a means to improve productivity. We have just begun to explore quality circles and participatory management in state government, but the results are already impressive. Workers say they feel a greater sense of "ownership" and pride in their jobs when they have a say in how their jobs are managed.

Our quality of work life effort, though also new, is bringing equally impressive results. Employees are now offered opportunities to attend state cultural facilities at reduced prices. They also have access to a confidential counseling program that helps them cope with job or family problems.

We already know that our quality of life is high—three of the top five places to live in the country are right here in North Carolina. No wonder so many people like calling North Carolina home!

Our progress in productivity reminds me of the story about a little girl who was trying to get her father's attention, while her father was reading the newspaper. He decided to give her something to do so that he could read his paper in peace and quiet. He took a picture of the world and cut it up into small pieces to make a puzzle. He then gave it to his daughter, assured, he thought, of an hour of quiet.

Five minutes later the little girl was back with the puzzle completed. The man looked up in surprise and asked her how she had put the puzzle together so quickly.

"There was a man on back," she said. "I just put the man together, and the world took care of itself."

We have seen the kind of success a comprehensive productivity program can have in North Carolina. Perhaps if other states were to follow our example, the country would take care of itself. I congratulate you on your efforts to bring productivity improvements to your work. It is essential to our economy that you be successful. I wish you a stimulating, and productive, conference.

---

[1]The *Fortune* series to which Hunt referred actually was entitled "Working Smarter"; the article by Main, "Why Government Works Dumb," appeared in the August 10, 1981, issue, pp. 146-158. The governor was quoted on p. 152.

[2]Dale Weldeau Jorgenson (1933-   ), native of Bozeman, Montana; resident of Cambridge, Massachusetts; A.B., 1957, Ph.D., 1959, Harvard University. Faculty member, University of California-Berkeley, 1959-1969; Harvard University economics professor, since 1969; author. *Who's Who in America, 1982-1983*, I, 1719.

MILITARY APPRECIATION DAY

MAY 22, 1984

[This address was delivered at Pope Air Force Base, Camp Lejeune Marine Base, Cherry Point Marine Corps Air Station, and Seymour Johnson Air Force Base, on May 22. It was also similar to one presented on April 13, 1984, at the North Carolina National Guard Association annual convention.]

I am delighted to be here with you today for Military Appreciation Day in North Carolina.

Just six months ago, I stood on a rainy, muddy field at Camp Lejeune as the president of the United States honored 200 Marines who died in Beirut. The hearts of all North Carolinians went out to those young men's wives and families. We also sympathize with the families of paratroopers from Fort Bragg who fought in Grenada that we saw on television waiting and worrying for news of their loved ones overseas.[1]

Today, pictures such as these have gone from television and the newspapers. They come readily to mind, however, as we celebrate Military Appreciation Day. They remind us that the military life is one of duty and sacrifice. They remind us that many pay the ultimate sacrifice to keep our nation free and a beacon of democratic light in a surrounding darkness of totalitarianism. We in North Carolina thank you for the sacrifices you endure. We are proud that you call North Carolina home.

North Carolina is home to a large military complement. There are more than 102,000 active military personnel, 13,000 national guardsmen, 6,000 reserves, and 660,000 veterans in North Carolina. More than a quarter of all active duty Marines live and train at Camp Lejeune and Cherry Point. The Eighty-second Airborne Division at Fort Bragg is a major part of our country's Rapid Deployment Force. Our forces at Seymour Johnson and Pope Air Force bases play key roles in tactical fighter support and worldwide military airlift capability.

As these military forces based in North Carolina play a key role in national defense, so do they play a key role in the economic well-being of this state. Few North Carolinians realize what a large role that is. U.S. Armed Forces expenditures in North Carolina for fiscal year 1982 were $3.1 billion. That figure includes $2.2 billion in payroll and $903 million in prime contracts for goods and services. I am certain the citizens and the merchants and businesses of this area join me when I say we appreciate this boon to our state's economy. We urge you to keep calling North Carolina home for a long, long time.

I very firmly believe in and support a strong American military to protect our interests in this hemisphere and abroad.

I have a vision of what is needed to maintain and increase our military strength.

I believe we must move quickly to strengthen our conventional military forces and improve their ability to respond when our interests are threatened around the world.

I believe we must modernize our strategic forces to maintain our deterrent against nuclear attack.

I believe we must increase defense spending and take the tough management steps we need to reduce waste, duplication, and cost overruns.

I believe we must strengthen vital relationships with our allies around the world, and I believe we must select tough negotiators, put them across the table from the Soviets, and get serious about finding a way to prevent the horrors of nuclear war.

This is a vision which will keep our nation strong and protect our interests around the world. It also is a vision which will promote peace in the world. Those who have fought in wars know the true purpose of military strength is peace. They know the objective of military strength is life, not death.

Dwight Eisenhower said once that our "true security problem is not merely man against man or nation against nation. It is man against war." Those words are as true today as when President Eisenhower first spoke them. You, the men and women of our armed forces, are the bulwark of our "true security." Yours is a noble calling, and it is appropriate that we set aside a special day to honor it. Thank you.

---

[1]Two hundred twenty-five U.S. Marines, guarding Beirut airport as part of a multinational peacekeeping contingent assigned to the Lebanese capital, were killed in a terrorist bombing attack on October 23, 1983. "Lebanon: High Risk in Staying In—or Getting Out," *U.S. News and World Report*, November 7, 1983.

Twelve hundred Marines and 700 U.S. Army Rangers assisted 300 soldiers from Antigua, Barbados, Dominica, Guadeloupe, Jamaica, Martinique, St. Lucia, and St. Vincent in an invasion of the island of Grenada at dawn on October 25, 1983. U.S. action was taken in response to an October 21 request, from the Organization of Eastern Caribbean States, expressing concern about the unstable political situation on Grenada; the mission was designed to evacuate Americans from the island and to remove the Cuban-Soviet presence there. The attack cost eighteen U.S. dead and eighty-nine wounded; Caspar Weinberger, secretary of defense, announced the cessation of hostilities on November 2. "Why Surprise Move in Grenada—and What Next," *U.S. News and World Report*, November 7, 1983, 31-34; "After U.S. Troops Pull Out of Grenada," *U.S. News and World Report*, November 14, 1983, 22.

STATEMENT ON U.S. SURGEON GENERAL

RALEIGH, MAY 25, 1984

[The economic importance of the tobacco industry in North Carolina provided the topic of a number of addresses the governor delivered during his second term. Among them were remarks welcoming members of the Flue-Cured Tobacco Cooperative Stabilization Corp., May 27, 1983; the kickoff of "Tobacco Day, U.S.A.," November 18, 1983; and the speech reprinted below. For Hunt's extemporaneous comments on this occasion, see *Raleigh Times*, May 25, 1984.]

Since I was first elected governor by the people of this state, my primary goal has been to lay a solid foundation today for continued growth and expanding opportunity in North Carolina tomorrow. That is why I've made educational excellence and economic development my top priorities. But North Carolina's economy also is heavily dependent upon tobacco, and I am determined that people in the rest of the country—particularly Washington, D.C.—understand that.

As governor of this state, I cannot remain silent when North Carolina farmers and workers and North Carolina products come under attack from a high administration official in Washington. Last Sunday, in a speech in Miami, the surgeon general of the United States, C. Everett Koop, said that this country's top health goal should become, and I quote, "a smoke-free society by the year 2000."[1] Dr. Koop has dared to say what the enemies of tobacco believe but have never had the nerve to say publicly: They want to institute a new form of prohibition against smoking.

Tobacco provides 147,000 jobs in North Carolina, nearly 7 percent of our labor force. It provides $1.6 billion in wages for North Carolina workers. The tobacco industry is a 400-year-old tradition in North Carolina. It is outrageous and irresponsible to suggest that the tobacco industry just disappear in the next sixteen years.

Now, I wonder if Dr. Koop, who is well known as a militant antitobacco crusader, has pondered the implications of his remark. It means economic ruin from one end of North Carolina to another, from the burley growers out west to the manufacturing plants in Winston-Salem and the tobacco heartland down east. It means that by the year 2000—just sixteen years from now—more than 40,000 North Carolina tobacco growers will be forced out of business. It means that our state's economy will lose over a billion dollars in cash from tobacco sales. And Dr. Koop's assault on tobacco spells unemployment for the nearly 23,000 cigarette workers in North Carolina, as well as economic hardship for the families they support.

If Dr. Koop gets his way, a long and perhaps permanent depression would settle on North Carolina's rural communities, and a way of life that we cherish will vanish. As governor of the nation's leading tobacco-producing state, I'm not going to stand by and watch as the destruction of tobacco becomes the official policy of the United States government. Dr. Koop's antitobacco zeal has blinded him to the fact that thousands upon thousands of North Carolinians depend on tobacco for their livelihood. In my judgment, Dr. Koop should be removed from his post by the president before he takes his antitobacco crusade any farther. I would hope that North Carolina's elected representatives in Washington will join me in calling for the dismissal of Dr. Koop.

---

[1] Charles Everett Koop (1916-   ), native of Brooklyn, New York; A.B., Dartmouth College, 1937; M.D., Cornell University, 1941. Surgeon-in-chief, Children's Hospital of Philadelphia, since 1948; University of Pennsylvania medical school professor, since 1959; U.S. surgeon general, since 1981. *Who's Who in the East, 1985-1986* (Chicago: Marquis Who's Who, Inc., 1984), 413. Koop also noted in a May 24 television interview that a smoke-free society was possible by the twenty-first century. *Raleigh Times*, May 24, 25, 1984.

The capabilities of one of the Fourth Tactical Fighter Wing's Phantom II F4-E aircraft were described to Governor Hunt during a visit to Seymour Johnson Air Force Base, Goldsboro. The stop was part of his 1984 Military Appreciation Day tour of armed services installations in the state.

Crew members in sixteenth-century dress guide Her Royal Highness the Princess Anne of Great Britain and Governor Hunt around the *Elizabeth II*, a replica of a vessel typical of the Roanoke voyages. The ship's commissioning on July 13, 1984, in Manteo, provided the climax of ceremonies over which the governor and the princess presided marking the official beginning of America's Four Hundredth Anniversary celebration. (Photograph by Joe Ernst, Eastman Kodak Co.)

FLUE-CURED TOBACCO
COOPERATIVE STABILIZATION CORPORATION

RALEIGH, MAY 25, 1984

[Concern over the impact, upon the state's economy, of increasing amounts of foreign flue-cured tobacco entering the country prompted Governor Hunt to seek aid from the Reagan administration in 1981 (see "Testimony at International Trade Commission Hearing on Scrap Tobacco," June 24, 1981, above). A worsening situation forced Hunt to repeat his request for presidential assistance three years later. On April 19, 1984, he asked Reagan to impose restrictions on cheap tobacco imports, noting that quantities of such leaf shipped to the United States rose 250 percent in 1983. That, coupled with the increase in the federal excise tax on cigarettes, resulted in a $25 million loss to North Carolina's farmers, the termination of 1,000 jobs, and threatened the future of the crop's price-support program, Hunt maintained. When the Venezuelan government announced its freeze on domestic tobacco prices the following July, the governor reminded President Reagan that the South American country banned imports of the U.S.-grown commodity and, once more, urged him to invoke the power to curb imports granted under section 22 of the Agriculture Adjustment Act. "News Release from the Governor's Office," April 19, July 27, 1984.

In a related matter, Hunt sent telegrams to major tobacco-purchasing companies, on at least two occasions, requesting that they buy American produce at fair prices. He warned that if the amount of the 1984 harvest destined for Stabilization Corporation warehouses had not diminished from levels reached in previous years, the tobacco quota for 1985 would be reduced and the per-pound assessment paid by farmers would increase. "News Release from the Governor's Office," August 1, October 8, 1984.]

As someone who grew up on a tobacco farm, as a farm state governor whose daughter and son-in-law are down on the farm in Wilson now happy about the rain we got the other day, I want to welcome all of you—our tobacco family—to the "City of Sir Walter Raleigh." This is an important day for tobacco and tobacco people. Decisions made here today could affect the future of the tobacco industry and the people who make their living from tobacco for many years to come.

Everyone here knows that since 1980 tobacco has been hit and hit hard. For flue-cured tobacco, the effective quota is down 30 percent. The support price is down 21 percent. Exports are down 19 percent. Imports are up a whopping 252 percent.

Stabilization stocks are up 48 percent. A few weeks ago I visited a Fuquay-Varina warehouse that was filled to the rafters. We can't export that good tobacco. We can't sell it domestically. It's just sitting there, the interest and storage costs are mounting, and that's the same story everywhere.

And that's not the end of it. I think we're going to have to build a bigger cigarette package to accommodate all the warning labels.

To top everything off, we now have a surgeon general in Washington, Dr. C. Everett Koop, who is calling for a "smoke-free society by the year 2000"—just sixteen years from today. What the enemies of tobacco really want is a new prohibition—this time on tobacco, not alcohol.

Dr. Koop finally said what the opponents of tobacco have felt all along: that they want to see a prohibition on tobacco.

What all this comes down to is that we are going to have to work harder now than ever before. We are going to have to bend our backs and work together because North Carolina and many other states have thousands of families who depend on tobacco for a living.

We have to work twice as hard to tell the tobacco story every day. The final line in that story is that, in North Carolina, the nation's number-one tobacco state, tobacco means jobs. Mr. Surgeon General, I respectfully suggest to you that America needs jobs; America needs tobacco.

We cannot lose hope. We cannot resort to fighting within our tobacco family. We must pull together, and I am very bullish on us leading the way with some changes that will be a real shot in the arm for tobacco.

First, we must bring down the crushing federal budget deficits that threaten to rob our society of its ability to grow. Because sky-high federal deficits are propping up high interest rates, our dollar is up 40 percent against the currency of our trading partners around the world. That means our exports are 40 percent less competitive in world markets. That is a burden we cannot afford to bear, and that is why I support a constitutional amendment to balance the federal budget.

Second, we need new policies that will support our agricultural products in a changing world economy. Today less than 2 percent of U.S. tobacco exports are included in government-sponsored export programs, down from 38 percent in 1970-1974. We must have export credit funds to move tobacco under international economic assistance programs. We must find out why the U.S. secretary of agriculture has not made these funds available for tobacco. We have to aggressively pursue profitable, long-term, bilateral supply agreements with good customers in the world market.

As the world economy changes, we need to change with the times. That's why I have proposed the creation of an Intermediate Term Credit Facility, which would guarantee three- to ten-year loans from commercial banks to overseas customers. This facility would help move agricultural commodities, including tobacco products, in countries unable to afford short-term commercial credit—and that is a lucrative market.

Dramatically increase our exports. Build new world markets.

Adapt to new financial realities around the world. Work harder on improving the quality of tobacco. These are some of the steps we need to take for tobacco in 1984. I am bullish on tobacco's future. I believe that if we work together, if we show some of the toughness, strength, and imagination that built this great industry, we are going to see brighter days for tobacco at home and around the world.

NORTH CAROLINA
SENIOR CITIZENS FEDERATION

Durham, June 8, 1984

I am really so delighted to be here with all of you today. I know this annual meeting is something that you look forward to, and I have been looking forward to it, too. Our older people are very special. You are the ones who fought in our great wars, and who gave so much of your wisdom and energy and love to building this state and this nation. You have contributed so much to our lives, but I am very concerned about what we are contributing to yours.

Right now, there are about 700,000 older people living in North Carolina. Many of them are living on very limited incomes. Poverty is hard enough when you're young and healthy. When you're older, poverty is impossible. Too many of our older people are living in or near poverty, and I'm very concerned about that. You deserve better. You deserve for this time in your life to be good. You deserve it to be a time that is free from worry about where your next meal is coming from, whether you make the next payment for your home, and what you are going to do about your medical bills.

Studies show that older people spend about one fifth of their income on medical care. Now if you're only getting a hundred or two hundred dollars, and you take a fifth of that away, you don't have much left. It is not enough to live decently, and we've got to do something about that.

I have been going around the state talking to people like you to find out just how they feel. One lady I talked with last week was telling me that when she got her last medical bill, it was for $174. And how much of that do you think Medicare paid for? Eight dollars. Just eight dollars. Now if you are living on a small, fixed income, where are you going to get $166? Something has to be done.

Medical costs in this country are rising at two to three times the rate of inflation. That hurts everyone. But our elderly, and especially our poor elderly, face the most serious threat.

We must put the brakes on these rising medical costs, and last week I announced a plan that would do that. My proposal would involve reimbursing hospitals according to a set fee. It would end the blank check approach that we have had that allows hospitals to charge whatever they wanted to. It would put hospitals on a budget. It would place the responsibility for sound health care management where it belongs: with the health care industry.

Now this principle has been tried. Several states are already doing it, and it works. The federal government has just begun to try it with Medicare through the Diagnosis Related Grouping plan.[1] If my proposal were put into effect beginning in 1986, it would reduce federal health care spending by over 2 billion dollars in a year.

I believe the choice is clear. Either we put the brakes on health care costs or you will end up paying. You will pay through reduced benefits or increased taxes or some other plan that takes money out of your pocket. I believe you don't have enough as it is. To take any more would be cruel and wrong.

My plan would hold the line on out-of-pocket costs for our elderly. It would reduce upward pressure on premiums and deductibles and copayments. It would eliminate the need for benefit cutbacks. *It would protect you*, and that is what I am concerned about.

I believe that our elderly need help and protection in other areas of their lives, too. We need to reduce crime, especially the kind that singles out the elderly.

We need to put Medicare on a solid footing. They tell us that if something isn't done, Medicare will be bankrupt by 1990. I believe it is vital, once and for all, to get Medicare on a sound and permanent financial basis, and we've got to do the same for Social Security. Both of these programs are vital to the elderly in this country. They have to be protected. Your quality of life must come first.

I am also concerned about long-term care. The day may come when some of you will need the type of care that you can get only in a nursing home or some other facility, but until that day comes, I want to make sure that you have all the help you need to stay in your own home. I think a lot of times where you are determines how you feel. If you are able to sleep in your own bed at night, and be around your own family and loved ones during the day, you will probably be in better health for a longer time. That's why I believe it is so important to make sure you have enough home care services and enough income to live at home.

Right now there is no national strategy for long-term care. That is a serious gap in our health care system. We need to do something about that. We need a program that will take into account *your* needs and *your* desires. We need a long-term care program designed with your best interests in mind.

I believe that each generation of Americans makes a contract with the next: to keep a system going that will provide every older person with a life of security and dignity. I believe that is a sacred trust and one that must be honored. You have given so much. You have fought for this state and this country to give us all a better life. Now it's our turn to fight for you.

---

[1] "An Act to Assure the Solvency of the Social Security Trust Funds, to Reform the Medicare Reimbursement of Hospitals, to Extend the Federal Supplemental Income Compensation Program, and for Other Purposes," 97 Stat. 65-172, was approved by President Reagan on April 20, 1983. See Title IV, "Prospective Payments for Medicare In-Patient Hospital Services," 97 Stat. 149-172.

STATEMENT ON UNITARY TAX

RALEIGH, JUNE 13, 1984

It is my pleasure today to welcome officials with some of Japan's largest corporations. They are members of the *Keidanren*, the most influential business organization in Japan. Members of that organization include the chairmen, presidents, and senior advisers of companies like Nissan, Hitachi, Nippon Steel, Komatsu, Sony, Bank of Tokyo, Toyota, Mitsubishi Electric, and Ajinomoto. Earlier today we discussed many issues of common interest. I reviewed for them our deep and sincere interest in continuing to attract Japanese business to North Carolina.

We now have thirty-five Japanese companies in North Carolina, from Asheville to Wilmington, including seventeen manufacturing operations. That compares with five Japanese-owned manufacturing companies in 1977. Total investment in North Carolina by Japanese companies has reached $300 million. Total employment by those companies in North Carolina is nearly 2,000 people. That will increase significantly when the Mitsubishi Electric and Sumitomo plants are in operation.

I've also reviewed for them our state's continuing commitment to the Japan Center.

One item of particular interest to the Japanese is the unitary tax. That tax has been established in one form or another by twelve states. It allows states to tax foreign or United States companies on their entire corporate profits worldwide, not just the share of their operation in the state.

I feel that is wrong. It is one of the most unrealistic and unfair forms of taxation by states. We have been able to make great progress in North Carolina without increasing corporate income taxes. That is a policy we should continue.

I have assured this prestigious delegation that North Carolina will not establish such a tax. They have met with leaders in our General Assembly and received the same commitment. A resolution to that effect has been introduced at my urging, and I am certain it will be overwhelmingly approved.[1]

In summary, I want to thank members of the delegation for visiting our state. We are honored to have you here. I want to assure you our state will continue to have the positive climate toward business that last year made us the most popular state in the nation for location of United States and foreign-owned companies. We look forward to your return.

---

[1]"A Joint Resolution Expressing the General Assembly's Disapproval and Rejection of the Unitary Method of Taxation whereby the Worldwide Earnings of a Multinational Business Enterprise are Subject to State Income Tax" was ratified June 22, 1984. *N.C. Session Laws, 1983, Extra and Regular Sessions, 1984*, Resolution 67.

NORTH CAROLINA CREDIT UNION LEAGUE

PINEHURST, JUNE 22, 1984

[Much of this material had been included in the governor's May 9, 1984, remarks to the North Carolina Federation of Chapters of the National Association of Retired Federal Employees.]

I want to thank Roger Honeycutt, of the State Employees Credit Union; your board chairman, Larry Wilson; and your president, Larry Johnson, for their kind invitation to speak at this fiftieth anniversary of the North Carolina Credit Union League.[1]

I am proud to be a member of your largest institution, the largest state-chartered credit union in the world: the State Employees Credit Union. But I know that 75 percent of North Carolina's credit unions have assets of less than $1 million; membership runs from 150,000 State Employee Credit Union members to some credit unions with less than 100 members and assets of less than $200,000. Yet no matter how large or small they may be, each credit union has the same philosophy, the same structure, the same purpose. And that, I believe, is your great strength.

Your guiding principle is not profit, but service. You serve members, not customers. Member participation, the ultimate in representative democracy, is your hallmark. Over 5,000 North Carolinians serve as volunteers on credit union boards. They set policy, they guide the affairs of the credit union, and they are accountable to their fellow members.

I was very proud to hear that a recent survey by your national association rated the North Carolina Credit Union Act as number two in the nation. I hope that rating holds as we move into a financial marketplace where some of the old lines will become blurred.

No matter how much financial deregulation we see in the years ahead, and no matter how many new competitors we see enter the financial marketplace, I don't expect the philosophy and structure of credit unions to change very much. I believe the expectations of your members, in terms of services, will certainly change—and I know you will meet those new expectations just as you have done over the past few years. But there are other factors in today's financial marketplace that will dramatically affect you and your members.

Credit unions were born in hard times. Many people couldn't save money. Reasonable credit was hard to find. The country faced an uncertain financial future. In other words, not much has changed because that's exactly the uncertain world we live in today.

Today you've got to deal with about a third of your funds as "rate-sensitive" money. In this hot financial shopping center, people will move their money overnight for as little as an eighth of a point. That kind of uncertainty erodes the possibility of secure, stable, long-term economic growth. It literally undercuts our nation's [ability] to grow.

I understand, for example, that when interest rates were high in 1980, lending by North Carolina credit unions went up only 3 percent. Last year when rates stabilized a bit, lending went up a whopping 22 percent.

That trend reflects a genuine financial fact of life: Our economy is sustained and made stronger by people and businesses borrowing money to grow. Unless we stabilize interest rates, our economy cannot grow strong; it can only grow stagnant. That's why I believe the most important task facing this nation in 1984 is to reach a broad, bipartisan agreement on how we can reduce the massive and growing federal deficits that have a stranglehold on our economy.

Last month, a Wall Street analyst described our situation as plain as day. He said: "The credit crunch is here." He was right on the money.

The federal government has traditionally absorbed about one quarter of all net new savings in our economy. But, during 1983, the situation was reversed, and the federal government took 75 percent of the total, leaving only 25 percent for private investment. This means the federal government is gobbling up money that is desperately needed for private investment in housing, plants and equipment, business expansion, and dozens of other areas.

America is now on an economic collision course. Private credit demands are thundering down the track toward the federal government's deficit funding requirements, a black hole that is swallowing up larger and larger chunks of this nation's available credit. Unless we put the brakes on this train, we are going to have a smashup.

And after the dust clears, we will be faced with higher interest rates, sluggish levels of investment, growing inflation, and the undermining of America's ability to compete in the world market.

We have got to get serious about reducing the bloated deficits that are propping up high interest rates, and that means Congress has to bite the balanced budget bullet the way we have here in North Carolina. That's why I support a constitutional amendment to balance the federal budget, and that is why our legislature made North Carolina one of the thirty-two states that have formally called for the amendment.

We don't need blind optimism. We don't need people determined to defend unrealistic, far-out positions. We need a reasonable partnership dedicated to genuine fiscal responsibility, and we need action now.

I have proposed a plan to cut the federal deficit by $80 to $100 billion in one year, fiscal year 1986. We can start by closing down unproductive tax shelters and loopholes. The Internal Revenue Service has one-quarter million cases under review now on questionable tax shelters; limitations should be placed on sale-leaseback transactions involving tax-exempt properties.

We need to go after tax cheaters. The Internal Revenue Service estimates that tax cheating reduces federal income tax revenues by 25 percent every year.

We need to restore fairness to our tax system. That means putting a cap on the third year of the [Reagan] administration's tax cut for those who make over $50,000 a year, limiting their tax cut to $700. Working people, people who make under $50,000 a year, have not received a fair shake on taxes, and they deserve their full tax cut.

The 1981 rollback in windfall profits taxes for oil companies must be repealed.[2] And while I support steady, sustainable military growth, we must attack wasteful military spending. When defense contractors charge the taxpayer $1,100 for a 25-cent plastic cap, something is very wrong.

I believe the impact of health care costs on the deficit can be reduced if the federal government and the states will develop new health care incentives that reward sound management. We need to eliminate the blank check system of paying hospitals and put them on a budget that ensures both excellent and economical health care.

That's the kind of progress we need this year, but there's more we need to do. I believe the strength of our future economy can be found in the revitalization of our schools. That's what we have been about here in North Carolina over the past years, but the challenges of a growing economy and a changing world demand that we make a dramatic improvement in our schools.

My education package is now before the General Assembly. I am proposing that we reward excellent teachers, make our school curriculum more rigorous, upgrade math and science teaching, and create business/education partnerships in every North Carolina community. I hope you will take the time to make your voice heard on this important legislation for our schools, our children, and our future.

I am proud of what we have built here in North Carolina. We are a state where tradition and technology prosper together. This is the best place in America to live, work, and raise a family. In fact, your slogan says it all:"Proud of our Past . . . Prepared for the Future." If we have the political will and national wisdom to bring this nation's finances into line and invest in education, then we will be on our way to a new future. Because I believe our faith is strong, because I believe in God's wisdom, I believe our best days are yet to come, and the great promise of America is still before us.

---

[1]Roger Bradley Honeycutt (1935-   ), native of Fuquay-Varina; resident of Raleigh; A.B., University of North Carolina, 1958; U.S. Army, 1959-1960. Professional baseball player, Chicago White Sox organization, 1959; employed by First Citizens Bank, 1960-1961; joined staff of State Employees' Credit Union, 1961, and became personnel vice-president, 1975. Roger Bradley Honeycutt to Jan-Michael Poff, February 21, 1986.

Larry T. Wilson (1947-   ), native of Rockingham County; resident of Raleigh; B.S., North Carolina State University, 1970. National director, Credit Union National Association; president, Atlantic States Financial, Inc.; chairman, North Carolina Credit Union League, 1980-1984; president, IBM Coastal Employees Federal Credit Union. Larry T. Wilson to Jan-Michael Poff, March 7, 1986.

Larry Gene Johnson (1940-   ), native of Rockingham County; resident of Greensboro; U.S. Air Force, 1959-1967. Manager, First Carolina Corporate Credit Union, 1968-1970; technical assistance director, North Carolina Credit Union League, Inc., 1970-1972; executive vice-president, 1972-1978, and president, since 1978, of the league and its affiliates. Larry Gene Johnson to Jan-Michael Poff, March 11, 1986.

[2]Approved by President Carter in April, 1980, the windfall profits tax on oil (PL 96-223) was expected to generate $227.3 billion in revenues for the federal government. The measure was relaxed under the Economic Recovery Tax Act of 1981 (PL 97-34). *Congressional Quarterly Almanac, 1980,* 473; *1981,* 94.

NORTH CAROLINA ASSEMBLY ON WOMEN AND THE ECONOMY

RALEIGH, JUNE 25, 1984

[The governor focused on many of the points, made below, in speeches presented to the Conference on the Changing Roles of Women in North Carolina, May 10, 1983; the Governor's Conference on Women and the Economy, October 31, 1983; and the North Carolina Federation of Business and Professional Women's Clubs, June 15, 1984.]

Last month the North Carolina Assembly on Women and the Economy presented to me its final recommendations on how to improve the economic status of women in North Carolina.[1] Many of you in this room, through the generous contributions of your businesses and organizations, helped to support the work of the assembly. At the October conference, over 1,000 people came to Raleigh to help share the more than 100 recommendations before you today. I want to thank you for your participation and for caring about the economic health of women in North Carolina. You have again demonstrated the business/government partnership that gives our North Carolina economy its competitive edge.

I want to suggest to you today that the issues before us now are not solely women's issues: equal employment opportunities; business development; financial security. We are not determined to make progress on these issues because they are solely women's issues. These are the economic issues of the 1980s. They are the issues and challenges that will shape this nation's future. That's why we are here today—to talk about the future well-being and vitality of an economy and society that needs the strength of all its people.

When this assembly met last October, I said that the bottom line in this state and nation is that we will never achieve our full economic potential until women are full economic partners. I believe that truth to be even more appropriate today. I am proud that North Carolina's economy has made tremendous progress over the past years. We have adapted to the rollercoaster ride of an American economy in transition, and we have prospered. Last year we were number one in the nation in new plant announcements by American businesses. We were number one in the nation in capital investment made in our state by overseas businesses. Since 1977 North Carolina has attracted $13.7 billion in new and expanding industries, creating almost 224,000 new jobs.

Because we have looked to the future and welcomed change, we have made progress. But I believe the tremendous changes we have endured will be nothing compared to what is now ahead of us. We are all witnesses to the beginning of a new American economy. It will be an economy based on technology, improved productivity, imaginative management, and the ability to adapt to a world where change is our constant companion. To cope with the dramatic change that will usher in this new American and world economy, we need every tool and resource available to us. And that means we need to bring the strength and talents of women into our economy.

Through its recommendations in four categories—employment, business development, financial security, and education—this assembly has given us a strong beginning.

In employment, we discovered this nation will see a new wave of women entering the work force. We found that in North Carolina, which has the nation's third-highest percentage of women in the work force, women accounted for 57 out of every 100 new workers during the last decade. In 1984 we estimate that two out of every three new workers in our nation will be women. But, on average, these women earn about 60 percent of the amount earned by men.

To narrow that wage gap, this assembly recommended that North Carolina employers and labor organizations review their pay schedules, personnel policies, and job classifications. The reasoning is straightforward: Uniform, fair pay makes for more productive workers. It's fair and it makes good business sense.

The budget just approved by the General Assembly last Friday contains a proposal to fund a $650,000 study on comparable worth in state government.[2] We need to make sure that all our employees are classified properly and that they are receiving pay that is comparable to other employees performing duties that require equal effort, skills, and responsibilities. I feel very strongly about this, and I believe state government should set the example.

I also feel strongly about matching the demands of the workplace and the home. As the chief executive officer of this state, I am proud to say that we have flexible work scheduling and leave time, that we offer permanent part-time work options, and we allow our employees to take unused sick leave to care for a sick relative. We have put these programs in place because our employees need them, and they are working.

We know family life is changing. To make ends meet, both parents are often working, and they want excellent day care for their children. But that kind of care is expensive. We found that day care expenses can average 10 percent of gross income for a working family. That makes day care the fourth largest family expense after housing, food, and taxes. Are we offering the quality, affordable day care our children deserve?

In business development, we know more and more women are looking to business for a career. We need to make sure they have an equal chance to acquire the skills and opportunities they need to open their own businesses. The assembly recommended that local chambers of commerce initiate training and leadership programs for women in business and women business owners. I saw such a program that was developed by the Asheville Chamber of Commerce.

Again, it makes good business sense. That's just one reason why I established within our state Department of Commerce a new high-level position: assistant secretary for women's economic development. Doris Cromartie is doing an outstanding job in that position.[3]

In the section on financial security the assembly offered several recommendations that address pension, annuities, and insurance plans. Those recommendations are designed to meet the tragic fact that poverty too often wears a woman's face.

In this age of plenty, it is incredible that the chances are one in three that a single-parent family headed by a woman will be in poverty. It is incredible that two out of every three older persons living in poverty are women. The broad implications of those trends, for our economy and for quality of life, are staggering.

Many of you in the private sector have already met the challenge of developing flexible benefits programs. We need to urge all companies to examine their benefits programs to make sure they meet different needs of the people they employ—single, married, parent, nonparent. The results can be worth the effort—improved attendance, better employee morale, and higher productivity. All we have to do is offer employees a choice.

Finally we come to education, the foundation of North Carolina's economic excellence. The General Assembly just passed the most far-reaching education reform package ever enacted in North Carolina. We're going to see a 15 percent salary increase for teachers, principals, superintendents, and other school personnel; reduction of class size in the critical learning grades of four through six; and many other changes in North Carolina's schools.

This assembly has recommended that government and the private sector make more financial assistance available to women for education and training. I hope you will give careful attention to this recommendation. We need to train more women for the jobs and opportunities of the future. We need their skills in business, engineering, government—every door must be opened if we are to restore the American economy to its role as the world's technological and economic leader.

In the years ahead, we cannot wonder what great business was not started, what medical breakthrough was passed by, what economic opportunities were lost in this nation, all because women were not full partners in the American economy. Our responsibility, our contract with our children, is to build for them a better world; to build a growing, prosperous economy; to guard a world that is at peace; to build a nation where everyone can reach their God-given potential.

That is our responsibility. That is the task we ask you to help us with today. You are the opinion makers and decision makers in your communities. You can turn these recommendations into reality. You can put these ideas to work for our economy. Together, we can build a more equal and excellent future for all our children.

---

[1] See: *Final Report of the North Carolina Assembly on Women and the Economy* (Raleigh: Office of Policy and Planning, North Carolina Department of Administration, May, 1984).

[2] The General Assembly approved the pay equity study in *N.C. Session Laws, 1983, Extra and Regular Sessions, 1984*, c. 971, s. 2, ratified June 25, 1984. However, the legislature terminated project funding less than a year later. *News and Observer*, April 26, 30, 1985.

[3] Doris Mingle Cromartie (1922-   ), native of Mifflintown, Pennsylvania; resident of Charlotte; attended Emory University, Queens College, and University of Michigan. North Carolina Democratic Executive Committee vice-chairwoman, 1960-

1963; Equal Opportunity Employment Commission senior compliance officer, 1966-1972; president, Employment Practices Associates, Inc., 1972-1979; State Banking Commission member, 1977-1983; Equal Employment Opportunity Programs director, 1979-1984, and corporate relations director, since 1985, Duke Power Co.; state assistant secretary of commerce for women's economic development, 1984-1985. Doris Mingle Cromartie to Jan-Michael Poff, September 30, 1983, and July 24, 1985; "News Release from the Governor's Office," January 31, 1984.

AMERICA'S FOUR HUNDREDTH ANNIVERSARY CELEBRATION

Manteo, July 13, 1984

[Between 7,000 and 10,000 people gathered on the Manteo waterfront, on July 13, to witness the ceremony marking the four hundredth anniversary of the landing of the first English explorers on Roanoke Island. Her Royal Highness the Princess Anne of Great Britain participated in the day's commemorative festivities and, with Governor Hunt, dedicated and toured the *Elizabeth II*. *News and Observer*, July 14, 1984. Statewide celebration of the quadricentennial of the Roanoke voyages was scheduled to continue through August 18, 1987, Virginia Dare's birthday.]

We have come to this place of history for one purpose: to celebrate what happened here four centuries ago. To our friends in England, that must seem like the day before yesterday, a time when their country already had more than a thousand years of history to remember. To native Americans, that might not seem like a long time, either, back to a time when their culture was already mature. But to many of us, 400 years ago seems a very long time, almost longer than we can imagine.

Why do we bother to extend our imaginations back to what happened then? The story is simple. English explorers sailed here. Colonists followed. The first colonists gave up and went home. The second group vanished. The remnants of their lives here are few and mysterious—outlines of a fort; bits of broken pottery; the story of a fragile infant, Virginia Dare, born in the wilderness. It's a story that could easily have been forgotten as the sand shifted, the waves crashed on the beaches, and the passage of time washed the recollection of this place from memory.

But that hasn't happened, because from the time the first word of the Roanoke voyages came back to England, people understood that what happened here was not an isolated event. It was a turning point in history, in which a growing power reached out for a new destiny. It set in motion exploratory forces which, more than twenty years later, sent settlers to Jamestown; and more than thirty-five years later, urged the Pilgrims on to Plymouth Rock.

Walter Raleigh sent those voyagers on their way. And in his

History of the World, Walter Raleigh captured the reason why we remember what happened a long time ago. He wrote, "History has triumphed over time."[1] I think he meant that events that matter will always have their place in memory. But I think he also meant that the people who record events that make up history and people who remember have a responsibility to pass the memory on.

North Carolinians have accepted that responsibility before today. In 1884 the state held an exposition in Raleigh that one observer said gave a new impulse to the development of the state. That same year the Roanoke Island Historical Association was founded. In the 1930s celebration of the 350th anniversary produced *The Lost Colony*, genesis of a new art form, outdoor symphonic drama.

Now in 1984, we celebrate 400 years with the honor of a royal visit; with the opening of a splendid ship, the *Elizabeth II*; with festivities for the next three years in every county. If a century ago, an exposition could give us a new impulse, think what this gathering of our minds and hearts will mean.

We gather in celebration of the past; we will reap the benefits of our pride and our achievement in our bright future.

---

[1] "[History] hath triumphed over time, which besides it nothing but eternity hath triumphed over," from Sir Walter Raleigh, *History of the World*, [1614], preface, quoted in Bartlett, *Familiar Quotations*, 199.

NAACP DINNER HONORING KELLY M. ALEXANDER, SR.

CHARLOTTE, AUGUST 18, 1984

[The following address is much like one delivered on June 4, 1984, as part of a tribute to Bishop John Hurst Adams of the African Methodist Episcopal church.]

I am proud to join with all of you tonight to honor a man who has dedicated his life to the cause of justice and freedom: Kelly M. Alexander, Sr.[1] We also honor the woman who has worked with him every step of the way: Margaret Alexander.[2]

Kelly Alexander's name is synonymous with the NAACP. He is both the conscience and heart of this organization. For decades, he has been a force in North Carolina life, a force committed to jobs, education, and opportunity for all North Carolinians. And I have been honored to call him my friend. It is, therefore, with great pleasure that I declare this "Kelly M. Alexander, Sr., Day" in North Carolina.

I see many other faces here tonight, the faces of friends who have stood with me over the past years. Since 1977 we have worked together in the legislature, in the Capitol, in the offices of state and local government. In education, health care, and jobs, North Carolina's progress has been our progress. Because of our partnership, the successes of this administration do not belong to me or to any one person. This has been *our* administration.

I know there have been many who have gone before us in this cause. For over fifty years the North Carolina NAACP has been a beacon of hope for those who have felt left out or shut out of this state's progress.

Those were not easy times. I can see the years of struggle on Kelly Alexander's face. His eyes have seen the days when free people could not sit together at a public lunch counter, or attend the same school, or drink from the same water fountain.

But because of people such as Kelly Alexander, Annie Flowers, Charles McLean, Ada Singleton, and Willie Mae Winfield, we have seen progress come to North Carolina.[3] Together, we have thrown open the doors of opportunity to those who were once locked out.

Just after I was elected governor, there were only 200 blacks elected to public office in North Carolina. Today, my best count tells me that there are over 600 black leaders elected to public office in this state—that makes us fifth in the country—and we have a great new leader here in Charlotte, Mayor Harvey Gantt.[4]

Today, twenty blacks sit on the bench as judges in North Carolina, more than most other states in the country. You know their names: state supreme court justice Henry Frye, federal judge Richard Erwin, judges Charles Becton and Clifton Johnson of the state court of appeals, judges Mike Todd and Terry Sherrill, district court judges here in Charlotte.[5]

I am particularly proud that over 500 black North Carolinians, including many of you, help to chart our state's future by serving on North Carolina boards and commissions. From our Advisory Budget Commission to the state Parole Commission, blacks are participating in the management of this state's government.

We have brought more blacks into the operations of state government: Harold Webb, our state personnel director, and Ben Ruffin,[6] my special assistant and right hand. And there are others.

So this is a night of celebration. A celebration of Kelly Alexander and his hard work, a celebration of the talent and resources his commitment—and the commitment of so many others—brought into the lifeblood of North Carolina and this nation. But this must also be a night of remembrance, for there are those who would have us turn back the clock of history on the progress we have made.

There are voices of prejudice and division in the land today. There are voices that would denounce the progress we have made, together, for North Carolina. Those voices ignore the traditions of Terry

Sanford and John Wheeler,[7] Fred Alexander[8] and Richardson
Preyer. They do not understand that North Carolina has become a
pluralistic state where we respect each other for what we are: all
equal, all North Carolinians.

Those voices demean and fear the contributions of the Reverend
Jesse Jackson.[9] Whether or not you agree with everything he says,
Jesse Jackson has brought excitement and enthusiasm to the
Democratic party and to the American political scene. I am proud
to be in a party that is broad and deep in its views, a party that
welcomes the contributions of all Americans, and I deplore the
party that says Jesse Jackson's voter registration effort is a "new
and potentially disastrous force at work."[10] I say voter registration
is democracy at work!

Those voices of division do not understand that a holiday
honoring Dr. Martin Luther King, Jr., would also honor Kelly
Alexander, President John F. Kennedy, and so many others. That's
why I supported the holiday—it honored not just one man, but the
contributions of millions who were committed to equality and
justice. They *all* had a dream!

Those voices of despair and division speak for the cause of the
comfortable and the wealthy. They do not speak for the child who
goes to bed hungry. They do not speak for the unemployed black
teenager or the child who cannot read. They do not speak for our
elderly. They do not speak for us. They do not speak for the people
here who have worked to make room in the American dream for
every American.

My friends, I have come here tonight to bring you a message of
determination and optimism. I bring you a new voice of hope. At
your side, I am *determined* to speak up for equal rights and [the]
civil rights of every North Carolinian and every American. I am
determined to see that this nation elects leaders who will speak for
and champion the cause of equality. I am *determined* to speak for
education, health care, Medicare, Social Security, farmers, and
small business. I am *determined* to speak for those whose voice may
be too weak or too tired from bearing the weight of oppression. I am
determined to carry forward North Carolina's agenda for progress,
and with your help, I am an optimist about our chances to give
North Carolina a new voice and a new direction in 1984.

We must put the brakes on America's eroding commitment to
equal rights and civil rights. We must make every citizen understand that if we divide this land, we conquer nothing, we gain
nothing. We cannot allow the voices of despair to build between us a
wall constructed not of bricks and mortar, but of fear and prejudice.
We cannot, and we must not, allow them to build that terrible wall.

It is with determination and optimism that I ask you to give me
your hand. Together, we will prove to the world what North
Carolina stands for. We stand for equal rights, civil rights, educa-

tion, jobs, health care, and opportunities for all our citizens; and we understand that unless you stand for something, you stand for nothing at all.

From a Birmingham jail cell in 1963, Dr. Martin Luther King wrote: "Injustice anywhere is a threat to justice everywhere." Together, we will put an end to injustice. My friends, for our children and grandchildren, for Martin Luther King, for Kelly Alexander and everyone who has a dream, for everything we cherish—let us join hands and march side by side until victory is won and North Carolina is lifted up as a home to justice and dignity that shines throughout this great land!

---

[1] Kelly Miller Alexander, Sr. (1915-1985), elected NAACP national board chairman, 1984. Previously identified in Mitchell, *Addresses of Hunt*, I, 701n; see also *Charlotte Observer*, April 4, 1985.

[2] Alexander married Margaret Gilreece in 1945. *News and Observer*, July 15, 1984.

[3] Charles A. McLean, a resident of Forsyth County, is state NAACP field director, emeritus. Mrs. Ada F. Singleton is president, Anson County Branch, NAACP. Carolyn Q. Coleman, North Carolina state field director, NAACP, to Jan-Michael Poff, March 12, 1986.

Willie Mae Winfield (1917-   ), resident of Roper; teacher. Previously identified in Mitchell, *Addresses of Hunt*, I, 163n.

[4] Harvey B. Gantt (1943-   ), native of Charleston, South Carolina; resident of Charlotte; attended Iowa State University, 1960-1962; Bachelor of Architecture, Clemson University, 1965; Master of City Planning, Massachusetts Institute of Technology, 1970. Architect; visiting lecturer, University of North Carolina at Chapel Hill, 1970-1972; visiting critic, Clemson University, 1972-1973; Charlotte city councilman, 1975-1979, mayor pro tem, 1981-1983, and mayor, since 1983. Harvey B. Gantt to Jan-Michael Poff, December 11, 1985.

[5] Henry E. Frye (1932-   ), native of Ellerbe; B.S., North Carolina A&T State University, 1953; J.D., University of North Carolina at Chapel Hill, 1959; U.S. Air Force, 1953-1955. Attorney; assistant U.S. attorney, Middle District of North Carolina, 1963-1965; North Carolina Central University law professor, 1965-1967; state House member, 1969-1980; state senator, 1981-1982; North Carolina Supreme Court associate justice, since 1983. *North Carolina Manual, 1983*, 777.

Richard C. Erwin (1923-   ), confirmed by U.S. Senate as U.S. District Court judge in 1980. Previously identified in Mitchell, *Addresses of Hunt*, I, 241n.

Charles L. Becton (1944-   ), native of Morehead City; B.A., Howard University, 1966; J.D., Duke University, 1969. Attorney; NAACP Legal Defense and Education Fund, Inc., lawyer, 1969-1970; visiting lecturer, since 1976, University of North Carolina law school; lecturer, Duke University law school, since 1980; appointed to North Carolina Court of Appeals in 1981. *North Carolina Manual, 1983*, 789.

Clifton E. Johnson (1941-   ), judge, North Carolina Court of Appeals, since 1982. *North Carolina Manual, 1983*, 789; also previously identified in Mitchell, *Addresses of Hunt*, I, 242n.

T. Michael Todd (1951-   ), native, resident of Charlotte; B.A., Duke University, 1973; J.D., Vanderbilt University, 1976. Assistant state attorney general, Special Prosecutions Division, 1977-1979; district court judge, 1979-1984, Twenty-sixth Judicial District; attorney in private practice since 1985. T. Michael Todd to Jan-Michael Poff, December 21, 1985.

Wilbert Terry Sherrill (1955-   ), native, resident of Charlotte; A.B., 1977, J.D., 1980, University of North Carolina at Chapel Hill. Assistant public defender, 1980-1983, and district court judge, since 1983, Twenty-sixth Judicial District. Wilbert Terry Sherrill to Jan-Michael Poff, December 4, 1985.

⁶Benjamin Sylvester Ruffin (1941-   ), named special assistant to Governor Hunt in 1978. Previously identified in Mitchell, *Addresses of Hunt*, I, 162n-163n.

⁷John Hervey Wheeler (1908-1978), director and secretary, Investments Committee, North Carolina Mutual Life Insurance Company. Previously identified in Mitchell, *Addresses of Hunt*, I, 177n.

⁸Frederick Douglas Alexander (1910-1980), native of Charlotte; A.B., Lincoln University, 1931. Housing management; Charlotte city councilman, 1965-1974, and mayor pro-tem, 1971-1973; state senator, 1975-1980. *North Carolina Manual, 1979*, 291; Mitchell, *Addresses of Hunt*, I, 708, 829.

⁹Jesse Louis Jackson (1941-   ), native of Greenville, South Carolina; resident of Chicago; attended University of Illinois, 1959-1960; B.A., North Carolina A&T State College (now University), 1964; ordained Baptist minister, 1968. A founder, 1966, national director, 1966-1971, of Operation Breadbasket; founder and director, since 1971, of Operation PUSH [People United to Save Humanity]; unsuccessful candidate for Democratic presidential nomination, 1984. *Who's Who in America, 1982-1983*, I, 1647.

¹⁰Alarmed at the number of black voters newly registered in North Carolina in 1984, state GOP chairman David T. Flaherty mailed a fund-raising letter to 45,000 recipients in hopes of winning financial backing for a counterregistration drive aimed at political conservatives. His message of early August characterized the voting of an estimated 77,020 minority, first-time registrants, many of whom were inspired by Jesse Jackson, as "frightening" and "potentially disastrous" to Republican candidates. Flaherty called the letter a "straightforward warning," but some of its readers took a dim view of its contents. W. Eugene Johnston, the state's Reagan-Bush reelection campaign chairman, criticized it as "more inflammatory than it needed to be" and said his organization's registration policy was color-blind. Irving L. Joyner, president of the North Carolina Association of Black Lawyers, denounced the appeal as "race-baiting as a tactic to win votes" and "an exercise in hate-mongering that is really offensive to black people." *News and Observer*, August 15, 1984.

STATEMENT ON POLITICAL TRAVEL

RALEIGH, SEPTEMBER 6, 1984

[State Republican party chairman David T. Flaherty filed a complaint with the Federal Election Commission (FEC) on April 20, 1984, claiming that the Governor's Office was contravening federal statutes by undercharging the Jim Hunt Committee—the governor's U.S. Senate campaign organization—for its use of state-owned aircraft. The same day, the Hunt administration halted billing to review the disputed policy. Jack L. Cozort, the governor's legal counsel, met with FEC attorneys and, on June 21, announced revised reimbursement guidelines. Implementation of the new procedures was not without error, however, as an investigation by the *News and Observer* revealed on September 5; at that time, the Governor's Office admitted it had found the revisions confusing and that mistakes had been made. The next day, Hunt issued the statement reprinted below. Tabulations by an independent accounting firm indicated that the Jim Hunt Committee still owed the state $185,939 for the governor's campaign trips, which it paid on September 21. In early October the FEC approved much of the repayment formula enacted the preceding June. Later, it fined Hunt $750 for violating a standard reimbursement plan for aircraft usage but also concluded that the state had been recompensed sufficiently. *News and Observer*, September 7, 22, October 3, 4, 1984, March 1, 1985.

The dispute over the use of state aircraft by public officials for private purposes had not been resolved by the time Hunt relinquished his duties as chief executive. Flaherty sued the governor on September 17, 1984, alleging that Hunt and his campaign aides shortchanged North Carolina taxpayers by failing to reimburse adequately the Department of Commerce for political travel in three of its helicopters and an airplane. The suit demanded that the committee pay "in excess of $100,000" in transportation costs and sought an injunction blocking the governor from making future unofficial trips in state aircraft. Citing Hunt's statement of September 6, a Democratic spokesman called the state GOP chairman's suit "a cheap political stunt"; the governor brought a countersuit charging that Flaherty, while serving as human resources secretary during the Holshouser administration, flew in state airplanes while on personal business. Ironically, legal procedure requires that if a state officeholder, in his official capacity, is named as a litigant, his successor must be, also. Republican governor James G. Martin consequently found himself on sides opposite Flaherty—whom he appointed as Employment Security Commission chairman in 1985—in two disputes, suing him in one instance and acting as defendant in another. *News and Observer*, September 18, October 4, 1984, March 1, 1985.]

Throughout my term as governor of North Carolina, I have been determined that not one cent of taxpayer money be used to pay for any of my travels that are political in nature. I have repeatedly instructed both the Governor's Office and my campaign to make certain that we completely complied with the laws regulating political travel. Should any questions arise, I have always instructed my staff to err on the side of paying too much.

Now that this campaign has entered its last two months, I have directed my office and my campaign to take the following steps to ensure full compliance with the law and to give the people of North Carolina confidence in my actions:

1. I will no longer use the state airplane or the state helicopter for any political travel. My campaign committee will charter private aircraft for those trips.

2. I have directed my staff to request a formal advisory opinion from the Federal Election Commission on whether the travel reimbursement guidelines that we have been using meet the full requirements of federal campaign laws. Such a request makes it mandatory that the FEC issue an opinion within twenty days. I have taken this action so that this matter will be resolved before election day.

3. I have directed my staff to retain an independent certified public accountant to make an accurate and objective determination of how much my campaign should reimburse the state for past political travels, if the FEC rules that a different method of reimbursement is required.

I believe that the actions I am taking will give the people of North Carolina confidence in the integrity of the process we have used to guarantee that all of my political travels be paid by campaign funds.

COMMUNITIES OF EXCELLENCE
AWARDS BANQUET

RALEIGH, SEPTEMBER 19, 1984

How many of you can remember what your community was like in 1977? I ask that question because I want to make a point tonight about how far our state has come in the last seven and a half years, and where it's going.

Since 1977, new and expanding industries have invested more than $14.5 billion in our state, creating about 238,000 new manufacturing jobs. Employment in new technology industries has reached more than 262,000. North Carolina exports have more than doubled. Per capita income has climbed from $4,900 to nearly $10,000 a year. Manufacturing wages have increased faster than the national average. Travel and tourism income has climbed from $1.7 billion to more than $4 billion a year. The American entertainment industry is now producing more than $35 million worth of major motion pictures in North Carolina each year, and one internationally recognized producer has set up permanent production facilities here.[1]

These are just a few examples of the tremendous economic growth we've seen in North Carolina in the last seven years. But what has that growth meant to individual communities? What has it meant to the towns and cities represented here tonight?

Just last week, it meant the announcement of 300 jobs and a new manufacturing operation for Union Corporation in Bryson City.

For Burnsville and Spruce Pine and Andrews, economic growth has meant more than $55 million worth of investment by Outboard Marine Corporation—three plants that will ultimately employ more than 500 people.

For Clinton, economic development has meant Fuji Cone—a $5 million investment and 80 jobs.

For Mooresville, it has meant Armitage Shanks and its $20 million ceramic fixtures plant—a plant that will eventually employ more than 135 North Carolinians.

For Warrenton, economic development has meant Owens-Illinois and a $20 million corrugated paper plant that is among the most modern in the world.

For Washington and Elizabeth City it has meant Donnelly Marketing Corporation and Hockmeyer Equipment Company.

For Zebulon, it has meant Glaxo.

Altogether, new and expanding industries in North Carolina's Communities of Excellence have announced more than $3.8 billion worth of industrial investments since 1977—investments that will create nearly 28,000 new jobs. But new jobs and investments aren't the only products of North Carolina's Community of Excellence program. In many communities, the program has fostered unity and spirit that didn't exist before; it has opened new pathways for communication and built partnerships capable of tackling other challenges. In Robbinsville, for example, Community of Excellence leaders were responsible for a downtown revitalization program. In Fuquay-Varina they played a major role in saving a community hospital. In Red Springs and Mount Olive, they helped rally efforts to rebuild their towns after a tornado.

Together with economic development efforts in larger cities and towns, the Communities of Excellence program has bettered the lives of thousands of families around our state. For some of these families economic development has meant a college education for their children; for others, a new home. And for those left unemployed by the ravages of recession, North Carolina's economic development programs have meant a chance to pick up the pieces, to learn new skills, and begin a new and more promising career.

Those are the end results, the down-to-earth benefits of the economic development effort you and I have led. But if we are to continue to bring new growth and development to North Carolina, I think we must understand the reasons behind our successes. I believe one of the most important factors has been our commitment to solid public education.

We have worked hard to improve the quality of our public schools. We have reduced class sizes in grades one through six and put teachers' aides in our primary grades. We have implemented a competency testing program for our high school graduates and a system of annual testing to help make sure students don't get behind in their earlier years. We've raised teachers' pay and provided new opportunities for practicing educators to sharpen their teaching skills. We've strengthened math and science education and committed ourselves to establishing computer laboratories in every school. We've established a statewide high school for students gifted in math and science, and we've continued strong support for arts in education. These commitments and others have brought North Carolina international recognition as a leader in the field of public education in the United States.

But we haven't stopped with the public schools. We've also worked to build a solid foundation for technological development in our community colleges and universities. In the present biennium alone, our state legislature has approved, at my urging, more than $160 million in expansion funding for technology-oriented programs.

There are allocations for new engineering and computer science buildings at three of our universities. We've funded new training equipment for our community colleges and increased support for new industry and high technology skills-training programs. We've provided increased funding for our microelectronics and biotechnology centers.

Those investments have paid off. Already the Microelectronics Center of North Carolina [MCNC] has helped attract such industry giants as General Electric, Wang laboratories, E. I. du Pont, and Verbatim. In all, new and expanding electronics companies have invested nearly $1 billion in North Carolina since we announced plans for the Microelectronics Center in 1980. And with this summer's dedication of MCNC's new world-class research and development facilities, I believe we can expect even greater returns on our investment in the years to come.

But those of us here tonight know that these new programs are only part of North Carolina's economic development success story. We also know that North Carolina's industrial recruitment successes are built on teamwork, on the great spirit of cooperation that has brought us here tonight. Working together, the people in this room made North Carolina the most successful state in the nation in 1983 when it comes to attracting new industrial investments. In 1983 more companies, both foreign and domestic, announced plans for new manufacturing facilities in North Carolina than in any other state in the nation.

Tonight, I am proud to announce that *Business Week* magazine will soon release still further evidence of North Carolina's appeal to growing industries. In its quadrennial corporate readership survey, *Business Week* asked executives of manufacturing companies which states they would most likely consider as a new plant site. The number-one answer was North Carolina.[2]

That *Business Week* survey says a lot about what we've accomplished for North Carolina since 1977. As governor, I'm proud to have been a part of that effort and deeply thankful for the opportunities I've had to work with so many of you here tonight. You are the people that have gone that extra mile to build a better future for communities across North Carolina. This is your night. North Carolina salutes you.

---

[1] In November, 1983, motion picture producer Dino De Laurentiis divulged plans to build a cinema studio complex in Wilmington. As envisioned, it would contain a special effects stage, three sound stages, property and wardrobe facilities, and offices. The producer's original intention had been to depart the state once the filming of his motion picture, *Firestarter*, had been concluded. However, De Laurentiis noted that "the assistance we have received from North Carolina's Film Office, and Governor Hunt's personal interest in the film industry, convinced us to set up permanent operations here." Hunt established the North Carolina Film Office during

his first administration. "News Release from the Governor's Office," November 23, 1983.

[2] *Plant Site Selection: A Survey of Management Subscribers in Industry* ([New York: *Business Week*, 1984]), 4, 14.

STATEMENT ON VELMA BARFIELD

RALEIGH, SEPTEMBER 27, 1984

[Governor Hunt denied clemency to two condemned murderers in 1984: James W. Hutchins and Velma M. Barfield. Hutchins, a textile worker who earlier had served a prison term for voluntary manslaughter in New Mexico, was convicted in Marion in 1979 for the shooting deaths of two Rutherford County sheriff's deputies and a state highway patrolman dispatched to Hutchins's home to investigate a domestic dispute. Hunt indicated on March 15 that he would not commute Hutchins's sentence to life imprisonment; Hutchins was executed the next day, the first death-row inmate to die in North Carolina in twenty-three years. *News and Observer*, January 5, 6, March 17, 1984.

Having gained a worldwide reputation as the "Death Row Granny," Velma Barfield was the first female to be executed in the United States since 1962 and the first in North Carolina since 1944. The Robeson County grandmother and Sunday school teacher, previously jailed for forgery, was found guilty in 1978 of having poisoned her fiancé. She also confessed to killing her mother and an elderly man and woman, whom she served as a nurse/companion, in the same manner, and surreptitiously obtained money from three of her eventual victims to support a decade-long addiction to prescription drugs.

Originally scheduled to die the last day of August, 1984, Mrs. Barfield received a stay of execution from the U.S. Supreme Court on July 2. In time, the stay was lifted. When superior court judge Giles R. Clark, a Holshouser appointee but a Democrat, announced he had rescheduled the execution for November 2, four days before the elections, speculation about the timing of the execution abounded. However, the governor's denial of clemency to Mrs. Barfield probably had little impact on the outcome of the 1984 Senate race. According to the results of a Carolina Poll conducted between February 17 and March 1, 1984, two out of three North Carolinians surveyed supported the death penalty. *News and Observer*, March 21, May 22, August 23, September 29, 1984; *Raleigh Times*, June 15, 1984.]

I have completed my review of the Velma Barfield case, and I am prepared to announce my decision.

I have given those who wanted to tell me what is on their minds and in their hearts the opportunity to do so, and what they have had to say has been very helpful to me. I have listened to supporters of Mrs. Barfield's request for executive clemency and have talked at length with her attorneys.[1] Two members of my staff, Jack Cozort[2] and Pam Gaither, recently interviewed Mrs. Barfield. I have also listened to the views of those who oppose clemency, including the district attorney who prosecuted the case,[3] and relatives and friends of Mrs. Barfield's victims. In addition, I have thoroughly reviewed trial transcripts, issues raised on appeal, and the formal request for clemency submitted to me by the defense attorneys.

The governor's powers of executive clemency are broad and extraordinary. No limits are placed upon me with respect to what facts and circumstances I may take into account. I have reviewed every piece of information made available to me. Accordingly, I have considered whether or not she received a fair trial, whether any new evidence has come to light since the trial, the nature of the crimes, and whether any new circumstances exist.

My review of the case raises no question as to her guilt. She received a fair trial, presided over by one of the state's best judges.[4] Her case has been reviewed in eight courts by twenty-one different judges, none of whom found reason to order a new trial or resentencing.

Supporters of Mrs. Barfield's request for clemency have not denied that she committed horrible crimes. Rather, they have focused their arguments upon the contention that she is a changed person who has helped redirect the lives of many of her fellow inmates. They contend society would best be served by her being allowed to continue that work. They also point to her use of prescription drugs at the time she committed these murders.

People on both sides are sincere in their convictions on this case. I am impressed by the depth of their convictions and their desire that the right thing be done.

After carefully studying all issues, I do not believe that the ends of justice or deterrence would be served by my intervention in this case. I cannot in good conscience justify making an exception to the law as enacted by our state legislature or overruling those twelve jurors who, after hearing the evidence, concluded that Mrs. Barfield should pay the maximum penalty for her brutal actions.

Death by arsenic poisoning is slow and agonizing. Victims are literally tortured to death. Mrs. Barfield was convicted of killing one person in this fashion; she admitted to three more, including her mother, and there was evidence of yet a fifth. Everybody associated with this case has undergone his own kind of emotional torture, the kind brought about by grief and despair. It has been a tragedy for an entire community, as well as our state.

It is my sworn duty as governor of this state to uphold the fundamental rule of law. I am satisfied that I have made a decision consistent with that duty.

---

[1] Mrs. Barfield's attorneys were James D. Little, of Raleigh, and Richard H. Burr III, of West Palm Beach, Florida. *News and Observer*, April 3, 1984.

[2]Jack Lowell Cozort (1950-   ), native of Valdese; resident of Raleigh; B.A., North Carolina State University, 1972; J.D., Wake Forest University, 1975. Associate attorney general, state Department of Justice, 1975-1977; legal counsel to Governor Hunt, 1977-1985; associate judge, North Carolina Court of Appeals, since 1985. Jack Lowell Cozort to Jan-Michael Poff, September 4, 1985.

[3]Joe Freeman Britt, district attorney for Robeson and Scotland counties, was the prosecutor in the Barfield case. *News and Observer*, June 14, 1984.

[4]Henry A. McKinnon, Jr. (1922-   ), native of Maxton; resident of Lumberton; A.B., 1943, LL.B., 1947, Duke University; U.S. Army, 1943-1945. Superior court judge, Sixteenth Judicial District, 1958-1980; superior court emergency judge, since 1980. Henry A. McKinnon, Jr., to Jan-Michael Poff, September 9, 1985.

STATEMENT ON INTERSTATE 40

WILMINGTON, OCTOBER 3, 1984

[Hunt repeated same announcement, later that day, at a roadside press conference near Warsaw.]

It is my distinct pleasure to announce today that construction contracts on an additional twelve miles of the Benson-to-Wilmington freeway will be let over the next few months. I am recommending that the state Board of Transportation use federal funds made available by the Highway Improvement Act of 1984 [1] to let contracts on twelve miles of the project in Duplin County at a cost of $16.7 million. This is made possible by a provision in the Highway Improvement Act that permits us to use funds specifically designated for the interstate system on the Benson-to-Wilmington project. We have never had that kind of flexibility before.

The contracts will be let in two stages, with five of the twelve miles going to contract before the end of this year, and the remaining seven miles in March of next year. This will extend the total work on the project all the way from Wilmington to U.S. 117 at Warsaw. With this addition, more than fifty miles of the 91.4-mile project will be under contract or under construction by early next year. That is a remarkable achievement for a highway project of this magnitude. When this administration came into office eight years ago, not even the first mile of right of way had been purchased.

We are able to put this new federal money to immediate use because we have done our homework. All of the right of way from Benson to Wilmington has been acquired, and we are far enough along with the necessary planning work to be able to react quickly to the availability of new funds.

I want to emphasize that this accelerated funding of the Benson-to-Wilmington freeway will not delay work on other interstate projects, nor will it delay other projects important to this area. I am referring to the four-laning of U.S. 74 in Brunswick County to the South Carolina state line. Construction has already begun on U.S. 74, and some right of way has been acquired for U.S. 17.

As everyone here knows, an interstate highway linking the port of Wilmington to the piedmont and west is of vital importance to the economic future of southeastern North Carolina and our entire state. This is a highway that has been talked about for generations. It isn't just talk anymore: We are building that road now, and we are more than halfway home. It is a road that will lead to new industry and good jobs, and I am proud of the contribution this administration has made to making it a reality.

---

[1]PL 98-229, "An Act to Apportion Certain Funds for Construction of the National System of Interstate and Defense Highways for Fiscal Year 1985 and to Increase the Amount Authorized to be Expended for Emergency Relief under Title XXIII, United States Code, and for Other Purposes," was signed March 9, 1984. 98 Stat. 55-57.

STATE GOALS AND POLICY BOARD

RALEIGH, DECEMBER 5, 1984

I want to first of all thank the members of the State Goals and Policy Board for the outstanding service they have given to the state of North Carolina. Governor Martin, this board is a statutory board and serves as the governor's chief citizen advisory board. You will be serving as its chairman.

These people here today have traveled hundreds of miles across this state to attend hearings, to listen to the concerns of our people, and to report back to me on their concerns. They have conducted long hours of research on issues of concern to the state and prepared policies which would benefit the people of this state. They have identified the kind of future the citizens of North Carolina want and have proposed goals to achieve that future. The work they have done in economic development, aging, children's issues, and government management and communication has greatly benefited this state and its people.

They have identified areas of public interest, informed the general public about the state's problems, and involved them in helping to solve those problems. Through regional hearings, task forces, public surveys, conferences, and special projects, such as North Carolina Tomorrow and North Carolina 2000, they have reached out to the people of this state, gotten their opinions on the issues facing this state, and have carried out the projects I assigned to them. In addition, they have monitored the progress of the policies set by this administration.

In our activities, the board has worked with more than 275,000 people and involved them in helping to solve the problems of the state.

Governor Martin, I will be turning this board over to you. You will have seven appointments to make to it in March, which will then make it "your board." The remaining members, whose terms expire in 1986 and 1987, will provide you with continuity as well as good leadership and ideas.

I would like to suggest three ways that this board might be of service to you:

—It can help to frame your policy agenda. The board will address the issues you think are most important and can involve the citizens of the state in the discussion of those issues.

—It can involve the citizens of the state in the policy process of the state of North Carolina by identifying areas of public interest and by proposing possible ways of involving the public.

—The board can help you to meet the governor's North Carolina 2000 statutory responsibilities. North Carolina 2000 was the most extensive public involvement project of the board. I know you are interested in planning, and this project sets the stage by identifying the major concerns of the citizens of this state. We have already begun to plan how to meet the challenges presented by those concerns. The issue papers in this notebook are an outgrowth of this project.

Now, I want Ruth Mary Meyer[1] to talk about the origins of the board and some of the major policy initiatives over the past decade, and then President Friday will tell you about the North Carolina 2000 process.

---

[1] Ruth Mary Meyer (1926-   ), native of Ann Arbor, Michigan; resident of Durham; B.A., Wellesley College, 1948; attended University of Geneva, Switzerland, 1948-1950. Bilingual secretary, General Agreement on Tariffs and Trade, Geneva, 1950-1952; president, Durham League of Women Voters, 1962-1965; registered lobbyist, 1969-1973, and president, 1975-1979, League of Women Voters of North Carolina; member, State Goals and Policy Board, 1977-1985, and of the North Carolina 2000 Commission, 1981-1982; first vice-president, 1982-1984, and president, since 1984, North Carolina Council of Women's Organizations. Ruth Mary Meyer to Jan-Michael Poff, January 31, 1986.

NEWS RELEASE FROM THE GOVERNOR'S OFFICE: HUNT PROPOSES TRANSFER OF DIX PROPERTY TO UNIVERSITY

RALEIGH, DECEMBER 17, 1984

Governor Jim Hunt Monday disclosed plans to transfer approximately 355 acres of the Dorothea Dix property to North Carolina

State University and recommended that the General Assembly transfer an additional 740 acres of the Dix property to the university.

The 355-acre tract, now controlled by the Department of Human Resources, will be transferred on Wednesday, December 19, during a meeting in the governor's Capitol office with university officials. At Hunt's direction, the land will be conveyed to the school by Secretary of Administration Jane Patterson. The other 740 acres is under the control of the North Carolina Farm Commission. That transfer will require the approval of the 1985 General Assembly, which is recommended in Hunt's 1985-1987 budget message to the legislators.

"Expansion of the university's main campus is limited on the east, north, and west by fully developed property," Hunt said. "Therefore, the only possible direction for expansion is to the south. The Dix property is the only property available for future expansion of the campus."

Hunt said the growth of the university is directly related to technological advances in such fields as engineering, agriculture, and computer science. "The university has enabled the entire state to attract high-technology industries. The future of the economy of North Carolina depends on the university's ability to continue to grow." Hunt said the university would use the newly acquired land exclusively for such educational and research purposes that are approved by the North Carolina State University Board of Trustees.

BUDGET BRIEFING

RALEIGH, DECEMBER 17, 1984

I want to commend to your attention today my final budget recommendations as governor of North Carolina.[1] This document contains some intriguing new initiatives, proposals that I believe will get a good reception in the General Assembly. But it is characterized by the same guiding principles as every other budget that I have submitted over the past eight years.

Those principles, simply put, are based upon economic growth, good jobs and better opportunities for our people, and the belief that the public schools are the gateway to economic progress. This budget is a road map to an even stronger North Carolina economy. Accordingly, it is also a road map to excellence in education.

The details of my budget proposals are spelled out in the summary and handouts that you have been given, but I will briefly mention some of the highlights, starting with the education items. These are based upon the recommendations of the Commission on Education for Economic Growth.

—In order to recruit the best minds into the teaching profession, I propose an improved compensation package, including a 5 percent cost-of-living increase for educators, restoration of step increases, funding for implementation of a career growth program, and salary adjustments for noncertified educational personnel.

—Reducing class size in grades seven, eight, and nine to one teacher for every twenty-six students, as we have already done in grades K through six.

—Increased pay for substitute teachers.

—Strengthening the curriculum by continuing to support the state Basic Education Program.

—Increased funds for professional development and funding for the establishment of a Center for the Advancement of Teaching at Western Carolina University. This would be modeled after the National Humanities Center at Research Triangle Park.

—Increased funding for textbooks to $20.00 per student.

—Special attention to risk students. This involves the establishment of a job placement center in every high school and dropout prevention programs in all middle schools.

—I also propose significantly increased funding for equipment needs, including the establishment of microcomputer laboratories in all public schools, and updated vocational, science, and math equipment.

To complement these programs for the public schools, I propose increased funding for the community college system. This would include support for enrollment increase, increased operating revenues, and expanding the Small Business and Cooperative Skills Training programs.

I am proposing major new funding to strengthen the finest state university system in America. This includes money for faculty salaries, equipment needs, and enrollment increases. One of the most significant capital recommendations for the system is a new building to house the School of Textiles at North Carolina State University.

There are several major items in the budget specifically tied to economic development. Among these are funds for development of biotechnology programs, continued support for the Microelectronics Center of North Carolina, and expansion of our Clean Water program.

The efficient operation of state government requires fair treatment of state employees. To that end, I propose a 5 percent salary increase, reinstatement of merit pay increases, and the addition of a tenth step in the salary schedule.

These are just some of the highlights of a two-year, $15 billion investment in human capital. To answer your questions about the details of this document, Betty Owen, my education adviser is here, along with Marvin Dorman [2] from the Budget Office.

I want to emphasize that while this is an ambitious budget, it is by no means extravagant. It is in keeping with my administration's eight-year commitment to balanced budgets and frugal use of the taxpayers' money. What we have tried to accomplish is to put scarce tax dollars into those programs that most directly relate to the economic vitality of our state. Judging by the enormous progress we have made in attracting good-paying jobs, ranging from microelectronics to movies, I think it is safe to say we have been successful in that effort.

We have laid a foundation for economic advancement in the years to come, and our quest for educational excellence is the most important part of that foundation. I respectfully submit the recommended budget for the 1985-1987 biennium to our citizens and to the members of the General Assembly.

---

[1] See State of North Carolina, *Summary of the Recommended Budget, 1985-1987 Biennium* ([Raleigh]: Office of State Budget and Management, December, 1984).

[2] Marvin K. Dorman, Jr. (1940-   ), native of Robeson County; resident of Raleigh; B.S., 1963, Master of Public Administration, 1977, North Carolina State University. Served with State Budget Office as analyst and supervisor; deputy state budget officer since 1977. Marvin K. Dorman, Jr., to Jan-Michael Poff, September 6, 1985.

STATEMENT ON ECONOMIC GROWTH

RALEIGH, JANUARY 3, 1985

I am extremely pleased that, in holding my last press conference as governor, I am able to share some very good news with the people of North Carolina: Our state set economic development records across the board in 1984. Such indicators as industrial development, jobs, travel and tourism, motion picture production, and international business recruitment all reached their highest levels in history.

New and expanding industries announced more than $2.67 billion in capital investment—a 25 percent increase over 1983, and easily surpassing the previous record of $2.2 billion set in 1980. Those investments will result in more than 46,000 new jobs, half of which will be in the advanced technology fields of instrumentation, chemicals, metalworking, [and] electrical and electronics products.

From 1977 through 1984, industrial investment in North Carolina totaled $15.5 billion, creating more than a quarter of a million new jobs.

Manufacturers of electrical and nonelectrical machinery led in new job announcements in 1984, creating more than 14,000 new employment opportunities, a new record for job announcements in those fields.

North Carolina's textile industry continued its tremendous modernization effort in 1984, announcing $537 million worth of capital investments—the largest such financial commitment in its history.

1984 was also a record year for international industrial recruitment in North Carolina. Sixty-three foreign firms announced plans for new or expanded manufacturing facilities in our state. Their combined investments will total nearly $467 million, a 35 percent increase over last year's record-breaking total. New job announcements by foreign firms totaled 5,783 in 1984, also setting a new record.

Finally, three other important indicators of economic growth saw dramatic increases in our state last year:

—Travel and tourism revenues climbed sharply. While final figures are not yet available, the state tourism division estimates visitor spending exceeded $4 billion for the first time ever in 1984, establishing a new record for the eighth consecutive year.

—State ports revenues hit an all-time high of $15.4 million on record-breaking tonnages.

—In motion picture production, our state Film Office estimates the economic impact of movie making rose to $115 million in 1984. And last month's announcement of Magder Studio's new multi-million-dollar production facility in Caswell County practically assures that 1985 will be another record-breaking year.

The numbers show that 1984 was a year of sweeping economic growth for North Carolina. It was also a year of quality in quantity. 1984's corporate newcomers to North Carolina include such internationally recognized companies as RCA in Asheville, BASF Wyandotte and Dynamit Nobel Silicon in the Research Triangle Park, Outboard Marine Corporation in Andrews, Owens-Illinois in Warren County, and many, many more.

These companies and others have come to North Carolina because they see here a burgeoning new center for high-technology development and economic growth for the future. That is a tribute to the people of North Carolina, people who understand the importance of good new jobs and who have supported us every step of the way in our economic development program. Together, we have built a more prosperous North Carolina and left a legacy of hope and opportunity for our children and generations to come.

OMITTED SPEECHES AND STATEMENTS, 1981-1985

[Any chief executive delivers more addresses and releases more statements, in a single term, than can possibly be reproduced in one volume. Therefore, in reviewing items available for potential inclusion in the final installment of the *Addresses of Hunt*, materials were chosen that emphasized the governor's goals and accomplishments, the issues confronting him, and developments in the state, during the period from January, 1981, to January, 1985. Speeches and official papers not reprinted herein are cataloged, by title, below; those either mentioned or excerpted in annotations accompanying Hunt's published remarks are denoted by an asterisk. Speaking engagements, indicated on the governor's weekly agenda but for which no prepared text was provided, have been incorporated into the following list and are marked by a dagger. Existing press copies of Governor Hunt's addresses and other public papers are housed at the Division of Archives and History, Department of Cultural Resources, Raleigh.]

1981

January 6, Adopt-a-School Workshop, Raleigh
January 8, Statement at News Conference, Raleigh†
January 9, Reliance Electric Announcement [Cleveland County], Raleigh
January 16, Greater Charlotte Chamber of Commerce, Charlotte
January 16, North Carolina Soybean Producers Association, Raleigh*
January 16, PRO '81 Conference, Nashville, Tennessee*
January 20, North Carolina Motor Carriers, Raleigh†
January 21, North Carolina Forestry Association, Raleigh†
January 21, Cooperative Council of North Carolina, Raleigh
January 22, Statement on Scrap Tobacco Imports, Raleigh*
January 22, Tenth Annual Gold Key Banquet, Rocky Mount
January 26, Sir Walter Cabinet, Raleigh
January 28, Opening Remarks, North Carolina Conference on Small Business, Raleigh*
January 29, Statement on North Carolina Conference on Delinquency Prevention, Raleigh
January 29, North Carolina Press Association Awards, Chapel Hill†
January 30, Statement on Bid Rigging, Raleigh*

---

*Referred to in headnote
†No press copy

January 30, North Carolina Dairy Products Association, Pinehurst

January 30, Imperial Spinning Mills Dedication, Wallace

February 2, Durham Chamber of Commerce 1981 Legislative Conference, Durham

February 3, Business and Professional Women Legislative Day, Raleigh

February 5, Statement at News Conference, Raleigh†

February 5, North Carolina Conference on Delinquency Prevention, Raleigh*

February 6, State Government Ombudsmen, Raleigh†

February 6, Swearing-in of Walter Johnson as Parole Commission Chairman, Raleigh†

February 7, North Carolina Jaycees Luncheon, Greensboro

February 11, Mitchell County "Dialogue '81," Raleigh

February 11, State Personnel Commission, Raleigh†

February 12, Statement at News Conference, Raleigh†

February 13, Small-Scale Hydropower Conference, Raleigh

February 13, County Agricultural Extension Councils Chairmen, Raleigh

February 16, Young Democrats of North Carolina, Raleigh†

February 16, Lions Club, Raleigh†

February 17, Appalachian State University Student Government Association, Boone†

February17, North Carolina Public Service Award Society Banquet, Raleigh

February 18, Governor's Task Force on Waste Management, Raleigh*

February 21, Conference on Technological Innovation for Economic Prosperity, Washington, D.C.*

February 25, Statement at News Conference, Raleigh†

March 2, Lord Corp. Announcement and Groundbreaking, Cary

March 4, State Personnel Commission, Raleigh†

March 5, Statement at News Conference, Raleigh†

March 5, Second Annual All-Industry North Carolina Insurance Day, Raleigh

March 6, Statement on Owens-Illinois, Inc., Manufacturing Plant, Eden

March 6, Owens-Illinois, Inc., Reception, Eden

March 11, Travel Council of North Carolina, Raleigh*

March 12, Statement on Federal Budget Cuts, Raleigh

---

*Referred to in headnote
†No press copy

March 12, Swearing-in of Colonel John Jenkins as Highway
Patrol Commander, Raleigh
March 13, WNCT Interview, "Carolina Today," Greenville†
March 17, North Carolina Traffic League, Raleigh*
March 17, Durham Jaycee Celebrity Roast Honoring Terry
Sanford, Durham
March 18, Statement on Legislation Providing Equitable
Distribution of Marital Property, Raleigh
March 19, North Carolina Association of Educational Office
Personnel, Raleigh
March 19, League of Municipalities Board of Directors,
Raleigh†
March 20, International Student Day, Raleigh*
March 20, Tobacco Associates, Inc., Raleigh
March 20, Carolina-Virginia Telephone Membership
Association, Inc., Raleigh
March 23, Wanchese Seafood Industrial Park Opening,
Wanchese†
March 23, Pasquotank County Courthouse Dedication,
Elizabeth City†
March 23, Waccacon Canoe Trail Dedication, Murfreesboro†
March 23, Burgwyn-Rogers Bridge Dedication, U.S. 258,
Halifax-Northampton County Line†
March 24, North Carolina Savings and Loan League, Raleigh
March 24, TRW, Inc., Announcement, Sanford
March 25, Statement at News Conference, Raleigh†
March 25, North Carolina Task Force for International Year of
Disabled Persons, Raleigh
March 26, North Carolina Aggregates Association, Pinehurst*
March 26, Kelly-Springfield Tire Co., Fayetteville*
March 27, North Carolina Student Legislature, Raleigh
March 28, Young Democrats State Convention, Raleigh*
March 30, Winston-Salem Chamber of Commerce, Raleigh†
March 31, Armed Forces Communications and Electronics
Association Exhibition, Raleigh
March 31, North Carolina State University Founders Day,
Raleigh
March 31, Cary Elementary School PTA, Cary
April 1, Statement on Transportation Needs, Greensboro*
April 1, Statement on Transportation Needs, Winston-Salem*
April 2, Statement on Transportation Needs, Raleigh*
April 2, North Carolina School Boards Association, Raleigh†
April 2, Western North Carolina Industries, Raleigh†

---

*Referred to in headnote
†No press copy

April 3, Statement on Transportation Needs, Charlotte*
April 3, North Carolina Association of Educators, Asheville*
April 3, Institute of Policy Sciences and Public Affairs Tenth
    Anniversary, Duke University, Durham
April 6, Davidson County Dinner, Lexington*
April 7, Yadkin River Preservation Committee, Raleigh
April 8, Leadership Workshop for Central Office School
    Personnel, Raleigh
April 8, North Carolina Bankers Association, Raleigh*
April 9, Statement at News Conference, Raleigh†
April 9, Reception, Business Council on the Arts and
    Humanities, Greenville†
April 9, Governor's Business Awards in the Arts and
    Humanities, Greenville
April 10, YMCA Youth in Government, Raleigh
April 11, Jefferson-Jackson Day Dinner, Raleigh
April 13, Statement at News Conference, Wrightsville Beach†
April 13, Governor's Conference on Travel and Tourism,
    Wrightsville Beach
April 13, Sales and Marketing Executives Club, Asheville*
April 14, North Carolina State Employees Association and
    North Carolina State Government Employees Association
    Membership Drive Luncheon, Raleigh*
April 14, Fuji Cone, Inc., Announcement [Clinton], Raleigh
April 15, North Carolina National Guard Senior Commanders
    Conference, Raleigh
April 16, Statement at News Conference, Raleigh†
April 16, Boy Scouts Crime Prevention Program
    Announcement, Raleigh*
April 21, Seminar on International Trade in Mexico, Chapel
    Hill*
April 22, Greater Raleigh Chamber of Commerce Small
    Business Council, Raleigh†
April 22, American Red Cross Exhibit Opening, North
    Carolina Museum of History, Raleigh
April 23, Statement at News Conference, Raleigh†
April 23, Conference on Public History, Raleigh
April 24, Eastern Regional Conference on Delinquency
    Prevention, Greenville*
April 24, Annual Assembly, Christian Church in North
    Carolina, Raleigh*
April 27, Address to the People on Highway Needs [televised],
    Raleigh*

---

*Referred to in headnote
†No press copy

April 28, Statement on Transportation Needs and Bid Rigging,
    Raleigh*
April 28, Fourth Annual Piedmont Industrial Show, Greensboro
April 29, Durham County Centennial Week Dinner, Durham
May 1, Stonewall Jackson Park Dedication, Concord†
May 2, Equal Rights Amendment March, Raleigh
May 4, Construction Career Awareness Fair, Raleigh
May 4, Charlotte Optimist Club, Charlotte*
May 5, Pig Picking, Executives' Tour of North Carolina,
    Raleigh
May 6, Opening Remarks, Governor's Commission on
    Governmental Productivity, Raleigh*
May 6, Telex Terminal Communications Board of Directors,
    Raleigh*
May 6, North Carolina Association of School Administrators,
    Raleigh
May 7, Governor's Commission on Governmental Productivity,
    Raleigh*
May 7, Statement at News Conference, Raleigh†
May 8, East Carolina University Commencement, Greenville
May 13, Forsyth Prison Chaplaincy, Winston-Salem
May 13, North Carolina Funeral Directors Association,
    Winston-Salem
May 13, Greensboro Community Leaders, Greensboro†
May 14, Statement on Resignation of Transportation Secretary
    Tom Bradshaw, Raleigh
May 14, National Transportation Week, Raleigh*
May 14, American Cancer Society, Raleigh
May 14, IBM Luncheon, Research Triangle Park
May 14, Lexington Chamber of Commerce, Raleigh
May 15, Northern Telecom Dedication, Research Triangle Park
May 15, Annual Awards, Governor's Advocacy Council for
    Persons with Disabilities, Raleigh
May 15, North Carolina Senior Citizens Federation, Raleigh
May 19, Soil and Water Conservation Board of Supervisors,
    Raleigh*
May 21, Statement Announcing Executive Order No. 65,
    Raleigh*
May 28, North Carolina Museum of Art Dedication, Raleigh
May 29, Wallace Murray Corp. Dedication, Asheville
May 30, Closing Ceremony, Bryan Center Dedication, North
    Carolina School of Science and Mathematics, Durham
May 31, Needham B. Broughton High School Baccalaureate
    Ceremony, Raleigh*

---

*Referred to in headnote
†No press copy

June 4, Statement at News Conference, Raleigh†
June 4, Luncheon for Congressional Staff Members, Raleigh*
June 6, North Carolina Memorial Hospital Perinatal Care
  Facility Dedication, Chapel Hill
June 8, State Government Interns, Raleigh†
June 8, North Carolina Annual Conference, United Methodist
  Church, Fayetteville*
June 9, IVAC Corp. Announcement, Creedmoor
June 10, PMA Peat-to-Methanol Plant Announcement
  [Washington County], Raleigh*
June 11, Statement at News Conference, Raleigh†
June 11, Texasgulf Chemicals Co. Dedication, Raleigh
June 12, Fortieth Anniversary National Tree Farm Dedication,
  Durham
June 12, Swearing-in of Inmate Grievance Commission,
  Raleigh
June 15, Worcester Controls Corp. Announcement, Liberty
June 15, Human Resources Volunteer Recognition Day, Raleigh
June 15, Genetics Societies of America and Canada, Raleigh
June 16, Israel Bonds Dinner, Greensboro*
June 18, Statement on Good Roads Program, Raleigh
June 19, Boys State, Wake Forest University, Winston-Salem
June 19, Girls State, University of North Carolina at
  Greensboro
June 19, Disabled American Veterans, Fayetteville
June 25, Statement on 1981 Legislative Session, Raleigh
June 27, Young Democrats of North Carolina Installation
  Banquet, Goldsboro
June 27, Miss North Carolina Pageant, Raleigh†
June 29, N.C. 93 [Elk Creek] Bridge Dedication, Alleghany
  County
July 20, Swearing-in of Wildlife Resources Commission,
  Raleigh
July 20, Walter B. Jones Bridge Dedication, U.S. 264, Hyde
  County
July 20, Swearing-in of William R. Roberson, Jr., as
  Transportation Secretary, Raleigh†
July 21, Luncheon Honoring Dr. John Slaughter, Raleigh
July 22, Rocky Mount Tobacco Market Opening, Rocky Mount
July 22, Biotechnology Luncheon, Raleigh
July 22, State Board of Education, Raleigh
July 23, North Carolina 4-H Congress, Raleigh*
July 24, Swearing-in of State Board of Transportation, Raleigh
July 25, Notes for Celebration, River Bend

*Referred to in headnote
†No press copy

July 28, Oxford Tobacco Market Opening, Oxford†
July 28, North Carolina Sheriffs Association, Boone
July 30, Statement at News Conference, Raleigh†
July 30, Emerson Electric Co., Murphy†
August 3, Merck and Co. Announcement [Wilson County],
    Raleigh
August 4, Western Democratic Party Rally, Asheville*
August 6, Data General Plant Dedication, Apex
August 13, Robeson County Elected Officials Luncheon,
    Lumberton*
August 14, Swearing-in of Rae McNamara as Prisons Division
    Director, and of Wymene Valand to Parole Commission,
    Raleigh
August 14, Statement Announcing Restructured State Board of
    Transportation, Raleigh*
August 14, North Carolina Association of County
    Commissioners, Winston-Salem*
August 20, Statement on Governor's Business Council on the
    Arts and Humanities, Raleigh
August 28, Education Commission of the States Annual
    Banquet, Cambridge, Massachusetts*
August 28, Acceptance of Nomination as ECS Chairman-Elect,
    Cambridge, Massachusetts*
August 31, West Charlotte High School Student Assembly,
    Charlotte
August 31, Taping, WTVI, Charlotte†
August 31, Central Piedmont Community College, Charlotte†
August 31, Visit to University of North Carolina at Charlotte
August 31, Johnson C. Smith University Freshman Assembly,
    Charlotte
August 31, Democratic Party Reception, Charlotte
September 2, Penn Elastic Co. Announcement [Jamesville],
    Raleigh
September 2, Groundbreaking for Nash Technical College
    Training Center, Whitakers†
September 2, Jobs for Progress Rally, Rocky Mount*
September 3, Statement on Federal Budget Cuts, Raleigh*
September 8, Committee to Save the Cape Hatteras Lighthouse,
    Raleigh
September 9, Northeast North Carolina Conference, Edenton
September 10, Statement on Federal Budget Cuts, Raleigh*
September 10, Public Service Co. Ribbon Cutting, Chapel Hill
September 10, Public Service Co. Luncheon, Chapel Hill

---

*Referred to in headnote
†No press copy

September 12, North Carolina State Government Employees
   Association, Asheville*
September 14, Swearing-in of State Board of Agriculture,
   Raleigh
September 15, Dalure Fashions, Inc., Dedication, Gatesville
September 15, Apex Chamber of Commerce, Apex
September 16, Energy Management Exposition IV, Raleigh*
September 16, National Restitution Conference, Raleigh*
September 16, Bulls Eye Barbecue, Raleigh
September 17, Statement on Crime Control, Raleigh
September 17, Solar and Energy Conservation House
   Dedication, North Carolina State University, Raleigh
September 17, Russell Walker Day, Seagrove*
September 18, IBM Plant and Laboratory Dedication,
   Charlotte
September 18, Democratic Women's Banquet, Wilson*
September 19, Mechanics and Farmers Bank Opening,
   Winston-Salem
September 19, North Carolina Agribusiness Council Awards
   Presentation, Raleigh
September 21, Southern Growth Policies Board, Raleigh
September 21, State Employees Combined Campaign Kickoff,
   Raleigh
September 22, Capital Area Visitor Services Committee,
   Raleigh
September 22, Butler Polymet, Inc., Dedication, Lenoir
September 22, St. Andrews College Twentieth Anniversary,
   Pinehurst
September 23, Statement on MGM Motion Picture *Brainstorm*,
   Raleigh
October 1, Statement on North Carolina 2000, Raleigh
October 1, Research Triangle Foundation, Research Triangle
   Park
October 2, Commissioning of GKN Alamance Facility, Mebane
October 3, Volunteer Recognition Ceremony, Asheville
October 8, Statement at News Conference, Raleigh†
October 8, North Carolina Economic Development Board, Nags
   Head†
October 10, Frank Porter Graham Child Development Center
   Rededication, Chapel Hill*
October 10, German-American Week Reception, Charlotte
October 12, National Association of Volunteers in Criminal
   Justice, Virginia Beach, Virginia*

---

*Referred to in headnote
†No press copy

October 14, Statement at News Conference, Raleigh†
October 15, Retired Senior Executives Program, Boone
October 15, Meredith-Burda, Inc., Dedication, Newton
October 15, Senior Executives Meeting, Asheville†
October 15, International Investors Conference, Charlotte*
October 15, Statement Announcing Appointment of Ernest
    Messer as Assistant Secretary for Aging, Asheville
October 17, North Carolina Textile Foundation, Raleigh
October 19, Bristol-Myers Co. Dedication, Morrisville
October 20, North Carolina Principals and Assistant Principals
    Association, Raleigh*
October 20, Merck, Sharp, and Dohme Groundbreaking, Wilson
October 20, United Carolina Bank Operations Center Opening
    and Dedication, Monroe
October 20, Union County Democratic Party Reception,
    Monroe*
October 22, Statement on Tobacco Program, Raleigh
October 22, Opening Remarks, Joint Meeting, Commission on
    the Future of North Carolina and the North Carolina 2000
    County Chairmen, Raleigh
October 22, Introduction of Slide Presentation, Joint Meeting,
    Commission on the Future of North Carolina and the North
    Carolina 2000 County Chairmen, Raleigh
October 22, Keynote Address, Joint Meeting, Commission on
    the Future of North Carolina and the North Carolina 2000
    County Chairmen, Raleigh
October 24, Kannapolis Seventy-fifth Anniversary Celebration,
    Kannapolis
October 26, Youth Involvement Day, Raleigh
October 27, Governor's Conference on Economic Development,
    Raleigh*
October 27, Communities of Excellence Awards Banquet,
    Raleigh†
October 28, Statement Announcing Appointment of Claud
    (Buck) O'Shields as Waste Management Board Chairman,
    Raleigh*
October 28, Governor's Statewide Volunteer Recognition
    Ceremony, Greensboro
October 28, North Central Piedmont Resource Conservation
    and Development Project, Burlington
October 29, North Carolina Comprehensive Community College
    Student Government Association, Raleigh

---

*Referred to in headnote
†No press copy

October 29, North Carolina Association of Community College
   Adult Educators and North Carolina Association of
   Community College Instructional Administrators, Raleigh
October 30, Western North Carolina Tomorrow, Cullowhee
October 30, Haywood County Library Dedication, Waynesville
October 30, Farm-City Week, Asheville
October 30, Swearing-in of Ernest Messer as Assistant
   Secretary for Aging, Asheville†
October 30, Statement Announcing Appointment of Tom
   Morrissey to Commission on the Future of North Carolina,
   Asheville
October 30, World's Fair Proclamation Signing Ceremony,
   Asheville
October 30, Robert G. Barr Expressway Dedication, West
   Jefferson
October 31, Dinner Bell Barbecue, Raleigh
November 2, Joint Meeting, Baptist State Convention of North
   Carolina and General Baptist State Convention, Greensboro*
November 3, Swearing-in of Arthur Cassell to Advisory Budget
   Commission, Raleigh†
November 4, Governor's Statewide Volunteer Recognition
   Ceremony, Raleigh
November 5, National School Volunteer Program, Washington,
   D.C.
November 9, Swearing-in of Board of Elections, Raleigh†
November 10, Travel Council of North Carolina, Charlotte
November 10, North Carolina Association of Educators,
   Division of Principals and Administrators, Greensboro*
November 10, Greensboro National Bank Opening, Greensboro
November 16, Southeast U.S.-Japan Association, Tokyo, Japan*
December 1, Commission for Mental Health, Mental
   Retardation, and Substance Abuse Services, Raleigh
December 2, Governor's Business Round Table on Children and
   Youth, Raleigh*
December 3, Statement on Second Economic Development
   Mission to Far East, Raleigh*
December 3, North Carolina Awards Dinner, Raleigh
December 5, Conference on the Parties and the Presidential
   Nominating Process, Harvard University, Cambridge,
   Massachusetts†
December 8, Wilson County Chamber of Commerce, Wilson
December 9, Statement at News Conference, Raleigh†

---

*Referred to in headnote
†No press copy

December 9, Capitol Outside Christmas Tree Lighting
Ceremony, Raleigh
December 10, Military Appreciation Day: Camp Lejeune
Marine Corps Base, Jacksonville; Cherry Point Marine Corps
Air Station, Havelock; Seymour Johnson Air Force Base,
Goldsboro; Pope Air Force Base-Fort Bragg Military
Reservation, Fayetteville
December 11, Wachovia Scholarship Announcement, Winston-
Salem
December 11, N.C. 86 Dedication [Hightowers-Prospect Hill
vicinity], Caswell County
December 11, Swearing-in of Superior Court Judge James A.
Beaty, Jr., Winston-Salem
December 14, Christmas Welcome, Official Capitol Christmas
Opening, Raleigh
December 19, National Association of Intercollegiate Athletics
Champions Bowl, Burlington
December 21, Statement Announcing $50,000 Grant for North
Carolina Symphony, Raleigh
December 23, Statement Announcing Appointment of R. W.
Wilkins, Jr., as Motor Vehicles Commissioner, Raleigh

1982

January 6, Swearing-in of Tony Rand as State Senator,
Fayetteville
January 6, School of the Arts Dinner, Raleigh
January 7, Swearing-in of Glenn Jernigan as Employment
Security Commission Chairman, Raleigh
January 7, Hotel Europa Grand Opening, Chapel Hill
January 11, Swearing-in of R. W. Wilkins as Motor Vehicles
Commissioner, Raleigh
January 11, Simon C. Sitterson, Jr., Appreciation Dinner,
Kinston
January 12, Takeda Chemical Announcement [New Hanover
and Pender counties], Raleigh
January 12, United Way Combined Campaign Reception,
Raleigh
January 12, Wilmington Industrial Development, Inc.,
Committee of 100, Wilmington

---

*Referred to in headnote
†No press copy

January 13, Swearing-in of Tom Bradshaw, Jr., as
   Environmental Management Commission Chairman,
   Raleigh
January 13, Small Business Advocacy Council, Raleigh
January 19, Juvenile Community Volunteer Program
   Conference, Raleigh
January 19, Canadian Days Announcement, Raleigh*
January 19, Governor's Advisory Committee on Travel and
   Tourism, Raleigh*
January 19, Governor's Award for Fitness and Health in
   Business and Industry, Raleigh
January 19, Presentation of Awards for Fitness and Health,
   Raleigh
January 20, Cooperative Council of North Carolina, Raleigh
January 25, Swearing-in of District Court Judge Acie L. Ward,
   Raleigh
January 26, North Carolina State University Conference on
   University-Industry Cooperative Research Center for
   Communications and Signal Processing, Raleigh
January 26, Small Business Advocacy Council, Raleigh
January 26, U.S. 220 Dedication, Greensboro
January 28, North Carolina Press Association Awards Dinner,
   Chapel Hill
January 29, "Jazz Is" Announcement, Winston-Salem
January 29, Winston Square Tour, Winston-Salem
January 29, North Carolina Alternative Energy Corporation
   Cogeneration Conference, Pinehurst
February 2, Swearing-in of Heman R. Clark as Crime Control
   and Public Safety Secretary, Raleigh
February 3, Swearing-in of North Carolina Supreme Court
   Associate Justice Burley B. Mitchell, Jr., Raleigh
February 4, Statement on Crime Prevention, Raleigh
February 4, St. Augustine's College Founders Day, Raleigh
February 8, Anson County Crime Watch Association,
   Wadesboro
February 9, Partners Breakfast, Charlotte
February 9, Charlotte Life Underwriters Association, Charlotte
February 9, North Carolina Hall of Natural History Dedication,
   Schiele Museum, Gastonia
February 9, Belmont Abbey College, Belmont*
February 10, Pine Hills Industrial Park Groundbreaking,
   Rockingham

---

*Referred to in headnote
†No press copy

February 10, Swearing-in of Tom Bradshaw, Jr., as
  Environmental Management Commission Chairman,
  Raleigh
February 11, Statement Announcing Creation of Governor's
  Task Force on Drunken Drivers, Raleigh*
February 12, Northeastern North Carolina Tomorrow,
  Elizabeth City
February 15, Five Points Coffee Club, Raleigh
February 18, Statement on Federal Block Grants, Raleigh
February 18, St. Augustine's College Luncheon, Raleigh
February 25, Jim Hunt Appreciation Dinner, Smithfield
March 1, Communications Workers of America District Three
  Convention, Raleigh
March 1, Introduction of Ike Andrews at Walter Mondale
  Dinner, Raleigh
March 4, Prayer Breakfast, Winston-Salem*
March 4, Piedmont International Trade Conference,
  Greensboro
March 4, North Carolina Agricultural Extension Leadership
  Update Conference, Raleigh
March 5, Seventh Annual Indian Unity Conference, Raleigh
March 8, Onslow County Day, Raleigh
March 8, Swearing-in of Governor's Advisory Committee on
  Education Block Grants, Raleigh
March 9, Democratic Party Sustaining Fund Patrons
  Breakfast, Raleigh
March 9, Capitol Grounds Statue Restoration Ceremony,
  Raleigh
March 9, EDA Grant Press Briefing, Raleigh
March 10, Opening Remarks, Second Annual North Carolina
  Conference on Delinquency Prevention, Raleigh
March 11, Governor's Conference on Leadership Development
  for Women, Raleigh*
March 12, Closing Remarks, Second Annual North Carolina
  Conference on Delinquency Prevention, Raleigh†
March 15, Vocational Education Award Ceremony, Pitt
  Community College, Greenville
March 15, World Trade Award, Coastal Plains Chapter, North
  Carolina World Trade Association, Greenville
March 17, North Carolina Conference on Transportation and
  Land Development, Raleigh
March 17, North Carolina Citizens Association, Raleigh
March 18, Statement on Block Grant Hearings, Raleigh

---

*Referred to in headnote
†No press copy

March 18, Taylor R. Kennerly Appreciation and Award
   Luncheon, Greensboro
March 19, Tobacco Associates Thirty-fifth Annual Meeting,
   Raleigh*
March 22, Reception for Governor Reubin Askew, Raleigh†
March 22, North Carolina State Florists Association
   Convention, Raleigh
March 23, State Building Construction Conference, Raleigh
March 23, Analog Devices Announcement, Greensboro
March 23, Business Round Table on Children and Youth,
   Greensboro
March 23, McDowell County Senior Citizens Center Dedication,
   Marion
March 23, Blue Ridge Terrace Project Dedication, Marion
March 24, Statement at News Conference, Raleigh†
March 24, North Carolina Association of Sheltered Workshops,
   Inc., Distinguished Service Award, Raleigh
March 24, National Conference of Christians and Jews, New
   York City
March 25, Governor's Business Council on the Arts and
   Humanities, Charlotte
March 25, Business Session, Governor's Business Council on
   the Arts and Humanities, Charlotte
March 25, Announcement on Recipients of Governor's Business
   Awards in the Arts and Humanities, Charlotte
March 30, Correctional Employees Meeting, Raleigh
March 30, Catawba Valley Hosiery Association, Hickory
March 31, WTVD Jefferson Awards [television appearance],
   Raleigh
March 31, WTVD Jefferson Awards Luncheon, Raleigh
March 31, North Carolina Rural Electric Cooperatives,
   Raleigh*
April 1, Statement at News Conference, Raleigh†
April 1, Union Carbide Technical Center Dedication, Research
   Triangle Park
April 1, Swearing-in of Superior Court Judge Charles Winberry,
   Nashville
April 1, North Carolina State Economic Development Board,
   Roanoke Rapids
April 2, Ajinomoto U.S.A., Inc., Dedication, Raleigh
April 2, Crimestoppers Conference, Raleigh
April 5, John Belk Freeway Dedication, Charlotte

---

*Referred to in headnote
†No press copy

April 7, Home Builders Association of Rocky Mount, Rocky
  Mount
April 8, Statement at News Conference, Raleigh†
April 8, Citizen Awareness Year Kickoff, Raleigh
April 14, NCSEA/NCSGEA Membership Kickoff Luncheon,
  Raleigh
April 14, David Kelly Day, Raleigh
April 15, Raleigh Chamber of Commerce, Raleigh
April 16, Davidson College Spring Convocation, Davidson
April 19, Governor's Advocacy Council for Persons with
  Disabilities, Raleigh
April 19, Young Men's Business Club, Birmingham, Alabama
April 20, Verbatim Corp. Symbolic Groundbreaking, Charlotte
April 20, North Carolina-Israel Visiting Scholar Dinner,
  Raleigh
April 21, North Carolina Holocaust Remembrance Observance,
  Raleigh
April 23, Sulzer Brothers Dedication, Kings Mountain
April 23, North Carolina World Trade Association, Wilmington
April 23, U.S.S. *Monitor* Artifact Exhibition Grand Opening,
  Fort Fisher
April 24, Jefferson-Jackson Dinner, Raleigh*
April 26, Terminal Dedication, Raleigh-Durham Airport, Wake
  County
April 26, Holiday Inn-Four Seasons Complex Dedication,
  Greensboro*
April 27, Dinner Honoring Arthur Cassell, Greensboro
April 28, Panel of Governors, Commission on the Future of
  North Carolina, Greensboro
April 28, *Charlotte News* All-Star Scholars Banquet, Charlotte
April 28, Statewide Conference on Child Passenger Safety,
  Clemmons
April 29, Statement at News Conference, Raleigh†
April 29, Terminal Dedication, Douglas Municipal Airport,
  Charlotte
April 29, Carl E. Bates Dormitory Dedication, Fruitland
  Baptist Bible Institute, Hendersonville
April 29, Recognition of Volunteers, Quality Forward, Asheville
April 29, Public Hearing, Governor's Task Force on Drunken
  Drivers, Asheville
April 29, Manufacturing Executives Association, Asheville
April 30, Asheville Chamber of Commerce, Asheville

---

*Referred to in headnote
†No press copy

April 30, Acceptance of Award, Great Smokies Council,
International Reading Association, Asheville†

April 30, U.S. 25-70 Dedication, Marshall

May 1, B. Everett Jordan Dam and Lake Dedication, Moncure

May 3, North Carolina Law Day, Raleigh

May 3, Acceptance of Award, Boy Scouts Distinguished Service
Award Banquet, Raleigh

May 4, Vance Senior High School Marketing and Distributive
Education Club, Henderson

May 6, Democratic Congressional Campaign Committee
Dinner, Asheville

May 7, Strawberry Festival, Chadbourn

May 9, Lenoir-Rhyne College Commencement, Hickory

May 10, Cambell University Commencement, Buies Creek

May 10, Raychem Dedication, Fuquay-Varina

May 11, Annie Penn Memorial Hospital Dedication, Reidsville

May 11, CPC North America Reception, Winston-Salem†

May 12, Small Business Advocacy Council, Raleigh

May 12, Inter-City Council, Greensboro†

May 13, Telex Corp. Dedication, Research Triangle Park

May 13, State Department of Transportation Division
Engineers and District Engineers, Raleigh

May 14, Wake County Schools Breakfast, Raleigh

May 14, Statement on School Dropouts, Raleigh*

May 16, Atlantic Christian College Commencement, Wilson

May 18, North Carolina Transportation Week Ceremony,
Raleigh

May 18, Armed Forces Communications and Electronics
Association Fifth Annual Communications Exhibition,
Raleigh

May 18, Reception for Governor's Award for Excellence
Recipients, Raleigh

May 18, Lexington Chamber of Commerce, Raleigh

May 19, Statement on Equal Rights Amendment, Raleigh*

May 24, State Government Interns Orientation, Raleigh

May 25, North Carolina Water Management Conference,
Raleigh

May 25, Four Hundredth Anniversary County Chairs
Reception, Raleigh

May 25, Western North Carolina Conference of the AME
Church, Raleigh

May 25, Statement at News Conference, Raleigh†

---

*Referred to in headnote
†No press copy

May 25, Goldsboro Chamber of Commerce Annual Banquet,
Goldsboro
May 26, American Political Process Class, Needham B.
Broughton High School, Raleigh
May 26, Hertford County Industrial Development Commission,
Ahoskie
May 27, Statement at News Conference, Raleigh†
May 27, North Carolina Social Services Association Annual
Conference, Raleigh*
May 27, Fayetteville Ambulatory Surgical Center Dedication,
Fayetteville
May 27, North Carolina Senior Citizens Association,
Fayetteville
May 28, North Carolina Day Ceremony, World's Fair, Knoxville
May 28, Ribbon Cutting, North Carolina Exhibit, World's Fair,
Knoxville
June 1, Public Transportation Advisory Council Ride-sharing
Awards Presentation, Raleigh
June 2, Southeastern Regional Child Welfare League, Winston-
Salem*
June 2, Southern Growth Policies Board, Research Triangle
Park
June 3, Statement at News Conference, Raleigh†
June 3, Four Hundredth Anniversary Reception, Raleigh
June 4, Frank Liske Park Dedication, Concord
June 5, Young Democrats of North Carolina Installation
Banquet, Charlotte*
June 10, North Carolina Merchants Association, Raleigh*
June 10, Statement on Public Utility Fuel Clause, Raleigh*
June 10, Community College Board Meeting, Raleigh†
June 10, Weyerhaeuser Scholarship Announcement, Raleigh
June 10, North Carolina Department of Human Resources
Volunteer Appreciation Day, Raleigh
June 11, Swearing-in of Louis Sewell to State Board of
Transportation, Raleigh
June 12, North Carolina School of Science and Mathematics
Commencement, Durham
June 12, North Carolina Democratic Party State Convention,
Raleigh
June 12, Unity Gala for Campaign '82, Raleigh
June 14, General Electric Microelectronics Center Dedication,
Research Triangle Park
June 14, Capitol Docents Luncheon, Raleigh

---

*Referred to in headnote
†No press copy

June 14, Grand Chapter of North Carolina, Order of the
  Eastern Star Seventy-seventh Annual Session, Raleigh
June 15, Child and Family Services Committee, Raleigh
June 16, State Future Farmers of America Convention,
  Raleigh*
June 17, Statement on 1982 Legislative Session, Raleigh
June 18, Girls State, University of North Carolina at
  Greensboro
June 18, Boys State, Wake Forest University, Winston-Salem
June 19, American Legion Annual Convention, Fayetteville
June 22, United Services for Older Adults, Greensboro
June 22, Mecklenburg County Democratic Party Dinner,
  Charlotte
June 23, Microelectronics Conference, Raleigh
June 24, Statement on Tobacco Price Supports, Raleigh
June 29, North Carolina Symphony Luncheon, Raleigh
June 30, Swearing-in of Betty S. Speir to State Board of
  Education, Raleigh
June 30, Bruce E. Whitaker School Dedication, John Umstead
  Hospital, Butner
June 30, "Jazz Is" Proclamation, Raleigh
July 1, North Carolinians United for ERA, Raleigh*
July 1, New York Times Affiliated Newspapers Dinner,
  Wrightsville Beach
July 13, Dropout Prevention Program Panel, Principals'
  Summer Conference, Wilmington
July 13, Principals' Summer Conference Keynote Speech,
  Wilmington*
July 19, North Carolina Chapter, National Association of
  Postmasters, Greensboro
July 19, Committee to Elect Democratic Governors, Democratic
  National Committee, Washington, D.C.
July 20, Fayetteville Street Mall Completion Celebration,
  Raleigh
July 20, Science and Technology Board Meeting, Raleigh†
July 21, Randolph Hospital Golden Anniversary, Asheboro
July 21, Lawn Party Honoring State Government Interns,
  Raleigh
July 22, Senior Democrats of North Carolina, Raleigh
July 22, Main Street Program Orientation Session, Raleigh
July 29, Statement Announcing Appointment of Donald S.
  Beilman as First President of Microelectronics Center of
  North Carolina, Raleigh

---

*Referred to in headnote
†No press copy

July 29, North Carolina Association of Minority Businesses, Raleigh

July 29, North Carolina Interfaith Coalition on Aging, Raleigh

July 29, Editors' Briefing, Four Hundredth Anniversary Celebration, Raleigh

July 29, International Connectional Council of the AME Zion Church, Charlotte

July 30, Southern Police Institute Alumni Association, Greensboro

August 3, Swearing-in of North Carolina Supreme Court Associate Justice Harry C. Martin, Raleigh†

August 3, Swearing-in of Judge Clifton E. Johnson to State Court of Appeals, Raleigh

August 17, Seminar on Economic Development, Portland, Oregon

August 20, Economic Development Conference, Seattle, Washington

August 20, Education Commission of the States Sixteenth Annual Meeting, Portland, Oregon*

August 24, Statement at News Conference with Congressman Charlie Rose, Fayetteville†

August 25, Ford Motor Company Assembly Plant Employee Rally, Norfolk, Virginia

August 26, Statement at News Conference, Raleigh†

August 27, School Friends Luncheon, Winston-Salem*

August 28, North Carolina Association of Minority Public Officials, Raleigh

August 31, Statement at News Conference, Raleigh†

August 31, Teachers' and State Employees' Comprehensive Major Medical Plan Board of Trustees, Raleigh

September 2, Statement at News Conference, Raleigh†

September 2, Governor's Task Force on Financing Public School Facilities, Raleigh

September 2, Child Care Resources, Inc., Dedication, Charlotte

September 2, Union County Crime Prevention Committees, Monroe

September 8, United Way Combined Campaign Kickoff, Raleigh

September 8, Dropout Prevention Conference, Raleigh

September 8, *Lexington Dispatch* One Hundredth Anniversary Celebration, Lexington

September 9, Statement Proclaiming 1982-1983 as "Year of the Public School" in North Carolina, Raleigh*

September 9, Central Prison Dedication, Raleigh*

---

*Referred to in headnote
†No press copy

September 10, Inauguration of Northern Telecom Annual
 Sculpture Exhibit, Research Triangle Park
September 10, North Carolina State Employees Association,
 Greensboro
September 11, Congressional Caucus for Science and
 Technology, Conference on the Status of Pre-College Science
 and Mathematics Education, Raleigh*
September 11, Presentation of Governor's Awards, North
 Carolina Agribusiness Council, Raleigh
September 13, General Federation of Women's Clubs Board of
 Directors, Raleigh
September 13, North Carolina State University Alumni
 Association, Raleigh
September 13, Department of Public Instruction Staff Meeting,
 Raleigh
September 14, Community Salute to Interfaith Council for
 Social Service, Chapel Hill
September 15, Statement on Legislation against Income Tax
 Violations, Raleigh*
September 16, Southeast U.S.-Japan Association, Nashville,
 Tennessee
September 17, Tribute to Frank Liske, Concord
September 17, Active Citizenship Training Class, Central
 Cabarrus High School, Concord
September 17, High School Assembly, Central Cabarrus High
 School, Concord
September 17, North Carolina AFL-CIO Convention, Charlotte
September 17, Reception for Jamie Clarke, Forest City
September 18, Linville Falls Recreation Trail Dedication,
 Linville Falls
September 18, U.S. 19 East Groundbreaking, Burnsville†
September 18, Yancey County Democratic Party Reception,
 Micaville
September 18, Representative Margaret Hayden's Barbecue,
 Sparta
September 20, Opening Remarks, Conference Board
 Contributions Council, New York City
September 20, Closing Remarks, Conference Board
 Contributions Council, New York City
September 21, Baker Perkins, Inc., Dedication, Goldsboro
September 21, Kickoff, Voters for Congressman Whitley,
 Goldsboro

---

*Referred to in headnote
†No press copy

September 21, North Carolina Association of Registers of
  Deeds, Wilmington
September 22, Cultural Resources Volunteers, Raleigh†
September 23, Governor's Task Force on Drunken Drivers,
  Raleigh
September 23, Fayetteville Little Theatre and Hastings
  [England] Theatre Guild, Raleigh†
September 23, Governor's Task Force on Science and
  Technology, Raleigh*
September 24, Bermuda Village Retirement Community
  Groundbreaking, Forsyth County
September 24, Robin Britt Luncheon [press copy dated
  September 23], Greensboro
September 24, Statement on U.S. 311, High Point
September 24, North Carolina State Government Employees'
  Association, Greensboro
September 24, Democratic Women of North Carolina,
  Hendersonville*
September 25, North Carolina-Nepal Day Celebration, Raleigh
September 25, Jaycees Action Legislature, Raleigh
September 25, Hiddenite Celebration of the Arts, Hiddenite
September 25, Jack Bass Roast, Hickory
September 27, Governor's Executive Cabinet on Juvenile
  Affairs, Raleigh†
September 27, Reception for Ike Andrews, Raleigh†
September 28, Eastern Secondary Mortgage Market
  Conference, Raleigh
September 28, AGA Gas Groundbreaking, Wake Forest
September 28, N.C. 86 Dedication, High Point
September 28, Women for [Robin] Britt, High Point
September 28, Statement at News Conference, Elon College†
September 28, Three Governors Dinner, Elon College
September 29, Legislative Issues Seminar, Raleigh
September 29, Wake Forest University Sesquicentennial
  Campaign, Raleigh
September 30, Statement at News Conference, Raleigh†
September 30, Jim Garrison Day, Badin†
September 30, Fayetteville State University, Fayetteville
September 30, District Seven Rally, Fayetteville
October 1, IVAC Corp. Dedication, Creedmoor
October 1, C. Grier Beam Truck Museum Ribbon Cutting,
  Cherryville
October 1, District Ten Rally, Lenoir

---

*Referred to in headnote
†No press copy

October 2, Volunteer Recognition Ceremony, Asheville

October 2, District Eleven Rally, Sylva

October 3, Sixth International Conference of Friendship Force, Asheville

October 4, Cooperative Council Breakfast, Asheville†

October 4, State Goals and Policy Board Retreat, Asheville

October 4, Madison County Democratic Party Reception, Marshall

October 4, Macon County Democratic Party Luncheon, Franklin

October 4, Remarks, Tour, Reception, Swain County Administration Building, Bryson City†

October 4, Cherokee Tribal Task Force, Cherokee

October 4, Statement on Cherokee Boys' Club, Cherokee

October 4, Cherokee Boys' Club Anniversary Program, Cherokee

October 4, Reception for Jamie Clarke, Waynesville

October 5, Buncombe County Democratic Leadership Breakfast, Asheville

October 5, Buncombe Alternatives, Asheville

October 5, Crime Prevention Awards Presentation, WWNC Radio, Asheville

October 5, McDowell County Democratic Party Reception, Marion

October 5, McGalliard Falls Recreation Park Dedication, Valdese

October 5, NAMCO Controls Dedication, Newton

October 5, Western Residence Association, Asheville

October 8, Statement at News Conference, Raleigh†

October 9, Terminal Dedication, Greensboro-High Point-Winston-Salem Regional Airport, Guilford County

October 9, North Carolina Chapter, American Society of Landscape Architects, Raleigh

October 9, District Four Rally, Raleigh†

October 11, American Society of Legislative Clerks and Secretaries [press copy dated October 10], Raleigh

October 11, "Emergency Medicine Today," Emergency Medical Services Conference, Raleigh

October 11, Reception for Sheriff John Baker, Raleigh

October 12, Tobacco Board of Trade, Durham

October 12, Child and Family Services Interagency Committee, Raleigh

---

*Referred to in headnote
†No press copy

October 12, North Carolina Division, United Daughters of the
Confederacy, Raleigh
October 13, Department of Transportation Achievements in
Management Conference, Raleigh
October 13, Opening Remarks, North Carolina Christian
Educators' Association Annual Convention, Raleigh
October 13, District Eight Rally, New London
October 14, Statement at News Conference, Raleigh†
October 14, Max Factor Dedication, Oxford
October 14, North Carolina-Israel Visiting Scholar Dinner,
High Point
October 15, North Carolina State Fair Opening, Raleigh
October 15, District One Rally, Kinston†
October 16, District Six Rally, High Point
October 18, Senior Citizens' Fun Festival, North Carolina State
Fair, Raleigh
October 18, Nash County Democratic Party Rally, Nashville
October 18, Northampton County Democratic Party Rally,
Jackson
October 19, Moore County Democratic Party Reception,
Southern Pines
October 19, James S. Melton Vocational Skills Center
Dedication, Coastal Carolina Community College,
Jacksonville
October 19, Onslow Business-Industry Association,
Jacksonville
October 20, Statement on Federal Unemployment Benefits,
Raleigh
October 20, Retired Senior Executives Program Meeting,
Raleigh
October 20, District Two Rally, Durham
October 21, Naegle's Fifth Annual Pig Pickin' and Open House,
Raleigh
October 21, Robin Britt for Congress, Lexington
October 22, North Carolina State Bar Association, Raleigh
October 22, Conference of Superior Court and District Court
Judges, Raleigh
October 25, North Carolina Association of Broadcasters,
Raleigh
October 25, Officers of Regional Investment Company of
Flanders-Belgium, Research Triangle Park†
October 25, District Five Rally, Wentworth

*Referred to in headnote
†No press copy

October 26, Opening Remarks, Governor's Western North
  Carolina Conference on School Dropouts, Morganton*
October 26, Osaka Transformer Co. Dedication, Charlotte
October 26, Volunteer Recognition Ceremony, Williamston
October 27, Statement at News Conference, Raleigh†
October 27, Charlotte-Mecklenburg Chamber of Commerce,
  Charlotte
October 28, Process Equipment Manufacturers Association,
  Research Triangle Park
October 29, Fountain Public Library Dedication, Fountain
October 29, Terminal Dedication, Pitt-Greenville Airport,
  Greenville
October 29, Brody Medical Sciences Building Dedication, East
  Carolina University, Greenville
October 29, Charlotte Business League Fifth Annual Awards
  Banquet, Charlotte
October 29, District Nine Rally, Charlotte
October 30, District Three Rally, Benson
October 30, Barbecue for Charlie Rose, Fayetteville
November 1, Robin Britt for Congress, United Services for
  Older Adults, Greensboro†
November 1, Rally for Robin Britt, Greensboro
November 1, North Carolina League of Municipalities,
  Greensboro
November 1, Statement Supporting Jamie Clarke for Congress,
  Asheville
November 2, North Carolina State University Honor Students,
  Raleigh
November 3, Youth Involvement Day, Raleigh
November 3, Expo Charlotte, Charlotte
November 3, Governor's Economic Development Conference,
  Raleigh
November 4, Statement at News Conference, Raleigh†
November 4, State Board of Education, Raleigh
November 4, Lorillard Tobacco Processing Facility Opening,
  Greensboro
November 4, North Carolina Awards Ceremony, Raleigh
November 5, Equal Employment Opportunity and Affirmative
  Action Conference, Raleigh
November 5, Inauguration of Emery Worldwide 727 Service,
  Raleigh-Durham Airport, Wake County
November 5, Volunteer Recognition Ceremony, Raleigh

---

*Referred to in headnote
†No press copy

November 12, Statement on Drunken Drivers, Raleigh
November 12, North Carolina Solar Energy Association, Raleigh*
November 15, National Institute of Environmental Health Sciences Research Facility Dedication, Research Triangle Park
November 15, One Park Center Site Dedication, Research Triangle Park
November 16, Governor's Conference on Drunken Drivers, Raleigh*
November 17, Washington County Chamber of Commerce, Plymouth
November 17, Roanoke Voyages Corridor Commission Luncheon, Nags Head
November 17, Dan Taylor Memorial Bridge Dedication, Sealevel
November 17, Carteret County Democratic Party, Morehead City*
November 18, Governing Board of the Council of State Governments, Raleigh†
November 19, Tobacco Growers' Association of North Carolina, Raleigh
November 19, Council of State Governments Executive Committee, Raleigh*
November 22, Outboard Marine Corp. Announcement, Burnsville
November 22, Thad Eure Day, Raleigh
November 23, Department of Transportation Appreciation Luncheon, Raleigh
November 23, Governor's Ride Sharing Task Force, Raleigh
November 24, Statement at News Conference, Raleigh†
November 24, Citizens Commission on Alternatives to Incarceration, Raleigh
November 29, Dolphin Systems Corp. Groundbreaking, Elizabeth City
November 29, Northeastern North Carolina Legislative Caucus, Williamston
November 30, North Carolina Citizens for Business and Industry, Raleigh†
November 30, Wake, Durham, and Granville Legislative Delegations, Research Triangle Park

---

*Referred to in headnote
†No press copy

December 1, Governor's Task Force on Coastal Water
Management, Raleigh

December 1, North Carolina Annual Older Americans
Volunteer Program Training Conference, Raleigh

December 1, United Way Combined Campaign Reception,
Raleigh

December 1, Unveiling, Cape Hatteras Lighthouse Painting by
Dimitrios Zografos, Raleigh

December 2, Oceanfront Development Conference, Wilmington

December 2, New Hanover County Resource Recovery Facility
Groundbreaking, Wilmington

December 2, Lexington Chapter, International Management
Council, Lexington

December 3, Bendix Corp. Groundbreaking, Rocky Mount

December 3, Conference on Day Care Issues, Raleigh

December 6, Wildlife Endowment Fund Ceremony, Raleigh

December 6, Opening Remarks, Conference on the Future of
North Carolina, Raleigh

December 6, North Carolina Farm Bureau Federation, Raleigh

December 6, Keynote, Conference on the Future of North
Carolina, Raleigh

December 7, Selmer Co. Dedication, Albemarle†

December 7, Stanly County Chamber of Commerce Reception,
Albemarle

December 7, Stanly County National Guard Armory
Dedication, Albemarle

December 7, Senator James B. Garrison Roast, Albemarle

December 8, Flame of Truth Award Dinner, Raleigh

December 9, National Conference of State Legislatures,
Washington, D.C.*

December 9, Statement on Education Commission of the States,
Washington, D.C.

December 9, Closing Remarks, Education Commission of the
States News Conference, Washington, D.C.

December 10, Governor's Crime Commission, Raleigh

December 10, Carolina Society of Association Executives Trade
Show Ribbon Cutting, Raleigh

December 10, Carolina Society of Association Executives,
Raleigh

December 13, Official Capitol Christmas Opening and Tree-
Lighting Ceremony, Raleigh

December 15, East-West Expressway Signing Ceremony,
Durham

---

*Referred to in headnote
†No press copy

December 15, State Highway Patrol Appreciation Luncheon,
   Garner
December 17, Highland Street Underpass Dedication, Mount
   Holly
December 23, Statement at News Conference, Raleigh†

1983

January 5, Briefing on Program against Drunk Driving,
   Raleigh
January 5, Swearing-in of E. V. Wilkins to State Board of
   Education, Raleigh
January 6, Briefing on Laws Regarding the Drunken Driver,
   Asheville
January 11, Public School Superintendents Winter Conference,
   Raleigh†
January 11, Briefing for Religious Leaders on DUI Legislation,
   Raleigh†
January 11, Wallace Chamber of Commerce, Wallace
January 13, Statement at News Conference, Raleigh†
January 13, Committee to Study Academic Credit for High
   School Volunteerism, Raleigh
January 14, North Carolina Bar Association, Raleigh
January 14, Human Relations Council Twentieth Anniversary,
   Raleigh
January 18, Budget Briefing, Raleigh†
January 18, Sir Walter Cabinet, Raleigh
January 18, University Place Development Contract
   Announcement, Charlotte
January 18, Laurinburg-Scotland County Area Chamber of
   Commerce, Laurinburg
January 19, Cooperative Council of North Carolina, Raleigh*
January 19, Statewide Conference for Community School
   Coordinators, Raleigh
January 20, Statement at News Conference, Raleigh†
January 20, Goodyear Tire and Rubber Co. Announcement,
   Asheboro
January 20, North Carolina Hospital Association, Raleigh*
January 26, Small Business Research and Development
   Conference, Raleigh
January 27, Statement at News Conference, Raleigh†

---

*Referred to in headnote
†No press copy

January 27, Swearing-in of State Board of Agriculture, Raleigh
January 27, Triangle Cities Better Business Bureau, Research
  Triangle Park
January 27, North Carolina Press Association Annual Press
  Institute and Awards Ceremony, Chapel Hill
January 28, North Carolina Association of Independent
  Schools, Durham County
January 28, Pamlico Nursing Center Dedication, Washington
January 28, First Congressional District Meritorious Service
  Dinner, Washington
January 31, Raleigh Rotary Club, Raleigh†
January 31, Park Broadcasting, Inc., Banquet and
  Management Meeting, Raleigh
February 3, Statement at News Conference, Raleigh†
February 3, Swearing-in of North Carolina Supreme Court
  Associate Justice Henry E. Frye, Raleigh†
February 4, Commission to Study Housing Programs in North
  Carolina, Raleigh
February 4, Governor's New Product Awards, Professional
  Engineers of North Carolina, Raleigh
February 4, Statement at News Conference, Greenville†
February 4, Greenville Waste Water Treatment Plant
  Announcement, Greenville
February 4, Installation of Chancellor John M. Howell, East
  Carolina University, Greenville
February 4, Annual Corporate Banquet, Elizabeth City State
  University
February 9, Local Government Advocacy Council, Raleigh†
February 10, Statement Announcing Public Hearings on
  Management of Hazardous Wastes, Raleigh
February 10, Commission for Mental Health, Mental
  Retardation, and Substance Abuse Services, Raleigh*
February 10, North Carolina Department of Community
  Colleges Luncheon Honoring Dr. and Mrs. Larry J. Blake,
  Raleigh
February 11, Local Government Advocacy Council, Raleigh
February 11, Governor's Award for Fitness and Health in
  Business and Industry, Raleigh†
February 12, Democratic Patrons Breakfast, Raleigh†
February 14, Southern Classified Advertising Managers
  Association, Raleigh†
February 15, Addisson H. Reese Building Dedication,
  University of North Carolina at Charlotte†

*Referred to in headnote
†No press copy

February 15, Charlotte Downtown Rotary Club, Charlotte†
February 15, Industrial Announcement, Norwood†
February 15, Joint Meeting, Southern Baptist Press
  Association and Association of State Baptist Executive
  Secretaries, Raleigh†
February 16, Governor's Advocacy Council on Children and
  Youth, Raleigh†
February 17, Statement at News Conference, Raleigh†
February 17, North Carolina State AFL-CIO Legislative
  Reception, Raleigh†
February 17, Goldsboro Charter Chapter, American Business
  Women's Association, Goldsboro†
February 18, Missouri Educational Policy Seminar, St. Louis,
  Missouri†
February 18, Guest Participant on "At Your Service," WMOX,
  St. Louis, Missouri†
February 18, Centerre Bank Reception, St. Louis, Missouri†
February 23, North Carolina Democratic Women, Raleigh
March 2, North Raleigh Hilton Grand Opening, Raleigh
March 3, Statement at News Conference, Raleigh†
March 4, Governor's Executive Cabinet on Juvenile Affairs,
  Raleigh†
March 4, American Horse Shows Association and American
  Morgan Horse Association's National Morgan Judges
  Seminar, Raleigh
March 7, Cape Hatteras Lighthouse Campaign Presentation,
  Charlotte†
March 8, North Carolina Council, International Reading
  Association, Winston-Salem
March 8, Governor's Eastern North Carolina Conference on
  School Dropouts, Greenville*
March 10, Statement at News Conference, Raleigh†
March 14, Alma Desk Co. Safety Award, High Point
March 14, Analog Devices Computer Laboratories Division
  Dedication, Greensboro
March 14, Western Steer, Inc., Annual Convention, Charlotte
March 15, North Carolina Extension Homemakers, Raleigh
March 16, State Goals and Policy Board, Raleigh*
March 16, Tobacco Associates, Inc., Raleigh
March 16, North Carolina Citizens for Business and Industry,
  Raleigh
March 17, Statement on Proposed Safe Roads Act, Raleigh

---

*Referred to in headnote
†No press copy

March 17, Statement on Cystic Fibrosis Research Center, Chapel Hill

March 17, National Cystic Fibrosis Foundation, Chapel Hill†

March 17, First Juried Exhibition of North Carolina Crafts, Raleigh

March 18, Advanced Leadership Program Services Seminar, Education Commission of the States, Chapel Hill*

March 21, Child and Family Services Interagency Committee, Raleigh

March 22, North Carolina Foundation for Alternative Health Care Programs, Research Triangle Park

March 22, North Carolina Criminal Justice Education and Training Standards Commission, Raleigh

March 23, International Student Day, Raleigh

March 23, Child Watch, Inc., Raleigh

March 24, Statement on Job Network Program, Raleigh

March 24, Greeting to Volunteers, Wilkesboro†

March 24, Business Session, Governor's Business Council on the Arts and Humanities, Wilkesboro

March 24, Award Presentation Banquet, Governor's Business Council on the Arts and Humanities, Wilkesboro

March 26, Governor's Conservation Achievement Awards Banquet, Raleigh

March 27, Billy Graham Parkway Dedication, Charlotte

March 28, Conference on Issues Shaping Public Education, East Carolina University, Greenville

March 28, Water Treatment Plant Dedication, Greenville

March 28, Order of the Golden Fleece Initiation Ceremony, University of North Carolina at Chapel Hill

March 29, Presentation of Frank Turner Award, State Building Construction Conference, Raleigh

March 30, Durham City Schools Reception, Durham

March 30, Retired School Personnel, Durham

March 30, Durham Chamber of Commerce Business and Education Conference, Durham*

March 31, Unveiling, "Mystery of the *Carroll A. Deering*," Cape Hatteras Lighthouse Campaign, Raleigh

March 31, North Carolina Fellows Program of the University of North Carolina at Chapel Hill, Raleigh

April 5, Business Preview and Luncheon, North Carolina Museum of Art, Raleigh

April 5, North Carolina Cable Television Association, Raleigh

---

*Referred to in headnote
†No press copy

April 6, Statement at News Conference, Raleigh†
April 11, Nash-Edgecombe Day Greetings, Raleigh
April 12, Halifax Day, Halifax
April 12, Northampton County Board of Education
    Administrative Building Ribbon Cutting, Jackson
April 12, Town Hall Restoration Dedication, Jackson
April 12, Charlotte Apparel-Related Shows Association,
    Charlotte
April 13, Statement on Mathematics Assessment, National
    Assessment of Educational Progress, Washington, D.C.
April 14, Workshop on Developing the Biotechnology
    Component of Engineering, Raleigh
April 14, Statement at News Conference, Raleigh†
April 14, North Carolina Museum of History Associates,
    Raleigh
April 14, North Carolina Retired School Personnel Association,
    Raleigh
April 15, J. C. Holliday Memorial Library Dedication, Clinton
April 15, Visit to Currituck County Schools, Coinjock
April 15, T. G. Joyner Highway Dedication, Hyde County
April 15, Northeastern Democratic Rally, Nags Head*
April 18, Verbatim Corp. Dedication, Charlotte
April 18, Eastern Correctional Center Dedication, Maury*
April 19, Raleigh Chamber of Commerce Leadership Institute,
    Raleigh
April 19, North Carolina Fellows Program of North Carolina
    A&T State University, Raleigh
April 19, Statement Proclaiming "Premium Bright Week,"
    Raleigh
April 20, North Carolina State University School of Veterinary
    Medicine Dedication, Raleigh
April 22, North Carolina National Guard Association,
    Greensboro
April 22, Roger L. Stevens Center Dedication, Winston-Salem
April 23, Jefferson-Jackson Dinner, Raleigh
April 24, American Association of Community and Junior
    Colleges, New Orleans, Louisiana
April 26, North Carolina Association of Distributive Education
    Clubs, Winston-Salem
April 26, Outboard Marine Corp. Announcement, Spruce Pine*
April 26, North Carolina Public Service Award Society
    Banquet, Raleigh
April 28, Statement on Education, Raleigh

---

*Referred to in headnote
†No press copy

April 28, Lumberton-Robeson County Chamber of Commerce, Raleigh

April 28, North Carolina Chapter, International Association of Personnel in Employment Security, Raleigh

April 29, Freshman Legislators Breakfast, Raleigh†

April 29, Statement on Pepsi-Cola's Eighty-fifth Anniversary, New Bern

April 29, Pepsi-Cola Anniversary Celebration Party, New Bern

April 30, Falls-of-the-Neuse Lake Project Dedication, Raleigh

April 30, Rotary International District 767, Asheville

April 30, Learning Resource Center Dedication, Southwestern Technical College, Sylva

May 2, Myrtle Wreath Award Acceptance Speech, Hadassah Southern Seaboard Region Spring Conference, Raleigh

May 6, Business Session and Closing Remarks, Education Commission of the States, Raleigh†

May 6, Lower Muddy Creek Waste Water Treatment Plant Groundbreaking, Clemmons

May 6, Unveiling of Winning Sculpture, Winston-Salem State University

May 6, Forsyth County Democratic Party Reception, Winston-Salem

May 9, Chapel Hill Chamber of Commerce, Chapel Hill

May 10, Conference on Changing Roles of Women in North Carolina, Raleigh*

May 10, North Carolina 2000 Hearing, Raleigh

May 10, Frank Holder Dance Company Tenth Anniversary, Greensboro

May 11, Governor's Conference on North Carolina Justice-Treatment Interface Project, Raleigh

May 11, Reliance Electric Dedication, Shelby

May 11, Teledyne Allvac Dedication, Monroe

May 11, Industrial Day for Burlington Industries, Dunn

May 11, Wake County Public Schools Education Foundation Banquet, Raleigh

May 12, "Save the Lighthouse" Promotion, Raleigh

May 13, Statement on Education Needs, Raleigh

May 15, Western Carolina University Commencement Address, Cullowhee

May 16, National Alcoholic Beverage Control Association, Miami, Florida

May 17, North Carolina Community College System Twentieth Anniversary, Raleigh

---

*Referred to in headnote
†No press copy

May 18, State Goals and Policy Board, Raleigh†
May 18, Dobbs School Open House, Kinston
May 18, Onslow Senior Center Dedication, Jacksonville
May 18, North Carolina Mental Health Association Tribute to
    Jim Hunt, Raleigh
May 19, Statement on Governor's Award for Excellence,
    Raleigh
May 19, National Transportation Week/Bicentennial Year of
    Flight Proclamation, Raleigh
May 19, State Employees Appreciation Awards Luncheon,
    Raleigh
May 19, North Carolina Close Up, Raleigh
May 19, Young Volunteers in Action Program, Raleigh
May 19, Council of Presidents of Youth Organizations, Raleigh*
May 20, North Carolina Bar Association, Raleigh
May 20, Industries of the Blind Fiftieth Anniversary,
    Greensboro
May 21, Campbell Soup Co. Dedication, Maxton
May 23, North Carolina Association of Volunteer
    Administrators, Winston-Salem
May 24, Statement on North Carolina Humanities Committee,
    Raleigh
May 24, Regional Forum, Governor's Task Force on Science and
    Technology, Wilmington
May 24, Greater Wilmington Chamber of Commerce Tribute to
    Garland Garrett, Wilmington
May 25, Statement on Industrial Growth, Raleigh
May 25, North Carolina Alliance for Public Education, Raleigh
May 25, Franklin County Courthouse Square Improvements
    Dedication, Louisburg
May 25, One-on-One Initiative in Franklin County, Louisburg†
May 26, North Carolina Close Up, Raleigh
May 27, Flue-Cured Tobacco Cooperative Stabilization Corp.,
    Raleigh*
May 27, Gala Dinner Honoring Billy Ray Cameron, Sanford†
May 28, Reception Honoring Solon Smart, Cliffside
May 28, *Stroker Ace* World Premiere, Charlotte†
June 1, State Government Summer Interns Welcome, Raleigh
June 1, Swearing-in of State Board of Agriculture, Raleigh
June 2, Statement at News Conference, Raleigh†
June 2, Springmoor Life Care Retirement Community Ribbon
    Cutting, Raleigh

---

*Referred to in headnote
†No press copy

June 3, North Carolina 2000 Public Hearing, Asheville
June 7, Industrial Engineering and Technologies Building
  Dedication, Durham Technical Institute
June 7, Wilson County Leadership Conference, Raleigh*
June 9, Carl Horn, Jr., Retirement Breakfast, Raleigh
June 9, Statement on Alcohol Law Enforcement, Raleigh
June 9, Job Training Coordinating Council, Raleigh
June 10, Pan American Airlines Announcement, Raleigh-
  Durham Airport, Wake County
June 10, Memorial Hospital of Alamance County Ancillary
  Services Wing Dedication, Burlington
June 10, North Carolina School of Science and Mathematics
  Threshold Campaign Victory Dinner, Durham
June 13, NCNB Management Awareness Series, Charlotte
June 13, University Memorial Hospital Groundbreaking,
  Charlotte
June 13, Hanes Wood-Fired Boiler Dedication, Morganton
June 13, Statement Announcing Establishment of Equipment
  Resource Center at University of North Carolina at Asheville,
  and Organization of North Carolina International Folk
  Festival, Asheville
June 13, Western North Carolina Regional Forum on Science
  and Technology, Asheville
June 14, Funeral Directors and Morticians Association of North
  Carolina, Inc., Raleigh
June 15, Carolina Power and Light Co. Mayo Plant Dedication,
  Roxboro
June 16, Statement on Resignation of Commerce Secretary
  Duncan M. "Lauch" Faircloth, Raleigh
June 16, North Carolina Public Manager Program, Raleigh*
June 16, Sales and Marketing Executives Club of Durham, Inc.,
  Durham
June 17, Senior Democrats Mini-Conference, Raleigh
June 17, American Legion Convention, Charlotte
June 21, Raleigh Chapter, National Association of Women in
  Construction, Raleigh†
June 21, GTE Engineering Center Announcement [Research
  Triangle Park], Raleigh*
June 21, North Carolina Industrial Developers Association,
  Wrightsville Beach
June 22, Statement on Task Force on Education for Economic
  Growth, Washington, D.C.*

---

*Referred to in headnote
†No press copy

June 23, Statement on Education, Raleigh*

June 23, Swearing-in of David L. Matthews as Highway Patrol
 Commander, Raleigh

June 23, Sumitomo Electric Industries Announcement
 [Research Triangle Park], Raleigh*

June 24, Swearing-in of C. C. Hope, Jr., as Commerce Secretary,
 Raleigh

July 5, Luncheon for British Ambassador Sir Oliver Wright,
 Research Triangle Park

July 6, Transatlantic Telephone Remarks to British Corporate
 Executives, Raleigh

July 7, Statement at News Conference, Raleigh†

July 9, Democratic Party State Executive Committee Meeting,
 Raleigh

July 12, Disposable Breath Analyzers Announcement, Raleigh

July 13, Bendix Automation Announcement, Bessemer City†

July 13, Bendix Automation Southeast Regional Center
 Announcement, Charlotte

July 14, Mitsubishi Semiconductor America, Inc.,
 Announcement [Durham County], Raleigh

July 18, Northern Telecom Expansion Announcement,
 Research Triangle Park

July 20, "Education for High-Technology Economy," Education
 Commission of the States, Denver, Colorado*

July 22, Presentation of James Bryant Conant Award to
 Congressman Carl Perkins, Education Commission of the
 States, Denver, Colorado

July 28, Statement on Microlectronics Facilities Recruiting,
 Raleigh*

July 28, Caldwell County Chamber of Commerce, Lenoir

July 28, I-26 Welcome Center Dedication, Polk County

July 28, Opportunity House Dedication, Hendersonville

July 29, NCAE Leadership Conference, Mars Hill*

July 29, Hot Springs Clinic Dedication, Hot Springs

July 30, Tenth Annual National Open Cribbage Tournament,
 Raleigh

July 31, Statement on Education Commission of the States
 Task Force on Education for Economic Growth, Portland,
 Maine*

August 3, Diversified Fuels, Inc., Announcement [Selma],
 Raleigh

August 3, Governor's Executive Cabinet on Juvenile Affairs,
 Raleigh†

August 3, American Honda Motor Co. Announcement
[Swepsonville], Raleigh

August 15, Eastern North Carolina Conference for the
Protection of the Family, Kinston*

August 16, Rocky Mount Bypass Dedication, Rocky Mount

August 16, General Cable Co. Dedication, Kenly

August 16, Wesley Long Community Hospital Expansion
Groundbreaking, Greensboro

August 17, Ciba-Geigy Announcement [Research Triangle
Park], Raleigh

August 17, Southern Regional Education Board Legislative
Workshop, Asheville*

August 24, Carolina Billets Dedication, Ahoskie

August 25, Statement at News Conference, Raleigh†

August 25, Cliff Benson Beltline Dedication, Raleigh

September 16, Induction of Earl B. Garrett into North Carolina
Agricultural Hall of Fame, Raleigh

September 19, Statement on Federal Aid Request on Behalf of
Drought-Stricken Farmers, Raleigh

September 20, Schools of Excellence Program, Raleigh

September 20, Volunteer Recognition Ceremony, Raleigh

September 22, Kickoff, North Carolina Museum of History
Campaign, Raleigh

September 23, North Carolina State Employees Association
Convention, Greensboro

September 23, Installation of Bruce Poulton as North Carolina
State University Chancellor, Raleigh

September 30, Statement on Safe Roads Act, Raleigh

September 30, New York Air Expansion Announcement,
Raleigh-Durham Airport, Wake County

September 30, Luncheon for Japanese Ambassador Yoshio
Okawara, Greenville

September 30, Tom Bradshaw Freeway Dedication, Raleigh

September 30, North Carolina Council on the Status of Women,
Raleigh

October 1, First Congressional District Black Leadership
Caucus, Elizabeth City

October 3, Greensboro Chapter, National Conference of
Christians and Jews, Greensboro

October 5, Prince Hall Grand Lodge Awards Banquet, Raleigh

October 6, Statement on *Brainstorm*, Raleigh

October 6, *Brainstorm* Premiere, Raleigh

---

*Referred to in headnote
†No press copy

October 7, North Carolina Association for Education of Young
Children, Winston-Salem
October 7, Howard Hawkins Wing Dedication, Eastern
Carolina Vocational Center, Greenville
October 8, Democratic Party Chairs and Co-Chairs Workshop,
Raleigh†
October 8, Hechinger Co. Ribbon Cutting and Log Sawing,
Durham
October 11, North Carolina Restaurant Association, Raleigh
October 11, State Computer Commission, Raleigh
October 11, Firetrol, Inc., Dedication, Cary
October 11, Asplundh Manufacturing Division Announcement,
Butner
October 12, Meeting of University of North Carolina and Duke
University Medical School Faculty Members, Chapel Hill
October 14, North Carolina State Fair Opening, Raleigh
October 14, North Carolina State Fair Vocational Education
Exhibit Opening, Raleigh
October 15, Governor's Bike-Along 1983 Kickoff, Raleigh
October 15, Welcome NASA Astronaut Dr. William Thornton,
Faison†
October 16, Senate Campaign Reception, Chapel Hill*
October 17, Involvement Council Chairpersons, Raleigh
October 17, Swearing-in of Hubert M. Leonard as Adjutant
General, Raleigh
October 17, North Carolina Association of Broadcasters,
Raleigh†
October 18, Statement at News Conference, Raleigh†
October 18, Awards Ceremony, Business Committee for
Mathematics and Science Education, Raleigh
October 18, Recognition Ceremony, Governor's Business
Awards in Mathematics and Science Education, Raleigh
October 18, Johnston County Baptist Association, Smithfield
October 19, State Goals and Policy Board Teleconference,
Raleigh†
October 19, du Pont Co. Announcement [Research Triangle
Park], Raleigh*
October 19, Governor's Economic Development Conference,
Raleigh
October 20, North Carolina Mutual Life Insurance Co. Eighty-
fifth Anniversary, Durham
October 21, North Carolina State Bar Association Fiftieth
Anniversary, Raleigh

---

*Referred to in headnote
†No press copy

October 22, Fall Southern Furniture Market, Hickory
October 22, Governor's Statewide Volunteer Awards, Asheville
October 22, Vance-Aycock Dinner, Asheville†
October 24, North Carolina Nurses Association, Raleigh
October 24, North Carolina Home Builders Association,
  Greensboro
October 25, Charlotte Downtown Rotary Club, Charlotte*
October 25, U.S. 521-James K. Polk Memorial Highway
  Dedication, Pineville
October 25, Greater Charlotte Chamber of Commerce,
  Charlotte†
October 25, Textile Olympics, Belmont*
October 25, Reception for Harvey Gantt, Charlotte†
October 26, Community Food Bank of North Carolina,
  Raleigh†
October 26, American Council on Education, Commission on
  Higher Education and the Adult Learner, Raleigh*
October 26, Blue Cross and Blue Shield of North Carolina
  Fiftieth Anniversary, Chapel Hill
October 27, Triangle J Council of Governments Horizons
  Unlimited Conference, Research Triangle Park*
October 27, New York Times Co. North Carolina Prize
  Presentation, Figure Eight Island
October 31, Governor's Conference on Women and the
  Economy, Raleigh*
October 31, Statement on Economic Growth, Asheville*
October 31, North Carolina League of Municipalities Seventy-
  fifth Anniversary Convention, Asheville*
November 1, North Carolina Travel Council Award Acceptance
  Speech, Chapel Hill
November 1, Charles B. Aycock Birthday Celebration, Fremont
November 1, Volunteer Recognition Ceremony, Williamston
November 2, Statement on Withdrawal of Water from Lake
  Gaston by Virginia Beach, and on Governor's Task Force on
  Science and Technology, Raleigh
November 2, Veterans' Employment Representatives
  Conference, Raleigh
November 3, Cumberland County Public Library Victory
  Celebration, Fayetteville
November 3, North Carolina Association of Colleges and
  Universities, Fayetteville
November 3, North Carolina Awards Dinner, Raleigh

---

*Referred to in headnote
†No press copy

November 4, Inauguration of Dr. Thomas K. Hearn as Wake
  Forest University President, Winston-Salem
November 4, Falcon Children's Home Annual Banquet, Falcon
November 5, University of North Carolina Board of Trustees,
  Chapel Hill†
November 7, Youth Involvement Day Breakfast, Raleigh
November 7, Launching of North Carolina Agricultural
  Extension Service "People's Plan," Raleigh
November 9, Statement at Interkama Trade Fair, Düsseldorf,
  West Germany*
November 14, Meeting of British Automotive Executives,
  London, England*
November 16, Induction of Dr. James Ralph Scales into
  Oklahoma Hall of Fame, Oklahoma City, Oklahoma
November 18, Tobacco Day, U.S.A., and Tobacco Growers'
  Association of North Carolina, Raleigh*
November 18, North Carolinians against Drug and Alcohol
  Abuse, Raleigh
November 21, North Carolina Motor Carriers' Association Safe
  Driver Award Presentation, Raleigh†
November 23, Statement on North Carolina Commission on
  Education for Economic Growth, Raleigh*
November 28, Regional Hearing, North Carolina Commission
  on Education for Economic Growth, Raleigh
November 29, Governor's Interagency Small Woodlot
  Committee Forum, Raleigh
December 1, Chase Brass and Copper Co. Announcement
  [Shelby], Raleigh
December 1, North Carolina Association for Home Care, Inc.,
  Raleigh
December 2, Statement on Establishment of Model Small Farm,
  North Carolina A&T State University, Winston-Salem
December 5, Catawba College Founders Day Convocation,
  Salisbury
December 5, Spencer Shops State Historic Site, Salisbury†
December 5, Rowan County Beautification Rally, Salisbury†
December 6, Regency Park Corp. Dedication, Cary
December 7, North Carolina State University Integrated
  Manufacturing Systems Institute, Raleigh
December 9, Statement on Impaired Driving, Raleigh
December 13, R. J. Reynolds Whitaker Park Facility Visit,
  Winston-Salem†
December 13, Winston-Salem Rotary Club, Winston-Salem*

---

*Referred to in headnote
†No press copy

December 13, State Christmas Tree Lighting Ceremony,
Raleigh†
December 14, State Computer Commission, Raleigh*
December 15, Regional Hearing, North Carolina Commission
on Education for Economic Growth, Asheville*
December 16, National Guard Thirtieth Infantry Brigade
Briefing, Raleigh†
December 21, Joe Grimsley Appreciation Night, Raleigh
December 22, Statement at News Conference, Raleigh†

1984

January 3, Council of State, Raleigh†
January 3, State Computer Commission, Raleigh
January 3, Swearing-in of James A. Summers as Natural
Resources and Community Development Secretary, Raleigh
January 3, Presentation of "Bicentennial Year of Methodism"
Proclamation, Raleigh
January 5, Statement on Economic Growth, Raleigh
January 5, Regional Hearing, North Carolina Commission on
Education for Economic Growth, Greenville*
January 6, Advisory Panel, North Carolina Commission on
Education for Economic Growth, Raleigh
January 7, New College Hall Dedication, Mount Olive College
January 9, Statement on Education Needs, Charlotte
January 10, Underwriters' Laboratories, Inc., Announcement
[Research Triangle Park], Raleigh
January 10, I-85 Dedication, Thomasville
January 10, Thomasville Furniture Industries, Thomasville
January 10, Surry County Public Health Building Dedication,
Dobson
January 10, Mount Airy Chamber of Commerce, Mount Airy*
January 12, Statement on James Hutchins, Raleigh
January 12, Mayor Bill Cox Appreciation Dinner, Hertford
January 16, Jim Hunt Dinner, Smithfield†
January 17, North Carolina Commission on Education for
Economic Growth, Winston-Salem
January 17, Statement on North Carolina School of the Arts,
Winston-Salem
January 19, Statement at News Conference, Raleigh†
January 19, State Goals and Policy Board, Raleigh
January 19, Tabor City Chamber of Commerce, Tabor City*

*Referred to in headnote
†No press copy

January 24, Conference on International Education, Raleigh
January 24, Women's Apparel Market, Carolina-Virginia
    Fashion Exhibitors, Charlotte
January 25, Greater Winston-Salem Chamber of Commerce,
    Winston-Salem†
January 26, Statement on Travel and Tourism, Raleigh*
January 26, Local Government Advocacy Council, Raleigh
January 28, "Leadership in the Successor Generation,"
    Jacksonville State University Centennial Symposium,
    Anniston, Alabama
January 30, Student Leaders Reception, Raleigh
January 30, Park Communications, Inc., Raleigh†
January 31, Advisory Panel, North Carolina Commission on
    Education for Economic Growth, Raleigh
January 31, Mitsubishi Semiconductor America, Inc.,
    Groundbreaking, Durham
January 31, Ahoskie Chamber of Commerce, Ahoskie*
February 1, Southern Farm Show, Raleigh*
February 2, Statement at News Conference, Raleigh†
February 4, Official Announcement for U.S. Senate, Wilson†
February 6, Formal Filing for U.S. Senate, State Board of
    Elections, Raleigh†
February 8, Statement at News Conference, Charlotte†
February 9, Statement at News Conference, Greenville†
February 9, Southeastern Speech and Hearing Services of
    North Carolina, Inc., Dedication, Fayetteville
February 10, Owens-Illinois, Inc., Announcement [Warren
    County], Raleigh
February 11, North Carolina Democratic Party Sustaining
    Fund Patrons, Raleigh†
February 11, North Carolina Association of Educators Winter
    Conference, Raleigh
February 13, Statement at News Conference, Wilmington†
February 14, Facet Enterprises Announcement, Greensboro
February 15, North Carolina State Government Employees-
    WRAL-Winn Dixie Model Health Fair, Raleigh
February 15, Statement at Democratic Headquarters, Raleigh†
February 16, Governor's Award of Excellence Presentation,
    Governor's Waste Management Board, Raleigh
February 16, Wilkes County Public Schools Education Fund
    Kickoff, Wilkesboro
February 17, Annual Farm Press, Radio, and TV Institute,
    North Carolina Farm Writers and Broadcasters Association,
    Raleigh†

*Referred to in headnote
†No press copy

February 18, Southeastern Livestock Market Dedication, Chadbourn

February 20, Executive Cabinet Awards for Management Excellence, Raleigh

February 21, Statement at News Conference, Asheville†

February 21, Economic Development Conference, Asheville*

February 23, Statement on Social Security Disability Benefits, Raleigh*

February 23, Swiss Bear, Inc., New Bern

February 24, North Carolina Democratic Club, Washington, D.C.*

March 1, Local Economic Development Conference, Raleigh*

March 2, Statement at News Conference, Raleigh†

March 3, Statement at Jim Hunt Headquarters, Charlotte†

March 3, Formal Opening, Jim Hunt Headquarters, Charlotte†

March 3, Young Democrats of North Carolina, Charlotte†

March 8, Awards Presentation, Governor's Business Council on the Arts and Humanities, Raleigh

March 9, Statement at News Conference, Elizabeth City†

March 9, Northeastern North Carolina Tomorrow, Elizabeth City

March 12, Southern Life Center Announcement, Greensboro

March 13, North Carolina Conference on Delinquency Prevention and Governor's Executive Cabinet on Juveniles, Raleigh

March 14, Statement at News Conference, Raleigh†

March 14, NCSEA/NCSGEA Membership Kickoff, Raleigh

March 14, Introduction of George Weissman, North Carolina Citizens for Business and Industry, Raleigh

March 15, Statement on James Hutchins, Raleigh*

March 15, Farm Bureau Women's Leadership Conference, Raleigh*

March 15, North Carolina Association of Electric Cooperatives, Raleigh

March 16, Indian Unity Conference, Raleigh

March 19, Union Carbide Groundbreaking, Cary

March 19, Union Carbide Luncheon, Cary

March 20, Local Economic Development Conference, Charlotte*

March 20, "Celebrate America Day," Kings Mountain Senior High School

March 20, Kings Mountain Bypass Dedication, Kings Mountain

March 22, Local Economic Development Conference, Hickory*

---

*Referred to in headnote
†No press copy

March 23, Statement at News Conference, Raleigh†
March 23, North Carolina Student Legislature, Raleigh
March 23, Swearing-in of Mary Mac Pope as Special Superior Court Judge, Raleigh†
March 23, Distinguished Women of North Carolina Awards, Raleigh
March 26, Memorial Service for Charlie Smith, Raleigh
March 26, Hardware Association of the Carolinas, Charlotte†
March 27, Local Economic Development Conference, Winston-Salem*
March 29, Local Economic Development Conference, Wilson*
March 30, Close Up Program, Canton†
March 30, Western North Carolina Development Association, Asheville
March 30, Statement at News Conference, Asheville†
March 31, United Methodist Men Annual Prayer Breakfast, Asheville
April 3, Phi Kappa Phi Symposium, East Carolina University, Greenville†
April 5, Statement on Education, Raleigh*
April 5, North Carolina Commission on Education for Economic Growth, Raleigh*
April 5, United Church Ministries of Wayne County, Goldsboro†
April 6, Owens-Illinois, Inc., Groundbreaking, Warren County
April 9, State Board of Community Colleges, Raleigh
April 9, Manteo Waterfront Redevelopment Section Groundbreaking, Manteo
April 9, Governor's Conference on Travel and Tourism, Nags Head*
April 10, Local Economic Development Conference, Jacksonville*
April 10, Groundbreaking, Harper Corp. of America, Charlotte
April 13, Statement at News Conference, Winston-Salem†
April 13, North Carolina National Guard Association, Winston-Salem*
April 13, Keep America/North Carolina Beautiful, Raleigh
April 14, Inauguration of James Hemby as President of Atlantic Christian College, Wilson
April 17, Announcement, Screening, Four Hundredth Anniversary Minutes, Raleigh
April 18, Chapel Hill High School Humanities Festival, Chapel Hill

---

*Referred to in headnote
†No press copy

April 19, Statement at News Conference, Charlotte†

April 24, Governor's Task Force on Drugs and Alcohol in the
Schools, Raleigh

April 25, Statement at News Conference, Raleigh†

April 26, Larkbeare House Dinner, Exeter, England

April 27, Council House Luncheon, Plymouth, England

April 27, Civic Reception, Plymouth, England

April 28, Raleigh Dinner at Buckland Abbey, Plymouth,
England

May 1, Briefing, North Carolina Commission on Education for
Economic Growth, Charlotte

May 2, Statement at News Conference, Raleigh†

May 2, Briefing, North Carolina Commission on Education for
Economic Growth, Smithfield

May 4, Briefing, North Carolina Commission on Education for
Economic Growth, Asheville

May 4, Greenhouse Dedication and Extension Center
Groundbreaking, Mountain Horticultural Research Station,
Fletcher

May 4, Avery County Senior Citizen Center Dedication,
Newland

May 4, Swearing-in of Special Superior Court Judge Charles C.
Lamm, Jr., Boone†

May 7, Department of Human Resources Volunteer Awards,
Raleigh

May 9, Lutravil Sales Co. Dedication, Durham

May 9, North Carolina District Council, Assemblies of God,
Inc., Southern Pines†

May 9, North Carolina Federation of Chapters, National
Association of Retired Federal Employees, Raleigh

May 10, Statement at News Conference, Raleigh†

May 10, Nonpublic Education Advisory Committee, Raleigh†

May 10, Small Business Awards Luncheon, Raleigh

May 11, Briefing, North Carolina Commission on Education for
Economic Growth, Greensboro

May 11, Fuji Foods Corp. Dedication, Greensboro

May 11, Kimberly-Clark Corp. Announcement, Lexington

May 11, South Brunswick Islands Chamber of Commerce,
Bolivia

May 14, Industrial Announcement, Raleigh†

May 14, Governor's Award for Fitness and Health in Business
and Industry, Raleigh

May 16, Statement at Democratic Headquarters, Raleigh†

---

*Referred to in headnote
†No press copy

May 16, Public Works Exhibit Opening, North Carolina
Museum of History, Raleigh
May 21, Department of Commerce Economic Development
Seminar, Asheville
May 21, Wang Laboratories, Inc., Announcement, Asheville
May 21, "Women Mean Business" Program Recognition,
Asheville†
May 22, Government-Industry Communications Exhibition
Opening, Fort Bragg
May 23, Economic Club of New York, New York City
May 30, Statement at News Conference, Raleigh†
May 30, Statement at News Conference, Greensboro†
May 31, Semiconductor Research Corp. and Semiconductor
Industry Association, Research Triangle Park
May 31, Statement at News Conference, Asheville†
May 31, Statement at News Conference, Charlotte†
June 1, Semicon, Inc., Announcement, Woodland
June 1, Welcome to State Government Interns, Raleigh
June 2, Third District Democratic Convention, Mount Olive†
June 3, British-American Festival, Durham
June 4, Soundolier Division Announcement, Laurinburg
June 4, Tribute to Bishop John Hurst Adams, Greensboro*
June 6, Governor's Blue-Ribbon Committee on Training
Schools, Raleigh
June 6, Onslow County Volunteer Awards, Jacksonville
June 6, Statement at News Conference, Jacksonville†
June 7, Statement at News Conference, Raleigh†
June 7, Hillsborough Old Town Cemetery Restoration
Celebration, Hillsborough
June 9, Roy A. Taylor Forest Dedication, Nantahala National
Forest, Haywood County
June 11, Cape Hatteras School Commencement Address,
Buxton
June 12, Microelectronics Center of North Carolina Dedication,
Research Triangle Park*
June 12, Elizabethtown-White Lake Chamber of Commerce,
Elizabethtown*
June 13, State Future Farmers of America Convention,
Raleigh†
June 14, Statement at Democratic Headquarters, Raleigh†
June 14, Carolinas Council on World Affairs, Charlotte†
June 15, Great Smoky Mountains National Park Fiftieth
Anniversary, Newfound Gap

*Referred to in headnote
†No press copy

June 15, North Carolina Federation of Business and
Professional Women's Clubs, Asheville*
June 16, State Democratic Convention Unity Breakfast,
Raleigh†
June 18, State Computer Commission, Raleigh
June 18, Book Preview, *North Carolina: Reflections of 400
Years*, Raleigh
June 19, Vance County Industrial Announcement [Eastern
Block, Inc.; Harper Prints, Inc.; Durham Drapery Co.;
Parkway Homes Co.; and one unnamed], Henderson
June 20, Salute to State Employees, Raleigh†
June 21, Statement at Democratic Headquarters, Raleigh†
June 23, Veterans of Foreign Wars, Charlotte†
June 25, North Carolina Chapter, National Association of
Postmasters of the United States, Raleigh
June 25, Tribute to William R. Roberson, Jr., Washington
June 25, Donnelly Marketing Dedication, Washington
June 28, Statement at Democratic Headquarters, Raleigh†
June 30, Disabled Veterans of America, Charlotte†
July 4, Fourth of July Celebration, Faith†
July 5, Statement at Democratic Headquarters, Raleigh†
July 10, BASF-Wyandotte Corp. Groundbreaking, Research
Triangle Park
July 10, Carolina Air Parcel Service, Inc., Groundbreaking,
Greensboro-High Point-Winston-Salem Regional Airport,
Guilford County
July 13, Cora Mae Daniels Basnight Bridge Dedication,
Manteo
July 13, America's Four Hundredth Anniversary Celebration,
Remarks No. 1 and No. 2, Manteo
July 25, Dynamit Nobel AG Announcement [Durham County],
Raleigh
July 26, Northern Telecom Dedication, Research Triangle Park
August 1, Kendall Complex [Employment Security
Commission] Dedication, Raleigh
August 3, Acceptance of James Bryant Conant Award,
Education Commission of the States, St. Paul, Minnesota
August 11, North Carolina Association of County
Commissioners, Asheville
August 24, North Carolina Poultry Federation, Raleigh†
September 8, North Carolina Grange Mutual Insurance Co.
Fiftieth Anniversary, Greensboro†
September 13, South Charlotte Street Dedication, Asheville†

---

*Referred to in headnote
†No press copy

September 13, U.S. 19-East Dedication, Burnsville†
September 13, Governor's 1984 Statewide Volunteer Awards
    Ceremony, Asheville†
September 14, Watauga Prison Chapel Dedication, Boone†
·September 16, Welcome for Bishop Carlton P. Minnick, Jr.,
    Raleigh
September 17, Hockmeyer Equipment Co. Dedication, Elizabeth
    City
September 24, Youth Involvement Day, Raleigh†
September 24, "Excellence in Education" Flag Raising,
    Needham B. Broughton High School, Raleigh†
September 24, Presentation of Ronnie Milsap Record, Cape
    Hatteras Lighthouse Benefit, Raleigh†
September 25, Merck, Sharp, and Dohme Dedication, Wilson
September 25, Governor's 1984 Statewide Volunteer Awards
    Ceremony, Williamston
September 26, Awards Ceremony, Governor's Program of
    Excellence in Education, Raleigh
September 28, Ciba-Geigy Biotechnology Research Unit
    Dedication, Research Triangle Park
September 28, State Employees of North Carolina Annual
    Convention, Winston-Salem
September 29, North Carolina Agribusiness Council Awards
    Presentation, Raleigh
October 2, Governor's 1984 Statewide Volunteer Awards
    Ceremony, Raleigh
October 3, Takeda Chemical Industries, Ltd., Ceremonial
    Groundbreaking, Wilmington
October 3, Statement on Interstate 40, Duplin County*
October 9, Wesley D. Webster Highway Dedication, Madison
October 9, Mayor's Council for the Employment of the
    Handicapped, Greensboro
October 12, University Day Convocation, University of North
    Carolina at Chapel Hill†
October 17, American Honda Dedication, Swepsonville
November 19, Executive Cabinet Awards for Management
    Excellence, Raleigh
November 19, Business Session, North Carolina Business
    Committee for Math-Science Education, Charlotte
November 19, Awards Banquet, North Carolina Business
    Committee for Math-Science Education, Charlotte
November 29, Acceptance of 1984 National 4-H Alumni Award,
    National 4-H Congress, Chicago, Illinois

---

*Referred to in headnote
†No press copy

November 30, One Hundredth Anniversary Celebration, Law
  Firm of Parker, Poe, Thompson, Bernstein, Gage, and
  Preston, Charlotte†
December 3, North Carolina Farm Bureau Convention,
  Winston-Salem*
December 3, Greetings, "Operation Raleigh," Raleigh†
December 4, Acceptance of North Carolina Association for
  Community Education Distinguished Service Award, Raleigh
December 5, Groundbreaking, North Carolina Museum of
  History, Raleigh
December 6, Nathan Yelton Portrait Unveiling, Raleigh
December 6, United Way-State Employees Combined
  Campaign, Raleigh
December 7, State Computer Commission, Raleigh†
December 7, North Carolina Vietnam Veterans Memorial
  Groundbreaking, Raleigh
December 10, Wildlife Endowment Fund Award Presentation,
  Raleigh
December 10, Involvement Council and Citizen Help
  Representatives, Raleigh
December 12, Capitol Christmas Tree Lighting Ceremony,
  Raleigh†
December 14, Statement at News Conference, Raleigh†
December 19, I-40 Dedication, Rocky Point†
December 20, U.S. 74 Bypass Dedication, Laurinburg
December 21, Magder Studios Announcement, Yanceyville

1985

January 2, State Board of Education, Raleigh†
January 2, Swearing-in of North Carolina Supreme Court
  Judge Earl Vaughn, Raleigh†
January 5, Introduction of Governor-Elect James G. Martin,
  Inaugural Ceremonies, Raleigh†
January 5, Passing of Great Seal of North Carolina, Raleigh†

*Referred to in headnote
†No press copy

EXECUTIVE ORDERS

[Governor Hunt issued fifty-four executive orders during his second term in office. Although space limitations prohibit the inclusion of each of these items in their entirety in this documentary, a listing of titles has been provided below. The complete texts of Hunt's executive orders, promulgated during the period from 1981 to 1985, are located as follows: numbers 60 through 73, *Session Laws of North Carolina, 1981*, 1735-1792; numbers 74 through 82, *Session Laws of North Carolina, 1981, Regular and Extra Sessions, 1982*, 329-356; numbers 83 through 98, *Session Laws of North Carolina, 1983*, 1397-1450; and numbers 99 through 114, *Session Laws of North Carolina, 1983, Regular and Extra Sessions, 1984*, 439-482.]

1981

Executive Order Number 60, Executive Memorandum to Regulatory Agencies, January 28

Executive Order Number 61, creation of the Governor's Study Commission on the Length of Sentences in North Carolina, March 20

Executive Order Number 62, creation of the North Carolina Management Program, March 25

Executive Order Number 63, establishment of the North Carolina Council on the Holocaust, April 29

Executive Order Number 64, creation of the Capital Area Visitor Services Committee, May 12

Executive Order Number 65, establishment of the County Transportation Efficiency Councils, May 21

Executive Order Number 66, establishment of the Commission on the Future of North Carolina, June 1

Executive Order Number 67, extension of Executive Order Number 54 authorizing the Advisory Council to the Governor's Office of Citizen Affairs through December 31, 1981, July 1

Executive Order Number 68, creation of the Highway Contract Oversight Commission, July 2

Executive Order Number 69, establishment of the North Carolina Ferry System Study Commission, July 3

Executive Order Number 70, amendment to Executive Order Number 53 creating the Governor's Commission for Recognition of State Employees, September 4

Executive Order Number 71, extension of the Judicial Nominating Committee for Superior Court Judges as created by Executive Order Number 12, amended by Executive Order Numbers 24, 30, and 52, until June 30, 1982, September 9

Executive Order Number 72, designation of the role of the

1983

Executive Order Number 89, creation of a new Advisory Committee for the North Carolina Public Manager Program to supersede Executive Order Number 32, January 11

Executive Order Number 90, revision of the membership of the Governor's Executive Cabinet on Juveniles created by Executive Order Number 63 and amended by Executive Order 76, January 11

Executive Order Number 91, creation of a new North Carolina Health Coordinating Council to supersede Executive Order Number 19 [Holshouser], February 28

Executive Order Number 92, direction to the secretary of crime control and public safety to enforce compliance with the federal law providing for twin trailers and the width of motor vehicles, April 1

Executive Order Number 93, systematization and coordination of the state job training policy, June 8

Executive Order Number 94, termination of the North Carolina Energy Institute created by Executive Order Number 17, and the Governor's Study Commission on Energy Loans created by Executive Order Number 57, June 10

Executive Order Number 95, creation of the Executive Cabinet Awards for Management Excellence, July 1

Executive Order Number 96, Conservation of Prime Agricultural and Forest Lands, August 23

Executive Order Number 97, directs the secretary of the Department of Human Resources to place a moratorium on terminating Social Security disability benefits, except in cases of fraud, September 7

Executive Order Number 98, creation of the Commission on Education for Economic Growth, October 13

Executive Order Number 99, certification of the office of Legal Counsel to the Governor as the agency to assist the chief executive in fulfilling his duties in clemency and extradition, November 1

1984

Executive Order Number 100, creation of the Advisory Council to the Friendship Force of North Carolina, January 3

Executive Order Number 101, declaration of State Affirmative Action Policy, February 13

Executive Order Number 102, proclamation that vehicles transporting emergency disaster relief supplies are permitted to carry the maximum weights as provided in N.C.G.S. 20-118, notwithstanding the load limit prescribed by the vehicle license, April 3

Executive Order Number 103, creation of the Special Advisory Committee for Improving Management in State Government, April 9

Executive Order Number 104, establishment of the Governor's Task Force on Alcohol and Drug Abuse among Youth and Teenagers, April 10

Executive Order Number 105, designation of the Department of Administration as the lead agency for the North Carolina Environmental Policy Act, May 7

Executive Order Number 106, creation of the North Carolina Women's Economic Development Advisory Council, May 10

Executive Order Number 107, creation of the Task Force on Missing Children, May 14

Executive Order Number 108, amendment of Executive Order Number 79 for the extension of the Judicial Nominating Committee for Superior Court Judges, June 28

Executive Order Number 109, creation of a new Board of Trustees of the North Carolina Public Employee Deferred Compensation Plan to supersede Executive Order Number 12 [Holshouser], July 31

Executive Order Number 110, proclamation of a private activity bond limit for Sampson County and the Sampson County Industrial Facilities and Pollution Control Financing Authority, September 4

Executive Order Number 111, establishment of the Planning Committee for the Center for the Advancement of Teaching, October 15

Executive Order Number 112, establishment of the North Carolina Missing Children's Information Center within the Department of Crime Control and Public Safety, October 25

Executive Order Number 113, proclamation on Industrial Development Bonds, October 30

Executive Order Number 114, creation of the State Commission on Child Support, November 30

APPOINTMENTS

Compiled by Rose P. Ennemoser, Trudy M. Rayfield, and Stephena K. Williams

[State law empowers the governor to appoint numerous persons to various advisory bodies, boards, commissions, and councils. This section lists the names of most of the appointees Hunt designated during his two terms as North Carolina's chief executive. Those included in the following roster appear under the heading of the board on which they served; the boards, in turn, are arranged either by the department of state government in which they functioned or under a general heading, as in the case of groups not directly affiliated with agencies of the executive branch. Departmental listings are presented first; next come judicial and related appointments, trustees of constituent institutions of the University of North Carolina system, independent commissions and miscellaneous statutory bodies, and licensing and examining boards.

The names and terms of office of Executive Cabinet secretaries whom Hunt appointed follow the appropriate department heading. Those elected to their posts, and therefore omitted from the ensuing listing, are James B. Hunt, Jr., governor; James C. Green, lieutenant governor; Thad Eure, secretary of state; Edward Renfrow, state auditor; Harlan E. Boyles, state treasurer; A. Craig Phillips, superintendent of public instruction; Rufus L. Edmisten, attorney general; James A. Graham, agriculture commissioner; John C. Brooks, labor commissioner; and John R. Ingram, insurance commissioner. The president of the Department of Community Colleges is not a member of the Executive Cabinet.

Position holders whose selection, according to state law, lay beyond the sole appointive powers of the governor were excluded from this section. Specifically, these consist of ex-officio board members and persons who either were recommended, nominated, or elected by a particular professional or special interest group and served with the governor's confirmation. Finally, in an attempt to conserve limited space, membership of nonstatutory bodies has not been provided herein; however, a listing of nonstatutory boards to which Hunt made appointments appears at the end of this section.

The information included in this section was derived from computer printouts generated and periodically updated by the Office of the Governor. The printouts, arranged by board, provide each appointee's position number, name, complete address, race, gender, a code indicating by whom he or she was chosen, date of appointment and expiration of term, county of residence, and, in many instances, a telephone number. Boards themselves are assigned code numbers, and most commission entries feature membership criteria and a general statute reference.

From the aforementioned types of data the compilers included, for each board contained in this section, the title, statutory reference, and code number of the commission; and the position number, name, post office, and dates of appointment and expiration of term of members listed thereunder. Entries lacking expiration dates indicate that either the individual served at the pleasure of the governor or that the information was missing from the printout; also, where no date of appointment was provided, none appears in this section. Readers are urged to consult the General Statutes for guidelines detailing the length of a board member's term of office as well as an explanation of a particular commission's purpose and composition.

Every effort was made, in compiling this list, to ensure its accuracy. Where the computerized rosters contained discrepancies in spelling or other information, the entry from the latest was employed. Regrettably, it must be noted that, in an undertaking of this magnitude, the potential for error and omission exists. The compilers monitored as many as fifteen computer-generated lists for each of the boards to which Governor Hunt assigned persons during his two terms in office; consider, also, that the printout for June, 1984, alone contained nearly 4,000 appointments, and the threat to precision becomes apparent. Furthermore, there is a chance that individual appointments, or even the membership of entire commissions, were never entered into the electronic record. Sincere apologies are extended to those persons who served their state but whose names do not appear in this section, for whatever reason.]

OFFICE OF THE GOVERNOR

NORTH CAROLINA HOUSING COMMISSION
G.S. 147-33.13 through -33.17/Board No. 0433

Position No.	Name of Appointee	Address	Date Appointed	Date of Expiration
01	Durwood Stephenson, *chairman*	Smithfield	10-11-83	06-30-86
02	James B. Garrison	Albemarle	10-11-83	06-30-85
03	David Weil	Goldsboro	10-11-83	06-30-85
04	Betty C. Rash	Charlotte	10-11-83	06-30-86
05	Wade Thomas	Asheville	10-11-83	06-30-86

NORTH CAROLINA HOUSING FINANCE AGENCY BOARD OF DIRECTORS
G.S. 122A-4/Board No. 0435

01	James K. Haley	Winston-Salem	08-10-78	06-12-82
			10-13-82	06-30-86
02	Sherrill H. Faw	North Wilkesboro	08-10-78	06-12-82
			10-13-82	06-30-86
	Eva M. Clayton	Littleton	08-03-84	06-30-86
03	George E. Carr, Jr.	Greensboro	02-07-78	06-12-81
			11-30-81	06-30-85
04	Robert D. Brown, *vice-chairman*	Gastonia	02-07-78	06-12-81
			11-30-81	06-30-85

COMMISSION TO STUDY THE HOUSING PROGRAMS IN NORTH CAROLINA
N.C. Session Laws, 1981, c. 950/Board No. 0436

01	Wade H. Thomas, Sr.	Asheville	09-30-81	02-01-83
02	Michael A. Stegman	Chapel Hill	09-30-81	02-01-83
03	Robert E. Harrington	Lewiston	09-30-81	02-01-83
04	David Weil	Goldsboro	09-30-81	02-01-83
05	William Breeze	Rougemont	09-30-81	02-01-83
06	Leslie J. Winner	Charlotte	09-30-81	02-01-83

LOCAL GOVERNMENT ADVOCACY COUNCIL
G.S. 143-506.14/Board No. 0543

05	Fred F. Bahnson, Jr.	Winston-Salem	04-26-78	04-19-80
			07-01-80	04-15-82
06, 05	Miriam P. Block	Raleigh	04-26-78	04-19-80
			07-30-82	04-19-84
			12-20-84	04-19-86
06	Aaron E. Fussell	Raleigh	07-01-80	04-15-82
			07-30-82	04-19-84
	Zander Guy	Jacksonville	12-21-84	04-19-86
07	George W. Dudley	Rocky Mount	04-26-78	04-19-80
			07-01-80	04-15-82
	Webster Lytle	Hickory	08-12-82	04-19-84
	Gwendolyn Burton	Wilson	05-15-84	04-19-86

NORTH CAROLINA BOARD FOR NEED-BASED MEDICAL STUDENT LOANS
G.S. 143-47.23/Board No. 0639

01	William J. Edwards	Stokes	08-11-82	07-01-86
	Ben Ruffin	Durham	12-31-84	07-01-86

NORTH CAROLINA BOARD FOR NEED-BASED MEDICAL STUDENT LOANS
(CONTINUED)

Position No.	Name of Appointee	Address	Date Appointed	Date of Expiration
02	Judy M. Stephenson	Garner	08-11-82	07-01-86
03	Billy O. Wireman	Charlotte	09-21-82	07-01-86

BOARD OF TRUSTEES OF THE TEACHERS' AND STATE EMPLOYEES' COMPREHENSIVE MAJOR MEDICAL PLAN
G.S. 135-39/Board No. 0554

01	Ray Sparrow, *chairman*	Raleigh	08-26-82	06-30-84
	Sam R. Noble	Lumberton	10-18-84	06-30-87
02	Maylon E. Little	Raleigh	08-26-82	06-30-84
			08-17-84	06-30-86
03	Donald Patterson	Chapel Hill	08-26-82	06-30-83
				06-30-85

NORTH CAROLINA TECHNOLOGICAL DEVELOPMENT AUTHORITY
G.S. 143B-471/Board No. 0891

01	Charles Cain, *chairman*	Greenville	10-31-83	07-01-87
02	Plato Pearson	Gastonia	12-19-83	07-01-87
03	Alexander Greenfield	Greensboro	11-07-83	07-01-87
04	William Veeder	Charlotte	10-31-83	07-10-87
05	Charles T. Byrd	Greensboro	10-31-83	07-01-87
06	P. S. Prasad	Greenville	10-31-83	07-01-87
07	E. Bruce Beasley	Raleigh	10-31-83	07-01-87
08	Jean D. O'Neal	Wilmington	10-31-83	07-01-87

DEPARTMENT OF STATE AUDITOR

BOARD OF TRUSTEES OF THE NORTH CAROLINA FIREMEN'S AND RESCUE SQUAD WORKERS' PENSION FUND[1]
G.S. 118-19/Board No. 0370

01	John P. Sykes	Rocky Mount	09-12-77	06-30-79
			12-03-79	06-30-83
	Bobby Joyner	Farmville	06-07-83	06-30-87
02	Carroll W. Hemphill	Marion	09-21-79	06-30-83
				07-01-87
03	Howard A. Shaw	Goldsboro	01-01-82	06-30-85
03, 04	Horace L. Browning, Sr.	Greensboro	12-03-79	06-30-83
				07-01-87

BOARD OF COMMISSIONERS OF THE LAW ENFORCEMENT OFFICERS BENEFIT AND RETIREMENT FUND
G.S. 143-166/Board No. 0530

01	Milford C. Hubbard	Brevard	04-19-77	
02	Conrad D. Wade	Greensboro	04-19-77	
03	Carl Gilchrist	Greenville	04-19-77	
04	Eugene F. Groce	Winston-Salem	04-19-77	
05	O. H. Leak	High Point	10-23-79	

---

1 Board formerly known as Board of Trustees of the North Carolina Firemen's Pension Fund. See *N.C. Session Laws, 1981*, c. 1029, ratified October 10, 1981, and G.S. 118-34.

DEPARTMENT OF STATE TREASURER

LOCAL GOVERNMENT COMMISSION
G.S. 159-3/Board No. 0540

Position No.	Name of Appointee	Address	Date Appointed	Date of Expiration
01	L. R. Morgan	New Bern	12-15-77	06-30-81
	Frederick E. Turnage	Rocky Mount	09-02-81	06-30-85
02	Gordon S. Myers	Asheville	12-15-77	06-30-81
			11-30-81	06-30-85
	Charles H. Mercer, Jr.	Raleigh	05-15-84	06-30-85
05	W. Raleigh Carver	Elizabeth City	12-15-77	06-30-81
			11-30-81	06-30-85
	James A. Weathers	Louisburg	06-22-84	06-30-85

LOCAL GOVERNMENT EMPLOYEES RETIREMENT SYSTEM BOARD OF TRUSTEES
G.S. 128-21, through -38/Board No. 0545

01	T. Bruce Boyette	Wilson	03-20-81	04-01-84
	Thomas Z. Osborne	Greensboro	05-12-82	04-05-85
	William H. Batchelor	Rocky Mount	06-22-84	04-05-85
02	Samuel M. Gattis	Hillsborough	04-09-81	04-05-85
	John S. Bone, Jr.	Manteo	10-16-81	04-05-84
	James N. Ziglar, Jr.	Winston-Salem	03-27-84	04-05-88

MUNICIPAL BOARD OF CONTROL[2]
G.S. 160A-6/Board No. 0610

01	Jones Norman	Eden	04-05-78	
02	James W. Cash	Clayton	03-26-81	

TAX REVIEW BOARD
G.S. 105-269.2/Board No. 0883

01	Thomas N. Brafford	Raleigh	02-12-80	06-30-83

TEACHERS' AND STATE EMPLOYEES' RETIREMENT SYSTEM BOARD OF TRUSTEES
G.S. 135-1 through -18.5/Board No. 0890

01	Lucius M. Cheshire	Hillsborough	08-22-78	04-05-80
	William C. Covington	Charlotte	07-20-81	04-04-84
	Sam Noble	Lumberton	12-31-84	04-01-88
02	T. Clyde Auman	West End	07-20-81	04-05-84
	V. Glenn Morton	Albemarle	03-17-83	04-05-84
			04-04-84	04-05-88
03	Linda Rader	Gastonia	06-28-79	04-05-83
				04-05-87
04, 06	Floyd J. Bass	Raleigh	05-20-77	04-05-79
			06-28-79	04-05-83
04	Horace Jernigan	Raleigh	10-19-79	04-05-83
				04-05-87
05	John P. Booker, Jr.	Raleigh	06-28-79	04-05-83
	Daniel W. Jones	Raleigh	04-15-83	04-05-87

2 G.S. 160A-6 through G.S. 160A-10 were repealed by *N.C. Session Laws, 1981, Second Session, 1982*, c. 1191, s. 63, ratified June 17, 1982, and became effective the following October 1.

TEACHERS' AND STATE EMPLOYEES' RETIREMENT SYSTEM BOARD OF TRUSTEES
(CONTINUED)

Position No.	Name of Appointee	Address	Date Appointed	Date of Expiration
06	Seddon Goode, Jr.	Charlotte	07-01-77	07-01-81
	R. Eugene Ballard	Lumberton	02-17-81	07-01-84
	Eugene M. White	Hudson	07-01-84	07-01-88
07	Minnie M. Brown	Raleigh	07-01-77	07-01-81
	Colleen C. Jakes	Cullowhee	06-16-82	07-01-85
08	Miss Ezra A. Bridges	Shelby	07-01-77	07-01-81
			04-13-82	07-01-85
11	Withers Davis	Garner	07-01-77	07-01-81
			04-06-82	07-01-85

DEPARTMENT OF PUBLIC EDUCATION

STATE BOARD OF EDUCATION
G.S. 115C-10/Board No. 0305

01	C. R. Edwards	Fayetteville	04-07-77	04-01-79
			06-07-79	04-01-87
	Elmer V. Wilkins	Roper	01-01-83	04-01-87
02	H. David Bruton, *chairman*	Carthage	05-04-77	04-01-85
	Mebane M. Pritchett	Chapel Hill	04-05-83	04-01-85
02, 09	C. D. Spangler, Jr.	Charlotte	08-12-82	04-01-85
				04-01-91
03	Prezell R. Robinson	Raleigh	05-07-81	04-01-89
04	John A. Pritchett	Windsor	06-07-79	04-01-87
	Betty S. Speir	Bethel	06-09-82	04-01-87
05	John L. Tart	Smithfield	05-04-77	04-01-85
06	Norma Turnage	Rocky Mount	09-06-79	04-01-83
				04-01-91
07	James B. Chavis	Pembroke	05-07-81	04-01-89
08	Barbara M. Tapscott	Burlington	05-07-81	04-01-89
10	Theda A. Moore	North Wilkesboro	06-07-79	04-01-87
11	Ben H. Battle	Cullowhee	05-04-77	04-01-85

COMMISSION ON CHILDREN WITH SPECIAL NEEDS
G.S. 120-58/Board No. 0197

01	Claudia H. Brinkley	Enfield	11-01-77	06-30-79
			10-05-81	06-30-83
			10-17-83	07-01-85
02	Calvin C. Davis	Charlotte	11-01-77	06-30-79
	Penny Tuttle	Lexington	10-05-81	06-30-83
			10-17-83	07-01-85
03	Carey S. Fendley	Raleigh	11-01-77	06-30-79
	Jeanne Fenner	Wilson	11-11-81	06-30-83
	Mary R. Bostick	Charlotte	11-18-83	06-30-85
10	Jane Luddington	Chapel Hill	11-18-83	06-30-85

COMPETENCY TEST COMMISSION
G.S. 115C-176/Board No. 0217

01	James J. Gallagher, *chairman*	Chapel Hill	08-10-77	07-01-81
	James Hemby	Wilson	07-01-81	06-30-85
02	Verna E. Bergemann	Weaverville	08-10-77	07-01-81
			07-01-81	06-30-85

COMPETENCY TEST COMMISSION (CONTINUED)

Position No.	Name of Appointee	Address	Date Appointed	Date of Expiration
03	Marian M. Boggs	Asheville	08-10-77	07-01-81
	Richard Warner	Greenville	07-01-81	06-30-85
	Florence H. Warren	Candler	09-25-84	06-30-85
04	Geraldine B. Deans	Wilson	08-10-77	07-01-81
			07-01-81	06-30-85
	Barbara K. Tillman	High Point	03-31-82	06-30-85
05	Charlotte R. Hampton	Charlotte	08-10-77	07-01-81
			07-01-81	06-30-85
	David Green	Durham	10-09-84	06-30-85
06	Andrew Haywood	Charlotte	08-10-77	07-01-81
	Sam Haywood	Charlotte	07-01-81	06-30-85
07	Mary G. Horton	Edenton	08-10-77	07-01-81
	George Welsh	Chapel Hill	07-01-81	06-30-85
08	Lenwood Padgett	Jacksonville	08-10-77	07-01-81
			07-01-81	06-30-85
09	Larry J. Poore	Chocowinity	08-10-77	07-01-81
	Phyllis Dunning	Winston-Salem	07-01-81	06-30-85
10	Judith L. Rochelle	Kinston	08-10-77	07-01-81
			07-01-81	06-30-85
11	Sam O. Jones	Greensboro	05-22-78	07-01-81
			07-01-81	06-30-85
12	Joseph W. Talley	Roanoke Rapids	08-10-77	07-01-81
	Vincent J. Colombo	Shelby	10-25-78	07-01-81
	Jay Robinson	Charlotte	10-25-78	07-01-81
			07-01-81	06-30-85
	Zane Eargle	Winston-Salem	08-16-84	06-30-85
13	Barbara M. Tapscott, *chairwoman*	Burlington	08-10-77	07-01-81
	Mary A. Chapin	Washington	07-01-81	06-30-85
14	Bert Westbrook	Raleigh	08-10-77	07-01-81
			07-01-81	06-30-85
15	Betty H. Pierce	Miller's Creek	08-10-77	07-01-81
	Roy Maynor	Pembroke	07-01-81	06-30-85
16	Julie C. Chiu	Charlotte	10-20-82	06-30-85
17	Leslie B. Troy	Chapel Hill	10-20-82	06-30-85

EDUCATION COMMISSION OF THE STATES
G.S. 115C-104/Board No. 0320

01	Marion D. Thorpe	Elizabeth City	06-09-77	
	E. K. Fretwell, Jr.	Charlotte	06-09-83	
02	H. David Bruton	Carthage	06-09-77	
	C. D. Spangler, Jr.	Charlotte	11-15-82	04-01-85
	Betty Owen	Cary	12-27-84	
03	Margaret R. Sanford	Durham	06-09-77	
	Frances M. Cummings	Lumberton	06-09-83	
	Cecil Banks	Raleigh	12-31-84	
04	A. Craig Phillips	Raleigh	06-09-77	

NORTH CAROLINA EDUCATION COUNCIL
G.S. 115C-105/Board No. 0323

01	Cameron West	Misenheimer	05-30-78	05-30-81
02	Craven Williams	Boiling Springs	05-30-78	05-30-81

NORTH CAROLINA EDUCATION COUNCIL (CONTINUED)

Position No.	Name of Appointee	Address	Date Appointed	Date of Expiration
03	Ruth Watkins	Rockingham	05-30-78	05-30-81
04	Kenneth R. Newbold	Greensboro	05-30-78	05-30-81
05	Patricia R. Keever	Asheville	05-30-78	05-30-81

COUNCIL ON EDUCATIONAL SERVICES FOR EXCEPTIONAL CHILDREN
G.S. 115C-121/Board No. 0327

01	R. McPhail Herring, Jr.	Clinton	07-07-78	06-30-80
			08-07-80	06-30-82
			07-07-82	06-30-84
			05-31-84	06-30-86
04	Benjamin D. Schwartz	Wilmington	08-07-80	06-30-82
	Barbara J. Stone	Lumberton	07-08-82	06-30-84
			05-31-84	06-30-86

PERSONNEL ADMINISTRATION COMMISSION FOR PUBLIC SCHOOL EMPLOYEES
G.S. 115C-328/Board No. 0681

01	Brooks M. Whitehurst	Aurora	12-02-80	08-30-81
			10-20-81	08-30-84
	Johnsie S. Perkins	Robersonville	10-20-81	08-30-84
	Jimmie D. Williams	Williamston	10-07-82	08-30-85
02, 07	Bonnie L. Rhodes................	Wilkesboro	12-02-80	08-30-81
			10-20-81	08-30-84
03	Jerilyn J. Lee.....................	Mt. Olive	12-02-80	08-30-81
03, 04	James I. Bolden	Durham	12-02-80	08-30-82
			10-07-82	08-30-85
	Michael P. Womble................	Sanford	10-20-81	08-30-82
			10-07-82	08-30-85
05	Don C. Cooper	Laurinburg	12-02-80	08-30-82
	Nancy M. Murray	Winston-Salem	09-13-83	08-30-86
06	Leonard R. Knox	Charlotte	12-02-80	08-30-82
	Judy W. Sellstrom	Charlotte	10-07-82	08-30-85
07, 08	Linda C. Winner	Asheville	12-02-80	08-30-83
			09-07-83	08-30-86
07	Ralph T. Steele.............	North Wilkesboro	10-08-82	08-30-84
	Ken Anderson	Newbold	08-26-83	08-30-84
08	Brank Proffitt	Burlington	12-02-80	08-30-83
09	Robert B. Lincks, *chairman*	Greensboro	12-02-80	08-30-83
			09-06-83	08-30-86

TESTING COMMISSION
G.S. 115C-191/Board No. 0042

01	J. Frank Yeager, *chairman*	Durham	07-01-77	07-01-79
	Edwin L. West, Jr., *chairman*	High Point	07-18-79	07-01-81
			07-01-81	06-30-83
	Johnny Presson	Shelby	11-07-83	06-30-85
02, 05	Jane P. Norwood	Boone	07-01-77	07-01-79
			07-18-79	07-01-81
			12-12-83	06-30-85
02	John McKnight	Greenville	07-01-81	06-30-83
			11-07-83	06-30-85

NORTH CAROLINA VOCATIONAL TEXTILE SCHOOL BOARD OF TRUSTEES
(CONTINUED)

Position No.	Name of Appointee	Address	Date Appointed	Date of Expiration
04	William D. Holt	Greensboro	06-01-78	07-01-79
			05-12-82	07-01-83
05	Lewis D. Davis	New Bern	11-19-79	07-01-83
	Chuck Hayes	Greensboro	12-20-84	06-30-87
06	Edward P. Schrum	Maiden	05-12-82	07-01-83
				07-01-87
07	John M. Harney, Jr.	Charlotte	06-01-78	07-01-81
			05-12-82	07-01-85
08	James H. Martin, Jr.	Gastonia	06-01-78	07-01-81
			05-12-82	07-01-85
09	Lewis S. Morris	Greensboro	06-01-78	07-01-81
	William O. Leonard, Jr.	Greensboro	06-30-82	07-01-85

DEPARTMENT OF JUSTICE

ALARM SYSTEMS LICENSING BOARD
G.S. 74D-4/Board No. 0025

01	Gregory D. Porter, *chairman*	Durham	12-28-83	10-01-86
	Jack Hill, *chairman*	Fayetteville	12-31-84	10-01-86
02	David W. Carter	Raleigh	09-28-83	10-01-86

NORTH CAROLINA CRIMINAL JUSTICE EDUCATION AND TRAINING STANDARDS COMMISSION
G.S. 17C-3/Board No. 0260

07	J. A. Faircloth, Jr.	High Point	01-18-80	07-01-83
			09-01-83	07-01-86
25	Clarence E. McLamb	Dunn	01-18-80	07-01-81
			11-11-81	07-01-84
			08-15-84	07-01-87

NORTH CAROLINA CRIMINAL JUSTICE EDUCATION AND TRAINING SYSTEM COUNCIL[3]
G.S. 17B-4/Board No. 0265

01	Dale P. Johnson	Clinton	09-28-77	09-01-78
				08-01-79
02	Ottis F. Jones	Fayetteville	11-30-77	09-01-78
				08-01-79
03	Ralph S. Knott	Louisburg	11-30-77	09-01-78
	Leon A. Lucas	Kenly	08-14-78	08-01-79
04	Joan J. Johnson	Benson	11-30-77	09-01-78
	Ronald G. Taylor	Elizabethtown	08-14-78	08-01-79
05	Delilah B. Blanks	Riegelwood	11-30-77	09-01-78
	Clarence E. McLamb	Dunn	08-14-78	08-01-79

---

3 G.S. 17B-1 through 17B-6 were rewritten in *N.C. Session Laws, 1979*, c. 763, s. 2, ratified June 4, 1979, and became effective on January 1, 1980. Chapter 17B was recodified as G.S. 17D-1 to 17D-4, under the heading "North Carolina Justice Academy."

CRIMINAL JUSTICE TRAINING AND STANDARDS COUNCIL[4]
G.S. 17A-3/Board No. 0270

Position No.	Name of Appointee	Address	Date Appointed	Date of Expiration
01	Jerry B. Grimes	Lexington	06-22-78	07-01-81
02	Donald M. Ellington	Pineville	08-01-77	07-01-80
14	Jack B. Lemons	Raleigh	06-28-78	07-01-79

GENERAL STATUTES COMMISSION
G.S. 164-14/Board No. 0400

01	William G. Smith	Wilmington	05-31-77	05-31-79
			05-09-79	05-31-81
			07-02-81	05-31-83
	James L. Nelson	Wilmington	08-15-83	05-31-85
02	Donald L. Weinhold, Jr.	Salisbury	05-31-77	05-31-79
			05-09-79	05-31-81
	Dale P. Johnson	Clinton	07-02-81	05-31-83
	Melvin L. Watt	Charlotte	08-25-83	05-31-85

PRIVATE PROTECTIVE SERVICES BOARD
G.S. 74C-4(b)/Board No. 0725

02	James Edwards	Hickory	09-21-77	06-30-81
08, 01	Albert Sorrells	Skyland	08-20-79	06-30-83

DEPARTMENT OF AGRICULTURE

BOARD OF AGRICULTURE
G.S. 106-2/Board No. 0010

01	Linwood P. Britton, Jr.	Ahoskie	07-06-77	05-04-81
	John L. Parker, Jr.	Colerain	07-15-81	05-04-83
				05-04-89
02	Benjamin D. Harrington	Raleigh	07-06-77	05-04-83
	L. Calvin Ross	Greensboro	05-20-83	04-04-87
03	Sam McLawhorn	Grifton	07-06-77	05-04-81
				05-04-83
				04-04-89
04	James L. Southerland, Jr.	Laurinburg	07-15-81	05-04-87
05	Vernon White	Winterville	07-15-81	05-04-87
	Larry B. Wooten	Currie	12-15-82	05-04-87
06	Wiley Shore	Yadkinville	07-15-81	05-04-87
07	John H. Canady	Richlands	06-06-79	05-04-85
08	James D. Speed	Louisburg	06-06-79	05-04-85
	Ronald V. Willard	High Point	12-15-82	05-04-85
09	John Guglielmi	North Wilkesboro	06-06-79	05-04-85
10	Evelyn M. Hill	Edneyville	06-06-79	05-04-85

---

4 G.S. 17A-1 through 17A-9 were rewritten in *N.C. Session Laws, 1979,* c. 763, s. 1, ratified June 4, 1979, and became effective on January 1, 1980. Chapter 17A was recodified as G.S. 17C-1 to 17C-12, under the heading "North Carolina Criminal Justice Education and Training Standards Commission."

NORTH CAROLINA AGRICULTURAL HALL OF FAME BOARD OF DIRECTORS
G.S. 106-568.14/Board No. 0015

Position No.	Name of Appointee	Address	Date Appointed	Date of Expiration
01, 09	A. W. Soloman	Raleigh	07-21-77	01-27-83
			02-22-83	01-27-89
02	Hill Carter	Ferguson	03-27-79	01-27-81
			03-10-81	01-27-87
03	Herbert L. Cameron	Yadkinville	12-12-79	01-27-85

GASOLINE AND OIL INSPECTION BOARD
G.S. 119-26/Board No. 0395

01	W. H. Kimball	Rocky Mount	09-12-77	
02	Randall H. Castleberry	Smithfield	09-12-77	
03	Archie M. Huggins	Laurel Hill	09-12-77	

ADVISORY COMMISSION FOR THE MUSEUM OF NATURAL HISTORY
G.S. 143-370/Board No. 0630

01	John D. Hobart	Smithfield	06-22-78	08-31-79
			02-13-84	08-31-85
02	O. W. Hooper, Jr.	Robbinsville	06-22-78	08-31-79
	Charles R. Pruden	Wilson	02-13-84	08-31-85
03	Arnold L. Daniels	Wanchese	06-22-78	08-31-79
	Lou Mitchell	Raleigh	02-13-84	08-31-85
04	Frank L. Reese	Taylorsville	06-22-78	08-31-79
05	James L. Dellinger, Jr.	King	06-22-78	08-31-79
06	Cornelia Graham	Linwood	06-22-78	08-31-79
07	Micou F. Browne	Raleigh	06-22-78	08-31-79
08	Kathryn Scotten	Siler City	06-22-78	08-31-79
09	Alda Jones	Nashville	06-22-78	08-31-79
10	Jack Faison	Seaboard	06-22-78	08-31-79
	Fred Lewis	Winston-Salem	03-06-84	08-31-85
11	Carey H. Bostian	Raleigh	11-02-78	08-31-79
	Danny Smith	Raleigh	03-13-83	08-31-85
12	James S. Lewis, Jr.	Goldsboro	11-02-78	08-31-79
13	Sue O. Fleetwood	Monroe	11-02-78	08-31-79
14	Wilma Woodard	Garner	12-04-78	08-31-79
15	William M. Wall	Raleigh	04-11-80	08-31-81

NORTH CAROLINA PESTICIDE BOARD
G.S. 143-436/Board No. 0685

01	Alfred S. Elder	Raleigh	09-12-77	07-01-81
	Melvin H. Hearn	Raleigh	09-18-81	07-01-85
02	Marshall Staton	Raleigh	09-12-77	07-01-81
	Tom Gilmore	Raleigh	07-18-80	07-01-81
	Ronald H. Levine	Raleigh	12-07-81	07-01-85
03, 05	H. A. Smith	Raleigh	09-12-77	07-01-81
			07-19-79	07-01-83
				07-01-87
03	Walton Jones	Raleigh	04-24-79	07-01-81
	James A. Summers	Raleigh	09-18-81	07-01-85
04	Morris L. McGough	Asheville	07-19-79	07-01-83
				07-01-87

NORTH CAROLINA PESTICIDE BOARD (CONTINUED)

Position No.	Name of Appointee	Address	Date Appointed	Date of Expiration
06	Leon G. Ballance .... Engelhard		07-19-79	07-01-83
				07-01-87
07	R. Earl Ogle, Sr. .... Raleigh		07-19-79	07-01-83
				07-01-87

NORTH CAROLINA PLANT CONSERVATION BOARD
G.S. 106-202.14/Board No. 0703

01	C. Ritchie Bell .... Chapel Hill		01-24-80	09-30-81
			05-17-82	09-30-85
02	James H. Horton .... Cullowhee		01-24-80	09-30-83
			06-29-84	09-30-87
03	Ralph C. Winkworth .... Raleigh		01-24-80	09-30-83
	C. Robert Grady .... Raleigh		05-29-80	09-30-83
			06-28-84	09-30-87
04	Emily H. Allen .... Winston-Salem		01-24-80	09-30-81
			05-17-82	09-30-85

NORTH CAROLINA RURAL REHABILITATION CORPORATION BOARD OF DIRECTORS
G.S. 137-31.3/Board No. 0800

01	John L. Parker .... Colerain		11-29-78	11-19-81
	James O. Buchanan .... Raleigh		09-25-81	11-30-84
			11-20-84	11-30-87
02	W. Bryan Oliver .... Jefferson		11-01-77	11-19-80
	Herbert L. Cameron .... Yadkinville		06-18-80	11-19-80
			02-13-81	11-30-83
			01-17-84	11-30-86
03	James E. Boyette, Jr. .... Louisburg		11-01-77	11-19-80
			02-13-81	11-30-83
			01-12-84	11-30-86
04	Joe M. Williams .... Olin		12-05-79	11-30-82
				03-04-86
	Melvin Hearn .... Raleigh		12-20-84	11-30-86
05	James L. Patrick, *president* .... Grifton		12-05-79	11-30-82
				03-04-86

STRUCTURAL PEST CONTROL COMMITTEE
G.S. 106-65.23/Board No. 0875

01	L. Arnold Hamm, Sr. .... Wilson		06-19-78	06-30-82
	Randolph M. Wilson .... Winston-Salem		08-23-82	06-30-86
02	Ralph Killough .... Charlotte		09-28-77	06-30-81
	Eugene Lynn .... Raleigh		07-15-81	06-30-85

DEPARTMENT OF LABOR

SAFETY AND HEALTH REVIEW BOARD
G.S. 95-135/Board No. 0805

01	Dewey A. Houston .... Conover		04-10-80	08-01-81
			12-07-81	08-01-87

SAFETY AND HEALTH REVIEW BOARD (CONTINUED)

Position No.	Name of Appointee	Address	Date Appointed	Date of Expiration
02	Michael A. Swann, *chairman*	Raleigh	11-19-79	08-01-85
	David W. Erdman	Charlotte	12-01-82	08-01-85
03	Michael K. Curtis, *chairman*	Greensboro	11-30-77	08-01-83
			03-13-83	08-01-89

DEPARTMENT OF INSURANCE

INSURANCE ADVISORY BOARD
G.S. 58-27.1/Board No. 0470

01	John N. Hackney, Jr.	Wilson	04-24-78	09-01-81
				09-01-85
02	John N. Chatham	Durham	04-24-78	09-01-81
				09-01-85
03	V. Lane Wharton, Jr.	Raleigh	04-24-78	09-01-81
				09-01-85
04	George B. Cherry, Jr.	Raleigh	01-29-80	09-01-83
	J. B. Gibson, Jr.	High Point	05-27-83	09-01-83
			12-27-84	09-01-87
05	Johnny Miller	Mooresville	01-29-80	09-01-83
	Charlie Grady	Raleigh	12-31-84	09-01-87
06	Irving Joyner	Raleigh	01-29-80	09-01-83
	Vernice Benton	Raleigh	02-22-83	09-01-87

BUILDING CODE COUNCIL
G.S. 143-136/Board No. 0150

01	Sam T. Snowden, Jr.	Laurinburg	09-28-81	07-31-87
02	Keith R. Harrod	Raleigh	02-01-80	07-31-85
03	John R. Adams	Raleigh	09-28-81	07-31-87
04	W. H. Gardner, Jr.	Durham	02-01-80	07-31-85
05	R. Glenn Agnew	Charlotte	02-01-80	07-31-85
06	Kenneth T. Knight	Raleigh	12-15-77	07-31-83
	Lewis M. Dibble	Washington	05-15-84	07-31-90
07	S. Ray Moore	Cary	12-15-77	07-31-83
	Scott Harrower	Asheville	05-15-84	07-31-90
08	John C. Ray	Fayetteville	02-01-80	07-31-85
09	Ronald L. Mace	Raleigh	09-28-81	07-31-87
10	Ralph P. Cochrane	Charlotte	12-15-77	07-31-83
11	Ray F. Debruhl	Raleigh	11-18-81	07-31-87
12	Thomas C. Lemonds	Greensboro	08-07-80	07-31-85

NORTH CAROLINA CODE OFFICIALS QUALIFICATION BOARD
G.S. 143-151.9/Board No. 0208

01	Edward A. Wyatt, *chairman*	Greenville	04-18-78	07-01-78
				07-01-82
	William B. Coleman	Pittsboro	06-28-82	07-01-86
02	S. Tony Jordan	Raleigh	04-18-78	07-01-80
	Bob Drakeford	Carrboro	04-30-81	07-01-84
	Ethel T. Clark	Spring Lake	10-02-84	07-01-88
03	Ruby Ramsey	Teachey	04-18-78	07-01-79
	Ross Persinger	Ayden	08-03-84	07-01-87

NORTH CAROLINA CODE OFFICIALS QUALIFICATIONS BOARD
(CONTINUED)

Position No.	Name of Appointee	Address	Date Appointed	Date of Expiration
	Willie B. Hopkins	Zebulon	05-19-82	07-01-85
04	Joe R. Hudson	Monroe	04-18-78	07-01-78
				07-01-82
	Harry Ritchie.	Lincolnton	09-13-82	07-01-86
05	D. Leonard McDonald	Rockingham	04-18-78	07-01-81
	L. M. Brinkley	Ahoskie	05-19-82	07-01-85
06	Lee Ball.	Greenville	04-18-78	07-01-79
	Ray Stepp	Asheville	05-19-82	07-01-83
				08-30-87
07	Henry A. Melvin	Fayetteville	04-18-78	07-01-80
			05-19-82	07-01-84
			08-03-84	07-01-88

NORTH CAROLINA HEALTH INSURANCE ADVISORY BOARD
G.S. 58-262.2/Board No. 0415

Position No.	Name of Appointee	Address	Date Appointed	Date of Expiration
01	Thomas B. Woodworth	Fayetteville	04-26-78	09-15-81
	Betty Snelson	Asheville	10-26-81	09-15-85
02	Paul Ellison	Shelby	04-26-78	09-15-81
				09-15-85
03	J. K. Sherron	Raleigh		09-15-87
04	Alice Ballance	Windsor	04-26-78	09-15-81
				09-15-85
05	Robert M. Stevenson	Lumberton	12-09-82	09-15-83
			09-15-83	09-15-87

MANUFACTURED HOUSING BOARD
G.S. 143-143.10/Board No. 0550

Position No.	Name of Appointee	Address	Date Appointed	Date of Expiration
01	Ralph Johnston	Fayetteville	11-11-83	09-30-84
02	Wilbur K. Boltz	Rockwell	11-11-81	09-30-84
	Wallace J. Connor	Morehead City	10-15-82	09-30-84
	Randy Miller	Morehead City	12-31-84	09-30-87

DEPARTMENT OF ADMINISTRATION
Secretaries
Joseph W. Grimsley, 1977-1979, 1980-1981
Jane S. Patterson, 1979-1980 (acting), 1981-1985

NORTH CAROLINA CAPITAL BUILDING AUTHORITY
G.S. 129-40/Board No. 0170

Position No.	Name of Appointee	Address	Date Appointed	Date of Expiration
02, 03	Wilburn C. Calton	Raleigh	07-18-77	06-30-79
			02-02-79	06-30-81
			08-11-82	06-30-83
			08-05-83	07-01-85
03	Larry Shaw	Fayetteville	08-16-82	06-30-83
			08-05-83	07-01-85
	James K. Polk	Charlotte	10-31-84	07-01-85
04	Judy M. Massey.	Zebulon	07-18-77	06-30-79
04, 03	Judy M. Stephenson	Raleigh	02-02-79	06-30-81
11	Alexander Biggs	Rocky Mount	08-05-83	07-01-85

CHILD DAY-CARE LICENSING COMMISSION
G.S. 143B-376/Board No. 0195

Position No.	Name of Appointee	Address	Date Appointed	Date of Expiration
01	Vivian M. Combs	Mooresville	04-24-78	12-31-83
			01-24-84	12-31-89
03	Pearl H. Wesson	Shelby	02-27-81	12-31-86
05	Robert Thompson	Lumberton	04-24-78	12-31-83
			01-24-84	12-31-89
07	Lesterine B. Whitehead	Rocky Mount	04-24-78	12-31-83
			01-24-84	12-31-89
08	Deborah D. Killian	Waynesville	02-27-81	12-31-81
				12-31-86
09	Sammie Jacobs	Bolton	04-13-82	12-31-82
	Francis B. Fry	Lexington	01-24-84	12-31-88
09, 12	Carolyn Turner, *chairwoman*	Greensboro	04-24-78	12-31-83
			01-24-84	12-31-89
10	Carol Spruill	Raleigh	04-13-82	12-31-84
			12-14-84	12-31-87
10, 13	Sylvia B. Campbell	Elizabethtown	02-27-81	12-31-81
			03-16-82	12-31-84
11	Beverly J. Martin	Asheville	03-18-82	12-31-83
	Jackie T. Smith	High Point	05-25-84	12-31-88
13	Ronald M. Thompson	Morganton	01-04-85	12-31-87

GOVERNOR'S ADVOCACY COUNCIL ON CHILDREN AND YOUTH
G.S. 143B-415/Board No. 0200

01	Herbert Stout	Raleigh	11-02-81	06-30-82
			10-07-82	06-30-86
02	J. Iverson Riddle	Morganton	07-19-76	06-30-82
			10-07-82	06-30-86
03	Betty Hinson	Greensboro	02-28-78	06-30-81
			11-02-81	06-30-85
04	Elijah Peterson	Hoffman	10-04-78	06-30-82
			10-29-82	06-30-86
05	Linda M. Roberts	Gastonia	02-28-78	06-30-81
	Richard C. Brake	Gastonia	11-02-81	06-30-85
06	Annie B. Cherry	Monroe	02-28-78	06-30-81
			11-02-81	06-30-85
07	Tillie Willis	Winston-Salem	01-02-85	06-30-85
	Linda D. Garrou	Winston-Salem	02-28-78	06-30-81
			11-02-81	06-30-85
08	Thelma K. Zaytoun	Cary	02-28-78	06-30-81
			11-02-81	06-30-85
09	John W. Eley, Jr.	Ahoskie	10-04-78	06-30-82
	Curtis E. Holloman	Ahoskie	10-22-82	06-30-86
10	Mark Holt	Fayetteville	02-28-78	06-30-81
	Donald E. Clark, Jr.	Durham	11-02-81	06-30-85
	Sara E. Sell	Southport	09-10-82	06-30-85
	John R. Peacock	Fremont	10-07-82	06-30-86
11	Cynthia Tompkins	Reidsville	11-11-81	06-30-82
	Robyn Radford	Louisburg	10-04-78	07-01-82
12, 13	Leslie Anderson	Asheville	10-07-82	06-30-86
14	Eva Marie Davis	Robbinsville	09-09-83	06-30-85

GOVERNOR'S ADVOCACY COUNCIL ON CHILDREN AND YOUTH
(CONTINUED)

Position No.	Name of Appointee	Address	Date Appointed	Date of Expiration
16	Jean F. Thompson	Wake Forest	06-07-77	07-01-78
				06-30-82
17	Sherri D. Watson	Raleigh	02-28-78	06-30-81
	Hannah A. Davis.............	Winston-Salem	11-13-81	06-30-85

NORTH CAROLINA DRUG COMMISSION[5]
G.S. 143B-212/Board No. 0290

01	Stephanie B. Murray	Greensboro	06-30-77	06-30-79
	Stephanie M. Walker	Greensboro	02-25-80	06-30-81
04	James A. Greene, *chairman*	Boone	04-11-78	06-30-79
			02-25-80	06-30-81
15	Frank G. Hickman..............	Wilmington	04-11-78	06-30-79
			02-25-80	06-30-81
16	Robert R. Henley	Hope Mills	04-11-78	06-30-79
	Juliette Wilkerson	Marion	02-25-80	06-30-81
17	Wayne J. Hurder	Raleigh	04-11-78	06-30-79
			02-25-80	06-30-81
18	John L. Goforth	Asheville	04-11-78	06-30-79
	Charles W. Rhoden, Jr...............	Shelby	06-02-80	06-30-81
19	L. Lionel Kendrick	Greenville	04-11-78	06-30-79
			02-25-80	06-30-81
20	Martha Y. Martinat	Winston-Salem	04-11-78	06-30-79
			02-25-80	06-30-81
21	R. Keith Bulla	Greensboro	04-11-78	06-30-79
			02-25-80	06-30-81
22	Jane G. Avent	Rocky Mount	04-11-78	06-30-79
			02-25-80	06-30-81
23	C. N. Simmons....................	Parkton	04-11-78	06-30-79
	Robert C. Rickman...................	Arden	02-25-80	06-30-81

STATE GOALS AND POLICY BOARD
G.S. 143B-372/Board No. 0870

01	Willie M. Whitfield	Roper	07-21-77	03-13-79
				03-15-83
			01-17-84	03-15-87
	Helen Gamble	Chadbourn	09-21-84	03-15-87
02	James G. Babb, Jr.................	Charlotte	07-21-77	03-13-81
	Carolyn Coleman................	Greensboro	09-15-81	03-15-85
03	Cecil C. Brooks	Cullowhee	07-21-77	03-13-81
			09-15-81	03-15-85
04	John Snow.......................	Murphy	07-21-77	03-13-82
	Larry B. Leake...................	Asheville	07-19-78	04-13-81
			09-15-81	03-15-85
05	Joseph M. Parker	Ahoskie	09-28-77	03-13-81
			09-15-81	03-15-85

---

5 G.S. 143B-212 was repealed under *N.C. Session Laws, 1981*, c. 51, ratified February 26, 1981. The new legislation, which became effective July 1, 1981, merged the North Carolina Drug Commission with the North Carolina Commission for Mental Health and Mental Retardation Services, the Mental Health Advisory Council, and the Alcoholism Advisory Council, to form the Commission for Mental Health, Mental Retardation, and Substance Abuse Services.

STATE GOALS AND POLICY BOARD (CONTINUED)

Position No.	Name of Appointee	Address	Date Appointed	Date of Expiration
06	Ruth M. Meyer	Durham	07-21-77	08-13-81
			09-15-81	03-15-85
07	Wade H. Hargrove	Raleigh	07-21-77	03-13-82
	Morris Speizman	Charlotte	08-08-79	03-15-82
			10-07-82	03-15-86
08	Florence B. Bryant	Charlotte	07-21-77	03-13-79
	Virgil McBride	Winston-Salem	08-08-79	03-13-83
	Elizabeth Y. Whittington	Fayetteville	09-15-81	03-15-83
	E. K. Fretwell	Charlotte	10-17-83	10-25-87
09	Arthur Cassell, *vice-chairman*	Greensboro	07-21-77	03-13-81
	James L. Mebane	McLeansville	09-15-81	03-15-85
	Thelma Roundtree*	Raleigh	00-00-00	00-00-00
10	Martha Davis	Winston-Salem	07-21-77	03-13-82
	Parker B. Grantham	Beaufort	09-21-79	03-13-82
	Nancy Davis	Charlotte	06-08-81	03-13-82
			10-07-82	03-13-86
11	Jamima P. Demarcus	China Grove	07-21-77	03-13-79
				03-15-83
			01-17-84	03-15-87
12	J. Marse Grant, *vice-chairman*	Raleigh	07-21-77	03-13-81
	Harvey R. Durham	Boone	08-08-79	03-13-81
			09-15-81	03-15-85
13	Lawrence Graves	High Point		03-13-82
	Kenneth Dews*	Winterville	06-08-81	03-15-82
			10-17-82	03-15-86
14	Jacqueline W. Thompson	Lumberton	05-31-78	03-15-82
	Winifred J. Wood	Camden	10-07-82	03-15-86
15	John G. Medlin	Winston-Salem	07-21-77	03-13-81
	Roy Cooper III	Nashville	08-08-79	03-13-81
			09-15-81	03-15-85

HUMAN RELATIONS COUNCIL
G.S. 143B-392/Board No. 0440

01	Jean Bennett	Murphy	06-01-77	
02, 01	William Chestnut	Tabor City	06-01-77	
			08-24-84	06-30-87
03	Howard L. Davenport	Creswell	06-01-77	
03, 02	Annie C. Dickens	Wilson	08-02-79	
			08-21-84	06-30-86
04, 03	Jerry Drayton, *chairman*	Winston-Salem	06-01-77	
			08-21-84	06-30-88
05, 04	Betty E. Eddleman	Concord	06-01-77	
			08-24-84	06-30-88
06	Lois G. Ellis	Bakersville	06-01-77	
06, 05	Daniel L. Stallings, Jr.	New Bern	02-01-82	
			09-07-84	06-30-85
07	Al Emma	Raleigh	06-01-77	
07, 06	Dee Aycock	Charlotte	11-11-81	
08, 07	Carolyn Ennis	Smithfield	06-01-77	

*Order of succession as indicated on printout.

HUMAN RELATIONS COUNCIL (CONTINUED)

Position No.	Name of Appointee	Address	Date Appointed	Date of Expiration
09	Geneva B. Hamilton	Goldsboro	06-01-77	01-24-78
	Joseph C. George	New Bern	01-30-79	
	Sylvester F. Lane	Goldsboro	08-21-84	06-30-85
10, 09	Judy Gilbert	Lincolnton	06-01-77	
			08-24-84	06-30-88
11	Ruby H. Hancock	New Bern	06-01-77	03-06-78
11, 10	Almetta Armstrong	Candor	02-14-79	
			08-21-84	06-30-85
12, 11	Solomon Jenkins	Halifax	06-01-77	
13, 12	Grady Locklear	Lumberton	06-01-77	
			10-09-84	06-30-85
14	Michael H. McGee	Charlotte	06-01-77	
14, 13	Robert J. Bingham	Boone	08-04-81	
			08-21-84	06-30-87
15	Grover Mooneyham	Asheville	06-01-77	
	Norman Silver	High Point	08-27-81	
15, 14	Susan Green	Greensboro	05-12-82	
			08-21-84	06-30-87
16, 15	Carroll Pledger	Durham	06-01-77	
			08-21-84	06-30-86
17, 16	Otha L. Sherrill	Raleigh	11-01-77	
			09-07-84	06-30-86
18, 17	Bertha B. Todd	Wilmington	06-01-77	
19, 18	Lillian Williams	Gastonia	06-01-77	
			08-21-84	06-30-87
20, 19	Bill Young	Morganton	06-01-77	

COMMITTEE FOR REVIEW OF APPLICATIONS FOR INCENTIVE PAY FOR STATE EMPLOYEES
G.S. 126-64/Board No. 0458

01	Martha Wilburn	Pilot Mountain	11-01-77	

NORTH CAROLINA STATE INDIAN HOUSING AUTHORITY
G.S. 157-68/Board No. 0461

01	Truex V. Carter	Charlotte	09-13-78	
02	James A. Hardin	Hope Mills	09-13-78	
03	Barbara S. Hammonds	Chadbourn	09-13-78	
04	Jeanette M. Freeman	Fairmont	09-13-78	
05	Julius Locklear	Greensboro	09-13-78	

NORTH CAROLINA INTERNSHIP COUNCIL
G.S. 143B-418/Board No. 0480

04	Frank L. Eagles, *chairman*	Wilson	02-24-78	06-30-79
			02-22-80	06-30-81
	Charles E. Russell	Greenville	09-15-81	06-30-83
			01-31-84	06-30-85
05	Hope M. Brogden	Southern Pines	02-24-78	06-30-79
	Thomas T. Williams	Southern Pines	02-22-80	06-30-81
			09-15-81	06-30-83
	Edith S. Cahn	Kinston	03-20-84	06-30-85

NORTH CAROLINA INTERNSHIP COUNCIL (CONTINUED)

Position No.	Name of Appointee	Address	Date Appointed	Date of Expiration
06	Lafayette Parker	Winston-Salem	02-24-78	06-30-79
	Donald E. Ensley	Greenville	02-22-80	06-30-81
			09-15-81	06-30-83
				06-30-85
07	Juanita Locklear	Pembroke	02-24-78	06-30-79
	Esther Jacobs	Pembroke	02-22-80	06-30-81
	Bhag S. Sidhu	Winston-Salem	07-22-81	06-30-83
				06-30-85
08	Donald B. Hayman	Chapel Hill	02-24-78	06-30-79
			02-22-80	06-30-81
			09-15-81	06-30-83
				06-30-85
09	Steve W. Panyan	Charlotte	02-24-78	06-30-79
	Timothy D. Mead	Charlotte	02-22-80	06-30-81
	Arthea Reed	Asheville	09-15-81	06-30-83
				06-30-85
10	Bonnie Bain	Durham	02-24-78	06-30-79
	Cameron West	Misenheimer	11-07-78	06-30-79
			02-22-80	06-30-81
	James Olliver	Misenheimer	09-15-81	06-30-83
				06-30-85
11	Thomas E. Kee	Raleigh	02-24-78	06-30-79
			02-22-80	06-30-81
			09-15-81	06-30-83
				06-30-85
12	Robert W. Appleton, *chairman*	Wilmington	02-24-78	06-30-79
			02-22-80	06-30-81
			09-15-81	06-30-83
				06-30-85
13	Ozell K. Beatty	Salisbury	02-24-78	06-30-79
	Grady Nelson	Salisbury	08-19-78	06-30-79
			02-22-80	06-30-81
	Robert Walton	Charlotte	09-15-81	06-30-83
	Diane O. Jones	Pembroke	03-06-84	06-30-85
14	Marie Capel	Raleigh	04-03-78	06-30-79
			02-22-80	06-30-81
			09-15-81	06-30-83
	Karen B. Peeler	Raleigh	11-01-81	06-30-83
	Dorothy K. Preston	Raleigh	10-07-82	06-30-83
				06-30-85
15	Melba Pridgeon	Greensboro	02-24-78	06-30-79
	John R. Murphy III	Elon College	02-22-80	06-30-81
	Wanda Campbell	Clarkton	09-15-81	06-30-83
	Chattie Broadnax	Raleigh	01-25-83	06-30-83
				06-30-85
	Lillie Clinton	Raleigh	12-21-84	06-30-85
16	David Ervin	Raleigh	02-24-78	06-30-79
	Mark Mann	Cary	02-22-80	06-30-81
	Kevin S. Bartlett	Raleigh	09-15-81	06-30-83
				06-30-85
17	Diana H. Middleton	Boone	02-24-78	06-30-79
	Georgette Smith	Raleigh	02-22-80	06-30-81
	Karen Long	Rutherfordton	01-24-84	06-30-85

NORTH CAROLINA COUNCIL ON INTERSTATE COOPERATION
G.S. 143B-380/Board No. 0485

Position No.	Name of Appointee	Address	Date Appointed	Date of Expiration
01	Jack Cozort	Raleigh	02-13-78	06-30-79
			07-01-79	06-30-81
			08-31-81	06-30-83
			11-18-83	06-30-85
02	Paul Essex	Raleigh	02-13-78	06-30-79
			07-01-79	06-30-81
			08-31-81	06-30-83
			11-18-83	06-30-85
03	Arnold Zogry	Raleigh	02-13-78	06-30-79
			07-01-79	06-30-81
			08-31-81	06-30-83
	Pat Shore	Washington, D.C.	11-18-83	06-30-85

GOVERNOR'S JOBS FOR VETERANS COMMITTEE
G.S. 143B-420/Board No. 0927

Position No.	Name of Appointee	Address	Date Appointed
01	Eli Anderson, Jr.	Fayetteville	07-15-78
02	O. Tom Blanks	Lumberton	07-15-78
03	Sam N. Brown	Tarboro	07-15-78
04	George Cade	Fayetteville	07-15-78
05	Steve Carver	Dunn	07-15-78
06	William A. Coward	Kinston	07-15-78
07	James Delemar	New Bern	07-15-78
08	Hazel Edwards	Kinston	07-15-78
09	Alease S. Gum	Haw River	07-15-78
10	William S. Gwynn	Reidsville	07-15-78
11	Ben B. Halterman	Wilmington	07-15-78
12	William R. Haynes	Mount Airy	10-11-78
13	Isaiah H. Hilliard	Weldon	07-15-78
14	Nomie C. Hooker	King	07-15-78
	Lillie P. Crews	Graham	09-27-80
15	David W. Jackson	Wilmington	07-15-78
16	Corl E. Koontz	Lexington	07-15-78
17	Robert A. Miskelly	Hays	07-15-78
18	Grady Moss	Salisbury	07-15-78
19	Dudley Robbins	Burgaw	07-15-78
20	Max Robinson	Jacksonville	07-15-78
21	Frederick K. Ruffin	Durham	07-15-78
22	J. C. Sossoman	Morganton	07-15-78
23	Arnold E. Tarr	Lincolnton	07-15-78
24	Robert A. Tart	Benson	07-15-78
25	Joe Thompson	Canton	07-15-78
26	Jim Wilson	Winston-Salem	07-15-78
27	Max L. Wallace	Shelby	07-15-78

ADVISORY COMMITTEE ON LAND RECORDS
G.S. 143-345.6(f)/Board No. 0522

Position No.	Name of Appointee	Address	Date Appointed	Date of Expiration
01	Irving Isaacson	Greensboro	03-10-78	06-30-81
			09-25-81	06-30-85
02	Harold D. Long, *chairman*	Waynesville	03-10-78	06-30-79
			02-18-80	06-30-83
			02-22-84	07-01-87

ADVISORY COMMITTEE ON LAND RECORDS (CONTINUED)

Position No.	Name of Appointee	Address	Date Appointed	Date of Expiration
03	Eunice H. Ayers, *vice-chairwoman*	Winston-Salem	03-10-78	06-30-79
	Betty J. Hayes	Hillsborough	02-18-80	06-30-83
			02-22-84	07-01-87

MARINE RESOURCES CENTER ADMINISTRATIVE BOARD
G.S. 143-347.11/Board No. 0557

01	Judith M. Spitsbergen	Beaufort	04-26-78	06-15-81
			08-23-82	06-15-87

NORTH CAROLINA MARINE SCIENCE COUNCIL
G.S. 143B-390/Board No. 0555

01	Charles C. Wells	Hampstead	04-23-82	06-15-87
02	B. J. Copeland	Apex	04-23-82	06-15-87
03	Donald W. Bryan	Nags Head	04-23-82	06-15-87
	Peggy Stamey	Raleigh	12-06-83	06-16-89
04	William H. Queen	Greenville	04-23-82	06-15-87
05	J. Stephen Barnes	Creswell	04-23-82	06-15-87
06	Mary Johrde	Edenton	04-23-82	06-15-87
07	John S. Bone, Jr.	Manteo	10-31-79	06-15-85
	Agnes H. Williams	Raleigh	12-31-84	06-16-89
08	Adrian D. Hurst	Wilmington	10-31-79	06-15-85
09	Melvin R. Daniels, *chairman*	Elizabeth City	10-31-79	06-15-85
10	J. Guy Revelle, Sr.	Conway	02-16-78	06-15-83
	Joe Landino	Columbia	12-12-83	06-16-89
	J. C. Jones	Raleigh	12-31-84	06-30-89
11	Frank B. Turner	Raleigh	02-16-78	06-15-83
	Frank H. Longino, Jr.	Greenville	12-06-83	06-16-89
12	Alphonse F. Chestnut	Morehead City	02-16-78	06-15-83
			10-25-83	06-16-89
13	Bruce Muga	Durham	02-16-78	06-15-83
14	Thomas J. Schoenbaum	Chapel Hill	02-16-78	06-17-83
	Jane S. Patterson	Raleigh	04-23-82	06-15-83
15	Theodore R. Rice	Beaufort	02-16-78	06-15-83
				06-16-89
16	Leon K. Thomas	Marshallberg	02-16-78	06-15-83
			10-25-83	06-16-89
17, 23	Leonard J. Langfelder	Raleigh	02-16-78	06-15-83
			10-25-83	06-16-89
18	James P. Lewis	Davis	02-16-78	06-15-83
			10-25-83	06-16-89
19	Mary T. Boyd	Morehead City	02-16-78	06-15-83
	Virginia Tillet	Manteo	12-06-83	06-16-89
20	Edith W. Marsh	Raleigh	02-16-78	06-15-83
	M. C. Henderson	Raleigh	12-06-83	06-16-83
21	Roy C. Bain	Wilmington	02-16-78	06-17-83
	Eugene W. Merritt, Sr.	Wilmington	04-23-82	06-15-83
	Sheila Davis	Wilmington	12-19-83	06-16-89
22	Victor W. Barfield	Raleigh	09-09-80	
23	Neil Grigg	Raleigh	09-04-79	
	Donald G. Brock	Morehead City	04-23-82	06-15-83
			10-25-83	06-16-89

NORTH CAROLINA MARINE SCIENCE COUNCIL (CONTINUED)

Position No.	Name of Appointee	Address	Date Appointed	Date of Expiration
24	Edward G. McCoy	Morehead City	01-10-77	
	Connell Purvis	Morehead City	01-10-77	
	Bob Mahood	Morehead City	05-31-84	06-16-89
25	Jacob Koomen	Raleigh	01-10-77	

ADVOCACY COUNCIL FOR THE MENTALLY ILL AND DEVELOPMENTALLY DISABLED[6]
G.S. 143B-399/Board No. 0577

01	Marian G. Grant, chairwoman	Raleigh	04-26-78	06-30-80
02	John E. Alston	Franklinton	04-26-78	06-30-80
03	Joan E. Belk	Charlotte	04-26-78	06-30-80
04	Mel Ellsweig	Greensboro	04-26-78	06-30-80
05	Katie O. Morgan	Lillington	04-26-78	06-30-80
06	Robert R. Reilly, Jr.	Raleigh	04-26-78	06-30-80
07	P. U. Watson	Raleigh	04-26-78	06-30-80

STATE PERSONNEL COMMISSION
G.S. 126-2/Board No. 0680

01	Elton R. Jeffries	Mebane	08-11-77	06-30-83
	Stephen Thomas	Burlington	01-09-79	06-30-83
				06-30-89
02	Lenora L. Carawan	Raleigh	08-11-77	06-30-83
				06-30-89
03	Polly W. Brewer	Charlotte	06-24-77	06-30-83
				06-30-89
04	Billy D. Horne	Stedman	01-27-78	06-30-81
			07-01-81	06-30-87
05	Earl H. Tate	Lenoir	01-27-78	06-30-81
			07-01-81	06-30-87
06	E. R. Carraway, chairman	Greenville	06-24-77	06-30-83
			07-01-79	06-30-85
	William H. Lyon	Durham	03-13-83	06-30-85
07	Robert F. Coleman	Wilson	06-24-77	06-30-83
			07-01-79	06-30-85

GOVERNOR'S ADVOCACY COUNCIL FOR PERSONS WITH DISABILITIES
G.S. 143B-403.2/Board No. 0683

01	Marian G. Grant, chairwoman	Raleigh	12-10-79	06-30-83
			07-16-84	06-30-86
02	Anna G. Butler, vice-chairwoman	Warrenton	12-10-79	06-30-83
	Patricia C. Walters	Charlotte	01-13-82	06-30-83
			07-16-84	06-30-86
03	Joan E. Belk	Charlotte	03-12-80	06-30-83
	Debby Casey	Winston-Salem	07-16-84	06-30-87
04	Theodore R. Bryant	Durham	03-12-80	06-30-81
			01-13-82	06-30-85

---

6 The council was abolished effective July 1, 1979, its functions transferred to the Governor's Advocacy Council for Persons with Disabilities. *N.C. Session Laws, 1979,* c. 575, ratified May 16, 1979.

GOVERNOR'S ADVOCACY COUNCIL FOR PERSONS WITH DISABILITIES
(CONTINUED)

Position No.	Name of Appointee	Address	Date Appointed	Date of Expiration
05	Mrs. Willie High	Raleigh	03-12-80	06-30-83
			07-24-84	06-30-87
06	Craig L. Johnson	Ayden	03-12-80	06-30-81
	Myree Hayes	Greenville	01-13-82	06-30-85
07	Caroline Livermore	Lumberton	03-12-80	06-30-83
			08-29-84	06-30-87
08	Carl S. McCulloch	Elizabethtown	03-12-80	06-30-81
	Don Ramsey	Marion	01-13-82	06-30-85
			08-15-84	06-30-87
09	John E. Alston	Franklinton	03-12-80	06-30-81
	Carey S. Fendley	Raleigh	01-13-82	06-30-85
10	Mel Ellsweig	Greensboro	03-12-80	06-30-83
	Hughelitta Edmiston	Lenoir	08-03-84	06-30-87
11	Johnsie Frye	Hamlet	03-12-80	06-30-81
12	James M. Keane	Charlotte	03-12-80	06-30-81
			01-13-82	06-30-85
13	Howard Kramer	Raleigh	03-12-80	06-30-83
	Robert R. Christie	Greensboro	02-18-81	06-30-83
	Mary Spaulding	Scotland Neck	08-03-84	06-30-85
14	Katie O. Morgan	Lillington	03-12-80	06-30-83
15	Judy R. Law	Reidsville	03-12-80	06-30-83
	Jim Wells	Greensboro	12-21-84	06-30-87
16	Ruth M. Easterling	Charlotte	03-12-80	06-30-81
			01-13-82	06-30-85
17	Ollie Harris	Kings Mountain	03-12-80	06-30-81
			01-13-82	06-30-85
18, 16	Joan W. Hollowell	Goldsboro	04-17-80	06-30-81
			01-13-82	06-30-85

BOARD OF TRUSTEES OF THE NORTH CAROLINA PUBLIC EMPLOYEE DEFERRED COMPENSATION PLAN
G.S. 143B-426.24/Board No. 3075

01	John A. Williams	Raleigh	05-13-77	
	---	---	---	---
	Myron C. Banks	Raleigh	03-14-83	
02	Donald Umstead	Raleigh	03-14-83	
04	Lacy H. Reaves	Raleigh	08-22-78	

PUBLIC RADIO ADVISORY COMMITTEE
G.S. 143B-426.12/Board No. 0748

01	Marie W. Colton, *chairwoman*	Asheville	05-01-80	06-30-83
			04-20-84	06-30-87
02	Priscilla Balaban	Wilmington	05-01-80	06-30-82
			09-27-82	06-30-85
03	Dolores Dough	Plymouth	05-01-80	06-30-82
			09-27-82	06-30-85
04	William A. McIntosh	Charlotte	05-01-80	06-30-83
			04-20-84	06-30-87
05	Joseph C. Ross	Fayetteville	05-01-80	06-30-82
			09-27-82	06-30-85
06	Norman Sefton	Durham	05-01-80	06-30-83
			04-20-84	06-30-87

Board of Public Telecommunications Commissioners
G.S. 143B-426.9/Board No. 0893

Position No.	Name of Appointee	Address	Date Appointed	Date of Expiration
01	George F. Bland	Raleigh	09-10-79	06-30-82
			08-24-82	06-30-86
02	Charles H. Crutchfield	Charlotte	09-10-79	
03	Joel L. Fleishman	Chapel Hill	09-10-79	06-30-80
			07-23-80	06-30-84
			08-13-84	06-30-88
04	Nathaniel N. Fullwood	Durham	09-10-79	06-30-84
	Frank Bright	Durham	12-14-84	06-30-88
05	Wade H. Hargrove	Raleigh	09-10-79	06-30-84
			08-13-84	06-30-88
06	James E. Heins	Sanford	09-10-79	06-30-80
			01-02-81	06-30-84
			12-07-84	06-30-88
07	Claudia Kadis	Goldsboro	09-10-79	06-30-80
			07-23-80	06-30-84
			08-13-84	06-30-88
08	Hugh H. Stevens, Jr.	Raleigh	09-10-79	06-30-80
			07-23-80	06-30-84
			08-13-84	06-30-88
09	John E. Thomas	Boone	09-10-79	06-30-80
			07-23-80	06-30-84
			08-13-84	06-30-88
10	Lee R. Wallenhaupt	Winston-Salem	09-10-79	06-30-82
	Norman A. Vogel	Research Triangle Park	08-24-82	06-30-86
11	Carrie C. Winter	Charlotte	09-10-79	06-30-82
	James A. Heavner	Chapel Hill	08-24-82	06-30-86

Southern States Energy Board[7]
G.S. 104D-2/Board No. 0855

Position	Name	Address	Date Appointed
01	Jimmie J. Wortman	Research Triangle Park	05-06-77
	James E. Gibson, Jr.	Raleigh	04-29-80
	Carson D. Culbreth	Raleigh	02-17-81

Standardization Committee[8]
G.S. 143B-398/Board No. 0865

Position	Name	Address	Date Appointed
03	R. F. Stoops	Raleigh	01-03-78
04	Charles E. Gordon	Raleigh	01-03-78
05	Ben W. Aiken	Raleigh	01-03-78
06	Eddie Knox	Charlotte	03-03-78
07	James B. Garrison	Albemarle	03-03-78

Veterans' Affairs Commission
G.S. 143B-400/Board No. 0925

Position	Name	Address	Date Appointed	Date of Expiration
01	William E. Bass, Sr., *chairman*	Hickory	05-17-77	06-30-82
				06-30-86
02	John Best	Asheville	02-03-83	06-30-85

7 Formerly known as Southern Interstate Nuclear Board.
8 G.S. 143B-398 was repealed under *N.C. Session Laws, 1983*, c. 717, ratified July 11, 1983.

VETERANS' AFFAIRS COMMISSION (CONTINUED)

Position No.	Name of Appointee	Address	Date Appointed	Date of Expiration
03	Billy R. Cameron	Sanford	09-27-80	06-30-84
04	Monroe Lowry	Pembroke	09-06-78	06-30-82
	Benjamin B. Halterman	Wilmington	01-12-83	06-30-85
05	Garfield C. Joyce	Mayodan	10-25-80	06-30-83
	Stacey Foster...................	Lexington	08-15-83	06-30-87
06	C. Marcelle Williams, *vice-chairman*......	Faith	09-12-77	06-30-81
			08-15-83	06-30-85
07	Horace A. Silver................	Charlotte	09-12-77	06-30-81
				06-30-85
08	William E. West..................	Kinston	09-12-77	06-30-81
	John Ocha.....................	Swansboro	01-12-83	06-30-85
09	Johnnie L. Bardin	Wilson	09-12-77	06-30-81
	Carl Duncan	Henderson	01-12-83	06-30-83
				06-30-85
10	Shade A. Wooten	Cary	09-12-77	06-30-81
				06-30-85
11	Robert F. McNeill.............	West Jefferson	09-12-77	06-30-81
				06-30-85

COUNCIL ON THE STATUS OF WOMEN
G.S. 143B-394/Board No. 0967

Position No.	Name of Appointee	Address	Date Appointed	Date of Expiration
00, 03	Patricia M. Eckerd	Greensboro	11-18-82	06-30-84
			12-21-84	06-30-86
01	William G. Smith...............	Wilmington	08-26-78	06-30-80
	James K. Polk	Charlotte	08-19-81	06-30-82
	Louise McColl	Wilmington	12-27-84	06-30-86
02	William E. Howell	Elm City	08-26-78	06-30-80
	Mercedith E. Bacon	Bryson City	08-19-81	06-30-82
			07-30-82	06-30-84
			12-21-84	06-30-86
03	Rachel G. Gray	High Point	08-26-78	06-30-80
			08-19-81	06-30-82
	Janet Y. Jacobs	Raleigh	12-21-84	06-30-86
04	Terry Sanford	Durham	08-26-78	06-30-80
	William E. Clark	Fayetteville	08-19-81	06-30-82
	Eula Miller	Durham	08-06-82	06-30-84
			12-21-84	06-30-86
05	Helen Mahlum..................	New Bern	09-15-77	06-30-79
				06-30-81
			08-19-81	06-30-83
			12-21-84	06-30-86
06	Martha C. McKay	Chapel Hill	09-15-77	06-30-79
				06-30-81
	William G. Moore................	Asheville	02-12-80	06-30-81
			08-19-81	06-30-83
			12-21-84	06-30-86
07	Maria Bliss	Asheboro	09-15-77	06-30-79
				06-30-81
			08-19-81	06-30-83
			12-21-84	06-30-86
08	Elizabeth D. Koontz	Raleigh	09-15-77	06-30-79
				06-30-81

COUNCIL ON THE STATUS OF WOMEN (CONTINUED)

Position No.	Name of Appointee	Address	Date Appointed	Date of Expiration
	Joyce B. Smith	Durham	09-18-81	06-30-83
			12-21-84	06-30-86
09	Patricia S. Dinken	Thomasville	09-15-77	06-30-78
				06-30-80
	Kay Sebian	Wilmington	08-19-81	06-30-82
			07-30-82	06-30-84
			12-21-84	06-30-86
10	Barbara F. Kamara	Greensboro	09-15-77	06-30-78
				06-30-80
	Rebecca S. Clark	Chapel Hill	01-04-80	06-30-80
	Carl J. Stewart, Jr.	Gastonia	09-18-81	06-30-82
			07-30-82	06-30-84
			12-21-84	06-30-86
11	Camilla H. Bain	Wilmington	09-15-77	06-30-78
				06-30-80
	Frances P. Walker	Moyock	08-19-81	06-30-82
			07-30-82	06-30-84
			12-21-84	06-30-86
12	Ruth H. Helms	Monroe	09-15-77	06-30-79
	Polly A. Richardson	Smithfield	01-04-80	06-30-81
			08-19-81	06-30-83
	Grace Vickery	Henderson	12-31-84	06-30-85
13	Nancy H. Griffin	Kinston	09-15-77	06-30-78
				06-30-80
	Della Maynor	Raeford	08-19-81	06-30-82
			07-30-82	06-30-84
14	Betty H. Wiser	Raleigh	09-15-77	06-30-79
				06-30-81
			08-19-81	06-30-83
	Eunice H. Grossman	Chapel Hill	12-31-84	06-30-85
15	Mazie S. Woodruff	Winston-Salem	09-15-77	06-30-79
				06-30-81
			08-19-81	06-30-83
	Sammie Chess	High Point	12-27-84	06-30-85
16	Bertha M. Holt	Burlington	09-15-77	06-30-79
				06-30-81
	Margaret B. Hayden	Sparta	08-19-81	06-30-83
	Fay S. Skidmore	Charlotte	08-06-82	06-30-84
			12-21-84	06-30-86
17	Natalie A. Cohen	Charlotte	09-15-77	06-30-78
				06-30-80
			08-19-81	06-30-82
	Braxton B. Townsend	Rocky Mount	05-03-83	06-30-84
			12-21-84	06-30-86
18	Helen R. Marvin, *chairwoman*	Gastonia	09-15-77	06-30-79
				06-30-81
			08-19-81	06-30-83
	Rita L. Ray	Asheville	05-03-83	06-30-85
19	Sondra Katzenstein	Gastonia	09-15-77	06-30-79
	Mabel D. Epps	Maxton	01-04-80	06-30-81
	Louise Muse	Oriental	05-03-83	06-30-85

COUNCIL ON THE STATUS OF WOMEN (CONTINUED)

Position No.	Name of Appointee	Address	Date Appointed	Date of Expiration
19, 20	Ruby Jones	Greensboro	08-19-81	06-30-83
			12-21-84	06-30-86
20	Bertha Saunooke	Cherokee	09-15-77	06-30-78
	Dorothy Roark	Shelby	08-26-78	06-30-80
			08-19-81	06-30-82

STATE YOUTH ADVISORY COUNCIL
G.S. 143B-386/Board No. 0970

01	Eula H. Miller, *chairwoman*	Durham	02-27-78	06-30-79
	Tom B. Rabon, Jr.	Winnabow	05-30-80	06-30-81
				07-01-85
	Isabella Cannon	Raleigh	11-11-81	06-30-83
02	Robert C. Owen	Clinton	05-30-80	06-30-81
	Anne E. Young	Hertford	08-24-83	07-01-85
03	Lawrence A. Miller	Durham	05-30-80	06-30-81
	Ruffin H. McNeill, Jr.	Lumberton	11-11-81	06-30-83
			08-26-83	07-01-85
04	David B. Smith	Mars Hill	05-30-80	06-30-81
	Bartow Houston	Manteo	11-11-81	06-30-83
				07-01-85
05	Harold Burrell	Tryon	10-08-78	06-30-80
	Deborah R. Morris	Charlotte	09-22-80	06-30-82
	Calvin Davis	Charlotte	08-26-83	07-01-85
06	Mrs. Shelby Shore, *chairwoman*	Yadkinville	02-27-78	06-30-80
			09-22-80	06-30-82
				07-01-85
07	James A. Gallaher	Winston-Salem	09-22-80	06-30-82
				07-01-85
08	L. O. Saunders	Morganton	10-08-78	06-30-80
			09-22-80	06-30-82
				07-01-85
09	Wayne Ashley	Hertford	02-27-78	06-30-80
	Jimmie W. Phillips	Lexington	09-22-80	06-30-82
	Michael T. Mills	Bolton	11-11-81	06-30-82
	Lillian P. Willingham	Jacksonville	08-26-83	07-01-85
10	Nancy K. Johnston	Jefferson	03-15-78	06-30-79
	David Maynard	Burlington	05-30-80	06-30-81
			11-12-81	06-30-83
				07-01-85
17	Lisa Milby	Fayetteville	11-13-81	06-30-82
	Brookes Parrish	Winston-Salem	08-24-83	07-01-84
18	Allen Nelson	Graham	11-11-81	06-30-82
	Cyrus W. Brame III	North Wilkesboro	08-26-83	07-01-84
19	Demarcus M. Pitt	Goldsboro	11-11-81	06-30-82
	Roderick L. Wilson	Durham	09-12-83	07-01-84
20	Muzette Fitts	Roanoke Rapids	11-11-81	06-30-82
			08-26-83	07-01-84

DEPARTMENT OF COMMERCE
Secretaries
Duncan M. Faircloth, 1977-1983
Clarence C. Hope, Jr., 1983-1985

NORTH CAROLINA ALCOHOLIC BEVERAGE CONTROL COMMISSION[9]
G.S. 18B-200/Board No. 0030

Position No.	Name of Appointee	Address	Date Appointed	Date of Expiration
01	Marvin L. Speight, Jr., *chairman*	Farmville	02-11-77	
02	Clark S. Brown	Winston-Salem	02-11-77	
03	Zebulon D. Alley	Waynesville	02-11-77	
	John A. Powell	Asheville	01-09-81	

STATE BANKING COMMISSION
G.S. 53-92/Board No. 0110

01	N. K. Dickerson	Monroe	10-27-77	04-01-81
	C. J. Mabry, Jr.	Shelby	08-11-81	04-01-85
	Alexander D. Guy II	Jacksonville	09-21-83	04-01-85
02	Donald A. Davis	Raleigh	10-27-77	04-01-81
			09-01-81	04-01-85
03	W. Frank Comer	Dobson	07-25-79	04-01-83
			09-21-83	04-01-87
04	Steven A. Hockfield	Charlotte	07-25-79	04-01-83
			09-21-83	04-01-87
05	J. J. Sansom, Jr.	Raleigh	10-27-77	04-01-81
			09-01-81	04-01-85
06	Doris M. Cromartie	Charlotte	10-27-77	04-01-81
			09-01-81	04-01-85
	Katherine Harper	Charlotte	09-01-81	04-01-85
07	Wallace N. Hyde	Asheville	10-27-77	04-01-81
	Gordon Myers	Asheville	09-24-80	04-01-81
	Helen A. Powers	Asheville	11-18-81	04-01-85
08	C. Frank Griffin	Monroe	10-27-77	04-01-81
			09-01-81	04-01-85
09	Rhone Sasser	Whiteville	07-25-79	04-01-83
			09-21-83	04-01-87
10	Lorimer Midgett	Elizabeth City	10-27-77	04-01-81
	Eunice Ayers	Winston-Salem	07-25-79	04-01-81
	Charles C. Bost	Newton	08-11-81	04-01-85
	Robert V. Owens, Jr.	Manteo	06-02-82	04-01-85
11	John C. Bolt, Jr.	Wilson	10-27-77	04-01-81
			09-01-81	04-01-85
12	James J. Scarlett	Greensboro	07-25-79	04-01-83
	Paul L. Jones	Kinston	09-21-83	04-01-87

COMMISSIONER OF BANKS
G.S. 53-92/Board No. 0105

01	Thomas N. Brafford	Raleigh	04-27-78	04-01-79
	James S. Currie	Raleigh	09-01-78	04-01-79
				04-01-83
				04-01-87

---

9 G.S. 18A-1 through 18A-69, inclusive, were repealed under *N.C. Session Laws, 1981,* c. 412, s. 1, ratified May 18, 1981, and became effective on January 1, 1982; see also c. 412, s. 6. The North Carolina Alcoholic Beverage Control Commission was formerly known as the State Board of Alcoholic Control.

NORTH CAROLINA MUTUAL BURIAL ASSOCIATION
G.S. 58-241.7/Board No. 0155

Position No.	Name of Appointee	Address	Date Appointed	Date of Expiration
01	Dennis W. Moody, Sr.	Mount Airy	12-21-81	12-01-85
	William E. Bass, Jr.	Hickory	08-05-82	12-01-85

NORTH CAROLINA CEMETERY COMMISSION
G.S. 65-50/Board No. 0177

01	Carolyn W. Dearborn	Charlotte	09-09-80	06-30-84
			06-28-84	06-30-88
02	Jyles J. Coggins, *chairman*	Raleigh	02-16-78	06-30-82
			08-18-82	06-30-86
03	Ona C. Mitchell, Jr.	Durham	02-16-78	06-30-82
			08-18-82	06-30-86
04	R. Glenn Helms	Goldsboro	09-09-80	06-30-84
	Wiley M. Davis	Raleigh	03-15-82	06-30-84
			12-31-84	06-30-88

CREDIT UNION COMMISSION
G.S. 143B-439/Board No. 0255

01, 05	Shirley T. Gibson	Red Springs	08-06-80	07-15-83
02	Roger A. Shelor, *chairman*	Charlotte	08-06-80	07-15-83
03	Ellen P. Lee	Lewisville	08-06-80	07-14-81
04	James Walker	Greensboro	02-28-78	07-14-81
	Sam M. Wilson	Fayetteville	03-30-81	07-14-81
			03-16-82	07-15-85
05, 01	J. L. Faulcon	Ahoskie	04-24-78	07-14-81
			03-16-82	07-15-85
05	Karen L. Young	Raleigh	12-31-84	07-15-87
06	W. Ed Greer	Raleigh	04-24-78	07-14-81
06, 03	Edward H. Pope	Durham	04-01-81	07-14-81
			03-16-82	07-15-85
06	Elizabeth N. Hamilton	Greensboro	03-16-82	07-15-85
07	William F. Shelton	Louisburg	08-06-80	07-15-83
	Melvin R. Daniels, Jr.	Elizabeth City	12-28-84	07-15-87

ECONOMIC DEVELOPMENT BOARD
G.S. 143B-434/Board No. 0299

01	Matthew Bacoate, Jr.	Asheville	08-24-77	07-01-81
			10-20-81	07-01-85
02	Philip A. Baddour, Jr.	Goldsboro	08-24-77	07-01-79
				07-01-83
	Oscar J. Ledford	Franklin	08-04-81	07-01-83
				07-01-85
				07-01-87
03	James S. Belk	Greensboro	08-24-77	07-01-79
				07-01-83
			08-05-83	07-01-87
04	Cliff L. Benson, Sr.	Raleigh	08-24-77	07-01-81
	James E. Humphreys, Jr.	Winston-Salem	01-11-79	07-01-81
	Ted Sumner	Charlotte	12-30-80	07-01-81
			10-20-81	07-01-85

ECONOMIC DEVELOPMENT BOARD (CONTINUED)

Position No.	Name of Appointee	Address	Date Appointed	Date of Expiration
05	Leo Brody	Kinston	08-24-77	07-01-79
				07-01-83
			08-05-83	07-01-87
06	D. M. Campbell, Sr.	Elizabethtown	08-24-77	07-01-79
				07-01-83
	Odell Williamson	Shallotte	09-25-81	07-01-83
				07-01-87
07	James B. Childress	Sylva	08-24-77	07-01-81
08	Bessie N. Culpepper	Elizabeth City	08-24-77	07-01-81
	Tom Campbell	Elizabeth City	10-20-81	07-01-85
	R. Timothy Brinn................	Hertford	06-24-83	07-01-85
	Bill Owens...................	Elizabeth City	11-28-84	07-01-85
09	R. Edward Davenport, Jr............	Farmville	08-24-77	07-01-79
				07-01-83
	Elisabeth G. Hair................	Charlotte	09-25-81	07-01-83
				07-01-87
10	Charles N. Fitts	Roanoke Rapids	08-24-77	07-01-81
			10-20-81	07-01-85
11	Raymond W. Goodman...........	Rockingham	08-24-77	07-01-81
			10-20-81	07-01-85
12	Katharine C. Lambeth	Thomasville	08-24-77	07-01-81
			10-20-81	07-01-85
13	Mabel C. Maddrey	Raleigh	08-24-77	07-01-79
				07-01-83
			08-05-83	07-01-87
14	John F. McNair III, *chairman* ...	Winston-Salem	08-24-77	07-01-79
				07-01-83
			08-05-83	07-01-87
15	Graham A. Phillips, Jr.	Wallace	08-24-77	07-01-81
			10-20-81	07-01-85
16	Sadie A. Wilder	Raleigh	08-24-77	07-01-81
	Maggie M. Sanders	Greensboro	11-12-81	07-01-85
17	Robert E. Siler	Rocky Mount	08-24-77	07-01-79
				07-01-83
			08-05-83	07-01-87
18	Miles J. Smith, Jr., *vice-chairman*.....	Salisbury	08-24-77	07-01-79
				07-01-83
			08-05-83	07-01-87
19	Hiram D. Southerland	Jacksonville	08-24-77	07-01-81
19, 07	William Debrule.................	Forest City	11-30-81	07-01-85
19	Edward P. Godwin III	Wilmington	05-25-82	07-01-85
20	Ben Tison	Charlotte	08-24-77	07-01-79
				07-01-83
			08-05-83	07-01-87
21	Elbert L. Whitley, Jr.	Albemarle	08-24-77	07-01-81
			10-20-81	07-01-85
22	Lynwood T. Smith	High Point	08-24-77	07-01-79
				07-01-83
			08-05-83	07-01-87
	Earl N. Phillips	High Point	12-21-84	07-01-87

EMPLOYMENT SECURITY COMMISSION OF NORTH CAROLINA
G.S. 96-3/Board No. 0345

Position No.	Name of Appointee	Address	Date Appointed	Date of Expiration
01	J. B. Archer, *chairman*	Raleigh	02-01-78	07-01-81
	Glenn R. Jernigan	Fayetteville	01-07-82	
02	A. Carroll Coleman	Wilson	02-14-78	07-01-81
			01-07-82	07-01-85
03	David W. Erdman	Charlotte	02-14-78	07-01-81
			01-07-82	07-01-85
	Henry Mann	Greensboro	12-15-82	07-01-85
04	John H. Taylor, Jr.	Greenville	02-14-78	07-01-81
	Ada F. Singleton	Wadesboro	11-14-79	07-01-81
			01-07-82	07-01-85
05	Charles L. Hunley	Monroe	11-14-79	07-01-83
			08-03-83	07-01-87
06	John R. Manley	Chapel Hill	09-18-79	07-01-83
			08-03-83	07-01-87
07	Dan B. Wortman	Lenoir	11-14-79	07-01-83
			08-03-83	07-01-87

ENERGY POLICY COUNCIL
G.S. 113B-3/Board No. 0353

01	William S. Lee	Charlotte	05-05-77	01-31-81
			12-15-81	01-31-85
	Donald H. Denton	Charlotte	03-09-83	01-31-85
02	Donald W. McCoy	Fayetteville	05-05-77	01-31-81
			12-15-81	01-31-85
03	Robert L. Mattocks II	Pollocksville	05-05-77	01-31-81
			12-15-81	01-31-85
04	John D. Neufield	Greensboro	05-05-77	01-31-81
	Colin C. Blaydon	Durham	12-31-81	01-31-85
05	Alice M. Welsh	Chapel Hill	05-05-77	01-31-81
	John S. Curry	Carrboro	10-09-79	01-31-81
			12-15-81	01-31-85
06	George E. Norman, Jr.	Greensboro	05-05-77	01-31-81
			12-15-81	01-31-85
07	Robert S. Cole	Weaverville	05-05-77	01-31-81
	Franklin G. Hart	Raleigh	07-29-81	01-31-85
13	Ruth D. Cherry	Rocky Mount	12-31-81	01-31-85
	Clarence E. Tucker	Reidsville	05-25-83	01-31-85
14	Hope Brogden	Southern Pines	02-01-82	12-31-85

NORTH CAROLINA INDUSTRIAL COMMISSION
G.S. 97-77/Board No. 0463

01	Charles A. Clay	Raleigh	09-18-81	05-01-87
02	Coy M. Vance	Raleigh	09-18-81	05-01-85
03	William H. Stephenson, *chairman*	Garner	05-01-77	05-01-83
				05-01-89

LABOR FORCE DEVELOPMENT COUNCIL[10]
G.S. 143B-438/Board No. 0516

Position No.	Name of Appointee	Address	Date Appointed	Date of Expiration
01	Howard Boudreau	Fayetteville	05-22-78	07-01-79
02	George Broadrick................	Charlotte	05-22-78	07-01-81
03	Elma Byrd......................	Windsor	05-22-78	07-01-80
04	William H. Cluck	New Bern	05-22-78	07-01-79
05	Ruth E. Cook	Raleigh	05-22-78	07-01-81
06	John R. Dossenbach, Jr.............	Sanford	05-22-78	07-01-81
07	Graham Flanagan, Jr.............	Greenville	05-22-78	07-01-80
08	William K. Hobbs................	Wilmington	05-22-78	07-01-81
09	Abraham Holtzman	Raleigh	05-22-78	07-01-81
10	Ruth P. Jones	Hendersonville	05-22-78	07-01-79
11	Douglas McMillan, Jr.	Lumberton	05-22-78	07-01-80
12	William J. Veeder.................	Charlotte	05-22-78	07-01-81

NORTH CAROLINA MILK COMMISSION
G.S. 106-266.7/Board No. 0585

01	Noel L. Allen	Raleigh	12-13-77	06-30-81
	Isabella W. Cannon	Raleigh	10-14-80	06-30-81
	Anna Butler.....................	Warrenton	09-09-81	06-30-85
	Albert A. Corbett, Jr.	Smithfield	03-29-83	06-30-85
02	Inez Myles.....................	Henderson	12-13-77	06-30-81
			09-09-81	06-30-85
03	Oren J. Heffner	Mocksville	12-13-77	06-30-81
	Charlie L. Hardee	Grifton	09-09-81	06-30-85
	Dewey L. Hill....................	Whiteville	01-14-83	06-30-85

MOREHEAD CITY NAVIGATION AND PILOTAGE COMMISSION
G.S. 76A-401/Board No. 3330

01	Paul H. Geer, Jr................	Morehead City	10-07-82	07-01-85
02	William M. Greene	Morehead City	10-07-82	07-01-84
03	Walter D. Phillips.................	Newport	10-07-82	07-01-83
				06-30-86
04	Ormsby Mann	Newport	10-07-82	07-01-83
				06-30-86

NORTH CAROLINA NATIONAL PARK, PARKWAY, AND FORESTS
DEVELOPMENT COUNCIL
G.S. 143B-447/Board No. 0625

01	Peggy A. Halsey	Jefferson	01-04-80	07-01-83
	Bob Sloan	Franklin	07-12-83	07-01-87
02	Charles D. Jaynes	Marion	10-12-79	07-01-83
	Margaret Blocker.............	Hendersonville	02-10-81	07-01-83
03	Madeline Patton	Candler	07-15-77	07-01-81
	Thomas L. Mallonee...............	Candler	07-21-81	07-01-85
	Edgar Israel	Brevard	08-16-83	07-01-87
04	David F. Felmet, *chairman*........	Waynesville	07-15-77	07-01-81
			07-21-81	07-01-85

---

10 G.S. 143B-438, establishing the Labor Force Development Council, was repealed under *N.C. Session Laws, 1981*, c. 380, ratified May 13, 1981.

NORTH CAROLINA NATIONAL PARK, PARKWAY, AND FORESTS DEVELOPMENT COUNCIL (CONTINUED)

Position No.	Name of Appointee	Address	Date Appointed	Date of Expiration
05	Marshall Smith	Bryson City	07-15-77	07-01-81
			07-21-81	07-01-85
	Bennett Arvey	Bryson City	07-12-83	07-01-85
06	R. V. Jenkins	Sylva	08-23-79	07-01-83
				07-01-87
07	Ralph J. Gwaltney	Banner Elk	10-12-79	07-01-83
				07-01-87

BOARD OF COMMISSIONERS OF NAVIGATION AND PILOTAGE FOR THE CAPE FEAR RIVER
G.S. 76-1/Board No. 0635

Position No.	Name of Appointee	Address	Date Appointed	Date of Expiration
01	Thomas Hodges, Jr.	Wilmington	05-20-77	04-15-81
			02-02-81	07-01-83
	Robert B. Rehder	Wilmington	07-07-82	07-08-83
			08-21-84	06-30-87
02	Joe Fox, *chairman*	Wilmington	05-20-77	04-15-81
	Edward E. Lee, Jr.	Wilmington	02-02-82	07-01-83
			08-15-84	07-01-87
03	Beatrice Clemmons	Wilmington	05-20-77	04-15-81
	Kenneth A. Shanklin	Wilmington	02-02-82	07-01-85
04	L. Gleason Allen	Wilmington	05-20-77	04-15-81
	Grover Gore	Southport	02-02-82	07-01-85
05	James R. Prevatte	Southport	05-20-77	04-15-81

NORTH CAROLINA STATE PORTS AUTHORITY
G.S. 143B-452/Board No. 0715

Position No.	Name of Appointee	Address	Date Appointed	Date of Expiration
01	Thomas F. Taft, *chairman*	Greenville	08-10-77	06-30-79
			06-30-79	06-30-85
02	J. F. Allen	Biscoe	08-10-77	06-30-83
	William C. Monk	Farmville	03-24-80	06-30-83
				06-30-89
03	William R. Williamson	Wilson	08-10-77	06-30-83
				06-30-89
04	Colin Stokes, *vice-chairman*	Winston-Salem	08-10-77	06-30-79
			06-30-79	06-30-85
	Lynwood T. Smith	High Point	12-21-84	06-30-85
05	Herman Cone, Jr.	Greensboro	02-16-82	06-30-83
				06-30-89
06	Furman K. Biggs III	Lumberton	08-11-81	06-30-87
07	William A. Clement	Durham	03-09-82	06-30-87
07, 05	Edward E. Crutchfield, Jr.	Charlotte	01-11-79	06-30-83
09, 06	Betty E. Williamson, *secretary*	Lumberton	08-10-77	06-30-81
10, 07	Elmer V. Wilkins	Roper	08-10-77	06-30-81

NORTH CAROLINA PORTS RAILWAY COMMISSION BOARD OF DIRECTORS
G.S. 143B-469/Board No. 0717

Position No.	Name of Appointee	Address	Date Appointed	Date of Expiration
01	Jyles J. Coggins..................	Raleigh	05-23-80	03-15-84
02	A. D. Guy	Jacksonville	05-23-80	03-15-84
03	Franklin Randolph	Bolivia	05-23-80	03-18-81
			02-17-82	03-15-85

NORTH CAROLINA PORTS RAILWAY COMMISSION BOARD OF DIRECTORS
(CONTINUED)

Position No.	Name of Appointee	Address	Date Appointed	Date of Expiration
04	Perley A. Thomas	High Point	05-23-80	03-15-82
05	R. F. Wilkes	Raleigh	05-23-80	03-15-83

NORTH CAROLINA RURAL ELECTRIFICATION AUTHORITY
G.S. 117-1/Board No. 0795

01	Russell C. Seawell, *chairman*	Bennett	10-20-77	06-05-81
	Heyward H. McKinney	Wadesboro	12-15-82	06-05-85
02	Emily G. Eason	Sanford	10-20-77	06-05-81
			07-23-82	06-05-85
03	George L. Huffman, Jr.	Hildebran	08-21-79	06-05-83
	Frank James	Crumpler	08-17-83	
04	Novile C. Hawkins	Mars Hill	08-21-79	06-05-83
	Richard H. Greene	Warrenton	08-10-82	06-05-83
				08-30-87
05	James S. Melton, *chairman*	Hubert	10-20-77	06-05-81
	Wilton O. Rowe	Snow Hill	02-19-81	06-05-81
			07-23-82	06-05-85
	A. William McDonald.	Elkin	12-21-84	06-05-85

SAVINGS AND LOAN COMMISSION
G.S. 54B-53/Board No. 0820

01	Walter Church	Valdese	10-28-77	07-14-81
			10-02-81	07-15-85
02	Donald T. Robbins	Granite Falls	11-08-79	07-15-83
	Frank S. Pittman.	Raleigh	10-25-83	07-15-87
03	Noah H. Bennett, Jr.	Durham	11-08-79	07-15-83
			10-25-83	07-15-87
04	M. W. Mullinix, Sr.	Richfield	11-08-79	07-15-83
			10-25-83	07-15-87
05	William F. McCray, *chairman*	Kannapolis	10-28-77	07-14-81
			10-02-81	07-15-85
	Janice L. Bryant	Brevard	07-23-82	07-15-85
06	Julian R. Sparrow	Raleigh	10-28-77	07-14-81
	Thomas L. Drew	Durham	11-08-80	07-14-81
	John W. McDevitt	Durham	02-19-81	07-14-81
	Robert B. Brannan.	Concord	10-02-81	07-15-85
07	Jack B. Kirksey	Morganton	11-08-79	07-15-83
	William G. Smith.	Lenoir	10-25-83	07-15-87

NORTH CAROLINA BOARD OF SCIENCE AND TECHNOLOGY
G.S. 143B-441/Board No. 0825

05	Joseph W. Grimsley	Raleigh	08-08-79	06-30-81
			07-30-81	06-30-85
	Jane S. Patterson	Raleigh	09-25-81	06-30-85
06	Leon Golberg, *chairman*	Research Triangle Park	08-08-79	06-30-81
			07-30-81	06-30-85
	Norman R. Cohen	Charlotte	01-24-84	06-30-87
10	Thomas E. Powell III	Burlington	08-08-79	06-30-83
	Sharon S. Exum.	Charlotte	01-26-84	06-30-87
11	Betty A. Knudsen.	Raleigh	08-08-79	06-30-81
			07-30-81	06-30-85

NORTH CAROLINA SEAFOOD INDUSTRIAL PARK AUTHORITY
G.S. 113-315.25/Board No. 0830

Position No.	Name of Appointee	Address	Date Appointed	Date of Expiration
01	Allen C. Barbee	Spring Hope	10-15-79	07-01-85
02	Thomas B. Gray, *chairman*	Buxton	10-15-79	07-01-83
03	W. T. Harris, *vice-chairman*	Charlotte	10-15-79	07-01-81
04	Wilda H. Hurst	Swansboro	10-15-79	07-01-81
05	Roger W. Jones	Newport	10-15-79	07-01-81
06	Charles F. Lovette	Winston-Salem	10-15-79	07-01-83
07	Randolph G. O'Neal, Jr.	Wanchese	10-15-79	07-01-83
08	C. A. Phillips	Edenton	10-15-79	07-01-81
09	Willie E. Sloan	Leland	10-15-79	07-01-83

NORTH CAROLINA UTILITIES COMMISSION
G.S. 62-10/Board No. 0920

Position No.	Name of Appointee	Address	Date Appointed	Date of Expiration
01	Edward B. Hipp	Raleigh	10-21-77	07-01-81
			07-01-81	07-01-89
02	Robert K. Koger, *chairman*	Raleigh	03-30-77	07-01-81
			07-01-81	07-01-89
03	Sarah L. Tate	Raleigh	04-15-77	07-01-85
04	Leigh H. Hammond	Raleigh	03-30-77	07-01-85
	Hugh A. Crigler, Jr.	Lexington	08-02-84	07-01-85
05	A. Hartwell Campbell	Wilson	07-02-79	07-01-87
06	John W. Winters, Sr.	Raleigh	04-29-77	07-01-83
	Ruth E. Cook	Raleigh	06-21-83	06-30-91
07	Robert Fischbach	Raleigh	03-29-77	07-01-85
	Douglas P. Leary	Wake Forest	12-20-79	07-01-85

EXECUTIVE DIRECTOR OF THE PUBLIC STAFF OF THE NORTH CAROLINA UTILITIES COMMISSION
G.S. 62-15/Board No. 0921

Position No.	Name of Appointee	Address	Date Appointed	Date of Expiration
01	Robert Fischbach	Raleigh	09-13-79	06-30-83
	Robert Gruber	Raleigh	06-21-83	06-30-89

DEPARTMENT OF COMMUNITY COLLEGES

STATE BOARD OF COMMUNITY COLLEGES AND TECHNICAL INSTITUTES
G.S. 115D-2.1/Board No. 0212

Position No.	Name of Appointee	Address	Date Appointed	Date of Expiration
01	Sam L. Wiggins	Waynesville	09-05-80	06-30-85
	Donald C. Eudy	Waynesville	01-03-83	06-30-85
02	Ronald E. Deal	Hickory	09-05-80	06-30-81
	Michael Claman	Taylorsville	01-12-82	06-30-87
	William C. Parton	Morganton	07-13-83	06-30-87
03	Melvin C. Swann, Jr.	Greensboro	09-05-80	06-30-85
04	Stacy Budd	Sanford	09-05-80	06-30-83
	Clyde J. Rhyne	Sanford	09-23-81	06-30-83
	Edward J. Snyder, Jr.	Albemarle	07-13-83	06-30-89
05	Martha Granger	Wilmington	09-05-80	06-30-81
			09-23-81	06-30-87
06	Charles E. Branford	Wilson	09-05-80	06-30-83
	Samuel Roebuck	Elizabeth City	03-06-84	06-30-89
07	Richard L. Daugherty	Raleigh	09-05-80	06-30-81
			09-23-81	06-30-87

BLADEN TECHNICAL COLLEGE BOARD OF TRUSTEES
(CONTINUED)

Position No.	Name of Appointee	Address	Date Appointed	Date of Expiration
03	Betsy S. Fields	Tar Heel	07-01-77	06-30-85
04	Sudie Sheridan	Elizabethtown	09-04-79	06-30-87

BLUE RIDGE TECHNICAL COLLEGE BOARD OF TRUSTEES
G.S. 115D-12(a)/Board No. 2035

01	Philip R. Milroy	Hendersonville	08-20-81	06-30-89
02	Sam H. McGuirt	Hendersonville	07-19-82	06-30-91
03	Edmond M. Walker	Hendersonville	07-01-77	06-30-85
04	Frank W. Ewbank, vice-chairman	Hendersonville	08-17-79	06-30-87

BRUNSWICK TECHNICAL COLLEGE BOARD OF TRUSTEES
G.S. 115D-12(a)/Board No. 2037

01	Durwood T. Clark, Sr.	Leland	09-20-79	06-30-81
			08-27-81	06-30-89
02	Cora Greene	Bolivia	09-20-79	06-30-83
			09-02-83	06-30-91
03	Robert R. Harris, chairman	Southport	09-20-79	06-30-83
	Edward D. Redwine	Shallotte	05-13-83	06-30-87
04	Allen C. Ward	Thomasboro	09-20-79	06-30-85
	James L. Johnson	Shallotte	01-23-81	06-30-85

CALDWELL COMMUNITY COLLEGE AND TECHNICAL INSTITUTE BOARD OF TRUSTEES
G.S. 115D-12(a)/Board No. 2040

01	T. Jack Fox	Lenoir	09-04-79	06-30-87
02	William M. Lovelace, Jr.	Hudson	07-01-77	06-30-85
03	Royal B. Everett	Lenoir	10-21-83	
04	Linda M. McGee	Boone	07-01-81	06-30-89

CAPE FEAR TECHNICAL INSTITUTE BOARD OF TRUSTEES
G.S. 115D-12(a)/Board No. 2045

01	Richard L. Burnett, chairman	Wilmington	08-27-79	06-30-87
02	Berry A. Williams	Wilmington		06-30-85
	Mary S. Bell	Currie	08-29-80	06-30-85
				06-30-89
03	Howard Holly	Burgaw	06-21-79	06-30-83
				06-30-91
04	Luther M. Cromartie	Wilmington	01-03-83	06-30-85

CARTERET TECHNICAL COLLEGE BOARD OF TRUSTEES
G.S. 115D-12(a)/Board No. 2050

01	Donald R. Croom	Swansboro	09-22-81	06-30-85
02	Holly M. Salter	Beaufort	06-30-83	06-30-91
03	D. Wayne West, Jr.	Newport	07-01-77	06-30-85
	Elsie D. Hunt	Morehead City	01-29-82	06-30-89
04	Ralph L. Thomas, Jr.	Beaufort	09-04-79	06-30-87

DAVIDSON COUNTY COMMUNITY COLLEGE BOARD OF TRUSTEES
G.S. 115D-12(a)/Board No. 2085

Position No.	Name of Appointee	Address	Date Appointed	Date of Expiration
01	Charles M. England	Lexington	06-22-83	06-30-91
02	Leroy Pearson	Lexington	07-01-77	06-30-85
03	Elvin M. Copple	Thomasville	08-17-79	06-30-87
04	Phyllis S. Penry	Lexington	08-25-81	06-30-89

DURHAM TECHNICAL INSTITUTE BOARD OF TRUSTEES
G.S. 115D-12(a)/Board No. 2090

01	W. Kimball Griffin	Durham		06-30-89
02	Jesse Anglin	Durham	06-30-83	06-30-91
03	Byron K. Hawkins	Durham	07-01-77	06-30-85
04	Sherrill R. High	Durham	07-27-79	06-30-87

EDGECOMBE TECHNICAL COLLEGE BOARD OF TRUSTEES
G.S. 115D-12(a)/Board No. 2095

01	James H. Long	Tarboro	08-17-79	06-30-87
02	J. B. Webb	Tarboro	07-01-77	06-30-85
03	Vivian M. Diggs	Tarboro	06-24-83	06-30-91
04	Margaret B. Quincy	Tarboro	09-04-81	06-30-89

FAYETTEVILLE TECHNICAL INSTITUTE BOARD OF TRUSTEES
G.S. 115D-12(a)/Board No. 2100

01	Thomas R. McLean	Fayetteville	10-26-81	06-30-89
02	Robert C. Lewis, Jr.	Fayetteville	06-09-83	06-30-91
03	Harry F. Shaw, *chairman*	Fayetteville	07-01-77	06-30-85
04	Mary A. McCoy	Fayetteville	08-27-79	06-30-87

FORSYTH TECHNICAL COLLEGE BOARD OF TRUSTEES
G.S. 115D-12(a)/Board No. 2105

01	Robert F. Joyce	Winston-Salem	06-02-80	06-30-83
02	W. Douglas Foster	Winston-Salem	07-01-77	06-30-85
	John P. Arrowood	Rural Hall	10-18-79	06-30-85
03	Velma G. Watts	Winston-Salem	07-01-77	06-30-79
			08-17-79	06-30-87
07	Ned R. Smith	Winston-Salem	08-31-81	06-30-89

GASTON COLLEGE BOARD OF TRUSTEES
G.S. 115D-12(a)/Board No. 2110

01	Earl T. Groves	Gastonia	08-03-81	06-30-89
02	Tom D. Efird	Gastonia	07-01-77	06-30-85
03	Charles A. Rhyne	Mount Holly	06-24-83	06-30-91
04	Linda M. Roberts	Gastonia	08-17-79	06-30-87

GUILFORD TECHNICAL COMMUNITY COLLEGE BOARD OF TRUSTEES
G.S. 115D-12(a)/Board No. 2115

01	Joanne W. Bowie	Greensboro	08-03-81	06-30-89
02	Nina K. Starr	Greensboro	06-07-83	06-30-91

ROANOKE-CHOWAN TECHNICAL COLLEGE BOARD OF TRUSTEES
G.S. 115D-12(a)/Board No. 2205

Position No.	Name of Appointee	Address	Date Appointed	Date of Expiration
02	A. M. Williams	Ahoskie	07-01-83	06-30-91
03	Robert E. Lee	Gatesville	07-01-77	06-30-85
04	Roberts H. Jernigan, Jr., *chairman*	Ahoskie	08-17-79	06-30-87

ROBESON TECHNICAL COLLEGE BOARD OF TRUSTEES
G.S. 115D-12(a)/Board No. 2210

01	Glenn A. Maynor	Lumberton	09-15-81	06-30-85
02	Luther H. Moore	Maxton	06-30-83	06-30-91
03	John M. Brooks	Pembroke	07-01-77	06-30-85
	John W. Oxendine	Lumberton	09-10-81	06-30-89
	Mable H. Revels	Lumberton	12-21-84	06-30-89
04	Robert E. Ballard	Lumberton	07-06-79	06-30-87
	Janie B. Silver	Lumberton	10-17-83	06-30-87

ROCKINGHAM COMMUNITY COLLEGE BOARD OF TRUSTEES
G.S. 115D-12(a)/Board No. 2215

01	Sue McMichael	Reidsville	02-01-82	06-30-89
02	Dwight Sparks	Madison	11-18-83	06-30-91
03	Julius J. Gwyn, *vice-chairman*	Reidsville	07-01-77	06-30-85
04	Sara B. Stultz	Eden	07-01-77	06-30-79
			08-17-79	06-30-87

ROWAN TECHNICAL COLLEGE BOARD OF TRUSTEES
G.S. 115D-12(a)/Board No. 2220

01	William S. Murdock	Salisbury	08-21-81	03-30-89
	Larry Ford	Salisbury	08-03-83	06-30-89
02	C. C. Brewer	Salisbury	03-22-78	06-30-83
			07-01-83	06-30-91
03	John E. Ramsey	Salisbury	07-01-77	06-30-85
04	Sarah B. Singer	Salisbury	04-08-77	06-30-87

SAMPSON TECHNICAL COLLEGE BOARD OF TRUSTEES
G.S. 115D-12(a)/Board No. 2225

01	Bobby R. Porter	Roseboro	08-03-81	06-30-89
02	Douglas Parsons	Clinton	07-01-83	06-30-91
03	Carmen M. Butler	Roseboro	07-01-77	06-30-85
04	Joseph Underwood	Clinton	09-10-79	06-30-87

SANDHILLS COMMUNITY COLLEGE BOARD OF TRUSTEES
G.S. 115D-12(a)/Board No. 2230

01	William E. Simmons	Pinehurst	08-27-79	06-30-87
	Leroy McMillan	Southern Pines	01-24-84	06-30-87
02	Ralph Monger, Jr.	Sanford	07-01-77	06-30-85
03	Robert Hunt	Pinehurst	07-01-83	06-30-91
04	J. E. Causey	Lakeview	07-01-81	06-30-89

Wake Technical College Board of Trustees
G.S. 115D-12(a)/Board No. 2267

Position No.	Name of Appointee	Address	Date Appointed	Date of Expiration
01	W. H. Holding	Wake Forest	08-17-79	06-30-87
02	James P. Swindell, *chairman*	Cary	07-01-77	06-30-85
03	Ralph E. Forrest	Cary	05-15-78	06-30-83
			07-01-83	06-30-91
04	Cliffornia Wimberley	Raleigh	01-10-79	06-30-81
			08-03-81	06-30-89

Wayne Community College Board of Trustees
G.S. 115D-12(a)/Board No. 2270

Position No.	Name of Appointee	Address	Date Appointed	Date of Expiration
01	Margie Shirley....................	Goldsboro	08-03-81	06-30-89
02	J. Field Montgomery	Goldsboro	07-01-83	06-30-91
03	Hal H. Tanner	Goldsboro	07-01-77	05-22-78
	R. Glenn Helms	Goldsboro	07-13-78	06-30-85
04	George E. Wilson	Goldsboro	09-04-79	06-30-87

Western Piedmont Community College Board of Trustees
G.S. 115D-12(a)/Board No. 2275

Position No.	Name of Appointee	Address	Date Appointed	Date of Expiration
01	Claude Sitton	Morganton	10-20-77	06-30-81
			07-01-81	06-30-89
02	Helen McDowell.................	Morganton	06-30-83	06-30-91
03	W. Stanley Moore	Morganton	07-01-77	06-30-85
	Robert R. Byrd..................	Morganton	01-19-81	06-30-85
04	Edward W. Phifer, Jr.............	Morganton	07-01-77	06-30-87
	Mary E. Phifer.................	Morganton	05-30-80	06-30-87

Wilkes Community College Board of Trustees
G.S. 115D-12(a)/Board No. 2280

Position No.	Name of Appointee	Address	Date Appointed	Date of Expiration
01	Bonnie L. Rhodes...............	Wilkesboro	08-03-81	06-30-89
02	Austin A. Adams	North Wilkesboro	07-01-83	06-30-91
03	Gordon E. Rhodes	North Wilkesboro	08-17-77	06-30-85
04	Judith B. Bloomfield.........	North Wilkesboro	08-17-79	06-30-87

Wilson County Technical Institute Board of Trustees
G.S. 115D-12(a)/Board No. 2285

Position No.	Name of Appointee	Address	Date Appointed	Date of Expiration
01	Robert H. Hackney.................	Wilson	08-03-81	06-30-89
02	Inez Bell	Wilson	08-05-83	06-30-91
03	Nelda M. Bertrand	Wilson	07-01-77	06-30-85
04	John Webb.......................	Wilson	08-17-79	06-30-87

DEPARTMENT OF CORRECTION
Secretaries
Amos E. Reed, 1977-1981
James C. Woodard, 1981-1985

Board of Correction
G.S. 143B-265/Board No. 0235

Position No.	Name of Appointee	Address	Date Appointed	Date of Expiration
01	Virginia Bass	Wilson	11-29-77	
	John R. McCall	Raleigh	02-19-81	

BOARD OF CORRECTION (CONTINUED)

Position No.	Name of Appointee	Address	Date Appointed	Date of Expiration
02, 03	Stafford G. Bullock	Raleigh	11-29-77	
03, 02	W. H. S. Burgwyn, Jr..............	Woodland	11-29-77	
04	W. H. McElwee.............	North Wilkesboro	11-29-77	
	Wilton O. Rowe	Snow Hill	11-09-79	
	Thomas H. Morrissey................	Arden	03-03-81	
05	Christie S. Price.................	Chapel Hill	11-29-77	
06	Willie J. Stratford	Charlotte	11-29-77	
07	Robert Weinstein	Raleigh	11-29-77	
08	Bernadette Gray-Little	Chapel Hill	11-29-77	
	John R. Ball..................	Greenville	10-25-83	

AREA INMATE LABOR COMMISSIONS
G.S. 148-26.2/Board No. 0466

01	Ralph C. Williams	Brevard	08-31-78	07-01-81
02	Marjorie T. Green..............	Rutherfordton	08-31-78	07-01-81
03	J. Earl Daniels.....................	Marion	08-31-78	07-01-81
	Samuel W. Noble, Jr.	Granite Falls	01-22-79	07-01-81
04	Betty P. Cooke	Hickory	08-31-78	07-01-81
05	Edwin Chapman	Morganton	08-31-78	07-01-81
06	Genelle T. Graham................	Graham	08-31-78	07-01-81
07	Melvin Marley	Asheboro	08-31-78	07-01-81
08	Robert G. Cox	Reidsville	08-31-78	07-01-81
09	Robert G. Hedrick	Lexington	08-31-78	07-01-81
10	Benny B. Hampton	Asheboro	08-31-78	08-31-79 07-01-81
11	Thomas J. Burgin	Lincolnton	08-31-78	07-01-81
12	Almetta Armstrong	Candor	08-31-78	07-01-81
13	David E. Lowe	Lincolnton	08-31-78	07-01-81
14	W. Davis Fort....................	Albemarle	08-31-78	07-01-81
15	Bill Bambach....................	Charlotte	08-31-78	07-01-81
16	George T. Young, Sr.................	Halifax	08-31-78	07-01-81
17	Jerry W. Adcock	Henderson	08-31-78	07-01-81
18	Hugh T. Ragland, Jr.	Oxford	08-31-78	07-01-81
19	W. P. Jones.....................	Warrenton	08-31-78	07-01-81
20	David H. Creech	Selma	08-31-78	07-01-81
21	Thomas E. Poole	Robbins	08-31-78	07-01-81
22	Jim McKinnon....................	Leland	08-31-78	07-01-81
23	Jim Pennington	Oxford	08-31-78	07-01-81
24	John Balfour	Lumber Bridge	08-31-78	08-31-79 07-01-81
25	Eddie B. Coleman	Troy	08-31-78	07-01-81
26	Bob Turner	Jarvisburg	08-31-78	07-01-81
27	John R. Thompson	Morehead City	08-31-78	07-01-81
28	J. G. McNeil.....................	Fairbluff	08-31-78	07-01-81
29	T. F. Leary.....................	Camden	08-31-78	07-01-81
30	Douglas Sawyer	Elizabeth City	08-31-78	07-01-81

STATE INMATE LABOR COMMISSION
G.S. 148-26.3/Board No. 0467

01	Daniel F. Finch, *chairman*	Oxford	10-04-78	07-01-81

PAROLE COMMISSION
G.S. 143B-267/Board No. 0675

Position No.	Name of Appointee	Address	Date Appointed	Date of Expiration
01	James C. Woodard, *chairman*	Selma	07-18-77	06-30-81
	Walter T. Johnson, Jr., *chairman*	Greensboro	03-06-81	06-30-81
			08-14-81	06-30-85
02	Jane G. Greenlee	Marion	07-18-77	06-30-81
			08-14-81	06-30-85
03	Joy J. Johnson	Fairmont	02-08-78	06-30-81
			08-14-81	06-30-85
04	Rae McNamara	Raleigh	07-18-77	06-30-81
	Wymene S. Valand	Raleigh	08-14-81	06-30-85
05	Henry W. Oxendine	Pembroke	07-18-77	06-30-81
			08-14-81	06-30-85
	Joe H. Palmer	Clyde	08-03-82	06-30-85

DEPARTMENT OF CRIME CONTROL AND PUBLIC SAFETY
Secretaries
J. Phillip Carlton, 1977-1978
Herbert L. Hyde, 1979
Burley B. Mitchell, Jr., 1979-1982
Heman R. Clark, 1982-1985

GOVERNOR'S CRIME COMMISSION
G.S. 143B-478/Board No. 0257

Position No.	Name of Appointee	Address	Date Appointed	Date of Expiration
01	Burley B. Mitchell	Raleigh	03-01-77	03-01-80
01, 03	John H. Baker	Raleigh	09-28-79	03-01-80
			04-11-80	03-01-83
01	Joy Hamilton	Raleigh	08-17-83	03-01-86
02	James R. Van Camp, *chairman*	Pinehurst	03-01-77	03-01-80
			04-11-80	03-01-83
				03-01-86
03	Carl H. Axsom	Wentworth	03-01-77	03-01-80
	T. Dale Johnson	Newton	10-23-78	03-01-80
			04-11-80	03-01-83
	Joe McQueen, Jr.	Wilmington	08-17-83	03-01-86
04	Manly Lancaster	Winston-Salem	03-01-77	03-01-80
			04-11-80	03-01-83
				03-01-86
05	Ralph L. Thomas	Beaufort	03-01-77	03-01-80
			04-11-80	03-01-83
			08-17-83	03-01-86
06	Darryl L. Bruestle	Wilmington	03-01-77	03-01-81
			09-18-81	03-01-84
			08-15-84	03-01-87
07	Trevor A. Hampton	Greensboro	03-01-77	03-01-81
			09-18-81	03-01-84
	C. M. Gilstrap	Goldsboro	11-02-84	03-01-87
08	William Clarence Owens	Elizabeth City	03-01-77	03-01-79
			05-15-79	03-01-82
			06-29-82	03-01-85
09	Jacob T. Hedrick	Southmont	03-01-77	03-01-80
	Robert T. Howard	Whiteville	12-03-79	03-01-80
			04-11-80	03-01-83
				08-17-86

GOVERNOR'S CRIME COMMISSION (CONTINUED)

Position No.	Name of Appointee	Address	Date Appointed	Date of Expiration
10	Betty S. Speir	Bethel	03-01-77	03-01-79
			05-15-79	03-01-82
10, 11	Drew T. Pledger	Winston-Salem	06-29-82	03-01-84
			08-15-84	03-01-87
10	Linda Hayes	Dunn	08-17-83	03-01-86
11	Barbara W. Sarudy	Greensboro	03-01-77	03-01-79
			05-15-79	03-01-82
	Steven J. Williams	Raleigh	05-21-81	03-01-82
12	Peter S. Gilchrist III, vice-chairman	Charlotte	01-26-78	03-01-80
			04-11-80	03-01-83
				03-01-86
13	Richard Whitted	Hillsborough	03-15-78	03-01-81
			09-18-81	03-01-84
				03-01-85
14	J. M. Lackey	Hiddenite	11-01-77	03-01-80
	Howard J. Hunter, Jr.	Murfreesboro	12-30-79	03-01-80
			04-11-80	03-01-83
	Gerald Fox	Charlotte	09-06-83	03-01-86
15	Elisabeth G. Hair	Charlotte	03-01-77	
	Tom Doughton	Sparta	09-28-79	03-01-81
	Jack Shore	Yadkinville	09-18-81	03-01-84
	Tommy Bardin	Tarboro	09-25-84	03-01-87
16	Beth D. Finch	Fayetteville	03-01-77	03-01-81
	Bob R. Braswell	Goldsboro	04-15-82	03-01-84
			11-02-84	03-01-87
17	W. A. Miles	Warrenton	03-06-78	03-01-81
	John H. Moss	Kings Mountain	09-18-81	03-01-84
	Robert A. Gibbons	Lenoir	10-02-84	03-01-88
18	Simon C. Sitterson, Jr.	Kinston	03-01-77	03-01-79
	W. Bruce Teachy, Jr.	Jacksonville	09-28-79	08-01-82
	Rex McLeod	Sanford	02-24-84	03-01-85
38	James H. Slaughter	Kannapolis	08-10-82	03-01-85
39	Anthony T. Lathrop	Chapel Hill	11-08-82	03-01-85

CRIME PREVENTION AND PUBLIC INFORMATION COMMITTEE OF THE
GOVERNOR'S CRIME COMMISSION
G.S. 143B-480/Board No. 3074

01	Jane Barkley	Fayetteville	08-21-78	03-01-79
			08-29-79	03-01-81
02	Miron Bentley	Wilkesboro	08-21-78	03-01-79
			08-29-79	03-01-81
03	Joyce F. Cashion	Kings Mountain	08-21-78	03-01-79
			08-29-79	03-01-81
04	Thomas R. Cloninger	Kure Beach	08-21-78	03-01-79
			08-29-79	03-01-81
05	Edith C. Everest	Winston-Salem	08-21-78	03-01-79
			08-29-79	03-01-81
06	Herman Ivey	Thomasville	08-21-78	03-01-79
			08-29-79	03-01-81
07	Lawrence Jackson, Jr.	Laurinburg	08-21-78	03-01-79
			08-29-79	02-01-81
08	Willoree Jobe	Burnsville	08-21-78	03-01-79
			08-29-79	03-01-81

CRIME PREVENTION AND PUBLIC INFORMATION COMMITTEE OF THE
GOVERNOR'S CRIME COMMISSION (CONTINUED)

Position No.	Name of Appointee	Address	Date Appointed	Date of Expiration
09	Robert E. McQueen	Kernersville	08-21-78	03-01-79
			08-29-79	03-01-81
10	Agnes P. Merritt	Louisburg	08-21-78	03-01-79
			08-29-79	03-01-81
11	W. C. Owens	Elizabeth City	08-21-78	03-01-79
			08-29-79	03-01-81
12	Agnes B. Sullivan	Jacksonville	08-21-78	03-01-79
			08-29-79	03-01-81
13	Bernard Walters	Louisburg	08-21-78	03-01-79
			08-29-79	03-01-81
	Roger Phillips	Thomasville	03-31-80	03-01-81
14	Eugene B. Walters, Jr.	Fuquay-Varina	08-21-78	03-01-79
			08-29-79	03-01-81
15	Norman W. Whitley	Smithfield	08-21-78	03-01-79
			08-29-79	03-01-81
16	Whittier Witherspoon	Elizabeth City	09-25-78	03-01-79
			08-29-79	03-01-81
17	Bill Cox, vice-chairman	Hertford	08-21-78	03-01-79
			08-29-79	03-01-81
18	Frank L. Todd	Hendersonville	08-21-78	03-01-79
			08-29-79	03-01-81
19	Manly Lancaster, chairman	Rural Hall	08-21-78	03-01-79
			08-29-79	03-01-81
20	Tom Morrissey	Arden	08-21-78	03-01-79
			08-29-79	03-01-81
21	E. Y. Ponder	Marshall	08-21-78	03-01-79
			08-29-79	03-01-81
22	William F. Southern	Walnut Cove	08-21-78	03-01-79
			08-29-79	03-01-81
23	Louise Stokes	Washington	08-21-78	03-01-79
			08-29-79	03-01-81
24	Troy Toppin	Edenton	08-21-78	03-01-79
			08-29-79	03-01-81
25	Dave Wiggins, Jr.	Bryson City	08-21-78	03-01-79
			08-29-79	03-01-81
26	Hazel M. Wiggins	Tryon	08-21-78	03-01-79
			08-29-79	03-01-81
27	Raymond Evans	Oxford	08-21-78	03-01-79
			08-29-79	03-01-81
28	Worth L. Hill	Durham	08-21-78	03-01-79
			08-29-79	03-01-81
29	Robert J. Todd	Yadkinville	08-21-78	03-01-79
			08-29-79	03-01-81
30	Rick E. Smith	Chapel Hill	08-01-78	03-01-79
			08-29-79	03-01-81
31	M. L. Stallings	Smithfield	08-21-78	03-01-79
			08-29-79	03-01-81
32	C. M. Gilstrap	Goldsboro	08-21-78	03-01-79
			08-29-79	03-01-81
33	Melvin L. Tucker	Asheville	08-21-78	03-01-79
			08-29-79	03-01-81
34	Lonnie D. Burton	Asheville	08-21-78	03-01-79
			08-29-79	03-01-81

CRIME PREVENTION AND PUBLIC INFORMATION COMMITTEE OF THE
GOVERNOR'S CRIME COMMISSION (CONTINUED)

Position No.	Name of Appointee	Address	Date Appointed	Date of Expiration
35	Michael D. Bellamy .... Wilmington		08-21-78	03-01-79
			08-29-79	03-01-81
36	Tami Purdue .... Raleigh		08-21-78	03-01-79
			08-29-79	03-01-81
37	David A. Swanson .... Buies Creek		08-21-78	03-01-79
			08-29-79	03-01-81
38	Clarence P. Deyton................. Raleigh		08-21-78	03-01-79
39	Wylie F. Hagler .... Raleigh		08-21-78	03-01-79
			08-29-79	03-01-81
40	H. Ted Harrison.................... Raleigh		08-21-78	03-01-79
			08-29-79	03-01-81
41	Max Powell .... Durham		08-21-78	03-01-79
			08-29-79	03-01-81
42	Francine Sawyer .... New Bern		08-21-78	03-01-79
			08-29-79	03-01-81
43	William F. Booth .... Roseboro		08-21-78	03-01-79
			08-29-79	03-01-81
44	William A. Taylor .... Cary		08-21-78	03-01-79
			08-29-79	03-01-81
45	Dewey L. Keesler .... Charlotte		08-21-78	03-01-79
			08-29-79	03-01-81
46	Tommy Hayes .... Southern Pines		08-21-78	03-01-79
			08-29-79	03-01-81
47	Gray Hutchins.................. Rural Hall		08-21-78	03-01-79
			08-29-79	03-01-81
48	Rollie Tillman .... Chapel Hill		08-21-78	03-01-79
			08-29-79	03-01-81
49	Preston Hill .... Charlotte		08-21-78	03-01-79
			08-29-79	03-01-81

STATE FIRE COMMISSION
G.S. 143B-481/Board No. 0367

03	David L. Cope .... Durham		11-01-77	06-30-80
			08-07-80	06-30-83

MILITARY AIDES-DE-CAMP
G.S. 127A-18/Board No. 0580

01	L. Wesley Ives .... Raleigh		04-15-77	
	Dewey T. O'Kelly, Jr. .... Raleigh		08-01-79	
02, 01	Douglas B. Whitley .... Wilson		04-15-77	
			08-01-79	
			03-06-81	
02	Wiley E. Andrews .... Smithfield		03-06-81	
03, 05	Joseph M. Parker .... Ahoskie		04-15-77	
			03-06-81	
03	Furman P. Bodenheimer .... Cary		03-06-81	
04	Jack W. Markham .... Durham		04-15-77	
	Joseph L. Jennings .... Durham		09-08-78	
05	Roy L. Brantley .... Kinston		04-15-77	
	Wayne L. Brantley .... Kinston		08-14-78	
06	Larry J. McGuire .... Andrews		04-15-77	

MILITARY AIDES-DE-CAMP (CONTINUED)

Position No.	Name of Appointee	Address	Date Appointed	Date of Expiration
07, 06	George R. Auten	Belmont	04-15-77	
			03-25-81	
07	Delores D. Adams	New Bern	03-25-81	
08	Fred Burt	Fuquay-Varina	04-15-77	
	Jack M. Jones	Cary	03-25-81	
09	Joe G. Creech	Garner	04-15-77	
	Leslie Y. Kirby	Edenton	03-25-81	
10, 04	Robert E. Gorham	Creedmoor	04-15-77	
			03-06-81	
10	Kenneth G. Tilley	Raleigh	03-25-81	
11	Paul B. Barbee	Forest City	04-15-77	
	William C. Owens, Jr.	Elizabeth City	10-29-81	
12	Joseph L. McGee	Middlesex	09-16-77	
	Karen Brooks	Kinston	04-27-82	

DEPARTMENT OF CULTURAL RESOURCES
Secretary
Sara W. Hodgkins, 1977-1985

AMERICA'S FOUR HUNDREDTH ANNIVERSARY COMMITTEE
G.S. 143B-86/Board No. 0041

Position No.	Name of Appointee	Address	Date Appointed	Date of Expiration
01	Frell M. Owl	Cherokee	02-01-78	06-30-81
	Charles B. Winberry, Jr.	Rocky Mount	12-05-80	06-30-81
			07-30-81	06-30-85
02	Paul Green	Chapel Hill	02-01-78	06-30-81
	Richardson Preyer	Greensboro	06-09-81	06-30-85
03	H. G. Jones, *chairman*	Chapel Hill	02-01-78	06-30-79
03, 04	Lindsay C. Warren, Jr., *chairman*	Greensboro	12-05-80	06-30-83
			01-17-84	01-30-87
03	Andy Griffith	North Hollywood, Ca.	04-02-81	06-30-83
			01-17-84	06-30-87
04	Elizabeth V. Moore	Edenton	02-01-78	06-30-79
05	Emma N. Morrison	Washington, D.C.	02-01-78	06-30-81
			07-30-81	06-30-85
	Lucille Winslow	Hertford	12-30-82	06-30-85
06	Herbert R. Paschal	Greenville	02-01-78	06-30-79
			04-17-81	06-30-83
	Marc Basnight	Manteo	12-30-82	06-30-85
07	William S. Powell	Chapel Hill	02-01-78	06-30-81
			07-30-81	06-30-85
08	David Stick	Kitty Hawk	02-01-78	06-30-79
			04-17-81	06-30-83
			01-17-84	06-30-87
09	Margot E. Tillett	Manteo	02-01-78	06-30-79
			06-23-81	06-30-83
			01-17-84	06-30-87
10	Charles B. Wade, Jr.	Winston-Salem	02-01-78	06-30-81
			07-30-81	06-30-85

ARCHAEOLOGICAL ADVISORY COMMITTEE
G.S. 143B-66/Board No. 0043

Position No.	Name of Appointee	Address	Date Appointed	Date of Expiration
01	William N. Still, Jr.	Greenville	03-07-79	06-30-81
				06-30-85
02	Pressley R. Rankin, Jr.	Ellerbe	03-07-79	06-30-79
				06-30-87

NORTH CAROLINA ART COMMISSION [11]
G.S. 143B-55/Board No. 0050

02	Abram Kanof.	Raleigh	06-18-79	07-01-84
05	Noah H. Bennett, Jr.	Durham		07-01-80
06	Jeanne Rauch	Gastonia	07-13-78	07-01-84

NORTH CAROLINA ART SOCIETY, INCORPORATED, BOARD OF DIRECTORS
G.S. 143B-89/Board No. 0070

01	Jean Fox	Oxford	11-30-77	07-01-80
	June G. Snow	Mount Airy	07-21-81	07-01-83
	Camma Merritt	Mount Airy	02-13-84	07-01-86
02	Louise W. Talley.	Raleigh	11-30-77	07-01-80
			04-13-81	07-01-83
			02-13-84	07-01-86
03	John B. Lewis, Jr.	Farmville	11-30-77	07-01-80
	Marcia W. Simon	Charlotte	04-13-81	07-01-83
	Sally Phillips.	High Point	09-14-84	07-01-86
04	Alma H. Brady	Salisbury	11-30-77	07-01-80
			04-13-81	07-01-83
			02-22-84	07-01-86
05	Wanda J. Garrett	Durham	11-30-77	07-01-80
	Mary A. Warlick	Jacksonville	04-13-81	07-01-83
			02-13-84	07-01-86
06	Jeanne E. Meiggs.	Shawboro	11-30-77	07-01-80
			04-13-81	07-01-83
	Lulu Robinson	Raleigh	06-18-84	06-30-85

NORTH CAROLINA ARTS COUNCIL
G.S. 143B-88/Board No. 0060

01	Frances F. Hobart	Smithfield	10-28-77	06-30-78
				06-30-81
			07-01-81	06-30-84
			11-19-84	06-30-87
02	Sallie W. Nixon	Denver	10-28-77	06-30-78
				06-30-81
	Roy Parker, Jr.	Fayetteville	07-01-81	06-30-84
			11-19-84	06-30-87
03	Patricia D. Dalton	Statesville	08-03-78	06-30-81
	Anna L. Cassell	Greensboro	08-28-84	06-30-87
	Nina K. Starr.	Greensboro	11-10-81	06-30-84

---

11 G.S. 143B-54 through 143B-57, inclusive, were repealed under *N.C. Session Laws, 1979, Second Session, 1980*, c. 1306, s. 5, ratified June 25, 1980, and became effective July 1, 1980.

North Carolina Arts Council (CONTINUED)

Position No.	Name of Appointee	Address	Date Appointed	Date of Expiration
04	Bernard W. Goss	West Jefferson	08-03-78	06-30-81
			07-01-81	06-30-84
			11-19-84	06-30-87
05	Mollie G. Blankenship	Cherokee	08-03-78	06-30-81
			07-01-81	06-30-84
			11-19-84	06-30-87
06	Wally Kaufman	Pittsboro	08-02-78	06-30-81
	Claude F. Howell	Wilmington	11-30-81	06-30-84
			11-19-84	06-30-87
07	Leo W. Jenkins	Morehead City	08-03-78	06-30-81
			07-01-81	06-30-84
			11-19-84	06-30-87
08	Michael Newman	Winston-Salem	08-03-78	06-30-81
			07-01-81	06-30-84
			08-28-84	06-30-87
09	H. Martin Lancaster, *chairman*	Goldsboro	10-28-77	06-30-80
	Mary P. Seymour, *chairwoman*	Greensboro	01-12-81	06-30-83
10	Henry Bowers	Raleigh	10-28-77	06-30-80
			01-12-81	06-30-83
11	Portia A. Mapp	Asheville	10-28-77	06-30-80
			01-12-81	06-30-83
12	Mellicent S. Adams	Dunn	10-28-77	06-30-80
			01-12-81	06-30-83
13	Samuel T. Ragan	Southern Pines	10-28-77	06-30-80
	Maxine Levine	Charlotte	01-12-81	06-30-83
14	Sydnor Thompson	Charlotte	10-28-77	06-30-80
			01-12-81	06-30-83
15	Roberts E. Timberlake	Lexington	10-28-77	06-30-80
	Elizabeth W. Cone	Greensboro	01-12-81	06-30-83
16	Annette Fairless	Edenton	10-28-77	06-30-80
	Jack Lewis	Farmville	01-12-81	06-30-83
17	Charles E. Brady	Salisbury	12-03-79	06-30-82
			09-21-82	06-30-85
18	Mary R. Andrews	Robersonville	11-09-79	06-30-82
			09-21-82	06-30-85
19	Beatrice Covington	Winston-Salem	11-09-79	06-30-82
			09-21-82	06-30-85
	Maya Angelou	Winston-Salem	12-07-84	06-30-85
20	Stacy L. Weaver, Jr.	Fayetteville	08-03-78	06-30-79
			11-09-79	06-30-82
			09-21-82	06-30-85
21	William T. McDaniel, Jr.	Greensboro	11-09-79	06-30-82
	Lana Henderson	Durham	01-12-81	06-30-82
			09-21-82	06-30-85
22	Martha Davis	Winston-Salem	12-19-79	06-30-82
	James H. Semans	Durham	09-17-82	06-30-85
23	Eve Smith	Raleigh	11-09-79	06-30-82
	Margaret Baddour	Goldsboro	09-17-82	06-30-85
24	Ralph A. Simpson	Lexington	11-09-79	06-30-82
			09-21-82	06-30-85

NORTH CAROLINA AWARDS COMMITTEE
G.S. 143B-84/Board No. 0095

Position No.	Name of Appointee	Address	Date Appointed	Date of Expiration
01	Mary Semans, *chairwoman*	Durham	07-07-77	
	Doris Betts	Chapel Hill	03-18-81	
02	Guy Owen, Jr.	Raleigh	07-07-77	
	Elizabeth D. Koontz	Raleigh	03-18-81	
03	Voit Gilmore	Southern Pines	07-07-77	
	Sam Ragan	Southern Pines	03-18-81	
04	Louise N. Sutton	Elizabeth City	07-07-77	
	Wilbert W. Johnson	Raleigh	04-11-79	
	H. F. Robinson	Cullowhee	03-18-81	
05	Mary L. Cecil	Asheville	07-07-77	
	Terry Sanford	Durham	03-18-81	

HISTORIC BATH COMMISSION
G.S. 143B-102/Board No. 0120

Position No.	Name of Appointee	Address	Date Appointed	Date of Expiration
01	Jackie O. Thompson	Aurora	12-07-77	06-30-82
	George D. Elliott, Jr.	Bath	08-24-82	06-30-87
02	E. Bruce Beasley III	Greenville	12-07-77	06-30-82
	Jane W. Page	Washington	08-24-82	06-30-87
03	Mary A. Chapin	Washington	12-07-77	06-30-82
	Thaddeus E. Tankard, Jr.	Bath	08-24-82	06-30-87
04	Emma N. Morrison	Washington	12-07-77	06-30-82
	Mary E. Parker	Rocky Mount	08-24-82	06-30-87
05	Odell L. Snow	Washington	12-07-77	06-30-82
			08-24-82	06-30-87
06	Ira M. Hardy	Greenville	07-15-81	06-30-86
07	Eve H. Smith	Raleigh	07-15-81	06-30-86
08	Robert B. Gwyn	Tulsa, Ok.	07-15-81	06-30-86
09, 16	Edgar S. Woolard, Jr.	Greenville, De.	07-15-81	06-30-86
10	Anice Tripp	Greenville	07-15-81	06-30-86
	Ruth B. Smith	Bath	12-14-84	06-30-86
11	James B. McMullan	Washington	11-20-80	06-30-85
12	Rose Herring	North Wilkesboro	11-20-80	06-30-85
13	Henry Humphreys	Washington	11-20-80	06-30-85
14	Frances M. Roberson	Washington	11-20-80	06-30-85
15	Patricia D. Duke	Farmville	11-20-80	06-30-85
16	Henry C. Bridgers	Tarboro	02-01-80	06-30-84
16, 09	Zelma M. Winfield	Washington	07-15-81	06-30-84
			10-18-84	06-30-89
17	Gwen Lamb	Washington	08-03-78	06-30-83
	Rachel F. Futrell	Washington	03-25-80	06-30-83
			09-19-83	06-30-88
18	Gino P. Giusti	Stanford, Ct.	02-01-80	06-30-84
			10-18-84	06-30-89
19	Beverly W. Harrington	Lewiston	02-01-80	06-30-84
	Judy Raper	Bath	10-02-84	06-30-89
20	Loonis McGlohon	Charlotte	02-01-80	06-30-84
			10-18-84	06-30-89
21	Catherine Lang, *secretary*	Greenville	02-01-80	06-30-84
			10-18-84	06-30-89
22	Herbert R. Paschal	Greenville	00-00-00	06-30-83

HISTORIC BATH COMMISSION (CONTINUED)

Position No.	Name of Appointee	Address	Date Appointed	Date of Expiration
	Donald R. Lennon*	Greenville	08-24-82	06-30-83
			09-19-83	06-30-88
23	Blake C. Lewis, Jr., *chairman*	Washington	08-03-78	06-30-83
			09-10-83	06-30-88
24	Milton P. Fields	Rocky Mount	08-03-78	06-30-83
			09-19-83	06-30-88
25	Leo W. Jenkins, *vice-chairman*	Greenville	08-03-78	06-30-83
	Jo Ann Davis	Kitty Hawk	09-19-83	06-30-88

EDENTON HISTORICAL COMMISSION
G.S. 143B-98/Board No. 0300

01	Vivian P. Bond	Edenton	11-18-77
02	Louis F. Hofermehl	Raleigh	11-18-77
03	Richard D. Dixon, Jr.	Edenton	11-18-77
04	Rebecca W. Drane	Edenton	11-18-77
05	Carrie M. Earnhardt	Edenton	11-18-77
06, 13	Trudy White	Elizabeth City	11-18-77
07, 14	George A. Byrum	Edenton	11-18-77
			12-17-81
08	John W. Graham	Edenton	11-18-77
09	Anna Bair	Elizabeth City	11-18-77
10, 15	Judy Earnhardt	Edenton	11-18-77
			12-17-81
11	Lena M. Leary, *secretary*	Edenton	11-18-77
12	Elizabeth V. Moore	Edenton	11-18-77
13	Jacqueline Nash	Tarboro	11-18-77
14	Anna Ragland	Raleigh	11-18-77
15	Gertrude Rosevear	Edenton	11-18-77
16	James G. Blount	Edenton	11-18-77
17	Nancy Campbell	Edenton	11-18-77
18	Lucille Winslow	Hertford	11-18-77
19	J. Gilliam Wood	Edenton	11-18-77
20, 18	Ruth Phillips	Edenton	11-18-77
			12-17-81
20	Frank Sellers	Edenton	02-28-83
21	L. F. Amburn, Jr.	Edenton	11-18-77
22	Marcia K. Crandall	Edenton	11-18-77
23	William B. Gardner	Edenton	11-18-77
	Frances T. Hollowell	Edenton	12-09-81
24	Cornelia J. W. Privott	Edenton	11-18-77
	April B. Lane	Edenton	12-09-81
25	John A. Mitchiner, Jr.	Edenton	11-18-77
	Betty L. Manning	Edenton	12-09-81
26	Richard H. Jenrette	New York, N.Y.	11-18-77
	Isaac R. Self	Edenton	12-09-81
27	Naomi Morris	Raleigh	11-18-77
	Katherine K. Busby	Edenton	12-09-81
28	J. Everette Fauber, Jr.	Lynchburg, Va.	11-18-77

*Order of succession as indicated on printout.

EDENTON HISTORICAL COMMISSION (CONTINUED)

Position No.	Name of Appointee	Address	Date Appointed	Date of Expiration
	Christopher Bean	Edenton	12-09-81	
29	Betty Silver	Raleigh	11-18-77	
	Tamar Clarke	Edenton	12-09-81	
30	Jack M. Pruden	Durham	11-18-77	
	Emily O. Brooks	Edenton	12-09-81	
31, 19	Lindsay Hornthal	Edenton	11-18-77	
32	William W. Foreman	Elizabeth City	11-18-77	
33	John G. Zehmer	Richmond, Va.	11-18-77	
34	Helen Stevenson	Raleigh	11-18-77	
35	Lloyd Griffin	Edenton	11-18-77	
36	C. Clement Lucas	Edenton	11-18-77	
			02-15-78	
37	Thomas B. Wood	Raleigh	11-18-77	
38, 21	Frances D. Inglis, *chairwoman*	Edenton	11-18-77	
39	William W. Shaw	Rocky Mount	11-18-77	
40, 22	Minnie L. Creech	Tarboro	05-03-78	

EXECUTIVE MANSION FINE ARTS COMMITTEE
G.S. 143B-80/Board No. 0360

01	Dee S. Pell	Charlotte	02-12-81	06-30-84
			12-13-84	06-30-88
02	Bessie B. Ballentine	Raleigh	01-16-80	06-30-81
			09-30-81	06-30-85
03	Anne R. Forsyth	Winston-Salem	01-16-80	06-30-81
	Mabel C. Maddrey	Raleigh	10-06-81	06-30-85
04	Lorraine Gayle	High Point	01-16-80	06-30-81
			09-30-81	06-30-85
05	Yvonne Hammonds	Durham	01-16-80	06-30-81
			09-30-81	06-30-85
06	Mary D. Semans	Durham	02-12-81	06-30-84
			12-13-84	06-30-88
07	Thomas S. Kenan III	Chapel Hill	02-12-81	06-30-84
			12-13-84	06-30-88
08	Nancy M. Jenkins	Greenville	12-18-81	06-30-84
			12-13-84	06-30-88
09	Margaret B. Harvey	Kinston	01-16-80	06-30-83
				06-30-87
10	Mae D. Hope	Charlotte	01-16-80	06-30-83
				06-30-87
11	Mary T. Pell	Pilot Mountain	01-16-80	06-30-83
				06-30-87
12	H. L. Riddle	Morganton	01-20-82	06-30-83
	Betty Y. Powell	Burlington	01-05-84	06-30-87
13	Claudia W. Belk	Charlotte	01-16-80	06-30-82
				06-30-86
14	Dixie I. Bost	Newton	01-16-80	06-30-82
				06-30-86
15	Anna L. Cassell	Greensboro	01-16-80	06-30-82
				06-30-86
16	Marjorie B. Debnam	Raleigh	01-16-80	06-30-82
				06-30-86

HISTORIC HILLSBOROUGH COMMISSION
G.S. 143B-106/Board No. 0427

Position No.	Name of Appointee	Address	Date Appointed	Date of Expiration
01	Betty P. McAllister	Hillsborough	11-16-77	10-01-83
	Jack E. Martin	Hillsborough	11-30-81	10-01-87
02	Lucius M. Cheshire	Hillsborough	11-16-77	10-01-83
	Hilda Winecoff	Hillsborough	01-02-85	10-01-89
03	James Webb	Greensboro	05-01-78	10-01-81
04	John P. Kennedy, Jr.	Hillsborough	11-16-77	10-01-83
	Robin C. Andrews	Chapel Hill	11-03-78	10-01-83
			12-27-84	10-01-89
05	Elizabeth T. Cates	Hillsborough	11-16-77	10-01-83
	J. L. Brown, Jr.	Hillsborough	01-01-83	10-01-85
06	Clarence D. Jones	Hillsborough	11-16-77	10-01-83
			12-27-84	10-01-89
07	Refford Cate	Reidsville	11-16-77	10-01-83
			01-02-85	10-01-89
08	Elizabeth R. Daniel	Chapel Hill	11-16-77	10-01-83
	Myra C. Markhum	Durham	01-02-84	10-01-89
09	Tempie H. Prince	Reidsville	11-16-77	10-01-83
	Grace J. Roberts	Hillsborough	01-02-85	10-01-89
10	Paul R. Williams	Hillsborough	11-30-81	10-01-87
11	Mary C. Engstrom	Chapel Hill	11-30-81	10-01-87
12	Minerva Kenyon	Hillsborough	11-30-81	10-01-87
13	Evelyn Patterson	Hillsborough	11-30-81	10-01-87
14	Randolph Riley	Raleigh	12-03-81	10-01-83
14, 03	Ann Sanders	Chapel Hill	11-30-81	10-01-87
15	Geneva W. Warren	Prospect Hill	12-03-81	10-01-87
17	Alonzo B. Coleman, Jr.	Hillsborough	12-01-81	10-01-87
18	Mary F. Vogler	Chapel Hill	11-30-81	10-01-87
19	Charles H. Blake	Hillsborough	01-10-80	10-01-85
	Margaret Moore	Hillsborough	01-01-85	10-01-85
20	Henry W. Moore	Hillsborough	01-10-80	10-01-85
21	Robert J. Murphy, Jr.	Hillsborough	01-10-80	10-01-85
22	Rocoe L. Strickland, Jr.	Hillsborough	01-10-80	10-01-85
23	Ronald G. Witt	Hillsborough	01-10-80	10-01-85
	Stephen H. Halkiotis	Chapel Hill	01-01-83	10-01-85
24	Leigh J. Cameron	Hillsborough	01-10-80	10-01-85
25	Evelyn Lloyd	Hillsborough	01-10-80	10-01-85
26	Evan H. Turner	Hillsborough	01-10-80	10-01-85
27	Bonnie B. Davis	Hillsborough	01-10-80	10-01-85
28	H. Marion Clark	Hillsborough	01-10-80	10-01-85
29	E. Wilson Cole	Hillsborough	01-10-80	10-01-85

NORTH CAROLINA HISTORICAL COMMISSION
G.S. 143B-63/Board No. 0430

01	Gertrude S. Carraway	New Bern	11-17-77	03-31-83
	Lala C. Steelman	Greenville	10-05-83	03-31-89
02	Thomas H. Gatton	Raleigh	11-17-77	03-31-78
			11-19-79	03-31-85
03	John E. Raper, Jr.	Fayetteville	11-17-77	03-31-81
	Clifton W. Everett, Jr.	Greenville	11-30-82	03-31-87
04	Julia Daniels	Raleigh	04-01-81	03-31-87

NORTH CAROLINA HISTORICAL COMMISSION (CONTINUED)

Position No.	Name of Appointee	Address	Date Appointed	Date of Expiration
05	Raymond Gavins	Durham	03-10-77	03-31-81
	Earl E. Thorpe	Durham	12-17-82	03-31-87
	Percy Murray	Durham	10-05-83	03-31-87
06	Harley E. Jolley	Mars Hill	09-12-79	03-31-85
07	Dick Brown	Laurinburg	10-02-79	03-31-85
08	Clyde M. Norton	Old Fort	11-17-77	03-31-81
			07-30-82	03-31-87
09	Samuel W. Johnson	Rocky Mount	11-17-77	03-31-83
	Betty Burton	Shelby	10-05-83	03-31-89
10	Sarah M. Lemmon, *chairwoman*	Raleigh	11-17-77	03-31-79
			11-20-79	03-31-85
	William S. Powell	Chapel Hill	10-05-83	03-31-89
11	H. G. Jones	Chapel Hill	11-17-77	03-31-83
			10-05-83	03-31-89

JOHN MOTLEY MOREHEAD MEMORIAL COMMISSION
G.S. 143B-115/Board No. 0595

Position No.	Name of Appointee	Address	Date Appointed	Date of Expiration
02	Martha F. Hawley	High Point	11-01-77	07-01-83
03	Catherine T. Bonner	Greensboro	11-01-77	07-01-83
04	Grace B. Hunt	Greensboro	11-01-77	07-01-83

STATE LIBRARY COMMISSION
G.S. 143B-91/Board No. 0535

Position No.	Name of Appointee	Address	Date Appointed	Date of Expiration
01	Flora W. Plyler, *chairwoman*	Wilson	01-20-78	07-01-83
			01-31-84	07-01-89
02	Margaret S. Parrott	Greensboro	01-20-78	07-01-83
			01-25-84	07-01-89
03	Artemis C. Kares	Greenville	07-29-81	07-01-87
04	Elizabeth R. Hill	Brevard	07-01-79	07-01-85
			02-24-84	07-01-89
05	Marguerite B. Heafner	Lincolnton	01-20-78	07-01-79
			08-07-80	07-01-85
	Sharon Porter	Clyde	06-06-84	07-01-85
06	Peggy C. Simmons	Lincolnton	09-12-78	07-01-81
			07-29-81	07-01-87

HISTORIC MURFREESBORO COMMISSION
G.S. 143B-110/Board No. 0615

Position No.	Name of Appointee	Address	Date Appointed	Date of Expiration
01	Catherine H. Jenkins	Murfreesboro	11-11-77	03-07-82
			04-13-84	03-01-87
02	W. H. S. Burgwyn, Jr.	Woodland	03-07-77	03-07-82
			04-13-82	03-01-87
03	Clarence J. Parker	Ahoskie	11-17-77	03-07-82
			04-13-82	03-01-87
	J. Harvey Pence	Murfreesboro	02-23-83	03-01-87
	Betsey Overton	Aulander	06-09-83	03-01-87
04	Virginia Smith	Raleigh	11-17-77	03-07-82
			04-13-82	03-01-87
05	Etheleen Underwood	Murfreesboro	11-17-77	03-07-82
			04-13-82	03-01-87

HISTORIC MURFREESBORO COMMISSION (CONTINUED)

Position No.	Name of Appointee	Address	Date Appointed	Date of Expiration
06	Henry K. Burgwyn	Murfreesboro	11-17-77	03-07-82
			04-13-82	03-01-87
07	Mildred Lackey	Murfreesboro	03-30-81	03-01-86
08	L. A. Bailey	Rocky Mount	09-11-78	03-01-83
	June D. Ward	Winston-Salem	06-09-83	03-01-88
09	Margaret L. Johnston	Weldon	03-30-81	03-01-86
10	Lillian Robinson	Littleton	03-30-81	03-01-86
11	Harry W. Whitley	Murfreesboro	03-30-81	03-01-86
12	Dorothy H. Brown	Murfreesboro	03-30-81	03-01-86
	Brenda Jordan	Raleigh	06-09-83	03-01-86
13	Benjamin F. Martin	Winston-Salem	04-23-80	03-01-85
14	Julia A. Fitts	Roanoke Rapids	04-23-80	03-01-85
15	Lindsay S. Newsom	Raleigh	04-23-80	03-01-85
16	Randy V. Britton	Ahoskie	04-24-80	03-01-85
17	Barbara Gillam	Windsor	04-23-80	03-01-85
18	Harry L. Thompson	Windsor	04-23-80	03-01-85
19	Rachel Pittman	Ahoskie	09-07-79	03-01-84
			06-06-84	03-01-89
20	John R. Jordan, Jr.	Raleigh	09-07-79	03-07-84
	James C. Pennington	Murfreesboro	04-24-80	03-01-84
21	E. Frank Stephenson, Jr.	Murfreesboro	09-07-79	03-01-84
			06-06-84	03-01-89
22	William S. Vann	Alexandria, Va.	09-07-79	03-01-84
			06-18-84	03-01-89
23	Gertrude J. Revelle	Murfreesboro	09-07-79	03-01-84
			06-18-84	03-01-89
24	Nancy S. Copeland	Murfreesboro	09-07-79	03-01-84
			06-06-84	03-01-89
25	Mildred Godwin	Raleigh	09-11-78	03-07-81
	Bob F. Hill, Sr.	Murfreesboro	06-24-81	03-01-86
26	Marie V. Cooke	Murfreesboro	09-11-78	03-01-83
				03-01-88
27	J. H. Stutts	Como	06-22-83	03-01-88
28	Lavinia S. Vann	Murfreesboro	09-11-78	03-01-83
				03-01-88
29	Thomas Parramore	Raleigh	06-09-83	03-01-88
30	Kenneth D. Wright	Wake Forest	09-11-78	03-01-83
			06-09-83	03-01-88

THE BOARD OF TRUSTEES OF THE NORTH CAROLINA MUSEUM OF ART
G.S. 140-5.13/Board No. 0049

No.	Name	Address	Date Appointed	Date of Expiration
01	Ivie L. Clayton	Raleigh	12-03-80	06-30-83
			08-26-83	06-30-89
02	Mary S. Froelich	High Point	12-03-80	06-30-86
03	Ruth B. Jones	Rocky Mount	12-03-80	06-30-83
	Douglas Covington	Winston-Salem	08-26-83	06-30-89
	John Dozier	Southern Pines	12-14-84	06-30-89
04	Mable P. McLean	Concord	12-03-80	06-30-86
05	Jeanne G. Rauch, vice-chairwoman	Gastonia	12-03-80	06-30-86
06	Sally Rhoades	Asheville	12-03-80	06-30-86
07	Mary D. B. Semans	Durham	12-03-80	06-30-83
	Alice Welsh	Chapel Hill	08-26-83	06-30-89

Tryon Palace Commission
G.S. 143B-72/Board No. 0910

Position No.	Name of Appointee	Address	Date Appointed	Date of Expiration
02	John E. Tyler	Roxobel	08-22-78	
08	Gary M. Rousseau	Wilkesboro	08-11-82	
11	J. Samuel Mitchener	Raleigh		
12	Gerald L. Lewis	Raleigh	03-09-81	
13	Ann O. Harvey	Kinston	01-02-78	
14	Anita Schenck	Greensboro	08-11-82	
15	Kay S. Hewitt, *recording secretary*	Newport	08-22-78	
22	Joseph E. Zaytoun	Cary	01-23-79	
24	Jean B. Noble	Lumberton	05-09-77	
25	Carroll H. Leggett	Washington, D.C.	08-22-78	

U.S.S. *North Carolina* Battleship Commission
G.S. 143B-74/Board No. 0125

01	Knox M. Barnes, *chairman*	Lumberton	04-04-77	04-04-79
			04-24-79	04-04-81
			08-07-81	04-04-83
				04-04-85
02	Alberta Boyd	Pineville	04-04-77	04-04-79
			04-24-79	04-04-81
			08-06-81	04-04-83
				04-04-85
03	Bess W. Finch	Asheboro	04-04-77	04-04-79
			04-24-79	04-04-81
			08-06-81	04-04-83
				04-04-85
04	J. D. Fitz	Morganton	04-04-77	04-04-79
			04-24-79	04-04-81
	William B. Whitehurst	Greenville	08-06-81	04-04-83
				04-04-85
05	L. Bennett Gram, Jr.	Ahoskie	04-04-77	04-04-79
			04-24-79	04-04-81
	David Redwine	Shallotte	08-06-81	04-04-83
	Anna Harper	Kinston	05-27-83	04-04-85
06	Mary Henson	Boone	04-04-77	04-04-79
			04-24-79	04-04-81
			08-06-81	04-04-83
				04-04-85
07	Elizabeth R. Hoyle	Smithfield	04-04-77	04-04-79
			04-24-79	04-04-81
			08-06-81	04-04-83
				04-04-85
08	Vivian E. Irving	Raleigh	04-04-77	04-04-79
			04-24-79	04-04-81
			08-06-81	04-04-83
				04-04-85
09	Richard B. Kepley, *treasurer*	Carolina Beach	04-04-77	04-04-79
			04-24-79	04-04-81
	R. Max Blackburn	Charlotte	07-25-80	04-04-81
			08-06-81	04-04-83
				04-04-85

U.S.S. *NORTH CAROLINA* BATTLESHIP COMMISSION
(CONTINUED)

Position No.	Name of Appointee	Address	Date Appointed	Date of Expiration
10	Elizabeth H. Maddrey	Eden	04-04-77	04-04-79
			04-24-79	04-04-81
			08-06-81	04-04-83
				04-04-85
11	Thomas V. Moseley	Wilmington	04-04-77	04-04-79
			04-24-79	04-04-81
			08-06-81	04-04-83
				04-04-85
12	Wallace C. Murchison............	Wilmington	04-04-77	04-04-79
			04-24-79	04-04-81
	Gleason Allen	Wilmington	08-06-81	04-04-83
				04-04-85
13	Sara S. Reece, *vice-chairwoman*	Statesville	04-04-77	04-04-79
			04-24-79	04-04-81
			08-06-81	04-04-83
	Michael Crowell	Winston-Salem	05-25-84	04-04-86
14	Shirley Spaeth	Elizabeth City	04-04-77	04-04-79
			04-24-79	04-04-81
			08-06-81	04-04-83
				04-04-85
15	Justis N. Willcox	Rocky Mount	04-04-77	04-04-79
			04-24-79	04-04-81
			08-06-81	04-04-83
	Bobby O. Wilder..................	Garner	06-30-83	04-04-85
16	Thomas H. Wright, Jr.	Wilmington	04-04-77	04-04-79
			04-24-79	04-04-81
			08-06-81	04-04-83
				04-04-85

DEPARTMENT OF HUMAN RESOURCES
Secretaries
Sarah T. Morrow, 1977-1984
Lucy H. Bode, 1985

BOARD OF HUMAN RESOURCES [12]
G.S. 143B-141/Board No. 0445

01	John K. Nelms	Oxford	03-05-78
02	George W. McCleary................	Asheville	04-18-77
03	W. T. Harris	Charlotte	04-18-77
04	Ruth S. Starnes	Monroe	04-18-77
05	Gary L. Levinson	Gastonia	03-05-78
06	James L. Hall	Clinton	04-18-77
07	Ginny L. Dees	Burgaw	04-18-77
08	C. Clement Lucas, Jr.	Edenton	04-18-77
	Eldora H. Terrell	High Point	05-30-80

---

12 The Board of Human Resources was abolished under *N.C. Session Laws, 1983,* c. 494, ratified on June 10, 1983.

GOVERNOR'S ADVISORY COUNCIL ON AGING
G.S. 143B-181/Board No. 0005

Position No.	Name of Appointee	Address	Date Appointed	Date of Expiration
02	Claude H. Farrell	Raleigh	09-08-77	06-30-81
	John T. Denning	Clinton	06-31-82	06-30-86
03	Edward M. Barnes	Wilson	09-08-77	06-30-81
			12-07-81	06-30-85
04	E. L. Hauser	Fayetteville	09-08-77	06-30-81
			12-07-81	06-30-85
05	Floyd Brown	Trenton	09-08-77	06-30-81
			12-07-81	06-30-85
06	Myrtle Garris	Garner	09-08-77	06-30-81
	Catherine Williamson	Chadbourn	12-15-81	06-30-82
			08-24-82	06-30-86
	Louise C. Siler	Wilmington	08-16-84	06-30-86
07	Madeline Jones	Hamlet	09-08-77	06-30-81
			12-07-81	06-30-85
08	Ellen B. Winston, *chairwoman*	Raleigh	06-02-77	06-30-80
			12-17-80	06-30-84
	Grady R. Galloway	Cary	08-22-84	06-30-88
09	Wallace Kuralt	Kitty Hawk	12-17-80	06-30-84
	Ann M. Johnson	Durham	06-30-84	06-30-88
10	L. H. Moseley	Garysburg	09-19-79	06-30-83
			09-23-83	06-30-87
11	Elsie B. Evans	Winston-Salem	09-19-79	06-30-83
			09-23-83	06-30-87
12	Elizabeth C. Corkey	Charlotte	09-22-78	06-30-82
	Monroe T. Gilmour	Charlotte	08-24-82	06-30-86
13	Ernest B. Messer	Canton	09-22-78	06-30-82
	Melba von Sprecken	Charlotte	12-08-81	06-30-85
14	Eleanor Rogers	Spruce Pine	12-17-80	06-30-84
15	H. L. Mitchell	Gatesville	08-24-82	06-30-86
16	Helen D. Jacobs	Cherokee	09-19-79	06-30-83
	Ethelyn A. Conseen	Cherokee	09-16-82	06-30-83
			09-23-83	06-30-87
21	Eula Vereen	Greensboro	09-15-82	06-30-86
22	Sara Hodgkins	Raleigh	08-29-83	
23	Stanley Moore	Raleigh	09-23-83	
24	John Noe	Raleigh	09-23-83	
25	Joel New	Raleigh	09-23-83	
26	L. D. Hyde	Raleigh	09-23-83	
27	John Ingram	Raleigh	09-23-83	
28	Edward N. Wilson	Raleigh	09-23-83	

COMMISSION FOR THE BLIND
G.S. 143B-158/Board No. 0130

01	H. Mozelle Jones	Raleigh	08-29-80	07-02-86
02	C. Coleman Cates, Jr.	Burlington	11-15-77	07-02-81
			10-21-81	07-01-87
03	Leon N. Falkner	Henderson	11-15-77	07-02-81
			10-20-81	07-01-87
05	W. Herbert Hollowell, Jr.	Edenton	12-22-77	07-02-83
			02-22-84	07-01-89

COMMISSION FOR THE BLIND (CONTINUED)

Position No.	Name of Appointee	Address	Date Appointed	Date of Expiration
06	J. Oattley Lee	Fayetteville	02-29-80	07-02-86
07	Marcus V. Ingram	Durham	11-15-77	07-02-83
			02-22-84	07-01-89
08	George D. Murphy	Hickory	11-15-77	07-02-80
			08-29-80	07-01-86
09	Rachel F. Rawls	Raleigh	11-15-77	07-02-83
			02-22-84	07-01-89
10	Charles A. Waller, Jr., *chairman*	Winterville	11-15-77	07-02-83
			02-22-84	07-01-89
11	Wallace I. West, Sr.	Wilmington	11-15-77	07-02-81
			10-20-81	07-02-87

BOARD OF DIRECTORS OF THE CONFEDERATE WOMEN'S HOME[13]
G.S. 143B-174/Board No. 0220

01	Josephine S. Boyd	Fayetteville	12-05-77	06-30-79
			06-30-79	06-30-81
02	Theresa Keith, *chairwoman*	Wilmington	12-05-77	06-30-79
			06-30-79	06-30-81
03	Ruth Davis	Elm City	12-05-77	06-30-79
			06-30-79	06-30-81
04	Kathleen Faulk	Lumberton	12-05-77	06-30-79
			06-30-79	06-30-81
05	Ruth Moring	Raleigh	12-05-77	06-30-79
			06-30-79	06-30-81
06	Viola Stevens	Asheville	12-05-77	06-30-79
			06-30-79	06-30-81
07	Mabel Darden	Fayetteville	12-05-77	06-30-79
			06-30-79	06-30-81

BOARD OF DIRECTORS OF THE NORTH CAROLINA SCHOOLS FOR THE DEAF
G.S. 143B-174/Board No. 0280

01	Cecil L. Porter, *chairman*	North Wilkesboro	12-09-77	07-17-81
			11-30-81	07-15-85
02	James G. Northcott, Sr.	Black Mountain	12-09-77	07-17-81
	J. Gresham Northcott, Jr.	Charlotte	07-01-80	07-17-81
			11-30-81	07-15-85
03	George M. Holt	Burlington	12-09-77	07-17-81
			11-30-81	07-15-85
04	Ray C. Fletcher	Valdese	12-09-77	07-17-81
			11-30-81	07-15-85
05	Seroba A. Aiken	Snow Hill	12-09-77	07-17-81
			11-30-81	07-15-85
06	Jane W. Smith	Lumberton	12-09-77	07-17-81
			11-30-81	07-15-85
07	Sue C. Hooks	Fremont	12-09-77	07-17-81
			11-30-81	07-15-85
08	James L. Lee	Wilson	12-09-77	07-17-81
	John D. Stockton, Jr.	Fairview	04-21-80	07-17-81
			11-30-81	07-15-85

13 The board was abolished, effective July 1, 1981, under *N.C. Session Laws, 1981*, c. 462, s. 7, ratified May 28, 1981.

BOARD OF DIRECTORS OF THE NORTH CAROLINA SCHOOLS FOR THE DEAF
(CONTINUED)

Position No.	Name of Appointee	Address	Date Appointed	Date of Expiration
09	James M. Dixon	Greensboro	12-09-77	07-17-81
	Sterling White	Winston-Salem	02-08-80	07-17-81
			11-30-81	07-15-85
10	Selena H. Hall	Rocky Mount	12-09-77	07-17-81
			11-30-81	07-15-85
11	Lillian W. Snipes	Greensboro	12-09-77	07-17-81
	William H. Worrell	Greensboro	11-30-81	07-15-85

COUNCIL ON DEVELOPMENTAL DISABILITIES
G.S. 143B-179/Board No. 0285

Position No.	Name of Appointee	Address	Date Appointed	Date of Expiration
01	Ralph H. Scott, *chairman*	Burlington	09-29-77	
			11-11-81	06-30-85
02, 18	Marilea R. Grogan	Charlotte	09-29-77	06-30-81
			11-11-81	06-30-85
02	Ann Gibbs	Greensboro	06-29-84	06-30-88
03, 19	Joseph P. Roberson	Washington	09-29-77	06-30-81
			11-11-81	06-30-85
03	Theodore Drain	Raleigh	10-09-80	
04	Ann P. Turnbull	Chapel Hill	09-29-77	06-30-81
	Richard A. Harrop	Raleigh	02-05-82	
05, 20	Lois P. Queen	Waynesville	09-29-77	06-30-81
			11-11-81	06-30-85
05	Lucy H. Bode*	Raleigh	00-00-00	
06	Felecia B. Greenfield	Charlotte	09-27-77	06-30-81
	Paul R. Perruzi	Raleigh	10-09-80	
07, 14	Juanita L. Howard	Greenville	09-29-77	06-30-81
			11-11-81	06-30-85
07	Mike Pedneau	Raleigh	10-09-80	
	Robert Fitzgerald**	Raleigh	10-09-80	
	Theodore R. Parrish	Raleigh	11-17-82	
08, 21	Jeanne T. Fenner	Wilson	09-29-77	06-30-81
			11-11-81	06-30-85
08	Don Taylor	Raleigh	10-22-82	06-30-86
09, 32	Albert J. Morton, Jr.	Charlotte	09-29-77	06-30-81
09	Thomas J. Vitaglione	Raleigh	10-05-83	06-30-86
10, 28	James E. Surratt	Burlington	09-29-77	06-30-81
				06-30-85
11, 04	Richard Urbanik	Raleigh	09-29-77	
			10-09-80	
12, 05	Minta M. Saunders	Raleigh	09-20-77	
12	Martha K. Walston	Raleigh	10-09-80	06-30-84
			06-29-84	06-30-88
13	William R. Windley	Raleigh	09-29-77	
	Steve Metcalf	Asheville	10-09-80	06-30-84
	Douglas A. Gibbs	Engelhard	11-11-81	06-30-84
	Joanne Murray	Raleigh	10-05-83	06-30-84
			07-24-84	06-30-88
14	Nettie D. Ellis	Raleigh	09-29-77	
15	Anne R. Sanford	Chapel Hill	10-11-78	06-30-79

*Date when Bode succeeded Queen in Position No. 5 not indicated on printout.
**Date and order of succession as indicated on printout.

Council on Developmental Disabilities
(continued)

Position No.	Name of Appointee	Address	Date Appointed	Date of Expiration
	R. Glenn Helms	Goldsboro	11-11-81	06-30-84
	Tom Jarrett	Goldsboro	06-29-84	06-30-85
16	Edsel L. Haney	Raleigh	09-29-77	
	Rolf R. Williams	Chapel Hill	10-09-80	06-30-82
	Deborah A. Sugg	Durham	03-29-82	06-30-82
	Kenny Jacobs	Maxton	10-22-82	06-30-86
17	Linwood E. Jennings, Jr.	Raleigh	09-29-77	
	Victor C. Hall	Raleigh	10-09-80	06-30-81
			11-11-81	06-30-85
18, 08	Ann F. Wolfe	Raleigh	09-29-77	
19, 09	Ronald H. Levine	Raleigh	09-29-77	
20, 10	Bob H. Philbeck	Raleigh	09-29-77	
21, 11	Joan C. Holland	Raleigh	09-29-77	
21, 32	Gale S. Swann	Morehead City	11-11-81	06-30-85
22	George A. Khady	Raleigh	09-29-77	
	Frank Johnson	Fayetteville	10-09-80	06-30-84
	Nancy Seymour	Asheville	10-05-83	06-30-84
			06-29-84	06-30-88
23	Robert W. Wynne	Raleigh	09-29-77	
	Doris Rosemond	Wilson	10-09-80	06-30-84
24, 02	T. Clyde Auman	West End	09-29-77	
24	Joanne E. Brown	Durham	11-17-82	06-30-86
25	James Ezzell	Rocky Mount	09-29-77	
	Jack B. Hefner	Charlotte	10-22-82	06-30-86
26, 29	Naomi Henry	Winnabow	04-15-77	06-30-80
			10-09-80	06-30-84
27	Vickie Kilimanjaro	Greensboro	10-09-80	06-30-81
			11-11-81	06-30-85
29	Pearl L. Finch	Bailey	11-18-82	06-30-84
			07-16-84	06-30-88
30	James R. Bachar	Chapel Hill	10-11-78	06-30-82
	Donald T. Austin	Charlotte	10-22-82	06-30-86
31	Harrie R. Chamberlin	Chapel Hill	10-11-78	06-30-82
			10-22-82	06-30-86
32, 24	Joseph M. Butterworth, Jr.	Bethel	10-11-78	06-30-82
33, 25	Charles E. Waddell	Skyland	09-29-77	06-30-82
34, 26	Mary L. Warren	Durham	09-29-77	06-30-80
			10-09-80	06-30-84
			06-29-84	06-30-88
35	Elly Hathcock	Raleigh	10-11-78	06-30-82
36	Alice Yates	Raleigh	09-29-77	06-30-79

Governor's Council on Employment of the Handicapped[14]
G.S. 143B-185/Board No. 0410

01	Carl S. McCulloch	Elizabethtown	06-07-77	06-30-79
02	Georgia T. Reinhardt	Conover	11-18-77	06-30-81
03	Judy R. Hartman	Reidsville	11-18-77	06-30-81
04	Albert L. Bumgarner	Hickory	10-08-75	06-30-79

---

14 G.S. 143B-412 and -413, formerly G.S. 143B-184 and -185, were repealed under *N.C. Session Laws, 1977*, c. 872, s. 2, ratified July 1, 1977.

GOVERNOR'S COUNCIL ON EMPLOYMENT OF THE HANDICAPPED
(CONTINUED)

Position No.	Name of Appointee	Address	Date Appointed	Date of Expiration
06	Johnsie Frye	Hamlet	11-18-77	06-30-81
07	Charles A. Gregory	Angier	11-18-77	06-30-79
08	Craig L. Johnson	Rocky Mount	11-18-77	06-30-81
09	Anna G. Butler, *chairwoman*	Warrenton	11-18-77	06-30-81
10	Ruth B. Stoner	Lexington	10-05-78	06-30-82
11	Edward T. Smith	Raleigh	10-05-78	06-30-82
12	Rhonda H. Byrd	Rocky Mount	10-05-78	06-30-82
14	James M. Keane	Charlotte	10-05-78	06-30-82
15	Theodore R. Bryant	Durham	10-05-78	06-30-82
16	Mrs. Willie High	Raleigh	10-05-78	06-30-82
17	Barney Williamson	Wilson	10-05-78	06-30-82
18	Susan G. Kelly	Raleigh	10-05-78	06-30-82

GOVERNOR MOREHEAD SCHOOL BOARD OF DIRECTORS
G.S. 143B-174/Board No. 0590

Position No.	Name of Appointee	Address	Date Appointed	Date of Expiration
01	Doris Simmons	Lillington	10-20-81	05-01-87
02	George C. Griffin	Williamston	11-04-77	05-01-83
			02-24-84	05-01-89
03	Alice E. Wilson	Tarboro	11-04-77	05-01-83
			03-26-84	05-01-89
04	Prudence L. Johnson	Cooleemee	11-04-77	05-01-83
	Avis Martin	Durham	03-26-84	05-01-89
05	Stanley R. Taylor	High Point	11-16-79	05-01-81
			10-20-81	05-01-87
06	Harvey Reid, Jr.	Wilson	10-20-81	05-01-87
07	Jane R. Purser, *chairwoman*	Raleigh	11-04-77	05-01-83
			02-24-84	05-01-89
08	Nina W. Fountain	Tarboro	11-16-79	05-01-85
09	Ben Eason	Raleigh	11-16-79	05-01-85
10	Lee J. Stone	Asheboro	11-16-79	05-01-85
11	Vance B. Taylor	Farmville	11-16-79	05-01-85

STATE COMMISSION FOR HEALTH SERVICES
G.S. 143B-143/Board No. 0420

Position No.	Name of Appointee	Address	Date Appointed	Date of Expiration
01	J. Marshall Sasser	Smithfield	08-01-79	05-01-83
	Thomas E. Smart	Hamlet	04-29-83	05-01-87
02	Betty Snelson	Asheville	11-29-77	05-01-81
	Frank C. Cockinos	Charlotte	04-29-83	05-01-85
	James F. Bivins	Asheboro	08-05-81	05-01-85
03	George Walker	Raleigh	11-29-77	05-01-81
	Mitchell Hatchell, Jr.	Fletcher	08-05-81	05-01-85
04	Glenn P. Deal	Taylorsville	08-01-79	05-01-83
				05-01-87
05	James M. Fry	China Grove	11-29-77	05-01-81
			08-05-81	05-01-85
06	C. R. Byrd, Jr.	Burlington	11-29-77	05-01-81
	Kimsey King, Jr.	Durham	08-05-81	05-01-85
07	Dot Preston	Raleigh	11-29-77	05-01-81
	Berline Graham	Riegelwood	08-05-81	05-01-85
08	Frances R. Eason	Rocky Mount	08-02-78	05-01-82
	Jacquelyn D. Pruett	Raleigh	07-30-82	05-01-86

BOARD OF DIRECTORS OF THE LENOX BAKER CHILDREN'S HOSPITAL
G.S. 143B-173, -174/Board No. 0185

Position No.	Name of Appointee	Address	Date Appointed	Date of Expiration
01	Martha Speed, *chairwoman*	Louisburg	01-11-78	07-10-83
02	Nancy D. Roberts	Durham	02-20-80	07-10-85
03	Carolyn Booth	Cary	08-26-82	07-10-85
04	Ava T. Albritton	Snow Hill	08-26-82	07-10-87
05	Mary L. Dennis	Durham	08-26-82	07-10-87
	Thomas O. Gilmore	Julian	01-02-85	07-01-87
06	Leona P. Whichard	Durham	07-17-78	07-10-83
			08-24-83	07-10-89
	Mary D. Bender	Pollocksville	01-11-78	07-10-84
07	Norvell T. Lee	Goldsboro	02-20-80	07-10-85
08	Elizabeth S. Fisher	Durham	01-11-78	07-10-83
			08-24-83	07-10-89
09	Richard J. Vinegar	Durham	08-26-82	07-10-87

NORTH CAROLINA MEDICAL CARE COMMISSION
G.S. 143B-166/Board No. 0560

02	David Jones	Mount Airy	09-16-80	06-30-84
			08-28-84	06-30-88
03	William L. Adcock	Raleigh	09-16-80	06-30-84
	Kathy A. Taft	Greenville	04-20-84	06-30-88
04	David S. Nelson	Winston-Salem	11-04-80	06-30-84
	Louie E. Woodbury	Wilmington	08-29-84	07-01-88
05	Douglas Covington	Winston-Salem	02-12-80	06-30-83
	Daniel D. Mosca	Raleigh	07-19-83	06-30-87
06	Orlando R. Stovall	Goldsboro	02-12-80	06-30-83
				06-30-87
08	Tom P. Phillips	Charlotte	02-12-80	06-30-83
				06-30-87
09	Charles D. Watts	Durham	09-15-78	06-30-82
	Vivian Chambers	Charlotte	12-20-82	06-30-86
	Gwendolyn Blount*	Greensboro		06-30-86
14	John T. Bode	Raleigh	02-03-78	06-30-81
			09-02-81	06-30-85
16	Jack V. Hill	Fayetteville	12-16-77	06-30-81
			09-02-81	06-30-85
17	James A. Johnson	High Point	12-16-77	06-30-81
			09-02-81	06-30-85

COMMISSION FOR MENTAL HEALTH, MENTAL RETARDATION, AND
SUBSTANCE ABUSE SERVICES
G.S. 143B-148/Board No. 0570

01, 06	Howard F. Twiggs	Raleigh	02-15-78	06-30-81
			02-16-81	06-30-85
01	Pam Joyner	Raleigh	11-30-84	06-30-85
02, 09	Donald J. Stedman	Chapel Hill	02-15-78	06-30-81
			09-16-81	06-30-84
			09-14-84	06-30-88
02	Betty S. Saunders	Charlotte	09-16-81	06-30-85
	Hugh H. Macaulay	Charlotte	07-18-83	06-30-85

*Order of succession as indicated on printout.

COMMISSION FOR MENTAL HEALTH, MENTAL RETARDATION, AND
SUBSTANCE ABUSE SERVICES (CONTINUED)

Position No.	Name of Appointee	Address	Date Appointed	Date of Expiration
03	John E. Shields	Winston-Salem	02-15-78	06-30-81
	J. Albert Greene	Banner Elk	09-16-81	06-30-85
04	Theodore R. Clark	Pinehurst	02-15-78	06-30-81
	Willie F. Everhart	Lexington	12-02-82	06-30-85
05, 11	Bruce E. Whitaker, *chairman*	Murfreesboro	02-15-78	06-30-81
			09-16-81	06-30-84
			09-21-84	06-30-88
05	Randolph Cloud	Raleigh	09-16-81	06-30-85
06, 14	Mabel Hatch	Raleigh	02-15-78	06-30-80
			08-29-80	06-30-84
			09-16-81	06-30-84
06	R. Edwin McClearen	Raleigh	05-13-83	06-30-85
07	Mary L. Morrissey	Arden	02-15-78	06-30-80
			08-29-80	06-30-84
			09-16-81	06-30-85
08, 01, 14	Moses W. Stancil	Selma	02-15-78	06-30-80
			08-29-80	06-30-84
			09-16-81	06-30-85
			11-30-84	06-30-88
08	Keith Bulla	Greensboro	09-16-81	06-30-84
			09-14-84	06-30-85
09, 04, 16	John W. Varner	Lexington	02-15-78	06-30-80
			08-29-80	06-30-84
			09-16-81	06-30-85
			11-19-84	06-30-87
12, 10	Thomas E. Curtis	Chapel Hill	02-15-78	06-30-79
			01-30-80	06-30-83
			09-16-81	06-30-84
12	Martha Martinat	Winston-Salem	09-16-81	06-30-84
			09-14-84	06-30-88
13, 20	Reuben J. Davis	Kinston	02-15-78	06-30-79
			01-30-80	06-30-83
			09-16-81	06-30-83
13	Allen T. Small	Concord	09-16-81	06-30-84
14	Odessa Hicks	Raleigh	02-15-78	06-30-79
			01-30-80	06-30-83
15	Helen A. Bell	Charlotte	02-15-78	06-30-79
			01-30-80	06-30-83
	Neil Dobbins	Asheville	09-16-81	06-30-83
			07-19-83	06-30-87
	Bobby James	Raleigh	11-19-84	06-30-87
16	Anita Gause	Wilmington	09-16-81	06-30-83
	Anita King	Roanoke Rapids	07-19-83	06-30-87
17	Peggy Alston	Carrboro	09-16-81	06-30-83
			07-19-83	06-30-87
18	Ludie White	Durham	09-16-81	06-30-83
			07-19-83	06-30-87
	Dorothy Hardy	Goldsboro	11-19-84	06-30-87
19	Florine Roberson	Durham	09-16-81	06-30-83
			07-19-83	06-30-87
20	Ralph P. Edwards	Greensboro	11-28-83	06-30-87
21	Eugene Gore	Southport	09-16-81	06-30-83
				06-30-87

Mental Health Advisory Council
G.S. 143B-183/Board No. 0575

Position No.	Name of Appointee	Address	Date Appointed	Date of Expiration
05	Rebie W. Crandol	Greenville		06-30-81
06	Vivian Burke	Winston-Salem		06-30-81
07	Mary A. Claud	Tryon	02-20-78	06-30-81
08	Helen C. Cooper	Windsor	02-20-78	06-30-81
09	Judy J. Harward	Durham	02-20-78	06-30-81
10	Andra Pond	Beaufort	02-20-78	06-30-81
11	Luther J. Prevatte, Jr.	Lumberton	02-20-78	06-30-81
12	Bonnie L. Rhodes	Wilkesboro	02-20-78	06-30-81
	Eugene Gore	Southport	10-23-78	06-30-81
13	Marcia W. Simon	Charlotte	02-20-78	06-30-81
22	Olivia B. Greeson	Charlotte		06-30-81
23	Norma J. Thompson	Pembroke		06-30-81
24	Richard F. Sherman	Rocky Mount		06-30-81
25	Mansfield Elmore	Pinehurst		06-30-81
26	Carlos Young	Shelby		06-30-81
27	Mel Daniels	Elizabeth City		06-30-81
28	Philip Nelson, *chairman*	Greenville		06-30-81
29	Myree Hayes	Greenville		06-30-81
30	Millie Keen	Morganton		06-30-81
31	Carolyn Ennis	Smithfield		06-30-81
32	Martha A. Strater	Highlands	02-20-78	06-30-81
33	F. L. Armstrong	Winston-Salem		06-30-81
34	Tom Elmore	Winston-Salem		06-30-81
35	Jenny Snead	Winston-Salem		06-30-81

North Carolina Orthopedic Hospital Board of Trustees [15]
G.S. 143B-174/Board No. 0665

01	Hector H. Henry II	Concord	02-08-78	04-04-83
02	Edith Marsh	Raleigh	02-08-78	04-04-83
03	Virginia A. Fincher	Matthews	02-08-78	04-04-83

The Governor's Council on Physical Fitness and Health
G.S. 143B-216.9/Board No. 0697

01	Robert S. Boal, *chairman*	Wake Forest	01-15-80	06-30-83
			08-15-84	06-30-87
02	Frank W. Clippinger	Durham	01-15-80	06-30-81
	Melvin H. Groomes	Greensboro	01-06-81	06-30-85
03	Michael A. Estrada	Statesville	01-15-80	06-30-80
			01-12-81	06-30-84
	Ben Tench	Raleigh	08-15-84	06-30-88
04	Frank J. Hielema	Durham	01-15-80	06-30-80
			01-12-81	06-30-84
			08-15-84	06-30-88
05	Joan B. Page	Chapel Hill	01-15-80	06-30-82
				06-30-86
06	Elaine Saleeby	Hope Mills	01-15-80	06-30-83

---

15 This board was terminated in *N.C. Session Laws, 1981*, c. 50, s. 2, ratified February 26, 1981.

THE GOVERNOR'S COUNCIL ON PHYSICAL FITNESS AND HEALTH
(CONTINUED)

Position No.	Name of Appointee	Address	Date Appointed	Date of Expiration
	Margot H. Raynor	Raleigh	11-21-83	07-01-87
07	Charles D. Waddell	Chapel Hill	01-15-80	06-30-81
	Caldwell W. Nixon	Denver	01-06-81	06-30-85
08	John Steinbaugh	Raleigh	03-28-80	06-30-82
	Ben J. Lawrence	Mount Airy	05-13-83	06-30-86

RADIATION PROTECTION COMMISSION
G.S. 104E-8/Board No. 0752

Position No.	Name of Appointee	Address	Date Appointed	Date of Expiration
01	James E. Watson	Chapel Hill	05-19-78	06-30-82
			07-21-82	06-30-86
02B	Patrick W. Howe	Raleigh	05-10-78	06-30-81
			09-18-81	06-30-85
02C	Milton E. McLain, Jr.	Wilmington	03-12-82	06-30-86
	Scott Murray	Wilmington	02-24-84	06-30-86
04	Raymond L. Murray	Raleigh	11-29-79	06-30-83
			11-27-83	06-30-87
07	Aaron P. Sanders, *vice-chairman*	Durham	11-29-79	06-30-83
	Donald G. Willhoit	Chapel Hill	06-22-83	06-30-87
08	Lonnie E. Moore	New Bern	05-19-78	06-30-81
10	Janice Keene	Chapel Hill	05-19-78	06-30-79
			11-29-79	06-30-83

COUNCIL ON SICKLE CELL SYNDROME
G.S. 143B-188/Board No. 0840

Position No.	Name of Appointee	Address	Date Appointed
01	James P. Green, *chairman*	Henderson	03-07-77
02	Ivestia H. Beckwith	Charlotte	03-07-77
03	Christine A. Johnson	Winston-Salem	03-07-77
04, 13	Nathaniel L. Rumph	Winston-Salem	03-07-77
04	Mary E. McAllister	Fayetteville	08-28-78
05	Shirley McQueen	Maxton	03-07-77
06	John W. Hatch	Durham	03-07-77
	Riddick E. Wilkins, Sr.	Warsaw	02-25-80
	Walter Faribault, Jr.	Hillsborough	01-12-83
07	Almita Woods	Jacksonville	03-07-77
08	Katie G. Dorsett	Greensboro	03-07-77
09	David R. Brewington	Jacksonville	03-07-77
	Jerry W. Wiley	Raleigh	01-02-85
10	Wendell Rosse	Durham	03-07-77
11	David K. Hall, Jr.	Asheville	03-07-77
	Carter T. Holbrook	Greenville	01-14-83
12	John R. Manley	Chapel Hill	03-07-77
	David D. Phoenix, Jr.	Pittsboro	01-12-83
13	Willie Sutton*	Bayboro	03-07-77
	Eugene C. Hines, Jr.	Clinton	01-12-83
14	Allene Drain	Wilmington	03-07-77
15	Leo Bradshaw	Greensboro	03-07-77
	Lucian Johnson	Asheville	01-14-83

*Rumph succeeded Sutton in Position No. 13.

SOCIAL SERVICES COMMISSION
G.S. 143B-154/Board No. 0845

Position No.	Name of Appointee	Address	Date Appointed	Date of Expiration
01	Helen R. Marvin	Gastonia	05-15-79	04-01-83
	Sammie L. Anderson	Newland	12-15-82	04-01-87
02	Doris S. Dees	Chadbourn	07-17-79	04-01-83
	Alice V. Oesen	Wilmington	03-31-83	04-01-87
03	James C. Spencer, Jr.	Burlington	05-15-79	04-01-83
				04-01-87
04	Jim Richardson, *chairman*	Charlotte	04-18-77	04-01-83
	George E. Battle	Charlotte	07-27-83	04-01-87
05	Rex A. Parramore	Nashville	04-18-77	04-01-83
	Helen C. Amis	Oxford	04-14-83	04-01-87
06	Leolia G. Spaugh	Raleigh	06-08-81	04-01-85
07	Charles T. Fort	Winston-Salem	04-23-81	04-01-85
08	Mozelle B. Stout	Wadesboro	06-21-77	04-01-81
			04-23-81	04-01-85
09	Betsy H. Johnson	Fremont	06-21-77	04-01-81
			04-23-81	04-01-85
10	Harvey J. Hyatt	Bryson City	06-21-77	04-01-81
	Martha G. Weir	Asheville	04-23-81	04-01-85
11	Marguerite Whitfield	Kinston	06-21-77	04-01-81
			04-23-81	04-01-85

NORTH CAROLINA CERTIFICATION BOARD FOR SOCIAL WORK
G.S. 90B-5/Board No. 0677

Position No.	Name of Appointee	Address	Date Appointed	Date of Expiration
01	Jean M. Evans	Goldsboro	10-11-83	07-01-84
02	Linwood Foust	Charlotte	10-11-83	07-01-85
03	William G. Henry	Waynesville	10-11-83	07-01-84
			12-21-84	07-01-87
04	M. Keith Fearing	Manteo	10-11-83	07-01-85
05	Carolyn Phillips	Lexington	10-11-83	07-01-86
06	Audreye E. Johnson	Durham	10-11-83	07-01-84
	Wilburn Hayden	Cullowhee	12-10-84	07-01-87
07	Kathy Rose	Jacksonville	10-05-83	07-01-84

NORTH CAROLINA SPECIALTY HOSPITALS BOARD OF DIRECTORS[16]
G.S. 143B-174/Board No. 0862

Position No.	Name of Appointee	Address	Date Appointed	Date of Expiration
01	Edwin A. Rasberry, Jr.	Wilson	10-26-77	04-29-83
02	James M. Hall, Jr., *chairman*	Asheville	10-26-77	04-29-83
03	Jane H. McPhaul	Southern Pines	10-26-77	04-29-83
04	Dorris R. Bryant	Rocky Mount	10-26-77	04-29-83

GOVERNOR'S WASTE MANAGEMENT BOARD
G.S. 143B-216.12/Board No. 0949

Position No.	Name of Appointee	Address	Date Appointed	Date of Expiration
01	Claud O'Shields, Jr., *chairman*	Wilmington	11-01-81	11-01-84
	Wayne McDevitt	Marshall	12-20-84	11-01-87
02	Charles Holt	Fayetteville	11-01-81	11-01-83
	James A. Summers	Cary	01-02-85	11-01-86

---

16 This board was terminated under *N.C. Session Laws, 1979, Second Session, 1980,* c. 1245, ratified July 1, 1980.

GOVERNOR'S WASTE MANAGEMENT BOARD (CONTINUED)

Position No.	Name of Appointee	Address	Date Appointed	Date of Expiration
02, 05	Michael R. Overcash	Raleigh	12-27-83	11-01-86
03	Virginia Newell	Winston-Salem	11-30-81	11-01-83
			01-19-84	11-01-86
04	Albert L. Canipe	Spruce Pine	11-01-81	11-01-82
			01-19-84	11-01-85
05	Bernard Greenberg	Chapel Hill	11-01-81	11-01-84
06	Bill Briner	Durham	11-01-81	11-01-83
			01-19-84	11-01-86
07	William L. Lewis	Sanford	11-01-81	11-01-82
			01-19-84	11-01-85
08	William E. Graham, Jr.	Raleigh	11-01-81	11-01-84
			12-20-84	11-01-87
16	David S. Citron	Charlotte	12-27-83	11-01-86
	Harold Imbus..................	Greensboro	12-27-84	11-01-86

NORTH CAROLINA WATER TREATMENT FACILITY OPERATORS BOARD OF CERTIFICATION
G.S. 90A-21/Board No. 0945

02	Jack Neel......................	Albemarle	09-28-83	07-01-85
03	Ronald L. Matthews................	Raeford	09-28-83	07-01-84
04	Robert F. Coleman	Wilmington	09-28-83	07-02-85
05	Marshall T. White	Riegelwood	09-27-83	07-02-86
06	Charles Smallwood	Raleigh	09-28-83	07-02-86
08	Dallas O. Tucker	Cary	10-24-83	10-24-86

YOUTH SERVICES ADVISORY COMMITTEE[17]
G.S. 143B-208/Board No. 0975

01	Bill D. Brittain, *chairman*	Raleigh	05-03-78	07-01-79
02	Ruth M. Wells	Brevard	05-03-78	07-01-79
03	Jeannette M. Council	Fayetteville	05-03-78	07-01-79
04	Robert F. Hunt..................	Pinehurst	05-03-78	07-01-79
05	Jean R. Donovan	Winston-Salem	05-03-78	07-01-79

DEPARTMENT OF NATURAL RESOURCES AND COMMUNITY DEVELOPMENT
Secretaries
Howard N. Lee, 1977-1981
Joseph W. Grimsley, 1981-1983
James A. Summers, 1983-1985

BOARD OF NATURAL RESOURCES AND COMMUNITY DEVELOPMENT
G.S. 143B-280/Board No. 0627

01	Lois M. Winstead..................	Roxboro	09-27-77	
	James E. Brown...................	Monroe	08-04-78	
	Marion Nichol	Durham	12-01-81	
02	James W. Boone.................	Jackson	09-27-77	

---

17 The Youth Services Advisory Committee was abolished under *N.C. Session Laws, 1981*, c. 50, s. 8, ratified February 26, 1981.

BOARD OF NATURAL RESOURCES AND COMMUNITY DEVELOPMENT
(CONTINUED)

Position No.	Name of Appointee	Address	Date Appointed	Date of Expiration
03	Edward P. Godwin III	Wilmington	09-27-77	
	L. J. McDougle	Shelby	12-05-78	
	Wiley Lash	Salisbury	12-01-81	
04	Samuel L. Phillips	Spruce Pine	09-27-77	
05	John G. Wood, *chairman*	Edenton	09-27-77	
	James Ferguson	Clyde	08-26-81	
	John M. Gilkey	Marion	11-05-81	
06	James P. Powers	Lumberton	09-27-77	
07	Inez C. Jones	Lenoir	09-27-77	
	Joseph L. Hill	Morehead City	12-01-81	
	Logan D. Delany	Asheville	11-18-83	
08	Melba G. Smith	Belhaven	09-27-77	
	Roberts H. Jernigan, Jr.	Ahoskie	11-05-81	
09	Marsha H. Cornelius	Mooresville	09-27-77	
	Beth Finch	Fayetteville	12-01-81	
10	Dorothy Jones	Reidsville	09-27-77	

AIR QUALITY COUNCIL
G.S. 143B-318/Board No. 0020

01	Guy H. Cheek	Greensboro	08-24-78	06-30-84
03	Virginia Anderson, *chairwoman*	Hot Springs	02-01-78	06-30-84
05	Robert Lee, Jr.	Murfreesboro	02-01-78	06-30-80
08	Joseph D. Weaver	Ahoskie	08-24-78	06-30-84

ATLANTIC STATES MARINE FISHERIES COMMISSION
G.S. 113-254/Board No. 0080

01	Edward A. O'Neal	Swan Quarter	09-11-78	06-30-81
	Gerald W. Gaskill	Cedar Island	09-27-83	06-30-84
			06-18-84	06-30-87

COASTAL RESOURCES COMMISSION
G.S. 113A-104/Board No. 0207

06	Charles D. Evans	Manteo	10-26-77	06-30-80
			08-28-80	06-30-84
10	Charles C. Wells	Wilmington	08-28-80	06-30-84
			11-29-84	06-30-88
13	Arthur W. Cooper	Raleigh	08-28-80	06-30-84

COMMERCIAL AND SPORTS FISHERIES ADVISORY COMMITTEE
G.S. 143B-326/Board No. 0210

01	Orville L. Woodhouse, *chairman*	Grandy	07-25-77	07-01-79
			04-01-80	06-01-83
02	Gilbert W. Bane	Wilmington	02-15-78	06-01-81
03	Norman C. Bellamy	Supply	02-15-78	06-01-81
04	A. F. Chestnut	Morehead City	02-15-78	06-09-81
	James A. McGee	Greenville	10-25-78	06-01-81
05	Monroe Gaskill	Cedar Island	02-15-78	06-09-79
	C. J. Belch, Jr.	Plymouth	11-01-78	06-09-79
			04-01-80	06-01-83

COMMERCIAL AND SPORTS FISHERIES ADVISORY COMMITTEE
(CONTINUED)

Position No.	Name of Appointee	Address	Date Appointed	Date of Expiration
06	Elward Jenette	Mesic	02-15-78	06-09-79
			04-01-80	06-01-83
07	Ray W. Nabors	Fayetteville	02-15-78	06-01-81
08	James L. Sutherland	Laurinburg	02-15-78	06-09-79
			04-01-80	06-09-83
09	Dorothy E. Thomas	Elizabeth City	02-15-78	06-01-81

COMMUNITY DEVELOPMENT COUNCIL
G.S. 143B-306/Board No. 0215

01	Grace H. Bonner, *chairwoman*	Aurora	03-31-78	06-30-81
			04-06-82	06-30-85
02	S. Leigh Wilson	Raleigh	03-31-78	06-30-81
			04-06-82	06-30-85
03	C. Ronald Aycock	Raleigh	03-31-78	06-30-81
			04-06-82	06-30-85
04	John S. Bone, Jr.	Manteo	03-31-78	06-30-81
	Linwood E. Mercer	Farmville	04-06-82	06-30-85
05	James E. Andrews	Raleigh	03-31-78	06-30-81
	E. A. Britt	Raleigh	04-06-82	06-30-85
06	Patricia A. Pierce	Raleigh	03-31-78	06-30-81
	G. Ray Cantrell	Hendersonville	04-06-82	06-30-85
07	John B. Gilliam III	Windsor	03-31-78	06-30-81
	Sampson Buie, Jr.	Greensboro	04-06-82	06-30-85
08	Thelma W. Ramseur	Newton	03-31-78	06-30-81
	Ferd Harrison	Scotland Neck	04-06-82	06-30-85
09	Ed N. Warren, *vice-chairman*	Greenville	03-31-78	06-30-81
	Robert L. Walton	Charlotte	04-06-82	06-30-85
10	Jesse G. Ray, Jr.	Asheville	03-31-78	06-30-81
	Roy Trantham	Asheville	04-06-82	06-30-85
11	Iris Davis	Raeford	03-31-77	06-30-81
			03-31-78	
			04-06-82	06-30-85

EARTH RESOURCES COUNCIL
G.S. 143B-303/Board No. 0293

07	Jimmy L. Morris	Vanceboro	08-15-78	06-30-82

NORTH CAROLINA EMPLOYMENT AND TRAINING COUNCIL
G.S. 143B-341/Board No. 0351

01	A. Craig Phillips	Raleigh	06-28-77	
	Charles J. Law	Raleigh	10-30-79	
02	J. B. Archer	Raleigh	03-22-78	
			10-30-79	
03	Sarah T. Morrow	Raleigh	06-28-77	
			10-30-79	
04	Wilbur Hobby	Raleigh	07-26-78	
	James M. Pierce	Charlotte	10-30-79	
05	Willie Harvey	Hertford	06-28-77	
			10-30-79	

North Carolina Employment and Training Council
(CONTINUED)

Position No.	Name of Appointee	Address	Date Appointed	Date of Expiration
06	James A. Summers, *chairman*	Salisbury	06-28-77 10-30-79	
	Gerald James...................	Wentworth	03-12-81	
07	R. D. Adams	Durham	06-28-77 10-30-79	
08	Howard N. Lee, *vice-chairman*	Raleigh	06-28-77 10-30-79	
09	Norris W. Daves	Gastonia	06-28-77 10-30-79	
	Walter Farabee...............	Winston-Salem	08-26-81	
10	Ronald D. Baker	Jacksonville	06-28-77 10-30-79	
11	Marion G. Follin III	Greensboro	06-28-77	
	Charles Trent....................	Raleigh	08-26-81	
12	Robert Person	Charlotte	06-28-77 10-30-79	
13	James R. Leutze...............	Chapel Hill	06-28-77	
	Alton W. Greenlaw	Winston-Salem	10-30-79	
14	Pat L. Everhart	Lexington	07-26-78 10-30-79	
15	Ben S. Eason	Raleigh	07-26-78 10-30-79	
16	Ben E. Fountain, Jr..................	Raleigh	06-28-77	
	Larry Blake	Raleigh	10-30-79	
17, 35	John C. Brooks	Raleigh	06-28-77 01-07-80	
17	N. D. McGinnis	Fayetteville	10-30-79	
18	D. M. Faircloth	Raleigh	06-28-77	
	Edward J. Dowd	Charlotte	10-30-79	
	Jerome Melton	Raleigh	08-26-81	
19	Margaret Hall	Hickory	06-28-77	
	Dewey G. Harwood, Jr...............	Raleigh	10-30-79	
20	Inez D. Bell	Wilson	06-28-77	
	Joseph S. Brake, Jr.	Beaufort	10-30-79	
21	Lester Moore	Burgaw	01-07-80	
22	William L. McLaurin, Sr.	Cary	01-07-80	
23	Mike Abernethy	Newton	01-07-80	
24	Richard A. Clack	Rocky Mount	10-30-79	
25	Beverly H. Moore	Reidsville	10-30-79	
26	Joyce F. Kinnison	Cary	10-30-79	
27	O. M. Graham, Sr.	Laurinburg	10-30-79	
28	Alice D. Pope	Seaboard	10-30-79	
29	Gwendolyn Worsley	Wilson	10-30-79	
30	Leon Taylor	Henderson	10-30-79	
31	William K. Hobbs.................	Wilmington	10-30-79	
32	Kevin B. Grealey	Raleigh	10-30-79	
33	Henry G. Capucille	Raleigh	10-30-79	
34	Thomas Council	Fayetteville	10-30-79	
	Bobby Lowery	Charlotte	08-26-81	
36	Douglas M. Davis	Greensboro	01-07-80	

ENVIRONMENTAL MANAGEMENT COMMISSION
G.S. 143B-283/Board No. 0355

Position No.	Name of Appointee	Address	Date Appointed	Date of Expiration
01	Marvin D. Gentry	King	10-13-77	07-01-83
			10-04-83	07-01-89
02	Clementine B. Shaw	Winston-Salem	10-13-77	07-01-83
	William T. Small	Durham	10-04-83	07-01-89
03	William G. Sullivan	Mount Olive	10-11-79	07-01-85
04	P. Greer Johnson	Asheville	10-11-79	07-01-85
05	Fred S. Barkalow, Jr.	Raleigh	10-11-79	07-01-81
			09-22-81	07-01-87
	Richard T. Barber	Beaufort	08-27-82	07-01-87
06	Brenda E. Armstrong	Durham	10-13-77	07-01-83
			10-04-83	07-01-89
07	James C. Wallace	Chapel Hill	10-13-77	07-01-83
			10-04-83	07-01-89
08	James E. Brown	Charlotte	09-22-81	06-30-87
09	Jerry D. Lewis	Shallotte	10-11-79	07-01-85
10	David H. Howells	Raleigh	10-11-79	07-01-85
11	Virgil McBride	Winston-Salem	10-15-81	07-01-87
12	Robert L. Harris, Jr.	Raleigh	12-31-82	07-01-87
13	Harry W. Whitley, *chairman*	Murfreesboro	10-13-77	07-01-83
	Thomas W. Bradshaw, Jr.	Raleigh	09-22-81	07-01-83
			10-04-83	07-01-89

FORESTRY ADVISORY COUNCIL
G.S. 143B-309 (1973)/Board No. 0385

Position No.	Name of Appointee	Address	Date Appointed	Date of Expiration
01	Edward Rizzoti	Wilkesboro	03-20-81	06-30-84
			12-21-84	06-30-88
02	William H. Utley	New Bern	08-09-78	06-30-82
				06-30-86
03	James H. Wheless	Louisburg	03-20-81	06-30-84
	Michael Evans	Nashville	12-07-84	03-30-88
04	James H. Sears	Gates	08-09-78	06-30-82
				06-30-86
05	Joseph W. Nowell	Belvidere	08-09-78	06-30-82
	James B. Hunt, Sr.	Lucama	03-30-81	06-30-82
				06-30-86
06	C. Siler Slagle	Franklin	08-09-78	06-30-82
				06-30-86
07	Wilbur W. Yeargin	Oxford	08-09-78	06-30-82
	Voit Gilmore	Southern Pines	03-10-83	06-30-86
08	Robert R. Richardson	Lake Waccamaw	03-20-81	06-30-84
			12-07-84	06-30-88
09	Lois Turner	Winston-Salem	03-20-81	06-30-84
			12-21-84	06-30-88
10	Garrett A. Smathers	Cullowhee	03-20-81	06-30-84
			12-07-84	06-30-88
11	Mack B. Ray	Burnsville	08-09-78	06-30-82
				06-30-86

JOHN H. KERR RESERVOIR COMMITTEE
G.S. 143B-329/Board No. 0515

Position No.	Name of Appointee	Address	Date Appointed	Date of Expiration
01	C. W. Wilkinson, Jr.	Oxford	08-30-79	07-26-83
02	William D. Turner, Jr.	Henderson	08-30-79	07-26-83
03	C. Thomas Peele....................	Norlina	08-30-79	07-26-83
	Charles A. Hayes	Warrenton	02-24-83	07-26-83
04	Robert P. Jones	Henderson	08-30-79	07-26-83
05	Doan B. Laursen	Oxford	08-30-79	07-26-83
06	Geri Curtis......................	Manson	09-20-78	07-26-79
			08-30-79	07-26-83
			03-20-83	07-26-85
07	Robert E. Hale, *vice-chairman*	Henderson	09-12-77	07-26-81
			08-30-79	07-26-83
08	Sherby G. Slaughter	Oxford	08-30-79	07-26-83
09	David J. Mitchell, *chairman*	Oxford	09-20-78	07-26-79
			08-30-79	07-26-83

NORTH CAROLINA LAND CONSERVANCY CORPORATION BOARD OF TRUSTEES
G.S. 113A-137/Board No. 0517

04	Lynwood Smith	High Point	07-01-79	04-13-83
05	Walton Jones	Raleigh	07-01-79	04-13-83

NORTH CAROLINA ADVISORY COMMITTEE ON LAND POLICY[18]
G.S. 113A-154/Board No. 0518

01	Herbert T. Mullen, Sr..............	South Mills	03-17-78
	N. Elton Aydett	Elizabeth City	11-02-78
02	C. Wiley Purvis	Robbins	03-17-78
03	Brady Angell, *vice-chairman*	Mocksville	03-17-78
04	Ruth Long	Hillsborough	03-17-78
05	Richard A. Scroggs	Hayesville	03-17-78
06	Gerald L. Anderson	New Bern	03-17-78
07	Dohn B. Broadwell..............	Fayetteville	03-17-78
08	Charles D. Owens	Forest City	03-17-78
09	Barbara Lee	New Bern	03-17-78
10	Mack Weeks.................	Willow Springs	03-17-78
11	Jonathan B. Howes, *chairman*	Chapel Hill	03-17-78
12	Richard C. Berne	Cullowhee	03-17-78

MARINE FISHERIES COMMISSION
G.S. 143B-287/Board No. 0552

01	Joseph T. Miller	Belhaven	09-23-83	06-30-86
02	Herman N. Hayden	Sparta	02-27-81	06-30-82
			07-01-82	06-30-88
03, 01	Ted M. Day, Jr.	Washington	08-06-80	06-30-86
04, 03	Alphonse F. Chestnut	Morehead City	09-28-78	06-30-84
			06-22-84	06-30-90

---

18 The North Carolina Advisory Committee on Land Policy was abolished under *N.C. Session Laws, 1981,* c. 881, ratified July 8, 1981.

Marine Fisheries Commission (continued)

Position No.	Name of Appointee	Address	Date Appointed	Date of Expiration
04	Roy B. Dixon	Grantsboro	08-10-82	06-30-88
05	Joseph J. Smith, Jr., *chairman*	Hampstead	05-31-84	06-30-90
06	John C. Graham, Jr.	Elizabeth City	08-06-80	06-30-86
	John Bell	Elizabeth City	12-04-84	06-30-86
07	W. M. Smith	Elizabeth City	01-16-79	06-30-80
	Joseph W. Nowell, Jr.	Belvidere	10-19-79	06-30-80
	James L. Sutherland, Jr.	Laurinburg	08-06-80	06-30-86
08	Ed Cross	Arapahoe	07-12-77	07-01-79
	Harold L. Stephenson	Oriental	02-25-80	06-30-85
09	Earl Smith	Edenton	07-12-77	07-01-79
			02-25-80	06-30-85
10	Carson Stout, *vice-chairman*	High Point	10-19-77	07-01-79
			02-25-80	06-30-85
	Wayland F. Vereen	Long Beach	08-06-80	06-30-85
11	John T. Bryant	Engelhard	10-19-77	07-01-79
	Edward A. O'Neal	Swan Quarter	05-20-80	06-30-85
	Murray Fulcher	Ocracoke	03-13-84	06-30-85
12	Ron K. Tillett	Wanchese	07-12-77	07-01-81
			11-11-81	06-30-87
13	Virginia Tillet	Manteo	10-19-77	07-01-81
	Cecil J. Belch	Plymouth	11-11-81	06-30-87
14	B. Frank Markham	Elizabeth City	10-19-77	07-01-81
	Monroe Gaskill	Cedar Island	09-28-78	06-30-81
	Frank T. Randolph	Washington	11-11-81	06-30-87
15	Clara M. Everett	Sneads Ferry	10-19-77	07-01-81
	Gerald W. Gaskill	Cedar Island	03-02-81	07-01-81
			11-11-81	06-30-87

Marine Fisheries Study Commission
N.C. Session Laws, 1981, c. 930/Board No. 0553

01	Rodney P. Cahoon	Beaufort	11-30-81	04-01-82
02	Thomas Baum	Wanchese	11-30-81	04-01-82
03	James B. Moore	Southport	11-30-81	04-01-82

North Carolina Mining Commission
G.S. 143B-291/Board No. 0587

02	John Dowdle	Madison	10-21-83	06-30-87
03	John F. Long	Cary	08-15-78	06-30-79
			03-17-80	06-30-85
04	Earl C. Van Horn	Newland	03-17-80	06-30-85
05	W. W. Woodhouse	Raleigh		06-30-87
06	Gale Billings	Greenville	08-15-78	06-30-83
	Stanley R. Riggs	Greenville	03-17-80	06-30-83
			09-10-83	06-30-89
07	Harry L. Salisbury, Jr.	Cullowhee	03-17-80	06-30-81
				06-30-87
08	P. Greer Johnson	Asheville	03-17-80	06-30-85
09	Fred S. Barkalow, Jr.	Raleigh	03-17-80	06-30-81
	Richard T. Barber	Beaufort	12-17-82	06-30-87

PARKS AND RECREATION COUNCIL
G.S. 143B-312/Board No. 0673

Position No.	Name of Appointee	Address	Date Appointed	Date of Expiration
01	J. Banks Garrison, Jr.	Albemarle	09-13-78	06-30-82
			10-30-82	06-30-86
02	Cliff H. Brown	Kannapolis	09-13-78	06-30-82
	Frank Timberlake	Raleigh	11-11-81	06-30-82
			10-13-82	06-30-86
03	Richard B. Dobbin	Spruce Pine	09-13-78	06-30-82
	James A. Saylor	Elkin	11-11-81	06-30-82
			10-13-82	06-30-86
	Thomas P. Burgiss	Laurel Springs	05-31-84	06-30-86
04	William E. Tyson	Hope Mills	09-13-78	06-30-82
	J. Burton Gillette	Wilson	10-13-82	06-30-86
05	David J. Mitchell	Oxford	08-30-79	07-26-83
06	Franklin Thomas	East Bend	09-13-78	06-30-82
			10-13-82	06-30-86
07	Thomas A. Stein	Chapel Hill	09-13-78	06-30-82
			10-13-82	06-30-86
08	Charles S. Hubbard, chairman	Pittsboro	01-22-79	06-30-82
			10-13-82	06-30-86
09	Helen R. Muldrow	Elizabeth City	09-13-78	06-30-82
			10-13-82	06-30-86
10	Mary P. Seymour	Greensboro	09-13-78	06-30-82
			10-13-82	06-30-86
11	Michael A. Boryk	Topsail Beach	09-13-78	06-30-82
	Jerome Parker	Cherokee	08-10-82	06-30-86
15	Laurie B. Cowan	Ahoskie	10-20-82	06-30-86
	Joseph E. Malcolm	Pembroke	10-20-82	06-30-86

SEDIMENTATION CONTROL COMMISSION
G.S. 143B-299/Board No. 0835

Position No.	Name of Appointee	Address	Date Appointed	Date of Expiration
04	Earl F. Stephenson	Raleigh	10-19-77	06-30-81
			03-07-80	06-30-83
06	W. W. Woodhouse	Raleigh	10-19-77	06-30-81
			12-03-81	06-30-84
				06-30-88
07	Robert J. Bowers	Sanford	07-03-78	12-13-80
				01-06-85
08	James C. Wallace	Chapel Hill	10-19-77	06-30-81
	David H. Howells	Raleigh	03-05-80	06-30-83
				07-01-86
09	Joseph A. Phillips, chairman	Raleigh	10-19-77	06-30-81
			12-03-81	06-30-84
				06-30-88
10	B. J. Hurst	Hubert	10-19-77	06-30-81
	Barden Lanier	Jacksonville	06-28-82	06-30-84
	Brantley Deloatche	Durham	12-31-84	06-03-88
11	Johnsie Setzer	Claremont	10-19-77	06-30-81
	Alice S. Byrd	Durham	05-05-80	06-30-81
			12-03-81	06-30-84
	Joseph W. Grimsley	Raleigh	12-31-84	06-30-87

SOIL AND WATER CONSERVATION COMMISSION
G.S. 143B-295/Board No. 0847

Position No.	Name of Appointee	Address	Date Appointed	Date of Expiration
01	Robert J. Bowers, *chairman*	Sanford	02-03-78	12-31-80
			11-17-82	01-06-85

SOUTHEASTERN INTERSTATE FOREST FIRE PROTECTION COMPACT ADVISORY COMMITTEE
G.S. 113-60.14/Board No. 0380

01	Joe H. Palmer	Clyde	08-17-78	10-31-79
02	Jeff H. Enloe, Jr.	Franklin	08-17-78	
03	Nelson Leggette	Rocky Mount	08-17-78	10-31-79
			06-29-81	10-31-83
			09-10-84	10-31-85
04	Clemmon L. Jacobs	Riegelwood	08-17-78	10-31-79
			06-29-81	10-31-83
			09-10-84	10-31-85

TRIAD PARK COMMISSION
G.S. 143B-342/Board No. 0907

01	Carson Bain, *chairman*	Greensboro	09-26-79	09-01-85

NORTH CAROLINA WILDLIFE RESOURCES COMMISSION
G.S. 143-241/Board No. 0965

10	Polie Q. Cloninger, Jr.	Dallas	07-25-77	04-01-81
			03-05-81	04-01-85
11	J. Robert Gordon, *chairman*	Laurinburg	07-25-77	04-01-81
			03-05-81	04-01-85

NORTH CAROLINA ZOOLOGICAL PARK COUNCIL
G.S. 143B-336/Board No. 0980

01	Ernst W. Greup	Durham	01-20-78	06-30-79
			01-29-80	06-30-85
02, 14	Clyde W. Lucas	Asheboro	02-14-80	06-30-85
			11-19-84	06-30-87
02	Pat Wilson	Winston-Salem	12-04-84	06-30-85
03	Leonard Kaplan.................	Greensboro	08-05-82	06-30-87
04	Carroll L. Mann, Jr..................	Raleigh	02-14-80	06-30-85
05	James D. Little	Wilson	01-20-78	06-30-83
	Fred F. Bahnson, Jr.	Winston-Salem	10-01-80	06-30-83
	Louise Bahnson	Winston-Salem	09-23-83	06-30-89
06	Mary C. Hopper	Charlotte	08-05-82	06-30-85
07	Samuel F. Rees	Siler City	01-20-78	06-30-83
	William R. Henderson	Cary	10-01-80	06-30-83
	James Culberson	Asheboro	09-19-83	06-30-89
08	Margaret W. Ransdell	Raleigh	01-20-78	06-30-83
	Pegge C. Newsome	Salisbury	09-19-83	06-30-89
09	Cullie M. Tarleton	Charlotte	02-14-80	06-30-85
10	John S. Lowery	Lincolnton	04-10-81	06-30-81
			08-05-82	06-30-87

North Carolina Zoological Park Council
(CONTINUED)

Position No.	Name of Appointee	Address	Date Appointed	Date of Expiration
11	C. J. Snow, *chairman*	Mount Airy	01-20-78	06-30-83
			09-19-83	06-30-89
12	Stanley Green, Jr.	Rocky Mount	02-14-80	06-30-85
	Josephine Clement	Durham	05-13-83	06-30-85
	L. B. Frasier	Durham	12-28-84	06-30-85
13	Lottie M. High	Rocky Mount		06-30-87
14	Charles A. Whitehurst	Greensboro	01-20-78	06-30-83
	D. Wescott Moser	Asheboro	02-11-80	06-30-83
	Sally Rhoades	Asheville	08-12-82	06-30-87

DEPARTMENT OF REVENUE
Secretary
Mark G. Lynch, 1977-1985

Property Tax System Study Committee
N.C. Session Laws, 1981, c. 943/Board No. 0741

01	Brenda W. Sumner	Enfield	09-10-81	02-01-83
02	Marshall West	Weaverville	09-10-81	02-01-83
03	Cecil Carlyle	Fayetteville	09-10-81	02-01-83
04	Jesse C. Alphin, Sr.	Dunn	09-10-81	02-01-83
05	Richard L. Thomas	Lexington	09-10-81	02-01-83

Property Tax Commission
G.S. 143B-223/Board No. 0740

01	Heywood Edmundson IV	Wilson	08-21-79	07-01-83
			08-15-83	07-01-87
02	John L. Turner	Winston-Salem	04-05-78	07-01-81
			07-17-81	07-01-85
03	John B. Lewis, Jr., *chairman*	Farmville	03-31-78	07-01-81
	Charles H. Mercer, Jr., *chairman*	Raleigh	02-08-80	07-01-81
	James E. Long	Graham	07-17-81	07-01-85
	Wiley Wooten	Burlington	12-21-84	07-01-85

DEPARTMENT OF TRANSPORTATION
Secretaries
Thomas W. Bradshaw, Jr., 1977-1981
William R. Roberson, Jr., 1981-1985

Board of Transportation
G.S. 143B-350/Board No. 0905

01	T. G. Joyner	Garysburg	07-28-77	01-14-81
			07-24-81	01-14-85
02	Joseph E. Thomas	Vanceboro	07-28-77	01-14-81
	John Halstead*	Elizabeth City	03-13-8?	01-15-85
02, 08	Joseph C. Hamme	Oxford	01-12-79	01-14-81
			07-24-81	01-14-85
03, 04	Garland B. Garrett, Jr.	Wilmington	07-28-77	01-14-81
			07-24-81	01-14-85

---

*Year in which Halstead succeeded Basnight in Position No. 2 is not indicated on printout.

BOARD OF TRANSPORTATION (CONTINUED)

Position No.	Name of Appointee	Address	Date Appointed	Date of Expiration
04	William C. Herring	Wilson	07-28-77	01-14-81
	Louis Sewell	Jacksonville	06-01-82	01-14-85
05, 07	Iley L. Dean	Durham	07-28-77	01-14-81
			07-24-81	01-14-85
05	Philip A. Baddour, Jr.	Goldsboro	07-24-81	01-14-85
06	Arthur Williamson	Chadbourn	07-28-77	01-14-81
07	Michael B. Fleming	Greensboro	07-28-77	01-14-81
08, 13	Martha B. Hollers	Candor	07-28-77	01-14-81
			07-24-81	01-14-85
09, 14	John K. Gallaher	Winston-Salem	07-28-77	01-14-81
			07-24-81	01-14-85
10, 15	John Q. Burnett	Charlotte	07-28-77	01-14-81
			07-24-81	01-14-85
10	Oscar N. Harris	Dunn	07-24-81	01-14-85
11, 17	Marvin R. Phillips	Boone	07-28-77	01-14-81
			07-24-81	01-14-85
11	Lenwood Rich III	Fairmont	07-24-81	01-14-85
12, 18	David W. Hoyle	Dallas	07-28-77	01-14-81
			07-24-81	01-14-85
12	Sanders Dallas, Jr.	High Point	07-24-81	01-14-85
13	John M. Gilkey	Marion	07-28-77	01-14-81
14	Oscar J. Ledford	Franklin	07-28-77	01-14-81
15, 03	George G. Harper	Kinston	07-28-77	01-14-81
			07-24-81	01-14-85
16, 06	Moses A. Ray	Tarboro	07-28-77	01-14-81
			07-24-81	01-14-85
17, 09	Jeanette W. Carl	Raleigh	07-28-77	01-14-81
			07-24-81	01-14-85
17	J. Bradley Wilson	Lenoir	08-01-82	01-14-85
18	Jack E. Bryant	Brevard	07-28-77	01-14-81
19, 02	Marc Basnight	Manteo	07-28-77	01-14-81
			07-24-81	01-15-85
19	Zeno H. Ponder	Marshall	07-24-81	01-14-85
20	Helen Little	Yanceyville	07-28-77	01-14-81
	James W. Daniels	Asheville	07-24-81	01-14-85
21, 16	Seddon Goode, Jr.	Charlotte	06-27-79	01-14-81
			07-24-81	01-14-85
21	Charles R. Jonas, Jr.	Charlotte	07-28-77	01-14-81
	Thomas E. Davis	Robbinsville	07-24-81	01-14-85

AERONAUTICS COUNCIL
G.S. 143B-357/Board No. 0001

Position No.	Name of Appointee	Address	Date Appointed	Date of Expiration
01, 10	Ted G. West	Lenoir	08-10-78	06-30-81
			07-30-82	06-30-85
02, 03	George W. Parker	Sanford	09-21-77	06-30-81
03, 04, 02	Robert T. Pifer	Durham	09-21-77	06-20-81
			07-30-82	06-30-87
03	William A. Christian	Sanford	07-30-82	06-30-85
04, 08	Rufus H. Honeycutt, Jr.	China Grove	09-21-77	06-30-81
			07-30-82	06-30-85
04	Regina McLaurin	Cary	08-24-82	06-30-85

AERONAUTICS COUNCIL (CONTINUED)

Position No.	Name of Appointee	Address	Date Appointed	Date of Expiration
05, 07	William M. Rowe	Wilmington	09-21-77	06-30-81
			07-30-82	06-30-85
06, 01	Daniel T. Lilley, *chairman*	Kinston	09-21-77	06-30-81
			06-30-79	06-30-83
			07-30-82	06-30-87
07, 02	Alexander Biggs	Rocky Mount	06-08-78	06-30-79
			06-30-79	06-30-83
08, 05, 13	Edward A. Smith, Jr.	Lexington	12-05-79	06-30-83
			08-05-83	06-30-87
08, 05	William N. Schultz, Jr.	Madison	07-30-82	06-30-83
				06-30-87
09, 06	Stanley Frank	Greensboro	06-30-79	06-30-83
			07-30-82	06-30-87
10, 09	Jack L. Dellinger	Lincolnton	12-05-79	06-30-83
				06-30-87
10	Brad Wilson.......................	Lenoir	12-20-84	06-30-85
11	Joseph R. Randall	Forest City	08-10-78	06-10-79
			06-30-79	06-30-83
				06-30-87
12	Robert L. Stallings	New Bern	08-04-83	06-30-87

ATLANTIC AND NORTH CAROLINA RAILROAD
G.S. 124-6/Board No. 0075

01	D. Livingstone Stallings, *president*	New Bern	07-05-77	08-00-79
04, 01	Edward S. Dixon, *president*	Morehead City	07-05-77	08-00-78
				08-00-79
			08-08-80	08-08-83
02	Vernon H. Rochelle, *secretary-treasurer*..	Kinston	07-05-77	08-08-83
03	George R. Kornegay, Jr., *attorney* ...	Mount Olive	07-05-77	08-08-83
04	James F. Shine, *expert*	New Bern		08-00-79
			08-08-80	08-08-83
05	Thelma B. Edmondson	Pollocksville	07-05-77	08-08-83
06	Geraldine W. Femia	Morehead City	07-05-77	08-08-83
07	E. B. Hale	Rocky Mount	07-05-77	08-08-83
08	M. D. Jones	New Bern	07-05-77	08-00-79
	Lonnie Pridgen	New Bern	08-08-80	08-08-83
09	Raymond A. Morris	Snow Hill	07-05-77	08-08-83
10	Lina M. Sanders	Smithfield	07-07-77	08-08-83
11	Josephine S. Taylor	Walstonburg	07-05-77	08-08-83
12	Thad Eure, *proxy*	Raleigh	07-05-77	08-08-83
13	Earl Laughinghouse	New Bern	08-08-80	08-08-83

NORTH CAROLINA RAILROAD BOARD OF DIRECTORS
G.S. 124-6, 147-12/Board No. 0755

01	John M. Alexander, Sr., *president*	Raleigh	07-14-77	07-10-85
02	Ralph H. Scott	Haw River	07-14-77	07-10-83
03	Kenneth R. Downs	Pineville	07-14-77	07-10-85
04	Fred J. Corriher	Landis	07-14-77	07-10-85
05	E. V. Wilkins	Roper	07-14-77	07-13-78
06, 05	Tom Barringer	Raleigh	07-14-77	07-10-83
07, 06	J. M. Lackey	Hiddenite	07-14-77	07-10-85

NORTH CAROLINA RAILROAD BOARD OF DIRECTORS
(CONTINUED)

Position No.	Name of Appointee	Address	Date Appointed	Date of Expiration
08, 07	Sarah Lefler	Willard	07-14-77	07-10-85
09, 08	Jack A. Moody, *secretary-treasurer*	Siler City	07-14-77	07-10-85
10, 09	Dot Mason	Murphy	07-14-77	07-12-80
09	Wilton R. Duke	Farmville	02-02-81	07-10-85
11, 10	Woodrow W. Gunter	Hamlet	07-14-77	07-10-83
12, 11	Carra Lyles	Concord	07-14-77	07-10-85

JUDICIAL OFFICIALS AND RELATED APPOINTMENTS

JUDGES OF THE SUPREME COURT [19]
G.S. 163-9/Board No. 0496

01	Joseph Branch	Raleigh	08-01-79	12-31-86
02	J. Phil Carlton	Raleigh	08-02-79	12-31-84
	Henry E. Frye*	Raleigh		12-31-84
03	Burley B. Mitchell, Jr.	Raleigh	02-01-82	12-31-82
06	David M. Britt	Raleigh	08-31-78	12-31-86
07	Louis B. Meyer	Wilson	01-09-81	12-31-86
	Harry C. Martin	Raleigh	08-03-82	12-31-82

JUDGES OF THE COURT OF APPEALS
G.S. 163-9/Board No. 0490

02	Willis P. Whichard	Durham	12-31-80	12-31-82
08	Burley B. Mitchell, Jr.	Raleigh	12-02-77	12-31-84
	Cecil Hill	Brevard	09-14-79	12-31-84
09	John Webb	Wilson	12-02-77	12-31-84
10	Richard C. Erwin	Winston-Salem	12-02-77	12-31-84
	Charles L. Becton	Chapel Hill	01-19-81	12-31-84
11	Harry C. Martin	Raleigh	09-01-78	12-31-82
12	J. Phil Carlton	Pinetops	01-02-79	12-31-82
12, 11	Hugh Wells	Raleigh	08-20-79	12-31-82
12	Clifton Johnson	Raleigh	08-03-82	12-31-82

JUDGES OF THE SUPERIOR COURT
G.S. 163-9/Board No. 0494

04	David E. Reid, Jr.	Greenville	11-23-77	12-31-86
05	Henry L. Stevens III	Kenansville	11-23-77	12-31-86
06	James R. Strickland	Jacksonville	11-23-77	12-31-86
09	Richard B. Allsbrook	Roanoke Rapids	12-22-77	12-31-82
10	Charles B. Winberry, Jr.	Rocky Mount	04-01-82	12-31-82
11	Franklin R. Brown	Tarboro	01-10-78	12-31-82
12	James D. Llewellyn	Kinston	11-30-80	12-31-86
13	R. Michael Bruce	Mount Olive	11-18-77	12-31-86
14	Robert H. Hobgood	Louisburg	11-30-80	12-31-86
18	Robert L. Farmer	Raleigh	11-23-77	12-31-86

19 The name of Earl W. Vaughn was not included among those of other judicial appointees listed on the computer printout. Hunt announced Vaughn's posting, as an associate justice, to the state Supreme Court on December 18, 1984. Lung cancer forced the judge to resign, effective July 31, 1985; he died the following April. *News and Observer*, April 3, 1986; "News Release from the Governor's Office," December 18, 1984.
*Order of succession as indicated on printout.

JUDGES OF THE SUPERIOR COURT (CONTINUED)

Position No.	Name of Appointee	Address	Date Appointed	Date of Expiration
19	Wiley F. Bowen . . . . Dunn		01-12-81	11-31-82
22	Coy E. Brewer . . . . Fayetteville		11-23-77	12-31-86
24	Anthony M. Brannon . . . . Durham		11-17-77	12-31-86
26	John C. Martin . . . . Durham		11-17-77	12-31-86
28	Gordon Battle . . . . Chapel Hill		11-22-77	12-31-86
29	Samuel E. Britt . . . . Lumberton		11-14-80	12-31-82
				12-31-86
35	James C. Davis . . . . Concord		11-22-77	12-31-86
37	William H. Helms . . . . Wingate		07-22-80	12-31-80
			01-01-80	12-31-82
38	F. Fetzer Mills . . . . Wadesboro		11-16-77	12-31-86
42	Peter W. Hairston . . . . Mocksville		11-23-77	12-31-86
45	Claude S. Sitton . . . . Morganton		07-23-80	12-31-80
			12-31-80	12-31-86
51	Clifton E. Johnson . . . . Charlotte		11-23-77	12-31-86
	Chase B. Saunders . . . . Charlotte		08-06-82	12-31-82
55	Cary W. Allen . . . . Asheville		09-29-78	12-31-86
57	Hollis M. Owens, Jr. . . . . Rutherfordton		07-18-80	12-31-80
			12-31-80	12-31-82
59	Melzer A. Morgan, Jr. . . . . Reidsville		09-01-81	
60	William H. Freeman . . . . Winston-Salem		12-18-81	12-31-82

SPECIAL JUDGES OF THE SUPERIOR COURT
G.S. 7A-45(a)/Board No. 0495

01	Samuel E. Britt . . . . Lumberton		07-17-79	06-30-83
	Charles B. Winberry . . . . Rocky Mount		12-19-80	06-30-83
	Russell G. Walker, Jr. . . . . Asheboro		06-03-82	06-30-83
02	Judson D. Deramus, Jr. . . . . Winston-Salem		07-17-79	06-30-83
	James A. Beaty, Jr. . . . . Winston-Salem		10-29-81	06-30-83
03	John R. Jolly, Jr. . . . . Rocky Mount		07-17-79	06-30-83
	John B. Lewis, Jr. . . . . Farmville		08-02-82	06-30-83
04	Donald Smith . . . . Raleigh		07-17-79	06-30-83
05	H. L. Riddle, Jr. . . . . Morganton		08-07-78	06-30-79
	William H. Freeman . . . . Winston-Salem		12-01-80	
	Thomas S. Watts . . . . Elizabeth City		06-25-82	06-30-83
06	Charles C. Lamm, Jr. . . . . Boone		07-17-79	06-30-83
07	Arthur L. Lane . . . . Fayetteville		07-17-79	06-30-83
08	Clarence P. Cornelius . . . . Mooresville		01-19-80	06-30-83

JUDGES OF THE DISTRICT COURT
G.S. 163-9/Board No. 0492

00	Acie Ward . . . . Raleigh		01-01-82	12-31-82
03	James W. Hardison . . . . Williamston		01-13-81	11-30-84
06	W. Lee Lumpkin . . . . Morehead City		08-13-82	12-31-82
07	James E. Martin . . . . Bethel		08-26-80	11-30-80
10	E. Alex Erwin III . . . . Jacksonville		08-09-77	11-30-80
			11-30-80	11-30-84
15	Charles E. Rice . . . . Wilmington		01-19-80	11-30-80
			11-30-80	11-30-84
	Samuel E. Cathey . . . . Statesville		10-19-79	12-05-82
17	Harold P. McCoy . . . . Scotland Neck		08-13-79	11-30-80
			11-30-80	11-30-84

Judges of the District Court (continued)

Position No.	Name of Appointee	Address	Date Appointed	Date of Expiration
21	James E. Ezzell, Jr.	Rocky Mount	02-01-80	11-30-80
			11-30-80	11-30-84
	John T. Kilby	Jefferson	07-20-78	12-05-82
22	Albert Thomas, Jr.	Wilson	11-30-80	11-30-84
23	George M. Britt	Tarboro	04-12-77	11-30-80
			11-30-80	11-30-84
26	Joseph E. Setzer, Jr.	Goldsboro	01-04-80	11-30-80
27	Paul M. Wright	Goldsboro	06-23-78	12-01-80
			11-30-80	11-30-84
29	William H. Scarborough	Henderson	02-01-80	11-30-80
31	J. Larry Senter	Louisburg	02-13-78	11-30-80
			11-30-80	11-30-84
34	Robert P. Johnston	Charlotte	10-01-82	12-31-82
37	Russell G. Sherrill III	Raleigh	01-09-79	11-30-80
			11-30-80	11-30-84
39	Kelly E. Greene	Dunn	01-01-79	11-30-80
			11-30-80	11-30-84
41	William A. Christian	Sanford	09-20-78	11-30-80
			11-30-80	11-30-84
43	Sol G. Cherry	Fayetteville	01-06-78	12-05-82
47	Lacy S. Hair	Fayetteville	05-15-78	12-05-82
52	William G. Pearson II.............	Durham	09-20-77	12-05-82
55	J. Kent Washburn	Burlington	11-30-80	11-30-84
56	W. S. Harris, Jr.	Graham	08-30-77	11-30-80
			11-30-80	11-30-84
59	Herbert L. Richardson	Lumberton	08-14-79	12-05-82
61	Patricia S. Hunt.................	Chapel Hill	11-03-81	12-05-82
64	Jerry C. Martin	Mount Airy		12-05-82
65	Peter M. McHugh................	Reidsville		12-05-82
69	Joseph R. John..................	Greensboro	07-02-80	11-30-80
			11-30-80	11-30-84
71	Joseph A. Williams	Greensboro		11-30-80
	Edmund Lowe	High Point	11-30-80	11-30-84
73	Frank A. Campbell	Greensboro	01-01-79	11-30-80
	Robert E. Boncini...............	High Point	11-30-80	11-30-84
75	Clarence E. Horton, Jr.............	Kannapolis	01-30-81	12-05-82
76	John R. Parker................	Elizabeth City	08-14-79	12-05-82
77	James E. Ragan III	Bayboro	08-13-79	11-30-80
			11-30-80	11-30-84
78	James N. Martin	Clinton	08-14-79	11-30-80
			11-30-80	11-30-84
79	Carter T. Lambeth	Wilmington	09-30-79	12-01-80
			11-30-80	11-30-84
80	Roy D. Trest....................	Shallotte	09-05-79	11-30-80
			11-30-80	11-30-84
81	Karen B. Galloway................	Durham	12-31-79	12-31-82
82	Philip O. Redwine	Raleigh	07-24-81	12-05-82

Judges of the District Court II
G.S. 163-9/Board No. 0493

Position No.	Name of Appointee	Address	Date Appointed	Date of Expiration
04	William H. Heafner	Asheboro	01-01-79	11-30-80
	William Neely	Asheboro	11-30-80	11-30-84
06	Ronald W. Burris	Albemarle	02-16-79	11-30-80

JUDGES OF THE DISTRICT COURT II (CONTINUED)

Position No.	Name of Appointee	Address	Date Appointed	Date of Expiration
	H. Horton Rountree	Greenville	11-30-80	11-30-84
09	Kenneth W. Honeycutt	Monroe	12-16-77	11-30-80
			11-30-80	11-30-84
21	John T. Kilby	Jefferson	07-20-78	12-01-78
24	L. Oliver Noble, Jr.	Hickory	05-02-77	12-05-82
26	Robert A. Mullinax	Newton	05-15-81	12-05-82
32	Walter H. Bennett, Jr.	Charlotte	11-23-77	11-30-80
35	Daphene L. Cantrell	Charlotte	01-11-78	11-30-80
42	George W. Hamrick	Shelby	07-01-78	11-30-80
			11-30-80	11-30-84
43	Earl J. Fowler, Jr.	Arden	10-02-78	12-05-82
46	Peter L. Roda	Asheville	04-04-79	12-05-82
53	T. Michael Todd	Charlotte	10-19-79	12-01-80
			11-30-80	11-30-84
54	James T. Bowen	Lincolnton	10-01-79	12-01-80
			11-30-80	11-30-84
57	C. Philip Ginn	Boone	09-03-81	12-05-82
58	Michael E. Beale	Southern Pines	08-18-81	12-05-82
59	Resa L. Harris	Charlotte	08-19-81	12-05-82
60	T. Patrick Matus	Charlotte	08-19-81	12-05-84

JUDICIAL COUNCIL
G.S.7A-400, -401/Board No. 0500

01	Gerald W. Hayes, Jr.	Dunn	11-01-77	06-30-79
			04-11-80	06-30-81
			08-27-81	06-30-83
02	Robert C. Hunter	Marion	11-01-77	06-30-79
	Ronald C. Brown	Asheville	08-27-81	06-30-83

JUDICIAL STANDARDS COMMISSION
G.S. 7A-375(a)/Board No. 0505

01	Susan Whittington	Wilkesboro	02-28-79	12-31-84
	Pamela S. Gaither	Raleigh	12-27-84	12-31-90
02	Veatrice C. Davis	Fayetteville	03-29-82	12-31-87

UNIVERSITY OF NORTH CAROLINA SYSTEM

APPALACHIAN STATE UNIVERSITY BOARD OF TRUSTEES
G.S. 116-31/Board No. 1010

01	James P. Marsh, *secretary*	Boone	07-17-79	06-30-83
				06-30-87
02	Charles D. Owens	Forest City	07-17-79	06-30-83
	M. Randolph Phillips	Boone	11-30-82	06-30-83
				06-30-87
03	George B. Collins	North Wilkesboro	07-01-77	06-30-81
			08-03-81	06-30-85
04	William S. Jones, *vice-chairman*	Greensboro	07-01-77	06-30-81
10	Mariam C. Hayes	Concord	08-03-81	06-30-85

North Carolina Central University Board of Trustees
G.S. 116-31/Board No. 1030

Position No.	Name of Appointee	Address	Date Appointed	Date of Expiration
01	Frank W. Ballance, Jr.	Warrenton	07-17-79	06-30-83
	Henry M. Michaux, Jr.	Durham	03-30-83	06-30-87
	Evelyn Shaw	Fayetteville	12-11-84	06-30-87
02	Alfred Whitesides, Jr.	Asheville	07-17-79	06-30-83
				06-30-87
03, 04	William A. Clement, *chairman*	Durham	07-01-77	06-30-81
03	Robinson O. Everett	Durham	08-02-79	06-30-81
	Theaoseus T. Clayton	Littleton	09-15-82	06-30-85
04	Grace S. Epps	Lumberton	07-01-77	06-30-81
	Charles V. Holland	Raleigh	09-05-81	06-30-85

North Carolina School of the Arts Board of Trustees
G.S. 116-31/Board No. 1080

Position No.	Name of Appointee	Address	Date Appointed	Date of Expiration
01	Jeanelle C. Moore	Raleigh	08-14-79	06-30-83
				07-01-87
02	James Goodmon	Raleigh	08-15-79	06-30-83
	Herman Blumenthal	Charlotte	11-13-81	06-30-83
				07-01-87
03	Linwood L. Davis, Jr.	Winston-Salem	07-01-77	06-30-81
	Linwood L. Davis III	Winston-Salem	08-03-81	06-30-85
04	James H. Semans, *chairman*	Durham	07-01-77	06-30-81
	Mary D. B. Semans	Durham	08-03-81	06-30-85

North Carolina School of Science and Mathematics Board of Trustees [20]
G.S. 116-233/Board No. 0559

Position No.	Name of Appointee	Address	Date Appointed	Date of Expiration
01	William G. Anlyan	Durham	11-28-78	06-30-84
	J. David Robertson	Durham	12-21-84	06-30-90
02	Lewis S. Branscomb	Armonk, N.Y.	11-28-78	06-30-82
			07-01-82	06-30-88
03	Dean W. Colvard, *chairman*	Charlotte	11-28-78	06-30-80
			02-12-81	06-30-86
04	James J. Gallagher	Chapel Hill	11-28-78	06-30-82
			07-01-82	06-30-88
05	Sarah Hamilton	Rockingham	11-28-78	06-30-80
			02-12-81	06-30-86
	Bland W. Worley	Charlotte	09-19-83	06-30-86
06	Wassily W. Leontief	New York, N.Y.	11-28-78	06-30-80
			02-12-81	06-30-86
07	Larry K. Monteith	Raleigh	11-28-78	06-30-84
			12-21-84	06-30-90
08	Henry O. Pollack	Summit, N.J.	11-28-78	06-30-82
			07-01-82	06-30-88
09	Frank Press	Washington, D.C.	11-28-78	06-30-80

---

20 G.S. Chapter 115C, Article 15, was repealed by the 1985 General Assembly, first session, and rewritten under Chapter 116. See *1985 Advance Legislative Service to the General Statutes of North Carolina, Pamphlet Number 4* (Charlottesville, Virginia: The Michie Company, 1985), c. 757, s. 206(a), ratified July 15, 1985. The revisions made therein also transferred the North Carolina School of Science and Mathematics to the University of North Carolina System.

Western Carolina University Board of Trustees
G.S. 116-31/Board No. 1065

Position No.	Name of Appointee	Address	Date Appointed	Date of Expiration
01	Robert J. McGinn, Jr.	Lexington	07-17-79	06-30-83
				06-30-87
02	Jack Abbott	Canton	07-17-79	06-30-83
	Robert L. Edwards	Marshall	06-24-83	06-30-87
03	Paul E. Cowan	Sylva	07-01-77	06-30-81
	Creighton W. Sossomon	Sylva	08-03-81	06-30-85
04	Avis Phillips, *secretary*	Robbinsville	07-01-77	06-30-81
			08-18-81	06-30-85

Winston-Salem State University Board of Trustees
G.S. 116-31/Board No. 1075

Position No.	Name of Appointee	Address	Date Appointed	Date of Expiration
01	Louise Smith	Winston-Salem	07-17-79	06-30-83
				06-30-87
02	Graham F. Bennett	Winston-Salem	07-17-79	06-30-83
				06-30-87
03	Nan Coffee.	Thomasville	07-01-77	06-30-81
	Aurelia G. Eller	Winston-Salem	08-03-81	06-30-85
04	John W. Davis III	Winston-Salem	06-05-78	06-30-81
			08-03-81	06-30-85

INDEPENDENT AGENCIES, REGIONAL BODIES, AND MISCELLANEOUS STATUTORY BODIES

Advisory Budget Commission
G.S. 143-4/Board No. 0145

Position No.	Name of Appointee	Address	Date Appointed	Date of Expiration
01	H. Edward Knox, *chairman*	Charlotte	02-23-77	
			06-06-81	
	Arthur Cassell	High Point	11-03-81	
02	James B. Garrison	Albemarle	02-23-77	
			02-06-81	
03	Liston B. Ramsey	Marshall	02-23-77	
	Betty R. McCain	Wilson	02-06-81	
04	Ralph H. Scott	Haw River	02-23-77	
	Henry E. Frye	Greensboro	02-06-81	
	Nilous Avery	Asheville	10-21-83	
05	C. C. Cameron	Charlotte	10-21-83	

North Carolina Alcoholism Research Authority
G.S. 122-120/Board No. 0035

Position No.	Name of Appointee	Address	Date Appointed	Date of Expiration
01	L. C. Bruce, *chairman*	Raleigh	02-01-80	02-01-86
02	George C. Edmonds	Apex	02-01-80	02-01-86
03	Philip G. Nelson.	Greenville	02-01-80	02-01-86
04	Erskine Bowles	Charlotte	02-01-78	02-01-84
	Margaret Tennille	Winston-Salem	08-08-79	02-01-84
	Martha Alexander	Charlotte	08-27-82	02-01-84
05	W. J. K. Rockwell	Durham	02-01-78	02-01-84
06	Nannette S. Henderson	Warrenton	02-01-78	02-01-84
07	Curtis R. Lashley	Greensboro	02-01-82	02-01-88
	Carol Cunningham	Winston-Salem	12-31-84	02-01-88

North Carolina Alcoholism Research Authority
(continued)

Position No.	Name of Appointee	Address	Date Appointed	Date of Expiration
08	Fred W. Ellis	Chapel Hill	02-01-82	02-01-88
	Sam Pennington	Greenville	12-31-84	02-01-88
09	Augustus M. Witherspoon	Raleigh	02-01-82	02-01-88

North Carolina Bar Council
G.S. 84-17, -18/Board No. 0119

01	Leander R. Morgan	New Bern	04-14-83	07-01-84
			06-29-84	07-01-87
02	Janice Ramquist	Cary	07-13-83	07-01-84
			06-29-84	07-01-87
03	J. Ralph Squires.................	Charlotte	04-21-83	07-01-84
			06-27-84	07-01-87

Disciplinary Hearing Commission of the North Carolina State Bar
G.S. 84-28.1/Board No. 0287

01	Mary C. Bridges................	Greensboro	05-10-79	06-30-82
			10-13-82	06-30-85
02	Nona McDonald..................	Asheville	03-26-79	06-30-80
			06-08-81	06-30-83
	Henry H. Sherwood	Wingate	10-13-82	06-30-83
			02-13-84	06-30-86
03	Fred M. Byerly...................	Dunn	03-26-79	06-30-81
	Alice W. Penny...................	Raleigh	07-22-81	06-30-84
			06-22-84	06-30-87

The Central Orphanage of North Carolina Board of Directors
G.S. 115C-135/Board No. 0180

01	Rosetta C. Amis..................	Oxford	04-10-78	05-09-81
			04-06-82	05-10-85
02	Charles F. Jones, Jr.................	Oxford	04-10-78	05-09-81
			04-06-82	05-10-85
03	Dorothy J. Roberson...............	Oxford	04-10-78	05-09-81
			05-19-82	05-10-85
04	Harold L. Culbreth.................	Stovall	04-10-78	05-09-81
			04-06-82	05-10-85
05	R. M. Currin, Jr....................	Oxford	04-10-78	05-09-81
	Willard W. King..................	Oxford	03-21-80	05-09-81
			04-06-82	05-10-85

Columbus-Brunswick Regional Housing Authority
G.S. 157-36/Board No. 0209

01	Velma Haley, *chairwoman*	Whiteville	05-28-80	04-20-85

North Carolina Courts Commission
G.S. 7A-506/Board No. 0250

01, 04	Parks Helms, *chairman*	Charlotte	03-17-80	06-30-83
			09-09-83	06-30-87
02	Charles Becton	Durham	03-17-80	06-30-81

NORTH CAROLINA COURTS COMMISSION (CONTINUED)

Position No.	Name of Appointee	Address	Date Appointed	Date of Expiration
03, 05	David M. Britt	Raleigh	03-17-80	06-30-81
			08-24-81	06-30-85
04, 06	Itimous T. Valentine, Jr.	Nashville	03-17-80	06-30-83
05, 07	Louise B. Wilson	Graham	03-17-80	06-30-81
			08-24-81	06-30-85
06	Dennis J. Winner	Asheville	09-09-83	06-30-87
08	Wade Barber, Jr.	Pittsboro	08-24-81	06-30-83
			09-09-83	06-30-85
	Ron Brown	Asheville	11-02-84	06-30-85
09	Daniel T. Blue, Jr.	Raleigh	08-24-81	06-30-85
10	George R. Kornegay, Jr.	Mount Olive	08-24-81	06-30-85
	Rebecca B. Hundley	Thomasville	10-21-83	06-30-87

EASTERN CAROLINA REGIONAL HOUSING AUTHORITY
G.S. 157-36/Board No. 0295

01	Oscar N. Harris	Dunn	04-02-80	04-10-85

STATE EDUCATION ASSISTANCE AUTHORITY BOARD OF DIRECTORS
G.S. 116-203/Board No. 0315

03	Judy A. Dorman	Fayetteville	12-03-79	01-18-83
04	Thomas J. Elijah, Jr.	Winston-Salem	12-03-79	01-18-83
05	D. Douglas Wade, Jr.	Rocky Mount	02-23-79	01-18-82
06	J. Russell Kirby, Jr., *chairman*	Wilson	10-01-78	01-18-81
	Benton T. Haithcock	Mount Gilead	04-15-80	01-18-81
07	Julia W. Taylor, *vice-chairwoman*	Raleigh	10-01-78	01-18-80

STATE BOARD OF ELECTIONS
G.S. 163-19/Board No. 0330

01	John L. Stickley, Sr.	Charlotte	06-07-77	05-01-81
	Robert W. Spearman, *chairman*	Raleigh	11-02-81	05-01-85
02	Allene Highsmith	Asheville	06-07-77	05-01-81
	Joann Smith	Raleigh	01-05-79	05-01-81
	Ruth T. Semashko	Horse Shoe	02-05-80	05-01-81
			11-02-81	05-01-85
03	R. Kenneth Babb, *chairman*	Winston-Salem	06-07-77	05-01-81
	William A. Marsh, Jr...............	Durham	11-02-81	05-01-85
04	Sydney F. C. Barnwell	New Bern	06-07-77	05-01-81
	Elloree Erwin	Charlotte	11-02-81	05-01-85
05	Shirley Herring	Kinston	06-07-77	05-01-81
	John A. Walker	North Wilkesboro	11-02-81	05-01-85
	Robert R. Browning	Greenville	04-08-82	05-01-85

LEGISLATIVE STUDY COMMISSION FOR STATE POLICIES ON THE MEETINGS OF GOVERNMENTAL BODIES[21]
G.S. 143-318/Board No. 0650

01	Gordon A. Aulis	Raleigh	01-26-78	

---

21 G.S. 143-318.1 through -318.8, inclusive, were repealed under *N.C. Session Laws, 1979*, c. 655, s. 1, ratified May 28, 1979, and became effective on October 1, 1979.

LEGISLATIVE STUDY COMMISSION FOR STATE POLICIES ON THE
MEETINGS OF GOVERNMENTAL BODIES (CONTINUED)

Position No.	Name of Appointee	Address	Date Appointed	Date of Expiration
02	Janice H. Faulkner	Greenville	01-26-78	
03	Robert A. Jones, *chairman*	Forest City	01-26-78	
04	Ailey M. Young	Wake Forest	01-26-78	

GOVERNMENTAL EVALUATION COMMISSION [22]
G.S. 143-34.15/Board No. 0405

01	Emanuel S. Douglas	Southern Pines	03-03-78	06-30-80
02	Wymene Valand, *chairwoman*	Raleigh	03-03-78	06-30-80
03	Jack D. Fleer	Winston-Salem	03-03-78	06-30-80
04	John S. Stevens	Asheville	03-03-78	06-30-80
	Janet Pickler	New London	03-28-79	06-30-80
05	Paul Vick, *chairman*	Durham	03-03-78	07-30-80
	Willie M. Carney	Bethel	04-10-80	06-30-83
06	Nancy Chase	Eureka		06-30-80

COMMITTEE ON INAUGURAL CEREMONIES
G.S. 143-533/Board No. 0459

01	James B. Garrison, *chairman*	Albemarle	11-24-80	00-00-00
02	Mary M. Bradshaw	Raleigh	11-24-80	00-00-00
03	Jeanette Carl	Raleigh	11-24-80	00-00-00
04	Henry E. Frye	Greensboro	11-24-80	00-00-00
05	John A. Walker	North Wilkesboro	11-24-80	00-00-00
06	Cliffornia G. Wimberley	Raleigh	11-24-80	00-00-00

JUVENILE LAW STUDY COMMISSION
G.S. 7A-740/Board No. 0510

01	Gilbert Burnett	Wilmington	03-24-81	07-01-83
			03-24-84	07-01-86
02	Leonard Van Noppen	Danbury	03-24-81	07-01-83
	Lota Greenlee	Marion	03-20-84	07-01-86
03	Nancy Patteson	Wilson	03-24-81	07-01-82
			10-18-82	07-01-84
			09-14-84	06-30-86
04	Rosa M. Jones	Charlotte	03-24-81	07-01-82
			10-18-82	07-01-84
			09-21-84	06-30-86
05	Lee Crites	Silva	03-24-81	07-01-82
			10-18-82	07-01-84
			09-14-84	06-30-86
06	Sue Glasby	Lillington	03-24-81	07-01-83
			03-20-84	07-01-86
07	Rankin Whittington	Wadesboro	03-24-81	07-01-83
			03-20-84	07-01-85
08	Don L. Pagett	Swannanoa	03-24-81	07-01-81
			07-01-81	07-01-82
			10-18-81	07-01-83

---

22 G.S. 143-34.15 was repealed under *N.C. Session Laws, 1981*, c. 392, s. 1, ratified July 10, 1981.

JUVENILE LAW STUDY COMMISSION (CONTINUED)

Position No.	Name of Appointee	Address	Date Appointed	Date of Expiration
	Steve Williams	Raleigh	11-20-84	07-01-85
09	Janet Crisp-Lacey	Greensboro	03-24-81	07-01-81
			07-01-81	07-01-82
			10-18-82	07-01-83
			03-20-84	07-01-85
10	Jayne K. Kent	Lenoir	03-24-81	07-01-81
			07-01-81	07-01-82
			10-18-82	07-01-83
11	John Dietrick	Charlotte	03-24-81	07-01-81
16	Michael J. McGee	Raleigh	10-18-82	06-30-83
			03-20-84	06-30-85
17	Joseph B. Parks	Winston-Salem	10-18-82	06-30-83
			03-20-84	07-01-85

BOARD OF TRUSTEES OF THE UNIVERSITY OF NORTH CAROLINA CENTER FOR PUBLIC TELEVISION
G.S. 116-37.1(b)(1)/Board No. 0749

01	Eli N. Evans	New York, N.Y.	03-06-80	05-31-84
02	Valeria L. Lee	Warrenton	03-06-80	05-31-82
			09-22-82	05-31-86
03	Charles G. Rose III	Washington, D.C.	03-06-80	05-31-84
	Arthur Cassell	High Point	12-18-84	05-31-88
04	A. Thomas Stewart	Washington	03-06-80	05-31-82
			09-22-82	05-31-86

SOUTHERN GROWTH POLICIES BOARD
G.S. 143-492/Board No. 0850

01	Carl J. Stewart, Jr.	Gastonia	12-16-77
02	Dean W. Colvard	Charlotte	03-24-77
03	Paul Vick	Durham	03-23-83

BOARD OF CONTROL FOR SOUTHERN REGIONAL EDUCATION
N.C. SESSION LAWS, 1957, Res. 27/Board No. 0860

01	Robert B. Jordan III	Mount Gilead	10-01-80	06-30-84
			08-22-84	06-30-88
02	William C. Friday	Chapel Hill	02-04-80	06-30-83
			10-04-83	06-30-87
03	Dwight W. Quinn	Kannapolis	07-12-78	06-30-82
			10-01-82	06-30-86
04	Carl J. Stewart, Jr.	Gastonia	08-01-77	06-30-81
			12-17-81	06-30-85

STATE PARKS STUDY COMMISSION
N.C. SESSION LAWS, 1977, c. 1030/Board No. 3385

01	Cy W. Brame, Jr.	North Wilkesboro	07-13-78
02	Ellen P. Hyams	Bryson City	11-08-77
03	E. S. Melvin	Greensboro	11-08-77
04	Charles T. Fort	Winston-Salem	11-08-77

LICENSING AND EXAMINING BOARDS

North Carolina Board of Architecture
G.S. 83A-2/Board No. 0045

Position No.	Name of Appointee	Address	Date Appointed	Date of Expiration
01	Herbert P. McKim .... Wilmington		09-01-77	04-08-82
			04-01-82	04-01-87
02	Lloyd G. Walter, Jr. .... Winston-Salem		12-21-81	04-01-86
03	Harvey B. Gantt .... Charlotte		05-30-80	04-01-85
04	Tai Y. Lee .... Hazelwood		10-08-79	04-01-84
			03-26-84	04-01-89
05	John L. Atkins III .... Durham		04-12-78	04-01-83
			03-23-83	04-01-88
06	C. J. Mabry, Jr. .... Shelby		10-08-79	
	John C. Laughridge .... Marion		12-21-81	
07	Wanda S. Caldwell .... Lake Junaluska		10-08-79	

North Carolina Auctioneers Commission
G.S. 85B-3/Board No. 0085

Position No.	Name of Appointee	Address	Date Appointed	Date of Expiration
01	Jackie Ball...................... Marshall		10-20-77	06-30-78
				06-30-81
	Ronald W. Faison .... Raleigh		08-19-81	06-30-84
			10-31-84	06-30-87
02	John H. Sutton.................. Salisbury		01-01-83	06-30-83
			07-07-83	06-30-86
03	Donald R. Abernathy .... Landis		02-14-78	06-30-80
			09-12-80	06-30-83

State Board of Barber Examiners
G.S. 86A-4/Board No. 0115

Position No.	Name of Appointee	Address	Date Appointed	Date of Expiration
01	Tim E. Gore...................... Shallotte		08-31-77	07-01-79
	Luther C. Oliver, Sr. .... Fayetteville		01-02-80	07-01-83
				06-30-86
02	Susan Patterson................. Mount Airy		07-01-81	07-01-84
			12-04-84	07-01-87
03	Tommy G. Lewis, *chairman* .... Raleigh		09-28-78	07-01-83
			07-13-83	06-30-86
04	John P. Robertson .... Red Springs		11-09-82	07-01-84
			12-04-84	07-01-87

State Board of Certified Public Accountant Examiners
G.S. 93-12/Board No. 0190

Position No.	Name of Appointee	Address	Date Appointed	Date of Expiration
01	Maylon E. Little.................... Raleigh		09-12-77	06-30-80
			10-17-80	06-30-83
02	E. Howard Cannon .... Winston-Salem		09-12-77	06-30-80
			10-17-80	06-30-83
	Edgar M. Johnson .... Kill Devil Hills		11-28-83	06-30-86
03	E. Graham McGoogan .... Charlotte		10-17-80	06-30-83
	William E. Self.................... Durham		11-28-83	06-30-86
04	Julius A. Grisette .... Valdese		01-11-80	06-30-82
			08-05-82	06-30-85
05, 01	William E. Perdew .... Wilmington		10-17-80	06-30-82
			11-28-83	06-30-86

STATE BOARD OF CERTIFIED PUBLIC ACCOUNTANT EXAMINERS
(CONTINUED)

Position No.	Name of Appointee	Address	Date Appointed	Date of Expiration
05	Carl M. Parnell	Raleigh	07-30-82	06-30-85
06	Madelyn C. Eve	Raleigh	11-13-80	06-30-83
	Barbara N. Stewart	Greensboro	07-13-83	06-30-86
07	Herman F. Fox	Greensboro	10-17-80	06-30-82
			08-05-82	06-30-85

STATE BOARD OF CHIROPRACTIC EXAMINERS
G.S. 90-139/Board No. 0205

07	William Y. Preyer, Jr.	Greensboro	05-24-79	03-06-83
	James C. Crates	Charlotte	01-11-84	03-06-86

STATE BOARD OF COSMETIC ART EXAMINERS
G.S. 88-13/Board No. 0245

01	Lee R. Amos	Greensboro	09-01-77	06-30-80
	Lillian W. Snipes	Greensboro	04-09-81	06-30-83
			02-13-84	06-30-86
02	Zada Noe, *chairwoman*	Beaufort	09-01-77	06-30-80
			04-09-81	06-30-83
			07-01-82	06-30-84
			11-19-84	06-30-87
03	Corena S. Smith	Asheville	09-01-77	06-30-80
			04-09-81	06-30-83
			07-06-82	06-30-85
04	Brenda M. Johnson	Zebulon	05-17-82	07-01-84
			11-19-84	06-30-87

BOARD OF DENTAL EXAMINERS
G.S. 90-22/Board No. 0281

01	Lucille McCall	Durham	10-12-82	07-31-84

STATE BOARD OF EXAMINERS OF ELECTRICAL CONTRACTORS
G.S. 87-39/Board No. 0335

01	Luther R. Herman	Raleigh	06-02-78	04-15-81
			07-23-81	04-15-88
	William T. Easter	Cary	11-30-82	04-15-88
02	Oscar Greene, Jr., *chairman*	Kinston	06-28-77	04-15-80
			11-03-80	04-15-87
03	John H. Garland	Asheville	08-22-78	04-15-79
			04-20-79	04-15-82
			11-30-82	04-15-89
06	Prince E. Graves	Greensboro	11-03-80	04-15-86
07	Joseph F. Martin	Franklin	11-03-80	04-15-86

STATE BOARD OF REGISTRATION FOR PROFESSIONAL ENGINEERS AND LAND SURVEYORS
G.S. 89C-4/Board No. 0354

01, 07	Chappell N. Noble	Lumberton	01-22-79	12-31-83
			02-24-84	12-31-87
01	George Paris	Red Springs	02-27-81	12-31-85

State Board of Registration for Professional Engineers and Land Surveyors (continued)

Position No.	Name of Appointee	Address	Date Appointed	Date of Expiration
02	Howard M. Loughlin	Hampstead	01-22-79	12-31-83
			02-24-84	12-31-87
03	Phillip L. Stanley	Cary	01-09-78	12-31-82
	Ronald H. Carpenter	North Wilkesboro	01-01-83	12-31-87
04	Guy H. Cheek	Monroe	01-20-82	12-31-86
05	Charles Y. Proffitt	Wilson	02-27-81	12-31-85
06	Robert E. Turner	Asheville	01-09-78	12-31-79
			02-01-80	12-31-84
	Gilbert R. Alligood	Washington	12-27-84	12-31-88
08	Charles B. Langston	Whiteville	02-27-81	12-31-83
			02-24-84	12-31-87
09	Marvin Raper	Murphy	02-27-81	12-31-84
	Larry D. Barnett	Laurinburg	12-27-84	12-31-88

State Board of Registration for Foresters
G.S. 89B-3/Board No. 0375

01	Fred M. White, *secretary*	Durham	06-20-80	06-30-84
	Otho C. Goodwin, Jr.	Raleigh	02-02-83	06-30-84
			07-10-84	06-30-89
02	Bernice H. Corpening	Asheville	02-16-78	06-30-82
	Thomas F. McClintock	Asheville	06-20-80	06-30-82
			09-27-82	06-30-87
03	Rufus Kimrey	Kinston	06-20-80	06-30-85
04	Joseph B. Brown	Raleigh	09-13-78	06-30-83
	Charles B. Davey	Raleigh	08-04-83	07-01-88
05	Tarlton R. Thompson, Jr.	New Bern	12-27-78	06-30-81
			10-19-82	06-30-86

State Licensing Board for General Contractors
G.S. 87-2/Board No. 0230

01	Richard R. Allen	Fayetteville	02-06-78	12-31-82
	Richard A. Mitchell	Durham	09-04-81	12-31-82
			01-27-84	12-31-87
02	Perry Greene, Sr.	Boone		12-31-86
03	J. S. Jacobs, Jr.	Gastonia	08-19-81	12-31-85
04	James L. Propst	Concord	02-29-80	12-31-84
	J. S. Evans, Jr.	Statesville	05-21-81	12-31-84
				12-31-89
05	Jimmy R. Flowers, *vice-chairman*	Clayton	03-26-79	12-31-83
			01-27-84	12-31-88
06	J. Ray Butler	Winston-Salem	04-29-80	12-31-81
			01-27-84	12-31-86
07	William W. Hill	Murfreesboro	04-02-80	12-31-83
	Marshall Dunn	Pinetops	03-13-83	12-31-88

North Carolina State Hearing Aid Dealers and Fitters Board
G.S. 93D-3/Board No. 0425

01	Roland C. Scott	Hillsborough	06-07-78	09-24-81
	James D. Mundell, Jr.	Winston-Salem	04-23-82	09-24-82
	Stan Deweese	Waynesville	02-02-83	09-24-85

NORTH CAROLINA STATE HEARING AID DEALERS AND FITTERS BOARD
(CONTINUED)

Position No.	Name of Appointee	Address	Date Appointed	Date of Expiration
02	Hubert Smith	Greenville	03-19-80	09-24-83
	James W. Mills	Asheville	04-30-81	09-24-83
03	Ray O. Bedsaul, *secretary*	Winston-Salem	10-17-78	09-24-82
04, 03	Harlan S. Cato, *president*	Greensboro	11-08-77	06-08-78
			04-23-82	09-24-84
04	W. Earl McCall	Rocky Mount	06-07-78	09-24-81
			01-12-81	09-24-84
05	Robert B. Jones	Wilmington	10-17-78	09-24-81
	Glenn E. Hair	Fayetteville	05-21-81	09-24-81
06	Carter S. Bagley	Asheville	10-17-78	09-24-81
07	Donald M. Ellington	Charlotte	04-23-82	09-24-84

NORTH CAROLINA BOARD OF LANDSCAPE ARCHITECTS
G.S. 89A-3/Board No. 0520

Position No.	Name of Appointee	Address	Date Appointed	Date of Expiration
01	Lindsay W. Cox	Greensboro	12-04-81	07-01-84
			12-31-84	07-01-88
02	Robert M. Jordan	Davidson	12-04-81	07-01-84
			12-31-84	07-01-88
03	C. Lamarr Bunn	Raleigh	12-04-81	07-01-83
	Leslie B. Wagle	Greensboro	07-29-83	07-01-87
04	Jerry M. Turner	Raleigh	04-19-78	07-01-81
			12-04-81	07-01-85
05	Henry C. Hammond	Raleigh	04-19-78	07-01-81
			12-04-81	07-01-85
06	Betty Burton	Shelby	12-04-81	07-01-83
07	Beverly Neilson	Charlotte	12-04-81	07-01-83
	Beatrice B. Matthews	Fayetteville	01-31-84	07-01-87

NORTH CAROLINA LANDSCAPE CONTRACTORS' REGISTRATION BOARD
G.S. 890-4/Board No. 0521

Position No.	Name of Appointee	Address	Date Appointed	Date of Expiration
01	George M. Coulter, Jr.	Charlotte	09-12-80	12-01-82
02	James Ferger	Wilmington	05-11-78	12-01-78
				12-01-80
	Richard C. Bell	Raleigh	05-25-82	12-01-83

NORTH CAROLINA MARITAL AND FAMILY THERAPY CERTIFICATION BOARD
G.S. 90-270.50/Board No. 0558

Position No.	Name of Appointee	Address	Date Appointed	Date of Expiration
01	Thomas E. Clark, *chairman*	Winston-Salem	03-10-80	09-30-83
			12-21-84	09-30-87
02	Sarah Y. Austin	Winston-Salem	03-10-80	09-30-82
			12-21-84	09-30-86
03	George D. Carter, Jr.	Morganton	03-10-80	09-30-81
	Elizabeth F. Little	Gastonia	02-12-81	09-30-81
			04-23-82	09-30-85
04	Edward W. Markowski	Greenville	03-10-80	09-30-81
			04-23-82	09-30-85
05	Roy L. Grant	Reidsville	03-10-80	09-30-81
			04-23-82	09-30-85
06	Arthaniel E. Harris, Sr.	Kinston	03-10-80	09-30-82
07	Nancy K. Johnston	Jefferson	03-10-80	09-30-83
			12-21-84	09-30-86

BOARD OF MEDICAL EXAMINERS
G.S. 90-2/Board No. 0561

Position No.	Name of Appointee	Address	Date Appointed	Date of Expiration
08	Martha Walston	Wilson	01-21-82	10-31-84
			08-22-84	10-31-87

NORTH CAROLINA BOARD OF MORTUARY SCIENCE
G.S. 90-210.18(b)/Board No. 0600

01	Stuart L. Cozort, Jr.	Troy	01-30-78	06-30-81
			12-09-81	06-30-85

NORTH CAROLINA BOARD OF NURSING
G.S. 90-159/Board No. 0640

01	Glenn Pickard	Chapel Hill	06-26-78	01-01-81
	Donna J. Thigpen	Beulaville	01-01-82	01-01-84
			01-05-84	01-01-87
02	Audrey J. Booth	Durham	01-07-77	01-01-81
	Juanita Yarborough	High Point	06-17-81	01-01-85
	Beth McAllister	Raleigh	01-01-82	01-01-83
	Joseph H. Nanny	Clyde	03-23-83	01-01-86
03	Bessie W. Funderburg.	Wilmington	04-01-78	01-01-82
04	Jane T. York	Badin	04-01-78	01-01-82
05	Nancy Cook	Mocksville	04-01-78	01-01-82
06	Judith B. Seamon, *chairwoman* . .	Morehead City	04-01-78	01-01-82
07	Jackie Stoker	Asheville	04-01-78	01-01-82
08	Russell E. Tranbarger	Greensboro	07-09-79	01-01-83
09	H. Hamilton Allen	Winston-Salem	07-09-79	01-01-83
10	John C. Blanton	Ahoskie	07-09-79	01-01-83
11	Robert L. Wall	Concord	01-16-80	01-01-84
12	Lois S. Isler	Greensboro	01-16-80	01-01-84

STATE BOARD OF EXAMINERS FOR NURSING HOME ADMINISTRATORS
G.S. 90-277/Board No. 0645

01	O. Wade Avent, Jr., *chairman*	Whiteville	08-25-78	06-30-81
	Daniel Tullock	Winston-Salem	07-29-81	06-30-84
			12-21-84	06-30-87
02	James R. Garrett, Jr.	Durham	07-01-80	06-30-82
	Gerald P. Cox	Rocky Mount	07-08-82	06-30-85
03	Sue B. Payne	Gastonia	07-29-81	06-30-84
04	Margaret R. Huffstetler	Burlington	08-25-78	06-30-81
	Frances T. Thomas	Raleigh	09-10-81	06-30-84
05	Kimsey King	Durham	04-10-78	06-30-81
	Howard A. Chubbs	Greensboro	07-01-80	06-30-82
			07-07-82	06-30-85
06	Augustus H. Tulloss	Rocky Mount	08-25-78	06-30-81
	Hector H. Henry II	Concord	07-01-80	06-30-81
			09-10-81	06-30-84
			12-21-84	06-30-87
08	Robert O. Hill, Jr.	Snow Hill	07-01-80	06-30-82
			07-07-82	06-30-85

NORTH CAROLINA STATE BOARD OF OPTICIANS
G.S. 90-238/Board No. 0655

Position No.	Name of Appointee	Address	Date Appointed	Date of Expiration
06	Charles G. Crawford	Maggie Valley	01-13-82	07-01-83
			06-29-84	07-01-86
07	Cora H. Hawkins	Warrenton	01-13-82	07-01-84
			06-27-84	07-01-87

NORTH CAROLINA STATE BOARD OF EXAMINERS IN OPTOMETRY
G.S. 90-116/Board No. 0660

06	Alfred M. Goodwin	Louisburg	11-18-81	05-01-86
07	Clarence Mace	Sanford	01-04-81	05-01-86

BOARD OF PHARMACY
G.S. 90-55/Board No. 0695

06	Joseph B. Roberts III	Gastonia	02-05-82	04-30-84
			06-28-84	04-30-89

NORTH CAROLINA BOARD OF PHYSICAL THERAPY EXAMINERS
G.S. 90-270.25/Board No. 0700

08	Shirley D. Wright	Jarvisburg	03-17-83	07-01-84
	George Hamilton	Greenville	12-27-84	01-01-87

STATE BOARD OF EXAMINERS OF PLUMBING AND HEATING CONTRACTORS
G.S. 87-16/Board No. 0705

01	Eugene A. Luquire, Jr.	Durham	10-08-80	04-25-87
02	Frank Seely	Raleigh	07-23-81	04-25-88
03, 04	Helen W. Thomas	Concord	04-15-82	04-25-82
				04-25-89
03	Leroy Adams	Lumberton	05-27-83	04-25-90
05	Emil T. Chanlett	Chapel Hill	07-21-77	04-25-84
06	James M. Fry	China Grove	03-20-79	04-25-85
07	Joseph M. Lee, Jr., *chairman*	Durham	04-25-79	04-25-86

NORTH CAROLINA STATE BOARD OF EXAMINERS OF PRACTICING PSYCHOLOGISTS
G.S. 90-270.6/Board No. 0720

06	James H. Stamey	Raleigh	12-31-85	07-01-86

NORTH CAROLINA REAL ESTATE LICENSING BOARD
G.S. 93A-3/Board No. 0765

01	Carolyn D. McCandlish	Charlotte	08-01-78	07-31-81
			08-19-81	07-31-84
	Lanelle K. Lilley	Wrightsville Beach	06-01-84	07-31-87
02	A. P. Carlton, Sr.	Greensboro	08-01-78	07-31-81
			08-19-81	07-31-84
			06-08-84	07-31-87
03	Brantley T. Poole, *chairman*	Raleigh	09-21-77	07-31-80
			08-07-80	07-31-83
				07-31-86

North Carolina Real Estate Licensing Board
(CONTINUED)

Position No.	Name of Appointee	Address	Date Appointed	Date of Expiration
04	William C. Stokes	Reidsville	09-21-77	07-31-80
	Fred Adams	Cary	08-11-81	07-31-83
	Lee R. Barnes	Durham	05-15-84	07-31-86
05	B. T. Bryson	Hendersonville	11-09-79	07-31-82
			09-30-82	07-31-85
06	B. Hunt Baxter	New Bern	11-26-79	07-31-82
			09-30-82	07-31-85
07	James A. Beaty, Jr.	Winston-Salem	11-26-79	07-31-82
	Thomas Council	Fayetteville	11-18-81	07-31-82
			09-30-82	07-31-85

State Board of Refrigeration Examiners
G.S. 87-52/Board No. 0775

Position No.	Name of Appointee	Address	Date Appointed	Date of Expiration
01	Charles C. Enscore	Raleigh	07-08-82	01-01-86
02	William L. Wester	Lumberton	07-08-82	01-01-85
			12-27-84	01-01-91
03	Thomas C. Hurley, *chairman*	Newton	09-27-77	01-01-84
			02-13-84	01-01-91
05	Parker C. Reist	Chapel Hill	10-06-82	01-01-89
06	James M. Lyndon	Wilson	10-06-82	01-01-88
07	Daniel Baucom	Raleigh	09-11-78	01-01-80
			07-06-82	01-01-87

State Board of Sanitarian Examiners
G.S. 90A-55(a)/Board No. 0815

Position No.	Name of Appointee	Address	Date Appointed	Date of Expiration
01	James Jones	Fayetteville	07-07-81	12-15-85
			02-03-84	12-15-87
02	Edward M. Wilkins, *secretary-treasurer*	Lumberton	08-02-80	12-15-83
			02-03-84	12-15-87
03	Jesse F. Williams	Fayetteville	09-12-78	12-15-82
			12-15-82	12-15-86
04	David Simpson	Franklin	02-28-79	12-15-82
	D. R. Baxley, Sr.	Taylorsville	11-30-82	12-15-86
05	Carlton S. Harrell	Burgaw	12-18-77	12-15-81
	Thomas F. Owens	High Point	10-08-82	12-15-85
06	Marshall Staton	Raleigh	01-25-78	12-15-81
	James F. Stamey	Raleigh	06-11-81	12-15-81
			10-08-82	12-15-85
07	Jesse S. Cannady, *chairman*	Fayetteville	09-12-78	12-15-81
	Charles E. Powell	Goldsboro	10-08-82	12-15-85

Board of Examiners for Speech and Language Pathologists and Audiologists
G.S. 90-303/Board No. 0863

Position No.	Name of Appointee	Address	Date Appointed	Date of Expiration
01	Robert G. Paul, *secretary-treasurer*	Durham	01-11-78	09-30-82
			10-01-82	09-30-85
02	Robert A. Muzzarelli	Greenville	08-24-82	09-30-84
03	Stanley Martinkosky	Chapel Hill	06-23-81	09-30-85
04	Charles M. Schlein	Morganton	08-24-82	09-30-84
			08-15-84	09-30-89

BOARD OF EXAMINERS FOR SPEECH AND LANGUAGE PATHOLOGISTS AND AUDIOLOGISTS (CONTINUED)

Position No.	Name of Appointee	Address	Date Appointed	Date of Expiration
05	W. Paul Biggers	Chapel Hill	08-24-82	09-30-84
07	Lewanna Stout	Raleigh	04-29-83	06-15-84
			07-24-84	06-15-89

NORTH CAROLINA VETERINARY MEDICAL BOARD
G.S. 90-182/Board No. 0930

01	Donald W. Lackey	Lenoir	12-16-77	07-01-82
03	William E. Plummer.	Goldsboro	07-01-80	07-01-85
04	Dennis L. Jackson	Fayetteville	11-29-79	07-01-84
	Ralph E. Gandy.	Rockingham	12-28-84	07-01-89
05	Mack S. Setser	Waynesville	07-05-78	07-01-83
			09-19-83	07-01-88
07	Jane Jernigan	Fayetteville	04-15-82	07-01-86

NORTH CAROLINA STATE BOARD OF EXAMINERS IN WATCHMAKING AND REPAIRING [23]
G.S. 93C-2/Board No. 0940

04	A. C. Fair.	Warrenton	09-11-78	07-01-82
05	Joseph C. Crooks, Jr.	Mooresville	09-30-77	07-01-81

STATE BOARD OF WATER WELL CONTRACTOR EXAMINERS [24]
G.S. 87-70/Board No. 0960

01	Vance J. Setzer	Shelby	03-23-78	12-31-80
02	Winston P. King.	Ahoskie	06-09-78	12-31-80
03	Charles W. Brinkley, Jr.	Teachey	06-09-78	12-31-80
04	Braxton Britt.	Wilson	07-14-78	12-31-80
06	Leland L. Layman	Raleigh	06-09-78	12-31-80

STUDY COMMISSIONS, ADVISORY COUNCILS, AND OTHER NONSTATUTORY BOARDS

Board Number	Title
3022	Committee for the Study of Abandoned Cemeteries
3003	Administrative Rules Study Commission
3002	Agriculture, Forestry, and Seafood Awareness
3005	Governor's Advisory Committee on Agriculture, Forestry, and the Seafood Industry
3007	Air Quality Legislative Study Commission
3008	North Carolina Alternative Energy Corporation
3009	Andrew Jackson Historic Memorial Committee
3020	Governor's Business Council on Arts and Humanities
3025	Advisory Council to the Governor's Office of Citizen Affairs
3030	Coastal Plains Regional Commission Agriculture and Forestry Advisory Committee

---

23 G.S. 93C-2 was repealed by c. 712, s. 1, *N.C. Session Laws, 1977*, to become effective July 1, 1979.
24 G.S. 87-70 was repealed by *N.C. Session Laws, 1977*, c. 712, s. 2, ratified July 1, 1977, and became effective July 1, 1979.

STUDY COMMISSIONS, ADVISORY COUNCILS,
AND OTHER NONSTATUTORY BOARDS (CONTINUED)

Board Number	Title
3040	Coastal Plains Regional Commission Environmental Task Force
3050	Coastal Plains Regional Commission Industrial Development Advisory Committee
3060	Coastal Plains Regional Commission Marine Resources Advisory Committee
3065	Commission on Code Recodification
3070	College Foundation, Incorporated, Board of Trustees
3067	Community College and Technical Institute Planning Commission
3250	Community Employment and Training Council [CETA]
3155	Interagency Council on Community Schools
3069	Conservation Law Study Committee of North Carolina
3072	Task Force on Security and Privacy of Criminal Justice Information
3071	North Carolina Criminal Justice Information System Board
3072	North Carolina Criminal Justice Information System Security and Privacy Board
3031	Criminal Justice Information Systems
3077	Governor's Task Force on Domestic Violence
3079	Governor's Task Force on Drunken Drivers
0309	Governor's Advisory Committee on Education Block Grants
3082	Electronic Town Hall Task Force
3084	Governor's Study Commission on Energy Loans
3085	North Carolina Board of Ethics
3100	Flue-Cured Tobacco Cooperative Stabilization Corporation Public Director
0386	Commission on the Future of North Carolina
3400	Governor's Commission on Governmental Productivity
3119	North Carolina Health Coordinating Council
3125	Governor's Commission on Highway Safety
3130	State Historical Records Advisory Board
3150	North Carolina Institute of Medicine
3156	North Carolina Job Training Coordinating Council
3160	Juvenile Code Revision Committee
3210	Law Enforcement Officers Liability Insurance Study Commission
3220	Learning Institute of North Carolina Board of Directors
3230	State Advisory Council to the Legal Services Corporation
3240	North Carolina Local Government Advocacy Council
3280	Mental Health Study Commission
3295	Governor's Advisory Commission on Military Affairs
3325	U.S.S. *Monitor* Research Council
3335	Board of Directors of the North Carolina Museum of History Associates, Incorporated
3087	Committee to Study the Facility Needs of the North Carolina Museum of History, North Carolina State Archives, and Other State Programs
3019	Committee for the Study of Mutual Burial Associations
3340	Board of Directors of the North Carolina Natural History Society
3350	North Carolina New Horizons Task Force
3353	Special Advisory Committee for Nonpublic Education
3362	Governor's Oversight Committee

STUDY COMMISSIONS, ADVISORY COUNCILS,
AND OTHER NONSTATUTORY BOARDS (CONTINUED)

APPENDIX

BLACK JACK FREE WILL BAPTIST CHURCH FAMILY FESTIVAL

MARCH 28, 1984

["Extending a helping hand to someone in need is God's work on earth. It is our foremost responsibility as individuals, and it is the most basic duty of government," said Hunt on March 4, 1982, at a Winston-Salem prayer breakfast. The governor addressed that theme on more than one speaking occasion during his two terms in office, and it reappeared in his message, below, at Black Jack Free Will Baptist Church, Greenville.

The following speech is essentially autobiographical; it touches on matters of personal faith and stresses the importance of the impact, upon a family and society, of shared moral values. But even though Hunt himself was a devout man, he also recognized that the church-state distinction must not be blurred. As he said in Winston-Salem, "No single religious doctrine should dictate to government, and, even more importantly, no government should impose its will on our religious institutions."

The following transcript was made from a tape recording supplied by Cedric D. Pierce, Jr., pastor of Black Jack Free Will Baptist Church, 1968-1971, 1978-1985. Hunt's notes for this address have been reprinted on pages 468-470, above. Although a comparison of the outline with the transcript will show that the governor closely followed the former, the latter was provided to give a more accurate and more colorful rendition of the speech. State Senator Vernon E. White introduced Governor Hunt to the congregation.]

Well thank you very much, Senator White,[1] that was a, a very nice introduction. I a, I'm honored and, and privileged that you would introduce me and say all those nice things about me. Sometimes when somebody goes on like that, and kind of stretches the truth maybe a little bit about me, but in a nice way, I say that I really wish that my wife and mother could've been here to have heard it—because my wife would've enjoyed it, and my sweet mother would've believed it!

I am delighted to be here with you all. This is a wonderful church. If you grew up in the Free Will Baptist denomination, as I did, you've heard of Black Jack all of your life. You've got a wonderful reputation for an active church, throughout North Carolina, and I have really been blessed tonight by being here with Dr. Cedric Pierce, my dear friend—a friendship that started the days he was at the children's home, when he and I worked together, and I worked as the attorney for the children's home, and we did a lot of things together, and became good friends.

I want to say to you all I've never in my life been in a church that has so many great singing groups. I know you're proud of 'em. I just—looking down here: the Youth Choir, the Black Jack Quartet that we've all heard of, the Son Light Singers, the Adult Choir, Mrs. Vicki Dixon—and Reverend Stacy Carter[2] told me there are ten more groups. But let me tell you something: They can't just anybody sing with your choir. Now, when I came in tonight, I came through the choir room, and they were all ready to come in, and I told them that I used to sing in the choir, and that, if they'd like for me to, I would sing bass with them tonight. They didn't take me up on it. But I have been thrilled and blessed from hearing them sing, and I, I want to say, I want to say to you, Cedric, I know you're a good preacher because I've heard you preach, but I expect in this church you could get by with a bad sermon every once in a while because people would go home with a blessing from the singing. And I want to commend your pianist and your organist—what wonderful musicians they are! Again, you, you truly make a joyful noise to the Lord, in this church, and you, and you use your talents that God gave us. Isn't just one or two people, it's a lot of people using their talents, and I think that's what we ought to be doing in life, and we surely ought to be doing it in our churches, and as I said, I'm awfully proud to be here with you.

I a, I did not get here in time—I did see the Scouts and I'm looking forward to having my picture made with them, and I sure hope you all are going to give me some of those Girl Scout cookies. I didn't get here in time for the supper, but a good friend's going to have packed me up some barbecue to take home with me. As, as an eastern North Carolina boy, I love that eastern North Carolina barbecue, so I'm going to take that home and, and enjoy it in the mansion.

You know, although it's been said you can't go home again, having grown up, as I said, in a Free Will Baptist church, I want to tell you that I do feel at home tonight. I am proud to be here, as a part of this Family Life Month in the Free Will Baptist denomination. You are my kind of people, the kind of people I grew up with and am a part of, and there's no place I'd rather be here than in, than in Dr. Pierce's church, and with all of you, and I appreciate you inviting me.

I want to just be sort of informal in talking with you all, tonight, just to kind of share with you some of how I feel about families, what my experience has been. Rather than give a speech on government programs, I want to, in the main, tell you what family means to me, and what I think it means in our society—for the Christian church, and Christian people, ought to be living in happiness. [Electrical failure.][3] I don't know if that's telling us something or not, but, a, . . . [Hunt's words unintelligible]. There's a storm watch out, a, tonight; now, Cedric, if you don't mind I'll just go ahead and preach in the dark. If you all would put some candles up here, that would be very nice. Any of you all in here remember when they used to have, a, mass in the church? I don't imagine you do, but we've got candles tonight.

I know I'm going to have to speak up a little more so all of you can hear me, but I grew up on a tobacco farm and a dairy farm, and I'm used to, I used to have to call in the cattle way back down on Contentnea Creek, so I can, I think, be heard from.

Let me say, first of all, to all of you tonight, that I think the family is important; that those of us who are Christian ought to be concerned about the family, because the family is really the bedrock of society. I don't think there's any accident that the first institution that God created was the home. I can tell you, as governor of the state, that the quality of all society, what we are like as a state, depends upon the health and the strength of the family. Of course, the strength of the family and the health of the family depends on what we do to make it that way. For example, tonight I went back to the mansion—I didn't have but about twenty-five minutes between the time I left my work and the time to leave and come down here, but I went back to the mansion so I could have my supper with my family tonight, with my wife and one daughter that we have left at home, who's been out of school the last two or three days with the flu, but I wanted to spend some time with them. I didn't get to see her this morning before I had to go to work.

It's important for us to spend some time with our families. I think the most important work that, that a church *or* a government can do, is to help families be all that God created them to be. Now, if we care about family, I think we must understand that it's important that we have an emphasis upon our economy. It's essential that families that are going to be strong, and provide for each other, be families in which mothers and fathers—if the mothers choose to work—have an opportunity to have good jobs and to take care of their children. Of course, you know that some families need help, and it's appropriate that churches give help to families in the community that need that. In fact, it's important for the government, at times, to give the kind of help that some people need. Turning our backs on needy families is contrary to the parable of the Good Samaritan.

Second, I believe that the family is essential in passing on the right values to the next generation. I've got a friend on my staff who used to be right far up in the Southern Baptist church in this state; his name is Dr. Charles Petty,[4] and he used to head the Family Life Commission in the Southern Baptist church. And he told me, one time, he said, "Governor, you know at the church that I go to with my family, I coach the track team." They have a track team amongst the churches there. And you have a lot of Scout troops here, and a wonderful program in softball; I saw your, your trophies as I came through with Dr. Pierce. He said, "My relay team wins the relay race every year." And he said, "You know how we win it? Not because our runners are the fastest, because a lot of times they're not." He said, "We win the relay race every single year because we know how to hand off the baton."

The secret in running a relay race is being able to hand it off without slowing down or stopping. They had learned that, and those of us in Christian families must understand that we "hand off" to our children the kinds of values that they will learn. I was fortunate to learn from my Christian parents the importance of belief in Jesus Christ, the importance of church attendance, of honesty, of hard work, of love, and justice, and discipline, of faithfulness and compassion, and stewardship for what we've been given. The Bible says, as we know, "Train up a child in the way he should go, and when he is old, he will not depart from it."

I suspect that many of you here this evening—I can remember that, being faced with hard decisions, I remember my parents' instructions. I can remember the biblical truths that I learned as a child. As a matter of fact, as I was sitting here this evening, I was remembering growing up in the Marsh Swamp Free Will Baptist Church, which was my home church, and I remember that in our church, during Sunday school—I don't know how you all do it here, you've got a, a much larger and nicer church than we had—but I remember we always congregated first in the, in the sanctuary, and we had a little opening service, and then the children were invited to come forward to the front of the church, and turn around and face the congregation, and recite that Sunday's Bible verse. And if you did that successfully for a whole year, you were presented with a Bible. I still have the first Bible that I earned in the Marsh Swamp Free Will Baptist Church.

Those things that our families teach us, that they have us learn in our Sunday school and our church, are the kinds of values that children will take with them throughout their lives. Of course, it is essential that we continue that church attendance, that Sunday school attendance. I'm thinking right now of the things that we had as our Sunday school lesson in our church this past Sunday, and of course in the church service, and I want to say to Dr. Pierce, and to Reverend Carter, and to all the Sunday school teachers in this congregation tonight: You should never underestimate the contribution that you are making by sharing God's truths every week with all of your congregation, but especially with the children. Those truths become our values upon which we base our actions. Those need to be instilled in, and reinforced in, our children.

Now, of course, we know that some children do not come from good homes. If that is the case, we have a special responsibility to to help those children learn those moral values. We need to teach right living as well as right learning. I think that even in the public schools, that we need to be concerned with more than just math and science and English. I think we ought to be teaching honesty as well as history; that we ought to be teaching equality as well as English, morality as well as math. Some of you have read in the last few days that we've had a statewide Commission on Education for Economic Growth. And they recommended a lot of things to improve our schools, to put our children in a position to hold a better job and to have a better future in their lives. But one of the things that they recommended that you may not have heard about was that we keep these values of honesty, and, and responsibility, and truthfulness, and compassion in our schools, and I think it's high time that we do that. I firmly believe that God gave us families, knowing we'd pass on those values which make us good and make us godly. Of course, every parent must set the right example, because in truth, our children will be following in our footsteps, whether those are good or bad footsteps.

Then a third reason that I believe families are so important is that the home is the place where we need to hear affectionate words. The home is the place where our children are nurtured, the place where they grow in spirit— not just the food that they eat; of course, we want to provide for them a good balanced diet, with plenty of good food; we want to make sure that they eat all that's on their plate and that they have the, the vitamins, and the minerals, and all those other things. My friends, what's more important than that food is that love, and that caring, that we give to our children. I think that the words that express love to them, that build up their self-image, that challenge them to become what they're capable of being, are the things that really give them a productive future. I know of family situations, as perhaps many of you do, where children never hear those words, "I love you"; where children are never hugged; where they're just really lucky to come out and be halfway-decent citizens.

The senator mentioned, tonight, in presenting me, that my wife and I work as volunteers every Monday in our public schools in Raleigh. For the last three years, I've been working in a dropout prevention program. You might be interested in knowing that, in the last five years, we have reduced the dropout rate in North Carolina by 17 percent. But the program that I work in is one in which we match up adult volunteers with young people who are having problems in their lives. Many of them come from broken homes. Many of them come from homes in which parents are alcoholics, or worse. Some of them are the subject of child abuse. But in far more cases, they aren't physically abused, they simply never get the kind of love and caring and encouragement and support that children need to have. So many young people are told that they can't make it, that they can't be somebody. They constantly hear words like "failure," or "loser." If you tell somebody something long enough, they'll, they'll believe it, and especially young people. If you expect nothing of a person, that is usually what that person will become. I think, with the members in this church—because I've had a chance to sing with you tonight, to see the kind of wonderful, enthusiastic, loving, and optimistic church you are—I believe if we are positive and optimistic about the future, and I think that Christians ought to be, because we know that with God's help we can accomplish things; we can be what we ought to be. There are so many negative people in the world; there are so many prophets of gloom and doom. All of us know that Jesus was different from that—we know the example of Jesus is being positive in talking about love, especially in talking about the children that he wanted to have come unto him, and forbid them not. That example of Jesus the Christ is probably the best example of the kind of human beings we ought to try to be, and the kind of way we ought to relate to our fellow man, and to help them and to encourage them and to care about them. I remember, as a boy growing up, I was very lucky to have parents who were open and who were generous with their affection. My wife Carolyn and I strive very hard, with our own children, to be that same way. Of course, the greatest example of all was, and is, God's love for us—so much that he gave his only begotten Son, and he gave his Son to live on this earth, to be an example for all of us, and then, of course, to die for our sins so that we might be saved. That love, that affection, that positive good news must be told over and over again, and our future, with God's help, can become the abundant life which the Bible talks about. If churches, and civic organizations, and government work together, the lives of all of our citizens can be positive, and can be abundant.

Let me conclude, tonight—and the storm is coming up, and the lightning and the rain—let me conclude by reminding you that good families don't just happen, they are the result of hard work. I believe that if there's anything that's true, it's that God wants us to have good families and he wants us to do that hard work it requires, the hard work of being good husbands and wives. Because unless we are that, unless we are true to each other and love each other, we cannot have families and we cannot raise up our children to be the kinds of people they ought to be. There is no way to repay the sacrifices that our parents made for us—that mine made for me on that farm just over in Wilson County, that your parents made for you. Churches and individuals need to make family relationships a very high priority. As governor, many people know that I have tried to take my family life seriously, as, as Vernon indicated. You know, I think that perhaps the greatest accomplishment during my public service is that after twelve years, serving as lieutenant governor and governor, I have a wife of twenty-six years who loves me and who supports me—and who even corrects me—and who gives that kind of love and support to our children. She's really the good parent in our family, and she takes that time. My wife is certain to be at home—and she has this opportunity and not all wives do—when our children come home from school, because that's the time when children need a lot of love and encouragement, and a lot of times they've got a lot of frustration. And those wives who work, of course, find that they need to do that when they get home from work, and do it . . . in preparing supper and all the other things, helping with the homework—it's a very, very big job. But that's what we need to do. We need to have those times together—Sunday is our time, and of course, we find other times as we can.

We're working hard, in our administration, to try to see that state government has policies that do not conflict with family life. We try to, to see that people who work in state government, and many of your congregation do, have the kinds of, of opportunities in their jobs that are consistent with whole families and that will help keep them together. My prayer is that we may be successful, as we give leadership in all of our state, in trying to help families that need help. I'm not sure how history will remember me, as governor, but I want to say this: I hope that, as a human being, that it will be said of Jim Hunt that he was a son who honored his father and his mother, and he was a husband and father who tried very hard to be a good one, for his wife and for his children.

I admire your work here in the Black Jack Free Will Baptist Church. I admire your work as Christian men and women and children, because the work of families is the work of all of us. I urge you to strive to continue to build families, in the way that God would have you do. This church stands here, as a great symbol of a vital Christian church in the community, in this county in eastern North Carolina, in the great Free Will Baptist denomination. Continue to let your light shine forward, whether it be a candle, as we have here tonight, or those beautiful lights that you have in this sanctuary, and let one of the testimonies of this church be not just your services, not only just your wonderful song service, but the work you do here in building families, in building children, in bringing about the kinds of people that God wants us to be. Would you please join me as we conclude with a moment of prayer:

Our heavenly Father, I thank you for this church, for this wonderful minister, for all of the ministers and robed leaders of the song services in this church. We thank you for the month of celebration of families that has been enjoyed here. We pray tonight that you would bless this church and bless every family here. Help them all—help *us* all—to rededicate ourselves to good families, to love our husbands and our wives more, to love our children and our parents more, to make our families first in our lives, and to make the family the very center of the church. We thank you for all the good things that you have given us, and help us, as members of Christian families, to do the work that you would have us to do in this world, to make this a place that you would be pleased with, to provide the kinds of opportunities that you want every man, woman, and child, as a member of a family, to have. This we pray in your holy name. Amen.

---

[1] Vernon E. White (1906-   ), native of Hertford County; resident of Pitt County; B.S., 1929, B.A., 1931, Wake Forest College (now University); World War II veteran. Farmer; teacher, principal, 1929-1940; Pitt County Board of Commissioners, 1963-1966, and board chairman, 1966; elected to state Senate in 1968, and returned in subsequent elections; chairman, Senate Committee on Agriculture. *North Carolina Manual, 1983*, 254.

[2] The Reverend Stacy Carter was youth director of Black Jack Free Will Baptist Church. Cedric D. Pierce, Jr., to Jan-Michael Poff, March 5, 1986.

[3]The power outage was caused by a tornado—one of many that ravaged southern and eastern North Carolina on the night of March 28, 1984—that struck Pitt County. After addressing the family festival, the governor surveyed Greenville-area storm damage. High winds took the lives of nine Pitt residents, injured more than 150 others, destroyed 400 homes, caused an estimated $15 million in damage, and left parts of the county without electricity for four days. Emergency coordinator Bobby Joyner reported that most of the destruction had been sustained in a twenty-two-mile-long, half-mile-wide swath affecting the county's Ayden, Simpson, Portertown, and Pactolus sections. *News and Observer*, March 31, April 7, 1984; *Raleigh Times*, March 29, 1984; see also "Local Economic Development Conference," April 2, 1984, above.

[4]Charles V. Petty (1940-   ), executive director, Governor's Office of Citizen Affairs. Previously identified in Mitchell, *Addresses of Hunt*, I, 39n.

INDEX